Yi-tag Wu

# Effective
# Reading
# Instruction, K–8

SECOND EDITION

# EFFECTIVE READING INSTRUCTION, K–8

DONALD J. LEU, JR.
Syracuse University

CHARLES K. KINZER
Vanderbilt University

Merrill, an imprint of
Macmillan Publishing Company
New York

Collier Macmillan Canada, Inc.
Toronto

Maxwell Macmillan International Publishing Group
New York  Oxford  Singapore  Sydney

*where , publisher.*

Cover photo: Jo Hall/Macmillan Publishing

Editor: Sally Berridge MacGregor
Developmental Editor: Linda James Scharp
Production Editor: Linda Bayma
Copy Editor: Mary Benis
Art Coordinator: Mark D. Garrett
Photo Editor: Gail Meese
Text Designer: Anne Daly
Cover Designer: Russ Maselli
Production Buyer: Pamela D. Bennett

This book was set in Clearface.

Photo credits: All photos by Charles K. Kinzer.
Macmillan Publishing Company
866 Third Avenue, New York, NY 10022
Collier Macmillan Canada, Inc.

**Library of Congress Cataloging-in-Publication Data**
Leu, Donald J.
  Effective reading instruction: K–8 / Donald J. Leu, Jr., Charles
K. Kinzer.
    p. cm.
  Rev. ed. of: Effective reading instruction in the elementary
grades. 1987.
  Includes bibliographical references and index.
  ISBN 0-675-21264-2
  1. Reading (Elementary)—United States. I. Kinzer, Charles K.
II. Leu, Donald J. Effective reading instruction in the elementary
grades. III. Title.
LB1573.L445   1991
372.4'1'0973—dc20                                      90-19149
                                                          CIP

Printing: 1  2  3  4  5  6  7  8  9     Year: 1  2  3  4

*To our families—*
*Alexandra, Debbie, Katie, Rita, and Sarah. Once again, with*
*gratitude for your understanding and support as we developed these*
*ideas during three years of late nights and weekends on the*
*computer.*

*To our preservice readers—*
*you are part of a very long and important chain that began with*
*your parents and teachers, includes your current professors, and will*
*continue as you enter the noblest of professions—teaching.*

*To our undergraduate and graduate students—*
*with appreciation for the opportunity to participate in your*
*development and for the ideas you shared which contributed to our*
*own development.*

*To teachers around the country—*
*with heartfelt thanks for allowing us to enter the special worlds you*
*create for children. Your insights have been especially helpful as we*
*seek to support the development of future teaching.*

# Preface

Developed as the basic text for preservice teachers in an elementary **Goals**
reading methods course, this book was written to develop insightful
teachers empowered to make logical, reflective decisions about reading
instruction. It is an integrative text, based on the assumption that effective
reading teachers must understand both what to do during instruction and why
it should be done.

This text translates the most consistent research findings into practice. It
presents the major perspectives in reading education, describes a comprehensive range of instructional practices, and shows teachers how to select and
modify practices that are consistent with their perspectives and the individual
needs of their students. Our goal is to provide a text that facilitates the development of teachers who can be reasoned decision makers within the school-
restructuring debate that promises to impact teacher empowerment in the
current decade.

The first edition noted that an explosion in reading research had oc-
curred in the 1970s and 1980s. Research findings on effective reading instruc- **Research Base**
tion, the reading process, readers' cognitive and linguistic processes, teacher
behavior and teacher cognition, classroom environments, interest and attitude, and different text structures resulted in a knowledge base with clear
instructional implications. Research efforts in these areas have continued,
augmented by research in emergent literacy, whole language, reading/writing
relationships, cooperative learning, reciprocal teaching, and portfolio and alternative assessment strategies. At the same time, changes in instructional
materials have taken place. Published reading programs now reflect a greater
emphasis on children's literature, and technological advances now go far beyond drill and practice.

In order to address these changes, substantive revisions have been made **Changes, Additions**
in each chapter, and several new chapters have been added.

- A full chapter about reading/writing relationships and major sections in
  several chapters about emergent literacy and whole language have been
  added.

- Sections on using literature in reading instruction have been expanded.
- Thematic lists of appropriate children's literature have been included in many chapters.
- Sections on product/process assessment and portfolio assessment have been added.
- Sections on questioning strategies such as QARs and comprehension strategies such as K-W-L have been added or enhanced.
- The treatment of linguistically and culturally diverse students has been expanded.
- Discussion of cooperative learning and its potential value to reading teachers has been added to several chapters.
- The section on computer literacy has been replaced with a broader focus on the use of technology, various types of software appropriate for reading instruction, and a discussion of technologies beyond microcomputers.
- Lists of software by category as well as by software publisher have been included.

These and other changes ensure that the text is as current as possible. References provide a comprehensive and up-to-date resource for students who will become our future teachers of reading.

**Model Lessons, Sample Activities**

Becoming an insightful, reflective teacher is not easy. We have written this text to be considerate of the needs of learners on their way to becoming professionals in literacy education. Part of this support structure comes from the model lessons provided for each major teaching procedure discussed and the more than 300 sample activities that are presented and highlighted for easier reference. Learning should also be facilitated by the early discussion of several different definitions of reading and a clear statement of the definition used in this book. In addition, end-of-chapter summaries, questions, and activities have been chosen to provoke further thought and to solidify important concepts presented in each chapter.

**Special Features**

Special attention has been devoted to the layout and design elements of this text in order to further support the needs of students—from initial reading through practicum and student teaching experiences. A relevant children's literature quotation captures each chapter's theme, followed by performance objectives that sharpen the reader's expectations and a list of key concepts that can function in a variety of ways. Instructors might use them in a prediscussion to build students' background, students might ask about definitions before they begin reading, or instructors and students together might focus on key concepts in postreading activities, perhaps constructing a concept or semantic map in class discussion.

To facilitate students' comprehension, key terms are highlighted in the text, and definitions appear as margin notes. In addition, major points are itemized at the end of each chapter. For easier access and reference during field experiences, model lessons and sample activities are highlighted by a unique design feature and a second color. Headings also have been clearly differentiated by a second color to promote previewing and studying.

Many chapters include an element called *Decision Point,* which presents issues being debated in the field and encourages students to think about their own responses. Instructors might use this feature in expanded class activities, for student research projects, or to promote student discussion. The end of each chapter contains a feature called *Making Instructional Decisions.* This is intended to encourage students' interaction with the text by providing projects, discussion questions, and hypothetical situations for student response. In addition, the brief annotated list for further reading at the end of each chapter allows interested readers to pursue a specific topic. These references also provide an initial source for literature searches as appropriate for class assignments. A comprehensive list of references cited concludes each chapter, and author and subject indexes appear at the end of the text.

Two additional features help make this text current and unique. First, extensive thematic lists of children's literature appear in many chapters. These lists allow students to choose appropriate literature selections during field experiences and allow instructors to more easily incorporate the use of literature in student assignments. Second, lists of software are provided by skill category and use (e.g., drill and practice through simulation), as is a list of software publishers.

Added to this edition are the comments of three experienced teachers: Mr. Burns, Emily Dodson, and Ms. Sanchez. Each teacher represents a different perspective about reading instruction, ranging from mastery of specific skills to whole language learning. In each chapter these teachers discuss how they use their perspectives to select and adapt the instructional materials and practices described in that chapter. Instructors should find these sections helpful in promoting a discussion of teacher decision making.

*Teacher Comments, Instructional Perspectives*

The text is divided into four major sections, the first of which contains three chapters. Chapter 1 provides an introduction to the field and presents various definitions of and perspectives toward reading. The second chapter presents the various materials and methods commonly used in reading instruction and describes the instructional frameworks within which they often appear. Comprehension is the subject of the third chapter. After exploring how a person reads and how reading ability develops, students identify how their own understanding of comprehension will affect their teaching decisions every day. As a whole, the first section assists students in developing their own instructional framework as they identify their perspectives toward reading. This framework will be enhanced and modified as readers proceed through the book and through their own teaching careers.

*Major Sections*

The second section includes seven chapters that develop the reader's knowledge base about reading and reading instruction. The chapters move from emergent literacy/reading readiness, decoding, and vocabulary through the comprehension of extended text. This section also includes separate chapters about using literature in a reading program, connecting reading and writing, and understanding the special reading and instructional demands of expository texts. Each chapter has a separate focus, yet each recognizes that fluent reading of "real" materials is the goal of effective reading instruction.

The third section consists of two chapters about determining and meeting instructional needs. Chapter 11 discusses methods of assessment in both individual and group situations with both formal and informal measures. The chapter considers product and process assessment, portfolio assessment, and the assessment of readers as well as reading materials. Chapter 12 looks at the instructional needs of special populations, including the learning disabled and the gifted. Special attention is given to instruction of children with diverse linguistic and cultural backgrounds.

The fourth section concludes the book with two chapters that present the physical patterns of reading instruction. Chapter 13 discusses instructional organization both between and within classes and addresses management issues related to effective teaching. Chapter 14 examines the changing patterns resulting from the impact of technology on reading instruction. This chapter moves beyond microcomputers to consider software types, videodisc technology, hypermedia, and simple, cost-effective uses of technology to facilitate disseminating information to parents and encouraging parental involvement.

**Instructional Sequence**

The chapters in this text have been ordered in a logical instructional sequence. We suggest that Chapters 1, 2, and 3 be read first, regardless of any reordering of subsequent chapters. These first three chapters explain the instructional consequences of various instructional frameworks and begin the process of helping readers develop their own personal frameworks. However, all chapters have been written to stand alone.

**Instructor's Guide, Blackline Masters, Test Bank**

Several ancillary materials have been developed for instructors who use this text. These materials can be requested from the publisher. An instructor's guide includes summaries of each chapter, as well as additional questions that are appropriate for cooperative learning activities, individual student projects, and prediscussion of chapters. The instructor's guide also contains blackline masters for each chapter, which incorporate many of the figures, diagrams, and summary lists in the text. These are intended for use with an overhead projector to facilitate class discussion. Finally, the instructor's guide includes an extensive test bank, complete with chapter questions, quizzes, and section tests. The test bank includes multiple-choice, true/false, short-answer, and essay questions and provides answer keys for multiple-choice and true/false questions.

**Videotape**

The final ancillary is a videotape that includes examples of major methods and topics discussed in the text. For example, short segments demonstrate a big book activity, a ReQuest procedure, a language experience activity, a directed reading-thinking activity, and so on. Although the segments are relatively short, they should enhance and promote class discussion and provide instructors with examples as well as points of departure for critiques.

**Request for Comments**

Nonetheless, even as this second edition goes to press, new research is appearing that has great potential for improving reading education. Future revisions will continue to incorporate the best, most current knowledge about effective reading instruction and will attempt to present it in a useful manner. To this end, we welcome comments and suggestions from both instructors and students who use this text. Comments on the first edition were most helpful to us in the revision process, and any recommendations for further improvements will be appreciated.

Working together has been an especially worthwhile experience for us. Neither the original text nor this second edition would have its depth of coverage without the combined knowledge of each author. The text is a joint effort in the fullest sense of a partnership, a coauthored text with both authors participating equally throughout the project. Author order was determined randomly.

A Personal Note

## ACKNOWLEDGMENTS

It is impossible to recognize or thank individually each of the many friends and colleagues who have contributed to this revision, and we beg the indulgence of any we might inadvertently fail to acknowledge. As in any major project, the quality of the finished product results from the efforts, encouragement, and sacrifices of many individuals. We greatly appreciate all who have supported our work.

This revision has benefited from an extensive review. The number of reviewers, their variety of perspectives, and their sharing of time and ideas have made this text current, complete, and accurate. More than 24 distinguished reviewers participated in this project and have our continuing gratitude for their professionalism and consideration. We especially thank the following friends and colleagues: Sara Ann Beach, University of California, Riverside; Janice Carson, Peabody College of Vanderbilt University; Sheila Cohen, State University of New York, Cortland; Karen Dahl, University of Cincinnati; Doris Walker Dalhouse, Moorhead State University; Penny Dyer, California State University, Fresno; Edward J. Earley, Kutztown University of Pennsylvania; Michael P. Ford, University of Wisconsin-Oshkosh; Beth Ann Hermann, University of South Carolina; Sylvia Hutchinson, University of Georgia; Rosie Webb Joels, University of Central Florida; Anita McClain, Pacific University; James Martin-Rehrman, Westfield State College; Judith P. Mitchell, Weber State College; Bill Oehlkers, Rhode Island College; Peggy E. Ransom, Ball State University; David Reinking, University of Georgia; Bob Rickelman, Millersville University; Deborah Rowe, Peabody College of Vanderbilt University; Jay Samuels, University of Minnesota; Ruth Sandlin, California State University, San Bernardino; Tim Shanahan, University of Illinois; Shelley Wepner, William Paterson College; Tom Wheat, Northern Illinois University; and James Wiley, Baylor University.

# Contents

*dialogue journal*

*KWL*

# ENTERING THE WORLD OF READING INSTRUCTION

PART
1

# The Problem, the Challenge, the Rewards

> *"What do you want to be when you grow up?" asked Fran Fox.*
> *"I want to be a doctor," said Billy Goat.*
> *"I want to be a banker," said Sam Snake.*
> *"I want to be someone special," said Irish Setter.*
> *"I want to be a teacher."*

From *Growing Up*, a language experience story by a second-grade class.

Teaching is a challenging and rewarding profession. Teachers often have a significant influence on their students' lives, and teachers of reading, especially, may have a lasting impact. The importance of reading is seen in every subject area and in nearly every aspect of life.

This chapter looks at reading instruction in a technologically changing world and introduces the concept of instructional frameworks, which can help you become an effective teacher of reading. Chapter 1 includes information that will help you answer questions like these:

1. Given the rapid technological advances that are occurring in our society, why do people argue that reading will continue to be important in the future?
2. How do different definitions of *reading* influence how reading is taught?
3. What is a personal framework of the reading process, and why is it important to you as a future teacher of reading?
4. What are instructional frameworks, and how do these affect teaching decisions in reading education?

## KEY CONCEPTS

comprehension framework
definitions of the reading process
instructional framework

interactive process
reading process

## TEACHING READING—A FUTURE NECESSITY

Let's assume that you will be teaching a first-grade class in two years. If we take this year's date and add 2 and then 12, we will have the year that your first students will graduate from high school. If we add 4 to that date, we will have the year that those students will graduate from college with an undergraduate degree if they choose to attend and go straight through. Keep in mind that the reading instruction (that you provide two years from now) will have to support those students throughout their school years and their adult lives.

During the past several years a tremendous change has taken place in education, in part because of the extensive development and rapid spread of technology in our society in general and in our schools in particular. This ever-increasing emphasis on technology has resulted in speculation that a number of school subjects may need to be taught differently if our students are to be educated most effectively. Certain traditional school subjects, such as reading and mathematics, will become obsolete, some say, since sophisticated and easy-to-use technology may soon read and calculate for us. The increasing acceptance and use of calculators in arithmetic classes and the potential of microcomputers with **synthetic speech** capabilities lend support to this line of thinking. Nonetheless, reading ability continues to concern parents, educators,

synthetic speech: Sounds generated electronically usually controlled by a computer.

and legislators alike. In fact, many primary-grade teachers measure their success against their students' literacy achievements. How should we resolve this seeming discrepancy between viewpoints? Will reading be relatively unnecessary in the future, or is reading ability the most important aspect of education?

In part, this discrepancy is associated with the way we understand reading. If our conception of reading is largely equated with pronunciation, then a talking computer might indeed make the intermediate step of looking at printed symbols unnecessary. But is that all there is to reading? In the case of a blind law student, the job of a paid reader is to read assigned class material to the student. Who would you say is reading—the sighted person who is pronouncing the material or the blind student who is comprehending it? Most people would agree that reading includes, but goes beyond, decoding symbols.

If we assume that reading goes beyond pronunciation and involves understanding, then we can see that the process of reading is more than a mechanical skill; it is active and internal. In fact, teaching reading may be thought of as teaching thinking, because readers must organize information, recognize cause and effect, assess the importance of what is being read, and fit the material into their own beliefs and knowledge base. The fact that technology is allowing ever-increasing access to information makes effective teaching of the reading process even more, not less, important. Individuals will be expected to perform more **higher-level reading comprehension tasks**—organizing available information, differentiating relevant from irrelevant facts, deciding how to use those facts, and much more.

higher-level reading comprehension tasks: Analysis and synthesis skills, such as organizing information and recognizing and using relevant facts.

In addition, talking machines do not allow certain common reading behaviors to occur easily. For example, have you ever gone back in your reading to check a fact? Perhaps you realized that an interesting point needed additional thought, or you missed an important word or phrase. Silent reading permits rereading. It is also faster and more efficient than listening when you want to absorb a large amount of information; you can proceed at your own pace or quickly scan an entire segment for a particular item. We use a telephone book in this way, quickly searching for one particular entry, rather than reading all of the page at the same speed.

Thus, we can conclude that there will continue to be a great need for reading, and it will not be effectively taught as an external skill. Sequential drills and repetitive practice may be appropriate for typing instruction, because the learner's major objective is to acquire an external, mechanical skill. However, in reading instruction the learner's major objective is to develop, refine, and use high-level thought processes—ultimately, to comprehend. Consequently, this text holds that comprehension must be taught throughout the reading curriculum. With that goal reading instruction will never become obsolete.

## Reading: A Useful Tool

Good readers often forget how difficult it may have been to learn to read. We may also take for granted the many times our reading ability is used. Look around you right now. How many things need to be read? At home there may be a newspaper, TV guide, cereal box, or mail. At school there may be a bulletin board, posters, books, or class notes. And think of all the things you have already read so far today. If we define reading as translating printed symbols into meaning, then you may have read your watch, the morning paper, road signs, a map or some other set of directions, or the numbers and letters on a dollar bill. Reading touches all aspects of life.

To a large extent, reading ability also influences our life-styles: how well we read is a key factor in determining employment opportunities. As a result, legislators are deeply concerned with literacy issues; adult literacy classes are one attempt to make people more self-sufficient, thus easing both the political and human costs of unemployment. In addition, reading can positively impact depression and boredom, as well as provide role models and inspiration. It can answer our questions and give us directions. It can teach and transform, provide pleasure, and stimulate original thought. It touches both our personal and our professional lives.

In school, too, reading cuts across every subject area; the ability to read a textbook, do research in the library, or read a teacher's notes on the chalkboard directly affects the quality of a student's learning. It is small wonder, then, that teachers and parents, as well as students, are so concerned that reading be effectively taught, even though there are many different perceptions about how to accomplish that task.

Reading is an important part of daily life and influences learning in all subject areas.

## ARRIVING AT A DEFINITION OF READING

### The Importance of Establishing a Perspective

Your view of reading—the factors involved, their relative importance, and the way the process takes place and develops—will have a direct and major impact on how you teach reading. That relationship between a personal view of reading and actual teaching practices has been discussed for some time.

> If we think of reading primarily as a visual task, we will be concerned with the correction of visual defects and the provision of legible reading material. If we think of reading as word recognition, we will drill on the basic sight vocabulary and word recognition skills. If we think of reading as merely reproducing what the author says, we will direct the student's attention to the literal meaning of the passage and check his comprehension of it. If we think of reading as a thinking process, we shall be concerned with the reader's skill in making interpretations and generalizations, in drawing inferences and conclusions. If we think of reading as contributing to personal development and effecting desirable personality changes, we will provide our students with reading materials that meet their needs and have some application to their lives. (Strang, McCullough, & Traxler, 1961, pp. 1–2)

Teachers are often left to discover their view of the **reading process** on their own and are not told how various viewpoints will affect their instructional decisions. This text provides guidance in transforming your view of reading into a framework on which you will ultimately make your instructional decisions. This approach allows you later to consciously modify your viewpoint and instruction as appropriate. First, however, we should look at how others have defined *reading* and how *reading* is defined in this text.

reading process: Active and internal operations involved in reading.

### Some Definitions of Reading

As our knowledge of the reading process has evolved, definitions of reading have become more complex. Although "getting meaning from print" is one way to define reading, such simplified definitions do not adequately present the complexity of the process, nor do they reflect the interaction of factors that enter into the reading act. Rudolf Flesch (1981) relates reading to a set of mechanical skills: "Learning to read is like learning to drive a car. . . . The child learns the mechanics of reading, and when he's through, he can read" (p. 3). Further, Flesch (1955) says we should teach the child phonics "letter-by-letter and sound-by-sound until he knows it—and when he knows it he knows how to read" (p. 121). However, Dechant (1982) believes that reading is more complex: "Reading cannot occur unless the pupil can identify and recognize the printed symbol, and generally the pupil must also give the visual configuration a name. Even so, it is only one aspect of the reading process. Meaning, too, is an absolute prerequisite in reading. Perhaps too much emphasis in reading instruction has been placed on word identification and not enough on comprehension" (p. 166).

psycholinguistic: Referring to the psychological and linguistic processes involved in language.

syntactic: Referring to the ordering of words that makes meaningful phrases and sentences.

semantic: Referring to the meanings of words.

pragmatic: Referring to the social appropriateness of speech acts in certain contexts.

Goodman (1976) relates reading to a type of guessing game based on an individual's knowledge of language: "Reading is a **psycholinguistic** guessing game. It involves an interaction between thought and language. Efficient reading does not result from precise perception and identification of all elements, but from skill in selecting the fewest, most productive cues necessary to produce guesses [about meaning] which are right the first time" (p. 498). Rumelhart (1986) states: "Reading is the process of understanding written language. It begins with a flutter of patterns on the retina and ends (when successful) with a definite idea about the author's intended message. . .a skilled reader must be able to make use of sensory, **syntactic, semantic,** and **pragmatic** information to accomplish his task. These various sources of information interact in many complex ways during the process of reading" (p. 722).

Other definitions describe reading within the more general context of literacy, focusing on the social, communicative nature of reading and writing. For proponents of such views, learning is thought to take place as children see the importance of communication, at which time requisite teaching occurs. Harste (1990), for example, notes that "language is a social event" (p. 317), and Shanahan (1990) stresses its communicative purpose.

> We read an author's words and are affected by the author's intentions. We write with the idea of influencing or informing others. . . . The fusion of reading and writing in the classroom offers children the possibility of participating in both sides of the communication process and, consequently, provides them with a more elaborate grasp of the true meaning of literacy. (p. 4)

The relationship between reading and writing, between readers and writers, has been called interactive by some, transactional by others. For example, Rosenblatt (1985, 1988) has described this relationship as a transaction between the text and the reader, during which both the text and the reader are changed, becoming more than the sum of their parts. Rosenblatt's transactional view has had a major impact on reader-response theory, that is, thoughts about how readers react to a text—socially, psychologically, and morally.

> The individual's share in language, then, is that part, or set of features, of the public system that has been internalized in the individual's experiences with words in life situations. The residue of such transactions in particular natural and social contexts constitutes a kind of linguistic-experimental reservoir. Embodying our funded assumptions, attitudes, and expectations about the world—and about language—this inner capital is all that each of us has to start from in speaking, listening, writing, and reading. We make meaning, we make sense of a new situation or transaction, by applying, reorganizing, revising, or extending elements drawn from, selected from, our personal linguistic-experimental reservoir. (Rosenblatt, 1988, p. 3)

All of these definitions present reading quite differently, ranging from a mechanical sounding-out process to a social and emotional experience, to an interaction between what is read and what is already known, which allows meaning to occur. Different teaching emphases result from these different definitions of reading. For example, a teacher who defines reading as strictly sounding out letters will spend more time at the early grade levels teaching letter-sound relationships and less time reading to students.

All definitions of reading are personal, based on an individual's view of the reading process and the way in which reading ability develops. The following definition has guided the writing of this text. It views reading in a broad sense, requiring learning as well as existing knowledge to arrive at meaning. We must remember, though, that any definition of reading is only a guide and must change as our knowledge of the reading process grows.

> Reading is a *developmental, interactive,* and *global process* that involves *learning.* It is a *personal process* specifically incorporating an individual's *linguistic knowledge* and can be both positively and negatively influenced by nonlinguistic *internal* and *external variables,* or factors.

The eight aspects of this definition that are italicized are briefly explained here and will become even clearer in the remaining chapters of this text.

- *Developmental process*. This aspect recognizes that reading ability develops over time and that readers read differently at different stages in their reading development. For example, a beginning reader attends more to individual letters, whereas a mature reader focuses more on words and general meaning.
- *Interactive process*. This aspect of the definition recognizes that reading is an interaction involving the reader, the writer, and the text being read. Meaning is not only in the mind of the person doing the reading, nor is it only in the text being read. Instead, it is the interaction between the text being read and a reader's existing knowledge and expectations, which determines the amount and type of comprehension that takes place. Because individual knowledge and expectations differ, different readers may interpret an identical text in different ways.
- *Global process*. This aspect recognizes that comprehension can occur at different levels of complexity yet as part of a comprehensive and organized process. For example, comprehension can occur at a letter, word, phrase, sentence, or entire discourse level, but all of these levels must function in a coordinated manner and with some sophistication for reading to occur.
- *Learning*. This aspect recognizes that reading ability develops over time; it also reflects our knowledge that instruction helps students learn to read. A reader must learn how to learn, acquiring certain strategies for reading as well as an understanding of when and how to use them.
- *Personal process*. This aspect recognizes the social and emotional dimensions of reading. In addition to the different interpretations noted earlier, readers' differing backgrounds and knowledge result in different emotional, moral, and psychological reactions to what is read.
- *Linguistic knowledge*. The inclusion of this aspect acknowledges that various language components influence reading ability: (1) phonic knowledge of

sounds and their relationship to symbols; (2) semantic knowledge of meanings; (3) syntactic knowledge of word patterns; and (4) discourse knowledge of how different written products are structured. This aspect also recognizes the effect of **metacognitive knowledge** on comprehension. Metacognitive knowledge allows a reader to monitor comprehension as it occurs and to choose strategies that result in rereading or asking for help when necessary.

metacognitive knowledge: A type of knowledge important for reading that includes the strategies used during reading and comprehension monitoring.

■ *Internal variables.* Factors such as physical and mental well-being, general intelligence, specific developmental handicaps, and interest in or attitude toward reading and reading content also influence the reading process. This aspect includes knowledge of pragmatics (the acceptability of speech acts in certain social contexts) and something called "world knowledge," or general knowledge or experience. For example, knowing what might be said acceptably in certain situations helps a reader interpret what a character in a novel might be saying; such knowledge might help a reader identify sarcasm. In addition, general knowledge of city life might boost comprehension of a story that is set in a large city.

■ *External variables.* This aspect recognizes that instructional and situational characteristics also influence the reading act. Such factors include the physical environment of the reader, the instructional program (including the materials used in instruction), the prereading home environment, teacher-student interactions in the classroom, and other influences that are neither controlled by or inherent to the reader.

Thus, this text views reading as more than recognition or pronunciation of printed squiggles on a page; it is a process in which the reader and print interact. From this perspective the material being read is a starting point from which the reader moves on, incorporating existing knowledge in order to reason, learn, react, and ultimately go far beyond the assimilated printed symbols. This view implies that all the knowledge that a reader already has can be used to comprehend symbols. And since reading is a language activity, preexisting language and language-related abilities are key factors in understanding and interpreting what is read. We must remember that children come to school with a wealth of language on which reading instruction can build. At the very least they know how to speak; they know that communication is possible and that its goal is to transmit meaning. Furthermore, all the sounds of the English language are already known, even if their relationship to specific printed symbols is not. Be sure not to overlook these highly developed communication skills in your classroom, whatever grade level you teach.

Throughout this text you will be reminded that your view of reading will determine how you teach. As you read through the following chapters, look back periodically at the definition we have just presented. Add to it or delete from it as your knowledge changes. Specifying a personal framework in order to develop and improve instructional strategies is an important part of being a reading teacher and will help you meet the challenges outlined here. Guiding you in this task is a major goal of this text.

## THE CHALLENGE OF TEACHING READING

As a teacher of reading, you will face one of the more challenging tasks in education. We have discussed how important reading is, and will continue to be, in our society. You will sense this importance as parents ask about their children's progress in reading, as administrators provide in-service workshops on reading instruction, as you see your school's reading test scores reported in the local newspaper, and especially as you look at the faces of your students, who want very much to learn to read. Many people consider reading an important part of the elementary curriculum and therefore pay close attention to reading instruction.

Teaching reading is also a challenge because reading is a complex developmental process. Consequently, teachers of reading must have some understanding of this complexity, as well as an understanding of effective instructional strategies. As you learn how to teach reading, you will be developing answers to a number of important questions.

What must readers know in order to comprehend complete stories, articles, and books? How can I help readers gain meaning from these and other kinds of writing?

What materials should be used to teach reading? How can I select and adapt appropriate materials for reading instruction?

What organizational patterns can be used to provide for the range of individuals in my classroom? How can I best organize my classroom?

What are the characteristics of effective teachers? What must I do to become an effective reading teacher?

Because there are so many different definitions of reading, there are different answers to each of these questions. No single, definitive answer exists that can apply to each individual situation.

A related aspect of the challenge of reading instruction is the diversity of the students. Some of your students will be far beyond their classroom peers in reading ability; others will be somewhat below the class average. All will have individual needs. Some may have difficulty with pronunciation in oral reading, others will need help understanding word meanings, and still others will require assistance in interpreting or evaluating what is read. This diversity of needs and abilities makes teaching in general, and the teaching of reading in particular, challenging and exciting.

The final challenge for you as a teacher of reading will be to make appropriate instructional decisions while you attend to the many events that take place during the course of a lesson. Learning to manage classroom activities to provide the best possible learning environment is part of becoming a teacher. Classroom management is not an impossible task. Can you remember how you felt when you were learning to drive a car? In that situation you were also confronted with important decisions that had to be made while you

In supportive environments children enjoy reading and, as they grow older, will encounter many different kinds of books.

attended to many other things—the cars in front of and behind you, the actions of your passengers, the condition of the road, and so on. You probably drive skillfully now, and any uneasiness has likely disappeared. With a solid knowledge base and concentrated practice, you can also master both the decision-making process and the management functions that will make your classroom a haven for learning.

As a reading teacher, then, you will face many challenges. To be successful, you will need a clear understanding of this complex subject, the ability to make informed decisions, and the management skill to accomplish your instructional goals in a busy classroom environment. Across the continent, teachers are meeting these and other challenges, giving North America one of the highest literacy rates in the world. When we compare the percentage of people who can read now to the percentage of 50 years ago, it is clear that teachers are learning to teach reading and are doing so effectively. With the help of this text and your own hard work and practice, you, too, can develop into a successful teacher of reading who will be rewarded over and over as your students become eager readers.

## INSTRUCTIONAL FRAMEWORKS AND DECISIONS

Teachers provide effective reading instruction in a busy environment by relying on different types of instructional frameworks. Such frameworks consist of the materials, methods, and beliefs about reading that teachers use to make their instructional decisions. Instructional frameworks guide teachers in planning and teaching their reading lessons in much the same way that road maps guide drivers in their travels or grocery lists guide shoppers at the supermarket. Instructional frameworks provide structure and reduce the number of conscious decisions that teachers must make during interactions with students. Frameworks help teachers decide both what to teach and how to teach.

### Three Types of Frameworks

Teachers use three types of frameworks to meet the challenges of reading instruction: frameworks based on a set of instructional materials, those based on instructional methods, and those based on an understanding of reading comprehension. A **material framework** is based on the materials and lesson planning information available in a published set of instructional tools, whether a kit of graded activity cards, computer software, or a complete reading program. Such a framework uses the detailed description of how a teacher is to teach reading that is provided in the given set of instructional materials, thereby reducing the number of instructional decisions that a teacher must make. Notice how many instructional decisions have been made for the teacher in the sample lesson presented in Figure 1–1. Adopting a material framework typically means becoming familiar with the teacher's manual for a particular reading program and following its directions quite closely. Many new teachers begin with a material framework because they have little time to develop or modify their own plans for instruction. Their willingness to accept the decisions of a teacher's manual does not suggest the absence of careful evaluation or conscious decision making. Rather, the guidelines provided by a set of materials provide the basis for the specific instructional decisions of teachers following a material framework.

> **material framework:** An instructional framework used to teach reading; based on a published set of materials and lesson-planning information.

Other teachers make instructional decisions primarily from a **method framework,** which hinges on the procedural steps of one or more instructional methods and the options that may be selected at each step. Once a method framework has been established, it becomes the basis for instruction across a wide variety of situations. Figure 1–2 presents an example of one type of method framework, a **directed reading-thinking activity (DRTA).**

> **method framework:** An instructional framework used to teach reading; based on procedural steps for teaching and options for completing each step.

A method framework provides a general description of the steps to follow during instruction and a general indication of the activities that might be used at each step. A method framework, however, is not usually tied to a specific set of materials; instead, it may be used with almost any set of materials, from selections found in published reading programs to selections written by teachers or provided by students. If the teaching procedures suggested by particular materials differ from a teacher's preferred method, then the teacher following

> **directed reading-thinking activity (DRTA):** A method framework used to assist students in predicting outcomes and drawing conclusions; involves predicting, reading, and proving.

FIGURE 1–1

A partial lesson plan from a published set of materials used to teach reading

---

**Unit 15**    How the Forest Grew    **Pages 208–217**      **Read**

## Guided Reading
**Pages 209–213**

### 1. Purpose Setting/Silent Reading

Have students read to the end of page 213. Tell them to read to find out about the first two stages of growth of a forest.

### 2. Guiding Comprehension

1. What are the first two stages of growth of a forest on land that has been cleared? . . . *(The first stage consists of sun-loving trees, like the white pine. In the second stage, the pines are succeeded by trees that like shade, such as ash, red oak, red maple, and tulip trees.)* [Developing Key Concepts—Literal]

2. Where did the seedlings that started the forest come from? . . . *(from seeds that the wind blew and birds dropped)* **Page 209** [Noting Details—Literal]

3. How did the animal life change with the different stages of the forest? . . . *(In the first stage, as the white pines grew, brush-dwelling birds moved onto the land, replacing the field dwellers that had been living there. Weasels and foxes made their homes in the thickets. In the second stage, when new trees succeeded the pines, meadow mice were replaced by white-footed mice; deer, squirrels, and chipmunks came to the land; cardinals, redstarts, and other birds perched in the trees.)* **Pages 210, 213** [Developing Key Concepts—Literal]

### 3. Thinking and Predicting

What kinds of trees do you think will succeed the ash, red oak, red maple, and tulip trees—trees that need a little shade or trees that need a lot of shade? . . . Why?

## Guided Reading
**Pages 214–216**

### 1. Purpose Setting/Silent Reading

Tell students to read the rest of the article to find out if their predictions are correct.

### 2. Guiding Comprehension

1. Were your predictions correct? . . . What kinds of trees succeeded the ash, red oak, red maple, and tulip trees? . . . *(trees that need deep shade—beeches and sugar maples)* **Page 214** [Developing Key Concepts—Literal]

2. How does decaying matter in the forest help trees to grow? . . . *(Decayed leaves and branches make humus. Bacteria, worms, and fungi turn humus into soil from which trees get food and water.)* **Page 214** [Cause–Effect—Inferential]

3. What is the understory? . . . *(the layer of smaller trees growing below the older trees)* **Page 214** [Noting Details—Literal]

4. Describe the forest in its final stage. . . . *(Beeches and sugar maples are kings of the forest. The forest is home to many wild animals and birds.)* **Page 215** [Summarizing]

15

**Source:** From *Houghton Mifflin Reading Flights* teacher's manual, p. 282 by William K. Durr et al. Copyright © 1989. Reprinted by permission of Houghton Mifflin Company.

FIGURE 1–2

A procedural outline for a directed reading-thinking activity   DRTA

1. *Predicting.* During this first step ask students what they expect to find when they read. At the beginning ask questions like, What will a story with this title be about? Why? Later in a story ask questions like, What do you think will happen next? Why? Each student should form a prediction and be able to support it.
2. *Reading.* During this second step ask students to read up to a specified point in the story and check their predictions. They may read either orally or silently. For example, tell students to read up to the end of a certain page and see whether their guesses were correct.
3. *Proving.* During this third step ask students to evaluate their predictions within the context of a discussion. Ask questions like, Was your guess correct? Why or why not? At the end of the discussion begin the procedural cycle again, and have students predict what will take place in the next portion of the story. Continue in a similar fashion until students finish reading the story.

a method framework would substitute the preferred method and appropriate activities.

Often teachers employ several different method frameworks, using each for different instructional purposes. For example, a particular method or set of methods might be preferred for teaching decoding skills; another combination might be preferred for teaching study skills. Some of the more frequently used method frameworks include directed reading activities, language experience activities, and activities associated with deductive and inductive instruction. These and other common method frameworks are presented in chapter 2.

A **comprehension framework** is the most powerful and flexible of the three frameworks discussed here; it is what most effective teachers strive toward. A comprehension framework is more abstract than either a material or method framework. It is based on an understanding of reading comprehension, and answers these questions: What are the components of the reading process? How do we read? and How does reading ability develop? Answers to these questions influence many instructional decisions—essentially why, what, and how we teach—and necessitate knowledge of a wide range of materials and methods. Experienced, effective teachers often arrive at their comprehension framework after being exposed to many materials and methods and drawing their own conclusions about how reading takes place and develops. Thus, a comprehension framework incorporates the knowledge base of a material and/ or a method framework.

comprehension framework: Beliefs about the components of reading comprehension, the way in which people read, and the way in which reading ability develops.

Comprehension frameworks are used in two major ways: first, to select appropriate materials and methods and second, to adapt methods and materials that are inconsistent with beliefs about reading comprehension. Thus, a teacher with a comprehension framework might adapt the lesson plans and activities in a set of materials and might select several different methods to teach a reading lesson. Each choice or decision would be deliberate and reasoned and would be consistent with that teacher's explanation of how a person reads and how reading ability develops.

Given the relative difficulty and complexity of developing a comprehension framework, why should teachers not be content with either a material or a method framework? Teaching from a comprehension framework is preferable for at least five important reasons.

1. A comprehension framework provides a clear sense of direction, especially as you decide how and when to modify instructional resources. All teachers adapt and supplement available instructional materials, and a comprehension framework guides the necessary decision making.
2. A comprehension framework provides more strategies for meeting individual needs. Within material or method frameworks individual needs are met by altering the pace of instruction and/or the amount of practice. Within a comprehension framework individual needs can also be met by altering instructional materials, methods, and even what is taught.
3. A comprehension framework helps explain why certain decisions are made during reading instruction, whereas frameworks based on materials or methods simply tell teachers what to do. Knowing why something is being done allows a teacher to alter instruction for particular students more effectively and to better evaluate the success of an instructional activity.
4. Comprehension frameworks can be used in many more situations than can frameworks based on materials or instructional methods. For example, specific material and method frameworks are helpful only if the teacher-preferred methods or materials are those favored by the school district in which they are to be used. A comprehension framework can be used in any instructional situation.
5. Comprehension frameworks offer more flexibility in instructional decision making than do either material or method frameworks. The illustration in Figure 1–3 indicates that teachers making decisions based on comprehension frameworks choose from the full range of methods and materials. Teachers with method frameworks are somewhat less flexible but are able to choose any materials that are appropriate to their chosen method(s). However, teachers with material frameworks are completely constrained by their chosen instructional materials.

Developing a comprehension framework is more difficult than developing either a material or a method framework, partly because of the broad knowledge base required. However, such wide-ranging knowledge will certainly make you a more effective teacher, and knowing in advance that you will probably develop a comprehension framework as you teach will facilitate that development. Knowing where you are going always makes the journey shorter and easier. Thus, learning about reading instruction from the perspective of a comprehension framework should make your learning process more effective and efficient.

FIGURE 1–3
An illustration of the inclusiveness of a comprehension framework

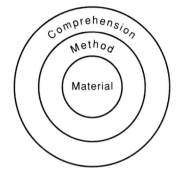

## Decision Making and the Modification of Frameworks

Instructional frameworks are not static devices; instead, they are modified as knowledge about materials, methods, and the reading process develops and changes. Teachers continually modify their frameworks according to what does and also what does not help children learn to read. In addition, with adequate knowledge of the reading process, goals, and students, teachers can shift from one framework to another or can use one framework predominantly, supplementing it with aspects of one or both of the other frameworks. Modification of instructional frameworks usually follows a cyclical routine, as described here and illustrated in Figure 1–4.

Step 1. Teachers use frameworks to help them make instructional decisions. Teachers with a material framework generally follow the directions in a teacher's manual. Teachers with a method framework choose instructional activities for the various steps in a procedural outline. Teachers with a comprehension framework select materials and methods consistent with their beliefs about how reading occurs and develops.

FIGURE 1–4
An illustration of the framework modification cycle

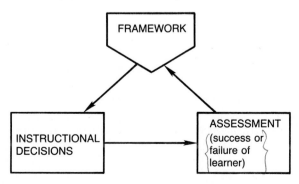

**Step 2.** Teachers evaluate the appropriateness of their instructional decisions. Successful activities are apparent in student performance, and both teachers and students share a feeling of accomplishment.

**Step 3.** Teachers modify their frameworks based on the success or failure of instructional decisions. Teachers with a material or method framework tend to repeat successful activities the next time that lesson is taught; unsuccessful activities are dropped or modified. Teachers with a comprehension framework find support for their beliefs in successful activities; unsuccessful lessons tend to alter beliefs about how reading occurs and develops.

**Step 4.** These confirmed or modified frameworks are used to make additional decisions, and the process repeats itself.

Figure 1–4 emphasizes the sequence of these steps. Assessment does not lead directly to instructional decisions. Instead, decisions are made by "filtering" the results of assessment through the controlling framework.

The decision-making process described here is similar to the process used by researchers or scientists. Just as researchers use a theory to make predictions, so teachers of reading use a framework to make instructional decisions. And as researchers test their predictions in an experiment, so teachers evaluate the appropriateness of their instructional decisions. Finally, just as researchers modify their theories based on the results of their experiments, so teachers modify their frameworks based on the results of classroom lessons. Thus, although teachers are not true scientific researchers, they are involved in decision-making processes that share many similarities.

Frameworks, then, are central to the decisions you will make as a teacher of reading. They will reduce complexity, allow you to make decisions quickly, and most importantly, help you meet the challenges encountered in reading instruction. As you learn about ways to teach reading effectively, you will define and clarify your own framework, which will guide your teaching decisions.

## WHAT ARE THE REWARDS?

Classroom teaching, particularly the teaching of reading, is not only challenging; it is also immensely rewarding. You will play a central role in helping children gain access to the pleasure and power of reading and thus will have a significant impact on their lives. Helping your students acquire needed skills and knowledge to develop into productive adults provides a feeling of reward and accomplishment that is rare in other professions. Perhaps it can best be described in the actual experiences of two students, whose teachers helped them enter the world of readers.

Helping children grow to love reading and books is a truly rewarding experience.

## Introducing Pat to Reading

Pat entered Mr. Nelson's first-grade class, eager to learn how to read. Her parents often read to her, and she knew that books had lots of interesting things in them. Pat was a gentle child, a little shy around other students. Although she knew some of the children in her class, many were strangers. Mr. Nelson knew that other children in his classroom were much like Pat, and he gave them lots of opportunities to get to know each other.

Mr. Nelson made a number of informal observations about Pat during her first week at school. She had very mature oral language abilities, as well as an extensive oral vocabulary. She explained her ideas clearly and asked interesting questions. She could identify most letters by name and enjoyed word games and rhyming activities. Mr. Nelson believed that Pat's reading-related skills were average to above average for her grade level, and he looked forward to helping her become a reader.

As the days and weeks went by, Mr. Nelson kept track of Pat's progress. She progressed normally through his reading program and looked forward to reading the short selections that were included. She particularly liked reading the short books that Mr. Nelson encouraged students to read on their own. At parent conference time Mr. Nelson found out that Pat proudly read words out loud, such as signs along the road, and Pat's parents were pleased with her progress. They had continued to read stories to Pat after she entered school, adding numerous books to her personal library.

By the end of the school year, Pat was independently reading books appropriate for her age level. Mr. Nelson was happy with her progress and knew that it would continue throughout her school experience. He looked back at Pat's reading ability when she entered his class and knew that he had been instrumental in teaching her both to read and to enjoy reading. He would miss Pat and the other students in his class, but he looked forward to the students that he would teach the next year. When he thought of the advantages that Pat's reading ability would provide for her, Mr. Nelson was happy with his teaching decisions.

## Making Jerry a Reader

Jerry was a third grader in Ms. Dye's room. He was a precocious youngster, the son of a university professor in a midwestern college community. Jerry was a very verbal child who knew a great deal about the world and communicated effectively orally. Jerry was having a hard time, though, keeping up with his peers in reading. On a **standardized, norm-referenced test** he scored in the bottom quarter of his class in word recognition, sentence comprehension, and story comprehension. Jerry was having trouble with almost all of the skills taught in his first two years of formal reading instruction and was having extreme difficulty with spelling and writing. He could spell only a small set of words correctly and never wrote more than a few sentences; writing was a struggle.

**standardized, norm-referenced test:** A published test with specific directions and procedures that bases scoring on a comparison to a peer group.

Jerry considered both reading and writing to be unimportant in his life. He was far more interested in things like fishing, hiking, dirt bikes, and sports. Consequently, during reading lessons Jerry was not attentive. Ms. Dye had to call on him often to keep him focused on the learning task. Jerry's answers were most often incorrect, but that fact did not distress him at all.

Because Ms. Dye was concerned about Jerry, she asked his parents to come for a conference to discuss the situation. Jerry's parents were equally concerned but noted that Jerry had always seemed more interested in the outdoors than in books. The conference resulted in a sharing of information but produced no specific solutions.

Ms. Dye's greatest concern was that Jerry would get so far behind in reading achievement that he would never reach his potential and, as he fell further and further behind, would eventually lose interest in school. Ms. Dye decided to use high-interest books to build Jerry's awareness that books could be sources of joy and important information.

Every day, immediately after lunch, Ms. Dye read aloud to the students in her room for about 20 minutes. She always selected quality literature that she thought would catch the students' interest and be meaningful. As she was finishing *Charlotte's Web,* she was amazed to see that Jerry had tears in his eyes, as did several other students in the class. They had obviously been touched by Charlotte's death.

Immediately after this session Ms. Dye took Jerry aside and asked whether he wanted to take the book home and share it with his parents. He seemed very interested in this possibility. Ms. Dye even suggested that Jerry's dad might reread the story aloud so that he could enjoy it, too. After school Ms. Dye called Jerry's home, explained what had happened, and suggested that Jerry's dad read a chapter aloud each night before Jerry went to bed. If this experience proved successful, she suggested that Jerry and his parents make regular trips to the city library for more books. She promised to provide a list of books that might be interesting for Jerry.

Meanwhile, at school Ms. Dye put Jerry in touch with books about fishing and backpacking and made time for him to browse through these books every day. Jerry very much enjoyed these new tasks, and his attention even improved in formal reading lessons. Within two weeks Jerry's parents called Ms. Dye to say that Jerry had brought books home from the library and was reading them with his dad. They commented on Jerry's new interest in reading and asked for a new list of titles to get from the library. Ms. Dye complied and told of Jerry's new interest at school also. Both teacher and parents agreed to maintain regular communication about Jerry's reading interests and performance.

By the end of the year Jerry was "hooked on books" and was reading as well as Ms. Dye's average third graders. Ms. Dye's only remaining concern was that Jerry's interests were very narrow, centered almost entirely on fishing and backpacking. However, she anticipated that with sufficient guidance and encouragement, this narrow focus could easily be expanded, now that Jerry was interested in reading.

## COMMENTS FROM THE CLASSROOM ■

### Emily Dodson

I'm a second-grade teacher at Tecumseh Elementary School, and my colleagues and I will be sharing comments about how our instructional frameworks influence our instructional decisions. Our comments will appear at the end of each chapter and will generally relate the topic of the chapter to our own classroom experiences.

The 25 students in my classroom range in ability and motivation. Some are reading well above their grade level in terms of standardized test scores. In fact, several students were reading well before entering school. Others are still struggling and are not yet considered readers. The majority are average second-grade students.

My students' home backgrounds also vary. Some come from middle and upper class backgrounds with parents that value schooling and reading, but other students from middle and upper income homes receive little parental support for literacy activities. There are also students who come from low socioeconomic backgrounds. Those students generally have little literacy experience and have few books or magazines in their homes. Some of their parents are nonreaders.

My comprehension framework, along with a knowledge of varied methods and materials, allows me to look at student progress and decide which blend of activities and methods is optimal for individual or small groups of students. It also allows me to modify my instruction effectively. I don't just repeat lesson plans each year unless I want to or think they're in the best interests of my students. I view teaching as a continuing challenge with rewards that give me personal satisfaction and allow me to continue to grow as a professional. I sure don't get bored!

**MAJOR POINTS**

■ Reading ability is important. It is a key factor in the job opportunities and quality of life for each one of us.

■ Reading is not a mechanical skill but is an interactive, problem-solving process. From this perspective the importance of reading and the teaching of reading will not become obsolete.

■ The teacher is an ongoing decision maker in the classroom, using observational skills to gather information with which to guide instruction.

■ A teacher's definition and perception of reading—that is, the framework of reading—determine how reading will be taught.

■ Teaching reading to children in the elementary grades is one of the most rewarding tasks anyone can perform. Teachers of reading have the potential to help young children achieve one of their most important and exciting accomplishments.

segmentchapterreadingsegment=Chapter 1 ■ The Problem, the Challenge, the Rewards     23

1. Specify as completely as possible your view of how people read. What factors do you think influence how effectively a reader translates abstract symbols into meaningful communication? How might your views influence your teaching? What aspects of reading would you emphasize in an instructional program?

2. Different teachers, using the same information about their students (e.g., test scores or observations), often arrive at different instructional decisions. How would you explain such differences?

3. Interview at least two teachers and two parents. Ask them (a) what they think reading is and (b) how important they think reading is now and will be in the future. Ask the teachers how their beliefs about reading and its importance influence their instructional decisions. Ask the parents what they would emphasize if they were teaching reading. What implications do any similarities or differences have for students and for teachers?

**MAKING INSTRUCTIONAL DECISIONS**

**FURTHER READING**

Aaron, I. E., Chall, J. S., Durkin, D., Goodman, K., & Strickland, D. (1990). The past, present, and future of literacy education: Comments from a panel of distinguished educators. Part I. *The Reading Teacher, 43,* 302–311.

Presents a discussion of trends in literacy and literacy education from various perspectives. Continues the discussion in *The Reading Teacher, 43,* 370–381.

Carroll, J. B. (1986). The nature of the reading process. In H. Singer & R. Ruddell (Eds.), *Theoretical models and processes of reading* (3rd ed., pp. 25–34). Newark, DE: International Reading Association.

Discusses the nature of reading. Points out that disagreement centers not on what is involved in reading, but on the order of the steps that are involved.

Diehl, W. A., & Mikulecky, L. (1980). The nature of reading at work. *Journal of Reading, 24,* 221–227.

Discusses reading demands in different jobs. Points out how these differ from what is expected in school.

Guthrie, J. T. (1983). Where reading is not reading. *Journal of Reading, 26,* 382–384.

Case studies of reading in 14 occupational settings.

Guthrie, J. T. (1986) Worldwide sources for information about primary education. *The Reading Teacher, 39,* 572–575.

Lists worldwide sources that present issues in primary education. Acquiring literacy is a key element discussed on an international basis.

**REFERENCES**

Dechant, E. (1982). *Improving the teaching of reading* (3rd ed.). Englewood Cliffs, NJ: Prentice Hall.

Fingeret, A. (1983). A new perspective on independence and illiterate adults. *Adult Education Quarterly, 33,* 133–146.

Flesch, R. (1955). *Why Johnny can't read.* New York: Harper & Brothers.

Flesch, R. (1981). *Why Johnny still can't read.* New York: Harper & Row.

Goodman, K. S. (1976). Reading: a psycholinguistic guessing game. In H. Singer & R. Ruddell (Eds.), *Theoretical models and processes of reading* (2nd ed., pp. 497–508). Newark, DE: International Reading Association.

Harste, J. C. (1990). Jerry Harste speaks on reading and writing. *The Reading Teacher, 43,* 316–318.

Heath, S. B. (1980). The functions and uses of literacy. *Journal of Communication, 30,* 123–133.

Miller, P. (1982). Reading demands in a high-technology industry. *Journal of Reading, 26,* 109–115.

Rosenblatt, L. M. (1985). The literary transaction: Evocation and response. *Theory into Practice, 21,* 268–277.

Rosenblatt, L. M. (1988). *Writing and reading: The transactional theory* (Tech. Rep. No. 416). Urbana, IL: Center for the Study of Reading.

Rumelhart, D. (1986). In H. Singer & R. Ruddell (Eds.), *Theoretical models and processes of reading* (3rd ed., pp. 722–750). Newark, DE: International Reading Association.

Samuels, S. J., & Kamil, M. L. (1984). Models of the reading process. In P. D. Pearson (Ed.), *Handbook of reading research* (pp. 185–224). New York: Longman.

Shanahan, T. (1990). Reading and writing together: What does it really mean? In T. Shanahan (Ed.), *Reading and writing together: New perspectives for the classroom* (pp. 1–18). Norwood, MA: Christopher-Gordon.

Strang, R., McCullough, C., & Traxler, A. (1961). *The improvement of reading* (3rd ed.). New York: McGraw-Hill.

# Using Material and Method Frameworks to Teach Reading

争論.辯論

- Material Frameworks
- The Controversy Surrounding Published Reading Programs
- Adapting a Published Reading Program to Teach Reading
- Method Frameworks: Procedural Routines for Instruction
- Using Individualized Reading, Cooperative Learning, and Other Method Frameworks

*Anne was curled up Turk-fashion on the hearthrug, gazing into that joyous glow where the sunshine of a hundred summers was being distilled from the maple cordwood. She had been reading, but her book had slipped to the floor, and now she was dreaming, with a smile on her parted lips.*

L. M. Montgomery, *Anne of Green Gables* (Toronto, Canada: McClelland & Stewart-Bantam, 1908), p. 238.

熱望的

One of the joys of teaching is helping youngsters develop into avid readers who devour books as Anne of Green Gables did. But classrooms are such complex and busy environments. How can teachers find the time and resources to develop such eager readers? This chapter prepares you to use both material and method frameworks in that endeavor. However, you must keep in mind that these frameworks are merely an instructional means to an end; they are not the end itself.                           努力

Chapter 2 includes information that will help you answer questions like these:

1. What are the distinguishing features of a published reading program?
2. What are the advantages and disadvantages of using a published program to teach reading?
3. How can a published reading program be adapted for use in a classroom?
4. What are the distinguishing features of a method framework?
5. How can different method frameworks be used to teach reading?

## KEY CONCEPTS
減除.    , 推論的,

cooperative learning groups
deductive instruction
directed reading activity
individualized reading
inductive instruction
        歸納的. 誘導的

language experience stories
material framework  骨架. 組織
method framework
published reading program

## MATERIAL FRAMEWORKS

material framework: An instructional framework used to teach reading; contains a published set of materials and lesson planning information.

published reading program: A comprehensive graded set of materials used to teach reading in grades K–6 or K–8.

The term **material framework** refers to a published set of instructional materials (that contains lesson planning information). In reading instruction the most common material framework is a **published reading program**. Such programs are comprehensive published sets of graded materials used to teach reading in kindergarten through Grades 6 or 8. They are sometimes referred to as basal reading programs, basal readers, or simply basals. According to some estimates, as many as 98 percent of elementary school classrooms have at least one published reading program available (Flood & Lapp, 1986). Many teachers use a published reading program in conjunction with method frameworks and a comprehension framework. Too frequently, the use of a published reading program is the only instructional framework used to guide reading instruction (Leu, 1986; Shannon, 1986).

Published reading programs reduce the complexity of classroom decisions in at least two ways. First, they systematically organize the reading materials that students and teachers will use. Second, they provide teachers with comprehensive directions for using those materials to teach reading. Published reading programs have been used to teach reading since 1836, when

McGuffey's readers first appeared in the United States. Even though other materials had been used earlier, the McGuffey series was the first comprehensive and graded set of materials used to teach reading in Grades 1 through 6 (Bohning, 1986). An example of a lesson from that early program can be seen in Figure 2–1. Compare it to a lesson in one of today's published reading programs, as seen in Figure 2–4 later in this chapter.

FIGURE 2–1
A first-grade lesson from one of McGuffey's readers

**LESSON XXVI.**

| fȧll | īçe | skātes | erȳ |
| wĭth | hăd | stōne | dĭd |

ȧ    ç    sk

The boys are on the ice with their skates.

There is a stone on the ice. One boy did not see it, and has had a fall.

But he is a brave boy, and will not cry.

**Source:** From *McGuffey's Eclectic Primer, Revised Edition* (New York: American Book Company, 1909), p. 31.

Published reading programs today are developed by numerous large publishing houses, including Economy Book Company; Silver Burdett and Ginn; Harcourt Brace Jovanovich; Harper & Row; D. C. Heath; Holt, Rinehart and Winston; Houghton Mifflin; Macmillan; Open Court; Riverside; and Scott, Foresman. Development of a published reading program is usually directed by a senior author who is a respected figure in reading education. Nonetheless, the program is typically referred to by the publisher's name. A major revision in any given program usually occurs every five to six years, coinciding with state adoptions in Texas and California, the two largest states that review published reading programs for their schools.

## Components

It is often mistakenly thought that a published reading program contains all of the materials necessary to teach reading in the elementary grades. If we looked at the comprehensive array of materials available in today's programs, we probably would not find that perception surprising. A published reading program usually includes the following components:

- *Teacher's manual.* The teacher's manual contains an extensive and precise set of directions to guide instruction. The manual usually includes the student material, along with discussion questions and correct answers. An example of one lesson in a teacher's manual can be seen in Figure 2–4.
- *Student's books.* These books contain the stories, articles, and other selections used in the program. Several graded books are common in each of the primary grades (first through third), whereas a single book is typical in each Grades 4–8.
- *Student workbooks.* These workbooks contain practice activities for the skills taught in the program.
- *Teacher's edition of the workbook.* This version includes an exact copy of the student workbook, along with additional directions and correct answers.
- *Tests.* Several types of assessment instruments may be available, including placement tests for making entry-level decisions at the beginning of the year and proficiency tests for assessing progress.
- *Duplicating and copying masters.* These masters contain additional practice activities like those in the student workbooks.
- *Picture and word cards.* Such cards are often used to teach decoding and vocabulary knowledge in the primary grades.
- *Pocket charts.* Pocket charts are sometimes included to hold and display picture and word cards during instruction.
- *Additional supplementary materials.* Programs often make additional materials available, such as read-along audio tapes, activity kits, language skills kits, filmstrips, and other ancillary materials.

Despite the comprehensive nature of the materials available in any single reading program, teachers are encouraged to modify published reading programs to best meet the unique needs of their students (Baumann, 1984; Good-

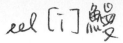

Published reading programs often include a variety of supplementary materials, such as sentence strips and charts.

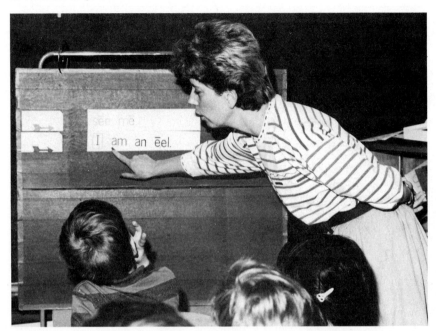

man, Freeman, Murphy, & Shannon, 1988). You will find other reasons, also, to modify a reading program: (1) to be more consistent with your personal beliefs about reading, (2) to raise student interest levels, (3) to integrate reading instruction with other subject areas, and (4) to include instructional activities known to be successful.

## Organization

**Levels.** Published reading programs are organized according to levels of difficulty, traditionally designated by grade levels. In kindergarten most children receive emergent literacy/readiness materials. First-grade students then typically experience five different levels of materials: three preprimers (PP), a primer (P), and a first reader. In second and third grades most students use a first semester reader and a second semester reader, identified by a numbering system such as 2.1 or 2–1, and so on. Finally, students in fourth through eighth grades generally read from a single level of materials. Recently, publishers have begun to replace grade-level designations with sequentially ordered numbers or letters. You can see both labeling systems in Figure 2–2.

**Skills.** Published reading programs are also organized around a set of reading skills developed in a particular sequence. The range of skills taught in any one program is referred to as the program's **scope;** the order in which skills are

scope: The range of skills taught in a traditional published reading program.

FIGURE 2–2
Two examples of grade-level equivalency tables

(a)

| K | Rise and Shine | Level K |
|---|---|---|
| Grade 1 | Away We Go Part A | Level 1A |
| | Away We Go Part B | Level 1B |
| | Taking Off | Level 2A |
| | Going Up | Level 2B |
| | On Our Own | Level 2C |
| | Hang OnTo Your Hats | Level 3 |
| | Kick Up Your Heels | Level 4 |
| Grade 2 | Rainbow Shower | Level 5 |
| | Crystal Kingdom | Level 6 |
| Grade 3 | Hidden Wonders | Level 7 |
| | Golden Secrets | Level 8 |
| Grade 4 | Sea Treasures | Level 9 |
| Grade 5 | Sky Climbers | Level 10 |
| Grade 6 | StarFlight | Level 11 |
| Grade 7 | Sun Spray | Level 12 |
| Grade 8 | Moon Canyon | Level 13 |

(a)

### HBJ BOOKMARK READING PROGRAM

#### Level-to-Grade Correspondences

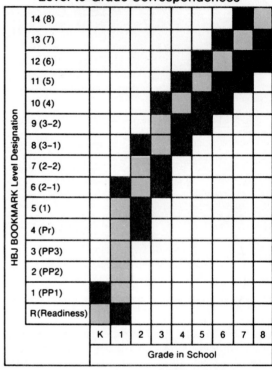

HBJ BOOKMARK Level Designation: 14 (8), 13 (7), 12 (6), 11 (5), 10 (4), 9 (3–2), 8 (3–1), 7 (2–2), 6 (2–1), 5 (1), 4 (Pr), 3 (PP3), 2 (PP2), 1 (PP1), R(Readiness)

Grade in School: K, 1, 2, 3, 4, 5, 6, 7, 8

☐ Levels used by a majority of students at each grade  ■ Levels used by some students at each grade

**Note:** The red blocks indicate the HBJ BOOKMARK materials used by a majority of children in each grade. However, children who are using materials from the levels marked red or gray for their grades are well within the normal progress range.

(b)

introduced is referred to as its **sequence**. Figure 2–3 shows a portion of a scope and sequence chart from one published reading program.

     The sequencing of skills may facilitate instruction, because students are able to build on what they already know. However, it also creates certain problems. At early levels the words in reading selections are often limited to vocabulary that has been previously taught. Consequently, selections may feature language that is different from the language young children use. And as a result, precisely because a sequenced set of skills has been incorporated into the reading program, stories may be more difficult for young readers to understand (Beck, Omanson, & McKeown, 1982).

     As an example, let's look at the following sentence from a first-grade reader (*Sun and Shadow,* 1985, p. 28):

> It is night. A man is very sick. The man comes here in a fast car.

The writers of this program chose to use the word *here* instead of *hospital* and *a fast car* instead of *ambulance*. Those decisions were made because the program had not yet taught students to recognize the words *hospital* and *ambulance*. We can see that children must infer the real meanings of these supposedly easier words, which have actually made the passage harder to understand.

## Teacher's Manuals

All published reading programs provide extensive lesson planning information in their teacher's manuals. Several structural characteristics are common to such manuals; for example, they contain at least two sections—an introduction and the teaching plans for each reading selection.

**The Introduction.** The first section of most manuals provides the teacher with an introduction to the reading program. The authors and their consultants are listed to provide a sense of the expertise that went into the program's development. In addition, a grade-level equivalency table is often included to help put each book into a developmental perspective. Frequently, the publisher also gives a scope and sequence chart in the first section. The complete range of materials used in the program is listed here—student books, student workbooks, a teacher's manual, duplicating and copying masters, test packets, and so on. And finally, the introductory section contains an overview describing the program: its general goals, the framework or philosophy behind the program, the structure of the teaching plans, and a suggested pace for movement through the materials.

**Teaching Plans.** The second section of most teacher's manuals contains teaching plans for each reading selection. To help you understand the organization of this second section, an example of a teaching plan for a first-grade lesson is included in Figure 2–4. You should refer to this example throughout the following discussion.

sequence: The order of skills taught in a traditional published reading program.

FIGURE 2–3
An example of a scope and sequence chart

## SCOPE AND SEQUENCE

| LEVEL 14 / PHONICS SKILLS | Teacher's Edition | Teaching Master | Workbook | Practice Master | Tested |
|---|---|---|---|---|---|
| Selection Vocabulary | | | 2, 5, 8, 12, 16, 19, 21, 26, 29, 32, 37, 41, 45, 47, 52, 55, 58, 62, 65, 68, 70, 75, 78, 81, 86, 89, 93, 95, 100, 103, 106, 110, 113, 116, 118, 123, 127, 130, 133, 136, 139, 141 | | • |
| **COMPREHENSION SKILLS** | | | | | |
| Selection Comprehension | | | 1, 4, 7, 11, 15, 18, 25, 28, 31, 36, 40, 44, 51, 54, 57, 61, 64, 67, 74, 77, 80, 85, 88, 92, 99, 102, 105, 109, 112, 115, 122, 126, 129, 132, 135, 138 | | |
| Cause and Effect | 71, 112, 128, 177 | 1, 8 | 3, 23 | 7 | • |
| Sequence | 110, 148, 163, 177 | 6, 13 | 9 | 13 | • |
| Referents | 162, 225, 265, 315 | 15, 20 | 20, 48 | 24 | • |
| Context Clues | 245, 281, 301, 316, 513, 518-520, 547, 562, 578 | 21, 27, 49, 55 | 33, 82, 97 | 31, 57, 58, 62 | • |
| Main Idea | 656, 700, 762, 853 | 66, 72 | 111, 142 | 83 | • |
| Stated Details | 800, 840 | 79, 84 | 134 | | |
| Supporting Generalizations | 91, 128, 176 | 5 | 22 | 8 | • |
| Inferred Sequence (Flashback) | 347 | | | 34 | |
| Identifying Unsupported Generalizations | 375, 415, 482, 577 | 35, 41 | 59, 96 | 52 | • |
| Inferred Cause and Effect | 533, 562, 624, 714 | 52, 58 | 87, 119 | 69 | • |
| Inferred Analogy | 784, 801, 840, 854 | 77, 80 | 131, 144 | 95 | • |
| Inferred Characterization | 839 | 83 | 140 | | |
| Author's Purpose | 228-230 | | | 21, 22 | |
| Figurative Language | 360, 400, 435, 450, 481, 515, 534, 565-567 | 33, 39, 45, 51 | 56, 76 | 49, 60, 64, 65 | • |
| Variations in Language | 699, 762, 801, 854 | 71, 76 | 117, 143 | 89 | • |

43

**Source:** From THE RIVERSIDE READING PROGRAM IN CONCERT by Leo Fay et al. Copyright © 1989. Reprinted by permission of Houghton Mifflin Company.

| COMPREHENSION SKILLS cont. | Teacher's Edition | Teaching Master | Workbook | Practice Master | Tested |
|---|---|---|---|---|---|
| Genre (Science Fiction) | 111, 148, 211 | 7, 14 | 10 | 16 | |
| Theme Mood | 163 | | | 15 | |
| Author's Purpose (Biased Language Persuasion) | 224, 265, 301, 316 | 19, 25 | 30, 49 | 30 | ● |
| Genre (Biography, Autobiography) | 414, 482, 498, 578 | 40, 46 | 66 | 53 | ● |
| Author's Point of View | 434, 498, 534, 578 | 43, 48 | 69 | 59 | ● |
| Story Setting, Story Plot | 515 | | | 56 | |
| Fiction and Nonfiction | 561, 624, 657, 715 | 57, 62 | 94, 120 | 72 | ● |
| Suspense, Foreshadowing | 641, 677, 700 | 63, 69 | 107 | 80 | |
| Suspense | 679-681 | | | 78, 79 | |
| Story Conflict and Resolution | 676, 745, 785, 853 | 68, 74 | 114 | 88 | ● |
| Punctuation Review | 90,128,163,177 | 4, 11 | 6, 24 | 14 | ● |
| **WORD STRUCTURE SKILLS** | | | | | |
| Prefixes *inter-, trans-, co-, post-, semi-* | 211 | | | 17 | |
| Prefixes *circum-, extra-, equi-, mal-* | 300, 361, 400, 451 | 29, 34 | 46, 71 | 43 | ● |
| Suffixes | 608, 643, 657, 715 | 59, 65 | 101 | 73 | ● |
| Suffixes *-ward, -ize, -some* | 762 | | | 84 | |
| **STUDY SKILLS** | | | | | |
| Title Page, Copyright Page, Table of Contents | 91 | | | 3 | |
| Following Written Directions | 399, 435, 498, 578 | 38, 44 | 63, 98 | 54 | ● |
| Footnotes | 497, 534, 562 | 47, 53 | 79 | 63 | |
| Bibliography | 546, 609, 624, 715 | 54, 60 | 90, 91, 121 | 70 | ● |
| City Maps | 112, 128 | 9 | | 9, 10 | |
| Road Maps | 127,163,225,316 | 10, 16 | 13, 14 | 19, 20 | ● |
| Signs, Symbols | 609 | | | 68 | |
| Tables | 623, 657, 660-663, 700 | 61, 67 | 104 | 76, 77, 81 | |
| Time Lines | 657 | | | 74 | |
| Thesaurus | 72, 91, 94-96, 177 | 2 | | 1, 5, 6 | ● |
| Dictionary Entries | 246, 281, 347, 451 | 22, 28 | 34, 35 | 32, 33 | ● |
| Library Card Catalog | 376, 415, 417-420, 435, 451 | 36, 42 | 60, 73 | 47, 48, 50, 51 | ● |

44

Increasingly, published reading series are organizing teaching plans around thematic units in children's literature. The opening paragraph of the teaching plan in Figure 2–4 tells us that the unit includes *Ira Sleeps Over,* as well as other literature selections that are consistent with the "Lights Out!" theme: *Who's Afraid of the Dark?; At Night,* and *Owl and Moon.*

Thematic units often contain suggestions for related learning activities that can provide meaningful and functional reading experiences. For example, on page 38 we can see the suggestions for conducting several read-aloud sessions with a different story related to the unit theme. In addition, there is a unit bibliography on page 39, suggestions for a bulletin board and a unit project on page 40, ideas for integrating the content of the reading selections into other subject areas which involve the children in several reading games and activities (p. 41), and possible approaches to meeting special and individual needs (pp. 42–43). Any of these suggestions can be used throughout this thematic unit.

You will find slight variations in the organization of individual lessons from series to series. Across all programs, however, you will notice that teaching plans are organized something like this:

I. Preview information for the teacher
 A. Summary of the selection
 B. New vocabulary
 C. Instructional objectives
 D. Instructional materials
II. Preparation activities
 A. Vocabulary development
 B. Skill development
 C. Defining a purpose for reading
III. Guided reading activities
 A. Reading the selection silently and then sometimes orally
 B. Discussion
IV. Skill development and practice activities
V. Extension activities

**preview information:** The first section of most teaching plans in a traditional published reading program.

**preparation section:** The second section of most teaching plans in a traditional published reading program; lists activities that prepare students to read the selection.

The first portion of most teaching plans contains **preview information** for the teacher. That information may include a summary of the story, a list of new vocabulary words that will appear in the story, a list of instructional objectives, and a list of necessary instructional materials. Such information allows teachers to understand the instructional purposes of a particular lesson and decide whether and how a lesson should be taught. It also permits teachers to collect and prepare the necessary materials for the lesson. The preview information for the lesson based on *Ira Sleeps Over* is shown in Figure 2–4 on pages 44 and 45. Note the summary of the selection, the list of new vocabulary words, miscellaneous additional information, the specific skill and language objectives of the lesson, and a list of the materials required for the various activities.

The second portion of most teaching plans is a **preparation section**. It

FIGURE 2–4
A lesson plan from a published reading program

UNIT 2

★ Lights Out!

**In This Unit**

. . . Bernard Waber introduces children to Ira, a young boy who likes to sleep with his teddy bear. Children will find out how Ira solves his conflict about whether to bring his teddy bear when "Ira Sleeps Over" at his friend Reggie's house. "Who's Afraid of the Dark?" Tina is, but not for long. Tina finds out that just about everyone is afraid of something. She learns how to deal with her fear of the dark when others share their secrets for dealing with fears. Then children read an article that describes the many ways in which people work and play in the city "At Night." In Arnold Lobel's tale of the "Owl and Moon," children will read about Owl, who believes his friend Moon follows him home.

**Introducing the Unit**

Have children open their books to page 43. Read the unit title, **Lights Out!**, to children, and explain that the phrase means bedtime or the time to turn the lights out and go to sleep. Call children's attention to the picture of the sleeping moon. *There are many things in this picture that tell you it is bedtime or time for lights out. What are they?* Help children identify these indications of bedtime in the picture: the moon and the stars in the sky, and the nightcap on the sleeping moon. *In this unit, you will read stories that tell about things that happen after dark. You will find out what happens to a teddy bear that belongs to Ira when Ira is invited to sleep over at his friend Reggie's house. Then you will meet a young girl who finds out how not to be afraid of the dark. You will read an article that tells about people who work at night. And you will find out some of the ways people have fun at night. Finally, you will read about Owl, who thinks that Moon is his friend when Moon follows him home and lights Owl's room all night.*

131

FIGURE 2–4
*continued*

## **L** iterature (Read-Aloud)

**Boris and the Monsters** by Elaine MacMann Willoughby and illustrated by Lynn Munsinger. Plan for three fifteen- to twenty-minute reading sessions.

### Summary

Every night after Boris goes to bed, he is tormented by monsters in his bedroom. No matter what his parents tell him, he cannot rid himself of them. One day Boris and his father go to buy a watchdog to protect him from the monsters. However, it turns out that the dog is more afraid of the dark than Boris, and Boris decides he will have to protect his pup from then on.

### Session 1

Ask children if they have ever imagined that there were monsters or the like in their bedroom at night. Explain that at night, things look different and shadows can look like things they are not. Then read the story up to page 16.

After reading, encourage children to discuss the story thus far. You may ask questions such as these:
1. Are there really monsters in Boris's room?
2. Can you think of an idea to help Boris fall asleep?
3. What would you do if you thought you saw monsters in your room?

Suggested Activities
1. Have children draw a picture of what they think a bedtime monster might look like.
2. Have children make a "No Monsters Allowed" sign that Boris can put up.

### Session 2

Before reading, encourage children to pay attention to how Boris overcomes his fear of monsters. Then read the rest of the story.

After reading, ask the following questions:
1. Why does Boris decide to get a dog?
2. Is Ivan afraid of the monsters?
3. Do you think the monsters will bother Boris anymore?

Suggested Activities
1. Have children draw a picture of a pet that could protect them.
2. Have children pretend they are Boris and have them write his friend a letter telling him all about Ivan.

### Session 3

Before reading, tell children to think about how they would feel if they were Boris. Then read the story.

After reading, discuss the story with children using the following questions:
1. When was Boris the most afraid?
2. Did you ever sleep with a nightlight on in your room? Do you think that a nightlight might have helped Boris? Why or why not?
3. Do you think that Boris's parents believed he saw monsters in his room? What do you think your parents would do if you told them there were monsters in your room at night?

Suggested Activities
1. Ask children to draw a picture of their pet or pets. If they don't have a pet, have them draw a picture of one they would like to have.
2. Have children suggest what the ending to the story might have been if Ivan had not been afraid. Encourage children to give as many endings as they can think of.

## Read Alone

Bang, Molly. **Ten, Nine, Eight**. Greenwillow, 1983. A countdown to bedtime as a little girl goes through the ritual that ends in warm, cozy sleep.

Richter, Mischa. **To Bed, to Bed!** Prentice-Hall, 1981. An almost wordless picture book. When the prince is told to go to bed, he finds ways to dilly-dally. Easy.

Schwerin, Doris. **The Tomorrow Book**. Pantheon, 1984. A child's night and anticipation of the next day.

## Read Together

Berenstain, Stan and Jan. **Berenstain Bears in the Dark**. Random House, 1982. Big Brother tries to scare Little Sister and later scares himself.

Bright, Robert. **Georgie**. Doubleday, 1959. Georgie the ghost decides he must move away from the Whittakers and find another house to haunt.

Brown, Margaret Wise. **A Child's Good-night Book**. Young Scott, 1950. A variety of topics to bring sleep to little children.

————. **Goodnight Moon**. Harper, 1947. In rhyme. A small rabbit says goodnight to the things in his room as it grows dark.

De Regniers, Beatrice Schenk. **Laura's Story**. Atheneum, 1979. A mother asks her daughter to tell her a story.

Hurd, Edith Thacher. **The Quiet Evening**. Greenwillow, 1978. Helps a child relax by focusing on a quiet place and winding down at the day's end.

Merriam, Eve. **Good Night to Annie**. Four Winds, 1980. An alphabet exercise book showing plants and animals at bedtime.

Moeri, Louise. **How the Rabbit Stole the Moon**. Houghton, 1977. A rabbit steals a piece of the sun to make the moon and stars.

North, Sterling. **Young Thomas Edison**. Houghton, 1958. Illustrated biography of the great American inventor.

Plath, Sylvia. **The Bed Book**. Harper, 1976. A delightful book of verse about beds that come in all shapes and sizes.

Russo, Susan, comp. **The Moon's the North Wind's Cooky**. Lothrop, 1979. A collection of poems about the child's experience of night.

Ryan, Chelo Duran. **Hildild's Night**. Macmillan, 1971. A woman tries to capture the night and put it into a bag.

Selsam, Millicent. **Night Animals**. Four Winds, 1980. A good introduction to animals that are active at night.

Showers, Paul. **Sleep Is for Everyone**. Crowell, 1974. How people and animals of different ages need different amounts of sleep.

## Audiovisual Resources

**Films/Videocassettes**
**Feelings/A Series**. Anger, sadness, loneliness, happiness, and fear are explored in animated sequences designed to help us understand our feelings. Churchill. Six films. Running time: 9 min. ea.

**The Owl and the Pussycat**. An original musical score enhances an animated version of the classic poem by Edward Lear. CRM/McGraw-Hill. Running time: 6 min.

**Paddington Bear—Series I and II**. The amusing adventures of the endearing toy bear who has a label around his neck reading "Please Look After This Bear." Filmfair. Fifty-six films. Running time: 5 min. ea.

**Sound Filmstrips**
**The Boy in the Moon**. Kereke pleads with his father to give him the moon because he wants it more than anything else in the world. A South Seas folktale. Clearvue. Running time: 9 min.

**Moon Mouse**. A curious mouse wants to know what the moon is made of and finds the answer much to his liking. Random House. Running time: 7 min.

FIGURE 2–4
*continued*

## B ulletin Board

Cover a bulletin board with dark blue or black paper. Arrange gummed stars in the patterns of simple constellations, such as the Big Dipper, the Little Dipper, and the Southern Cross. Connect the stars with chalk to show the outlines of the constellations. Children might enjoy hearing the stories and myths that explain how the constellations got in the sky. Title the bulletin board Star Light. Add to the display the titles of books and magazines that children can look at that tell about the stars. Leave room under each title for children to sign their names. Explain to children where they can find the books and magazines. Encourage them to look at these and see what they can find out. When they have had a chance to look at a book or magazine, have them write their name on the bulletin board under the appropriate title. Later give children the opportunity to discuss the books they found and share with the class what they learned.

STAR LIGHT

## U nit Project

Have children collect and draw pictures of things that produce light. Suggest that children begin by finding or drawing pictures of the things named in each story. Then they can add their own ideas, such as candles, headlights, a fireplace, and so on. Help children paste each cutout on a sheet of paper. Then ask children to put the cutouts and drawings into different categories, such as indoors/outdoors or daytime/nighttime. Promote a discussion of which type of light is best in different circumstances. Begin with a discussion of nighttime inside. Ask children to think about all the possible ways to get light in the nighttime inside. As children make suggestions, print them of the chalkboard. Challenge children to think of as many ideas as they can. Then, as children express their preferred method of lighting, urge them to say why they have made their choices. Use this procedure with other conditions—daytime, outdoors, and so on.

Tell children that they are going to need to make some recommendations of the best bedtime stories. First have children discuss what kind of stories they like best to hear or read at bedtime. After many children have a chance to state their preference, suggest that children think of categories of stories. Begin by suggesting funny stories. As children suggest categories, list them on the chalkboard. Then have children work in small groups to think of all the stories they know about in each category. Assign each group one or two categories and have them design an award for the best book in each category. Have children list all the stories and books they can think of for each category. Then assign the groups the lists and have them decide which story they think should be awarded the prize for the best book in the category. Try to obtain copies of the award-winning books for children to look through in class.

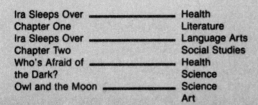

# Integrated Content

Encourage children to apply the information from the Unit Project to a dramatic-reading project. Ask children to recall the kinds of bedtime stories the class preferred. Ask children if they have ever read or told a bedtime story to a younger child. Write the following sentence: **When he was in bed, Robin could see the moon.** Tell children to pretend they are reading a story about Robin. Ask why the moon might be important in the story. Ask how Robin might feel abut seeing the moon when he is in bed. Elicit diverse interpretations. Then have volunteers read the line aloud to fit their interpretation. For example, a child who thinks this might be a line from a science fiction story might read the line with the excitement Robin would feel if he were in a space ship nearing the moon. Have children choose a story to prepare for oral reading. Over several days, give individuals help in interpreting the book. Then have children take turns doing a reading.

# Reading Games and Activities

**Yes or No**
Give each child one piece of paper or one index card. Have each child print the word **yes** on one side of the card and **no** on the other side. Have children place their cards on their desks. Pronounce pairs of words. Have children repeat the words, listening for the initial sound in each word. If the words begin with the same sound, they are to hold up the side of the card showing yes. If the words begin with different sounds, they are to hold up the side of the card showing no. Check to see that all children have selected the correct side of the card. Assist any child having difficulty. Continue by pronouncing other pairs of words. The following words may be pronounced: giant—gem, city—car, goat—general, cent—cymbal, germ—gym, ceiling—celery, gate—garage, cat—coat.

**Cross Over the Bridge**
Have children stand in a row on one side of the room. Choose one child to be the bridge keeper and to stand in the center of the room. Tell children that in order for them to cross the bridge, they must name a word that begins with the same sound as **glove** or **block**. The first child goes to the bridge keeper and says, "May I cross your bridge?" The bridge keeper says, "You may cross over my bridge if you can name a word that begins with the same sound as **glove** (or **block**)." If the child answers correctly, he or she may cross over the bridge and stand on the other side of the room. If incorrect, he or she goes back to the row of children and waits for another turn.

**Sentence Sounds**
Read children a sentence that contains words with clusters. Have them listen carefully to determine which words in the sentence begin with clusters. Then have them name the letters that stand for each cluster. Repeat the sentence, if necessary.
1. Our grass is brown and dry.
2. His grand crown is priceless.
3. Get a drink of milk and some bread.
4. Frame a picture from Tracy's trip.

FIGURE 2–4
*continued*

# M eeting Special Needs

## Language Development

### Previewing Vocabulary

Read the following sentences aloud. Then repeat the words in dark type. Ask children to tell you what each word means or to use the word in a sentence of their own.

1. My mother **decided** to read us another story after we begged her to.
2. I was afraid that I would be very lonely **without** my pet dog.
3. My dentist says you **should** always brush your teeth after eating.
4. If you leave early enough, you shouldn't have to **worry** about being late.
5. Losing my homework on the way to school was a big **problem.**
6. Luke likes to live in the **city.**
7. A **giant** glass of milk would taste good right now.
8. After he climbed the **stairs** to the second floor, he remembered the book was in the garage.
9. I'm afraid you won't keep your **promise** to help me with my work.
10. Do you **know** the names of all the states in the United States?
11. Kim must be **brave** to climb so high.
12. I was frightened when I **heard** a noise coming from the basement.
13. It was getting very dark in the house so I turned on a **light.**
14. Rosa was very **proud** when she won the long-distance race.
15. Our family has special rules to follow when we are at home **alone.**

### Initial Clusters

Initial clusters can be a problem for non-English speakers because the particular combination does not appear in the child's first language. The l-clusters and r-clusters are particularly problematic for native speakers of some Asian languages. Provide practice in producing these sounds and discriminating among them for all children having difficulty.

Prepare a set of picture cards using pictures whose names begin with the following clusters: **fr** (frog), **gr** (grapes), **dr** (dress), **br** (bread), **tr** (train), **pr** (present), **bl** (block), and **gl** (glove). Place the cards in a pile face down on a desk or table. Each child takes a turn by picking up a card, naming the picture, and then naming another word that begins with the same sound as the picture name.

Have children repeat the following pairs of words with you:

| br, bl | bread—bled, blade—braid, bland—brand, blue—brew |
|---|---|
| cr, cl | crown—clown, cram—clam, cloud—crowd, climb—crime |
| fr, fl | fry—fly, flame—frame, frank—flank, flesh—fresh |
| gr, gl | glass—grass, glade—grade, glow—grow, glue—grew |
| pr, pl | prod—plod, plowed—proud, pray—play, plied—pride |

Children may practice these tongue twisters:
Fred flew from France.
Brett blends black bread.
Glen grinds grain.
Priscilla plays pranks.
Brenda blames Brad.
Flags fly freely.
Clowns crowded Claudia.
Please plan proper programs.
Gretchen glides gracefully.
Craig claimed the crown.

After practicing the tongue twisters, have children listen carefully as you read each slowly. Have them raise their hands each time they hear the initial cluster change in the tongue twister.

To check children's ability to discriminate among these clusters, have children stand at the chalkboard and print the cluster they hear as you read a list such as this: **brag, plane, fright, climb, gray, gloss, blast, flips, price, crow.**

### Extending Vocabulary

Print the words listed below on the chalkboard. Read them aloud and ask children to tell you a word that means the opposite of each word you read.

| dark | yes | afraid | start |
|---|---|---|---|
| without | good | brave | light |

After children have named opposites for the listed words, ask them to name other pairs of opposites that they know. If time permits, children might enjoy working in pairs to act out sets of opposites.

# M eeting Individual Needs

<table>
<tr><th colspan="3">*S A F</th></tr>
</table>

## Story Content

| | S | A | F |
|---|---|---|---|
| **Vocabulary** | | | |
| Workbook 18, 22, 26 | ● | ● | ● |
| Review: Workbook 29 | ● | ● | ● |
| **Comprehension** | | | |
| Workbook 17, 21, 25 | ● | ● | ● |

## Phonics

| | S | A | F |
|---|---|---|---|
| **Initial Consonants c (celery), g (gym)** | | | |
| Teaching Master 15 | ● | ● | ● |
| Workbook 19 | ● | ● | ● |
| Teaching Master 23 | ● | ● | ● |
| **Initial Clusters br, pr, tr** | | | |
| Teaching Master 21 | ● | ● | ● |
| Workbook 23 | ● | ● | ● |
| Teaching Master 27 | ● | ● | |
| **Vowel Diphthong ou (cloud)** | | | |
| Teaching Master 25 | ● | ● | ● |
| Workbook 27 | ● | ● | ● |
| **Initial Clusters gl, bl** | | | |
| Teaching Master 17 | ● | ● | |
| Practice Master 15 | ● | | |
| Review: Workbook 31 | ● | ● | ● |
| **Final Cluster nt** | | | |
| Teaching Master 19 | ● | ● | |
| **Consonant Generalization** | | | |
| Teaching Master 18 | ● | ● | |
| Practice Master 14 | ● | | |
| Review: Workbook 30 | ● | ● | ● |
| **Initial Clusters sk, st** | | | |
| Practice Master 17 | ● | | |
| **Final Cluster nk** | | | |
| Teaching Master 28 | ● | ● | |

## Comprehension

| | S | A | F |
|---|---|---|---|
| **Stated Details** | | | |
| Teaching Master 20 | ● | ● | ● |
| **Context Clues (Missing Words)** | | | |
| Teaching Master 24 | ● | ● | ● |
| **Commas in Direct Address** | | | |
| Teaching Master 29 | ● | ● | |
| **Pronoun Referents** | | | |
| Practice Master 18 | ● | | |
| **Quotation Marks and Commas in Dialogue** | | | |
| Practice Master 20 | ● | ● | |

## Word Structure

| | S | A | F |
|---|---|---|---|
| **Compound Words** | | | |
| Teaching Master 16 | ● | ● | ● |
| Workbook 20 | ● | ● | ● |
| **Syllables** | | | |
| Teaching Master 22 | ● | ● | ● |
| Workbook 24 | ● | ● | ● |
| **Abbreviations** | | | |
| Practice Master 19 | ● | | |
| Review: Workbook 32 | ● | ● | ● |

## Study Skills

| | S | A | F |
|---|---|---|---|
| **Alphabetizing by First Letter** | | | |
| Teaching Master 26 | ● | ● | ● |
| Workbook 28 | ● | ● | ● |

## Language Extension (Writing)

| | S | A | F |
|---|---|---|---|
| Practive Master 16 | ● | ● | ● |

*S = Slower-achieving students   A = Average-achieving students   F = Faster-achieving students

FIGURE 2–4
*continued*

## LESSON 5
## Ira Sleeps Over— Chapter One

### Selection Objectives

Student Text pages 44-51
Literature: Realistic fiction
Purpose: To entertain

### Selection Vocabulary

**Instructional Words**
dark, fine, games, if, decided, mother, story, very, without, worry, problem, should

### Selection Information

**Author**
Bernard Waber is both an author and an illustrator. The youngest of four children, Waber was born and grew up in Philadelphia, Pennsylvania, where a love of books, libraries, and the Saturday cinema were the focus of his childhood. His first exposure to art came through the drawing interests of an older sibling. His first drawings were sketches of film stars. After serving in World War II, Waber joined the art department of *Life Magazine,* married, and with his wife, Ethel, began a family. Subsequently, his interest in picture books grew out of evening read-aloud sessions with his three children. Waber's *House on East 88th Street* was a New York Herald Honor Book. He lives in Baldwin, Long Island.

### Literature
In opening the unit Lights Out!, this story by Bernard Waber relates a child's fears about his first night away from home.

### Selection Summary
Ira, a young boy, is about to spend the night away from home with a friend for the first time. His older sister teasingly asks Ira whether he plans to take Tah Tah, his teddy bear. Ira wants to take the bear, but he is afraid his friend will think him babyish if he admits he still sleeps with a stuffed animal.

### Decoding Strategies

Learn New Words
Student Text page 44
Teacher's Edition page 140

Selection Vocabulary
Workbook page 18
Home-Study Master 4

### Comprehension Strategies

Read for Meaning/Get Set to Read
Teacher's Edition page 140

Selection Comprehension
Think About It
Teacher's Edition page 144
Workbook page 17

### Language Lab

Student Text pages 232-233
Teacher's Edition pages 145-146
Module: Choosing the Right Words
Lesson: Classification, Using an Idea Web
Writing Journal pages 10-12

### Cultural Literacy

The stuffed animal known as the teddy bear is named after the twenty-sixth President of the United States. Theodore Roosevelt, or Teddy, spared the life of a bear cub on a hunting trip. That event led the toy industry to create the teddy bear.

### Integrated Content

Health: Solving problems
Literature: Winnie the Pooh

## PLANNING GUIDE--Objectives & Materials

| SELECTION | Learn New Words | Get Set to Read | Think About It |
|---|---|---|---|
| Student Text pages 44 - 51 | TE page 140 | TE page 140 | TE page 144 |

| SKILL OBJECTIVES | | Teacher Directed | Guided Practice | Independent Practice | Tested |
|---|---|---|---|---|---|
| Phonics: Initial Consonants c (celery), g (gym) | △ ○ ☆ | Direct Instruction TE page 148 | Teaching Master page 15 | Workbook page 19 | Unit 3 |
| Word Structure: Compound Words | △ ○ ☆ | Direct Instruction TE page 149 | Teaching Master page 16 | Workbook page 20 | Unit 4 |
| Phonics: Initial Clusters gl, bl | ○ ☆ | Reteach TE page 150 | Teaching Master page 17 | | Unit 2 |
| Phonics: Consonant Generalization | ○ ☆ | Reteach TE page 150 | Teaching Master page 18 | | Unit 2 |
| Phonics: Final Cluster nt | ○ ☆ | Reteach TE page 151 | Teaching Master page 19 | | Unit 5 |
| Comprehension: Stated Details | ○ ☆ | Practice - 1 TE page 151 | Teaching Master page 20 | | Unit 3 |

| LANGUAGE OBJECTIVES | Teacher Directed | Cooperative Learning | Independent Activity | Other Resources |
|---|---|---|---|---|
| Language Lab Classification, Using an Idea Web Student Text pages 232 - 233 TE pages 145 - 146 | X | X | X | |
| Extend TE page 147 Listening: Vocabulary | X | X | | Writing Transparency 2 |
| Writing: Dialogue | X | X | | |
| Speaking: Expression | X | X | | |

**Supplementary Materials**
Phonics Picture Cards: celery, 20; gym, 59
Word Cards: dark, 314; fine, 317; games, 318;
if, 322; decided, 315; mother, 328; story, 337;
very, 340; without, 341; worry, 342; problem, 330;
should, 333
Pocket Chart
Story Big Book

Story Take-Home Book
Read On Take-Home Book
Literature Book Box
Oral Language Transition Program
  Story Time Tapes, Level 6
  Picture Time Cards, Level 6
  Chanting Time Sentences, Level 6
  Sounding Time Manipulatives
Tutorial Program, Level 6

**Meeting Instructional Needs**
△Faster-Achieving Students
☆Slower-Achieving Students
○Average-Achieving Students
  or Whole Group Instruction

139

FIGURE 2–4
*continued*

Ira Sleeps
Over—
Chapter
One

**Learn New Words**

1. We could not see in the **dark** house.  dog
2. You look **fine** in your new hat.  fish
3. We will play many **games**.  goat
4. I will be happy **if** you can go, too.  insects
5. Have you **decided** what to do?  dog
6. Then my **mother** said, "I can take you with me."  monkey
7. I will tell you a **story**.  stamp
8. The boy was **very** sad.  violin
9. Do not go out **without** your hat.  wagon
10. I will not **worry** about him.  wagon
11. I will help you with your **problem**.  present
12. What **should** I do?  shoe

44

aloud. Use this procedure with the remaining new words.

**Special Words**
Before children read the story, print these character names on the chalkboard and pronounce them: **Ira, Reggie, Tah Tah.**

Then print the words **ghost, hmm,** and **teddy**. Point to each word; read the context sentence aloud, omitting the new word; and help children use phonics and context clues to identify it.
*I wore a **ghost** costume.*
*"**Hmm,** I will have to think about the answer," said Lucy.*
*My friend has a **teddy** bear.*

**Get Set to Read**

*Before we read, let's review the steps we use to read for meaning.*

**How to Read for Meaning**

1. Set a purpose.
2. Read the story.
3. Answer the question.

*Let's use these steps with today's story. A boy named Ira is planning to sleep overnight at his friend Reggie's house. What are some of the things that friends take with them when they spend the night at each other's houses?* Encourage discussion. *Ira has something special that he is deciding whether to take. In reading this story, our purpose will be to find out: What special thing was Ira trying to decide whether to take to Reggie's house? After we read the story, we will be able to answer the purpose question.*

**Student-Directed Purposes**
Have children tell what kinds of things they would not like to bring along to their friend's house and tell why. Then have them read the story to compare their feelings with those of Ira.

**P** **Preteach**

**Learn New Words**

**Applying Initial d**
*We will use the sentences on this page to learn new words for the story.* Hold up a student book. Point to the word **dark** in the first sentence. *What is the first letter?* (D.) *Remember, the letter **d** stands for the beginning sound in the Key Word **dog**. This word begins with the same sound. Let's read the sentence together: We could not see in the* (pause) *house. What word begins with the sound **d** stands for and makes sense in this sentence?* (Dark.) *Let's review the steps we use to learn new words.*

**How to Learn New Words**

1. Look at the letters in the word.
2. Think of the sound clues.
3. Use the sentence clues.
4. Read the word.

Use the steps with the word **fine**. *Find the underlined word in the second sentence. Look at the letters in the word and think of the sound clues. What is the first letter?* (F.) *This letter stands for the beginning sound in the Key Word **fish**. Use the sentence clues. Let's read the sentence together: You look* (pause) *in your new hat. What word begins with the sound **f** stands for in **fish** and makes sense in the sentence?* (Fine.) Use Key Words (see list, page 516) to help children with the other phonic elements in the word. Have the sentence read

## Read

The questions beside the reduced student pages are designed to guide silent or oral reading. Questions under Think About It should be used after the whole selection has been read.

**Page 45**

**L**  Story Plot
*What is Ira going to do?* (Sleep over at Reggie's house.)

**C**  Inferred Characterization
*Why do you think Ira is so happy?* (Answers will vary.)

**C**  Inferred Characterization
*What could Ira's problem be?* (Answers will vary.)

**Page 46**

**L**  Stated Details
*Find what Ira says when his sister asks if he is taking his teddy bear to Reggie's house. Read the sentences aloud.* ("Taking my teddy bear? To my friend's house? I would never take my bear there.")

**I**  Inferred Characterization
*Why doesn't Ira want to take his bear to Reggie's house?* (Answers may vary. Suggestion: He doesn't want Reggie to know he sleeps with a teddy bear.)

**I**  Drawing Conclusions
*Why does Ira's sister feel he may have a problem if he doesn't take his bear?* (He might not be able to sleep without it.)
- *Does Ira always sleep with a teddy bear?* (Yes.)
- *Is Ira planning to sleep without the bear for the first time?* (Yes.)
- *Might Ira have a problem getting to sleep because of this change?* (Yes.)

# IRA
# SLEEPS
# OVER

by BERNARD WABER

**CHAPTER ONE**

I was going to sleep over
at Reggie's house.
Was I happy!
But I had a <u>problem</u>.

45

My sister said, "Are you taking
your teddy bear?"

"Taking my teddy bear?" I said.
"To my friend's house?
I would never take my bear there."

She said, "But you never sleep
without your teddy bear.
How will you feel sleeping without him
for the <u>very</u> first time, hmm?"

"I will feel <u>fine</u>.
I will love sleeping without my bear.
Do not <u>worry</u> about it," I said.

"Who is worrying?" said my sister.
"It is <u>your</u> problem."

46

FIGURE 2–4
*continued*

Page 47

**I** Inferred Characterization
*Look at the picture on page 47.
How do you think Ira is feeling at
the moment?* (Worried and
concerned.)

**L** Cause and Effect
*Who has caused Ira to worry
about his bear?* (His sister.)

**L** Story Conflict and
Resolution
*Find the questions that Ira asks
himself. Read them aloud.* (What
if I didn't like sleeping without my
teddy bear? What if I missed him
a lot? Should I go without my
teddy bear?)

**Purpose** Before children read
the next page, ask them to predict what Ira will decide to do.

Page 48

**L** Story Conflict and
Resolution
*What do Ira's mother and father
think Ira should do?* (Take the
bear.)

**I** Drawing Conclusions
*Why does Ira think Reggie will
laugh?* (Suggestion: Because Ira
is too old to be sleeping with a
teddy bear; because Ira's sister
said Reggie would laugh.)

But now she had me worrying
about the problem.
What <u>if</u> I didn't like sleeping
without my teddy bear?
What if I missed him a lot?
<u>Should</u> I go without my teddy bear?

47

"Take him," said my <u>mother</u>.

"You should take him," said my father.

"But Reggie will laugh," I said.

First, my mother said,
"He will not laugh."

Next, my father said,
"He will not laugh."

Last, my sister said,
"He <u>will</u> laugh."

I decided not to take
my teddy bear.

**L** Stated Details
*What is Reggie looking forward to doing when Ira sleeps over? (Playing games, having fun, telling a ghost story.)*

**I** Inferred Characterization
*Why do you think Ira asks Reggie what he thinks of teddy bears? (He still wants to take his teddy bear, but he is afraid of what Reggie will think.)*
- *What does Ira really want to do about his bear? (He wants to take it.)*
- *What is Ira afraid that Reggie will do when he sees the bear? (Laugh.)*
- *Would Reggie laugh if Reggie himself still sleeps with a teddy bear? (Probably not.)*

**L** Sequence*
*When does Reggie plan to tell a ghost story? (After the house is dark.)*

Page 50

**I** Inferred Cause and Effect
*Why do you think Ira asks Reggie if his house will be very dark? (He probably feels a little frightened or nervous.)*

**L** Story Plot
*What happens when Ira asks Reggie again how he feels about teddy bears? (Reggie doesn't answer the question because he has to leave.)*

**I** Inferred Characterization
*How can you tell that it is important to Ira to know how Reggie feels about teddy bears? (He asks Reggie more than once.)*

That day, I played with Reggie.
Reggie said, "When you come over,
we are going to have fun, fun, fun!
We will play many games."

"Great!" I said.
"I like games."
Then I asked, "What do you think
of teddy bears?"

Reggie went on talking as if I had
never said a thing about teddy bears.
"I will tell you a ghost story
when the house is dark," he said.
"A ghost story is great to tell
in the dark."

49

I thought about my teddy bear.
"Will your house be very dark?" I asked.

"Very, very dark," said Reggie.

"What do you think of teddy bears?"
I asked again.

But all Reggie said was,
"I have to go home.
See you."

"See you," I said.

50

49

FIGURE 2–4
*continued*

Page 51

**I** Inferred Cause and Effect
*Why do you think Ira changes his mind and decides to take his bear?* (He might not be so afraid if he has his bear.)

**L** Stated Details
*Find what Ira's sister says. Read the sentences aloud.* ("What if Reggie asks what your teddy bear's name is? Did you think about how he will laugh at a name like Tah Tah?")

**I** Inferred Cause and Effect
*What makes Ira change his mind again and decide not to take his bear?* (His sister's making fun of the bear's name.)

**C** Predicting Outcomes
*The name of this unit is* **Lights Out!** *When the lights go out in the story, do you think Ira or Reggie will be more scared? Why?* (Answers will vary.)

**Note** Tell children they will read the second part of "Ira Sleeps Over" in the next lesson.

### Think About It

These questions are designed for general discussion. Answers may vary for many of them. Some possible answers are given.

**L** Story Conflict and Resolution
*What special thing was Ira trying to decide whether to take to Reggie's house?* (His teddy bear.)—Purpose

**I** Inferred Characterization
*Why was he having trouble making this decision?* (He really wanted to sleep with his bear, but he was afraid Reggie would laugh.)

I decided to take my teddy bear.

"Fine," said my mother and my father.

But my sister said, "What if Reggie asks what your teddy bear's name is? Did you think about how he will laugh at a name like Tah Tah?"

I decided not to take my teddy bear.

51

**I** Making Generalizations
*How did Ira's sister make it harder for him to decide about taking his teddy bear?* (She kept teasing him about the bear and saying that Reggie would laugh.)

**C** Extending Interpretation
*What are some feelings that young people might have about staying overnight at a friend's house for the first time?* (Answers will vary.)

**C** Predicting Outcomes
*What do you think Ira is going to do about his teddy bear? Why?* (Answers will vary.)

**■** For work with selection comprehension and vocabulary, use Workbook pages 17 and 18.

## L Language Lab

Module: Choosing the Right Words
Lesson: Classification, Using an Idea Web

### Prewriting

*This part of the Language Lab is about choosing the right words.* Lead a discussion of when it might be important to choose the right words.

Before children read the lesson, print the word **which** on the chalkboard. Point to the word and read the context sentence aloud, omitting the new word. Help children use phonics and context clues to identify it: *I don't know which one to use, the red pencil or the blue pencil.*

Print the words **color** and **animal** on the chalkboard. Read the words aloud. *Each of these words is the name of a group. I will say some other words. I want you to tell me which group each word belongs in— animal or color.* Call on volunteers to identify the correct category for each word you say. Print the word under that heading. *Listen to these words: **red, cat, blue, orange, dog, horse, green, rabbit.*** When all the words have been printed, have children read the words in each group. *You can call a group of things by one name if they are alike in some way.*

Have children turn to page 232 in their books. Have a volunteer read the title of this lesson. *Today we are going to talk about things that make us happy and things that make us sad.*

Allow time for children to read the sentences silently. *The words **fun, play,** and **games** are underlined because these are things that make us happy.* Copy the idea web on the chalkboard. *What are the names of some of the things that make you happy?* As volunteers suggest words, print them around the key word, connecting them to the web. Follow this procedure with the idea web on page 233. Have children copy the webs into their Journals, and then have them look at the words at the bottom of page 233. Have them add any word from this list that is not already on the chalkboard to their webs.

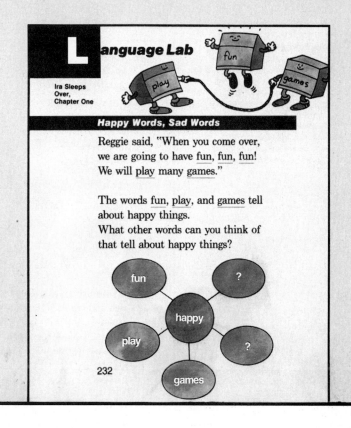

## L anguage Lab

Ira Sleeps
Over,
Chapter One

### Happy Words, Sad Words

Reggie said, "When you come over,
we are going to have <u>fun</u>, <u>fun</u>, <u>fun</u>!
We will <u>play</u> many <u>games</u>."

The words <u>fun</u>, <u>play</u>, and <u>games</u> tell
about happy things.
What other words can you think of
that tell about happy things?

232

51

FIGURE 2–4
*continued*

### Composing

Have children write a happy or sad story using the words from their webs.

### Creative Sharing

Have children come to the Sharing Place and read their stories. Have others listen for the happy and sad words.

■ Have children add words from this lesson to their Word Banks.

**Additional Suggestions for Cooperative Learning**
Before Composing, have children form pairs and choose the **happy** or **sad** idea web to work on. Have them compose a sentence for each word in the web and then think of other sentences that use two of the words. Children may continue to work in pairs to write their stories.

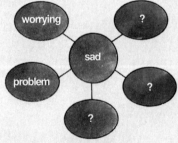

But now she had me worrying about the problem.

The words worrying and problem tell about sad things.
What other words tell about sad things?

worrying   ?
problem    sad    ?
?

Which words go with the word happy?
Which ones go with the word sad?

    laugh    lost    glad
    hurt    funny    mean

Use the words to write a happy story or a sad story.

146    LESSON 5

233

## E Extend

### Listening

#### Vocabulary

Tell children that you are going to read a selection that has words in it they may not know. Ask children to listen carefully as you read the selection. Tell them they will be asked to try to figure out what some words mean.

*Ira walked slowly up the stairs to his room. There, lying on the bed, was Tah Tah, his teddy bear. Ira* **gazed** *down at Tah Tah for a few minutes. He saw Tah Tah's torn ears. He picked him up and looked at the stuffing coming out of Tah Tah's right leg. He* **clasped** *Tah Tah in his arms and hugged him tightly. "Would you miss me very much?" he asked Tah Tah. "Would you feel very* **lonesome** *if I left you here to sleep all by yourself tonight?"*

1. *If you* **clasp** *something in your arms, are you holding it tightly or loosely?* (Tightly.)
2. *If you feel* **lonesome,** *are you usually with many people or are you all by yourself?* (All by yourself.)
3. *When you* **gaze** *at something, are you looking directly at it or looking away from it?* (Looking directly at it.)
4. *What is another word that means the same as* **gaze**? (Answers may vary. Suggestion: Stare, watch.)

● For additional work with vocabulary, use Transparency 2.

### Writing

#### Dialogue

*Let's turn to page 46 in our books. We can tell from the way the words are printed and from the picture at the bottom that two people are talking. What other clue do we have that people are talking?* (Quotation marks.) *Such words as* **said, answered,** *and* **asked** *are also clues that two or more people are talking in the story. Look at page 46 carefully. Who is the first person to talk on this page?* (Ira's sister.) *What clue word do you see?* (Said.) Ask for three volunteers, one to take the part of Ira, one to take the part of his sister, and one to read the narration. Have the three read the page for the class. To prevent confusion, point to each child as it becomes his or her turn to read. Repeat the process with page 48 to allow more children to participate.

*Now let's write some dialogue of our own. We'll pretend that Bill and Jane are talking.* On the chalkboard write: Jane said, "Bill, why did the chicken cross the road?" *What shall I write next? Does anyone know what the second line should be?* (Bill answered, "To get to the other side.") Use any answer suggested. Print it on the chalkboard, asking children to tell you where to put quotation marks. Ask what word indicated that the lines are dialogue. (Answered.) Underline the words **said** and **answered.**

### Speaking

#### Expression

Have children turn to page 46 and look at the picture of Ira and his sister. *Ira's sister sometimes likes to make fun of him. Think about how Ira's sister would say this sentence: Are you taking your teddy bear?* Call on a volunteer to say the sentence the way Ira's sister might. If necessary, demonstrate how a person who is making fun of another person might say the sentence. (In a haughty, taunting way; in a sly, challenging way.)

Next, have volunteers read the rest of the sentences on this page, with one child reading Ira's lines and another reading his sister's lines. Remind them that throughout this conversation, she is making fun of him.

● For work with vocabulary, use the Home-Study materials from the Teacher's Resource Book.

FIGURE 2–4
*continued*

 **Skills**

**Direct Instruction**

## Phonics: Initial Consonants c (celery), g (gym)

**Focus**
Show Phonics Picture Card **cel-ery.** *Besides being able to stand for the beginning sound in the word* **car,** *the letter* **c** *can also stand for the sound you hear at the beginning of the word* **celery.** Then show Phonics Picture Card **gym.** *Besides being able to stand for the beginning sound in the word* **goat,** *the letter* **g** *can also stand for the sound you hear at the beginning of the word* **gym.**

**Stated Objective**
*We will listen for words in which the letter* **c** *stands for the sound you hear at the beginning of* **celery** *and for words in which the letter* **g** *stands for the sound you hear at the beginning of* **gym.**

**Explanation** (Modeling)
Print the word **celery** on the chalkboard and underline the letter **c.** *Listen to the beginning sound as we say the word* **celery.** Repeat the word with children. *In some words, the letter* **c** *stands for the sound you hear at the beginning of* **celery.** Then print the word **gym** on the chalkboard and underline the letter **g.** *Listen to the beginning sound as we say the word* **gym.** Repeat the word with children. *In some words, the letter* **g** *stands for the sound you hear at the beginning of* **gym.**

**Checking for Understanding**
*I will read some sentences. Raise your hand when you hear a word that begins with the same sound as* **celery.** As each soft **c** word is identified, print it on the chalkboard and underline the initial **c.** Read these sentences.

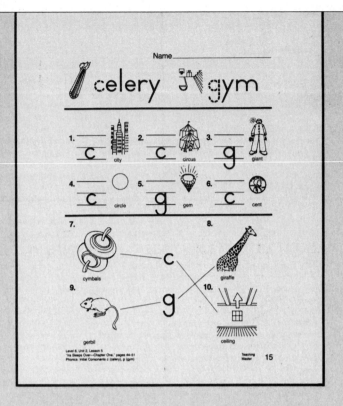

*I went to the circus.* (Circus.) *Jim walked around the city.* (City.) *A penny is one cent.* (Cent.)

*I will say four words. Raise your hand when you hear a word that begins with the same sound as* **gym.** As each soft **g** word is identified, print it on the chalkboard and underline the initial **g.** Say **giant, game, gem, giraffe.** The letter **g** stands for the beginning sound of **gym** in the words **giant, gem,** and **giraffe.**

**Guided Practice**
Distribute Teaching Master 15. Point to the celery. *Who can name this picture?* (Celery.) *The letter* **c** *can stand for the sound at the beginning of* **celery.** *Trace the dotted-line letter* **c** *to finish* **cel-ery.** Repeat this procedure for **gym.** Then point to the picture of the city. *This picture shows a city. Does the word* **city** *begin with the*

*same sound as* **celery** *or* **gym?** (Celery.) *What letter stands for the beginning sound in* **city** *and* **celery?** (Letter **c.**) *Print a* **c** *on the lines.* Continue the procedure for other pictures in the section.

Point to the letters **c** and **g** in the bottom section. *Who can name these letters?* (Letters **c, g.**) Point to the picture of the cymbals. *This picture shows a pair of cymbals. Which letter stands for the beginning sound in* **cymbals?** (Letter **c.**) *Draw a line from the cymbals to the* **c.** Repeat procedure for other pictures.

**Independent Practice**
▣ For more work with initial **c** (celery) and **g** (gym), assign Workbook page 19.

**Evaluation**
When children have finished the activity, review answers.

148    LESSON 5

54

## Word Structure: Compound Words

**Focus**
Print the word **rain** on the chalkboard. *Who can read this word?* (Rain.) Print the word **coat**. *Who can read this word?* (Coat.) Then print the word **raincoat** and point to it. *This word is **raincoat**. The word **raincoat** is called a compound word. Say **compound word** after me. A compound word is made by putting two words together to make a longer word.*

**Stated Objective**
*Today we will learn to recognize and decode compound words.*

**Explanation** (Modeling)
Point to the word **raincoat** again. *The compound word **raincoat** is made by putting together the words **rain** and **coat**. Many words you read, such as **raincoat**, are compound words.*

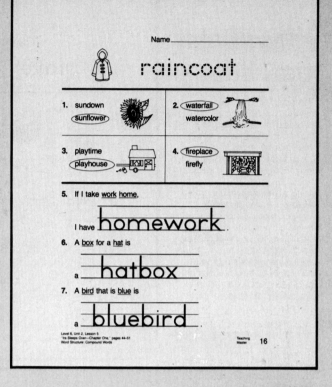

Print the words **fireplace, something, without, lookout** on the chalkboard. Help children read each word and then identify the two words that were put together to make the compound word. *What do we call a longer word that is made by putting two words together?* (A compound word.)

**Checking for Understanding**
*I will say four words. Raise your hand when you hear a compound word.* As each compound is identified, print it on the chalkboard and have volunteers name the two words that make it up. Say **rabbit, outside, radio, barnyard**. *The words **outside** and **barnyard** are compound words.*

**Guided Practice**
Distribute copies of Teaching Master 16. Point to the picture of the raincoat. *Who can name the picture at the top of the page?*

(Raincoat.) *Raincoat is a compound word. What two words have been put together to make raincoat?* (Rain, coat.) *Trace the dotted-line letters to complete the compound word **raincoat**. Remember, a compound word is made by putting two words together to make a longer word.* Point to the words in the first box. *Who can read these words?* (Sundown, sunflower.) *Look at the picture after the words. Which word describes the picture?* (Sunflower.) *Circle the word **sunflower**.* Repeat this procedure for the remaining pictures.

Point to sentence 5. *Look at this sentence. A word is missing from it. Who can read the words before the lines?* (If I take work home, I have —.) *Look at the underlined words in the sentence. Who can read these words?* (Work, home.) *How can these two words be put*

*together to make a compound word that fits into the sentence?* (Homework.) Print **homework** on the lines. *Now, who can read the sentence?* (If I take work home, I have homework.) Repeat this procedure.

**Independent Practice**
▣ For further work with compound words, have children complete Workbook page 20.

**Evaluation**
After the activity has been completed, review the answers. *Remember, a compound word is made by putting two words together to make a longer word.*

149

55

FIGURE 2-4
*continued*

### Reteach

#### Phonics: Initial Clusters gl, bl

Distribute Teaching Master 17. Point to the glove picture. *Who can name this picture?* (Glove.) *The letters **gl** together stand for the beginning sound in **glove**. Trace the dotted-line letters **gl** to finish the word **glove**. In many words, the letters **gl** stand for the sound you hear at the beginning of **glove**.* Repeat procedure for the word **block**. Point to the blouse picture. *Who can name this picture?* (Blouse.) *Which letters, **gl** or **bl**, stand for the beginning sound in **blouse**?* (Letters **bl**.) *Print **bl** on the lines next to the blouse picture.* Identify the pictures and let children finish the page.

### Reteach

#### Phonics: Consonant Generalization

Distribute Teaching Master 18. *When you read, you sometimes see the same consonant letter either at the beginning, in the middle, or at the end of words. The letter usually stands for the same sound wherever it appears.*

Now point to the letter **m** in the first row. *Look at the pictures in this row. The sound the letter **m** stands for can be heard in each picture name. Who can name these pictures?* (Drum, moon, hammer.) *Say **drum**. Do you hear the sound **m** stands for at the beginning, in the middle, or at the end of **drum**?* (At the end.) *Look at the three boxes under the picture. To show that the letter **m** stands for the ending sound in **drum**, make an X in the last box.* Repeat this procedure for the rest of the pictures in this row and for the remaining rows.

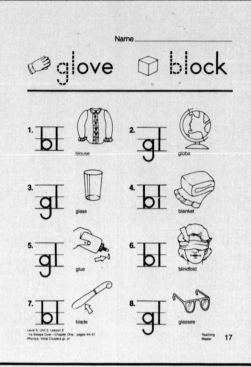

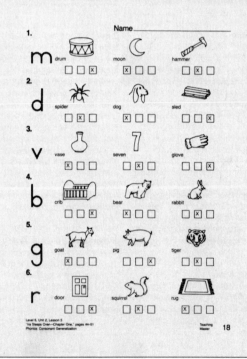

## Phonics: Final Cluster *nt*

Distribute Teaching Master 19. Point to the picture of the tent. *Who can name this picture?* (Tent.) *The letters **nt** together stand for the ending sound in **tent**. Trace the dotted-line letters **nt** to finish the word **tent**. In many words, the letters **nt** stand for the sound you hear at the end of **tent**.* Now point to the picture of the cent. *This picture shows a cent. Say the words **tent** and **cent**. Do they have the same ending sound?* (Yes.) *What two letters stand for this sound?* (Letters **nt**.) *Print the letters **nt** on the lines to finish the word **cent**. When the letters **nt** do not finish the picture name, leave the lines blank.* Repeat this procedure for the remaining pictures or, after identifying the pictures, let children finish the page on their own. Then discuss answers.

## Comprehension: Stated Details

Distribute copies of Teaching Master 20. *Here is another story about Ira. We are going to read the story. Then we will answer some detail questions about the story.* Ask volunteers to read the story aloud. Have the first question and the answer choices read aloud. *Look at the story to find the answer to this question. Look again at the three answer choices. Which of them answers the question?* (Answer **b.**) *To show that this is the correct answer, draw a circle around the letter **b**.* Let children finish the page on their own. Discuss answers.

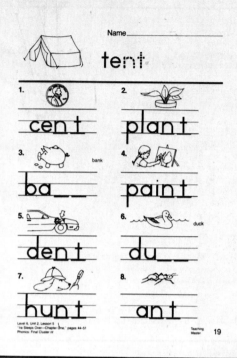

Name_____

tent

1. cen t

2. plan t

3. ba___ bank

4. pain t

5. den t

6. du___ duck

7. hun t

8. an t

Level 6, Unit 2, Lesson 5
"Ira Sleeps Over—Chapter One," pages 44–51
Phonics: Final Cluster *nt*

Teaching Master 19

Name_____

Ira was going to visit his new friend Adam.
Ira asked his mother, "How long will
the bus take to get there?"
"It will not be as fast as going in a car,"
said Mother.
"But it will not take long."
"I will miss you," said his father.
"But I am glad you are going.
You will have fun.
I will pick you up at the bus stop tomorrow."

1. Where is Ira going?
   a. to visit his mother
   b. to visit Adam
   c. to visit the zoo

2. How will Ira get there?
   a. on a train
   b. in a car
   c. on a bus

3. How does Ira's father feel about the visit?
   a. He is glad.
   b. He is sad.
   c. He does not want Ira to go.

4. When is Ira coming back to his house?
   a. today
   b. tomorrow
   c. never

Level 6, Unit 2, Lesson 5
"Ira Sleeps Over—Chapter One," pages 44–51
Comprehension: Stated Details

Teaching Master 20

FIGURE 2-4
*continued*

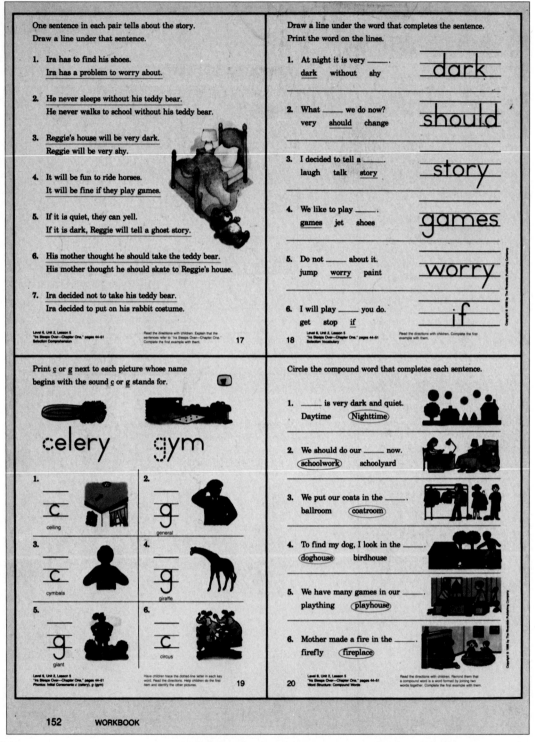

One sentence in each pair tells about the story.
Draw a line under that sentence.

1. Ira has to find his shoes.
   Ira has a problem to worry about.

2. He never sleeps without his teddy bear.
   He never walks to school without his teddy bear.

3. Reggie's house will be very dark.
   Reggie will be very shy.

4. It will be fun to ride horses.
   It will be fine if they play games.

5. If it is quiet, they can yell.
   If it is dark, Reggie will tell a ghost story.

6. His mother thought he should take the teddy bear.
   His mother thought he should skate to Reggie's house.

7. Ira decided not to take his teddy bear.
   Ira decided to put on his rabbit costume.

Level 6, Unit 2, Lesson 5
"Ira Sleeps Over—Chapter One," pages 44–51
Selection Comprehension

Read the directions with children. Explain that the
sentences refer to "Ira Sleeps Over—Chapter One."
Complete the first example with them.

17

---

Draw a line under the word that completes the sentence.
Print the word on the lines.

1. At night it is very ____.
   dark    without    shy

   dark

2. What ____ we do now?
   very    should    change

   should

3. I decided to tell a ____.
   laugh    talk    story

   story

4. We like to play ____.
   games    jet    shoes

   games

5. Do not ____ about it.
   jump    worry    paint

   worry

6. I will play ____ you do.
   get    stop    if

   if

Level 6, Unit 2, Lesson 5
"Ira Sleeps Over—Chapter One," pages 44–51
Selection Vocabulary

Read the directions with children. Complete the first
example with them.

18

---

Print c or g next to each picture whose name
begins with the sound c or g stands for.

celery    gym

1. c
   ceiling

2. g
   general

3. c
   cymbals

4. g
   giraffe

5. g
   giant

6. c
   circus

Level 6, Unit 2, Lesson 5
"Ira Sleeps Over—Chapter One," pages 44–51
Phonics: Initial Consonants c (celery), g (gym)

Have children trace the dotted-line letter in each key
word. Read the directions. Help children do the first
item and identify the other pictures.

19

---

Circle the compound word that completes each sentence.

1. ____ is very dark and quiet.
   Daytime    (Nighttime)

2. We should do our ____ now.
   (schoolwork)    schoolyard

3. We put our coats in the ____.
   ballroom    (coatroom)

4. To find my dog, I look in the ____.
   (doghouse)    birdhouse

5. We have many games in our ____.
   plaything    (playhouse)

6. Mother made a fire in the ____.
   firefly    (fireplace)

Level 6, Unit 2, Lesson 5
"Ira Sleeps Over—Chapter One," pages 44–51
Word Structure: Compound Words

Read the directions with children. Remind them that
a compound word is a word formed by joining two
words together. Complete the first example with them.

20

---

152    WORKBOOK

58

provides a set of activities designed to prepare students for reading the selection. New vocabulary words are listed, along with suggestions for how the new words should be taught. The lesson in Figure 2–4 presents its new words in the section called "Learn New Words" (see p. 46).

Often, specific reading skills are also developed during the preparation section. Such skills as phonics, recognition of compound words, study skills, and so on are usually related directly to some aspect of the reading selection. The reading program in Figure 2–4 is somewhat unusual in that its suggestions for skill development appear at the end of each lesson, not at the beginning (see p. 54). Teachers may choose to teach those skills before the selection, after the selection, or not at all. In addition, the preparation section defines a purpose for reading. In Figure 2–4 most of this information is contained in the section labeled "Get Set to Read" (see p. 46).

The third section of most teaching plans suggests how to conduct a **guided reading** of the passage. Directions usually call for students to read the passage silently and then sometimes orally. In addition, discussion questions and appropriate answers are given. The guided reading portion of our example lesson begins on page 47. This activity usually takes place in one of two ways. Often, students read the entire selection silently, and then the teacher initiates a discussion that may or may not include an oral reading of portions of the story. An alternative strategy has students read the story silently, a page or two at a time. After each portion is read, the teacher initiates a discussion that, again, may or may not include an oral reading. In both cases students have an opportunity to read stories silently before they are asked to read them aloud (Harris & Sipay, 1990).

guided reading: The third section of most teaching plans in a traditional published reading program; gives directions for guiding silent and sometimes oral reading.

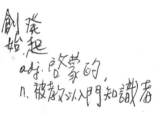

We can see in our sample lesson that questions are presented along the side of the page to assist the teacher in discussion. This particular program provides information in two ways. First, the letters *L, I,* and *C* tell whether a question requires readers to use literal information (L) in the story, make an inference (I), or make a critical judgment (C) about something they have read. Second, the skill area of each question (e.g., story plot, characterization, stated details) is indicated. Teachers usually select the discussion questions they find most important and appropriate for their students; they may also develop their own questions.

After the guided reading section, many teaching plans provide suggestions for **skill development and practice**. These sections often consist of workbook activities for students to complete independently at their desks. On page 50 in Figure 2–4 teachers are directed to workbook pages 17 and 18 "for work with selection comprehension and vocabulary." The actual activities can be seen on page 58.

skill development and practice: The fourth section of most teaching plans in a traditional published reading program; provides directions for specific skill instruction.

Finally, **extension activities** are often included for teachers; functional and enjoyable activities related to the content or the skills associated with a selection. In Figure 2–4 you can find this information listed under "Language Lab" (pp. 51 and 52) and "Extend" (p. 53). Also, a teacher could use any of the thematically related activities described at the beginning of the unit (see pp. 38–42).

extension activities: The fifth section of most teaching plans in a traditional published reading program; contains review and enrichment activities.

## THE CONTROVERSY SURROUNDING PUBLISHED READING PROGRAMS

One of the more controversial issues in reading instruction today is whether teachers should use a published, or basal, reading program to assist them in reading instruction. The comments that follow appeared on the front page of the International Reading Association newspaper (*Reading Today,* September 1989):

> Ask yourself, "What are my curricular goals in the language arts?. . ." The critical question then becomes, "Can basal readers, with their workbooks, skill packs, and assessment procedures, accomplish these goals for all children?" The answer clearly is "no." (Norma Mickelson, professor, Victoria, British Columbia)

> A well-constructed basal is an excellent teaching tool; all students have the same material and can follow along as the teacher demonstrates and guides them in practice sessions. (Carla R. Heymsfeld, reading specialist, Vienna, Virginia)

> Basals. . .are only what teachers and children make of them as they negotiate the language curriculum together. Empowerment in teaching comes when teachers make personal and professional decisions about instruction, and these decisions may include the use of the basal. Perhaps the most difficult thing of all is to respect the empowered reading professional who differs with my empowered opinion! (D. Ray Reutzel, associate professor, Provo, Utah)

Who decides whether to use a published reading program? In many situations that decision is made by the local school district or the building principal. In the past the vast majority of schools required or strongly encouraged the use of a published reading program. Increasingly, however, teachers are actively seeking a voice in the decision-making process. That trend is reflected in the recommendations made in the *Report Card on Basal Readers,* written by the recent Commission on Reading of the National Council of Teachers of English. Those recommendations are listed in Figure 2–5.

Teachers who object to the use of a published reading program often believe that children learn best by reading self-selected material to accomplish personal, meaningful, and functional tasks. These teachers find that published reading programs provide students with too few opportunities to make personal reading choices; they believe that such programs also teach too many skills, provide too many drills, and isolate the teaching of reading from other subject areas. These teachers prefer self-selected children's literature from the school or classroom library, and they encourage students to read their own writing in classroom projects.

Teachers who value published reading programs believe in the importance of direct instruction in teaching reading skills or strategies. In addition, they argue that published reading programs provide important support and direction for new teachers. Such programs save them from having to put together all of their own reading materials and activities. Also, these teachers note that many published reading programs have recently changed and now include literature selections organized within thematic units. Several pro-

FIGURE 2–5
Recommendations from the National Council of Teachers of English

Teachers should develop, individually or with others, a clear position of their own on how reading is best taught.
- They should continually examine this position as they work with children.
- They should examine policies and instructional materials from this professional perspective.
- They should keep themselves well-informed about developments in research and practice.
- They should communicate to administrators their own professional views.

Teachers individually and collectively need to take back the authority and responsibility to their classrooms for making basic decisions.
- They need to make their own decisions about how they use materials including, or not including, basals to meet the needs of their pupils.
- They need to be willing to take risks while asserting their professional judgments.

Teachers, through their organizations, should reject use of materials, including basals, which make them less than responsible professionals.

Teachers should communicate to administrators, publishers, and others their professional judgments about what they need in the way of resources.
- They should make clear to publishers the strengths and weaknesses of programs as they work with them.
- They should plan material purchases with administrators.
- They should demand a voice in text adoption decisions and policies.

**Source:** From K. S. Goodman, Y. Freeman, S. Murphy, and P. Shannon, *Report Card on Basal Readers* (Evanston, IL: National Council of Teachers of English, 1988).

grams are actually anthologies of children's literature and include classroom libraries of children's books. Finally, these teachers argue that published reading programs have decreased instruction in isolated skills and increased the integration of reading with other subject areas.

As you can see, the decision of whether to use a published reading program is closely associated with beliefs about reading. Teachers who believe that children learn best by reading self-selected materials to accomplish meaningful and functional tasks do not value published reading programs. Teachers who believe that children learn to read best through direct instruction do value published reading programs. Teachers who believe that children learn best through a combination of these approaches value a published reading program used in conjunction with additional reading and writing experiences.

Whatever your beliefs are, or come to be, about reading instruction, published reading programs will continue to be widely available in schools. Thus, it is important to carefully consider both their advantages and their disadvantages as you decide about their role in your classroom. Some of the major, recent conclusions about published reading programs are presented in Table 2–1.

TABLE 2–1
Advantages and disadvantages associated with the use of published reading programs

| Advantages | Disadvantages |
|---|---|
| Published reading programs save time. Having a complete set of stories, instructional activities, assessment instruments, and answer keys means that teachers do not have to spend large amounts of time developing or acquiring each of these components (McCallum, 1988). | Selections in published reading programs often lack educational content. Stories and articles are often selected to teach a particular skill rather than to provide children with substantive knowledge about their environment (Schmidt, Caul, Byers, & Buchmann, 1984). |
| Published reading programs include a comprehensive set of reading skills (Osborn, 1984). | Selections in published reading programs are often uninteresting. They tend not to interest young readers to the same extent as quality children's literature (Goodman, Freeman, Murphy, & Shannon 1988). |
| Published reading programs provide for regular and systematic review of skill development (Harris & Sipay, 1990). | Published reading programs direct teachers to assess children's performance more frequently than they teach children how to read (Durkin, 1981). |
| Published reading programs provide support for new teachers. They are thought by some to be more important than university courses in educating new teachers in reading instruction (McCallum, 1988). | Published reading programs are associated with an abdication of responsibility for classroom decisions. Teachers often believe that these materials must be correct because professionals prepared them (Shannon, 1986). |

## ADAPTING A PUBLISHED READING PROGRAM TO TEACH READING

Should you use a published reading program, it is essential to keep in mind this important point: *no teacher should ever attempt to accomplish everything that is included in any particular plan.* Lesson plans in teacher's manuals are intended to provide a range of suggestions. They should never be followed methodically from beginning to end. There are two general models for adapting those plans. The first is appropriate for teachers who value a systematic presentation of skill development. The second is appropriate for teachers who wish to supplement or replace specific skill lessons with functional reading and writing activities. Figure 2–6 summarizes the adaptations made within each model.

### Model I

If you value a systematic presentation of reading skills, you will use many of the lessons and teaching plans in a published reading program because you will not want your students to miss instruction in important skill areas. Sometimes, though, you will choose to skip a story selection and its related teaching plan when you believe that your students have adequately developed the skill(s) that are the focus of that particular lesson. For example, the sample lesson for *Ira*

FIGURE 2–6
Adapting teaching plans in published reading programs

## Model I
### Teachers Who Value a Systematic Presentation of Reading Skills

Many lessons and stories are used.

Lessons are completed in the sequence in which they appear.

Lessons are skipped when students are proficient at using the major skill(s) introduced or reviewed in the lesson.

Within each lesson instructional activities are usually completed in the general sequence in which they appear. The teacher may choose, however, to introduce or review a skill before students read the story selection rather than after they read it.

Teachers focus instruction on vocabulary development, skill development, reading and discussions, and practice activities. Extension activities are less frequently used.

An instructional activity within a lesson is skipped when the teacher knows the students to be proficient in this area.

Instructional activities within a lesson are modified when the teacher knows a better way of presenting a concept or skill or wants to try out a different method.

Usually, activities are added when a teacher wishes to provide additional practice in a particular skill area.

## Model II
### Teachers Who Wish to Supplement or Replace Specific Skill Lessons with Functional Reading and Writing Activities

Fewer lessons and stories are used.

Lessons and stories are more frequently completed out of sequence.

Lessons are skipped when students are proficient at using the major skill(s) introduced or reviewed in the lesson *or* when the selection is not particularly engaging.

Within each lesson instructional activities are not always completed in the general sequence in which they appear. Often teachers precede the reading of a story selection with an activity from the extension section of the lesson rather than an activity designed to introduce or review a skill.

Teachers focus instruction on vocabulary development, reading and discussions, and extension activities.

Instructional activities in lessons are often skipped, especially skill development sheets or workbook pages. These are replaced by more functional reading and writing activities.

Instructional activities within a lesson may be modified when the teacher knows a better way of presenting a concept or skill or wants to try out a different method.

Usually, activities are added when a teacher wishes to provide more meaningful and functional experiences in reading and writing.

*Sleeps Over* develops initial consonant skills (*c* and *g*) and compound word skills. If your students didn't need instruction in those areas, you would probably skip that entire lesson.

For the lessons that you do teach, you will be apt to make three types of changes in the specific lesson plans of published reading programs. First, you may skip an instructional activity when you know your students to be proficient in that area. In Figure 2–4, for example, you might skip the workbook activities if your students did well with comprehension and the vocabulary of the story. Or you might ask only those discussion questions that were necessary to assure you that students understood the story. In addition, you might skip the phonic skill development lesson on page 54 if your students understood those phonic generalizations. It is not uncommon for teachers to skip activities in published lesson plans.

Second, you may modify an instructional activity within a lesson when you know a better way of presenting the focus of the activity or want to try out a different method. For example, instead of following the teaching suggestions in the sample lesson for presenting new words, you might choose to have individual students read each sentence aloud and then explain which strategies they used to figure out the word in bold print. You might also conduct the guided reading of the story differently by having students work in several small groups, with each student in a group taking the part of one character in the story. Modifying instructional activities in published reading programs is quite common.

Finally, you may add an activity when you wish to provide additional practice in a particular skill area. For example, you might choose to add the "Yes or No" game listed on page 41 to provide additional practice on initial consonant skills (*c* and *g*). Or you might want to have students make compound pictures from compound words to provide additional practice on this skill. The pictures could then be put up in a bulletin board display on compound words. Teachers frequently add instructional activities to lessons in published reading programs.

## Model II

You will use fewer of the lesson planning suggestions in a published reading program if you wish to supplement or replace specific skill lessons with functional reading and writing activities. You might replace an entire lesson with some of the functional reading and writing activities described later in this chapter. Because you care less about completing each and every lesson in a published reading series, you will choose to skip lessons when students are already proficient in the major skill(s) taught in the lesson *or* when the selection is not engaging. It is likely, though, that you would have students read the story *Ira Sleeps Over* since it is such an engaging selection. It is also likely that you would make a number of changes in the lesson presented in the teacher's manual.

Teachers may wish to supplement or replace specific skill lessons with more functional reading/writing activities.

There are several ways for you to adapt the beginnings of lessons in published reading programs. One approach is to use an activity from the extension section of the lesson. Such a section often contains the type of functional activities that are important to you and that are effective in developing background knowledge about a selection (Reutzel, 1985). Alternatively, you could begin a lesson with a functional reading and writing activity that you create yourself. For example, you might brainstorm with your students about how to write an invitation to a friend to sleep overnight. You could write their suggestions for each sentence on the blackboard and then develop the invitation together. By talking about what to take on an overnight sleep over and what feelings are involved, you could develop important background knowledge for the story.

After that activity you might choose to introduce the new vocabulary words (page 46), set the purpose for reading (page 46), and then have students read the story silently. After students have read the story, you might wish to pursue some of the discussion questions on pages 47 to 50. Or you might have students work in small groups on a common task related to the story. For example, you could ask them to discuss and write down their group's prediction about how Ira will solve his problem. These predictions could then be shared before students read the conclusion to the story the next day.

You could also use any of the "Language Lab" or "Extend" activities listed on pages 51 to 53, since these represent the type of functional reading experience you favor. Another option would be to create your own type of extension activity. For example, you might wish to have students work on one of the "Unit Project" suggestions described on page 40. Or you might have students color and decorate their own teddy bear bookmarks for use with bedtime stories. (Blank masters could be cut out of heavy paper stock with lines running across the back.) As students and parents finish reading a bedtime book, they could write down the title on the back of the bookmark and then have it posted in a bulletin board display in the classroom.

Thus, for the Model II teacher, most skill activities are replaced or supplemented with functional reading and writing activities. These generally come from one of three sources: the extension activities at the end of a lesson, the thematic activities suggested at the beginning of a lesson, or the teacher's own creative and inventive mind.

---

## DECISION POINT ➤

What if you were teaching in an elementary school where the principal, facing accountability pressure from the district administration, requires all teachers to use the Houghton Mifflin reading program? You are allowed to replace, supplement, or skip lessons in the program, but student growth is regularly measured by the skill tests that accompany this program, and teachers are held accountable for their students' progress. You believe, however, that basals teach too many isolated skills.

This situation, one of the most common facing reading teachers today, has been described as putting teachers between a rock and a hard place (Mosenthal, 1989). What would you do? Would you follow lesson plans in the program closely? Or would you adapt the lessons, and if so, how? How do you think teachers should handle this type of situation? How do you think principals should handle it?

---

## METHOD FRAMEWORKS: PROCEDURAL ROUTINES FOR INSTRUCTION

method framework: An instructional framework used to teach reading; contains procedural steps for teaching and options for completing each step.

Another way to structure reading experiences for youngsters is through the use of a **method framework**. Method frameworks consist of two common elements: procedural steps for completing an activity and options for completing each of the procedural steps. Teachers employ method frameworks when they use routinized procedures to guide instructional decisions. Listen to several teachers talking about the method frameworks they use in their classrooms, and see whether you can determine the procedural steps in each.

> We're doing a language experience story today. We do one almost every day. It's easy. First we do an activity. Then we talk about it. As they tell me about it, I write their words down on the blackboard. Then I use their words to teach reading. Watch me. (A first-grade teacher preparing her student teacher for the first day of class)

> We do the writing process in our class. First we prewrite. Then we write a draft. Next we revise. Then we proofread. And last we publish. The writing process helps the reading process, you know. I use it as often as possible. (A fourth-grade teacher overheard at a state reading conference)

SQ3R helps my students really pay attention to their reading every time they read in their subject area classes. I tell them to survey the material, raise questions before they read, read to find the answers, recite the answers, and then review the information periodically. (A middle-school teacher enrolled in a university course on reading)

Why are method frameworks so pervasive in reading instruction? Method frameworks allow teachers to attend to the more important aspects of reading instruction. Knowing automatically what the next instructional step will be permits them to pay closer attention to individual students' needs—a student's inability to understand a particular word, another student's failure to make an inference, or a different student's limited range of reading interests. In short, method frameworks free teachers to make appropriate instructional decisions for individual students in busy classrooms.

## USING INDIVIDUALIZED READING, COOPERATIVE LEARNING, AND OTHER METHOD FRAMEWORKS

This section presents six common method frameworks. In addition, it provides model lessons to demonstrate how each method framework can be used to help youngsters develop into avid and proficient readers. Many more method frameworks are presented throughout the rest of this book.

### Individualized Reading Experiences with Literature

**Individualized reading,** or individualized developmental reading, is a method framework that is often used in place of a published reading program. It can also be used to supplement a published reading program. Individualized reading relies on self-selected literature to develop reading ability, a practice that has shown impressive results (Tunnell & Jacobs, 1989). Individualized reading is described in a variety of ways but often includes the following steps:

individualized reading: A method framework containing these four steps: selecting a book, reading it independently, having a conference, and completing a project.

1. The student selects a book to read from the classroom or school library.
2. The student reads the book independently, seeking assistance from the teacher or peers as required.
3. The student has a conference with the teacher about what was read.
4. The student has the option of completing a culminating project to share the book with others.

The first step in individualized reading is student selection of reading materials. Students determine what they will read, based on their own interests and achievement levels. Teachers, however, help children identify interest areas and put students in touch with a range of books in each area. Usually it is suggested that teachers have available four to five books for each student in the class in order to begin an individualized reading program (Harris & Sipay, 1990). This number should provide the necessary variety.

FIGURE 2–7

A sample conference record for individualized reading

Name _____    Date _____

Book _____    Status _____

Comprehension: _____

_____

_____

_____

_____

_____

_____

Other Observations: _____

_____

_____

_____

_____

_____

How will the book be shared? _____

_____

Ideas for additional assistance: _____

_____

Teachers have many options in implementing this first step, especially terms of how much support they wish to provide as students make th selections. For example, they might discuss possibilities with individual s dents, or they might ask that all students read a particular type or variet genre: perhaps poetry, historical fiction, contemporary fiction, or biograph is most common, however, to leave the choice entirely up to the student.

The second step in individualized reading takes place as students read their selections independently, and again, many options are possible. For example, teachers might provide instructional assistance whenever students request it, or they might ask students to meet with them every few chapters in order to keep track of their reading and provide assistance if necessary. Another possibility is to meet periodically only with students who are thought to need additional support.

The third step in individualized reading is the conference, which usually takes place after students have finished reading their selections. Sometimes teachers have an appointment chart so that students may sign up in advance. In other cases teachers arrange for conferences as students require them. During the conference session teachers informally assess through discussion questions how well students have comprehended the selection. Teachers might also ask that a favorite section be read aloud, and teachers and students might discuss what books will be read next.

In some cases the conference also includes a discussion of how students plan to share their books with the class—the optional fourth step in the individualized reading procedure. The project might be something as simple as a short oral report or an illustration of a central scene. It might be a crossword puzzle to be completed by the next student reading the book. It could also be something as elaborate as a diorama with a written synopsis of the book. Individual progress can be recorded on a form similar to the one in Figure 2–7. Suggestions for projects are listed in Figure 2–8 and in Table 2–2. In addition, the model lesson that follows describes how individualized reading is used in one classroom.

## Individualized Reading in Ms. Sanchez's Room

**The Student Selects a Book to Read.** In this classroom, students may select their books from the classroom library, the school library, or the local library. Students choose selections based on their own interests. Ms. Sanchez expects each student to complete at least three books each month. She has taught her second-grade students the five-finger guide to determining the difficulty level of a book. They are to read any page and put down one finger for each word they cannot read. If they have put down all five fingers before they get to the end of the page, the book is probably too difficult.

**MODEL LESSON**

**The Student Reads the Book Independently.** In this classroom, students usually read at their desks or in one of the bean bag chairs in the reading corner. Students seek each other's or their teacher's assistance as they require it. Every week or so, Ms. Sanchez schedules a read-it-and-share-it day. On these days students read a favorite part of their books to a friend and explain why the books are good to read. Students also make predictions about how their stories will end. Then they reverse roles. Ms. Sanchez knows that these activities provide students with rich oral language experiences and also expose them to possible reading selections for the future.

**The Student Has a Conference with the Teacher.** Ms. Sanchez has each student sign up on a schedule located on her desk. Students must sign up at least one day before the conference, listing their name and the book they have read. This gives Ms. Sanchez a chance to prepare herself for the conference. During conferences she asks students to read their favorite parts, while she checks for oral reading fluency. Then she asks several questions about the story and discusses a project that might be completed. She concludes by discussing possible reading selections to follow.

**The Student Completes a Culminating Project.** Students in this class complete one project for every two or three books they have read. The nature of the project is decided jointly by Ms. Sanchez and each student, in keeping with each student's interests and needs. Around the room are several recent projects: a poster advertising the book *I Was A Second Grade Werewolf* by Daniel Pinkwater, a diorama of a scene from *Sarah's Unicorn* by Bruce Coville, and a crossword puzzle made by one student and completed by another after each had read *Patrick's Dinosaur* by Carol Carrick.

## Language Experience Stories

language experience stories: A method framework containing these four steps: providing a vivid experience, eliciting oral language, transcribing oral language, and helping students read what was transcribed.

**Language experience stories** are a second method framework commonly found in elementary classrooms. Such stories are often used to supplement or replace a published reading program (Baumann, 1984). In addition, they may be used to prepare young children before they begin using a published reading program. Language experience stories are most commonly used in kindergarten and first-grade classrooms to develop beginning concepts about reading. They may also be used among older students experiencing difficulty in reading (Heller, 1988); they are especially useful in conjunction with classroom writing activities (Coate & Castle, 1989; Karnowski, 1989). When using language experience stories, teachers often follow these procedural steps:

1. Provide students with a vivid experience.
2. Elicit oral language from students that describes the experience.
3. Transcribe the students' oral language.
4. Help students read what was transcribed.

To begin a language experience story, teachers must first provide students with a vivid experience, which then provides the content for the story.

FIGURE 2–8
Generic activities that might be used to conclude any individualized
reading experience

1. Make a crossword puzzle using vocabulary words found in your reading selection. You may wish to use a computer program to help you. Have the next person reading this book attempt to complete the puzzle, with your help if necessary.

2. Make an advertisement for your book that tries to sell others on reading it. Put your ad up with others on a bulletin board labeled "Great Buys on Great Books."

3. Come to school dressed as one of the major characters in your book. When people ask you about your character, be certain to describe what the person did and how he or she acted.

4. Write a different ending to your reading selection. Make it the final chapter.

5. Create a shoebox diorama illustrating one of the scenes from your reading selection. Attach a 5-x-7 card to it listing the author, title, and publisher of the book, as well as a description of the scene you have created.

6. Write a letter to one of the characters in your reading selection. Put this with letters from other students on a bulletin board labeled "Letters to Characters in Books We Have Read."

7. Write a letter to the author of your reading selection; send it in care of the publisher.

8. Read several other books by the same author. Then write one review of all of the books. Post your review on a bulletin board labeled "Critics' Corner."

9. Read several books on the same theme written by different authors. Then write one review of all of the books. Post your review on a bulletin board labeled "Critics' Corner."

10. Read aloud to the class an exciting episode from your selection. Do not tell the other students what the ending is but encourage them to read the book for themselves.

Teacher options for this first step are limitless—a field trip, a leaf walk, a visit from a neighborhood helper (such as a firefighter), a movie, a filmstrip, a classroom pet.

The second procedural step is to elicit oral language from the students to describe the experience. Again, teachers have a wide variety of options. The entire class might orally compose a description of the experience. Or students might individually draw a picture of something that happened during the experience. At the same time the teacher might circulate, asking students to tell what they have drawn.

The third procedural step requires the teacher to transcribe the students' oral language. If the class dictated a story or a letter together, the teacher could

**TABLE 2–2**
Specific activities that might be used to conclude a particular individualized reading experience

| Selection | Activity |
|---|---|
| *The Little Prince* by Antoine de Saint-Exupery | Make a papier-maché model of the asteroid where the Little Prince lived. Use a balloon to mold the basic shape. |
| *Little House in the Big Woods* by Laura Ingalls Wilder | Write a book of pioneer recipes using the descriptions found in this book. Possible entries include head cheese, smoked ham, and sugar snow. |
| *The Very Hungry Caterpillar* by Eric Carle | Start making a "book caterpillar" around the walls of your classroom. Cut out a pattern for a segment of the caterpillar's body. Then have students write the title and author of each book they read on one of these segments and post them on the wall. Have the first student who reads a book make the head. Your caterpillar can even go out into the hallway, announcing your reading to the rest of the school. |
| *Alexander and the Terrible, Horrible, No Good, Very Bad Day* by Judith Viorst | Write a book with a similar pattern, entitled *Alexander and the Outstanding, Perfect, Beautiful, Very Good Day.* |
| *James and the Giant Peach* by Roald Dahl | Make a papier-maché model of the peach on which James flew away with all his insect friends. Use a balloon to mold the basic shape. Then cut out an opening and show James and his friends inside their home. |
| *Frog and Toad Are Friends* by Arnold Lobel | Draw a picture of your favorite story, and write a sentence underneath the picture describing what happened. Post this with other illustrations on a bulletin board entitled "Friendship." |
| *Where the Wild Things Are* by Maurice Sendak | Make a map describing the route Max took to get to the place of the "wild things." |

transcribe each student's sentence on the chalkboard. Another option would be to transcribe the story on chart paper, to produce a more permanent record of events in the classroom. The teacher could also transcribe the story by means of a computer program designed for language experience activities. If students drew individual illustrations, the teacher could transcribe their comments right on the illustration (e.g., "Here is the puddle Mike fell into").

The final step is to help students read what was transcribed. Even if youngsters have not learned to recognize any words, teachers can use this step to build important concepts about reading. With very young students, teachers

Language experience stories are often used to supplement or replace a published reading program.

can show how sentences are read from left to right. They can also read sentences aloud, stopping before each student name in the story and asking that individual to read his or her own name. Another option is to read all of a sentence except the last word and have a student complete it (e.g., "We went on a trip to an apple farm and picked _____"). Students will have enough background knowledge about the experience to fill in the final word in most sentences. The model lesson on page 74 illustrates the language experience approach.

## Cooperative Learning Groups

**Cooperative learning groups** are a third method framework that is used in conjunction with or in place of a published reading program. Cooperative learning groups may also be used when students are reading in individual subject areas (Harp, 1989; Herber, 1978; Maring, Furman, and Blum-Anderson, 1985; Uttero, 1988). This method framework goes by many different names: cooperative learning, collaborative learning, cooperative learning strat-

cooperative learning groups: A method framework containing these four steps: defining the learning task, assigning students to groups, having students complete the learning task in their groups, and letting the groups share their results.

**MODEL LESSON**

A Language Experience Story in Ms. Brown's Room

**Provide Students with a Vivid Experience.** It is the first day of school. Ms. Brown wants to start the year off right by providing her first-grade students with a positive reading experience. She has brought her pet rabbit, Fluffy, into the classroom, and she introduces Fluffy to the class. She explains how to feed and care for the rabbit. She gives each student a chance to pet Fluffy and feel her soft fur. Then Ms. Brown puts Fluffy back into her cage and explains that Fluffy will be visiting their room for one month. She concludes by answering each student's questions about this new member of the class.

**Elicit Oral Language That Describes the Experience.** Ms. Brown then has the students sit on the rug in front of a large piece of chart paper taped to the wall. She tells the students that they are going to tell a story together and that she will write down their words. She asks for a title for a story that will describe what they just did. Tomas suggests "Fluffy the Bunny." Other students contribute a sentence each until a story is formed, describing their experience.

**Transcribe the Students' Oral Language.** As each student contributes a sentence, Ms. Brown writes it down on the chart paper with a felt-tip pen. The completed story looks like this:

Fluffy the Bunny

Ms. Brown brought her bunny to our class.
Its name was Fluffy.
Fluffy has pink eyes and white fur.
Her fur is REALLY soft.
Fluffy bit Alexandra.
But Fluffy didn't mean to hurt her.
She thought Alexandra's finger was a carrot.
We get to keep Fluffy in our class.

THE END

**Help Students Read What Was Transcribed.** Ms. Brown uses two strategies today. First, she reads the title aloud and points out the word *Fluffy*. Then she asks students to find this word at other points in the story. ("Who can find another word that looks just like this? What does it say?. . . My, you can read so well already. Did you read books over the summer? Now, can anyone else find another word that says 'Fluffy'? Read it for us. Very good.") Several students get to come up and point to the word *Fluffy* in the story. Ms. Brown's second strategy is to read each sentence aloud, running her finger under each word but stopping before the last word in each sentence. Then she asks for volunteers to read that word. Ms. Brown concludes the lesson by praising her students for getting off to such a good start in reading this year.

egies, cooperative integrated reading and composition, cooperative reading teams, or collaborative learning groups. Depending on the definition, cooperative learning may also have many different sets of procedural steps. This text uses the term *cooperative learning groups* to refer to a method framework with these procedural steps:

1. The teacher defines a learning task.
2. The teacher assigns students to groups.
3. Students complete the learning task together through cooperative group activity.
4. The results of the learning task are shared with the other groups.

The first procedural step is to define a learning task for students. Teacher options are nearly limitless but must be related to instructional goals. For example, cooperative learning groups might be used to complete the guided reading portion of a story in a published reading program, having each member of a group read one character's part, as described earlier. Or each group could be given a set of statements and asked to decide whether the story or article they had read supported, or did not support, each of the statements (Herber, 1978). In addition, the group might be required to record its answer and the evidence from the story that supports its decision. An alternative task might be something as lengthy as having a group read material independently about setting up an aquarium and then summarize their information on a single data sheet. The sheet might be organized around questions such as these:

What type of fish can live together in our aquarium?

What kind of food do these fish need to eat?

How often should they be fed?

What should the water temperature be for these fish?

How do we get the aquarium ready for new fish?

Should we get natural or artificial plants? Why?

What special things should we do to prevent sickness?

Can we raise baby fish? How?

Figure 2–9 provides other examples of tasks that might be used within cooperative learning groups.

Teachers have the option of forming several groups to accomplish the same task. For example, three different groups might be assigned the task of deciding the most logical conclusion to a story. Or each of several groups could receive a page containing a set of statements related to a chapter in social studies. The students might then be directed to read the chapter individually and decide in their groups which statements could be supported from the information in the chapter and which could not. Each group's results could then be shared with the entire class.

FIGURE 2–9

Learning tasks that might be completed in cooperative learning groups

1. Before they read a particular passage, give students a list of words that may be unfamiliar. Have each cooperative learning group try to define the words and generate a sentence that uses each correctly. Then get back together and compare definitions and sample sentences.

2. After they have read a chapter in a subject area text, give students a list of statements about the topic of the chapter. Have each group determine whether the various statements are supported by the information in the chapter. Also have them record any supporting information.

3. After they have read a chapter in a subject area text, give students a list of statements about the topic of the chapter. Have each group determine whether the various statements are explicitly supported by information in the text or whether they require inferences to be made.

4. Before they read a story or article on a particular topic, have students in each group list all of the information they already know about this topic. Then get back together and compare notes.

5. After they have read a story, have students work together in groups to complete the workbook pages from a published reading program. Have one student appointed the recorder/reporter to write down why that group answered each item in the way that it did. Get back together and compare the reasons for the answers.

6. After they have read a story, have students work in their groups to develop a short script from one portion of the selection. Let them practice reading their parts several times before sharing the scripts with the rest of the class.

Teachers also have the option of assigning different tasks to different groups or a single task to just one group. For example, one group might prepare a TV advertisement for a book the students have read. Another group might prepare a book cover for the door of the classroom, advertising the book to the rest of the school. Another approach would be to ask a single group to complete the guided reading of a story by having each student read one character's part. Or a single group might complete the workbook pages in a lesson from a published reading program. Many possibilities exist for cooperative learning groups.

The second procedural step requires the teacher to assign students to groups, usually three to five students per group. Cooperative learning groups almost always consist of students with a range of reading abilities. Heterogeneous grouping allows students to benefit from the unique insights of each group member. It also avoids the motivational problems that result when lower-achieving students are placed in a single group. Often cooperative learning groups change composition with every task; at other times more stable teams are formed.

Learning in cooperative groups and then sharing with other groups is a useful method framework.

During the third procedural step students complete the learning task together in their groups. One element in this step is often fixed: each group usually designates one person to serve as a recorder/reporter. This individual keeps a written account of the group's decisions. This function is important because the results of the group's work are often shared in a brief oral report to the rest of the class.

The fourth step, sharing the results of the learning task with the entire class, is not always required. If the task is to read different parts of a story aloud, nothing needs to be reported. On most tasks, though, some sort of report is shared to permit the groups to compare their work.

## A Cooperative Learning Group in Ms. Gallagher's Room

**The Teacher Defines a Learning Task.** Ms. Gallagher spends about half of the year using a published reading program with her fifth-grade class. During the next three weeks, however, she will have the class working in five different interest groups, which are organized around the most popular interest areas of the students in her class. The students in one group, the Mysteries Group, will be required to read at least one mystery from the class or school library. During the final three days of the time period, members of this group will share the books they have read, select an exciting episode from one of the mysteries, practice acting it out, and then perform it for the entire class. A second group, the Hamster Group, will research the se-

**MODEL LESSON**

lection and care of hamsters. After reading everything they can find in the school library, these students will present a group report to the class. The third and fourth groups will do similar projects on mice and tropical fish. Then the second, third, and fourth groups will each send one member along with Ms. Gallagher on a lunchtime field trip to a pet store to select the new pets for the class. The fifth group, the Olympics Group, will read materials from the school library on the upcoming Olympics and then complete a fact sheet prepared by Ms. Gallagher. After collaborating on this fact sheet, each member will prepare a written report. This group will then organize a class-room Olympics to take place at the end of the three-week period.

**The Teacher Assigns Students to Groups.** Two days before the groups are assigned, Ms. Gallagher explains the group projects and puts out sign-up sheets for each group. Because these are interest groups, students select the project on which they wish to work. However, Ms. Gallagher limits each group to five members.

**Students Complete the Learning Task Together.** During the three weeks Ms. Gallagher circulates through the classroom during reading time, assist-ing students with their particular needs. She does a short lesson for some students on the use of the library's card catalog. She helps others use the index in their books to find specific information. She helps others select an interesting mystery. Ms. Gallagher remains available to help as students near completion of their group's project.

**The Results of the Learning Task Are Shared with the Entire Class.** At the end of the three-week period, time is set aside for each group to display the results of its work. The other fifth-grade class in the school is invited to this session, too.

---

## Directed Reading Activity

directed reading activity (DRA): A method frame-work containing these four steps: preparation, guided reading, skill development and practice, and enrich-ment.

A **directed reading activity (DRA)** is the method framework commonly used to structure reading lessons in published reading programs. However, it can also be transferred to other contexts. The procedural steps in a DRA follow the structure of lessons in published reading programs:

1. preparation
2. guided reading
3. skill development and practice
4. enrichment

During the preparation portion of a DRA, teachers introduce any new vocabulary that might be unfamiliar to students. In addition, the purpose for reading is set. Unlike the preparation portion of lessons in a published reading program, during this step of a DRA teachers themselves decide which words to teach, how to teach them, and how to define the purpose for reading.

Many options are available to teachers during this first procedural step. New words are typically selected on the basis of their centrality to the meaning of the passage and the difficulty they will cause students. Teachers may introduce vocabulary words in a variety of ways. They may directly teach the meanings, or they may allow students to induce the meanings from sentences in which the words occur. In addition, teachers may wish to design a cooperative learning task to promote understanding of these new words. Teachers also have considerable freedom in defining the purpose for reading.

The second step of a DRA, guided reading, usually takes place silently first. Then selected portions of the passage may be read and discussed. Teachers may wish to focus discussion on certain types of questions, such as inferential or predictive questions. As you have already seen, cooperative reading groups can also be used to accomplish this procedural step.

After guided reading, the next procedural step is skill development and practice. With published reading programs this step is usually accomplished with workbook pages. Without such programs, teachers may wish to create practice pages on their own that are designed to review information in the passage, new vocabulary, or particular skill areas. As an alternative, teachers might design a task that could be completed within a cooperative learning group.

The final procedural step in a DRA consists of an enrichment or extension activity. The nature of the activity depends on the passage that students have read. If they have read a chapter in social studies about Christopher Columbus's voyage of discovery, the teacher might ask students to write a diary entry for different days of Columbus's journey. These entries could then be put together to create a diary of Columbus's trip. If, instead, students have read a chapter in science about Madame Curie, the teacher might ask them to imagine that she is still alive and that they can ask her any question they want. Students might write their questions in letters addressed to Madame Curie, which could then be posted for all to read and enjoy. There are many ways to create enrichment activities.

---

## A Directed Reading Activity in Ms. Simonetta's Room

**Preparation.** On Fridays Ms. Simonetta devotes one hour to reading and discussing the *News Explorer,* a newspaper containing articles on current events of interest to students in the fourth grade. This week the newspaper is focused on the upcoming elections. Yesterday, Ms. Simonetta read through the articles and selected the following words that she thought might not be clear to her students: *electoral college, popular vote, electoral vote, Senate, House of Representatives, Speaker of the House,* and *cabinet.* At the beginning of the lesson, she writes each word on the chalkboard,

**MODEL LESSON**

along with the sentence in which it appears. Volunteers read each sentence and attempt to define the targeted word. Ms. Simonetta clarifies meanings and then lets the class members decide their purpose in reading the newspaper. They decide to see whether there is information in the newspaper with which they are unfamiliar.

**Guided Reading.** Everyone reads the paper silently. Then Ms. Simonetta suggests that the students form cooperative learning groups and list the new information they learned from reading the articles. Ms. Simonetta forms five different groups and reminds each to appoint a recorder/reporter to keep a written account of the new information. Ms. Simonetta circulates through the classroom, observing each group's progress. After each group is finished, she calls the groups together and asks each recorder/reporter to report back to the class. These reports produce a number of interesting issues that get clarified as a result of the discussion.

**Skill Development and Practice.** Ms. Simonetta uses this opportunity to review the concept of a main idea and supporting details. She defines each term and uses the lead article to give examples. She then gives each cooperative learning group a new task: to pick one article in the newspaper and determine its main idea and three supporting details. The groups complete the task and then get back together again to report their results.

**Enrichment.** Ms. Simonetta's class just completed its own election of class officers last week. Students ran for different offices, made campaign posters, presented campaign speeches, and had an election. Ms. Simonetta has decided to have each student write a newspaper article about some aspect of the election. She reminds them that their article should contain a main idea and several supporting details. After brainstorming possible topics, students complete their rough drafts. Ms. Simonetta then announces that the articles are to be edited and revised. Final copies will be put into a class newspaper about the election, which will be circulated throughout the school. Since this is the first issue, Ms. Simonetta announces that she will serve as editor but appoints an associate editor to assist. The associate editor will become the editor of the next issue and will get to pick an associate editor.

## Deductive Instruction

deductive instruction: A method framework containing these four steps: stating the skill or rule, providing examples, providing guided practice, and providing independent practice.

**Deductive instruction** is a method framework most commonly associated with phonic instruction in reading. However, it may be used to teach any skill, rule, or generalization. It is especially useful for lessons with small groups of students who need assistance in a specific area of reading. Deductive instruction contains four procedural steps:

1. State the skill or rule.
2. Provide examples of the skill or rule.

3. Provide guided practice.
4. Provide independent practice.

The first procedural step is to state the skill or rule that students should learn. For instance, a teacher might decide to present a phonic generalization (e.g., "When the letters *ow* appear together, they often represent the sound at the end of the word *cow* or the word *row*"). Or a teacher might decide to present a strategic skill useful to readers (e.g., "With an informational article it is often useful to read the introduction, skim the body of the text, and then read the conclusion before reading the entire article").

The second procedural step of deductive instruction is to provide examples of the skill or rule being taught. In the phonic generalization just mentioned, the teacher might choose to write these examples on the chalkboard:

| Cow | Row |
|-----|-----|
| town | low |
| clown | slow |
| bow | bow |
| how | glow |
| now | grow |
| wow | tow |

The third procedural step is to provide guided practice in using the skill or rule. When teaching this phonic generalization the teacher might provide students with additional words (*gown, plow, flown, crow*) and help them use the rule to determine the correct pronunciation. Or perhaps cooperative learning groups could sort through a list of *ow* words and determine the type of vowel sound made in each.

The final procedural step in deductive instruction is to provide independent practice. It is important that each practice opportunity be closely related to the lesson objectives (Blair & Rupley, 1988). One option is to have youngsters read a story or article in which the rule is required. For example, students might read a story containing words with both types of *ow* sounds. Or the teacher might select (or create) a skill page, with which students could practice this rule independently at their seats. This option is common in published reading programs. Examples of such skill pages can be seen on pages 56 to 58.

## Deductive Instruction in Mr. Burns's Room

**State the Skill or Rule.** Several students in Mr. Burns's second-grade class are experiencing difficulty with words containing the initial letter *c*—words like *candle, can,* and *come*. Mr. Burns decides to teach a lesson to these students, using a deductive framework. As he stands at the chalkboard, with six students sitting before him on the rug, Mr. Burns states the rule: "Today we are going to learn one of the sounds represented by the letter *c*. When the letter *c* is followed by *a, u,* or *o,* it usually represents the sound /k/, as it does at the beginning of the word *cat.* Look at these examples."

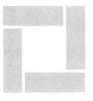

**MODEL LESSON**

**Provide Examples of the Skill or Rule.** Next, Mr. Burns reads and then has students read the following words:

| | | |
|---|---|---|
| cat | cut | cot |
| can | cup | corn |
| cap | cub | come |

As the words are read, Mr. Burns shows that in each case the letter *c* is followed by *a, u,* or *o*. He also points out that the letter *c* represents the /k/ sound in each word.

**Provide Guided Practice.** Next, Mr. Burns presents a new set of words to see whether the students have acquired the rule. He reminds them of the rule and assists with pronunciation when students have difficulty. The words in this second list are these:

| | | |
|---|---|---|
| cab | curl | cold |
| car | cure | cod |
| camp | curb | coal |

**Provide Independent Practice.** Mr. Burns explains how to complete the activity that he has prepared. Because he isn't confident that everyone can complete it independently, he changes this step slightly. He decides to have the students complete the task in a cooperative learning group. Mr. Burns gives directions to the students and then goes over their work when they have completed the activity. The page he gives them looks like this:

> Draw a circle around every word in which the letter *c* represents the same sound as the beginning sound in *kite*.
>
> 1. Can you come to the party?
> 2. Certainly. What should I bring?
> 3. Bring a bunch of cinnamon cookies.
> 4. Bring a knife, too, so I can cut my cake.
>
> Which letters follow *c* when it sounds like *k*? Write them here.
>
> ———   ———   ———

## Inductive Instruction

inductive instruction: A method framework containing these four steps: providing examples, helping students discover the skill or rule, providing guided practice, and providing independent practice.

**Inductive instruction** is another method framework commonly associated with phonic instruction. However, it, too, may be used to teach any skill, rule, or generalization. Inductive instruction is especially useful for lessons with small groups of students who need assistance in a specific area of reading. Inductive instruction contains four procedural steps:

1. Provide examples of the skill or rule.
2. Help students discover the skill or rule.

3. Provide guided practice.
4. Provide independent practice.

You may have noticed that the procedural steps in inductive instruction are identical to those in deductive instruction with one exception—the order of the first two steps is reversed. Inductive instruction begins with examples and then uses those examples to help students discover the rule.

Thus, the first step in an inductive framework is to provide students with examples of the rule they are to learn. To teach the phonic generalization about *ow* described earlier, a teacher might provide students with the following examples:

| | | | |
|---|---|---|---|
| cow | row | wow | low |
| plow | slow | bow | bow |
| how | glow | now | grow |

The second step in an inductive framework is to use these examples to help students discover, or induce, the targeted rule. For example, a teacher might ask students how many different sounds occur at the end of the listed words. Then students could sort the words into two sets: one for words like *cow* and one for words like *row*. Finally, the teacher might ask them to state a rule about the sounds of *ow* and help them do so: "When the letters *ow* appear together, they often represent the sound at the end of the word *cow* or the word *row*."

The third procedural step of inductive instruction is the same as that of deductive instruction—to provide guided practice in using the skill or rule. As before, the teacher might provide students with additional words and help them see whether their rule applied to the new words. Or a cooperative learning group could sort through a list of *ow* words and determine the type of vowel sound in each.

The fourth procedural step is also identical to that of deductive instruction—to provide independent practice. As before, the teacher might have youngsters read a story or article in which *ow* words appear. Or a skill page could provide independent practice for students at their seats.

---

## Inductive Instruction in Ms. Brown's Room

**Provide Examples of the Skill or Rule.** Ms. Brown has several first-grade students who are making good progress in reading but have difficulty reading words beginning with the letter *c,* such as *can, could,* and *cup.* Ms. Brown decides to teach the same rule that Mr. Burns taught, but she has decided to use an inductive framework instead. To begin, she puts the following words on the board for her students to analyze, and reads each one:

**MODEL LESSON**

| | | |
|---|---|---|
| cat | cut | cot |
| can | cup | corn |
| cap | cub | come |

**Help Students Discover the Skill or Rule.** Ms. Brown asks questions to help students notice both the consistent sound represented by the letter *c* and the environment in which it occurs. "What is the same in all of these words? Yes, they all begin with the letter *c*. Is the sound for *c* the same in all these words? What sound does *c* make in these words? Do you notice anything else about these words? What letters follow the letter *c*? I wonder if the letter *c* always makes the sound of *k* when the next letter is an *a, u,* or *o*? Let's see." Then Ms. Brown begins to put other words on the board with the letter *c* followed by *a, u,* or *o*: *cucumber, call, coconut*. She also puts up words in which *c* is followed by other vowels to show that the /k/ sound occurs only after *a, u,* or *o*: *city, cent, cyclone, center, cinder*. Finally she asks students to make up a rule to account for these observations. She helps them state it and then writes it on the board: a *c* followed by an *a, u,* or *o* usually represents the sound of /k/.

**Provide Guided Practice.** Next, Ms. Brown presents a new set of words to see whether students have acquired the rule. She reminds them of the rule and assists with pronunciation when they have difficulty. The words in this list are these:

| | | |
|---|---|---|
| cab | curl | cold |
| car | cure | cod |
| camp | curb | coal |

**Provide Independent Practice.** Ms. Brown also decides to try a cooperative learning group and borrows Mr. Burns's activity page. Ms. Brown provides directions and has her group complete the page at the round table in the corner. She goes over their work when they have completed the activity.

## COMMENTS FROM THE CLASSROOM ■

Emily Dodson

At Tecumseh Elementary School, Mr. Burns, Ms. Sanchez and I all started teaching second grade here four years ago, and we still try to have lunch together so we can compare notes on our teaching. Each of us teaches reading a little bit differently. Mr. Burns is the most structured in the way he approaches it. He believes that students benefit most from direct instruction in reading skills, and so he spends more time than either Ms. Sanchez or I with the published reading program our school uses. Frequently, he modifies skill activities in the program to be consistent with deductive instruction, his favorite method framework.

Ms. Sanchez spends the least amount of time with our reading program. Most of the time she has her students reading books they choose on their own. She uses individualized reading a lot.

I fall somewhere between Mr. Burns and Ms. Sanchez. If anything, I'm probably closer to Ms. Sanchez than I am to Mr. Burns. Like Ms. Sanchez, I believe that students learn by reading to accomplish meaningful and functional tasks. At the same time, though, I believe that they benefit from direct instruction about reading. On any given day my classroom probably shows a blend of both material and method frameworks.

Today, for instance, I was working with a group of students who have been having difficulty with inferential reasoning. Inferential reasoning requires that readers use information in the text together with knowledge they already have about the world to make a reasoned assumption about meaning. Some people refer to it as reading between the lines. In class, we had read and discussed *Amelia Bedelia* by Peggy Parish, a literature selection in our published reading series. That story is perfect for learning about inferences because Amelia interprets everything literally. If the owner of the house says to dust the furniture, poor Amelia gets out the dusting powder and sprinkles it all over. If the owner of the house says to draw the curtains, Amelia gets out her sketch pad and a pencil. After this group had talked about how important it is to read between the lines, I had the students complete several activities suggested in the teacher's manual. However, instead of following the manual's suggestions, I had the students work in cooperative learning groups.

At the same time other students were working in a corner of the room on another cooperative learning activity. They had been reading about how to set up the empty aquarium in the classroom. Today they were discussing and recording what they had learned. They're scheduled to make an oral report to the class at the end of the week. Then they'll get to set up the aquarium and take care of it. These students have had to read to accomplish a meaningful and functional task, and as a result, I know that each student in the group has learned something important. For one it may have been how to use an index. For another it may have been how to organize information.

At the very same time, another group in the room was working with self-selected literature from our classroom library. Some were reading, and others were talking about how they would share their books with the class. Still others were preparing their presentations. It seems that someone in my class is always engaged in individualized reading. I like that method framework a lot. It helps students learn about reading while they're accomplishing something that's personally meaningful and functional.

I've acquired these different frameworks over a period of time, and I'm pleased with the combination I'm using right now. Teaching from several method frameworks as well as a material framework allows me to provide the individual attention that's so important to my young students.

---

MAJOR POINTS

■ Teachers use a material framework when they use a published reading program for reading instruction. Published reading programs are comprehensive published sets of graded materials used to teach reading in kindergarten through Grades 6 or 8. They are sometimes referred to as basal reading programs, basal readers, or simply basals. Lesson plans in these programs have a common structure.

■ One of the more controversial issues in reading instruction today is whether teachers should use a published, or basal, reading program to assist them in reading instruction. There are both advantages and disadvantages associated with the use of published reading programs. The decision to use or not to use a published reading program is often associated with beliefs about reading.

■ There are at least two models for adapting lesson plans in a published reading program. One is for teachers who value a systematic presentation of skill development. The other is for teachers who wish to supplement or replace specific skill lessons with functional reading and writing activities.

■ Method frameworks consist of two common elements: procedural steps for completing an activity and options for completing each one of the procedural steps. Method frameworks, like material frameworks, are used by teachers to reduce the complexity of instructional decision making in busy classrooms.

■ Each of the following method frameworks is commonly used to teach reading: individualized reading, language experience stories, cooperative learning groups, directed reading activities, deductive instruction, and inductive instruction. You should be familiar with the procedural steps for each.

## MAKING INSTRUCTIONAL DECISIONS

1. You might find yourself in a school district that requires you to use a published reading program like the one illustrated in this chapter. If you want to be sure that you provide students with functional and meaningful reading experiences, where would you look for those types of activities in the teacher's manual? Identify the appropriate pages in Figure 2–4.

2. If, instead, teachers in your school district are allowed to decide for themselves whether to use the published reading program in Figure 2–4, what will you as a first-grade teacher choose to do with your class? Why? In order to make this decision, you will first need to define your beliefs about reading at this point in your development. Do children learn best through direct instruction or through self-selected materials to accomplish meaningful and functional tasks, or through a combination of both?

3. Having defined your beliefs about reading, what adjustments would you make if your school district required you to use the published reading program illustrated in this chapter? Describe the lesson that you would develop for the story *Ira Sleeps Over*, referring to the lesson in Figure 2–4 as necessary.

4. If you want to spend some time with a small group of students in your class who are having difficulty with inferences, which method framework(s) would you select for your other students so that you can spend time with this smaller group? Explain.

**5.** If you are not using a published reading program, how would you order the method frameworks described in this chapter in terms of probable frequency of use? Explain.

Baumann, J. F. (1984). How to expand a basal reader program. *The Reading Teacher, 37,* 604–607.

Shows how to modify a basal program with language experience activities, individualized reading, and other language arts activities, including the use of parent aides and peer tutors.

Blanton, W. E., Moorman, G. B., & Wood, K. D. (1986). *The Reading Teacher, 47*(3), 263–269.

Presents a seven-step method framework for teaching specific reading skills: exploration, explication, translation, modeling, guided practice, application, closure. Also provides an example of a lesson.

Karnowski, L. (1989). Using LEA with process writing. *The Reading Teacher, 42*(7), 462–465.

Explains how the procedural steps of language experience activities (LEA) and language experience stories may be combined with a process approach to teaching writing. Presents many examples of young students' writing. This technique is especially appropriate for kindergarten and first-grade students who are just beginning to learn to read and write.

Madden, L. (1988). Improve reading attitudes of poor readers through cooperative reading teams. *The Reading Teacher, 42*(3), 194–199.

Describes cooperative learning groups as especially effective in motivating weaker readers. Presents many specific activities in reading that may be accomplished within such a framework.

McCallum, R. D. (1988). Don't throw the basals out with the bath water. *The Reading Teacher, 42*(3), 204–209.

Argues that published reading programs play a key role in supporting instructional decision making and in developing knowledgeable teachers.

Tunnell, M. O., & Jacobs, J. S. (1989). Using "real" books: Research findings on literature-based reading instruction. *The Reading Teacher, 42*(7), 470–477.

Draws a number of important conclusions from an extensive review of the research on literature-based programs, many of which used individualized reading. Also describes the basic elements of successful programs.

**FURTHER READING**

Baumann, J. F. (1984). How to expand a basal reader program. *The Reading Teacher, 37,* 604–607.

Beck, I. L., Omanson, R. C., & McKeown, M. G. (1982). An instructional redesign of reading lessons: Effects on comprehension. *Reading Research Quarterly, 17,* 462–481.

Blair, T. R., & Rupley, W. H. (1988). Practice and application in the teaching of readi~ *Reading Teacher, 41,* 536–539.

Bohning, G. (1986). The McGuffey Eclectic Readers: 1836–1986. *The Readi~* 263–269.

Coate, S., & Castle, M. (1989). Integrating LEA and invented spelling in ki~ *Reading Teacher, 42*(7), 516–519.

Durkin, D. (1981). Reading comprehension instruction in five basal reader series. *search Quarterly, 16,* 515–544.

Fay, L. (1989). *The Riverside reading program: Teacher's edition, Level 6.* Chicago: ~

Flood, J., & Lapp, D. (1986). Types of texts: The match between what students read in ~ what they encounter in tests. *Reading Research Quarterly, 21*(3), 284–297.

**REFERENCES**

Goodman, K. S., Freeman, Y., Murphy, S., & Shannon, P. (1988). *Report card on basal readers*. Evanston, IL: National Council of Teachers of English.

Harp, B. (1989). What do we put in the place of ability grouping? *The Reading Teacher, 42*(7), 534–535.

Harris, A. J., & Sipay, E. R. (1990). *How to increase reading ability* (9th ed.). New York: Longman.

Heller, M. F. (1988). Comprehending and composing through language experience. *The Reading Teacher, 42*(2), 130–135.

Herber, H. (1978). *Teaching reading in content areas* (2nd ed.). Englewood Cliffs, NJ: Prentice Hall.

Karnowski, L. (1989). Using LEA with process writing. *The Reading Teacher, 42*(7), 462–465.

Leu, D. J., Jr. (1986). *Understanding three heuristics used during reading instruction: Material, method, and comprehension frameworks*. Paper presented at the National Reading Conference, San Diego, CA.

Maring, G. H., Furman, G. C., & Blum-Anderson, J. (1985). Five cooperative learning strategies for mainstreamed youngsters in content area classrooms. *The Reading Teacher, 39*(3), 310–313.

McCallum, R. D. (1988). Don't throw the basals out with the bath water. *The Reading Teacher, 42*(3), 204–209.

Mosenthal, P. B. (1989). The whole language approach: Teachers between a rock and a hard place. *The Reading Teacher, 42*(8), 628–629.

Osborn, J. (1984). Workbooks that accompany basal reading programs. In G. G. Duffy, L. R. Roehler, and J. Mason (Eds.), *Comprehension instruction: Perspectives and suggestions*. New York: Longman.

Reutzel, D. R. (1985). Reconciling schema theory and the basal reading lesson. *The Reading Teacher, 39*(2), 194–205.

Schmidt, W. H., Caul, J., Byers, J. L., & Buchmann, M. (1984). Content of basal text selections: Implications for comprehension instruction. In G. G. Duffy, L. R. Roehler, & J. Mason (Eds.), *Comprehension instruction: Perspectives and suggestions*. New York: Longman.

Shannon, P. (1986). The use of commercial reading materials in American elementary schools. *Reading Research Quarterly, 19*, 68–85.

*Sun and Shadow*. (1985). Orlando, FL: Harcourt Brace Jovanovich.

Tunnell, M. O., & Jacobs, J. S. (1989). Using "real" books: Research findings on literature-based reading instruction. *The Reading Teacher, 42*(7), 470–477.

Uttero, D. A. (1988). Activating comprehension through cooperative learning. *The Reading Teacher, 41*, 390–395.

# Developing a Comprehension Framework

- Comprehension Frameworks: Developing a Personal Perspective
- The Components of Reading Comprehension
- How Does a Person Read?
- How Does Reading Ability Develop?
- Using a Comprehension Framework to Guide Instructional Decisions

極桌、頂桌

*And so to completely analyze what we do when we read would almost be the acme of a psychologist's achievements, for it would be to describe very many of the most intricate workings of the human mind, as well as to unravel the tangled story of the most remarkable specific performance that civilization has learned in all its history.*

E. B. Huey, *The Psychology and Pedagogy of Reading* (Cambridge, MA: MIT Press, 1908), p. 6.

A comprehension framework provides insight into the reading process and the different components of reading. As a result, it helps teachers make reasoned decisions about two important issues: what to teach and how to teach it. In this chapter you will begin to develop a comprehension framework of your own.

Chapter 3 includes information that will help you answer questions like these:

1. What is a comprehension framework?
2. What are the major components of the reading comprehension process?
3. How does a person read?
4. How does reading ability develop?
5. How can a comprehension framework guide instructional decision making?

## KEY CONCEPTS

| | |
|---|---|
| affective aspects | metacognitive knowledge |
| decoding knowledge | reader-based explanation |
| discourse knowledge | reading readiness |
| emergent literacy | specific skills explanation |
| holistic language explanation | syntactic knowledge |
| integrated explanation | text-based explanation |
| interactive explanation | vocabulary knowledge |

## COMPREHENSION FRAMEWORKS: DEVELOPING A PERSONAL PERSPECTIVE

As a teacher you will make hundreds of decisions every day that affect the students in your classroom. The beliefs you develop about reading will be crucial to those decisions. It will be useful for you to consider your current beliefs about reading and then to reflect on those beliefs as you read on. To help you identify your beliefs, read the 15 statements in Figure 3–1 about how a person reads and the 15 statements in Figure 3–2 about how reading ability develops. After reading those statements, mark the 5 statements in Figure 3–1 and the 5 statements in Figure 3–2 that best represent your preliminary beliefs about reading. *Do this now before you read any further.* Then, when you finish reading this chapter, complete activities 1(a) and 1(b) on pages 122–123 to determine the nature of your own comprehension framework.

comprehension framework: Beliefs about the components of reading comprehension, the way in which people read, and the way in which reading ability develops.

A **comprehension framework** includes personal beliefs on three important issues:

1. what the components of reading comprehension are
2. how a person reads
3. how reading ability develops

FIGURE 3–1
Beliefs about how a person reads

1. For comprehension it is important that children be able to read most words correctly.

2. Children's knowledge about the world plays a central role in their comprehension of what they read.

3. When children cannot recognize a word, a useful strategy for them is to try to sound it out.

4. Before young children read about something, it is helpful for them to share an experience similar to that depicted in the reading passage.

5. There is usually only one best answer to each of the questions about a story that children have read.

6. When children cannot recognize a word, a useful strategy for them is to read the sentence again, look at the first letter of the difficult word, and make a guess.

7. Teachers should spend roughly equal amounts of time teaching students how to decode words and how to make reasonable guesses about words.

8. Comprehension is usually a joint product of the meaning in the text and the meaning a reader brings to the text.

9. Teachers should expect each child to have a different interpretation of a story.

10. The meaning of a text is more in the text itself than in the meaning brought to the text by the reader.

11. Teachers should always find out what children know about the topic of a story before asking them to begin reading.

12. When we think about comprehension, it is important to keep in mind that the meaning an author intended is usually what children should take away from their reading experience.

13. During the reading process guesses are often as important as accurate recognition of words.

14. Authors and readers understand a text in their own ways.

15. When children cannot recognize a word, a useful strategy for them is to read the sentence again and make a guess.

Table 3–1 summarizes how each portion of the framework guides instructional decision making. Being familiar with the components of reading comprehension and understanding how each contributes to the reading process can provide powerful insight into *why* different aspects of reading are taught. That foundation then permits reasoned decisions about what to teach and how to teach it.

FIGURE 3–2

Beliefs about how reading ability develops

1. It is important for teachers to provide clear presentations about important skills during reading instruction.

2. Children should receive many opportunities to select and read materials unrelated to specific school learning tasks.

3. Reading instruction should include teacher-directed lessons as well as student-directed learning tasks.

4. Children learn more about reading when they are engaged in meaningful, self-directed, and functional experiences with reading and writing.

5. A good reading program has a carefully designed scope and sequence of reading skills.

6. Children should be periodically tested to determine whether they have learned what was taught. Such tests should match very closely the skills that were taught in the reading program.

7. Some children seem to learn about reading best by reading widely and often; others seem to learn best through more structured experiences.

8. Children should be read to frequently while they are young so that they acquire a feel for what reading is like.

9. Teachers need to create personally meaningful experiences with reading to provide children with a reason to read.

10. Teachers need to regularly determine which children will benefit from more teacher-directed instruction and which children will benefit from more self-directed reading experiences.

11. Teachers should have a minimal list of specific reading skills appropriate for their grade level and ensure that their students acquire these skills.

12. Much of what children learn about reading can be attributed directly to what a teacher has taught in the classroom.

12. It is important to individualize reading instruction as much as possible by taking into consideration individual needs and the way such needs can best be met.

14. Children learn a great deal about reading by watching their parents at home.

15. No single reading program will fit each child perfectly. Teachers need to modify their programs to meet each child's needs.

The second portion of a comprehension framework, a personal perspective about how a person reads, assists in determining *what* to teach and emphasize in reading. For example, a teacher who believes that a person reads by sounding out words wants to spend more time helping students recognize words. On the other hand, a teacher who believes that a person reads by using background knowledge to predict upcoming words wants to spend more time

TABLE 3–1
Impact of personal beliefs on instructional decision making.

| Personal Beliefs | Instructional Impact |
|---|---|
| What the components of the reading comprehension process are | Can understand why each component of the reading process is taught |
| How a person reads | Can decide what to teach and emphasize |
| How reading ability develops | Can decide how to teach |

helping students develop vocabulary concepts and prediction strategies. A teacher who believes that a person reads by both sounding out words and effectively using background knowledge tries to spend relatively equal time helping students recognize words as well as develop vocabulary concepts and prediction strategies.

A comprehension framework, which includes beliefs about how a person reads and how reading ability develops, helps a reading teacher decide both what and how to teach.

The third portion of a comprehension framework, a personal perspective about how reading ability develops, assists in determining *how* to teach reading. Several different theories have been proposed to account for the development of reading proficiency, and each theory has different consequences for how reading is taught. For example, a teacher who believes that students learn best by being taught specific skills wants to provide direct instructional experiences in those skills. A teacher who believes that students learn best by reading to accomplish meaningful and functional tasks wants to create many meaningful and functional opportunities for students to read. A teacher who believes that students learn best with both specific skills and meaningful and functional tasks looks for ways to integrate those experiences.

Thus, each of these three issues is important for you to consider. Understanding the components of reading comprehension will help you understand *why* you teach different aspects of reading. Understanding how a person reads will help you decide *what* to teach. And understanding how reading ability develops will help you decide *how* to teach. Your knowledge of all three issues will empower you to make reasoned and appropriate decisions to benefit your students.

## DECISION POINT ➤

Because they are directly accountable to parents, school boards, and district superintendents, principals often discourage teachers from implementing their own comprehension frameworks during reading instruction. Instead, principals frequently require all teachers at a school to teach from a consistent perspective, often using a single set of materials. To what extent do you think that a teacher's comprehension framework should be sacrificed for consistency in a school reading program? What types of questions would you ask during a job interview to determine whether a prospective employer shared your reading perspective? How important will this issue be in your job search?

## THE COMPONENTS OF READING COMPREHENSION

The seven major components of the reading comprehension process exist in the mind of a reader and are central to the process. They are illustrated in Figure 3–3.

Much of reading instruction consists of activities designed to develop those components. For example, in chapter 2 we saw that teachers often discuss the meanings of unfamiliar words before asking students to read a selection. Those teachers are helping students develop vocabulary knowledge, one component of the process, in order to assist the students' comprehension of the upcoming story or article. Similar instructional activities are used to develop each of the other components.

*top-down*

## FIGURE 3–3
Major components of reading comprehension

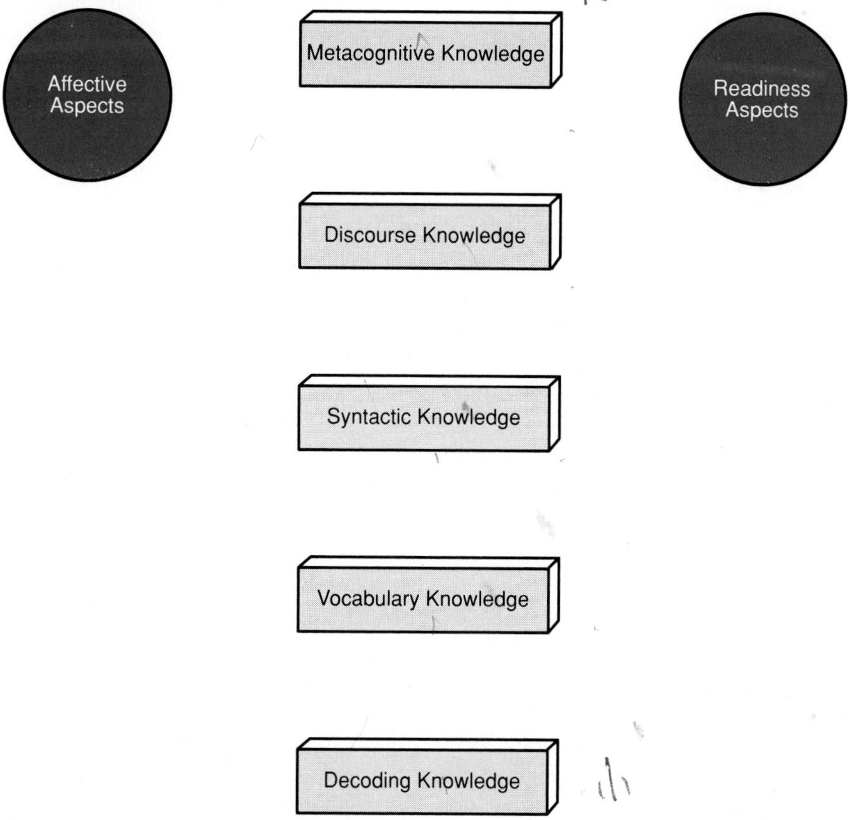

Affective Aspects

Metacognitive Knowledge

Readiness Aspects

Discourse Knowledge

Syntactic Knowledge

Vocabulary Knowledge

Decoding Knowledge

## Decoding Knowledge

**Decoding knowledge** is the knowledge that readers use to determine the oral equivalent of a written word. When we sound out an unfamiliar word, we are using decoding knowledge. Sometimes decoding knowledge is important for comprehension; at other times it is not. It is important when the sound of a word can help a reader identify its meaning. This situation frequently exists for beginning readers, who know the meanings of many words they hear but are less familiar with the printed version of those words. Thus, knowing how to decode a common word enables a beginning reader to determine its meaning. However, decoding knowledge is not important for comprehension when a word's sound does not help a reader identify the word's meaning. For example, knowing the oral equivalent of the word *ethmoid* is probably not an aid to comprehension.

Development of decoding knowledge is almost always included in instructional programs. It is an important part of beginning reading instruction

decoding knowledge: The knowledge that readers use to determine the oral equivalent of a word.

(Anderson, Hiebert, Scott, & Wilkinson, 1985; Chall, 1983). Teachers use activities such as the following to develop decoding knowledge.

**SAMPLE
ACTIVITIES**

**Inductive Decoding Instruction.** Use an inductive method framework to teach students that -*ake* usually represents the sound /ache/.

1. *Provide examples of the rule.* Present riddles in which the answers rhyme with *make* and end in -*ake*. For example, "I'm thinking of a word that rhymes with *make* and is something you eat at a party." (cake) "I'm thinking of a word that rhymes with *make* and is something that crawls in the grass." (snake) As students guess each riddle, write the answers on the board until you have four or five words that end in -*ake: cake, snake, rake, lake, bake.*
2. *Help students discover the rule.* Help students see that all of the words on the board end in *ake* and sound like /ache/. Use the words on the board to help students induce the decoding generalization: the letters -*ake* usually represent the sound /ache/.
3. *Provide guided practice.* Help students apply this generalization to read other, similarly spelled words such as *take, fake,* or *wake.*
4. *Provide independent practice.* Provide independent practice or a cooperative learning group task that allows students to practice this generalization. This activity may include the reading of a short literary selection containing the -*ake* pattern or an idea like the one described next.

**Card Matching.** To provide additional guided or independent practice on previously taught letter-sound patterns, prepare two sets of cards: one with initial consonant letters (*t, l, m, f,* and so on) and one with final letter patterns (*ake, ime, ame, ight*). Pass out the cards to a small group of students, and have them find partners with whom to join cards and make a word. Have each pair of students read their word to the group. If this activity is used as a cooperative learning group task, have each recorder/reporter write down all of the words each group is able to form. Then have the groups report their results to the rest of the class and compare their lists.

## Vocabulary Knowledge

vocabulary knowledge: The knowledge that readers have of word meanings; includes the ability to use context to determine word meanings.

**Vocabulary knowledge** includes both a knowledge of word meanings and an ability to use context to determine the meanings of unfamiliar words. Both elements are essential to the reading comprehension process, for we must understand the meanings of most of the individual words we read if we hope to understand an entire passage. For example, consider this first sentence in a brief passage:

Joan's problem is with her ethmoid.

Unless you know the meaning of the final word in this sentence, you cannot understand the sentence. Vocabulary knowledge is crucial.

One way to determine the meaning of a word is simply to recall familiar concepts. Sometimes, though, the meaning of the word is not known. In such a situation the surrounding words, or context, may help determine the meaning of the unfamiliar word. For example, the context of the second sentence in this brief passage can help you determine the meaning of *ethmoid:*

She broke her ethmoid at the point where the nose joins the skull.

The other words in this sentence, not your knowledge of the word *ethmoid,* probably helped you discover that this word refers to a bone connecting the nose and the skull. Thus, knowing word meanings and being able to use context are both important elements of vocabulary knowledge.

Helping students develop vocabulary knowledge is important at all grade levels (Harris & Sipay, 1990; Johnson & Pearson, 1984). However, it is particularly important as children explore less familiar subject areas that use specialized vocabularies. Before students read an article about the developmental stages of a butterfly, for example, the teacher should explain the meanings of unfamiliar words (e.g., *chrysalis, pupa,* and *metamorphosis*) in order to increase the students' ability to understand the article. Activities such as the following may also help students develop vocabulary knowledge.

**Making a Synonym Tree.** On a bulletin board put up the outline of a large tree made from construction paper. Cut out blank word cards in the shape of a leaf. Write difficult words on the word cards (one per card). Then pin each card on the tree. As students discover synonyms in their reading, have them write them on blank word cards and pin them to the original words on the tree. This activity can also be used for independent practice or as a cooperative learning group activity on synonyms.

**SAMPLE ACTIVITIES**

**Using Context.** When teaching students how to determine an unfamiliar word's meaning from context, provide them with several sentences such as the following:

Jim said, "The message is not clear. This message can mean either that Tom is hurt or that he is well. It seems *ambiguous* to me."

*Ambiguous* is likely to mean _____

_____ .

Write another sentence using the word *ambiguous.*

_____ .

Model your reasoning aloud as you complete the first example so that students can follow your strategies. Have students complete similar sentences in cooperative learning groups. Then have the groups report to the class the reasoning behind their answers.

## Syntactic Knowledge

syntactic knowledge: The knowledge that readers have of the word order rules that determine the meaning of sentences.

In addition to decoding knowledge and vocabulary knowledge, readers use **syntactic knowledge,** which is the knowledge of word order rules that determine meaning within sentences. That knowledge of sentence syntax, or word order, is crucial to the comprehension process (Irwin, 1986).

Syntactic knowledge often permits a reader to determine the grammatical function of a word and, as a result, its meaning and pronunciation. For example, consider your ability to read and understand the following sentence:

Sarah will lead the miners to the lead.

*contributions* ①

In this sentence syntactic knowledge enables you to determine the difference in meaning and pronunciation between two words that are spelled exactly the same but appear in different sentence positions. Syntax indicates that the third word (*lead*) is a verb meaning "to direct" and is pronounced /leed/. It also determines that the last word (*lead*) is a noun meaning "a heavy metal" and is pronounced /led/.

② Syntactic knowledge also contributes to comprehension in a second way. It allows readers to understand the relationships that exist between different

Sentence strips and sentence-combining activities can help build syntactic knowledge.

words or phrases in a sentence. For example, consider the following sentence:

Bill, Tom's dad, went outside.

Syntax should tell adults that Tom's dad is named Bill. However, most five-year-olds who saw and heard that sentence would think that two people went outside: Bill and Tom's dad. Their response suggests that most five-year-olds do not yet understand that appositive phrases clarify the meaning of the noun that directly precedes them.

Children's oral language ability is fairly well developed when they come to school, at five or six years of age. Nevertheless, a number of complex syntactic patterns that appear in print are unfamiliar to them, and they need to develop an understanding of how those patterns affect meaning.

Understanding more complex syntactic patterns becomes especially important as readers mature. Teachers often use activities such as the following to help students develop their syntactic knowledge.

**SAMPLE ACTIVITIES**

**Paraphrasing Appositives.** Teach the form and meaning of appositive phrases. Then have students practice by writing or reciting paraphrases of sentences like this:

Robert picked out a car, the red one with black trim, before he checked with his father.

*Paraphrase:* Robert picked out a red car with black trim before he checked with his father.

I caught a lot of fish, a nice mix of trout and salmon, on our trip to British Columbia.

*Paraphrase:* I caught a lot of trout and salmon on our trip to British Columbia.

Have students work individually, in pairs, or in small groups. Have them explain the reasoning behind their responses.

**Using Passive Forms.** Teach the function and structure of passive verb constructions. Then provide guided or independent practice by having students write (or tell) the passive equivalent for each active verb construction.

| Active | Passive |
| --- | --- |
| Joshua ate the apple. | The apple was eaten by Joshua. |
| Tomas rode the bike. | _____ |
| Rebecca painted the door. | _____ |
| Roberto saw the zebra. | _____ |

## Discourse Knowledge

discourse knowledge: The knowledge that readers have of the language organization that determines meaning beyond a single-sentence level; includes knowledge of different types of writing.

**Discourse knowledge** is the knowledge of language organization in units more complex than single sentences. It includes a knowledge of structural differences in various types of passages, such as narratives, memos, and newspaper articles. Discourse knowledge helps a reader determine whether a passage is fiction or nonfiction. It also suggests where to look for particular information, such as the solution to a mystery, and it builds expectations about upcoming information. For example, when readers see or hear the four words "Once upon a time . . . ," discourse knowledge leads them to expect the following:

- This will be a story, not a chapter in a social studies book.
- The story will not be true.
- The location is likely to be a kingdom "long ago and far away."
- There is apt to be a prince and princess as well as a king and queen.
- There will be some conflict that the hero or heroine will resolve.
- There will be a happy ending, perhaps with a message for young children.

Thus, knowing the structural organization of different types of writing is useful to reading comprehension.

Discourse knowledge receives greater instructional emphasis at higher grade levels, as students encounter a wider variety of written forms. The method framework known as individualized reading is very useful for encouraging students to read many different types of writing. In addition, teachers may use activities such as these to develop discourse knowledge.

**SAMPLE ACTIVITIES**

**Inductive Instruction in Discourse Knowledge.** Follow the procedural steps of an inductive method framework to teach the structural characteristics of a particular discourse form, such as a fable.

1. *Provide examples of the rule.* Read one fable aloud each day for several consecutive days. Briefly discuss each fable.
2. *Help students discover the rule.* Ask students to help you list the characteristics that are common to all; for example, animals are the main characters, the animals talk and act like people, there is usually a lesson (moral) at the end of each story, the stories did not really happen.
3. *Provide guided practice.* Read, or have students read, another fable to see whether the same structural elements also appear in it.
4. *Provide independent practice.* Have students read another fable and discuss its characteristics. You might even have them write a fable themselves, being sure to incorporate the structural elements of this type of writing.

**Deductive Instruction in Discourse Knowledge.** Follow the procedural steps of a deductive method framework to teach students that newspaper articles usually tell who, what, when, where, and why.

1. *State the rule*. Explain to students that most newspaper articles are written to inform readers about important current events. Explain that this form of writing usually tells who, what, when, where, and why.
2. *Provide examples*. Read two short articles, identifying each of these elements (who, what, when, where, and why) in the articles.
3. *Provide guided practice*. Provide students with a short article and have them underline each type of information.
4. *Provide independent practice*. Provide cooperative-learning groups with a headline. Then have each group write an appropriate newspaper article, including each type of information. Have them use a microcomputer if available. Have the reporter/recorder for each group share the results with the class.

## Metacognitive Knowledge

**Metacognitive knowledge** includes an awareness of the mental resources and strategies necessary to read effectively. It also includes the control and appropriate use of those factors during reading (Baker & Brown, 1984; Palincsar & Ransom, 1988). Thus, metacognitive knowledge is usually thought to include two elements: strategic knowledge and comprehension monitoring. Together these factors enable the reader to take charge and be certain that the information acquired makes sense.

metacognitive knowledge: A type of knowledge important for reading that includes the strategies used during reading and comprehension monitoring.

Let's consider first the use of strategic knowledge. You may have decided to start reading this chapter by first reading the summary at the end to get a sense of its content. Or perhaps you leafed through the pages, looking at the sequence of section headings. You may even have decided to read this page again if you got to the end of it and did not understand parts of what you had read. All of these strategies reflect your strategic knowledge.

Strategic knowledge is very useful for comprehension; it allows the efficient acquisition of information. Reading is not a linear process that begins with the first word and continues with each separate word in turn. Instead, good readers regularly use a range of strategies as they attempt to understand a passage. As already mentioned, they may start with the summary, or they may skim the contents of the entire passage. As they read, good readers stop to look at a figure or a table, to decode an unfamiliar word, to reread a troublesome sentence, to think about what they have read, to underline important information. Each of these decisions involves strategic knowledge.

The second aspect of metacognitive knowledge is comprehension monitoring, whereby the reader makes certain that the material being read makes sense. Comprehension monitoring allows the reader to continuously check the text against a developing understanding of its meaning; it prevents the reader from reaching the end of a passage and being unable to remember what was read. The development of metacognitive knowledge is usually thought to be a later-developing skill (Harris & Sipay, 1990). Metacognition requires readers to step back from their reading and consider their own reading process, a hard task for young children. Teachers use activities such as the following to teach metacognitive knowledge.

**SAMPLE ACTIVITIES**

**Learning to Use an Index.** Follow the procedural steps of a directed reading activity to organize a lesson in your students' social studies book. During the third procedural step, skill development and practice, teach students how an index can be used to locate specific information.

1. *Preparation*. Determine which words in this chapter will be difficult for your students to understand. Put each of the difficult words into a sentence on the blackboard. Help students read the sentences, and clarify the meanings of any words with which students need help. Introduce the topic of the chapter, and engage students in a brief discussion to determine what they already know about this subject.
2. *Guided reading*. Have students read the chapter independently. Help those who request assistance. When students have finished, form cooperative-learning groups, and give each student a set of statements about the chapter. Have the cooperative-learning groups determine whether each statement is true or false, based on the information in the chapter, and then have each group report its results to the entire class.
3. *Skill development and practice*. Explain to students that an index may be used to locate specific information in a textbook. Show students the index at the end of their social studies book. Demonstrate that the items are listed alphabetically and that each entry is followed by the number of the page where it can be found. Locate several entries in the chapter they have read.
4. *Enrichment*. Have individuals or groups practice using their index. Make up a set of questions from the next chapter and have students use their index to find the answers. If cooperative learning groups are used, have the reporter/recorder for each group share the results with the class.

**Monitoring Reading.** Write a page of text containing several deliberate mistakes in content. Have students read and attempt to find each of the errors. Use this activity to discuss the importance of checking comprehension. Discuss rereading strategies that might be used for this purpose.

emergent literacy: A recent view of reading as a continuously emerging and evolving ability that results from children's experiences and experiments with language in literacy contexts.

## Emergent Literacy/Readiness Aspects

Emergent literacy and readiness refer to two different, but related, concepts. According to an **emergent literacy** view, reading is a continuously emerging and developing ability. It is believed that even very young children can benefit from learning about reading, as long as reading instruction is defined appropriately for their developmental level. For example, all youngsters beginning school are ready to engage in a language experience story, all will benefit from being read to, and all can enjoy listening to a story book on tape, regardless of whether they are ready for more traditional and formal types of reading instruction.

**Reading readiness,** on the other hand, is a more traditional concept of early reading instruction. According to a readiness perspective, a young child must develop a number of skills before beginning formal reading instruction. Such skills include the following (Aulls, 1982; Clay 1980a, 1980b; Ollila, 1976):

reading readiness: Traditionally, the period of time in which students acquire the skills and abilities that allow reading to take place.

- knowing letter names
- knowing left-to-right sequence in writing
- being able to see similarities and differences in shapes
- having language proficiency
- being able to hear similarities and differences in sounds
- being able to work cooperatively in groups
- being able to work independently

Recently, this traditional notion of reading readiness has been criticized for two shortcomings (Teale & Sulzby, 1986, 1989). First, it assumes a clear line of demarcation between the times when a child is able and unable to read. Sometimes this dividing line prevents young students from engaging in experiences that might be helpful to their literacy development.

A second shortcoming of the reading readiness concept is that it fails to consider writing. Reading and writing are thought to be reciprocal processes (Tierney & Pearson, 1983). Therefore, learning about reading assists the development of writing, and learning about writing assists the development of reading. A more inclusive term, such as *literacy,* captures the reciprocal nature of this relationship.

Regardless of one's beliefs about the nature of early reading development, it is clear that the level of a child's development influences the manner in which that child comprehends written text. Activities such as those shown on page 106 may be used to develop either the emergent literacy or the reading readiness of youngsters.

## Affective Aspects

Much of the preceding discussion has focused on aspects of reading related to language skills. However, the child who has these skills but does not want to read shows us that reading is not only a language process; it is also an affective process. The **affective aspects** of comprehension include a reader's attitude toward and interest in reading.

All readers at all grade levels comprehend better when they are interested in reading, and the difference is especially noticeable among less proficient

affective aspects: Elements such as interest and attitude that increase motivation and facilitate comprehension.

**SAMPLE
ACTIVITIES**

**Reading from Left to Right.** Follow the procedural steps of a language experience story. During the final step show students how to read from left to right.

1. *Provide students with a vivid experience.*
2. *Elicit oral language that describes the experience.*
3. *Transcribe the students' oral language.*
4. *Help students read what was transcribed.* As you read the story to the students, run your finger from left to right under each of the words. After you have finished, ask students whether they noticed the direction in which your finger moved. Have a brief discussion about the left-to-right direction of print. Then reread the story, again running your finger from left to right under each of the words.

**Reading Predictable Texts.** Read predictable texts aloud to your young students. Predictable texts are story books that contain a repeated element—a sentence pattern, a rhyming pattern, or some other pattern—that makes the language highly predictable. Examples include *The Cat in the Hat, The Little Red Hen, Henny Penny, The House that Jack Built, The Gingerbread Boy,* and *Brown Bear, Brown Bear.* When you read predictable texts aloud to your students, they will quickly notice the repeated pattern. As they do, occasionally leave out the repeated pattern, and have students complete it for you. Afterwards, place that book out on a table for your students to enjoy. Even your weakest readers will be able to read many such books on their own as soon as they discover the predictable pattern.

---

readers. Many teachers of reading remember students who have had difficulty comprehending typical classroom assignments but have had no difficulty reading something of their own choosing. Consequently, another way to facilitate comprehension is to make reading and reading instruction as interesting and enjoyable as possible, never forgetting students' attitudes and interests in our attempt to develop their ability to read. Teachers use activities such as the ones found on page 107 to improve or increase students' attitude toward and interest in reading.

## A Historical Perspective

Because of extensive work conducted by researchers since the late 1800s, most people today agree that decoding knowledge, vocabulary knowledge, syntactic knowledge, discourse knowledge, metacognitive knowledge, emergent literacy/ readiness aspects, and affective aspects are all important to the reading process and need to be included in any reading program. People might disagree about how these components should be labeled, how they are related, how they develop, or how important they are; but there is little controversy about in-

**SAMPLE ACTIVITIES**

**Read-Alouds.** Conduct regular read-aloud sessions. Spend a short portion of each day reading books that you enjoy and that you think your students might enjoy. Model your interest and enthusiasm for books in the way you share them with others. Occasionally, stop reading a story at the most exciting part, and suggest that students finish the book on their own.

**Storybook Character Days.** Periodically, designate a day as Storybook Character Day. Encourage your students to come dressed as their favorite character in a book they have recently read. Come dressed as a character yourself. Have a contest to see who can identify the greatest number of characters. Encourage the youngsters to talk about their characters and the books from which their characters come. Such an activity will lead students to books they might not have considered reading.

cluding them in the reading process. As a result, this first portion of a comprehension framework—understanding the components of the reading process—is the easiest part to acquire.

## HOW DOES A PERSON READ?

The other two parts of a comprehension framework are harder to acquire. They require that we evaluate information and take positions on controversial issues in reading. However, they relate to decisions about two of the most important issues teachers face: what to teach and how to teach it.

A decision about how a person reads helps a teacher decide what to teach and emphasize. Of the different explanations that exist, the three most common are shown on the continuum in Figure 3–4.

Providing time to browse in the library and to check out books can positively impact affective aspects of reading.

FIGURE 3–4

Explanations of how a person reads

| Text-Based Explanations | Interactive Explanations | Reader-Based Explanations |

However, you should remember that explanations do exist at other points along the continuum, and your own beliefs may not fall neatly at one of the three points identified there. As you read each explanation, remember the five statements you selected at the beginning of this chapter in Figure 3–1, and try to define your own beliefs about how a person reads.

## (—) Text-Based Explanations

**text-based explanation:** Belief that people read by translating print into sounds as they determine the meaning in a text.

Some individuals adopt a **text-based explanation** of how one reads (Gough, 1986). They suggest that a person reads by decoding, or sounding out, the words on a page. According to text-based explanations, readers translate print into sounds to uncover the meaning that exists in a text. Text-based explanations assume that (1) meaning exists more in the text than in what a reader brings to a text; (2) reading consists of translating printed words into sounds and sounds into meanings; and (3) readers begin by using the lowest knowledge source (decoding) and then sequentially applying higher knowledge sources (vocabulary, syntactic, discourse, and then metacognitive knowledge).

One way to understand this type of explanation is to think about how we might read words like *Roskolnikov, Ekaterinburg,* or *Fedorachovna* in a novel. Many readers would find themselves attempting to sound out these difficult Russian names, hoping that hearing them would help the readers remember them. Such an approach, translating the print into sounds, supports a text-based explanation.

Figure 3–5 depicts the reading process according to a text-based explanation. In this example the reader has read the beginning of a fairy tale—"Once upon a time, a princess kissed a. . ."—and is now ready to read the word *frog*.

According to a text-based explanation, the reader first uses decoding knowledge to determine the oral equivalent of this word. Once the sound /frog/ has been determined, the reader uses that sound to search vocabulary knowledge and locates two meanings: (1) "a small green amphibian" and (2) "of or pertaining to a frog" (e.g., frog legs). Both meanings are passed on to syntactic knowledge, which decides that the word *frog* is being used as a noun, not an adjective. Consequently, the first meaning of the word is chosen. At this point discourse knowledge concludes that the selection is a fairy tale because the beginning is consistent with that story type. Finally, metacognitive knowledge is activated: comprehension monitoring lets the reader know that all this makes sense, and strategic knowledge directs attention to the first word of the

## FIGURE 3–5
A text-based explanation of reading comprehension

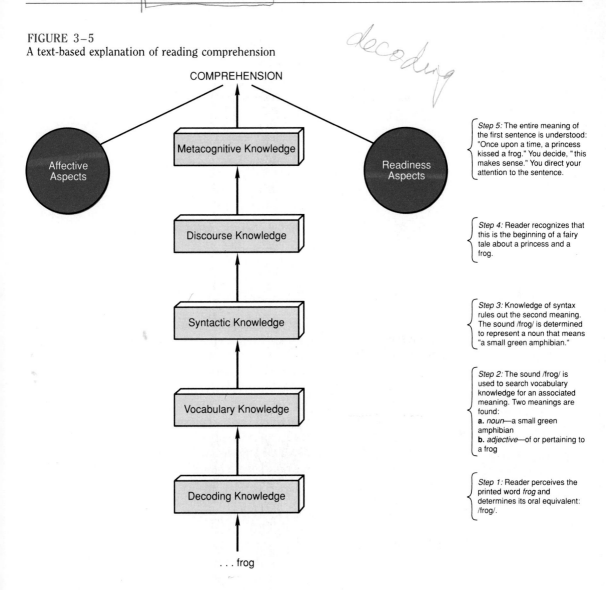

*decoding*

COMPREHENSION

Affective
Aspects

Readiness
Aspects

Metacognitive Knowledge

Discourse Knowledge

Syntactic Knowledge

Vocabulary Knowledge

Decoding Knowledge

. . . frog

*Step 5:* The entire meaning of the first sentence is understood: "Once upon a time, a princess kissed a frog." You decide, "this makes sense." You direct your attention to the sentence.

*Step 4:* Reader recognizes that this is the beginning of a fairy tale about a princess and a frog.

*Step 3:* Knowledge of syntax rules out the second meaning. The sound /frog/ is determined to represent a noun that means "a small green amphibian."

*Step 2:* The sound /frog/ is used to search vocabulary knowledge for an associated meaning. Two meanings are found:
**a.** *noun*—a small green amphibian
**b.** *adjective*—of or pertaining to a frog

*Step 1:* Reader perceives the printed word *frog* and determines its oral equivalent: /frog/.

next sentence, to see what is going to happen next. Thus, the reading process continues, moving always from lowest to highest knowledge source.

## Reader-Based Explanations

Other individuals adopt a **reader-based explanation** of how a person reads (Goodman, 1986; Smith, 1988). They believe that readers do not sound out each and every word they read; instead, readers use background knowledge and the evolving meaning of a text to make predictions about upcoming words. According to this view, readers first make a prediction about the meaning of a word and only then perceive the word's letters. Thus, reader-based explana-

reader-based explanation: Belief that people read by using background knowledge to predict upcoming words as they read.

tions assume that (1) meaning exists more in what a reader brings to a text than in the text itself; (2) reading is based more on predictions of upcoming words than on the translation of words into sounds; and (3) readers begin by using knowledge sources associated with meaning (discourse, syntax, and vocabulary) and only then apply decoding knowledge. Thus, according to reader-based explanations, readers continuously predict upcoming words and, when necessary, look at the letters in those words to see whether their predictions were correct.

One way to understand this type of explanation is to consider how we might read a popular romance novel. Before we begin reading, we probably have clear expectations about the story structure. Our expectations of the plot are strong, and most of the words are familiar. We do not even notice the words, let alone the letters in those words, at the end of a sentence (e.g., "Susi dove into her swimming _____ "). We fly through the story, skimming the incidental portions to get to the more interesting sections. Indeed, we may finish the book in a single night.

A reader-based explanation is depicted in Figure 3–6, again focusing on the final word in the sentence "Once upon a time, a princess kissed a. . . ." Initially, the comprehension monitoring element of metacognitive knowledge indicates that the sentence makes sense up to the final word. Then, strategic knowledge directs the reader to think about how this sentence might end and what the final word might be. Next, several expectations are generated from discourse knowledge: first of all, this story is probably a fairy tale. Moreover, the beginnings of most fairy tales contain information about the main characters. And since a princess is about to kiss someone, the reader can expect the second character to be mentioned next.

Expectations from discourse knowledge limit the expectations from syntactic knowledge: the reader can expect a noun, the recipient of a kiss. In turn, syntactic expectations limit the expectations from vocabulary knowledge. The word must belong to a limited set of nouns that are potential main characters in a fairy tale and are likely to be kissed by princesses. This set includes kings, queens, and princes. It also includes frogs if the reader is familiar with the princess-kisses-a-frog-and-finds-a-prince pattern of some fairy tales.

Finally, vocabulary knowledge limits the expectations of decoding knowledge. The reader analyzes the text for the graphic representation of one of the expected nouns, finds *frog,* and concludes that this is the final word. Sometimes, readers have such strong expectations that they do not even look at the final word. Instead, they continue reading until some evidence in the story indicates that their prediction was wrong. In any event the reader continues to read by using background knowledge and the evolving meaning of the text to make additional predictions about upcoming words.

**interactive explanation:** Belief that people read by simultaneously translating print into sounds and using background knowledge to predict upcoming words as they read.

## Interactive Explanations

Other individuals adopt an **interactive explanation** of how a person reads (Anderson, Hiebert, Scott, & Wilkinson, 1985; Rumelhart, 1976; Stanovich,

*consider both ways not just one of th...*

FIGURE 3-6

A reader-based explanation of reading comprehension

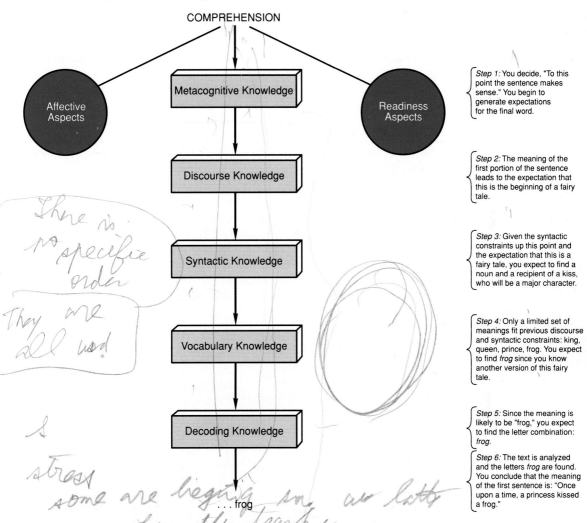

COMPREHENSION

Affective Aspects

Metacognitive Knowledge

Readiness Aspects

Discourse Knowledge

Syntactic Knowledge

Vocabulary Knowledge

Decoding Knowledge

... frog

*Step 1:* You decide, "To this point the sentence makes sense." You begin to generate expectations for the final word.

*Step 2:* The meaning of the first portion of the sentence leads to the expectation that this is the beginning of a fairy tale.

*Step 3:* Given the syntactic constraints up this point and the expectation that this is a fairy tale, you expect to find a noun and a recipient of a kiss, who will be a major character.

*Step 4:* Only a limited set of meanings fit previous discourse and syntactic constraints: king, queen, prince, frog. You expect to find *frog* since you know another version of this fairy tale.

*Step 5:* Since the meaning is likely to be "frog," you expect to find the letter combination: *frog*.

*Step 6:* The text is analyzed and the letters *frog* are found. You conclude that the meaning of the first sentence is: "Once upon a time, a princess kissed a frog."

*There is no specific order*

*They are all used*

*stress some are beginning on or later for the teacher*

1980). They suggest that we read by simultaneously sounding out words at the same time we form expectations from vocabulary, syntactic, discourse, and metacognitive knowledge. An interactive explanation assumes that (1) meaning is located both in the text and in the meaning that readers bring to the text, (2) reading consists of both translation and expectation, and (3) reading proceeds as each knowledge source interacts simultaneously with the print on the page and with other knowledge sources. Thus, reading comprehension is a product of the interaction between text and reader.

One way to understand an interactive explanation is to consider your own reading behavior. When your background knowledge is extensive, reading is easy, and you are able to anticipate the words that come next. In this case, the meaning that you bring to the page closely matches the meaning that exists on the page. However, when your background knowledge is limited, reading is somewhat difficult, and you may attempt to sound out unfamiliar words like *metacognitive* to see whether their oral equivalent might help you recall their meaning. Readers who shift quickly back and forth between expectations and decoding are reading in an interactive fashion.

Let's once again consider, this time from an interactive perspective, how a young reader is apt to read the final word in the sentence "Once upon a time, a princess kissed a. . . ." Readers who lack prior knowledge of the topic will read the word *frog* in a text-based fashion, as depicted in Figure 3–5. Children who are unfamiliar with fairy tales and who have never heard the princess-kisses-a-frog-and-finds-a-prince pattern must depend more on decoding and vocabulary knowledge. On the other hand, readers with an extensive prior knowledge of the topic will read the word *frog* in a reader-based fashion, as depicted in Figure 3–6. Children who are familiar with fairy tales and with the princess-kisses-a-frog-and-finds-a-prince pattern can generate accurate predictions. Consequently, they will depend more on metacognitive, discourse, syntactic, and vocabulary knowledge and will use decoding knowledge only to check predictions. Thus, from an interactive perspective, the nature of the reading process varies from text to text and from word to word, depending on a reader's background knowledge.

## A Historical Perspective

The issue of how a person reads was very controversial during the 1970s. At that time people's beliefs tended to fall at either end of the continuum illustrated in Figure 3–4. Most individuals had either strong text-based or strong reader-based explanations for the reading process. Today, this issue is not nearly so divisive, and most people's beliefs fall somewhere near the center of the continuum, suggesting an interactive explanation. Increasingly, people have concluded that neither a text-based nor a reader-based explanation is sufficient to explain how we read. At times, especially with unfamiliar or difficult texts, the evidence suggests that we read more by sounding out words; at other times, especially with familiar or easy texts, we read more by making predictions about upcoming words. Only an interactive explanation seems to account for both types of evidence.

## HOW DOES READING ABILITY DEVELOP?

A decision about how reading ability develops helps a teacher decide how best to teach reading. Of the different explanations that exist, the three most common are shown on the continuum in Figure 3–7. At one end of this continuum are explanations based on the idea that students best learn to read by learning specific reading skills that are taught directly by the teacher. At the other end

FIGURE 3–7
Explanations of how reading ability develops

| Specific | Integrated | Wholistic Language |
| Skills | Instruction and | Learning |
| Explanations | Learning | Explanations |
| | Explanations | |

are explanations based on the idea that students best learn to read in a holistic manner that they themselves control as they engage in meaningful and functional reading tasks. Somewhere in the middle are explanations based on the idea that students best learn to read through an appropriate combination of teacher-directed instruction and student-directed learning.

Again, as you read these explanations, remember the five statements you selected at the beginning of this chapter in Figure 3–2, and consider where your own beliefs might be located on this continuum. They may not fall neatly at one of the three points identified in this figure, but it will be helpful for you to locate your personal position.

## Specific Skills Explanations

A **specific skills explanation** of how reading ability develops is based on two assumptions: (1) reading ability develops to the extent that students master specific reading skills, and (2) reading ability develops to the extent that these skills are taught directly by the teacher in an explicit, and frequently **deductive,** fashion. Thus, students are assumed to learn best when the development of reading skills is directed by the classroom teacher.

Programs based on a specific skills explanation often contain a hierarchy of reading skills, organized according to level of difficulty. Easier reading skills are taught first; harder reading skills are taught last. A reading program based on this explanation might target skills like these:

1. The student will be able to correctly pronounce words that begin with both hard *c* and soft *c* sounds.
2. The student will be able to correctly interpret cause-and-effect relationships within a sentence.
3. The student will be able to identify the main idea in a paragraph.

Such skills are usually taught separately from the reading of stories and articles. The reading experiences are viewed either as opportunities to practice the specific skills that have been taught or as opportunities to develop a positive attitude toward and interest in reading.

In addition, a specific skills explanation assumes that reading ability develops best when students are taught in a direct, and frequently deductive, fashion. Thus, children are expected to learn best when teachers provide direct instruction on each separate skill. In short, a specific skills explanation of development is skill-specific and teacher-directed.

specific skills explanation: Belief that reading ability develops as students master the specific skills taught directly and deductively by a teacher.

deductive: Refers to learning that is direct, explicit, and teacher-directed; begins with a rule or principle and then demonstrates how it is applied.

## Holistic Language Explanations

holistic language explanation: Belief that reading ability develops as students direct their own learning in holistic, meaningful, and functional literacy experiences.

A **holistic language explanation** is at the opposite end of the continuum from a specific skills explanation. A holistic language explanation is based on very different assumptions about how reading ability develops: (1) reading ability develops as students engage in holistic, meaningful, and functional experiences with print, and (2) students learn best in an inductive fashion. Reading comprehension is perceived to be a holistic and unified entity that is difficult to break down into a fixed set of separate skills. And students are believed to induce most of the important skills required for reading during their self-directed experiences with print and their observations of others interacting with print.

Supporters of holistic language explanations believe that reading comprehension is not easily separated into a hierarchy of distinct skills (Clay, 1980b; Goodman, 1986; Goodman & Goodman, 1979; Holdaway, 1979). They argue that comprehension is a holistic process and that separating the reading process into isolated skills gives young children inappropriate information about the nature and purpose of reading.

inductive: Refers to learning that results from a student's self-discovery; uses experiences to generate a rule or principle.

Advocates of a holistic language explanation assume that written language skills (reading and writing) and oral language skills (speaking and listening) develop similarly (Weaver & Shonhoff, 1984). In fact, there is fairly clear evidence that oral language skills develop in an **inductive** fashion, as a result of meaningful and functional language interactions (Slobin, 1979). Chil-

Teachers with a holistic language explanation of how reading ability develops closely link reading and writing and provide many opportunities for writing to occur.

dren induce the rules of their language as they listen to it and speak it, not as a result of direct instruction in specific skills.

Advocates of a holistic language explanation believe that written and oral language proficiencies develop similarly since both are language processes. According to this explanation, children should be presented with a rich written-language environment, examples of others engaged in literacy tasks, and a functional need to communicate in writing. If these conditions exist, children will induce all the necessary generalizations they need to become proficient readers. Reading, like oral language, should develop in a very natural manner. In short, a holistic language explanation is skill-general and student-directed.

限制，控制

## Integrated Explanations

Teachers who support an **integrated explanation** believe that both specific skills and holistic language explanations are, alone, too limited to explain the nature of reading development among diverse students. These teachers believe that a specific skills perspective confines students too narrowly to mastery of isolated reading skills. Although some students benefit from this structure, others become bored and lose interest in reading. On the other hand, a holistic language perspective places too much responsibility on students for their own development. Although some students benefit from this freedom, others get lost in the opportunities for self-development.

An integrated explanation combines aspects of both previous explanations. According to this perspective, the development of reading occurs best in an integrated manner that includes both direct instruction by the teacher and self-generated, inductive learning by the student. An integrated explanation makes these assumptions: (1) reading ability develops to the extent that students learn specific reading skills and engage in meaningful, functional, and holistic experiences with print, and (2) reading ability develops as a result of both teacher-directed deductive experiences and student-generated inductive experiences.

Thus, teachers following an integrated explanation of reading development include elements from both specific skills and holistic language perspectives. They provide students with a rich written-language environment, examples of others engaged in literacy tasks, and a functional need to communicate in writing. In addition, they provide students with direct instruction in reading skills that they determine to be necessary.

**integrated explanation:** Belief that reading ability develops as students engage in both teacher-directed deductive learning and self-directed inductive learning.

## A Historical Perspective

There is far less agreement about how reading ability develops than there is about how a person reads. In fact, the question of how reading ability develops is currently one of the more controversial issues in the field of reading instruction. Individual explanations can be found at nearly every point on the continuum. The specific skills perspective has long had a strong influence on the field of reading; traditionally, students have been thought to learn best when presented with a skill-based curriculum taught directly by a teacher. The composition of most published reading programs tends to reflect the assumptions of this perspective. It is also found in instructional recommendations that emphasize direct teaching in specific skill areas (Bauman & Schmitt, 1986).

During the past decade, however, evidence has demonstrated that children acquire literacy skills through self-directed reading (and writing) experiences (Goodman, 1986; Harste, Woodward, & Burke, 1984). As a result, many teachers are associating themselves with what has come to be known as a whole language point of view, and that movement is powerfully influencing the development of new instructional materials and methods. The state of California, for example, has recently created a list of recommended literature selections and has circulated it widely throughout the state's schools, many of which are using these literature selections as the core of their reading programs. Other states are taking similar actions in an attempt to provide students with more self-directed learning experiences involving both literature and writing activities.

The term *whole language,* however, is quickly coming to represent many things to many people. For some, it represents an extreme position on the continuum, characterized by classrooms rich in literacy experiences and students who induce from these self-directed experiences the generalizations necessary to learn to read. For others, the term *whole language* represents the middle of the continuum, characterized by classrooms that combine students' self-directed learning experiences with direct instructional experiences whenever students experience difficulty in a particular aspect of reading.

## USING A COMPREHENSION FRAMEWORK TO GUIDE INSTRUCTIONAL DECISIONS

Developing a comprehension framework is not easy; reading comprehension is an abstract and complex concept. Nevertheless, a comprehension framework is a practical tool that can provide assistance with the instructional choices that you as a teacher of reading will need to make.

### Understanding Why Different Aspects of Reading Are Taught

Knowing how each component of reading contributes to the comprehension process will help you understand why you teach different aspects of reading and how your teaching can help your students. For example, knowing the role of syntactic knowledge is useful when youngsters misunderstand the meaning of an appositive phrase. Knowing the function of discourse knowledge is useful when students meet their first social studies textbook and are unfamiliar with its organization. Knowing about metacognitive knowledge is useful when students are able to decode words fluently but are unable to recall what they have read because they have failed to monitor their comprehension. Understanding the interaction of these various components of reading comprehension will help you make informed decisions about how to further your students' development as readers.

## Deciding What to Teach and Emphasize

Understanding how a person reads will help you decide what to teach and emphasize during reading instruction. Text-based, reader-based, and interactive explanations lead to different conclusions, which are summarized in Table 3–2. Teachers with a text-based explanation stress the acquisition of decoding knowledge more than any other type of knowledge, believing that strong decoding skills lead to successful translation of text meaning. Instruction, especially for younger readers, emphasizes activities like those described earlier under decoding knowledge.

Teachers with a reader-based explanation of how a person reads stress the acquisition of metacognitive, discourse, syntactic, and vocabulary knowledge, believing that adequate higher-level knowledge leads to accurate expectations of upcoming meaning. As a result, instruction emphasizes activities like those described earlier under metacognitive knowledge, discourse knowledge, syntactic knowledge, and vocabulary knowledge. Any activity designed to help students generate expectations is especially valued, such as the reading of predictable texts.

Teachers with an interactive explanation of how a person reads devote relatively equal attention during instruction to the acquisition of decoding, vocabulary, syntactic, discourse, and metacognitive knowledge. These teachers believe that readers need to determine the oral equivalent of words as well as develop expectations of upcoming words. All activities described earlier in this chapter might be used by these teachers.

TABLE 3–2
Instructional consequences of beliefs about how a person reads

| Beliefs | Instructional Consequences |
|---|---|
| Text-based | Decoding knowledge is emphasized, especially at younger levels. |
|  | Less time is spent developing metacognitive, discourse, syntactic, and vocabulary knowledge. |
| Reader-based | Metacognitive, discourse, syntactic, and vocabulary knowledge is emphasized. |
|  | Less time is spent developing decoding knowledge. |
| Interactive | Approximately equal attention is devoted to all knowledge sources: decoding, vocabulary, syntactic, discourse, and metacognitive knowledge. |

## Deciding How to Teach

Understanding how reading ability develops will help you decide how to teach reading. Specific skills, holistic language, and integrated explanations lead to different conclusions, which are summarized in Table 3–3. Teachers with a specific skills explanation provide students with direct instruction on progressively more difficult reading skills. Deductive learning is emphasized. Published reading programs are a popular material framework for these teachers because the programs are often organized around specific reading skills taught directly by the teacher. Also, two particular method frameworks are frequently used by these teachers: directed reading activities (DRA) and deductive instruction, both of which develop reading proficiency through direct instruction of specific reading skills.

　　Teachers with a holistic language explanation of how reading develops provide opportunities for students to see literacy skills in action, always in the context of real-world situations, and to both read and write so that they may induce the generalizations required for proficient reading. Reading skills are not taught directly. Instead, self-generated, inductive learning is emphasized. If these teachers are required to use a published reading program, they often supplement or replace specific skill lessons with functional reading and writing activities, as described in chapter 2. Four particular method frameworks are frequently used by these teachers: individualized reading, language experience stories, cooperative learning groups, and inductive instruction, all of which

TABLE 3–3
Instructional consequences of beliefs about how reading ability develops

| Beliefs | Instructional Consequences |
|---|---|
| Specific skills | Specific reading skills, organized hierarchically, are usually taught. |
|  | Teacher-directed, deductive instruction is common. |
|  | Directed reading activities and deductive instruction are two common method frameworks. |
| Holistic language | Reading is learned as an entity. |
|  | Student-directed, inductive learning is common. |
|  | Individualized reading, language experience stories, cooperative learning groups, and inductive instruction are common method frameworks. |
| Integrated | Reading is learned as an entity and as a product of specific skills. |
|  | Student-directed, inductive learning is combined with teacher-directed, deductive learning. |
|  | All method frameworks may be used. |

provide meaningful and functional experiences with print and allow students to direct their own inductive learning.

Teachers with an integrated explanation of reading development provide opportunities for students to see literacy skills in action and to both read and write so that they may induce on their own the generalizations that are required for proficient reading. In addition, these teachers give direct instruction on specific skills as students need such support. These teachers often use a published reading program to organize instruction but supplement or replace specific skill lessons with functional reading and writing activities. All of the method frameworks described in chapter 2 are used by these teachers during reading instruction; they shift between teacher-directed and student-directed learning experiences as appropriate to meet particular student needs.

Thus, a comprehension framework can be extremely helpful when you need to make instructional decisions. It provides insight into the reading process, helping you understand why you teach different components of reading and supporting reasoned decisions about what to teach and how to teach it. Figure 3–8 shows the grid that results when beliefs interact regarding how a person reads and how reading ability develops. Since both issues are represented by a continuum, innumerable combinations are possible. What is im-

FIGURE 3–8
A matrix illustrating the various types of comprehension frameworks that are possible

**How Does One Read?**

|  | Text-Based Explaations | Interactive Explanations | Reader-Based Explanations |
|---|---|---|---|
| Specific Skills Explanations |  |  |  |
| Integrated Instruction and Learning Explanations |  |  |  |
| Wholistic Language Learning Explanations |  |  |  |

How Does Reading Ability Develop?

portant to remember is that each reading teacher represents one of those combinations—reflecting a position on each continuum.

In the classroom comments section that follows, the three different teachers represent three different positions on the grid. See whether you can place them appropriately. Then, after you work through the instructional decisions at the end of this chapter, determine your own position on the grid. Finally, as you read the rest of this text, keep your comprehension framework in mind.

## COMMENTS FROM THE CLASSROOM ■

### Emily Dodson

Comprehension frameworks sound a bit complex, but they're really quite easy to understand. Mine helps me a lot as I work with students. Basically, I see the reading process and reading development from an interactive, integrated perspective.

I think each component of the reading comprehension process is equally important to develop. Last week, for instance, I devoted some time to inferencing skills, especially as they're needed with multiple-meaning words such as *dust, draw,* and *dress.* I also used an inductive method framework and several riddles to teach this same group of students that the letters *ake* were often pronounced /ache/. This decoding skill appeared in our published reading program and was important for reading one of the literature selections in that program. But the next day I included several short lessons on metacognitive knowledge since I noticed that a number of students were decoding words nicely but were not monitoring the meaning of what they were reading. Over the course of the year I probably spend roughly equal amounts of time developing decoding, vocabulary, syntactic, discourse, and metacognitive knowledge.

I think students learn to read best through both self-directed and teacher-directed experiences with print. I'm especially concerned that

students have opportunities to direct their own reading experiences, so I use individualized reading, which allows them to select their own reading experiences and direct their own learning. I also use cooperative learning groups a lot. At the same time, though, I am almost always working with a small group of students in learning activities that I direct. In those sessions I focus on specific skills and often use our published reading program because it saves time. I usually make several modifications, though.

All in all, I guess I use all three types of instructional frameworks—material, method, and comprehension. But my comprehension framework is probably the most helpful because it guides me in selecting and adapting both materials and methods.

### Mr. Burns

I think that decoding knowledge is the most important type of knowledge in reading. In fact, the first thing I say when one of my students is having difficulty with a word is "Let's look at that first letter and sound it out." But that doesn't mean that I completely ignore the other types of knowledge. Just the other day, for example, I worked with my students on discourse knowledge as we studied the organization of newspaper articles, just before we read our weekly newspaper. We had a lot of fun with that activity and even decided to start our own classroom newspaper to send home to parents each month. Writing and reading our newspaper should give the students some excellent practice.

Nonetheless, I do think it's most important for my second graders to have strong decoding skills. I guess I view the reading process from more of a text-based perspective, and from what I see of the reading program at our school, students don't receive much help in decoding after they leave second grade. I want to be sure my students can sound out any word they encounter.

I spend a lot of time in our published reading program because I really like the sequenced activities that teach specific skills, often deductively. That's how I think my students develop their reading ability best—by learning the specific skills that are involved in reading. And I firmly believe that direct instruction with clear explanations makes it easier for them to understand and acquire those skills. In addition, all the practice opportunities in the reading program really help the students achieve mastery. At the end of each unit I use the test in the reading program to be sure of their progress.

When I create my own lessons, I often use a deductive method framework as a guide. I also use directed reading activities fairly frequently. For instance, last week when we were reading in our social studies books, I taught a lesson on using the index. Recently, I've started using individualized reading, too. My students get to read their own self-selected library books, but only after they complete their regular reading assignments in our published reading program.

## Ms. Sanchez

I believe that it's most important for readers to develop metacognitive, discourse, syntactic, and vocabulary knowledge—the knowledge sources most associated with prior knowledge. I don't spend much time at all developing decoding knowledge. I'm more concerned that students make reasonable predictions about words they're reading than struggle over the sounds of the letters. In fact, the first thing I say when students are having difficulty with a word is always "Make a guess about what you think it might be." I look at reading as more of a reader-based process—greatly influenced by what the reader brings to the text.

I also think that students learn best by having many self-directed reading experiences, so I spend much of my time using individualized reading. I believe very strongly that the best way to learn to read is by reading, not by studying about reading. And I work writing activities in whenever I can because I think my students' reading ability develops better when they learn about language holistically.

I spend very little time in our published reading program. If our principal didn't require us to use it, I probably wouldn't. When I do use it, I turn many of the lessons into cooperative learning group activities.

I know my colleagues and I have very different views about reading, but we're still interested in each other's work. And none of us is so tied to our beliefs that we're unwilling to try out a new idea, especially one that seems to work for someone else. We do try to stay lighthearted about our differences. We always tell Mr. Burns that he needs to loosen up a bit in class, and we give Ms. Dodson a hard time about not being able to make up her mind about anything. I get teased about when I'm finally going to teach my students something about reading. What we all have in common, though, is that we're always looking for better ways to teach our students, even if it means adjusting our comprehension frameworks and our instructional practices.

■ A comprehension framework is a personal perspective toward reading. It addresses three issues: what the components of reading comprehension are, how a person reads, and how reading ability develops.

■ The reading comprehension process involves a number of important components: decoding knowledge, vocabulary knowledge, syntactic knowledge, discourse knowledge, metacognitive knowledge, emergent literacy/readiness aspects, and affective aspects. Reading instruction promotes the development of these components through carefully designed learning activities.

■ Explanations of how a person reads exist along a continuum ranging from text-based to reader-based, with interactive explanations somewhere near the middle.

■ Explanations of how reading ability develops exist along a continuum ranging from specific skills to holistic language, with integrated explanations somewhere near the middle.

■ Understanding the components of reading comprehension will help you understand why you teach different aspects of reading. Developing a perspective about how a person reads will help you decide what to teach and emphasize. A perspective about how reading ability develops will help you decide how to teach reading.

**MAKING INSTRUCTIONAL DECISIONS**

1. (a) At the beginning of this chapter you selected five statements from Figure 3–1 with which you most agreed. Return to that figure, and see whether your beliefs about how a person reads have changed. You may change your selections, but be sure to keep a record of both your initial and your revised selections. Then follow the directions here to determine your perspective on how a person reads.

   *Directions:* Figure 3–1 contains five statements that are consistent with each of the three explanations of how a person reads: text-based, reader-based, and interactive. The text-based statements include items 1, 3, 5, 10, and 12. The reader-based statements include items 2, 4, 9, 11, and 15. The interactive statements include items 6, 7, 8, 13, and 14. Use this information to determine how many text-based, reader-based, and interactive statements you selected from Figure 3–1 before you read this chapter. If you selected a majority of statements from any one category, you probably shared that perspective on how a person reads. If your statements were distributed among all three categories, you probably held an interactive perspective. If you revised any of your selections after you read the chapter, perform this same analysis on those selections.

   Given your current perspective on how a person reads, what will you teach and emphasize in your reading program?

(b) At the beginning of this chapter you selected five statements from Figure 3–2 with which you most agreed. Return to that figure, and see whether your beliefs about how reading develops have changed. You may change your selections, but be sure to keep a record of both your initial and your revised selections. Then follow the directions here to determine your perspective on how reading ability develops.

*Directions:* Figure 3–2 contains five statements that are consistent with each of the three explanations of how reading ability develops: specific skills, holistic language, and integrated. The specific skills statements include items 1, 5, 6, 11, and 12. The holistic language statements include items 2, 4, 8, 9, and 14. The integrated statements include items 3, 7, 10, 13, and 15. Use this information to determine how many specific skills, holistic language, and integrated statements you selected from Figure 3–2 before you read this chapter. If you selected a majority of statements from any one category, you probably shared that perspective on how reading ability develops. If your statements were distributed among all three categories, you probably held an integrated perspective. If you revised any of your selections after you read the chapter, perform this same analysis on those selections.

Given your current perspective on how reading ability develops, how will you teach reading? Which material and method frameworks might you use?

2. Imagine that you are using a published reading program and need to make decisions about which of the skill areas you will emphasize in your class. These are some of the skill areas included in the program:
   a. Knows the sounds represented by the consonant digraphs *ch, sh, th, wh*.
   b. Recognizes types of literature: autobiography, historical fiction, informational article.
   c. Relates word order to sentence meaning.
   d. Recognizes multiple meanings of words.
   e. Knows left-to-right and top-to-bottom progression of print.
   f. Knows efficient study strategies.
   g. Enjoys reading.

   You will need to determine which component of the comprehension process each skill area addresses before you can make your decision. Match each skill area with the component in the comprehension process that it is most likely to promote.

3. Which skill areas listed in Item 2 would you emphasize if you followed a text-based explanation of how a person reads? a reader-based explanation? an interactive explanation? Why?

4. Some instructional programs teach discourse knowledge about the structural characteristics of a fable (e.g., the characters in a fable are animals,

these animals have human characteristics, a conflict is resolved to the advantage of one of the animals, a moral or lesson is explicitly stated at the end, and so on). How would you develop this knowledge if you followed a specific skills explanation of how reading ability develops? a holistic language explanation? an integrated explanation? Which material and method frameworks would you use? Why?

5. How would you modify a published reading program if you had each of the following comprehension frameworks: text-based with specific skills explanation, interactive with integrated explanation, and reader-based with holistic language explanation? Which method frameworks would you combine with the use of a published reading program?

## FURTHER READING

Blachowicz, C. L. Z. (1984). Showing teachers how to develop students' predictive reading. *The Reading Teacher, 36,* 680–684.

Describes a method framework that can be used to help readers generate and test their expectations of upcoming meaning. Very consistent with reader-based or interactive explanations of how reading takes place.

Goodman, K. (1986). *What's whole in whole language?* Portsmouth, NH: Heinemann.

Describes the nature of the whole language movement and the assumptions behind this perspective. Also provides examples of whole language programs in operation.

Goodman, K., Bird, L., & Goodman, Y. (1990). *The whole language catalogue.* Santa Rosa, CA: American School Publishers.

A start-anywhere-and-read-in-any-direction compendium of information about whole language.

Samuels, S. J., & Schachter, S. W. (1984). Controversial issues in beginning reading: Meaning versus subskill emphasis. In A. J. Harris & E. R. Sipay (Eds.), *Readings on reading instruction* (3rd ed.). New York: Longman.

Specifies the two extreme explanations of how reading develops: holistic language and specific skills. Also discusses instruction that is consistent with each competing explanation.

Slaughter, H. B. (1988). Indirect and direct teaching in a whole language program. *The Reading Teacher, 36,* 30–38.

Describes ways to combine both teacher-directed and student-directed instructional activities in an integrated classroom reading program.

Stahl, S. A., & Miller, P. D. (1989). Whole language and language experience approaches for beginning reading: A quantitative research synthesis. *Review of Educational Research, 59* (1), 87–116.

Reviews two decades of studies comparing the use of published reading programs and whole language/language experience approaches. The authors conclude that, overall, these two approaches are approximately equal in their effects, with several exceptions: whole language/language experience approaches are more effective in kindergarten than first grade, they produce stronger effects on decoding knowledge than on comprehension, and they produce weaker effects with populations labeled as disadvantaged. More recent studies show a trend toward stronger effects for the use of published reading programs.

## REFERENCES

Anderson, R. C., Hiebert, E. H., Scott, J. A., & Wilkinson, I. A. G. (1985). *Becoming a nation of readers: The report of the commission on reading.* Washington, DC: National Institute of Education.

Aulls, M. W. (1982). *Developing readers in today's elementary school*. New York: Allyn & Bacon.

Baker, L., & Brown, A. (1984). Metacognitive skills and reading. In P. David Pearson (Ed.), *The handbook of reading research*. New York: Longman.

Bauman, J. F., & Schmitt, M. C. (1986). The what, why, how, and when of comprehension instruction. *The Reading Teacher, 39*, 640–645.

Chall, J. S. (1983). *Stages of reading development*. New York: McGraw-Hill.

Clay, M. M. (1980a). *The early detection of reading difficulties: A diagnostic survey* (2nd ed.). New York: Heinemann.

Clay, M. M. (1980b). *Reading: The patterning of complex behavior* (2nd ed.). London: Heinemann.

Duffy, G. (1982). Fighting off the alligators: What research in real classrooms has to say about reading instruction. *Journal of Reading Behavior, 14* (4), 357–373.

Goodman, K. S. (1986). Reading: A psycholinguistic guessing game. In H. Singer & R. Ruddell (Eds.), *Theoretical models and processes of reading* (3rd ed.). Newark, DE: International Reading Association.

Goodman, K. (1986). *What's whole in whole language?* Portsmouth, NH: Heinemann.

Goodman, K. S., & Goodman, Y. M. (1979). Learning to read is natural. In L. B. Resnick & P. A. Weaver (Eds.), *Theory and practice of early reading* (Vol. 1). Hillsdale, NJ: Erlbaum.

Gough, P. B. (1986). One second of reading. In H. Singer & R. Ruddell (Eds.), *Theoretical models and processes of reading* (3rd ed.). Newark, DE: International Reading Association.

Harris, A. J., & Sipay, E. R. (1990). *How to increase reading ability* (9th ed.). New York: Longman.

Harste, J., Woodward, V., & Burke, C. (1984). *Language stories and literacy lessons*. Portsmouth, NH: Heinemann.

Holdaway, D. (1979). *The foundations of literacy*. Exeter, NH: Heinemann.

Huey, E. B. (1968). *The psychology and pedagogy of reading*. Cambridge, MA: MIT Press. (Original edition published by Macmillan in 1908).

Irwin, J. W. (1986). *Teaching reading comprehension processes*. Englewood Cliffs, NJ: Prentice Hall.

Johnson, D. D., & Pearson, P. D. (1984). *Teaching reading vocabulary* (2nd ed.). New York: Holt, Rinehart & Winston.

Ollila, L. O. (1976). Reading: preparing the child. In P. M. Lamb & R. O. Arnold (Eds.), *Reading: Foundations and instructional strategies*. Belmont, CA: Wadsworth.

Palincsar, A. S., & Ransom, K. (1988). From the mystery spot to the thoughtful spot: The instruction of metacognitive strategies. *The Reading Teacher, 41*, 784–789.

Rumelhart, D. (1976). *Toward an interactive model of reading* (Report No. 56). La Jolla, CA: University of California, San Diego, Center for Human Information Processing.

Slobin, D. (1979). *Psycholinguistics* (2nd ed.). Glenview, IL: Scott, Foresman.

Smith, F. (1988). *Understanding reading: A psycholinguistic analysis of reading and learning to read* (4th ed.). Hillsdale, NJ: Erlbaum.

Stanovich, K. E. (1980). Toward an interactive-compensatory model of individual differences in the development of reading fluency. *Reading Research Quarterly, 16*, 32–71.

Teale, W. H., & Sulzby, E. (Eds.). (1986). *Emergent literacy: Writing and reading*. Norwood, NJ: Ablex.

Teale, W. H., & Sulzby, E. (1989). Emergent literacy: New perspectives. In D. S. Strickland & L. M. Morrow (Eds.), *Emerging literacy: Young children learn to read and write*. Newark, DE: International Reading Association.

Tierney, R. J., & Pearson, P. D. (1983). Toward a composing model of reading. *Language Arts, 60*, 568–580.

Weaver, P., & Shonhoff, F. (1984). Subskill and holistic approaches to reading instruction. In A. J. Harris & E. R. Sipay (Eds.), *Readings on reading instruction* (3rd ed). New York: Longman.

# DEVELOPING A
# KNOWLEDGE BASE

PART

2

# Emergent Literacy/Readiness and Comprehension

## Chapter 4

- The Concepts of Emergent Literacy/Reading Readiness
- Emergent Literacy: An Evolving Philosophy
- Factors Affecting Emergent Literacy/Reading Readiness
- Evaluating the Beginning Reader
- Using a Comprehension Framework to Guide Emergent Literacy/Readiness Instruction

*"When will I read?" Jim asked.*
*"Soon," the teacher said.*
*"But when?" said Jim.*
*"You know what the signs in our room say," the teacher said.*
*"Yes," said Jim. . . .*
*"You can read your name," the teacher said.*
*"But that's not really reading," said Jim. . . .*
*"Don't worry," the teacher said. "There's no hurry. You will read when you are ready."*
*"But when will I be ready?" Jim asked.*
*"You are getting ready all the time," she said.*

C hildren have well-developed language abilities before they enter kindergarten or first grade. Although many children, like Jim in the opening quotation, do not think that what they do counts as reading, teachers are increasingly viewing young children's literacy abilities as part of a continuum rather than as skills that are separate from "real" reading activities. In this chapter you will learn about traditional readiness programs as well as about programs based on emergent literacy viewpoints. Chapter 4 includes information that will help you answer questions like these:

1. How do traditional views of reading readiness differ from emergent literacy/whole language perspectives?
2. What literacy abilities do children have when they enter school, and how might a reading teacher capitalize on those abilities?
3. How do teachers evaluate beginning readers, and how might that information be used?
4. How might instructional frameworks guide instruction in an emergent literacy/readiness program?

## KEY CONCEPTS

auditory perception/discrimination
auditory-visual integration
big books
cognition/cognitive factors
emergent literacy
functional reading/writing (literacy)
    tasks
holophrastic speech
invented spelling

language experience approach
observational (informal) data
prereading activities
reading readiness
telegraphic speech
think-alouds
visual perception/discrimination
whole language program

## THE CONCEPTS OF EMERGENT 現出的、意外的 LITERACY/READING READINESS

Although children learn a great deal about reading and writing in school, much has already been learned before they enter kindergarten or first grade. Before formal schooling begins, children have the perceptual abilities to discriminate among different letters, words, and sounds. They also are already good users of their native language and are able to understand almost all basic types of English sentences, including questions, statements, and exclamations. In addition, children in the early elementary grades have highly developed speaking 感 vocabularies. Early studies indicated that a first grader's vocabulary averaged 業 about 2,500 words; more recent studies have put that estimate as high as 8,000 0 words (Anderson & Freebody, 1985; Dale, 1965). Teachers use these language-related abilities to advance their students' reading development. 呼 喊

As a mature reader, you probably take for granted your **fluent reading** ability. To remind yourself of some of the things that beginning readers are learning, study each of the following examples. See what things you can discover that are a help or a hindrance to reading.

> fluent reading: Reading unhindered by word identification or comprehension problems.

1. !@ #$# $@%©! &*$$*™#$ ®<§§ <§§¶$!©*!# $%># %~ !@ &©%/§#>$ †@<§[©#] ~*†# ®@#] §#*©]<]™ !% ©#*[:

2. ?seldoop ekil uoy oD .reh rof ynapmoc doog si eldoop ehT .ti ot desu eb tsum ehS .eciton t'nseod ehs syas robhgien ym tub ,tol a skrab tI .eldoop a sah robhgien yM

3. dogsareinterestinganimalseventhoughtheycanbenuisancesattim estheyareusuallyfriendlyandarenicetohavearounddoyou- haveadog

4. Somepeopledon'tlikedogs. Myfriend,forexample,isa"catperson." Hesaysthatdogsaredumbandthatcatsaremuchmoresophisticated. Whatdoyouthink?

Most people who try to read the first example agree that reading difficulty results from not knowing symbol-sound relationships. With the key provided here, it is possible to puzzle out the meaning of that sentence and thus to gain some idea of what beginning readers face.

| a | = | * | f | = | - | m | = | > | s | = | $ |
|---|---|---|---|---|---|---|---|---|---|---|---|
| b | = | / | g | = | ™ | n | = | ] | t | = | ! |
| c | = | † | h | = | @ | o | = | % | u | = | ¶ |
| d | = | [ | i | = | < | p | = | & | w | = | ® |
| e | = | # | l | = | § | r | = | © | . | = | : |

Understanding symbol-sound relationships is part of a **decoding** process. For traditional readiness programs, decoding is preceded by the more basic step of understanding that a relationship exists between a symbol and a sound, between oral and written language.

> decoding: A reader's process of determining the oral equivalents of words.

Example 2 violates a **convention** that proficient readers take for granted but that beginning readers must learn: English print is read from left to right and top to bottom on a page. Try reading Example 2 from right to left and bottom to top. It is entirely possible to read this way—we simply do not do so in English. The left-to-right sequence is something that is taught in all **emergent literacy**/readiness programs.

> convention: A common way that language is used by a particular group of people.

> emergent literacy: A view that literacy develops continually through children's playing with and exploring writing and reading.

Example 3 may have caused you some difficulty because there are no spaces between the words. In fact, this written representation can be compared to speech, in which there is no white space around individual words to signal where one word begins and another ends. Individuals reading this example are often confused when they get to *animalseven,* reading the words initially as *animal seven* rather than the intended *animals even.* Thus, we can see that white space around words provides important clues to pronunciation and meaning. Good readers are aware of what white space on a page can tell, but the concept of a word is something that beginning readers must learn (Allen, 1982; Hare, 1984; Hiebert, 1983).

In Example 4 the uppercase letters and punctuation probably allowed you to divide the passage into sentences. However, many beginning readers have not yet learned upper- and lowercase letters, nor do they realize that punctuation can signal meaning, making a passage easier to read.

These examples should have helped you understand some of the underlying knowledge that is necessary for reading to occur—for example, awareness that symbols stand for sounds; left-to-right progression; the concept of word and sentence; and discrimination between upper- and lowercase letters. These items are incorporated in the following general behavioral goals that are often targeted by reading programs for beginning readers (Durkin, 1987).

- to acquire an understanding of what reading and learning to read are all about
- to learn to want to be a reader
- to learn what is meant by *word*
- to understand the function of empty space in establishing word boundaries
- to learn about the left-to-right, top-to-bottom orientation of written English (pp. 110–111)

As this list implies, current emergent literacy/readiness programs do not wait for readiness to occur spontaneously in young children. Years ago, however—beginning in the early 1920s and continuing for 15 to 20 years—readiness was defined by mental age, largely because of the work of Morphett and Washburn (1931). It was thought that a child without a mental age of 6.0 to 6.5 was not ready to read and instruction would be wasted. Mental age was determined by this formula:

$$\text{mental age} = \text{intelligence quotient (IQ)} \times \text{chronological age (CA)} \div 100$$

Gradually, readiness for reading came to be viewed as something that could be developed rather than awaited, and measures of mental age stopped being used as a criterion for entry into kindergarten. Today, there is increasing emphasis on the idea that literacy develops continually and emerges from a child's ongoing exploration of the environment and of print, a concept known as emergent literacy.

## EMERGENT LITERACY: AN EVOLVING PHILOSOPHY

reading readiness: Traditionally, the time when a prereader acquires the skills and knowledge needed for reading instruction.

Traditionally, **reading readiness** identifies that period of time in which students acquire the specific skills and abilities that allow reading to take place. *The Dictionary of Reading and Related Terms* (Harris & Hodges, 1981) defines *readiness* as "preparedness to cope with a learning task" and goes on to state that readiness for learning of any type at any level is determined by a complex pattern of intellectual, motivational, maturational, and experiential factors in each individual, which may vary from time to time and from situation to situation (p. 263). A term related to reading readiness is **prereading activities,** which describes activities designed to result in fluent reading.

Traditional views often present reading readiness as a stage that children pass through before they become readers. In effect, proponents of this view look at nonreaders as not having required skills or abilities that are necessary for reading to occur. Consequently, traditional readiness programs attempt to provide activities that are aimed at developing those prereading skills and often do so with deductive methods.

In contrast, proponents of emergent literacy believe that *all* literacy-related activity is part of the reading and writing process. For example, scribbling is viewed as writing, especially if the child thinks that it is. Children's scribbles and descriptions of pictures in a book are seen as part of an evolution toward mature reading and are not separated from "real" literacy activities. Instruction from an emergent literacy perspective usually occurs in functional situations, without segmenting or isolating skills, and is usually based on inductive strategies and **functional literacy experiences.**

Some have argued that there is little theoretical difference between traditional and emergent literacy philosophies in terms of belief that children's literacy is developing, or emerging, from less mature to more mature forms of reading and writing (Harris & Sipay, 1990). Others disagree, citing the theoretical base of emergent literacy, which stresses the social nature of literacy acquisition (Luria, 1976; Vygotsky, 1978, 1986) and the emotional and psychological responses, included in reader-response theory, that are a part of reading and writing (Rosenblatt, 1988; Willinsky, 1988; Galda, 1988; see also Robeck & Wallace's 1990 presentation of the similarities and differences between Piaget's and Vygotsky's views). Indeed, emergent literacy views of reading development have brought into sharp focus the social, communicative nature of literacy (Rowe, 1989) and have made reading teachers look at the continuum of literacy activities, especially writing activities, as evolving through definable stages. Nonetheless, a major difference between traditional views of reading readiness and emergent literacy perspectives is in the instructional frameworks (deductive vs. inductive) that influence reading instruction.

The fact that oral language evolves in clear stages, from babbling to mature speech, has been accepted by language and educational theorists for some time. Teachers and parents generally accept toddlers' halting and incorrect verbalizations as attempts at communication and call these attempts talking. Until recently, however, there was little formal recognition that reading and writing might also proceed through stages. Teachers and parents were often unwilling to call young children's scribbles writing. Few teachers were ready to acknowledge work such as that pictured in Figures 4–1 and 4–2 as meaningful attempts at writing. More recently there has been increasing evi-

prereading activities: Activities that aid comprehension and take place before a selection is read.

functional literacy experiences: Literacy tasks and activities that are meaningful, not artificial.

FIGURE 4–1
Preschool writing products

(a)

(b)                    (c)                    (d)

dence that even very young children participate in and even initiate literacy-related play in an environment that includes adult models answering questions and encouraging children's curiosity about reading and writing (J. Goodman, in press; Harste, Woodward, & Burke, 1984; Teale & Sulzby, 1986, 1989). Such play can include writing activities that appear quite distant from what adults perceive as real writing yet are part of the experimentation common to all learning.

Trial and error during literacy learning are especially visible in writing, which has many subcomponents. For example, mature writing is thought to consist of legible penmanship and attention to correct grammar and spelling, straight lines of text, consistent margins and indentation of paragraphs, punc-

FIGURE 4–2
Samples of emergent writing: (a) a preschooler's shopping list, (b) a kindergartner's
note to a classmate ("I got a haircut"), and (c) the classmate's response ("I hope you
had a good time—I hope I can come")

(a)          (b)          (c)

tuation, and capitalization. As children experiment with writing, many or all of
these items may be missing or incomplete, yet one essential component is
present—the products have meaning and are intentionally created as a form
of expression and literary activity (Teale & Sulzby, 1986; Rowe, in press). In
other words, even young children are not randomly scribbling; they are intentionally writing products that have clear meaning to them.

　　Thus, an emergent literacy perspective implies that children's experiments with language are communicative acts that are evolving. Figure 4–1(a)
shows a letter that Lauren (age: 3 years, 2 months) wrote to her grandmother.
Lauren had just spent time watching her parents write a series of letters and
Christmas cards. She then asked for an envelope and went to her room. When
she returned, she gave her parents her letter and addressed envelope, read her
letter to them, and asked that it be mailed along with those her parents were
writing. When asked to reread her letter about 30 minutes later, she did not
deviate from her earlier reading. Thus, even though adults would not be able
to read Lauren's letter or addressed envelope, for her they were meaningful and
had a purpose.

In the samples shown in Figure 4–1(b) and 4–1(c), Alexandra (age: 2 years, 8 months) has drawn an apple tree and signed her name. The drawing in 4–1(b) preceded the finished product in 4–1(c), and when questioned, Alexandra explained. She had rejected the practice tree in 4–1(b) for several reasons; when finally satisfied, she signed her name. The sample in Figure 4–1(d) also shows **intentionality**. Alexandra had stated that she was going to practice making a list using *As, Os,* and *Ps;* and although the letters are by no means perfectly formed, it is easy to see that she is practicing these letters and that her completed list fulfills her goal.

Figure 4–2 shows other examples of children's written work. The sample in 4–2(a) shows a shopping list (student age: 2 years, 6 months), whereas 4–2(b) and 4–2(c) show two kindergartners' correspondence with each other. Even though they could not read their friend's note, they read their own notes to each other and happily kept their friend's note. All these examples demonstrate that children express meaning in their written work, regardless of how unpolished it might seem to an adult. Clearly, these children have conceptualized and used certain literacy conventions: Lauren's letter and envelope are in correct form (the envelope even has a stamp on it), the signature with the apple tree is in a suitable location, the shopping list is in list form, and so on. Such conventions will be refined through further practice.

## Instructional Implications

The concept of emergent literacy has resulted in an instructional approach that has been loosely defined as **whole language** (see chapter 3). In short, this term is meant to convey that instruction is based on all aspects of language—speaking, listening, and writing—and it implies that literacy instruction is holistic; that is, it does not break language learning into isolated skill components. Instead, language learning occurs in the context of meaningful literacy activities; for example, reading and writing skills are often taught within the context of complete stories. Thus, children's literature plays a large part in reading instruction in a whole language setting, and traditional published reading programs, which are viewed as fragmenting skills, are deemphasized. However, this recent emphasis on whole language instruction has resulted in several published reading programs that are largely based on anthologies of children's literature and involve fewer worksheets and less teaching of isolated skills (chapter 2 presents a discussion of such series).

In whole language kindergarten classrooms many reading activities center around **big books,** which usually reproduce in large format (sometimes as large as chart paper pads) children's literature selections. Big books are colorful and motivational and are found increasingly in traditional readiness programs as well. Even though big books are complete stories and are longer than language experience stories, teachers often read them to their students in much the same way that they read language experience stories—running their hands under the print as they read, commenting on a particular word, or

**intentionality:** The purposefulness of an activity, in contrast to random behavior or accidentally occurring responses that might be appropriate.

**whole language:** The philosophy that all literacy and language processes interact and thus can be used to reinforce each other.

**big books:** Children's literature selections reproduced in large format.

Big books, which are often used in beginning reading instruction, can be purchased or created as a class project, with the teacher printing the story and students illustrating appropriate pages.

asking children to read a word or phrase if they can. Big books are available from publishers but can also be created by teacher and students, with the teacher writing down on chart paper what children dictate (perhaps suggesting story lines that the children can refine).

All of the literacy-related activities in whole language classrooms are intended to be relevant and meaning-based. Such activities need not always be shared, however. For example, a child might want to write a very private fantasy story that would not be shared even with friends or parents. For that child the writing activity would be meaningful and motivational even without sharing. On the other hand, literacy activities certainly can be shared. Writing activities, especially, might lead to student conferences in which student writers share their "work-in-progress" with other students, eliciting comments, reactions, and suggestions from friendly but knowledgeable readers (Calkins, 1983; Graves, 1983). The resulting dialogue between writers and readers can lead to significant insights for each about both reading and writing. Meaningful activities can also be teacher-assigned tasks that are purposeful rather than purely artificial. For instance, if students are dictating a letter that the teacher transcribes, the letter should be delivered or mailed to a real person and the response shared and posted. In this way, students learn that writing is purposeful, and motivation for both writing and reading remains high.

A favorite technique that uses literacy in a meaningful way is the morning message (e.g., see Kawakami-Arakaki, Oshiro, & Farran, 1989). This is typically the first instructional activity of the school day and comes right after attendance is taken. Students watch the teacher write on the chalk board or on chart paper the date and several short messages or announcements pertaining to the day's activities. At the beginning of the school year the messages are relatively short, increasing in length as the year goes on.

**MODEL
LESSON**

## Morning Message

After taking attendance, the teacher writes the following message on chart paper, reading each word as she writes it.

> November 4
> Today is Thursday. Mr. Paolo will be here during story time. He will tell us a story about Brazil. You can take your art projects home today!

After the message is complete, the teacher reads it to the class. The children are encouraged to read along if they are able. The teacher runs her hand under the words as she reads them. Then the whole message is read in chorus (most of the children will be able to repeat it from memory at this point).

The teacher asks whether the children notice anything interesting about the written message itself. Tom says that the first letter is the same as the first letter of his name. Janie notices the exclamation mark and says that the message doesn't end "in a dot." The teacher uses this input to draw the parallel between *Tom, Today,* and *Thursday*. She explains that these words begin with capital *T*s and also points out the lowercase *t*s in *story-time*. Then she explains why she used an exclamation mark instead of a period (the artwork is so good that she's excited about letting them take it home). Finally, the message itself is discussed. Mr. Paolo heard some interesting folktales while he was in Brazil recently, and he is coming to share those stories with the class.

---

The concept of emergent literacy also implies that students' written products are communicative acts in a state of evolution, thus students' written work should be considered meaningful and should be encouraged, shared, and highlighted. Teachers in whole language classrooms encourage children to ask questions as they work and to elaborate orally on what they are attempting to convey through their writing. According to an emergent literacy view, teachers should also be tolerant of variations in form as children write and read their work. Nonstandard handwriting, spacing, margins, letter formation, and spelling are considered a part of the developmental process; and through teacher modeling, instruction, and continued attempts by the child, such variations will continue to more closely approximate traditional forms until the correct form appears. In short, variations in form are treated as normal stages of learning; and as in all learning, mistakes are made along the way toward expertise. Figure 4–2 shows some of the **invented spelling** that children use as their writing evolves.

**invented spellings:** Children's spellings that are meaningful to them but are inconsistent with the spellings accepted as correct by mature readers and writers.

Many of these instructional implications are immediately apparent in a whole language environment. Classroom walls are often covered with students' writing and illustrations, and students often have their own bulletin board. In addition, the classroom probably has many things conducive to reading and writing in plain view and in use by the students: mobiles, reading corners, writing corners, and, in particular, much print everywhere—on the walls, in books on bookshelves, in magazines on tables, and in the artwork area.

## The Continuing Debate

Whole language instruction is making a significant impact on literacy education, especially in kindergarten and primary grades. However, some questions are being raised with regard to the whole language approach.

First of all, there may be little difference between what are now being called whole language programs and what have been known as good teaching practices for the past two decades. For example, good teachers have usually incorporated writing with reading activities in meaningful contexts, often at the suggestion of basal reader programs, which McCallum (1988) cautions may be discarded prematurely. Others argue that there is little difference between whole language programs and language experience approaches if the LEA lesson is expanded to encompass more of the instructional program (see Stahl & Miller, 1989, for a discussion of differences between language experience and whole language approaches). In addition, an increasing number of theorists believe that terminology such as *emergent literacy* and *whole language* is problematic since in fact *all* approaches hold that literacy acquisition is developmental or emergent (Bransford, 1988; Rowe, 1989; Rowe & Harste, 1990). An associated concern is the lack of consistent, comparative evidence regarding the value of whole language as opposed to that of other approaches; according to Catterson's (1989) and Stahl & Miller's (1989) views of research evidence, whole language programs appear no more effective than traditional programs.

Another area of discussion related to whole language instruction focuses on whether reading and writing should be equally stressed in kindergarten programs or whether writing should receive greater emphasis. Durkin had this to say:

> I find particularly troublesome the assumption that *all* children should do a lot of writing right away. . . . what one child finds easy and meaningful and is successful with is not going to be the same for another child. That's why I find articles with titles like "Write First, Read Later" objectionable. . . . there are lots of unanswered questions about the connection between reading and writing and about the effects of early writing, for instance, and of invented spelling. . . . I think we're a little lopsided now about the way we look at some things. I think we need to be vigilant about unverified assumptions about reading and writing and the reading and writing connections. (Aaron, Chall, Durkin, Goodman, & Strickland, 1990, p. 305)

Strickland responded to Durkin's comments by affirming the close relationship between reading and writing but agreed that to "place undue emphasis on one or the other is probably misplaced. . .offering opportunities for both reading and writing is very different from pressuring or requiring that children engage in writing early on." (Aaron et al., 1990, p. 305).

In summary, whole language programs appear to have benefits in motivation and in the amount of writing and reading accomplished by students. As a result, both intuition and research suggest that literacy development should be facilitated by whole language approaches (Mason, 1989). Indeed, there have been many descriptions of children learning to read and write in whole language settings, both at home and in preschool and first-grade programs, and their success stories cannot be ignored (e.g., see DeFord, 1986; Harste, Woodward, & Burke, 1984; Holdaway, 1979; Wells, 1986). Furthermore, these and other researchers have linked a whole language approach to theories of learning, classroom management, and functional, communicative uses of literacy. And those theoretical links are leading to further research into the relative effectiveness of the approach. Those interested in reading more about both the background and the implementation of whole language/emergent literacy programs are referred to McGee and Richgels (1990) and Shanahan (1990), both of which are included in the reference section at the end of the chapter.

Providing an experience, using any or all of the senses, can be the basis for a later language experience activity.

---

## DECISION POINT ➤

An ongoing debate in early childhood education centers around the curricular content of kindergarten programs. Some educators believe that kindergarten should only prepare children for later schooling, focusing on the social skills and curricular background necessary for instruction in first grade. According to this line of thinking, kindergarten should provide children with opportunities to scribble, draw, look at picture books, and explore literacy as their interests dictate. Others believe that kindergarten should more formally teach some basic reading content, which usually relates specifically to letter names, letter sounds, and discrimination of both upper- and lowercase letters. What do you think kindergarten instruction should accomplish? How does your comprehension framework relate to this debate?

---

## Broader Applications

Even though emergent literacy/readiness concepts are most often applied to beginning readers, they can also relate to proficient readers. For example, even mature readers are apt to have difficulty comprehending the following passage:

> Comprehensive allocation is more consistent with the accounting for liabilities than roll over, such as accounts payable. New accounts payable continually replace accounts being paid, much the same as originating timing differences replace timing differences that reverse. Each creditor's account is accounted for separately, even though aggregate accounts payable continue to roll over. Consistency requires that timing differences related to a particular asset or liability likewise be accounted for separately. (Davidson, Stickney, & Weil, 1980, pp. 20–26)

To see how well you comprehended the important concepts in the passage, try to answer the following questions:

1. Why is comprehensive allocation more consistent with liabilities than roll over?
2. What is the concept of timing differences, and what is their importance to accounts payable?
3. What is the paragraph about? Explain it in your own words.

You may be a fluent reader, yet you may not have been ready to read such a passage from an accounting text (an accountant would have had no difficulty with it). You could probably have used some prereading activities—perhaps some additional background knowledge, definitions of new vocabulary, and maybe discussion of overall meaning. The point is that emergent literacy/readiness does not stop with the acquisition of decoding knowledge. A broader view acknowledges that we all may encounter text that we are unprepared to read, given our current level of knowledge.

## FACTORS AFFFECTING EMERGENT LITERACY/ READING READINESS

A number of factors interact to affect literacy development. Some, such as cognitive factors, are internal; others, such as home environment, are external. All, however, influence prereaders and continue to influence their reading throughout life. These interacting factors are presented separately here for ease of discussion.

### Cognitive Factors

cognition: Knowing; thought processes.

All human beings have the capability of progressing through four levels of **cognition:** sensorimotor, preoperational, concrete operational, and formal operational (Inhelder & Piaget, 1964; Piaget, 1963). Table 4–1 identifies the approximate age ranges and particular behaviors associated with these four cognitive levels.

cognitive development: Growth in mental abilities and thought processes.

Research has provided insight into the relationship between **cognitive development** and the behaviors or abilities necessary for mature reading. However, too often poor performance is excused as a lack of emergent literacy/ readiness. Good instructional practice can do much to facilitate children's language behaviors, and educators should not simply wait until students are ready to acquire a skill.

seriation: The ability to order a set of objects logically.

Among the cognitive operations related to reading are these (Almy, Chittenden, & Miller, 1966; Bybee & Sund, 1982; Waller, 1977): **seriation,** ordering, **temporal relations, conservation,** one-to-one correspondence, spatial relations, classification, and number relations. Seriation and ordering, for example, play a part in learning left-to-right progression and in realizing that letters and words go together in sequence. One-to-one correspondence is a factor in learning letter-sound relationships, and classification relates to such tasks as learning upper- and lowercase letters. Text comprehension relies on all of these operations.

temporal relations: A relationship based on either the passage of time or a particular interval of time.

conservation: The ability to keep an unchanging property of something in mind when perceptual conditions are changed.

In order to understand the importance of these cognitive operations, let's first consider the following sentences:

> The boy was hungry. He stole some food. He hid under a table that had a large pot of flowers on it.

Then let's answer these related questions, for which Bybee and Sund (1982) have identified the required cognitive operations.

> What happened first—the boy's being hungry or his stealing the food? (seriation, ordering, and temporal relations)
>
> What do you think the boy will do next? (ordering)
>
> Where was the food at the end of the story? (spatial relations)

Questions like these are often asked by teachers without adequate attention being given to the cognitive demands involved. Although questions that

TABLE 4–1
Cognitive levels and associated ages and behaviors/abilities.

| Cognitive Level | Age (years) | General Behaviors or Abilities |
|---|---|---|
| Sensorimotor | 0–2 | No concept of space, time, cause and effect, or self; no object permanence; reflexive actions |
| Preoperational | 3–7 | Awareness of past, present, and future; fairly broad concept of space; ego-centric awareness of self; egocentric language; ability to conceptualize some cause-and-effect relationships |
| Concrete operational | 8–11 | Conceptualizes and relates temporal order and duration; conserves, or holds constant, quantity, number; seriation; recognizes multiple-class membership; exhibits logical, reversible thought related to concrete situations; understands cause and effect in concrete problems; displays reduced egocentrism |
| Formal operation | 12+ | Comprehends relative space and time; exhibits combinatorial logic; controls and separates variables in complex problems; can deal with abstractions and "ideal" situations; understands others' viewpoints; uses abstract language and concepts |

extend and appropriately challenge students are necessary for learning, questions that are too difficult can frustrate and prompt students to give up prematurely. Thus, teachers must be careful not to use concepts that are beyond the level of beginning readers. Most emergent literacy/readiness programs try to provide activities to build many of the concepts that adults take for granted—such as *before, in front of,* or *under*. Teachers can demonstrate such concepts in everyday teaching routines. For example, there are ample opportunities for students to stand *beside* one student but *in front of* another. Students can also be asked to manipulate objects, placing them on, under, and around other objects. Or they might perform a sequence of activities, allowing other students to describe the order of events.

Following directions is another potentially difficult cognitive task. However, teachers frequently ask students to do several things at once—for example, "Put your pencils down, close your books, and pass your papers forward before you line up for recess"—forgetting that children may have difficulty grasping multiple directions. Emergent literacy/readiness programs should provide specific activities targeting listening skills and following directions. A simple game such as Simon Says is an appropriate activity, as is a classroom treasure hunt that requires students to follow instructions precisely. Other activities related to important cognitive operations are noted here.

**SAMPLE ACTIVITIES**

**Observing Writing.** Ask students to point to the places on a page of chart paper where you should start and stop writing. Then ask them to watch as you write—perhaps transcribing a simple story or sentence they dictate to you. Draw their conscious attention to where you start and stop each line.

**Picture-story Sequencing.** Cut simple cartoon strips into individual frames. Then, have the children arrange the frames from left to right so that the story is told. After the frames are arranged, have students tell the story in their own words, frame by frame, pointing to each frame as appropriate.

**Meaning Match.** Have the children draw lines from left to right between two pictures that, when joined, make sense. For example, pictures on the left might show a squirrel, a car, and a boat; pictures on the right, a nut, a garage, and a lakeshore. Say to the children, "Help the squirrel [car, boat] get to the nut [garage, water] by drawing a line from left to right between the two."

Sequencing and Following Directions Games

- Supply students with pictures, and ask them to follow specific, sequential instructions (e.g., "Put an *X* below the house and then circle the dog").
- Provide motor activities such as drawing pictures to certain specifications (e.g., "Draw a man in one corner, two dogs in the middle, and a car between the man and the dogs"). Then help students label their pictures.
- Have students give directions to you or another student to perform a simple task.
- Present a simple board game and explain the directions. Have students repeat the directions to check for understanding. After they have played the game, change the directions, and discuss the effect on the game.
- Teach the importance of directions by bringing a simple recipe to class (e.g., popcorn or Jell-O). Make the item by reading and following the directions step by step. Discuss how important the directions were.

Vygotsky's work (1978, 1986) has significantly influenced emergent literacy/reading readiness instruction. Specifically, Vygotsky believed that cognitive development, including the development of language, is greatly affected by an individual's social interaction with others. In other words, mediators, such as teachers or parents, influence a child's cognitive and language skills.

Thus, emergent literacy/readiness is viewed as an evolving stage, or phase, that is influenced by teachers, rather than a static stage that a learner progresses through independently.

One of Vygotsky's major contributions is the zone of proximal development, which represents the difference between what learners can do on their own and what they can accomplish with guidance. Within that zone concepts are maturing; that is, they are being refined through social interaction, but they are not yet sufficiently developed to be applied without help. Vygotsky believes that learners can do more with appropriate mediation than by themselves; thus, a teacher's actions are viewed as critical in a child's cognitive development. The instructional implications of Vygotsky's concepts include these suggested behaviors:

1. Identify the learner's zone of proximal development. This area lies immediately beyond the area in which the learner can function without help.
2. Present tasks that the child can do with the help of others who are able to complete the tasks on their own. The tasks should be completed through social interaction and participation. The child should not simply watch others complete the task but should actively collaborate in completing it.
3. Monitor the learner's ability to complete tasks. The zone of proximal development shifts to a higher level whenever the child is able to complete tasks previously performed only with help.

Another of the implications of Vygotsky's work is the use of modeling within social situations. The social, sharing nature of the reading activity makes this an excellent time for modeling to occur, especially through a procedure known as a **think-aloud** (Davey, 1983; Fitzgerald, 1983). A think-aloud is a method framework (detailed in chapter 7) in which the teacher reads a passage aloud and talks through the processes used to make sense of what is being read, thereby modeling the thought processes and application of background knowledge necessary to understand the text.

think-aloud: A procedure whereby a reader states aloud the thought processes and decisions that occur while reading.

## Think-Aloud Procedure

The teacher wants to use a modified think-aloud procedure with the book *Ten Little Caterpillars* (Martin, 1967), which includes the following lines of text on four different pages:

> The first little caterpillar crawled into a bower.
> The second little caterpillar wriggled up a flower.
> The third little caterpillar climbed a cabbage head.
> The fourth little caterpillar found a melon bed. (pp. 3, 5, 7, 9)

First, the teacher reads the title and says, "I wonder what this will tell me about the ten caterpillars. It could tell about how they live together or

**MODEL LESSON**

about what they do." After the first line the teacher says, "*Bower*. Now that's a word I haven't seen before. I wonder what it means. Maybe I can find out by looking at the picture on this page or by reading farther. If not, I might have to ask someone or look in the dictionary." After the second line the teacher says, "This sentence tells me about the second caterpillar. I wonder if the rest of the sentences will tell me about what the other caterpillars do."

After the third line the teacher says, "It sure looks like each sentence is going to tell about a different caterpillar. How many of you think so? Thumbs up if you do, down if you don't. I have a picture in my mind of a caterpillar climbing into a cabbage head. It's easy to think of a cabbage head because I sometimes buy them in the grocery store and because they grow in my neighbor's garden. I wonder if she has caterpillars in her garden." After the fourth line the teacher says, "The first part of each sentence is pretty much the same. That makes it easier to read. I wonder what a melon bed looks like. The bed I sleep in is a place to lie down. A melon bed is probably a place where the melon sits in the garden."

The teacher continues in a similar fashion. Finally, at the end of the story the teacher wraps it up by saying, "Well, after the title I predicted that we might find out about how the caterpillars live or what they might be doing. It looks like the book is mostly about what they are doing. I never did find out the meaning of *bower*. I think I'll go look it up in case I see it again."

---

Think-alouds should be an occasional part of oral reading activities. They should not be done continually.

## Oral Language Factors

The language base of beginning readers is critically important to their learning to read; a solid oral language foundation allows them to generalize from what they already do well. Consequently, children who do not have well-developed aural and oral language skills have more difficulty learning to read.

Early oral language progresses through three basic stages: babbling, holophrastic speech, and telegraphic speech. In the initial babbling stage, the infant generates random sounds. Although it is generally thought that these sounds are not an attempt to actively communicate, the infant does appear to be experimenting with the vocal system. The sounds that are generated include, but go beyond, the sounds that will eventually make up the infant's native language. Only later, when children learn which sounds make up the language of the communicating group to which they belong, are unnecessary sounds dropped. Perhaps because of lack of need and practice, adult speakers have great difficulty pronouncing and even hearing sounds that are not used in their native language.

After the babbling stage the infant appears to apply words to events, apparently using single words logically and consistently to label complete thoughts. For example, a single word such as *milk* or *doll* might be used to communicate thoughts like "I want more milk" or "Give me the doll." This stage, beginning midway to late in the first year of the infant's life, features what is called **holophrastic speech**. Early in this stage parents might hear the child say *papa* or *mama,* even when the adult is not the father or the mother. At a certain stage of cognitive development, children do overgeneralize. In addition, it appears that early sound combinations are the ones that are farthest apart in the **vocal tract**. Thus, it seems easy to rock back and forth between the two sounds of *mama* or *papa:* both the /m/ and the /p/ are formed at the front of the vocal tract with the mouth closed, whereas the /ɑ/ is formed at the back with the tract open.

holophrastic speech: A stage of early language acquisition when a child uses a single word to express a thought.

vocal tract: Speech organs used to make sounds.

Soon after the holophrastic stage, the child begins to string two or three words together in **telegraphic speech**. Examples of such utterances are "Milk here," "All gone milk," or "Baby milk." The child's speech is not yet in the form of complete sentences, yet thoughts seem to be grouped in sentence form. One problem with interpreting an expression like "Milk here" is that we really have no way of knowing whether the child means "Bring the milk here," "The milk has spilled over here," "Here is the milk," or something quite different. In many instances what adults think a child means is not, in fact, the intended meaning. This problem also applies to the speech of kindergarten and first-grade students, and teachers must be careful not to impose their adult interpretation on what their young students say.

telegraphic speech: A stage of oral language development when all but essential words are omitted.

It is very important that parents and teachers provide many opportunities for oral expression. Storytelling by children is a beneficial activity, as is the recapping or retelling of a story that has been told to them. Structured oral language activities should form an ongoing part of an emergent literacy/readiness instructional program. Such activities can range from dictating a story to the teacher, to explaining or describing an event, to planning a class play. Teachers should also provide opportunities for students to build conversational skills, such as turn-taking, listening, and **intonation.**

intonation: The rise, fall, and stress in a voice and the pauses in speaking.

---

**Picture/Sequence Story.** Show a picture or a sequence of two or three pictures, and have students tell a story about what is shown.

**Expressing Emotions.** Have students pretend that they are certain animals or objects in a given situation and talk about their feelings.

**Activity Sequence.** Have students think of a specific sequential activity, such as getting ready for school in the morning, going home from school, or getting from the classroom to the library. Then have students tell a partner or a group the specific directions to follow to perform the activity. If the activity has not been stated, other students can try to guess it from the set of directions.

**SAMPLE
ACTIVITIES**

**Relating Intonation and Mood.** Tell a story to your students. Then tell it again, varying your tone of voice and general expression. Discuss how the different readings made the story seem scarier, happier, and so on. Have students try to vary their own expression on sentences that they repeat after you. Other students can guess the moods that are being expressed.

**Build a Story.** Have students sit in a circle. Begin a story with one sentence and have each student add another sentence until the story gets back around to the teacher. If the session is tape-recorded, transcribe the whole story while the students watch. Later, let students illustrate the story and post it on the classroom bulletin board.

**Show and Tell.** Ask students to bring something special with them from home. Let them show the item and talk about it (i.e., show and tell).

language experience approach: A method framework for teaching reading that is based on children's language and experiences.

**The Language Experience Approach.** Many individuals have attempted to demonstrate the power of oral language and personal experiences in helping children learn to read (Allen & Allen, 1976; Ashton-Warner, 1963, 1972; Nessel & Jones, 1981; Stauffer, 1980). The generic term **language experience approach** (LEA) has come to represent those efforts to teach reading that use children's language and experiences as a base. At beginning levels the language experience approach uses transcriptions of children's oral language to help them learn about reading. The most common language experience activity at this level is an experience story, which is detailed in chapter 2. Essentially, a language experience story begins with a memorable experience. Then the teacher elicits a description, or story, of the experience from the children and transcribes each student's contribution on paper or a chalkboard. When the story is completed, the teacher uses it to teach a variety of reading-related concepts.

In an emergent literacy/readiness program a teacher might simply read back the language experience story, moving a hand under each word as it is read. The teacher might also comment about frequently occurring words or point out the left-to-right progression of the words. Another approach is to read a portion of the story and then stop before a word that is highly predictable and ask someone to "read" the word. Later on, a letter-sound pattern might be pointed out. If the stories are saved over a period of time, students and teacher can go back together and reread these enjoyable accounts of memorable experiences.

An experience story is not the only language experience activity that can be used at beginning levels. Other examples are listed on page 150.

A Language Experience Story

Teacher:  Boys and girls, let's write a story about our field trip today. We can use it to practice our reading, and then we can put it in the hall to tell the rest of the school where we went and what we did. What do you think we should call our story? What should be the title?

Jaime:   I know. Let's call it "Apples, Apples, Everywhere!"

Teacher:  [Writing.] Good, Jaime. I like that. Look at these capital letters. Titles always have capitals at the beginning of each word. Now, how shall we start our story?

**MODEL LESSON**

Maggie:  I want to start: We had a special day. We had an apple day.

Teacher:  [Writing.] Good. Now what shall we say?

Tom:     We went to Beak and Skiff Apple Farm. [Teacher writes.]

Pam:     And we got to ride on the tractor. [Teacher writes.]

Katie:   We got to pick apples. [Teacher writes.]

Jason:   And we got to eat apples. [Teacher writes.]

Sarah:   And Tom got his shoes wet. [Teacher writes.]

Kerrie:  We saw bees. [Teacher writes.]

Del:     When we got back, we were tired, and we got ready to go home. [Teacher writes.]

The teacher explains to the students that they can sometimes use other words to help them read. She reads the first two sentences, stopping at the last word.

We had a special day. We had an apple _____ .

The teacher lets the students read the last word together. Then she gives them a chance to practice using context as she reads each sentence and lets the students supply the last words. Sometimes students say an entire sentence along with the teacher or "read" a sentence on their own, especially if it is the sentence that they contributed to the story. At the end the teacher restates the generalization about context use.

The teacher then has each student draw a picture of the trip. As she walks around the room, she helps some students copy words or a short sentence from the experience story to serve as a caption for their picture. With other students the teacher transcribes their dictated sentences or words on the bottom of their pictures. Finally, the teacher places the experience story on the bulletin board in the hall and surrounds it with the students' pictures.

**SAMPLE
ACTIVITIES**

**Student Name Cards.** Make name labels for all the students in your class. Allow them to place the labels on their desks on the first day of school.

**Labeling.** Have students give the names of important items in the classroom and watch you as you make labels for those objects. A similar activity is having students suggest labels for magazine pictures. Have them watch as you make the labels. Post the pictures and labels around the classroom or on a bulletin board.

**Word Walk.** Take the students on a walk around the playground or around the block. Talk about what is around them. Later, make up word cards about some of the things they saw. Use the word cards as triggers for oral language. Let students randomly pick a card, think of the walk, and talk about the specific word on the card. Be ready to read the card for some students.

**Art-Based Stories.** When children come to school in the fall (or after winter vacation), have them draw a picture of an exciting summer (or winter) experience. Circulate and ask students to dictate a sentence or two about their pictures. Write their sentences on their pictures, ask students to read their sentences, and then bind the art stories into a book for the reading center.

**Class Diary.** Keep a regular class diary, making entries each day. Include photos of class activities wherever you can. Keep the diary in the reading center for children to read and remember class events.

**Helper Chart.** Construct helper charts with movable name tags. Rotate names regularly.

**Dictated Letter Writing.** Write class-dictated letters to authors of books that you have read to your students.

## The Home Environment

internalized: Made a part of one's existing knowledge.

correlated: Showing a relationship to something else.

Before students come to school, they have had vast learning experiences. They have learned how to communicate and have **internalized** a set of language rules, in addition to acquiring a sophisticated awareness of the behaviors necessary for effective communication (e.g., turn taking, intonation, gestures, and facial expressions). During those formative years several home environment factors are highly **correlated** to reading achievement. Through interviews with parents of early readers, Durkin (1966, 1974–1975) has identified these common elements:

■ Parents of early readers spend much time in conversation with their children.

- Early readers ask many questions, and their parents take the time to answer those questions.
- A frequent question asked by early readers is "What's that word?"

The importance of home environment and parental involvement has also been noted by the Commission on Reading (Anderson, Hiebert, Scott, & Wilkinson, 1985; see also Mason, 1980):

> Parents play a role of inestimable importance in laying the foundations for learning to read. Parents should informally teach preschool children about reading and writing by reading aloud to them, discussing stories and events, encouraging them to learn letters and words and teaching them about the world around them. These practices help prepare children for success in reading. (p. 57)

Other factors related to children's later reading success include

- the value that adults in the home place on literacy
- the amount of reading done by adults in the home (modeling)
- the amount of reading material available in the home

Providing early experiences with print, including reading to a child and sharing an interest in books, positively influences later success in reading and writing.

■ the number of language-based games and activities in the home
■ the availability of personal reading materials for the child

There are literally thousands of books available for the preschool child, ranging from colorful picture books, with and without story lines, to fairly complex stories. One type of book that is popular with young children contains highly predictable patterns of language—perhaps rhyming patterns, repeated words and phrases, or predictable concepts. Such books are highly motivational because they allow children to begin quickly to read along with a parent or teacher, using prior knowledge to predict and thus aid understanding, just as mature readers do. An example of a predictable text is *Ten Little Caterpillars,* which was cited and excerpted in the model lesson on pages 145–46. Other predictable texts are included in the more extensive discussion of such books in chapter 9.

Reading to children from an early age plays such an important role in establishing later success in reading that parents often ask their children's kindergarten or first-grade teacher to suggest appropriate reading materials. Numerous reference sources provide titles, critiques, and suggestions for parents about reading to their children at home. Here are several.

■ M. H. Arbuthnot, M. M. Clark, H. G. Long, & R. M. Hadlow, *Children's Books Too Good to Miss* (7th ed.) (New York: University Press Books, 1979)
■ B. E. Cullinan and D. R. Stoll, *Magazines for Children* (Newark, DE: International Reading Association, 1990)
■ A. Flowers (Ed.), *The Horn Book Guide to Children's and Young Adults' Books* (Boston: Horn Book, 1990)
■ L. L. Lamme, V. Cox, J. Matanzo, and M. Olson, *Raising Readers: A Guide to Sharing Literature with Young Children* (New York: Walker, 1980)
■ J. Trelease, *The New Read-Aloud Handbook* (New York: Penguin, 1989)

Additionally, the International Reading Association (800 Barksdale Road, Newark, DE 19711) publishes informational material for parents, including *Children's Choices* and *Teacher's Choices,* which are annual compilations of children's and teachers' favorite books.

Good reading habits are built when children are read to with appropriate intonation and evident pleasure and when their attention is drawn to the reading material. Reading a wide variety of materials to children helps to build their discourse knowledge, use of syntax, and use of context. As parents use specialized reading vocabulary (e.g., "Let's turn the page" or "Isn't that a funny title?"), children learn terms that will serve them well in school reading.

The activity described in the model lesson that follows is appropriate for use with young children. However, parents should be cautioned not to force their children but to wait until they exhibit an interest in such an activity. Teachers, too, might want to use this kind of interaction with their young students.

Fostering Discourse Knowledge and Predicting Outcomes

1. Choose an interesting story to read, and divide it into two parts. Have paper or a chalkboard available.

2. Read the first part of the story, and discuss it. Ask for suggestions about what might come next, that is, what might happen in the rest of the story. Record responses. Ask for reasons to support the predictions. Be ready to help clarify the information in the text that provides the bases for the predictions.

3. Read the next section of the story.

4. Go back to the predictions. Discuss them. Talk about why some predictions may not have appeared in the story.

**MODEL LESSON**

Beyond actual reading, many games and activities allow young children to classify ("Let's put all the blocks with the big letters together"), to match items ("Let's see if this puzzle piece will fit into this slot"), to discriminate ("Let's see if we can find what's wrong in this picture"), or to build concepts of *same* and *different* ("Let's see if we can find a word that looks the same"). A guessing game like I Spy can enhance children's manipulation of language as well as their visual and auditory discrimination skills ("I spy something with a color that rhymes with *bed*"). All of these activities can be done at home, and all aid in the successful completion of future reading tasks.

Perceptual Factors

Perception deals with the senses and is divided into visual (seeing), auditory (hearing), tactile (touching), olfactory (smelling), and tasting categories. In traditional readiness programs the most emphasis is placed on **visual** and **auditory perception** because the normal reader depends on vision to read print (Braille readers depend on tactile perception instead), and hearing is instrumental in matching sounds to symbols. In whole language programs perceptual and discrimination activities are deemphasized in favor of more integrated reading and writing activities.

visual perception: In reading, the ability to see the characteristics of such things as letters, words, or lines of print.

auditory perception: Awareness of the presence of sound.

Four terms are important to remember in a discussion of perceptual factors.

■ *Acuity*. The strength of the signal. Related questions include, How well does the child hear? and How good are the child's eyes?
■ *Discrimination*. The ability to notice similarities and differences.
■ *Recognition*. Awareness that something being experienced is the same as something previously experienced. Visually recognizing a word signals an awareness that the word has been seen before.
■ *Identification*. Deals specifically with identifying, or grasping, meaning.

These definitions are consistent with those found in the *Dictionary of Reading and Related Terms* (Harris & Hodges, 1981).

**Visual Perception.** Basically, visual perception is the ability to notice that there are lines and squiggles on a page. Normal reading is impossible in total darkness because visual perception is impossible, but light intensity can vary widely without affecting reading. Can you think of the variety of lighting conditions under which you have managed to read over the years? The more important aspect of visual perception is discrimination, which allows recognition that letters and words differ. Appropriate activities to build the concept of sameness and differentness include matching words, letters, or combinations of words and letters in different sizes, shapes, and colors. Normal classroom surroundings can also provide such practice. For example, even identifying a chair that is the same as the teacher's can promote an understanding of sameness and differentness. Because the goal in emergent literacy/readiness programs is to facilitate later fluent reading, it is best to provide activities that use reading-related items, such as words and letters. If the underlying concept of sameness and differentness is taught with objects in addition to words and letters, activities should move more and more into reading-related items once the target concept has been established.

---

**MODEL
LESSON**

### Print-Based Visual Discrimination Activity

To teach visual discrimination in a small-group setting using children's language and background, you might take target words from a language experience story like the one developed after a visit to an apple farm and included in an earlier model lesson in this chapter.

1. Print selected words on 3″-x-5″ cards.

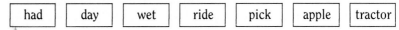

| had | day | wet | ride | pick | apple | tractor |

2. Reread the experience story (previously printed on chart paper) with the children.

3. Then give one 3″-x-5″ word card to each child, and tell the children to look carefully at the words on their cards.

4. Point to a word in the story. Ask whether any child has a card with the same word that you are pointing to. Ask students to hold up their cards whenever they match the word you are pointing to. Then read the target word aloud. If a child raises a card with a word that does not match the target word, ask the child to identify what is similar and different about the two words (e.g., beginning letter, ending letter, or shape), and then ask again whether the words are the same.

5. Ask the child with the matching card to hold it under the word in the story. Have the child verify the match and say the word, with your help if necessary.

6. Then ask whether there are any more words in the story that look exactly like the one on the card. If the word appears more than once in the story, repeat the preceding step.

7. Continue until every child has had a chance to match a word. Finally, write the children's names on their cards and attach them to the chart paper story under the matching word.

---

To truly build the concepts of sameness and differentness, you must move beyond children's answers to the reasoning behind them. This approach helps both the children with correct answers (by forcing an examination of their mental processes), and those with incorrect answers (by showing where their logic broke down).

Careful questioning can clarify similarities and differences, as demonstrated in this short exercise with *m, n,* and *mother.*

> Trace *m* and *n.* Are they the same?
> Do both have straight lines? Where?
> Do both have curved lines? Where? How many?
> Are the curved lines the same? How are they different?

Such questioning helps students differentiate between particular features of letters and allows them to examine the details that make up overall configurations.

One way to help children internalize the similarities and differences they perceive is to have them copy or trace print-based material—letters, letter combinations, and words. Such activities focus students' attention, are print-based, and force children to attend to all parts of an item. However, since the goal is to develop visual discrimination, not writing skills, the activity should include a discussion of the similarities and differences among the items being traced or copied.

---

**Word-Matching Games.** Divide a piece of poster paper into large rectangles. Print a word in each rectangle. Make a matching set of rectangular word cards. Then have students cover the words on the paper with the appropriate word cards. You can turn this activity into a bingo game by having students, perhaps in pairs, cover the words that you point to on your "bingo card." You might also make labels for objects around the classroom and attach an envelope below the label on each item. Then give children a set of word cards that include the labeled items and have them place their word cards in the envelopes under the appropriate labels. If children's names are on their word cards, you will have a quick check of who is having difficulty matching cards to labels.

**SAMPLE ACTIVITIES**

**Letter-matching Games.** Using plastic or paper letters, arrange groups of letters that are the same except for one that is obviously different.

$$C\ C\ X\ C\ C\qquad F\ S\ F\ F\ F$$

Ask children to replace the one that is different so that all the letters are the same. Gradually increase the similarity of the letters.

$$C\ C\ O\ C\ C\qquad F\ F\ E\ F\ F$$

**Discriminating Letter Features.** Help children perceive the differences among letters by discussing and pointing out the features of letters—curved lines, straight lines, and height. Present two letters with color on the parts that make them different.

**Discriminating Word Features.** Ask children to discriminate between similar words, drawing a circle around the part(s) that are different (e.g., *near/rear, rat/rut, window/widow*). Also, discuss similarities and differences between words of clearly different shapes and lengths. For example, write *mow* and *motorcycle* on the board or on chart paper. Discuss how they are the same and different (e.g., one is longer, two of the letters in *mow* are in *motorcycle,* one word has a letter with a "tail," and so on).

---

auditory discrimination: The ability to hear likenesses and differences among sounds.

**Auditory Perception.** Auditory perception is basically the ability to notice the presence of sound. More important for reading, however, is the ability to discriminate between the sounds of various letters, syllables, and words. Controversy continues to surround what should be taught in the **auditory discrimination** component of emergent literacy/readiness reading programs. For example, according to Gibson and Levin (1980),

> Auditory perceptual analysis of words is an important skill for learning to read, and training in it helps and does show transfer, at least in the initial stages of learning to read. . . . Clapping for each unit, marking (with dashes), deleting sounds, producing omitted sounds, and substituting sounds are successive stages of training, with apparently successful results in kindergarten and first grade. (p. 260)

Burns, Roe, and Ross (1988) agree, noting that environmental sounds (e.g., the scraping of a desk across the floor, the closing or opening of a window) can teach the concepts of sameness and differentness, as can activities that deal with hearing rhyming words; identifying similarities and differences in word endings, beginnings, and middles; and blending individual sounds into a whole word.

However, Durkin (1983, 1989) disagrees with the value of some of these activities "because they do not contribute to success with reading" (1983, p. 73). She objects especially to activities like distinguishing among musical and environmental sounds. Aulls (1982) is even more definite, citing a number of studies that support his conclusion.

> Emphasizing reading tasks such as sounding out words or emphasizing phonics may be a waste of time for many kindergartners. . . .[although] there does appear to be justification for teaching auditory segmentation to those children

who have naturally begun to sound out words and who have already begun to read. (p. 99)

One benefit of auditory discrimination activities is that they provide a common terminology for both teacher and student, as has been clearly demonstrated in teacher's guides for some time.

> The purpose of giving practice in listening for beginning sounds is not to teach children to "hear" sounds or to distinguish sounds from one another. Children who understand and reproduce their language do this automatically. However, many pupils in kindergarten or first grade have trouble with the concept that a word has a beginning because they think of a word as one undifferentiated sound. Since children will be taught in a later lesson that one sound to use in decoding is the sound "at the beginning of a word," they need to know exactly what this expression means. (*Getting Ready to Read,* p. 21)

As in visual discrimination, later transfer to print is better when auditory discrimination tasks center around reading-related materials.

---

**Picture-Sound Match.** Provide magazines and blunt scissors. Have students find and cut out pictures of objects that have names beginning with the same sounds that the students' own names begin with. Then have them say the names of the pictures they have cut out, and let the other students determine whether the beginning sounds are the same.

**Key-Word Banks.** Take cut-out pictures, and place them in a box. Also, provide containers that are labeled, each with a single word. Have students take the pictures out of the box and place each in a container that has a label beginning with the same sound as that particular picture.

**Tongue Twister Sounds.** Find or make up simple tongue twisters (e.g., "Six silly sheep saw a slippery snake"). Have students repeat the twisters after you, first slowly, then slightly faster. Put several twisters into a box, and have students choose ones for you to say. Then have them suggest other words that might make each tongue twister longer (e.g., "Saw a slippery snake *sliding*").

**Key-Word Spaceship.** On a large piece of posterboard draw a spaceship on Earth, aimed toward the Moon. Present a target word, and have children provide words or pictures with a sound similar to that of the target word. For every three correct words, move the ship closer to the Moon. Dividing students into teams makes this a motivational game.

**Key-Word Match.** Present key words that begin or end with a specified sound. Provide students with other words and ask them to decide whether the sounds are the same.

**SAMPLE ACTIVITIES**

**Auditory/Visual Integration.**  Beginning readers learn that oral language can be represented in symbolic form, that sounds and symbols are linked, and that the purpose of reading is to acquire meaning. Activities that build these concepts relate to **auditory/visual integration**. In such activities children are presented with both visual material and the sound(s) represented. They must see and hear both at the same time, perhaps naming an item aloud with the teacher while they look at it or following along as the teacher reads and telling what word might come next.

Thus, activities to promote auditory/visual integration differ somewhat from those noted earlier in that students need to hear and see the stimulus at the same time. For example, whereas a purely auditory activity might ask students to repeat the beginning sound in *baby*, a corresponding auditory/visual integration activity would present the visual image of the word while the teacher pronounced it. Students might be asked to repeat the beginning sound or point to the part of the word that has the /b/ sound *as the teacher says the word*. Such activities build the association between specific sounds and specific parts of a word and can be used with sounds in beginning, medial, and ending positions, as well as with units larger than single letters.

## Affective Factors

We have all experienced tasks that seemed to be completed in record time, whereas others dragged on and on. If we think back to tasks of both types, we will probably find that those we found pleasant flew by, whereas those we did not enjoy moved slowly. Your affective set—the way you felt about the tasks—influenced your motivation and performance. This principle applies equally to the reading task.

Many children come to school eager to learn to read; they view reading as potentially exciting (Downing et al., 1979). Much of that feeling comes from having had interesting and exciting stories read to them at home, which leads, in turn, to the dual realization that their pleasure originated in books and that learning to read would be a real mark of independence. Thus, we can conclude that reading to students must be a vital part of any emergent literacy/readiness program that intends to foster a desire to read.

Teachers should read to beginning readers often—sometimes individually, sometimes in small groups or in whole-class situations. In addition, it is important to allow time for discussion of what was read, pointing out pictures and interesting drawings and thereby fostering positive attitudes as well as story comprehension. Encouraging students to talk about personal experiences that relate to the reading selection is also highly motivational, especially with beginning readers, who are often **egocentric**.

Issues of motivation are closely tied to feelings. Is a specific activity liked or disliked? Our response is called **attitude**. A closely related term is **interest,**

*Margin glossary:*

**auditory/visual integration:** The linking or association of sound and sight.

**egocentric:** Describing the self-centeredness of children, who are unable to take another's point of view.

**attitude:** The way a person feels about something.

**interest:** Intentional focusing of attention on something as a result of motivation.

which indicates the importance we place on pursuing a given topic or activity. To illustrate how these two affective factors interact, it is possible to dislike something yet be interested in finding out more about it. For example, someone might have an intensely negative attitude toward snakes but have a strong interest in finding out more about them—perhaps where they are most likely to be found. Conversely, it is possible to feel very positive about something but have no interest in studying it further. Someone might find Gothic architecture visually pleasing but at the same time have no interest in studying its history or specific characteristics.

In emergent literacy/reading readiness programs, as in all instruction, teachers need to be aware of both the interests and the attitudes of their students. Often, students' attitudes toward learning to read may be positive, but their interest in performing specific instructional tasks may be quite low. To generate interest in required assignments, teachers must make each task motivational, thereby fostering a positive attitude toward the task being performed. And for young children, long-term goals do not provide strong motivation. Telling students that they need to complete a task so that they will eventually become good readers is not conceptually relevant for them. The immediate task must, in itself, be motivational.

A short attitude survey can help teachers choose instructional tasks and materials to motivate their students. Heathington (1976) has developed attitude scales for use in both primary and intermediate grades. The answer sheets for the Heathington primary scale ask students to show how they feel about various things by marking a set of faces that range from smiles to frowns. The scales provide a variety of pertinent questions—for example, "How do you feel. . .when you go to the library?"—but teachers sometimes supplement with their own questions. What do you like to do most? What are your favorite TV shows? Do you have (want) any pets? Your favorite story is. . .? The best day of the week is. . .? When you grow up, you'd like to be. . .? (Further discussion and more examples of attitude and interest assessment are included in chapter 11.)

Even though an attitude/interest inventory can be a valuable tool, teachers must recognize that young children have short attention spans and their interests can change fairly quickly. Consequently, it is important to talk to young students often to keep abreast of their current interests. Furthermore, with students who have somewhat poor attitudes toward reading, teachers should make a special effort to identify motivational materials. They should pick stories likely to be of high interest to such students and should spend extra time reading to them and discussing their interest in the stories.

## EVALUATING THE BEGINNING READER

Teachers are decision makers, who continually make instructional choices based on the information around them. For beginning readers that information is gathered in three ways: formal and informal tests, observations of student behavior and abilities, and information from parents and students. The characteristics of formal and informal tests are discussed in some depth in chapter 11, as are assessment procedures appropriate across grade levels. The discussion here looks at testing specifically within the context of emergent literacy/readiness classrooms and includes special considerations for teachers who are assessing literacy development in young children.

## Formal Tests

Four areas appear to predict success in reading: knowledge of letter names, general oral vocabulary knowledge, recognition of whole words, and visual discrimination ability (Barrett, 1965; Bond & Dykstra, 1967; Loban, 1963; Richek, 1977–1978; Silvaroli, 1965). Although some studies have failed to show that these four areas are predictive of later reading ability (Calfee, Chapman, & Venezky, 1972; Olson & Johnson, 1970; Samuels, 1972), they are generally included in formal emergent literacy/readiness tests. Such tests usually measure the following abilities:

- auditory perception
- auditory discrimination
- visual perception
- visual discrimination
- auditory/visual integration
- concepts of *same, different, over,* and *under*
- motor skills
- awareness of left-right sequence
- letter identification and recognition
- oral sentence or short passage comprehension
- word identification and recognition

Formal tests at this level range from paper-and-pencil tests given to groups of students, to tests administered individually. Figure 4–3 presents examples of different kinds of test activities.

Generally, emergent literacy/readiness tests require that students match pictures, words, letters, or shapes to either visual or auditory stimuli. Children might be asked to listen to or look at an item and then find that item in a series of choices, or they might complete an item to match a stimulus. Even with seemingly simple tasks, teachers must be careful that young students clearly understand test directions, for beginning readers easily confuse some test items and may be unable to grasp certain types of instructions (e.g., "From the pictures on the right, mark the one that is the same as the one on the left"). In addition, teachers should be sure that a test clearly relates to what is being measured. For example, it should not evaluate a student's ability to follow directions unless that is the specific objective of the test.

Another caution regarding the testing of young children relates to their attention spans. Teachers must be sure that testing tasks are within a child's attention span. A kindergarten or first-grade student is often a bundle of energy, unused to sitting still and focusing attention for extended periods. Most formal tests contain time lines, beyond which rest periods or other activities are suggested. Teachers should never ignore such instructions.

**FIGURE 4–3**
Sample pages from a traditional readiness test

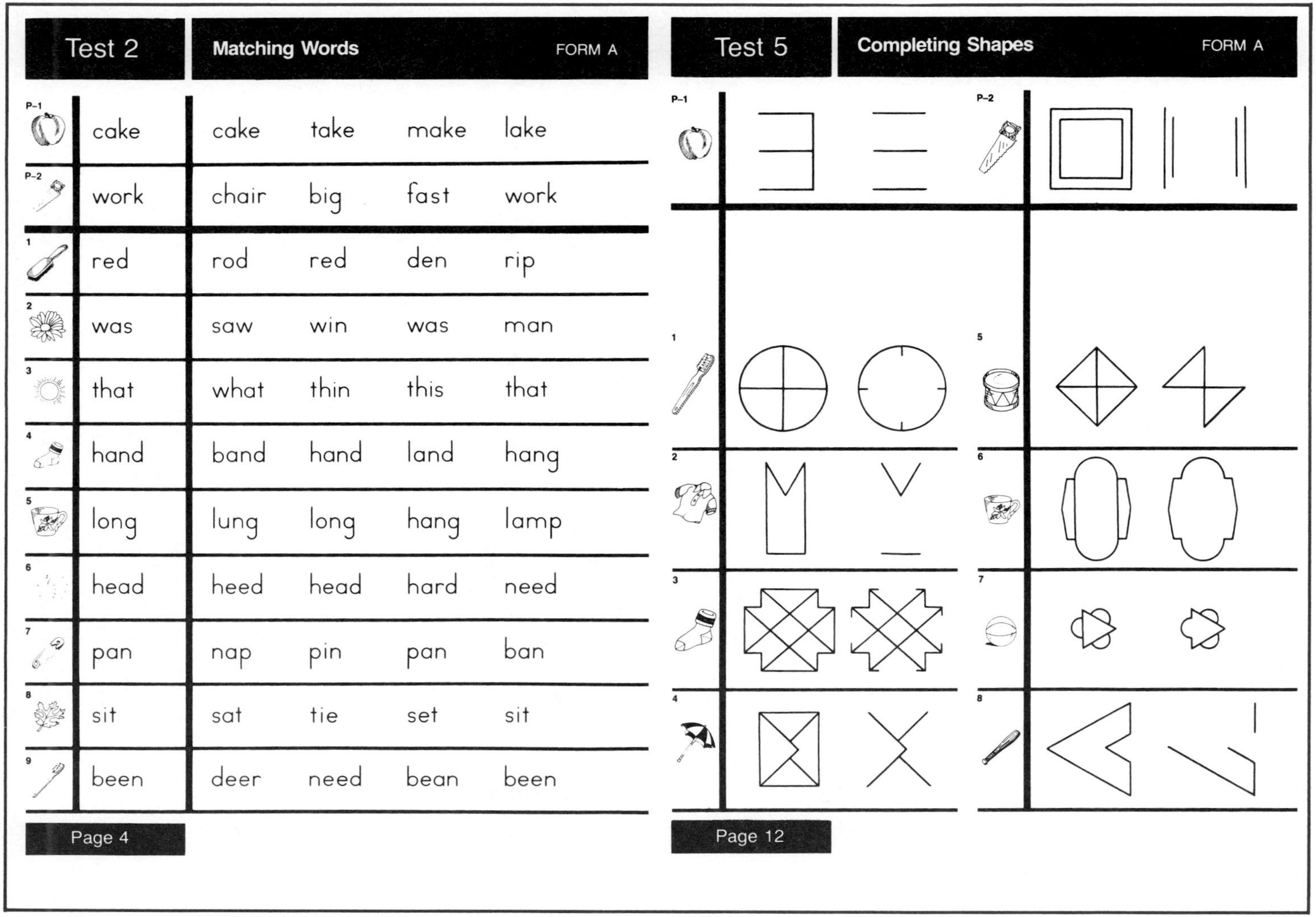

**Source:** From T. Clymer and T. Barrett, *Clymer-Barrett Readiness Test* (Form A) (Santa Barbara, CA: Institute for Reading Research, 1983), pp. 4,12. Reprinted by permission.

161

Before deciding on a formal test, teachers should answer the following questions:

- What exactly do I want to measure, and why?
- What exactly does this test measure, and how?
- Does the test measure what it says it is measuring?
- Is there a close relationship between what I want to measure and what the test measures?

To answer these questions, teachers must become familiar with a particular test, taking the time to examine it carefully and to read the test manual completely. A test manual contains valuable information on administration procedures and the intent of the test. With that information teachers should decide whether they wish to spend potential instructional time on testing. If they do select a test and administer it, they must then be sure to keep careful records.

Formal tests in this area were developed mainly from the 1920s to the 1950s. They have been less popular in recent times, partly because studies have shown that the predictive power of such tests is fairly low. In other words, a good score on a formal emergent literacy/readiness test does not always predict with a high degree of certainty how well a student will learn to read. For this reason many now advocate using more informal and observational measures at this level (Durkin, 1987; Goodman, Goodman, & Hood, 1989; Sulzby, 1990).

Teachers in whole language programs may have special difficulty assessing students with traditional, formal tests (see Stallman & Pearson, 1990, for a discussion of formal readiness tests and their incompatibility with shifting views of literacy development). Since whole language programs generally do not structure teaching within skill units, formal assessment instruments (which usually measure independent or isolated skills) may be inappropriate. Students taught within whole language programs may be better assessed through observational and informal measures and through an ongoing compilation of student work. Such compilations, or portfolios, can be useful in documenting students' progress. In addition, tests such as *Sand: The Concepts About Print Test* and *Stones: The Concepts About Print Test* (Clay, 1972, 1979) measure more global aspects of literacy—aspects that are learned through interaction with print rather than through direct teaching of isolated skills (Clay, 1980a, 1980b). Thus, such tools may be more valuable in whole language programs than traditional tests.

## Observational and Informal Data

A school environment provides a wealth of opportunity for the observant teacher to informally assess student abilities, interests, attitudes, and social skills. Assignments, oral responses to questions, student-initiated questions, attention span, speed of task completion, and patterns of correct/incorrect responses all provide data on which to base instructional decisions. The checklist presented in Figure 4–4 can help draw attention to specific behaviors and

FIGURE 4–4
Informal checklist of behaviors and abilities

Student's name: _____    Date: _____

Age:  Years  _____    Months  _____

Use the following scale in the decision column:   1 = yes, 2 = somewhat, 3 = no.
Comments should be added whenever possible, especially if the decision is "somewhat."

|  | Decision | Comments |
|---|---|---|
| 1. Knows alphabet (can say it with little or no help) | _____ | |
| 2. Can write alphabet | _____ | |
| 3. Can distinguish between upper- and lowercase letters | _____ | |
| 4. Recognizes written letters by name | _____ | |
| 5. Can rhyme words | _____ | |
| 6. Can count to 20 | _____ | |
| 7. Can state numbers from written form | _____ | |
| 8. Can write numbers | _____ | |
| 9. Recognizes and matches items that are the same | _____ | |
| 10. Knows relational words (before, after, back, front, under, above, until) | _____ | |
| 11. Can describe (tell) a picture-based story | _____ | |
| 12. Can appropriately order a simple picture-story (i.e., a cartoon strip) | _____ | |
| 13. Can read common words (stop, dog, run) | _____ | |
| 14. Can read own name when written by teacher | _____ | |
| 15. Can write own name | _____ | |
| 16. Knows own age | _____ | |
| 17. Can repeat sequence of events in a simple story | _____ | |
| 18. Speaks in sentences rather than in words or phrases | _____ | |
| 19. Knows simple reading terms (page, word, story) | _____ | |

General comments (e.g., attentiveness, concentration, ability to follow directions, shyness, pronunciation of words/sounds, general verbal fluency):

_____

_____

_____

Observing students during games and other activities is part of informal assessment and can provide valuable information.

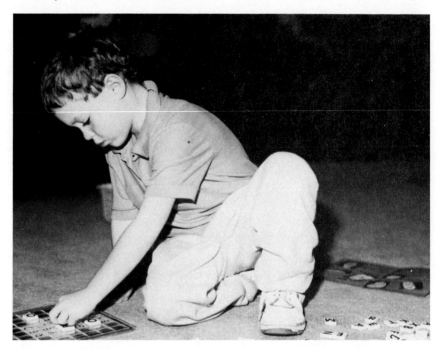

abilities. Some of the items can be deduced by observation; others require input from parents or students. Such a checklist gives an informal indication of which students might be grouped for various instructional activities. It can also suggest activities or items that might be motivational and can identify students who might need a little special consideration because of a personality trait. As with any informal evaluation instrument, teachers should modify checklist items to fit particular instructional situations.

Group activities and observation of playground behavior can also provide valuable information. Is the child an active participant in games? Does the child take leadership or passive roles? In what kinds of activities? Is the child shy or more of a bully? How do other students react to the child? Answers to such questions provide valuable insights. Informal observations should be recorded along with formal test data, for together these pieces of information enable teachers to plan instructional activities according to student needs.

## Parental Input

Informal discussions with parents can prove to be very productive, providing valuable information about students. Through parent conferences, parent-teacher association (PTA) meetings, and notes or questionnaires sent to parents, teachers can learn about students' siblings, motivating factors, attitudes toward school, and home reading environment. Parents can also be a tremendous help in more direct instructional aspects of an emergent literacy/readiness program. Usually, parents are aware of the value and importance of good reading abilities and are willing to help in whatever way they can. Having parents function as storytellers, give demonstrations, or help with class activities can provide valuable assistance and can extend regular classroom learning, especially when that parental involvement is used as a base for oral, written, or art experiences. In addition, young children are typically proud when their parents visit their classes and thus try hard to do their best. Parental involvement often helps foster positive student attitude and motivation.

Working parents who are unable to come to class during school hours might be able to arrange an interesting field trip to their business or place of work. Or perhaps they have a hobby that can be brought to school and left for the teacher and students to discuss whenever it is appropriate. These types of parental involvement can form the basis for highly motivating lessons that build experiential background, oral language, and vocabulary.

## USING A COMPREHENSION FRAMEWORK TO GUIDE EMERGENT LITERACY/READINESS INSTRUCTION

The way that you implement emergent literacy/readiness instruction will depend on your comprehension framework. If you believe that reading takes place through exact pronunciation of what is written, you may stress perceptual, discrimination activities in your program. Such an approach has as its goal the direct teaching of sound-symbol relationships, and you would provide many activities aimed at helping students understand that letters and sounds are related. If you believe, instead, that reading takes place as readers sample text to confirm or reject their predictions, then you may stress more meaning-based activities, such as language experience activities or functional writing tasks.

Although few would argue that emergent literacy/readiness programs should teach exclusively either sound-symbol relations or extraction of meaning from print, there is disagreement about the degree of emphasis of either component. Some advocate a focus on sound-symbol relationships and decoding processes (Chall, 1979, 1989; Liberman & Shankwiler, 1980). Others believe that decoding is not central to reading and imply that emergent literacy/readiness programs should focus on meaning (Goodman & Goodman, 1979; Smith, 1980; Carbo, 1988). Still others argue that reading is an interactive process between text and reader and that a reader's initial focus therefore depends on factors such as overall reading ability, the reader's purpose for reading, and the difficulty of the text. (Danks & Fears, 1979; Fredericksen, 1982). Those who hold this interactive view suggest that both perceptual- and meaning-based instructional activities should receive equal attention.

## COMMENTS FROM THE CLASSROOM ■

Emily Dodson

Although we teach second grade, Mr. Burns, Ms. Sanchez, and I have been asked to comment on how we would teach kindergarten students. This might be somewhat easier for me, since I taught kindergarten for several years.

What I remember most is the mix of students I had in my kindergarten classes: Hispanic, black, white, and a Korean student whose parents spoke little English at home. Although the majority of my kindergarten students had a keen interest in learning to read, several had relatively poor attitudes toward school in general. Several others were already reading simple storybooks independently when they started kindergarten.

When I taught kindergarten, my school offered both half-day and whole-day sessions. I chose to teach the whole-day class and have recreated here the general structure of my classroom time. From what other teachers tell me, my structure was fairly common.

| | |
|---|---|
| 8:30–9:00 | Getting started. I took attendance and discussed with students what might have happened since the last class meeting. I also introduced any special activities for the day. |
| 9:00–9:30 | Whole group time. I announced any major event or news to the group—for example, a student's birthday, someone's new pet, any new books or magazines, and so on. |
| 9:30–11:00 | Group activity time. I worked with one group while three other groups had their choice of work centers (music, art, listening, dramatic play, reading, writing, and so on). The children moved through the cen- |
| | ters at about 20 minute intervals. We also had snacks at about 10:30. |
| 11:00–11:20 | Story time. |
| 11:20–12:00 | Outdoor play. At 11:50 a small group of students (a different group each day) helped to set the table for lunch. |
| 12:00–12:30 | Lunch. |
| 12:30–12:45 | Clean up. The children also brushed their teeth at this time. |
| 12:45–1:30 | Table games and activities (e.g., LEGOS, puzzles, etc.). |
| 1:30–2:30 | Nap/rest time. |
| 2:30–3:00 | Snack time. |
| 3:00 | Dismissal. |

Because of my comprehension framework, my classroom included a wide range and variety of materials, and I made sure I was familiar with a wide range of methods, too. I did everything from teaching specific things like letter and word discrimination to targeting more holistic literacy skills. I tried to choose the activities that were appropriate for my students' needs. I remember I attended several workshops then and read lots of articles about what were fairly new concepts at that time—emergent literacy and whole language. And I worked those points of view into my teaching also.

As I said, my instructional materials came from a variety of sources. At times I used stories and activities from a published program, but I usually modified the suggestions in the teacher's guide. I also used kits that allowed students to match letters and words, and I went through *lots* of chart paper with language experience stories. Those stories also gave me lots of words to use in creating my own word-matching games for the students. Overall, I spent relatively equal time working on specific skills like discriminating letter and word sounds and helping students develop their emerging literacy skills.

Thus, I didn't use any one program but adapted activities from a range of materials and techniques to meet the needs of my students. It wasn't unusual to see children in different parts of the room pursuing different activities. Students with poor motor skills might have been tracing felt letters with their fingers, while those with better-developed fine motor skills might have been tracing the letters on paper, and others might have been illustrating language experience stories that I'd reproduced on paper. Of course, at some time all my students got to work on illustrating and writing, just as they all got to work on letter knowledge. I tried very hard to change my instructional tasks as students' abilities grew.

I used our story time to ask high-level questions aimed not only at story comprehension but also at story structure, and we spent time playing with sentences and language. Even though most of my students weren't readers, their listening and conversational skills were well developed, so I asked questions that applied to oral language but would reappear later in reading activities. We talked about opinions, cause and effect, sequence, main ideas, and the relationship of stories to personal experiences.

I do remember using a formal test, although I paid more attention to informal measures and observation. I kept a journal on each student and was always careful to record my informal observations regularly. That really helped clarify formal test information, especially when I had to discuss certain students with the principal or the students' parents.

## Mr. Burns

As I said before, I spend most of my instructional time with a published reading program, and I'd do the same thing in kindergarten—hopefully with a program that provided a firm foundation in decoding. Although I'd never ne-

glect reading to my students or providing them with writing activities and language experience stories, I know I'd emphasize letter, sound, and word discrimination activities more than my colleagues. And since I think phonics is so important later, I'd probably give extra attention to auditory discrimination activities.

I'd probably spend some of the first week of school testing, like I do now, using the test included in the published program to determine which students needed practice on specific skills. Then I'd group my students according to their needs, and I'd teach each of the important readiness skills, probably deductively. I'd test at the end of each unit, however the program suggests.

I'd also supplement the published program with a variety of workbooks so that my students could practice their skills. I'd choose workbooks that were colorful and motivational, and I'd try hard to match specific workbook activities to the specific skills taught in our core program. I'd select well-designed materials and then would follow them fairly closely. Also, after reading to my students, I'd discuss with them what was stated in the story and help them figure out what the author was trying to say. I think it's important for students to understand early that reading involves getting the meaning out of what's written.

My instructional day would probably follow whatever is a normal kindergarten routine, and I'd be sure to get in all the different activities. Of course, I'd emphasize activities that would lead to decoding, and I'd always keep a published program as my base. But that's just my emphasis—I'd still be reading to my students and giving them opportunities to write.

## Ms. Sanchez

If I had to teach kindergarten, I doubt that I'd use a published program. Instead, I'd base the whole environment on the children's oral language, on literacy activities related to their writing and artwork, and on a lot of reading aloud to them. I'd spend very little time in isolated decoding activities; instead, I'd emphasize language experience activities, and I'd do a lot of modeling. Specifically, I'd use the think-aloud method framework to show how background knowledge can help a reader guess the meanings of words and predict endings.

I'd be sure that even my kindergarten students participated in real uses of literacy. I'd start with a morning message, and then I'd let them help with administrative functions, such as attendance checks or progress charts. I think I'd put their progress charts on the classroom walls, and let students update them under my supervision. I'd also have a wide variety of posters, pictures, and item labels in my classroom, and I'd have lots of students' work displayed—simple drawings and colorings, as well as stories the students had dictated.

I think most of my literacy activities would be based on my students' oral language and personal experiences. I might start the school day with a story and then ask students to tell each other or the whole class a story of their own. Sometimes I might use a tape recorder to capture a student's story, or I might write someone's story on the chalkboard or on a piece of chart paper as the student tells it. I'd use their stories as the basis of discussion and as a stimulus for illustrating and drawing activities. In fact, my students' oral language and background experiences would underlie almost all other activities. And since I believe that all language skills are related, I'd link oral and written language whenever possible.

For assessment I'd rely on compilations of students' work, with journal comments about their progress. I'd avoid formal tests because they generally fragment overall processes into isolated skills, and they don't agree with my holistic explanation of how reading ability develops. However, I'd have to be careful to document my students' progress so that I could explain it to parents who have difficulty understanding that invented spellings and other variations from traditional writing are a natural part of learning.

## MAJOR POINTS

- Traditional readiness programs for prereaders stress auditory and visual perception, emphasize the relationship of sounds and symbols, and build an understanding of reading-related concepts. Deductive methods are most common.  推論. 演繹

- Kindergarten programs based on emergent literacy or whole language viewpoints teach traditional readiness aspects in a more integrated manner, using inductive methods and functional reading and writing experiences.

- Readiness is not a fixed point in time, but refers equally well to beginning or proficient readers who are not able to read selections because of experiential background or other factors.

- A number of factors interact to affect literacy development: cognitive development, oral language, home environment, perceptual factors, and affective factors.

- Emergent literacy/readiness activities for prereaders are most effective when they deal specifically with print-related items (e.g., letters, letter groups, words, sentences, stories, and concepts such as *page*).

■ Beginning readers should be read to often; given opportunities to trace and copy letters, letter groups, and words; allowed to use their oral language skills; and provided with many chances to experiment with print.

■ Informal measures and observational data, in addition to more formal emergent literacy/readiness tests, form an integral part of the assessment of prereaders.

MAKING INSTRUCTIONAL DECISIONS

1. Design a traditional readiness lesson in each of the following areas: auditory discrimination, visual discrimination, following directions, and auditory/visual integration. Then explain how you would teach each of these aspects from a whole language perspective.

2. If possible, visit two kindergarten classrooms to observe what is taking place. Try to visit one traditional class and one whole language class. Discuss with each teacher how activities are planned, which seem to be most appropriate for the students, and why.

3. Make a list of what you think a child entering first grade might already know that would help in learning to read. Tell how the things you have identified relate to reading ability. How would you capitalize on what the child already knows in your emergent literacy/readiness program?

4. Differentiate between attitude and interest. How do you think the terms are related? How do they differ? How might aspects of both affect your emergent literacy/readiness instruction?

5. Examine a formal and an informal readiness test (these are probably available in your curriculum library). What similarities and differences do you see, both in terms of structure and focus of evaluation? How would you use the information from each in an emergent literacy/readiness program?

FURTHER READING

Ellis, D. W., & Preston, F. W. (1984). Enhancing beginning reading using wordless picture books in a cross-age tutoring program. *The Reading Teacher, 37,* 692–698.

    Discusses the value of wordless picture books and describes how they were used in a tutoring program with fifth and first graders. Provides a list of 162 wordless picture books published in the United States.

Lass, B. (1982). Portrait of my son as an early reader. *The Reading Teacher, 36,* 20–28.

    Provides a brief overview of research on characteristics of early readers and provides a timeline of emerging reading behaviors.

McCormick, S. & Collins, B. M. (1981). A potpourri of game-making ideas for the reading teacher. *The Reading Teacher, 34,* 692–696.

    Points out general guidelines for the use of games (e.g., they should provide academic learning, not busywork, and they should teach, not test) and provides a list of supplies generally needed to construct instructional materials, as well as where to get them and what to do with them.

McGee, L. M., & Richgels, D. J. (1989). "K is Kristen's": Learning the alphabet from a child's perspective. *The Reading Teacher, 43,* 216–225.

> Discusses case studies of children's and parent's dialogues and games that lead to development of children's alphabet knowledge. Provides guidelines for classroom adaptations.

Sampson, M. R. (Ed.). (1986). *The pursuit of literacy: Early reading and writing.* Dubuque, IA: Kendall-Hunt.

> A short volume containing representative articles from a variety of experts familiar with emergent literacy and whole language. A good introduction for teachers wanting information in this area. Very readable articles.

Strickland, D. (1988). Some tips for using big books. *The Reading Teacher, 41,* 966–968.

> A chart presenting an overview of what the teacher does, what the child does, and what the objectives are for big book activities.

Strickland, D. S., & Morrow, L. M. (1989). *Emerging literacy: Young children learn to read and write.* Newark, DE: International Reading Association.

> A series of short articles on emergent literacy, from theory to classroom implementation.

Tovey, R. T., & Kerber, J. E. (Eds.). (1986). *Roles in literacy learning: A new perspective.* Newark, DE: International Reading Association.

> A selection of short articles discussing the roles and responsibilities of parents, teachers, children, administrators, and researchers in literacy acquisition.

Vukelich, C. (1984). Parents' role in the reading process: A review of practical suggestions and ways to communicate with parents. *The Reading Teacher, 37,* 472–477.

> Points out the most frequent suggestions made to parents and provides suggestions, methods, and activities to involve parents.

## REFERENCES

Aaron, I. E., Chall, J. S., Durkin, D., Goodman, K., & Strickland, D. S. (1990). The past, present, and future of literacy education: Comments from a panel of distinguished educators, Part I. *The Reading Teacher, 43,* 302–311.

Allen, K. K. (1982). The development of young children's understanding of the word. *Journal of Educational Research, 76,* 89–92.

Allen, R. V., & Allen, C. (1976). *Language experience activities.* Boston: Houghton Mifflin.

Almy, M., Chittenden, E., & Miller, P. (1966). *Young children's thinking: Studies of some aspects of Piaget's theory.* New York: Teachers College Press.

Anderson, R. C., & Freebody, P. (1985). Vocabulary knowledge. In H. Singer & R. B. Ruddell (Eds.), *Theoretical models and processes of reading* (3rd ed., pp. 343–371). Newark, DE: International Reading Association.

Anderson, R. C., Hiebert, E. H., Scott, J. A., & Wilkinson, I. A. G. (1985). *Becoming a nation of readers: The report of the commission on reading.* Washington, DC: National Institute of Education.

Ashton-Warner, S. (1963). *Teacher.* New York: Simon & Schuster.

Ashton-Warner, S. (1972). *Spearpoint.* New York: Knopf.

Aukerman, R. C. (1984). *Approaches to beginning reading instruction* (2nd ed.). New York: John Wiley & Sons.

Aulls, M. W. (1982). *Developing readers in today's elementary schools.* Boston: Allyn & Bacon.

Barrett, T. C. (1965). Visual discrimination tasks as predictors of first grade reading achievement. *The Reading Teacher, 18,* 276–282.

Bond, G. L., & Dykstra, R. (1967). The cooperative research program in first grade reading instruction. *Reading Research Quarterly, 2,* 5–142.

Bransford, J. D. (1988, August). Personal communication.

Burns, P. C., Roe, B. D., & Ross, E. P. (1988). *Teaching reading in today's elementary schools* (4th ed.). Boston: Houghton Mifflin.

Bybee, R. W., & Sund, R. B. (1982). *Piaget for educators*. Columbus, OH: Merrill.

Calfee, R., Chapman, R., & Venezky, R. (1972). How a child needs to think to learn to read. In L. Gregg (Ed.), *Cognition in learning and memory* (pp. 139–182). New York: John Wiley & Sons.

Carbo, M. (1988). Debunking the great phonics myth. *Phi Delta Kappan, 70,* 226–237.

Catterson, J. (1989). Reflections: An interview with Jane Catterson. *Reading-Canada-Lecture, 7,* 40–49.

Caulkins, L. (1983). *Lesson from a child*. Exeter, NH: Heinemann.

Chall, J. S. (1979). The great debate: Ten years later, with a modest proposal for reading stages. In L. B. Resnick & P. A. Weaver (Eds.), *Theory and practice of early reading* (Vol. 1, pp. 29–55). Hillsdale, NJ: Lawrence Erlbaum.

Chall, J. S. (1989). Learning to read: The great debate 20 years later—A response to "Debunking the great phonics myth." *Phi Delta Kappan, 70,* 521–538.

Clay, M. M. (1972). *Sand: The Concepts About Print Test*. Exeter, NH: Heinemann Educational Books.

Clay, M. M. (1979). *Stones: The Concepts About Print Test*. Exeter, NH: Heinemann Educational Books.

Clay, M. M. (1980a). *The early detection of reading difficulties: A diagnostic survey* (2nd ed.). New York: Heinemann Educational Books.

Clay, M. M. (1980b). *Reading: The patterning of complex behavior* (2nd Ed.). New York: Heinemann Educational Books.

Dale, E. (1965). Vocabulary measurement: Techniques and major findings. *Elementary English, 42,* 895–901, 948.

Danks, J., & Fears, R. (1979). In L. B. Resnick & P. A. Weaver (Eds.), *Theory and practice of early reading* (Vol. 3). Hillsdale, NJ: Erlbaum.

Davey, B. (1983). Think-aloud—Modeling the cognitive processes of reading comprehension. *Journal of Reading, 27,* 44–47.

Davidson, S., Stickney, C. P., & Weil, R. (1980). *Intermediate accounting concepts: Methods and uses*. Hinsdale, IL: Dryden Press.

DeFord, D. E. (1986). Classroom contexts for literacy learning. In T. E. Raphael & R. E. Reynolds (Eds.), *The contexts of school-based learning* (pp. 163–190). New York: Random House.

Downing, J., Dwyer, C. A., Feitelson, D., Jansen, M., Kemppainen, R., Matihaldi, H., Reggi, D. R., Sakamoto, T., Taylor, H., Thakary, D. V., & Thomson, D. (1979). A cross-national survey of cultural expectations and sex-role standards in reading. *Journal of Research in Reading, 2,* 8–23.

Durkin, D. (1966). *Children who read early: Two longitudinal studies*. New York: Columbia University, Teachers College Press.

Durkin, D. (1974–1975). A six-year study of children who learned to read in school at the age of four. *Reading Research Quarterly, 10,* 9–61.

Durkin, D. (1983). *Teaching them to read* (4th ed.). Boston: Allyn & Bacon.

Durkin, D. (1987). *Teaching young children to read* (4th ed.). Boston: Allyn & Bacon.

Durkin, D. (1989). *Teaching them to read* (5th ed.). Boston: Allyn & Bacon.

Fitzgerald, J. (1983). Helping readers gain self-control. *The Reading Teacher, 37,* 249–253.

Fredericksen, J. R. (1982). A componential theory of reading skills and their interaction (Tech. Rep. No. 242). Champaign, IL: University of Illinois, Center for the Study of Reading.

Galda, L. (1988) Readers, texts, and contexts: A response-based view of literature in the classroom. *New Advocate, 1,* 92–102.

*Getting Ready to Read* (teacher's ed.). (1979). Boston: Houghton Mifflin.

Gibson, E. J., & Levin, H. (1980). *The psychology of reading* (3rd ed.). Cambridge, MA: MIT Press.

Goodman, J. (in press). *A naturalistic study of the relationship between literacy development and sociodramatic play in five-year-old children*. Unpublished doctoral dissertation, Peabody College of Vanderbilt University, Nashville, TN.

Goodman, K. S., & Goodman, Y. M. (1979). Learning to read is natural. In L. B. Resnick & P. A. Weaver (Eds.), *Theory and practice of early reading* (Vol. 1, pp. 137–154). Hillsdale, NJ: Erlbaum.

Goodman, K. S., Goodman, Y. M., & Hood, W. J. (Eds.). (1989). *The whole language evaluation book*. Portsmouth, NH: Heinemann.

Graves, D. H. (1983). *Writing: Teachers and children at work*. Exeter, NH: Heinemann.

Hammill, D. D., & McNutt, G. (1981). *The correlates of reading: The consensus of thirty years of correlational research*. Austin, TX: Pro-Ed Books.

Hare, V. C. (1984). What's in a word? A review of young children's difficulty with the construct *word*. *The Reading Teacher, 37*, 360–364.

Harris, A. J., & Sipay, E. R. (1990). *How to increase reading ability* (9th Ed.). White Plains, NY: Longman.

Harris, T. L., & Hodges, R. E. (Eds.). (1981). *A dictionary of reading and related terms*. Newark, DE: International Reading Association.

Harste, J. C., Woodward, V. A., & Burke, C. L. (1984). *Language stories and literacy lessons*. Portsmouth, NH: Heinemann.

Heathington, B. S. (1976). Scales for measuring attitudes. In J. E. Alexander & R. C. Filler (Eds.), *Attitudes and reading* (pp. 27–32). Newark, DE: International Reading Association.

Hiebert, E. H. (1983). Knowing about reading before reading: Preschool children's concepts of reading. *Reading Psychology, 4*, 253–260.

Holdaway, D. (1979). *The foundations of literacy*. Exeter, NH: Heinemann.

Inhelder, B., & Piaget, J. (1964). *The early growth of logic in the child*. New York: Norton.

Kawakami-Arakaki, A. J., Oshiro, M. E., & Farran, D. C. (1989). Research into practice: Integrating reading and writing in a kindergarten curriculum. In J. M. Mason (Ed.), *Reading and writing connections* (pp. 199–218). Needham Heights, MA: Allyn & Bacon.

Liberman, I. Y., & Shankwiler, D. (1980). Speech, the alphabet, and teaching to read. In L. B. Resnick & P. A. Weaver (Eds.), *Theory and practice of early reading* (Vol. 2). Hillsdale, NJ: Erlbaum.

Loban, W. D. (1963). *The language of elementary school children*. Urbana, IL: National Council of Teachers of English.

Luria, A. R. (1976). *Cognitive development: Its cultural and social foundations*. Cambridge, MA: Harvard University Press.

Martin, J. B., Jr. (1967). *Ten Little Caterpillars*. New York: Holt Rinehart & Winston.

Mason, J. M. (1980). When do children learn to read: An exploration of four-year-old children's letter and word reading competencies. *Reading Research Quarterly, 15*, 203–223.

Mason, J. M. (Ed.). (1989). *Reading and writing connections*. Needham Heights, MA: Allyn & Bacon.

McCallum, R. D. (1988). Don't throw out the basal with the bathwater. *The Reading Teacher, 42*, 204–209.

McGee, L. M., & Richgels, D. J. (1990). *Literacy's beginnings: Supporting young readers and writers*. Boston: Allyn & Bacon.

Morphett, M. V., & Washburn, C. (1931). When should children begin to read? *Elementary School Journal, 31*, 496–503.

Nessel, D., & Jones, M. (1981). *The language experience approach to reading*. New York: Teachers College Press.

Ollila, L. O. (Ed.). (1981). *Beginning reading instruction in different countries*. Newark, DE: International Reading Association.

Olson, A. V., & Johnson, C. (1970). Structure and predictive validity of the Frostig Development Test of Visual Perception in grades one and three. *Journal of Special Education, 4*, 49–52.

Piaget, J. (1963). *The origins of intelligence in children*. New York: Norton (Original edition by International Universities Press, 1952).

Richek, M. A. (1977–1978). Readiness skills that predict initial word learning using two different methods of instruction. *Reading Research Quarterly, 13*, 209–221.

Robeck, M. C., & Wallace, R. R. (1990). *The psychology of reading: An interdisciplinary approach* (2nd ed.). Hillsdale, NJ: Erlbaum.

Rosenblatt, L. M. (1988). *Writing and reading: The transactional theory*. (Tech. Rep. No. 416). Urbana, IL: Center for the Study of Reading.

Rowe, D. W. (1989). Author/audience interaction in the preschool: The role of social interaction in literacy learning. *Journal of Reading Behavior, 21,* 311–350.

Rowe, D. W. (in press). *Preschoolers as authors: Literacy learning in the social world of the classroom.* Norwood, NJ: Ablex.

Rowe, D. W., & Harste, J. C. (1990). Learning how to write. In R. Tierney, S. Greene, & N. Spivey (Eds.), *Writing, learning and knowing: Social-cognitive perspectives.* Unpublished manuscript.

Samuels, S. J. (1972). The effect of letter-name knowledge on learning to read. *American Educational Research Journal, 9,* 65–74.

Shanahan, T. (Ed.). (1990). *Reading and writing together: New perspectives for the classroom.* Norwood, MA: Christopher-Gordon.

Silvaroli, N. J. (1965). Factors in predicting children's success in first grade reading. In J. A. Figure (Ed.), *Reading inquiry international* (Vol. 10, pp. 296–298). Newark, DE: International Reading Association.

Stahl, S. A., & Miller, P. D. (1989). Whole language and language experience approaches for beginning reading: A quantitative research synthesis. *Review of Educational Research, 59,* 87–116.

Stallman, A. C., & Pearson, P. D. (1990). Formal measures of early literacy. In L. M. Morrow & J. K. Smith (Eds.), *Assessment for instruction in early literacy* (pp. 7–44). Englewood Cliffs, NJ: Prentice Hall.

Stauffer, R. (1980). *The language experience approach to the teaching of reading* (2nd Ed.). New York: Harper & Row.

Sulzby, E. (1990). Assessment of emergent writing and children's language while writing. In L. M. Morrow & J. K. Smith (Eds.), *Assessment for instruction in early literacy* (pp. 83–109). Englewood Cliffs, NJ: Prentice Hall.

Teale, W. H., & Sulzby, E. (Eds.). (1986). *Emergent literacy: Writing and reading.* Norwood, NJ: Ablex.

Teale, W. H., & Sulzby, E. (1989). Emergent literacy: New perspectives. In D. S. Strickland & L. M. Morrow (Eds.), *Emerging literacy: Young children learn to read and write* (pp. 1–15). Newark, DE: International Reading Association.

Vygotsky, L. S. (1978). *Mind in society.* Cambridge, MA: Harvard University Press.

Vygotsky, L. S. (1986). *Thought and language.* (A. Kozulin, Ed. & Trans.). Cambridge, MA: MIT Press (Originally published 1962).

Waller, G. T. (1977). *Think first, read later! Piagetian prerequisites for reading.* Newark, DE: International Reading Association.

Wells, G. (1986). *The meaning makers: Children learning language and using language to learn.* Portsmouth, NH: Heinemann.

Willinsky, J. (1988). Recalling the moral force of literature in education. *Journal of Educational Thought, 22,* 118–132.

# Decoding and Comprehension

- What is Decoding Knowledge?
- Developing Context Knowledge
- Developing Phonic Knowledge
- Developing Sight Word Knowledge
- Using a Comprehension Framework to Guide Instructional Decisions about Decoding

*Miss Binney. . .was standing in front of the class holding up a brown paper sack with a big T printed on it. . . "Now who can guess what I have in this bag with the letter T printed on it? Remember it is something that begins with T. Who can tell me how T sounds?"*

*"T-t-t-t-t," ticked the kindergarten.*

*"Good," said Miss Binney. "Davey, what do you think is in the bag?" Miss Binney was inclined to bear down on the first letters of words now that the class was working on the sounds letters make.*

*"Taterpillars?" said Davey hopefully.*

K nowing how to determine the oral equivalents of words is often helpful during reading. We refer to this component of the reading comprehension process as decoding knowledge. As the opening quotation indicates, knowing the relationship between letters and sounds is especially important in the younger grades. But decoding knowledge is not limited to letter-sound relationships. This chapter discusses three different types of decoding knowledge and presents instructional activities to develop each type.

Chapter 5 includes information that will help you answer questions like these:

1. What does decoding knowledge include, and when does it contribute to comprehension?
2. What instruction is appropriate to develop context knowledge?
3. What instruction is appropriate to develop phonic knowledge?
4. What instruction is appropriate to develop sight word knowledge?
5. How can a comprehension framework be used to guide instructional decisions about decoding?

**KEY CONCEPTS**

analytic approach
cloze tasks
consonant blend
consonant clusters
consonant digraphs
context knowledge
decoding knowledge
deductive method framework
individualized word banks

inductive method framework
long vowel sound
short vowel sound
sight word envelopes
sight word knowledge
silent letter combinations
synthetic approach
traditional whole-word method
vowel digraphs

## WHAT IS DECODING KNOWLEDGE?

decoding knowledge: The knowledge that a reader uses to determine the oral equivalent of a word; includes context knowledge, sight word knowledge, and phonic knowledge.

**Decoding knowledge** is the knowledge a reader uses to determine the oral equivalent (i.e., pronunciation) of a written word. We use decoding knowledge when we read aloud. We also use it at various other times during reading, such as when we encounter an unfamiliar word and attempt to determine its pronunciation. Decoding knowledge contributes to the comprehension process when a printed word is within the listening vocabulary of the reader. Decoding knowledge does not contribute to comprehension when the targeted word and its meaning are both unfamiliar to the reader.

Decoding knowledge is especially important to beginning readers (Chall, 1983). Because they know the meanings of most words they encounter in print, determining the oral equivalent of a printed word gives them a reasonable opportunity to determine its meaning. Consequently, instruction in decoding knowledge receives the greatest attention in the primary grades (kindergarten through third).

Readers use three different types of decoding knowledge to determine the oral equivalent of a written word: context knowledge, phonic knowledge, and sight word knowledge. Decoding instruction helps children develop each of these types of knowledge.

## DEVELOPING CONTEXT KNOWLEDGE

**Context knowledge** refers to a reader's ability to use information from the text in conjunction with background knowledge to assist the reading process. Readers often use context knowledge to determine the oral equivalent and meaning of a word.

context knowledge: One element of decoding knowledge; the reader's ability to use information in the text along with background knowledge to assist the reading process.

For example, notice how you decode the italicized words in the following sentence:

Alexandra will *read* the book after you have *read* it.

Context knowledge, which allows readers to use what they know together with information in the text, is often used during decoding.

Even though the same word appears twice, you decoded it differently. You first decoded the word as /reed/ and later as /red/. In each case you relied on the information from the text in conjunction with your background knowledge to determine the appropriate oral equivalent and meaning. In other words, you used context knowledge. For the first use of the word the information in the text suggests a future tense verb. Your background knowledge told you that the word *read* is pronounced /reed/ in the future tense. For the second use of the word the text suggests a past tense verb. Your background knowledge told you that the word *read* is pronounced /red/ in the past tense. Readers frequently use context knowledge like this to determine the oral equivalent and meaning of words.

Sometimes readers use context knowledge so proficiently that they do not even perceive certain words. Consider this sentence with a missing word.

Sarah, an only child, had always wanted a sister or a _____.

In this example you could again rely on the information from the text along with your own background knowledge to determine that the missing word is *brother*. The text indicates that the word is something that an only child wants. It is also a noun and must fit with *sister*. Your own background knowledge tells you that the word *brother* fits all these conditions and is therefore a likely candidate. Thus, readers are able to use context knowledge to predict upcoming words when the readers possess sufficient background knowledge and when text information is sufficiently rich.

## Instructional Methods

Even before children learn how to read, they have developed context knowledge from their oral language experiences. Children have learned how to use the information in spoken messages along with background knowledge to help them recognize speech sounds. Thus, helping children use context knowledge during reading builds on a skill they already have. Several instructional practices can help students see the utility of using context knowledge during reading: cloze tasks, inductive instruction, and deductive instruction.

cloze tasks: Used to develop context knowledge; challenge the reader to determine a missing word by using text information and background knowledge.

**Cloze Tasks. Cloze tasks** present a reader with writing that contains at least one missing word. The reader's task is to use the information in the text along with background knowledge to determine the word that is missing. The following sentence gives just one example.

My mother comes home late at _____.

A cloze task is probably the most common technique used to develop context knowledge. It forces students to rely on contextual knowledge, as they must when they are unable to recognize a word from its spelling.

To prepare a lesson with cloze tasks, teachers can select commercial materials or make their own. For instructional purposes any one of several

*[handwritten annotations in top margin: "for K. 1 grade, don't read silently. let them"]*

*[handwritten annotations in right margin: "I will read. I read."]*

elements associated with the task can be varied: the length of the passage, the location of the target word, the information available at the target word location, or the nature of the available contextual information.

By varying the length of the cloze passage, teachers can use single sentences to provide instruction in syntactic and vocabulary context and longer selections to provide instruction in discourse context. Longer passages are easier to complete than single sentences because more information is provided in the text, as illustrated in the following examples from *Curious George* (Rey, 1952).

He knew how to ride a _____, but he had never had one of his own. (p. 6)

He took George out to the yard, where a big box was standing. George was very curious. Out of the box came a bicycle. George was delighted; that's what he had always wanted. He knew how to ride a _____, but he had never had one of his own. (p. 6)

A second element that can be varied is the target word location. Putting the target word at the end provides practice in using preceding context to recognize a word; putting it near the beginning helps teach students how to use contextual information that follows an unknown word. Notice the different reading strategies that are required in these two examples:

A _____ is a person who delivers mail.

A person who delivers mail is a _____.

A third element that can be varied is the information available at target word locations. Traditionally, only a blank space is provided. However, the task can be made easier by providing the first letter or two of the target word. It can be made easier still by placing two or more words underneath the blank and having students choose the correct word. Notice that the task becomes progressively easier in each of the following examples:

We went to the _____.
We went to the st_____.
We went to the _____.
(run, store)

When only a blank space is provided, students receive practice using context knowledge alone to recognize words. If the first letter or two are provided, students can practice using context knowledge while also attending to letter-sound information. When several words are available, students must pick the best letter-sound combination to fit the context.

A fourth element that can be varied is the nature of available contextual information. Certain sentence patterns provide useful clues to readers attempting to identify a word: patterns of definition, comparison, contrast, and example. Definition patterns define the meaning of a word within the sentence.

consonants | vowels
single " | single "
(b,d,c,g,r,v,f) | ⌐ long
 | ∟ short

cluster | clusters
– blends | – dipth,
(str, pl, bl) | (oi, oy, ou, ow)

– digraphs | – ea, ou
(ph, sh, ch)

Often the meaning is provided in a clause or appositive phrase that follows the troublesome word. However, students must know enough to read beyond the troublesome word to find the clue. The following examples illustrate this pattern:

_____ is a force that keeps you from floating out into space.

The plane was _____, or made late, by the weather.

The _____ (a person who flies airplanes) enjoyed his job.

Comparison patterns compare one word or phrase with another. Such patterns feature two locations with important and related information. Often, students can use the information in one location to identify a troublesome word in the other. Comparison patterns may also require readers to read past a troublesome word.

My ancient car is as _____ as the earth.

I _____ going to bed early. In fact, I hate it.

Contrast patterns also feature two locations with important and related information. However, with contrast patterns one word or phrase is contrasted with another. Again, students can use the information in one location to identify a troublesome word in the other.

My sister is _____, unlike her noisy brother.

It is _____ during our winters, unlike the warm weather that you enjoy.

Example patterns provide examples after the troublesome word. Students must learn to read past the troublesome word and use the examples to identify it.

We went up into several _____ in New York City, but the Empire State Building was the tallest.

There are seven _____: Europe, Asia, North America, South America, Africa, Australia, and Antarctica.

**Inductive Instruction.** Inductive instruction is often used with cloze tasks to develop context strategies. As presented in chapter 2, inductive instruction follows four procedural steps. Initially, the teacher provides students with several examples of the skill that is to be learned. Second, the teacher guides students to discover and articulate the skill or rule. Third, students receive guided practice experiences. And fourth, students receive independent practice experiences. Table 5–1 illustrates how inductive instruction can help students learn to read past a troublesome word and search for useful context clues.

**Deductive Instruction.** Deductive instruction can also be used with cloze tasks to develop context strategies. Also presented in chapter 2, deductive instruc-

TABLE 5–1
Inductive instruction used to teach students how to look for context clues

| Procedural Step | Activity |
| --- | --- |
| Provide examples. | Show students several cloze tasks in which important contextual information follows the blank. Definition, comparison, contrast or example patterns might be used. |
| Help students discover the skill. | Ask whether any students can determine the missing words in the cloze tasks. If so, ask them to explain how they solved the tasks. Write their solutions on the board. |
| Provide guided practice. | Have individuals practice the new strategy with several different sentences. Encourage students to share their reasoning aloud as they read past the target word to find the clues. |
| Provide independent practice. | Give students a practice page containing cloze tasks in which the useful information follows the missing words. Divide students into cooperative learning groups to complete the page. |

tion contains four procedural steps. First, the teacher states a rule. Second, the teacher shows students several examples of how that rule operates. Third, students receive guided practice. Fourth, students receive independent practice. Table 5–2 shows how deductive instruction can help students learn to identify an unknown word when it appears in an example pattern.

TABLE 5–2
Deductive instruction used to teach students how to use context knowledge in example patterns

| Procedural Step | Activity |
| --- | --- |
| State the skill you want students to learn. | Show students several sentences containing example patterns. Tell them that these are example patterns, which require reading past the target word to find useful clues in the examples. Write this strategy on the board. |
| Provide examples. | Show students several new sentences containing example patterns and target words that are difficult to recognize. Demonstrate how to read past the target words and use the examples as clues. Explain your thinking aloud to students. |
| Provide guided practice. | Have individuals practice this strategy with several new example patterns. Encourage students to share their reasoning aloud. |
| Provide independent practice. | Provide students with a practice page containing cloze tasks within example patterns. Have students complete the page in cooperative learning groups. |

**Integrating Context Use into Daily Classroom Activities.** Often the best way to provide instruction on context use is to incorporate this aspect of decoding knowledge into ongoing reading experiences, thus encouraging students to make context use a habit. Several examples of this approach are included in the activities that follow.

**SAMPLE ACTIVITIES**

**Oral Cloze Tasks.** Use oral cloze tasks during read aloud experiences. While reading children's literature aloud to your class, periodically omit the last word in a sentence. Then ask students to complete the sentence for you. This experience is especially enjoyable with younger readers and predictable texts. Try using any of these selections with first-grade students:

*The Very Hungry Caterpillar* by Eric Carle

*Drummer Hoff* by Barbara Emberly

*Brown Bear, Brown Bear, What Do You See?* by Bill Martin

*Fire! Fire! Said Mrs. McGuire* by Bill Martin

*The House That Jack Built* by Janet Stevens

*Too Much Noise* by Ann McGovern

**Cloze Tasks with New Vocabulary Words.** Present each new vocabulary word in a cloze task, and see whether students can guess its meaning from the context.

When they fight, pirates use sharp _____.

The pirates had to pull up the _____ before their ship could leave.

Encourage students to describe their own successful strategies. You may wish to keep a running list of these strategies posted in your room.

**Oral Reading Strategies.** Help students use context strategies during oral reading. When children have difficulty recognizing a word, suggest that they read the sentence over from the beginning, looking for clues as to what the troublesome word might be. Then encourage them to make a guess, consistent with their clues and with the initial letter of the troublesome word.

## DEVELOPING PHONIC KNOWLEDGE

phonic knowledge: Knowledge of letter-sound relationships and the ability to blend the sounds represented by letters.

**Phonic knowledge** consists of two elements: (1) knowledge of the relationship between letters and sounds and (2) the ability to put together, or blend, the sounds represented by letters. Letters in English do not always represent a single sound; nevertheless, knowledge of the more regular letter-sound rela-

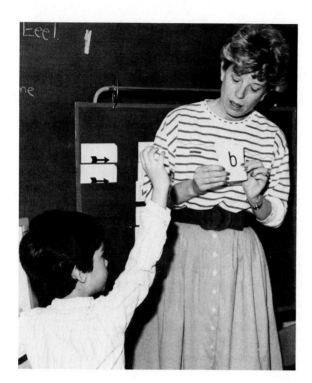

Teachers build students' phonic knowledge by relating letters to sounds and then blending those sounds into words.

tionships helps us recognize many of the words we encounter. Understanding the essential elements of phonic knowledge is especially important for teachers of beginning readers.

No other topic in reading inspires more controversy and less agreement than that of phonics instruction (Adams, 1990; Chall, 1983). Some have argued against the utility of extensive phonics instruction because English does not contain a perfect one-to-one relationship between letters and sounds (Hittleman, 1988; Smith, 1988). These individuals tend to have reader-based beliefs about how a person reads. On the other hand, there is enough regularity in the relationship between English letters and sounds that other individuals support phonics instruction (Durkin, 1983; Harris & Sipay, 1990; Resnick & Beck, 1984). These individuals tend to have a text-based or interactive belief about how a person reads.

Even the experts who advocate phonics instruction, however, have different ideas about which letter-sound relationships need to be taught. This text describes those relationships that are most consistently included in instructional programs (Clymer, 1963; Lesiak, 1984). The consonant generalizations are presented first, followed by the vowel generalizations. Durkin (1983) and Burmeister (1983) provide more extensive treatment of this topic.

## Consonants

In English, single consonants contain the most consistent relationship between letters and sounds. As a result, those relationships are usually taught to beginning readers. Figure 5–1 presents the single consonant relationships that are included in most instructional programs. The letters *c* and *g* are unique single consonants; the sound for each is dependent on the vowel that follows. These rules are often used for the sounds of *c* and *g*.

> *c* represents the sound /s/ when it is followed by the letters *e, i,* or *y.* When *c* is followed by *a, o,* or *u,* it represents the sound /k/.

| Soft *c* /s/ | Hard *c* /k/ |
|---|---|
| cent | cat |
| city | coat |
| cymbal | cut |

> *g* often represents the sound /j/ when it is followed by the letters *e, i,* or *y.* When *g* is followed by *a, o,* or *u* it often represents the sound /g/.

| Soft *g* /j/ | Hard *g* /g/ |
|---|---|
| gem | game |
| ginger | go |
| gym | gun |

Exceptions: finger, get, forget, give, forgive, girl

**consonant clusters:** Two or three consonant letters that often appear together.

**consonant digraphs:** A type of consonant cluster in which two different consonants together represent a single sound.

In addition to single consonants, there are **consonant clusters,** which consist of two or three consonant letters that often appear together. Three different types of consonant clusters are consonant digraphs, silent letter combinations, and consonant blends. **Consonant digraphs** are two different consonant letters that together represent a single sound. Some consonant digraphs represent sounds not usually associated with either letter—for example, *ch* (*child*), *ng* (*sing*), *ph* (*phone*), *sh* (*fish*), and *th* (*thin*). Other

FIGURE 5–1
Letter-sound relationships for the single consonants included in most instructional programs

| | | | |
|---|---|---|---|
| *b* as in *boy* | *j* as in *job* | *r* as in *rat* | *w* as in *we* |
| *c* as in *cent* | *k* as in *king* | *s* as in *sat* | *x* as in *six* |
|      *cat* | *l* as in *like* |      *has* |      *exam* |
| *d* as in *did* | *m* as in *make* |      *sure* |      *xylophone* |
| *f* as in *feet* | *n* as in *no* |      *measure* | *y* as in *yes* |
| *g* as in *gem* | *p* as in *pan* | *t* as in *time* | *z* as in *zoo* |
|      *go* | *q* as in *queen* | *v* as in *very* | |
| *h* as in *home* |      *bouquet* | | |

consonant digraphs represent sounds associated with one of the letters—for example, *kn* (*knit*), *wr* (*write*), *ck* (*check*), *gn* (*sign*), *mb* (*comb*), or *gh* (*ghost*). Because the other letter is silent, these digraphs are often called **silent letter combinations**.

A third type of consonant cluster is called a **consonant blend**. It contains two or more consonant letters, each with a separate sound that is blended together. Consonant blends include the following:

|            |            |              |
|------------|------------|--------------|
| *bl* as in *blue*  | *pl* as in *play*    | *sq* as in *squirrel* |
| *br* as in *brick* | *pr* as in *present* | *st* as in *still*    |
| *cl* as in *close* | *sc* as in *scare*   | *str* as in *street*  |
| *cr* as in *cream* | *scr* as in *scream* | *spr* as in *spring*  |
| *dr* as in *drop*  | *sk* as in *skip*    | *sw* as in *swim*     |
| *fl* as in *fly*   | *sl* as in *sleep*   | *thr* as in *three*   |
| *fr* as in *free*  | *sm* as in *small*   | *tr* as in *tree*     |
| *gl* as in *glass* | *sn* as in *snow*    |                       |
| *gr* as in *green* | *sp* as in *spot*    |                       |

> silent letter combinations: A type of consonant cluster in which two consonants express the sound of only one of the letters.

> consonant blend: A type of consonant cluster in which two or more consonants blend together their separate sounds.

## Vowels

Vowels include the letters *a, e, i, o, u,* and sometimes *y* and *w.* Like consonants, vowels are divided into single vowels and vowel clusters. Single vowels include long vowels, short vowels, and *y* when it functions as a vowel. A **long vowel sound** is identical to the vowel names of the five traditional vowel letters—*a, e, i, o,* and *u.* Long vowel sounds occur most frequently in two positions: (1) when a vowel occurs at the end of a syllable, as in *mē, nō, pā·per, cē·dar,* and *cī·der;* and (2) when a vowel is followed by a consonant and the letter *e,* as in *māne, thēme, tīme, rōpe,* and *cūte.* The final *e* in this pattern is usually silent.

> long vowel sound: A sound identical to the name of each of the five traditional vowels: *a, e, i, o,* and *u.*

Each of the five traditional vowel letters also has a **short vowel sound**. These sounds are usually learned with a set of key words, each with a short vowel sound at the beginning.

> short vowel sound: One of the five vowel sounds found at the beginning of each of these words: *apple, egg, ink, octopus,* and *umbrella.*

*a* as in *ăpple*
*e* as in *ĕlephant*
*i* as in *ĭnk*
*o* as in *ŏctopus*
*u* as in *ŭmbrella*

Often, first-grade classrooms contain pictures of these key words to remind students of the appropriate short vowel sounds (see Figure 5–2). Short vowel sounds occur most frequently in syllables that end in a consonant or consonant cluster, such as *hăp·py, lĕt, wĭn, ŏt·ter,* or *fŭn.*

*Y* functions as both a consonant and a vowel. It functions as a consonant in words like *yes, yellow,* and *yet.* There are two positions, however, when *y* functions as a vowel: (1) when *y* appears at the end of a word with more than one syllable, it usually represents a long *e* sound, as in *sandy, baby,* or *sixty;* and (2) when *y* appears at the end of a word with only one syllable, it usually represents the long *i* sound, as in *try, my,* or *cry.*

FIGURE 5–2
Key words to help students remember short vowel sounds

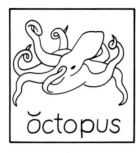

vowel clusters: Two or three vowels that often appear together.

vowel digraphs: A type of vowel cluster in which two different vowels together represent a single sound.

diphthongs: A type of vowel cluster in which two or more vowels blend together their separate sounds.

Like consonants, vowels also appear in clusters. **Vowel clusters** consist of two or three vowel letters that often appear together, such as *ou, ee, ai, ew,* and *oy.* Notice that both *w* and *y* can function as vowels when they appear in a vowel cluster. **Vowel digraphs** are two different vowel letters that together represent a single sound—for example, *oo (boot), au (caught), ea (each),* and *oa (boat).* Some vowel digraphs represent sounds not usually associated with either vowel letter: *oo (shoot), ew (new), aw (saw), au (auto).* Other vowel digraphs represent sounds usually associated with one of the letters: *ay (say), ea (beach), ee (see), oa (coat), ai (bait),* or *ei (sleigh).* Vowel blends, or **diphthongs,** are two vowel letters that represent a blending of the sounds often associated with each letter: *oi (soil), oy (toy), ou (mouse),* and *ow (cow).*

Instruction ⟨ *synthetic approach*
            *analytic approach*

Phonics instruction usually employs a wide variety of commercial materials. Sometimes these materials are part of a published reading program; at other times a separate set of phonics materials is used. In either case it is important to remember that phonic knowledge is merely a means to an end, which is comprehension. In addition, certain principles of instruction apply, regardless of framework or approach.

■ *Provide many opportunities for students to apply phonic generalizations in functional reading experiences.* Make sure students have opportunities to read widely and often outside regular instructional materials.

- *Be consistent.* Students benefit from consistency in the selection of ir. tional terms and in the expression of phonic generalizations.
- *Encourage students to be flexible in their application of phonic strateg* Students need to know that exceptions exist to every rule. They should ai try alternative letter-sound relationships when the application of one gen eralization fails to yield a familiar word.
- *Spend more time on consonants than on vowels.* Consonants have more consistent letter-sound relationships than vowels do. Consonants also carry more information about words, as can be seen in the examples that follow. The same sentence is shown first with only its vowels and then with only its consonants.

$$\_\,\_e\_\_ \quad \_o\_e \quad \_i\_e \quad o\_ \quad \_o\_\_o\_a\_\_\_!$$
$$Sp\_nd \quad m\_r\_ \quad t\_m\_ \quad \_n \quad c\_ns\_nants!$$

- *Be sure that students can actually use a phonic generalization.* Do not assume that they can use a generalization when they are able to verbalize it. The point of learning any phonic generalization is not to parrot back a verbal rule, but to have a strategy for determining the pronunciation of a difficult word.

Several instructional practices are used to develop phonic knowledge.

**Synthetic Approaches.** A **synthetic approach** to phonics instruction first teaches a number of separate letter-sound relationships, using either an inductive or a deductive method framework. Then children are taught how to blend individual sounds to recognize a word. According to Resnick and Beck (1984), this instruction in blending sounds should follow a five-step method framework.

**synthetic approach:** An approach to phonic instruction that first teaches separate letter-sound relationships and then teaches how to blend sounds to decode a word.

1. Model the blending procedure. Point to each letter separately, indicating the sound for each (e.g., c = /k/, u = /u/, t = /t/). Then slide your finger under the first portion of the word (*cu*), and say this blended sound (/ku/). Slide your finger under the final portion of the word (*t*), and say this sound (/t/). Then slide your finger under the entire word, and say the blended sound (/kut/). Circle the word with your finger, and say, "The word is *cut*."
2. Have children imitate the model with you. Maintain your use of verbal cues and finger cues to assist them.
3. Repeat Step 2 but do not say the sounds or the blends. Have students say these as you continue the verbal cues and finger cues.
4. Repeat Step 3 but this time give only finger cues.
5. Provide independent blending practice. Have children independently or in cooperative learning groups perform the pointing, sounding, and blending steps.

**Analytic Approaches.** An **analytic approach** to phonics instruction proceeds in an opposite direction. Analytic approaches first teach students how to recognize a basic set of words (e.g., *cat, dog, on*) and then use that knowledge to

**analytic approach:** An approach to phonic instruction that first teaches whole words and then uses those words to demonstrate letter-sound relationships.

illustrate letter-sound relationships. For instance, "The letter *c* often represents the sound at the beginning of the word *cat*. The letter *o* often represents the sound at the beginning of the word *on*. The letter *t* often represents the sound at the end of the word *cat*. The letter *d* often represents the sound at the beginning of the word *dog*." Finally, knowledge of the separate letter-sound relationships is used to recognize new words, such as *cot* and *dot*. This approach seldom isolates sounds or teaches blending ability as a specific skill.

**Inductive Instruction.** Inductive instruction is often used within either a synthetic or an analytic approach to phonics. The model lesson that follows illustrates how Ms. Dodson used inductive instruction to teach students that *y* sometimes functions as a vowel. Several of her second-grade students had been confused about the two sounds of *y* at the ends of words. Consequently, she decided to bring them together for a short lesson on that phonic skill.

**MODEL
LESSON**

Inductive Instruction in Ms. Dodson's Room

**Provide Examples of the Skill or Rule.** Ms. Dodson began by writing the following words on the chalkboard for her students to analyze. She read each word aloud as she wrote it.

|       |         |
|-------|---------|
| try   | baby    |
| my    | rapidly |
| cry   | sticky  |
| sky   | pretty  |

**Help Students Discover the Skill or Rule.** Ms. Dodson asked questions to help students notice the two sounds of *y* at the ends of words. "Which letter is at the end of all these words? That's right! *Y* is at the end, isn't it? Now, which sounds do you hear at the ends of these words? Yes, we hear the sound /I/ at the end of the word *try* and the sound /E/ at the end of the word *baby*. Can anyone state a rule that would apply to these words?" Ms. Dodson helped the students state the rule and then wrote it on the board: "When *y* is at the end of a word, it can have two sounds: /I/ as in *try* or /E/ as in *baby*."

Then Ms. Dodson asked questions to help the students notice where each of those sounds occurred. "What is the same about all these words in the first column, where *y* has the long *i* sound? That's right! They are all short words, aren't they? How many syllables does each word have? Right, only one syllable. Now look at the second column, where *y* has the long *e* sound. What is the same about all of these words? That's right! They all have more than one syllable. Can anyone help us change our rule to include this new information?" Ms. Dodson helped the students state the new rule and then wrote it on the board: "When *y* is at the end of a word, it can have two sounds: /I/ as in *try* or /E/ as in *baby*. Y has the /I/ sound at the end of a word with one syllable. Y has the /E/ sound at the end of a word with more than one syllable."

**Provide Guided Practice.** Ms. Dodson then presented a new set of words to see whether students had acquired the rule and to show them how the rule applied to other words: *pry, why, fry, quickly, rainy,* and *sunny*. She asked individuals to read each new word aloud, tell the group which column it should go in, and explain why. Ms. Dodson helped when students had difficulty.

**Provide Independent Practice.** Ms. Dodson then provided her students with a short cooperative learning group task, using a worksheet she had made and duplicated. She gave each student a copy of the page but explained that it should be completed by the group. She appointed one student to serve as the leader of the discussion and asked that they all share their work with her when they were finished. The page she gave them looked like this:

> Put each of the following words in the correct column according to the sound of *y* at the end of each word.
>
> | happily | shy | spy | runny | sly |
> | dry | silly | cry | Christy | windy |
>
> Words like <u>My</u>          Words like <u>Baby</u>
>
> _____          _____
> _____          _____
> _____          _____
> _____          _____
> _____          _____
>
> When does *y* sound like long *i?*
> _____
>
> When does *y* sound like long *e?*
> _____

**Deductive Instruction.** Deductive instruction can also be used to develop phonic knowledge. The model lesson that follows illustrates how Mr. Burns used deductive instruction to teach the same concept—that *y* sometimes functions as a vowel.

**MODEL
LESSON**

Deductive Instruction in Mr. Burns's Room

**State the Skill or Rule.** Mr. Burns began by stating the phonic generalization: "Sometimes you will find words ending with the letter *y*. *Y* has the /I/ sound at the end of a word with one syllable. *Y* has the /E/ sound at the end of a word with more than one syllable. Look at these examples."

**Provide Examples of the Skill or Rule.** Mr. Burns wrote the following words on the board.

|     |        |
|-----|--------|
| try | baby   |
| my  | rapidly|
| cry | sticky |
| sky | pretty |

He read some of the words aloud and asked students to read others. As they read the words, Mr. Burns pointed out that the one-syllable words ending in *y* had the /I/ sound, whereas the words with more than one syllable had the /E/ sound.

**Provide Guided Practice.** Mr. Burns then presented a new set of words to his students: *pry, why, fry, quickly, rainy,* and *sunny.* He wanted to be sure that his students had acquired the rule, and he also wanted to show them how the rule applied to other words. He asked individual students to read each new word aloud, tell the group which column it should go in, and explain why. Mr. Burns helped when students had difficulty.

**Provide Independent Practice.** Mr. Burns then gave his students the same cooperative learning group task that Ms. Dodson gave her students (see previous model lesson). Mr. Burns gave each student a copy of the page but explained that it should be completed by the group. He appointed one student to serve as the leader of the discussion and asked that they all share their work with him when they were finished.

---

**Integrating Phonic Instruction into Daily Classroom Activities.** Creating your own instructional activities permits you to design learning experiences to meet the precise needs of your students. Several activities that develop phonic knowledge are described on page 191. You might use them as models with which to create your own.

**DECISION POINT ➤**

Phonics instruction has probably generated more debate over the years than any other area of reading. How do you see the role of phonics in a primary grade classroom. What should be taught? How should it be taught? Why?

**Letter-Sound Boxes.** Make letter-sound boxes for your students. Each day place a different consonant on the front of a box. After introducing the target sound, give students old magazines and have them cut out pictures that begin with that sound. Have them place their pictures in the box. Periodically, take out the pictures and check them with the class.

**Sound Bags.** Make sound bags for your students, each with a consonant on the outside and one object inside that begins with the sound of that letter (e.g., a book for *b*, a cup for *c*, a doll for *d*). Each day introduce a new bag, and have children guess what might be inside. Write all of your students' guesses on the chalkboard so that they can see all the words beginning with the target letter. At the end of the day take out the object, and see whether anyone correctly guessed what it was.

**Vowel Volumes.** Make vowel volumes with your class. Start by making ditto masters of each vowel letter and running off enough copies for each student. Each page should contain one vowel letter and several words that begin with either the long or the short sound of that letter. Give the children old magazines and have them cut out pictures that contain the target vowel sound. Then have them paste those pictures on the correct page. You, or your students, may wish to label each picture. When pages for all the vowels are completed, make a book cover and staple the pages together. Have students write titles on their books, like *Samantha's Short Vowel Volume* or *Jerry's Long Vowel Volume*. This activity is an excellent way to combine reading and writing with younger students as you develop decoding knowledge (see chapter 9).

**SAMPLE ACTIVITIES**

## DEVELOPING SIGHT WORD KNOWLEDGE

**Sight word knowledge** refers to the ability to recognize the pronunciation of words automatically, without conscious application of other decoding strategies. Mature readers recognize most words by relying on their extensive sight word knowledge. Beginning readers have far less sight word knowledge, and some readers have none at all. If beginning readers knew that they had to recognize so many different words by sight, they might give up. Memorizing the pronunciation of thousands of separate items would be a tremendous challenge.

Fortunately, however, two considerations reduce the difficulty of developing extensive sight word knowledge. First, a small set of words appears frequently in writing. By knowing how to recognize these 200 to 400 words by sight, readers can immediately recognize 50 to 65 percent of the words in nearly any reading selection (Harris & Sipay, 1990). Second, most of the other words that become part of sight word knowledge are acquired experientially over a period of time. Initially, readers attempt to recognize each new word by

sight word knowledge: One aspect of decoding knowledge; the ability to recognize the pronunciation of words automatically, without conscious use of other decoding strategies.

Many commercial materials are available to help teach phonic knowledge, in addition to teacher-created activities that may more precisely meet the needs of individual students.

using either a phonic or a context strategy. However, after a number of such experiences with a particular word, a reader becomes able to recognize it automatically, without using a conscious strategy to determine its pronunciation (Samuels & Eisenberg, 1981). Many more sight words are acquired from reading experience and use than from deliberate instruction. With beginning readers, then, it is not our goal to teach automatic recognition of all of the words in our language. The sight word knowledge necessary for beginning readers consists of a limited set of words that share several characteristics.

- *High frequency.* Words taught as initial sight words should appear frequently in print. Thus, words like *is, a, the, to,* and *she* should be taught, but not words like *excavation*.
- *Familiar meanings.* The meanings of initial sight words should be familiar to beginning readers; that is, they should know the words from their oral language. Thus, words like *car, come, good,* and *school* are better candidates than words like *oyster* or *nucleus*.
- *Phonic irregularity.* Words taught as initial sight words often cannot be recognized by applying phonic generalizations. Words like *one, said, where,* and *some* are thus more appropriate for early instruction than words that can be identified by applying common phonic generalizations.

Which specific words, then, should be taught to beginning readers? Published reading programs usually have their own list of words that students are expected to learn as sight words. In addition, there are several different lists of sight words that are based on a wider range of reading material. Some of the lists sample selections in several published reading programs to determine the most frequent words; others sample an even wider range of reading material. The list in Figure 5–3 includes words that appear frequently in the oral language of kindergarten and first-grade students and in a variety of published materials. Other lists by Fry (1980), Dolch (1960), and Harris and Sipay (1990) can also be consulted.

## Instruction

Whenever possible, sight word instruction should take place within sentence contexts, because children are more certain about a word's meaning when it appears in a sentence or phrase. Confusion about meaning can be great among words that look or sound alike, and it is important to establish the habit of using context to identify words. These examples illustrate the potential for confusion.

The book was *red*. The book was *read*.

That play was *close*. That play will not *close*.

A second reason for teaching sight words in context is to more closely approximate the reading task. Presenting words in isolation sometimes leads children to think that reading is simply a process of recognizing the pronunciations of separate words. Slow, inefficient, word-by-word reading without attention to meaning is often the result.

**Integrating Sight Word Development into Daily Classroom Activities.** There are many ways to develop sight word knowledge. An aphorism known to most reading teachers is that "the best way to learn to read is to read." This advice is sound because the more opportunities students have to read real texts, the more they encounter the high-frequency words in our language. It is important, therefore, for them to have many opportunities to read during daily classroom activities. Reading promotes the development of sight word knowledge, and sight word knowledge, in turn, promotes the development of reading.

Creating a literacy environment in the classroom can do much to develop sight word knowledge. Labeling objects, pictures of objects, and art work provides excellent exposure to the sight words students should know. Teachers might also consider prominently displaying weather charts, calendars, and job charts. In addition, writing activities such as those described in chapter 9 are particularly useful for providing exposure to high-frequency words. These sample activities on page 195 offer further suggestions.

**Using Individualized Word Banks.** Sight word knowledge can also be developed by using **individualized word banks**. Such banks consist of index card

**individualized word banks:** One means of developing sight word knowledge; uses words written on index cards and filed in index card boxes.

FIGURE 5–3
Johnson's first- and second-grade word lists

## Johnson's First-Grade Words

| | | | | | | |
|---|---|---|---|---|---|---|
| a | day | had | let | off | so | under |
| above | days | hand | like | old | some | up |
| across | did | hard | little | one | something | very |
| after | didn't | has | look | open | soon | want |
| again | do | have | love | or | still | wanted |
| air | don't | he | make | out | table | was |
| all | door | help | making | over | than | way |
| am | down | her | man | past | that | we |
| American | end | here | may | play | the | well |
| and | feet | high | me | point | then | went |
| are | find | him | men | put | there | what |
| art | first | home | miss | really | these | when |
| as | five | house | money | red | they | where |
| ask | for | how | more | right | think | which |
| at | four | I | most | room | this | who |
| back | gave | if | mother | run | those | why |
| be | get | I'm | Mr. | said | three | will |
| before | girl | in | must | saw | time | with |
| behind | give | into | my | school | to | work |
| big | go | is | name | see | today | year |
| black | God | it | never | seen | too | years |
| book | going | its | new | she | took | yet |
| boy | gone | it's | night | short | top | you |
| but | good | just | no | six | two | your |
| came | got | keep | not | | | |
| can | | kind | now | | | |
| car | | | | | | |
| children | | | | | | |
| come | | | | | | |
| could | | | | | | |

## Johnson's Second-Grade Words

| | | | | |
|---|---|---|---|---|
| able | different | idea | of | take |
| about | does | knew | office | tell |
| almost | done | know | on | their |
| alone | each | last | only | them |
| already | early | leave | other | thing |
| always | enough | left | our | things |
| America | even | light | outside | thought |
| an | ever | long | own | through |
| another | every | made | part | together |
| any | eyes | many | party | told |
| around | face | mean | people | town |
| away | far | might | place | turn |
| because | feel | morning | plan | until |
| been | found | Mrs. | present | us |
| believe | from | much | real | use |
| best | front | music | road | used |
| better | full | need | same | water |
| between | great | next | say | were |
| board | group | nothing | says | west |
| both | hands | number | set | while |
| bought | having | | should | whole |
| by | head | | show | whose |
| called | heard | | small | wife |
| change | | | sometimes | women |
| church | | | sound | world |
| city | | | started | would |
| close | | | street | |
| company | | | sure | |
| cut | | | | |

**Source:** From *Teaching Reading Vocabulary*, second edition by Dale D. Johnson and P. David Pearson. Copyright © 1984 by CBS College Publishing. Reprinted by permission of Holt, Rinehart and Winston, CBS College Publishing.

**The Naming Game.** Play the naming game with kindergarten or first-grade students. Each day label three new objects in your classroom before your students arrive. At the end of each day see whether anyone has found and can read all three new labels. In the beginning this task will be easy. Quickly, though, as labels begin to cover the room, it will be difficult to find the three new objects. The real benefit of this activity is that students are continually reading the names of objects in the room as they search for the three new labels each day.

**SAMPLE ACTIVITIES**

**Predictable Texts.** Have your beginning readers read many predictable texts with repeated sentence patterns. High-frequency words are repeated in such patterns, and exposure to those high-frequency words in predictable texts has been demonstrated to significantly increase sight word knowledge. Predictable texts that are especially useful for developing sight word knowledge include these:

*Drummer Hoff* by Barbara Emberly

*Brown Bear, Brown Bear, What Do You See?* by Bill Martin

*The House That Jack Built* by Janet Stevens

*The Very Busy Spider* by Eric Carle

*The Three Billy Goats Gruff* (several versions)

boxes (shoe boxes make an inexpensive substitute) with cards inside. Words that children have not yet learned completely are written on those cards; on one side the words may be written in isolation, and on the other side, in a sentence context. The words can be practiced individually or with a partner. In addition, cooperative learning group activities can be designed using these boxes. When a sufficient number of words are accumulated, the cards can be organized alphabetically, to develop familiarity with alphabetical order in a functional learning experience. Figure 5–4 shows an example of a word bank.

Often individualized word banks are used in student-centered programs in which the students themselves decide which words they need to practice and learn (Ashton-Warner, 1963). In conjunction with writing activities, a teacher might write a new word on a card whenever a student asks for its spelling. That word card could then go into that student's word bank after it was used in the writing activity.

**Using Sight Word Envelopes. Sight word envelopes** can also be used to develop initial sight word knowledge. To develop a set of sight word envelopes, a teacher must first prepare blocks of sight words (perhaps three across and four down) on ditto masters (see Figure 5–5). On one side of the page the sight words should appear in isolation; on the other side they should be written in

sight word envelopes: One means of developing sight word knowledge; keeps sight words in envelopes for practice until they are known.

Many sight words are acquired through repeated encounters during reading.

sentence context. The pages are then duplicated, and the individual sight words are cut apart and placed by sets in separate envelopes for each student.

Sight word envelopes help students develop their sight word knowledge. They also help teachers monitor the students' developing knowledge. Students

FIGURE 5–4
A word bank for sight words

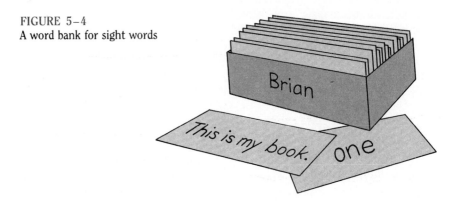

FIGURE 5–5
Word cards for a sight word envelope

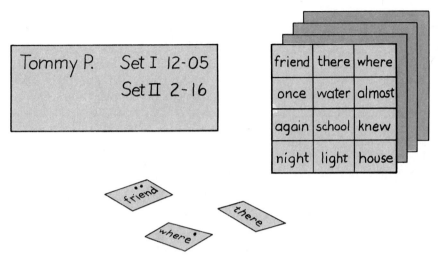

can practice reading the individual words and the sentences alone or with a friend. The teacher then regularly checks the students' ability to quickly recognize the words in their envelopes. When a student correctly recognizes one of the words, the teacher places a small dot in the corner of that piece of paper. When a student has correctly recognized a word twice and two dots appear in the corner, that slip can be removed from the envelope. When all of the sight words are removed, the name of the set and the date are recorded on the student's envelope.

**A Traditional Whole-Word Method Framework.** In some first- or second-grade classrooms initial sight word instruction follows a **traditional whole-word method**. This method framework presents new words to beginning readers as whole units. According to Durkin (1983), whole-word methods follow several procedural steps.

traditional whole-word method: A method framework used to develop sight word knowledge.

1. Present the new word in sentence context for children to see.
2. Help children read the entire sentence. Have several individuals read the new word.
3. Point to the new word. Have students read, spell, and reread it.
4. Check to be sure the meaning is understood.
5. List words that appear similar. Discuss the similarities and differences.
6. Erase everything but the new word. Have students read, spell, and reread it.

It is important with this approach to be sure that students actually look at each complete word as it is presented. Calling their attention to the spelling of the word helps focus their attention on it. Usually no more than three or four words are presented in a single session, and some type of independent practice or cooperative learning group activity should be provided.

## USING A COMPREHENSION FRAMEWORK TO GUIDE INSTRUCTIONAL DECISIONS ABOUT DECODING

You will face two basic decisions as you consider decoding instruction. First, you will need to decide what to teach and emphasize in order to develop your students' decoding knowledge. In addition, you will also need to decide how to teach decoding knowledge to your students. Your comprehension framework will guide you in both these decisions.

### What to Teach and Emphasize

To guide your decisions regarding what to teach and emphasize about decoding, you should consider that portion of your comprehension framework that tells how a person reads. Table 5–3 summarizes how that explanation can be used to guide your content decisions in this area.

**Text-Based.** If you follow a text-based explanation of how a person reads, you believe that reading consists largely of translating words into sounds, for which task readers use decoding knowledge before any other knowledge sources. As a result, you will probably decide to spend much time on the development of decoding knowledge, especially with beginning readers. And you will probably emphasize phonic and sight word instruction, rather than development of context knowledge. Instruction in both phonic and sight word knowledge facilitates the translation of printed words into sounds.

**Reader-Based.** If you follow a reader-based explanation of how a person reads, you believe that reading consists largely of expectations for upcoming words. Thus, you believe that extensive prior knowledge leads to successful reading because readers are able to accurately predict upcoming words. As a result, you will probably spend little time on the development of decoding knowledge. The limited time that you do spend will be devoted to developing context knowledge, and you will encourage children to use contextual analysis strategies to decode words.

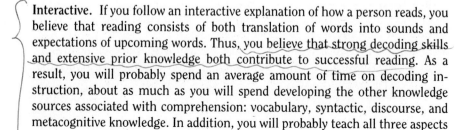

**Interactive.** If you follow an interactive explanation of how a person reads, you believe that reading consists of both translation of words into sounds and expectations of upcoming words. Thus, you believe that strong decoding skills and extensive prior knowledge both contribute to successful reading. As a result, you will probably spend an average amount of time on decoding instruction, about as much as you will spend developing the other knowledge sources associated with comprehension: vocabulary, syntactic, discourse, and metacognitive knowledge. In addition, you will probably teach all three aspects

可能的
大概的.

TABLE 5–3

Summary of how a comprehension framework guides decisions about what to teach in decoding instruction

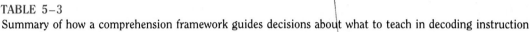

| Explanation of How a Person Reads | Related Assumptions | Probable Time Spent on Decoding Instruction | Probable Emphasis in Decoding Instruction |
|---|---|---|---|
| Text-based | Meaning exists more in the text. Reading is translation. Reading begins by using decoding knowledge. | Much | Phonic knowledge Sight word knowledge |
| Reader-based | Meaning exists more in what the reader brings to the text. Reading hinges on expectations of upcoming words. Reading begins with prior knowledge (vocabulary, syntactic, discourse, and metacognitive knowledge). | Little | Context knowledge |
| Interactive | Meaning exists in both the text and the reader. Reading is both translation and expectation. Reading uses all knowledge sources simultaneously. | Average | Context knowledge Phonic knowledge Sight word knowledge |

of decoding knowledge—context, phonics, and sight words—with a balanced emphasis.

## How to Develop Decoding Knowledge

To guide your decisions about how to teach decoding knowledge, you should consider that portion of your comprehension framework that tells how reading ability develops. Table 5–4 summarizes how that explanation can be used to guide your decisions about instructional methods and activities in this area.

**Specific Skills.** If you follow a specific skills explanation of development, you favor learning experiences that are deductive in nature and that focus on specific skills. As a result, you will probably use deductive methods to teach context and phonic knowledge and a traditional whole-word method to develop sight word knowledge. You might use sight word envelopes also since they help

TABLE 5–4
Summary of how a comprehension framework guides decisions about how to teach decoding knowledge

| Explanation of How Reading Ability Develops | Related Assumptions | Probable Instructional Activities |
|---|---|---|
| Specific skills | Reading ability develops as students learn specific reading skills. | Deductive method framework to teach context and phonic knowledge |
|  | Students learn best as a result of teacher-directed deductive experiences. | Traditional whole-word method framework and sight word envelopes to develop sight word knowledge |
| Holistic language | Reading ability develops as students engage in holistic, meaningful, and functional experiences with print. | Inductive method framework to teach context and phonic knowledge |
|  | Students learn best as a result of self-directed inductive experiences. | Individualized word banks and integrated daily classroom activities for sight word development |
| Integrated | Reading ability develops as students learn specific reading skills and as they engage in meaningful, functional, and holistic experiences with print. | Both inductive and deductive method frameworks to teach context and phonic knowledge |
|  | Reading ability develops as a result of both teacher-directed deductive experiences and self-directed inductive experiences. | Traditional whole-word method framework, individualized word banks, sight word envelopes, and integrated daily classroom activities for sight word development |

students master specific sight words. In general, you will organize your direct instruction around a set of specific decoding skills.

Holistic Language. If you follow a holistic language explanation of development, you favor learning experiences that are inductive in nature. As a result, you will probably use inductive methods to teach context or phonic knowledge and will integrate sight word development into daily classroom activities, perhaps by using individualized word banks and letting your students determine the words to enter into the banks. You may also provide functional literacy activities to encourage your students to read widely and interact with print, again to develop extensive sight word knowledge. In addition, you will probably consider writing experiences to be especially appropriate for the development of decoding knowledge.

*Integrated.* If you follow an integrated explanation of development, you will use both deductive and inductive methods to develop context or phonic knowledge. To develop sight word knowledge, you will probably use some combination of individualized word banks, sight word envelopes, a traditional whole-word method, and integrated daily classroom activities.

## COMMENTS FROM THE CLASSROOM ■

### Emily Dodson

When my colleagues and I talk about decoding instruction, we get into some of our most heated discussions. Mr. Burns believes that decoding is the most important part of the comprehension process, and he spends much of his time teaching phonics and sight words. He spends very little time on context; according to him, we shouldn't be telling students to guess what words are when we can help them sound them out or recognize them by sight. Mr. Burns usually uses a deductive method to teach phonics, and he uses a traditional whole-word method to teach sight words. He also likes to use sight word envelopes since they help him keep track of which words each student knows. He has a different parent volunteer come in each day to work with individual students on the words in their sight word envelopes.

Ms. Sanchez is at the opposite end of the continuum. She believes that prior knowledge is far more important than decoding skills. Consequently, she spends very little time teaching decoding, and most of that she devotes to context strategies. She teaches her students how to predict upcoming words by paying attention to the meaning of the sentence and then guessing words that make sense. She uses an inductive method to help students who are having trouble with context strategies. As far as phonics, she teaches students only initial consonant sounds. According to her, students can almost always guess what a word is if they know the sentence context and the first letter of the word. Why waste time on phonics?

Because Ms. Sanchez believes that reading ability develops through holistic language experiences, she has her students read and write frequently. She incorporates word banks into their writing experiences so that they learn the sight words that are important to them when they are writing. She always seems to find new ways to integrate sight word development into daily classroom activities.

As for me, I believe that we need to sound words out sometimes—usually when we're reading material on an unfamiliar topic. But at other times I think our guesses about words help us more than our ability to sound them out, especially when we know something about the topic. So I spend an average amount of time on decoding, and I teach it all—context, phonics, and sight words.

In the process I use both inductive and deductive methods to teach context and phonics. For sight words I use the traditional whole-word method for any students who need it, but more often I rely on reading and writing experiences. And I do use word banks and sight word envelopes for high-frequency sight words. All in all, I think I have quite a wide range of strategies to use with my students.

MAJOR POINTS

■ Decoding is the process that readers use to determine the oral equivalent of written words. Decoding knowledge includes context knowledge, phonic knowledge, and sight word knowledge. Decoding contributes to the comprehension process when a word's pronunciation helps a reader determine its meaning. Decoding knowledge is especially important for beginning readers.

■ Several instructional practices can be used to develop context knowledge: cloze tasks, inductive instruction, and deductive instruction.

■ Several instructional approaches are used to develop phonic knowledge: synthetic approaches, analytic approaches, inductive instruction, and deductive instruction.

■ Sight word knowledge can be developed by integrating sight word activities into daily classroom routines, using individualized word banks or sight word envelopes and/or employing a traditional whole-word method framework.

■ A comprehension framework can be used to guide decisions about the content and manner of decoding instruction. An explanation of how a person reads can help determine what to teach. An explanation of how reading ability develops can help determine how to teach.

MAKING INSTRUCTIONAL DECISIONS

1. Consider the following list of decoding skills that are taught in one particular reading program. Identify the type of decoding knowledge represented by each listed skill: context knowledge, phonic knowledge, or sight word knowledge.

   a. Recognizes mastery words in isolation and in context.
   b. Decodes the appropriate sound for *f*.
   c. Uses picture context.
   d. Uses meaning and syntax to recognize words.
   e. Knows that one sound is represented by different letters.
   f. Recognizes these common words: *the, a, one, he, she, here, we, run,* and *goes*.

2. Develop a lesson to teach some aspect of context use, such as reading past a troublesome word. Use an inductive method framework. Then develop another lesson using a deductive method framework to teach that same aspect.

3. Define your own comprehension framework. Then specify the range of phonic skills you will include in your instructional program. Will you teach letter-sound relationships for consonants? Which ones? Will you teach letter-sound relationships for vowels? Which ones? Explain how your comprehension framework determines the phonic instruction you will include.

4. Specify how you will develop sight word knowledge in your instructional program. Which methods and activities will you use? Explain how your comprehension framework has guided your decision making.

5. Describe the comprehension framework of a second-grade teacher who makes these decisions about decoding instruction:

   a. Decoding will receive far less attention than the development of vocabulary, syntactic, or discourse knowledge.
   b. Context knowledge will receive greater emphasis than the development of phonic or sight word knowledge.
   c. Inductive methods will be used to develop context knowledge.
   d. Sight word knowledge will be developed through writing experiences, the use of sight word boxes, and the integration of sight word activities into daily classroom routines.

   Explain how this teacher's comprehension framework has guided these instructional decisions.

**FURTHER READING**

Dowhower, S. L. (1989). Repeated reading: Research into practice. *The Reading Teacher, 42,* 502–507.

Describes a useful technique for developing fluency in decoding processes. Summarizes research showing how repeated reading contributes to both automatic decoding and improvements in comprehension.

Fry, E., & Sakiey, E. (1986). Common words not taught in basal reading series. *The Reading Teacher, 39,* 395–398.

Identifies several hundred common words not taught in basal reading programs. Teachers may wish to include these words in their sight word programs.

Jacobson, J. M. (1990). Group vs. individual completion of a cloze passage. *Journal of Reading, 33,* 244–250.

Describes a study in which students completed cloze tasks individually and in cooperative learning groups. Results favored the use of cooperative learning groups for completing cloze passages.

Johnson, D. D., & Pearson, P. D. (1984). *Teaching reading vocabulary* (2nd ed.). New York: Holt, Rinehart & Winston.

Describes a wide range of instructional activities for promoting the development of decoding and vocabulary knowledge. Quite readable and useful.

Maclean, R. (1988). Two paradoxes of phonics. *The Reading Teacher, 41,* 514–517.

Discusses two interesting paradoxes associated with phonics instruction. Notes that phonics is an important component of reading even though phonic skills have little to do with the processes of reading acquisition. Suggests that phonics may be quite important in getting students started on the path to reading.

**REFERENCES**

Adams, M. J. (1990). *Beginning to read: Thinking and learning about print.* Champaign, IL: Center for the Study of Reading.

Ashton-Warner, S. (1963). *Teacher.* New York: Simon & Schuster.

Burmeister, L. E. (1983). *Foundations and strategies for teaching children to read*. Reading, MA: Addison-Wesley.

Chall, J. S. (1983). *Stages of reading development*. New York: McGraw-Hill.

Cleary, B. (1968). *Ramona the pest*. New York: Scholastic Book Services.

Clymer, T. (1963). The utility of phonic generalizations in the primary grades. *The Reading Teacher, 16,* 252–258.

Dolch, E. W. (1960). *Teaching primary grade reading*. Champaign, IL: Garrard Press.

Durkin, D. (1983). *Teaching them to read* (4th ed.). Boston: Allyn & Bacon.

Fry, E. (1980). The new instant word list. *The Reading Teacher, 34,* 284–289.

Harris, A. J., & Sipay, E. R. (1990). *How to increase reading ability* (9th ed.). New York: Longman.

Hittleman, D. R. (1988). *Developmental reading* (3rd ed.). Columbus, OH: Merrill.

Lesiak, J. (1984). There is a need for word attack generalizations. In A. J. Harris & E. R. Sipay (Eds.), *Readings on reading instruction* (3rd ed.). New York: Longman.

Resnick, L. B., & Beck, I. L. (1984). Designing instruction in reading: Initial reading. In A. J. Harris & E. R. Sipay (Eds.), *Readings on reading instruction* (3rd ed.). New York: Longman.

Rey, H. A. (1952). *Curious George rides a bike*. Boston: Houghton Mifflin.

Samuels, S. J., & Eisenberg, P. (1981). A framework for understanding the reading process. In F. J. Pirozzolo & M. C. Wittrock (Eds.), *Neuropsychological and cognitive processes in reading*. New York: Academic Press.

Smith, F. (1988). *Understanding reading* (4th ed.). Hillsdale, NJ: Erlbaum.

*[Handwritten annotations:]*

Deictic Terms
[ˈdɑɪˌdɪk]
↓ it's a problem for youngsters

a reader-based explanation of reading comprehension.

comprehension
↓
metacognitive knowledge — step 1 → readiness aspects
← affective aspects
↓
discourse    " — step 2
↓
syntactic    " — step 3   explicit
tacit
↓
vocabulary    " — step 4 — conceptual / procedural
real
↓
decoding    " — step 5 — phonic / sight word / context

step 6

Instr.   Framework

Material          Compr-ehension              method

How does   read?                    How does reading ability deve.?

what to teach

- TB ———— phonic          How to teach
- I        sighted         - S.S.
- RB      contextual

- I.

- HLL

# Vocabulary and Comprehension

- The Meanings of Words
- Building Concepts
- Deciding What to Teach
- Deciding How to Teach
- Two Special Cases

*"Dictionopolis will always be grateful, my boy," interrupted the king, throwing one arm around Milo and patting Tock with the other. "You will face many dangers on your journey, but fear not, for I have brought you this for your protection."*

*He drew from inside his cape a small heavy box about the size of a schoolbook and handed it ceremoniously to Milo.*

*"In this box are all the words I know," he said.*

N. Juster, *The Phantom Tollbooth* (New York: Random House, 1961), p. 98. Reprinted by permission.

Vocabulary knowledge is one of the most important factors in comprehending written passages. Not knowing the concept represented by a particular word makes it difficult, if not impossible, to understanding the author's intended meaning. This chapter examines the importance of vocabulary in reading comprehension. It also looks at the complexity of meaning acquisition and a variety of effective instructional strategies.

Chapter 6 includes information that will help you answer questions like these:

1. What is the role of concept development in teaching and learning new vocabulary?
2. How are pronunciation and meaning determined in reading?
3. How does vocabulary teaching differ across primary and intermediate grades?
4. What are effective techniques to teach new meanings for already-known words?

KEY CONCEPTS

content vocabulary                          learning center
content-specific vocabulary                 morphemes
feature analysis                            multiple response card
function vocabulary                         semantic map/web
homonyms/homophones/homographs  schema
instantiation

## THE MEANINGS OF WORDS

Good speakers and readers of English almost unconsciously select the appropriate meanings of words from a large number of possibilities. Even the simplest words often have more than one meaning, as well as numerous shades or gradations of meaning. Look at these examples.

Copper is a good *conductor* of electricity.
Give your ticket to the *conductor*.
The orchestra *conductor* was quite young.

The *staple* went into his finger.
Corn was a *staple* in some Native Americans' diet.

The *frog* jumped into the pool.
He started coughing because he had a *frog* in his throat.

The sunset was fiery *red*.
She has *red* hair.
The fire engine was bright *red*.

The first three sets of examples show that words can have more than one meaning; the last set demonstrates that a word can have multiple shades of meaning, too. Did you not visualize a different color in each of the last three sentences? Almost all words in our language have multiple meanings, yet we use most of them appropriately from a very young age. In fact, we are usually not even aware of our own skill in distinguishing among the possible variations. Think of the common word *up*.

Look *up* at the moon.
Look *up* the word in the dictionary.
Lock *up* the car.
The drain is stopped *up*.
He can't join us because he's tied *up*.

In order to help students develop and expand their vocabularies, teachers must understand how words and their meanings are learned. In addition, they must understand how concepts are stored in memory and how they are accessed for use in appropriate situations.

*Trigger (槍的) 扳机*

## The Relationship of Words and Concepts

In chapter 1 it was noted that words themselves have no meanings; words are simply labels for concepts. When we read, we attempt to match a printed label to a concept in memory; it is the concept that has meaning. The word-label can be thought of as a trigger to access the concept. Thus, a concept must be present before a word for that concept should be taught.

This line of reasoning raises several questions. Can we know something without a language label? For example, can we have a concept for a *chair* and can we access it without using a language label? In other words, is it possible to have an internalized concept in memory without thinking of it in language-related terms? Such questions are important and have led to perspectives that advocate teaching word-labels and concepts together, as opposed to learning the concept first and later attaching a label to it.

Have you ever had the experience of trying to say something and not being able to do so, even though you knew clearly what you were trying to say? Often we say that something is on the tip of our tongue even though we are unable to verbalize it at that moment. This **tip of-the-tongue phenomenon** has been studied and supports the belief that we do have internalized representations of concepts that can be accessed, or triggered, by language (Brown & McNeill, 1966). Thus, the implication is that we can and do know things without a labeling term being accessible at all times. Some theorists argue that thought and language interact (e.g., Vygotsky, 1962), but many others believe that thought precedes language and that concepts are well established before they are labeled (Dehaven, 1988; Ginsburg & Opper, 1969).

*internal 内在的、本質的*

"tip-of-the-tongue" phenomenon: Having a concept and a word in memory, but being unable to access that knowledge at that time.

*接近*

**Primary and Intermediate Grade Level Concerns.** Vocabulary knowledge changes throughout our lives, with new concepts being learned and others

*for primary*

being increasingly refined. Teachers need to be sure that the concept for a new word is known when they attempt to link the word and its concept. In the primary grades students usually have a concept in their speaking vocabulary before they are taught its printed form. Because beginning readers have not yet learned to use decoding strategies, they are still attempting to understand what the "squiggles" on the page represent, and oral vocabulary can be a bridge between written words and concepts. For this reason the vocabulary in traditional published reading programs is controlled to focus on the speaking vocabulary of young children. Thus, vocabulary lessons in the primary grades generally teach the written forms of known concepts. Teachers need to be sure that those words are actually in the children's speaking vocabulary before introducing them in print, but it is not usually necessary to teach the underlying concepts. Although some would argue that such lessons are an exercise in word recognition, most published reading programs label them vocabulary lessons, especially if decoding or word analysis strategies are not included in the instruction.

In later grades children are relatively competent decoders and are confronted with new concepts as well as new word-labels for those concepts, especially in subject areas such as social studies, mathematics, and science. In the intermediate grades and beyond, therefore, teachers must build the new concepts in addition to forging the link between words and concepts. Figure 6–1 illustrates the difference between vocabulary lessons in primary and higher grades. For clarity the figure represents concepts as being either known or unknown, even though in reality students may have a partial idea about what something means. It is really the degree to which something is known that determines whether the concept needs to be taught.

## Factors in the Communication of Meaning

Theorists have noted that it is the commonality of shared experiences within a culture or a social group that allows communication to take place (Carroll, 1964a, 1964b). In other words, individuals communicate by referring to their common experiences. When society accepts a word-label to refer to a particular experience or concept, everyone familiar with that word is then able to access that concept. However, if society has not agreed on a word-label, then communication regarding that concept is difficult or impossible. In addition, if the continuing experiences of different groups cause an underlying concept to be differently perceived, then even a shared word-label may cause confusion!

Thus, when communication fails, any of several factors may be responsible. For example, someone from France and someone from the United States attempting to communicate about a furry domestic animal that meows may not understand each other for one or more of these reasons:

■ There may be no shared experience with such an animal.
■ The two societies or cultures may have evolved a different word-label for such an animal.

FIGURE 6–1
Basic difference in vocabulary instruction in primary (concept known) and
intermediate grades (concept unknown)

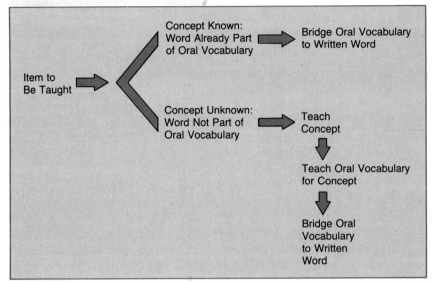

■ The same word-label may represent different concepts in the different societies.

In this case the second reason is the most likely explanation since we know that
people in France also keep cats as pets, and the two countries do speak different
languages. In France such a creature is called *le chat*. Thus, because the two
individuals do not share the same word-label, communication does not take
place.

     In your classroom, you may find students who have difficulty with vo-
cabulary for any of these three reasons: they may not have the relevant concept
as part of their knowledge base; they may have a different label for the targeted
concept; or they may have a somewhat different meaning for the label. Effective teachers must be aware of the diversity in their students' backgrounds and
must ensure that vocabulary lessons are related to students' prior knowledge
and shared experiences.

## BUILDING CONCEPTS

### The Importance of Examples

Examples, which can take many forms, allow students to experience and clarify
meaning and integrate it into existing knowledge (Duffelmeyer, 1985). Teachers should use concrete examples whenever possible and appropriate, and

should provide the opportunity for students to see, touch, smell, and otherwise experience concepts. For abstract concepts, such as truth or beauty, concrete examples may be difficult to provide. In such cases teachers often let character actions from literature serve as examples.

**Experience.** Experience is the most concrete way of teaching a new concept. Often, teachers take their classes on field trips and point out things that will form the basis of a vocabulary lesson when the class returns to school. A field trip need not be an expensive outing; it can be a walk around the block. Direct experience can also be provided by bringing an object into the classroom. It is critical, however, to focus the students' attention; they must actively perceive the object, not simply look at it. As appropriate, the students should have opportunities to touch, see, smell, and otherwise experience the object; and they should be helped to identify features that link the new concept to a familiar one.

**Facsimile.** Often, it is not possible to provide hands-on experience for a new concept. In such cases providing a facsimile can be nearly as effective. Common facsimiles are drawings, photographs, filmstrips, videotapes, and audiotapes related to the object or concept under discussion. Teachers must remember, however, to build the concept actively and not to allow students to be passive observers.

**Discussion.** Although less concrete than experience or a facsimile, a meaningful discussion can lead to understanding and acquisition of a new concept. The discussion must relate to things already a part of students' knowledge, while focusing on the unique features of the new concept. For example, a teacher needing to teach the concept gorilla might begin by asking whether anyone knew of an animal that lived in trees in the jungle. If students suggested a monkey, the teacher might build on that knowledge in further questions: What is a monkey like? What makes a monkey a monkey and not an elephant? The class could then discuss the similarities between monkeys and gorillas and could conclude by establishing similarities and differences between gorillas and other animals.

## Feature Analysis

As infants interact with the world, they encounter many new things, and each new experience adds to conceptual understanding and memory. Initially, however, such concepts may be overgeneralized. If you have had experience with a young child, you may have noticed that for a little while all furry, four-legged animals were called "doggie." The child may have seen a particular furry, four-legged animal that was called doggie and may have generalized that set of features to include any furry, four-legged animal. Later, as the child gained experience with different kinds of animals and focused on finer discriminations, features such as barking, having a cold nose, and chewing bones may have been added, and doggies may have come to include only the appropriate animals.

To see how we use features to discriminate among related items, let's work through a sample exercise. In the blank to the right of each feature, write *all possible* choices from the word list.

dog    cat    horse    poodle    toy dog

1. Has four legs: _____
2. Is alive: _____
3. Eats meat: _____
4. Barks: _____
5. Has a long nose and is often trimmed to have a ball of fur at the end of its tail: _____

This example is not intended as a completely accurate representation of how we identify perceived items, but it illustrates that internalized features do provide a basis for classification. As more features of an item are identified, classes of objects become more narrowly defined. This same process is what enables infants to make fewer overgeneralization errors as they recognize more features.

What you did in the preceding example is a type of **feature analysis**. When linguists analyze words to determine differences in meaning, they often use feature analysis, employing plus and minus signs to indicate the presence or absence of a given feature (Katz, 1972; Leech, 1974; Lyons, 1977).

**feature analysis:** A linguistic method that specifies differences between concepts; can aid understanding of new vocabulary concepts.

| Boy | Man | Girl |
|---|---|---|
| + alive | + alive | + alive |
| + male | + male | − male |
| − adult | + adult | − adult |

A feature analysis chart, developed in a class discussion, often aids students' understanding of a new concept by relating it to concepts they already know. Anders and Bos (1986) point out that feature analysis can be very used in content-area reading with content-specific concepts. Usir proach at various stages (before, during, and after reading) allows relate their already-acquired knowledge to new concepts and inc interest in the selection.

To use feature analysis effectively, teachers need to provide ples that focus on important features of the concept to be acquir should include both positive and negative examples of the con define its boundaries and show how it is both similar to and d already-known concepts. For example, if the concept goblet is to teacher might show and discuss several kinds of drinking vesse also show things similar to but different from goblets—per glasses and bowls. In addition, teachers should be aware that

continually refined as features are identified and clarified; they are not learned on a one-shot basis. Thus, teachers should revisit concepts periodically, both within and across grades.

## Discussion of Features

In this lesson a teacher is trying to relate her students' prior knowledge about different kinds of boats to the new word *canoe*. The word to be learned was chosen because it appears in a story to be read after the vocabulary lesson.

**MODEL LESSON**

1. The teacher shows the class a picture of a rowboat. Pointing to the rowboat, she asks, "Who can tell me what this is?" She writes the students' response on the chalkboard: "boat."
2. Pointing to a picture of a canoe, the teacher says, "Raise your hands if you know what this is called." Three of the eight students in the instructional group raise their hands.
3. The teacher asks one of the students to name the item and receives the response "canoe." She writes *canoe* on the chalkboard beside the word *boat*.
4. The teacher shows the students a picture of a sailboat and asks whether this is also a boat. With a little guidance the students decide that the original word *boat* is not specific enough. They should have called the first boat a rowboat; this one a sailboat. The teacher erases the word *boat* from the chalkboard and replaces it with *rowboat*.
5. The teacher says, "Let's list how a rowboat and a canoe are the same and how they're different. Tell me how they're the same."
6. As the students provide responses, the teacher writes them on the chalkboard in the appropriate columns.

|  | rowboat | canoe |
|---|---|---|
| Same: |  |  |
| Different: |  |  |

Near the end of the discussion, the teacher may write the word *sailboat* to the right of the other two words and ask which of the features already identified apply to the sailboat.

7. The students generate sentences using the word *canoe*. The sentences must reflect the word's meaning and be specific enough that a reader would not confuse it with another kind of boat.

## Use of Context

If we keep in mind that the goal of reading instruction is the comprehension of text, then teaching words as isolated units seems inappropriate. Children need to see that vocabulary is useful. Furthermore, using new vocabulary in meaningful context teaches students that words have particular shades of meaning and play different roles in sentences. Words must therefore be used very carefully.

Context can also be a powerful tool to help readers derive meanings for unfamiliar words. However, we must not assume that all students will understand new concepts simply because they have been used in written context. Contextual interpretations require good language facility and appropriate background knowledge, both of which allow students to relate new, unknown terms to what they already know. Thus, an effective teacher provides or makes explicit appropriate background information before students are expected to use the context clues embedded in a sentence or story.

The three following examples illustrate the limitations of context in clarifying meaning.

1. A common practice, especially when the salvage value is assumed to be zero, is to apply an appropriate percentage, known as the depreciation rate, to the acquisition cost in order to calculate the annual charge (Davidson, Stickney, & Weil, 1980, pp. 13–17).
2. The giraffe, a tall animal with a long neck, lives in Africa.
3. John, the basketball player, is really quite skinny and has red hair and a fair complexion. His friend Sam, however, is corpulent.

If the concepts of salvage value and depreciation rate are not already a part of your background knowledge, it is unlikely that the context clues embedded in the first example will help you with the concept of annual charge. Furthermore, if you know what a giraffe is and have the word in your speaking vocabulary, then the context clues in the second example will probably help. However, if you know nothing about giraffes, you will probably need a picture to acquire the concept. Finally, in the third example there are simply too many possible meanings for *corpulent*. The contrast might be implying that Sam is dark complexioned, does not have red hair, or is not a basketball player, in addition to the correct implication that Sam is overweight.

Despite these limitations, context can be a valuable aid in developing concepts. In addition, as mentioned earlier, it teaches something beyond a word's basic meaning; it shows the way a particular meaning is used in a sentence. Figure 6–2 presents several context exercises to help students internalize a word's function.

It is interesting to note that the instructions in Figure 6–2 never actually state that *clock* is a noun. Memorizing a word's part of speech does little to facilitate proper use of a word and may be confusing and faulty if the word is

FIGURE 6–2
Examples of context exercises to teach the word *clock*

---

1. Modified cloze (fill-in-the blank) procedure:

   Instructions to students: A clock is something used to tell time. It is used in sentences in the same way that the word *boy* is used. Write the word *clock* wherever it appropriately completes the sentence.

   a. Don't touch the _____.
   b. My house is _____.
   c. Bring me the _____.
   d. Where is the _____?

2. Categorization exercises:

   Instructions to students: Circle all the words that can be used in sentences (a) and (b). Underline all the words that can be used in sentences (c) and (d).

          sit   eat   clock   jump   dog   table   go   spoon

   a. She is looking at the _____.
   b. The _____ is in the kitchen.
   c. He will _____ soon.
   d. Don't _____ in the bedroom.

3. Correcting exercises:

   Instructions to students: Put a check mark in front of each sentence in which *clock* is used properly. If *clock* is not used properly, cross it out, choose a word from the following list, and write it on the blank in front of the sentence.

          sit   jump   eat   go

   _____ a. He will <u>clock</u> on the chair.
   _____ b. The <u>clock</u> was on the table.
   _____ c. Look at the <u>clock</u>!
   _____ d. She wants to <u>clock</u> the candy.

---

later used in a different context. If the goal of instruction is students' proper use of new vocabulary in good sentences, then practice in context will be of far more value than memorized parts-of-speech definitions. The activities that follow promote the use of both concrete examples and context. Memorizing parts-of-speech definitions will not transfer easily into students' use of new vocabulary in real-world situations. Use of new words in context will aid such transfer.

*given example is very powerful.*

**Experiencing New Concepts.** Have students see, touch, smell, taste, and use an item as appropriate, and then discuss the name and the features of the item being experienced.

Have students walk around the school yard with you. Stop periodically to write a word on a notepad, and discuss it before moving on. Follow up by using these words in language-related classroom activities. (This activity can be done as part of any field trip.)

**SAMPLE ACTIVITIES**

**Using Facsimiles.** Using a picture, videotape, movie, audiotape, or other secondary source, have students focus closely on the features of the item in the facsimile. Discuss the item's size, looks, possible uses, and so on.

**Using Context.** During discussion of a new vocabulary item, have students close their eyes. Present a detailed, verbal picture of the concept. Then, after students open their eyes, link the concept to the written form of the word. Finally, give sentences with the target word omitted, and let students supply it to see how the word is used in context.

*computer*

*concepts term ⟹ teach vocabulary { classic, property — machine*
*feature — math, record*
*examples — IBM PC*

## DECIDING WHAT TO TEACH

### Types of Words

Vocabulary can be divided into two general types: function words and content words. Figure 6–3 illustrates these two categories and a subcategory called content-specific words and provides examples of each.

**Function Words.** **Function words** are often called the glue that holds a sentence together. Frequently occurring words such as articles (e.g., *a, an, the*), conjunctions (e.g., *and, but, or*), prepositions (e.g., *at, into, over,*), and auxiliary verbs (e.g., *could* run, *had* snowed) are function words. They make a sentence cohesive, linking words and phrases so that understanding can occur. Function words are frequently irregular in spelling and/or pronunciation. And if taught out of context, they can be difficult for young children to conceptualize, because the concepts they represent are not concrete. Although there are times when it is appropriate to present words in isolation (e.g., when discussing the "context" of a prefix), this text advocates teaching all vocabulary in context. Context generally serves to clarify meaning.

function words: Words that facilitate comprehension by connecting other words and phrases.

**Content Words.** **Content words** such as nouns (e.g., *house, car*), pronouns (e.g., *I, his, they*), verbs (e.g., *run, swim*), adjectives (e.g., *hot, sticky*), and adverbs (e.g., *then, neatly, suddenly*) have concrete meanings. Everyday content words, such as *dog* or *car,* are sometimes called general vocabulary words.

content words: Words with definitions in general use in everyday language.

② *procedure term : procedure steps*

FIGURE 6–3
Different categories of vocabulary

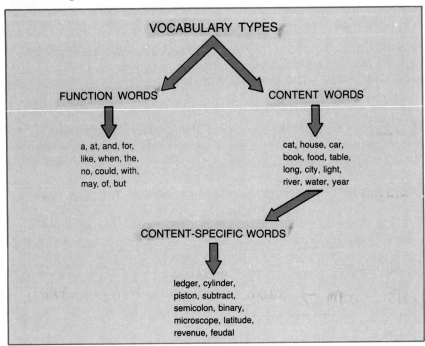

However, the same word can have both general and specific meanings, depending on the context in which it is used.

> The *race* was run yesterday.
> The Asian *race* has a long and fascinating history.

Again, vocabulary requires context to clarify meaning, and teachers cannot assume that students know any meanings other than those they appropriately demonstrate in context.

**content-specific words:** Words with definitions specific to a content area; words that are not used in everyday language.

**Content-Specific Words. Content-specific words** always have specialized meanings within a particular subject area and must be learned within the context of that area. For example, *beaker* and *isotherm* do not have general-meaning counterparts; they have meaning only in their subject area—in this case, science. Especially in the middle grades, teachers should spend time teaching their students the meanings of words that are apt to be encountered in their reading material. In subject areas like science, social studies, and mathematics, words often have content-specific meanings, and not knowing those meanings can make comprehension impossible. Chapter 10 deals with this issue in more depth.

When reading, students encounter function words, content words, and content-specific words.

## Selection of Vocabulary Items

In general, teachers select the vocabulary they will teach from three sources.

1. graded word lists
2. words that students will encounter in current reading materials
3. words used by students in their natural, oral language

Although teachers may use all three sources, they generally draw from one most heavily.

There are many published word lists available that indicate the frequency of words encountered by students at specific grade levels. These lists are usually developed from an analysis of reading materials, including textbooks, that children are expected to read in each grade. Teachers who systematically use such a list generally construct pretests and then teach the specific words that students do not know. Some common lists are identified here:

E. Dale and J. O'Rourke, *Living Word Vocabulary: The Words We Know* (Elgin, IL: Dome, 1976)

E. B. Fry, J. K. Polk, and D. Fountoukidis, *The New Reading Teacher's Book of Lists* (2nd ed.) (Englewood Cliffs, NJ: Prentice Hall, 1985).

A. J. Harris and M. D. Jacobson, *Basic Reading Vocabularies* (New York: Macmillan, 1982)

R. J. Marzano and J. S. Marzano, *A Cluster Approach to Elementary Vocabulary Instruction* (Newark, DE: International Reading Association, 1988)

Word lists can provide much useful information, such as the number of students at a given grade level who do not know a specific word or a frequency ordering of words encountered by students in elementary reading materials. There are also lists of roots, prefixes, suffixes, synonyms, antonyms, homophones, commonly misspelled words, and so on. Such lists can provide words that are conceptually or semantically related (e.g., Marzano & Marzano's list) as well as words that might be specific to regional or cultural areas (e.g., Gunderson, 1984). Systematic teaching from a list, however, means that the words taught may not match the words students find in their reading.

The second source of vocabulary items is based on the philosophy that vocabulary is best learned and retained when the items to be learned occur in real, meaningful situations. Consequently, vocabulary identified as critical to students' understanding of an upcoming passage or story is pretaught. With this approach someone must determine which words in the text are important for overall understanding of the passage. Sometimes this task is accomplished for the teacher; for example, teacher's guides often present a list of words introduced in each unit or each story, with the expectation that teachers will focus on those new and important words.

One possible disadvantage of using this vocabulary source is that not all reading materials introduce the same vocabulary at identical grade levels. In fact, Harris and Jacobson (1982) showed that words introduced in different basal readers can vary by as much as five grade levels. In our highly mobile society, where a significant number of children change school districts and instructional materials from one year to the next, differences in vocabulary acquisition can easily occur. Thus, teachers must always remember that students will have been taught using a variety of materials, and will not have been exposed to a similar or core set of vocabulary.

The third vocabulary source centers around the students' use of oral language and is closely related to the language experience approach discussed in chapter 3. A teacher might have a student dictate a story, which the teacher writes down. That story then forms the basis of vocabulary instruction. The teacher can point out synonyms that might be appropriate substitutions for some of the student's words. In addition, having the child attempt to read the dictated story may show that certain words are in the student's speaking but not reading vocabulary and should therefore by targeted for instruction. This approach is highly motivational and helps forge a link between already-known concepts and print. Nonetheless, using a child's oral language as a base for vocabulary lessons is sometimes criticized because only known concepts are used. The sample activities that follow are intended to expand a child's vocabulary while using oral language as a foundation.

**Logical Cloze.** Transcribe a story provided by a student(s). Then present logical replacements for some of the original words, teach and discuss the new words and ask the children to place them in the appropriate blanks. For example, the words to be taught might be *morning, cape, previous,* and *annoyed*.

**SAMPLE ACTIVITIES**

字典, 百科全書
[θɪˈsɔrəs]

The girl was on her way to school. It was a rainy day _____, and she had her raincoat _____ and her umbrella with her. She hoped that she wouldn't forget her umbrella at school like she did the last _____ time. Her mother was upset _____ with her when she didn't bring her umbrella home.

**Thesaurus Detective.** After students have mastered the skills necessary to use a thesaurus, cut pages out of a newspaper and have students work in pairs. Within each pair have one student circle five familiar words that the other student is to replace with words found in a thesaurus. Then have students read the words to each other one at a time, with the listener attempting to provide the meaning of the synonym and the original word.

## Pretesting

Since students do not have identical needs when it comes to vocabulary instruction, a quick and informal pretest of new or necessary terms may help identify those students who will benefit from instruction. Although it may be desirable to reinforce previously taught vocabulary, it is not a good use of time or resources to teach already-known words. Thus, pretesting makes teaching more effective, interesting, and relevant, and it also helps to prevent student boredom or frustration. Here are several ways to quickly test students' vocabulary knowledge.

**Oral Question.** Who knows what _____ means? (This is perhaps the most common, yet least effective, approach because not all students respond.)

**Oral (or Written) Expression.** Say (or write) _____ in a sentence.

**Matching Activity.** Match the word with the meaning.

**SAMPLE ACTIVITIES**

    a. house _____      1. grows in the garden
    b. flower _____     2. a place to live

**Fill in the Blank.** Using the choices provided, write the appropriate word in each sentence.

house          flower

a. The _____ grows in the garden.

b. The _____ has three bedrooms.

**Multiple Choice.** Choose the best meaning for each word.

house

a. a place to live

b. something to eat

c. a large animal

---

Once pretest results are known, it may be difficult to decide how to group students for instruction. One student may not know any of the words to be taught, another may know all but three, and still another may know all but a different three. Logistically, it is impossible to teach individual vocabulary lessons to each student, but groups can be formed to minimize the ratio of known to unknown words. For example, let's imagine that five words are to be taught (1, 2, 3, 4, 5) to a group of five students (A, B, C, D, E). The teacher performs a brief pretest and decides on this arrangement.

| Student | Unknown Words | Group Placement |
|---------|---------------|-----------------|
| A | 1, 2 | 1 |
| B | 3, 4, 5 | 2 |
| C | 1, 2, 3 | 1 |
| D | 1, 3, 5 | 2 |
| E | 4 | 1 |

With this grouping, students in Group 1 are exposed to a maximum of two already-known words; those in Group 2, only one. Teaching the five students as one group would have resulted in exposure to as many as four already-known words (for student E).

This example shows that pretesting does not result in perfect matches, but it can help target vocabulary instruction. The example may seem unrealistic because of the relatively low number of already-known words included in the grouping arrangements. But in reality, when more words are presented to a greater number of students, grouping does substantially reduce the number of already-known words that are taught.

## DECIDING HOW TO TEACH

### General Principles

There are some general principles that apply to all vocabulary instruction, regardless of grade level. Nagy (1988) points out that effective vocabulary instruction has three components.

1. *Integration.* Teaching strategies must use methods that integrate the concept to be learned with existing knowledge.
2. *Repetition.* Teaching strategies should provide sufficient practice so that meaning is accessed automatically, without the need to decode the word during reading. This level of familiarity requires many encounters with a new word—certainly far more than the number of repetitions necessary just to learn a definition.
3. *Meaningful use.* Teaching strategies should provide opportunities for students to use a new concept and word in context rather than in isolation. This approach facilitates inferencing and allows for repetitive practice that is interesting and motivational.

Other common strategies include revisiting words that are learned over a period of time. Although words receive the greatest attention during the initial teaching phase, students need to revisit them periodically. This task is simplified if students collect vocabulary words in some form as they are learned. For example, students might maintain a **word bank** or a special section of a notebook. Periodically, then, teachers could remind students to use words from their word banks or notebooks in their writing or in other meaningful activities.

**word bank:** A place to organize word cards and a means to help develop decoding and vocabulary knowledge.

Certain differences are apparent in the vocabulary instruction in whole language classrooms. Teachers in those classrooms often present vocabulary instruction as an **incidental learning** experience, consciously using new vocabulary during morning message time (see chapter 4), story reading, conversations, or functional writing activities, for example. Students' attention is then drawn to the new words, and follow-up activities—writing tasks, dictation, and other literacy activities—allow students to practice writing, seeing, and hearing the words in context (see Noyce & Christie, 1989, for a discussion of the value of copying and dictation activities).

**incidental learning:** Learning that takes place without direct instruction, often as part of everyday routines.

**DECISION POINT ➤**

Some people believe strongly that incidental learning is very effective, especially as practiced in whole language classrooms. Although it is not yet possible to say whether vocabulary instruction is more or less effective in whole language classrooms, there is some evidence that first-grade children in such classrooms generate vocabulary at least comparable to that used in published reading programs (Shapiro & Gunderson, 1988) and that listening to stories contributes significantly to vocabulary acquisition (Elley, 1989). However, there is also evidence suggesting that direct instruction in word meanings should be combined with such approaches (Jenkins, Matlock, & Slocum, 1989). Given the lack of any clear directive from research, how will you choose to teach vocabulary?

## Conceptual Links

Research does indicate that certain concepts are closely linked with each other (Adams & Collins, 1979; Anderson, Reynolds, Schallert, & Goetz, 1977). For example, if people are asked to say the first word that comes to mind when they are presented with List A, most will respond with the words in List B.

| A | B |
|---|---|
| mother | father |
| boy | girl |
| man | woman |
| dog | cat |
| day | night |

schema theory: A theory about knowledge that says objects and their relationships form a network in memory.

Moreover, research in **schema theory** implies that there are sets, or networks, of concepts that appear to help trigger each other (Anderson & Pearson, 1984; Anderson, 1985). For instance, a person given the stimulus word *restaurant* is more apt to respond with *menu, food,* or *waiter* than with *car* or *television*.

Notice that although the words in the lists are opposites, they are in the same domain—that is, parents, children, and so on. This supports the notion that associated concepts might be stored in memory as being related, and that accessing one concept in a linked network helps to access others that are associated with it. Nagy and Scott's (1990) research in word schemas also implies that schemas for words in general are applied to the learning of new words and their parts of speech. Thus, these research findings support instructional practices that attempt to link words into meaningful networks rather than teaching each word separately. This can be done in a variety of ways, but one common option is teaching in thematic units, as discussed below.

thematic units: Conceptual clusters used in vocabulary instruction.

**Thematic Units.** The fact that concepts seem to cluster—that is, that one concept seems to facilitate access to related concepts—implies that vocabulary might be effectively presented in **thematic units**. Figure 6–4 presents a thematic practice activity that is common in commercially available materials. This activity is intended for children in kindergarten or beginning first grade; their task is to match the picture to the appropriate word and then write that word in the puzzle. Such activities are worthwhile since they allow the matching of word-labels and picture clues, and also provide an opportunity for students to write the words even though teachers will need to add contextual activities. It is also important to relate words to each other within sentences and stories. The model lesson that follows presents one popular and effective way of teaching vocabulary by linking meanings within a coherent context.

FIGURE 6-4
A thematic practice activity

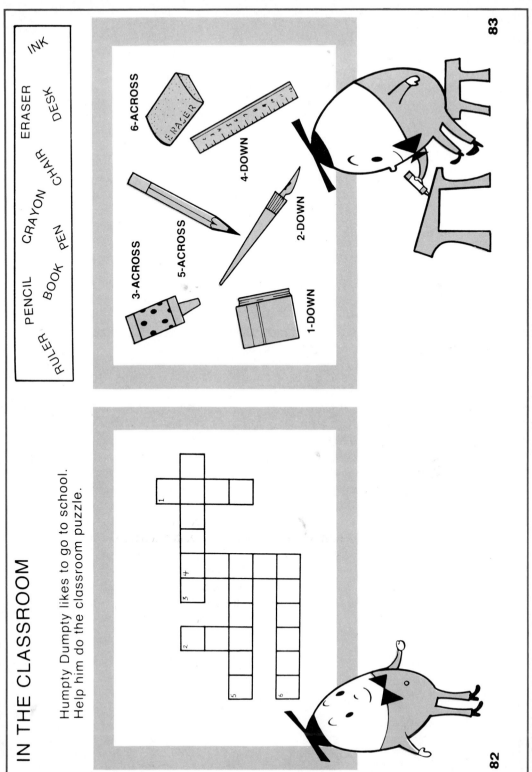

# IN THE CLASSROOM

Humpty Dumpty likes to go to school.
Help him do the classroom puzzle.

RULER  PENCIL  CRAYON  ERASER  INK
BOOK  PEN  CHAIR  DESK

3-ACROSS
5-ACROSS
6-ACROSS
4-DOWN
2-DOWN
1-DOWN

82

83

**Source:** From Gilda Waldman, *The Big Book of Puzzles* (New York: Playmore, 1976), pp. 82–83. Reprinted by permission.

**MODEL
LESSON**

Linking Vocabulary in Thematic Contexts

1. Discuss the following words with students—what they mean, how they might be related to each other, and so on.

    barn    difficult    handle    horse    cheerful

2. Have students write a brief story, as a class or individually, that uses the target words. The example included here was suggested by a group of four first-grade students. As each student presented the teacher with an oral sentence, the teacher wrote it on the chalkboard, and the students copied it in their notebooks. The last sentence was provided by the teacher; the title was determined after the story was completed.

### The Cheerful Horse

There was a cheerful horse who lived in a barn. The horse was cheerful because he got to live in a big barn and had lots to eat. There was a big handle on the door of the barn. It was difficult to turn. The horse was cheerful because his barn was beautiful.

3. Have students underline the vocabulary words. Discuss the words' appropriate contextual use.

---

**Concept Webs.** Webs of related concepts can also be use to present vocabulary. For example, restaurant terms might be diagrammed as a web, with the central component being the most general or generic concept and outlying components representing increasing detail or specificity. The amount of detail in such a concept, or semantic, web varies according to the level of students. The following is a reasonably complex semantic web.

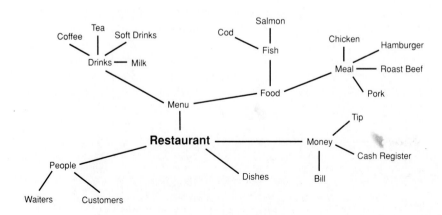

Discussion based on a concept web, which visually links concepts, is an effective vocabulary-teaching technique.

Semantic webs are most effective when discussion specifically relates to students' background knowledge, explains the concepts behind the words used, and corrects students' misunderstandings (Stahl & Vancil, 1986). In addition, a concept web can contain both known and new concepts, allowing connections to be highlighted between the two (Johnson, Pittleman, & Heimlich, 1986). Teachers interested in concept webs should find Marzano and Marzano's (1988) cluster approach helpful. Those authors have organized more than 7,000 words into semantically related clusters, and they present a number of webbing approaches to the teaching of those words. Additional approaches to semantic webbing have been provided by Heimlich and Pittleman (1986).

**Synonyms.** We know that individuals use their interpretive abilities to remember things that were not specifically stated in what they read. For example, look at the following sentence:

The woman was outstanding in the theater.

Readers who are presented with such a sentence often believe that the word *actress* was used in the sentence. Their response suggests that readers remember the essence of what they have read, not the particulars. The process of remembering the key idea as it fits the context has been called **instantiation** (Anderson, Pichert, Goetz, Schallert, Stevens, & Trollip, 1976). Related research has provided a rationale for using synonyms—in addition to appropriate, logically related examples—in vocabulary instruction. If you were teaching the word *hammer,* for instance, you might say something like this:

> He hit the nail with a _____ .
> What word fits in the blank? What other words could be used? Which is most appropriate? Why? What do all the words have in common?

You might also approach it this way:

> He hit the nail with the hammer.
> What other words could be used instead of *hammer* (e.g., *rock, wrench,* and so on)? Why could we use those other words? Why might *hammer* be the best choice? Where might a hammer be found?

Such discussion methods use children's prior knowledge and help them place the new concept into a network of similar items (e.g., tools, or items used to hammer), thus facilitating learning.

**Analogies and Continuums.** Analogies and continuums use known concepts to build new ones, implying that knowledge is organized in a series of related, linked concepts. Using analogies to teach students new words and their uses is appropriate at all grade levels. Students are presented with items such as these:

> *Pipe* is to *water* as *conductor* is to *electricity.*

> *Dog* is to *puppy* as *horse* is to *foal.*

Used with discussion, analogies foster concept development because they show the relationship between known items and incorporate one unknown item (in these examples *conductor* and *foal*) in such a way that students are able to infer the unknown meaning. Teachers must be sure that all other words in the analogy are known and should focus discussion on the relationship within the familiar half of the analogy. Questions about the relationship on the other side of the analogy should then follow naturally.

Continuums, which include meanings that are known as well as one or more to be taught, also facilitate vocabulary development by using prior knowledge. For example, students might be shown the following:

> scream        shout        speak        murmur        whisper

Discussion of the change in gradation of meaning from left to right presents a scheme in which students can fit the new term—in this case, *murmur.*

## Use of Word Parts

Although knowledge of word parts aids word recognition, it also helps readers discover the meanings of words and thus expand their vocabularies. When readers use word parts as clues to meaning, they are using their knowledge about affixes (prefixes and suffixes) and root words. **Morphemes,** the smallest meaningful parts of language, include prefixes, suffixes, and root words. For example, these words each contain one morpheme:

morphemes: Prefixes, suffixes, and roots.

play       run       cow

These words contain two morphemes each:

playful       rerun       cows

Knowing the meanings of common prefixes and suffixes can help determine word meanings. For instance, knowing that the prefix *non-* means "not" or "no" helps a reader understand words like *nonprofit, nonsense,* and *nonstop*.

Prefixes, suffixes, and roots are often taught as vocabulary items in reading instruction. Although teaching all affixes and roots is impossible, teaching the most common ones is worthwhile. There are many published lists that contain the most useful morphemes—for example, Fry, Polk, and Fountoukidis's *The New Reading Teacher's Book of Lists* (Englewood Cliffs, NJ: Prentice Hall, 1985). In addition, you will be able to use activities such as the following to teach affixes and roots.

---

**Affix Deletion.** Write several sentences containing words with the same affix.

He had to <u>reheat</u> the food because it had cooled down.

After she used the towel, Mary had to <u>refold</u> it.

Since the color came out of his shirt when it was washed, Sam had to <u>redye</u> it.

Have students state the meaning of each underlined word. Then cross out the affix and discuss how the meaning of the word has changed. Finally, agree on the meaning of the affix.

**Affix Addition.** Change the previous activity by using the key words without affixes and requiring the students to add them. Present the activity like this:

*Re-* is a prefix that means again. Use it to revise the underlined words in the sentences.

1. He had to <u>heat</u> the food <u>again</u> because it had cooled down.
2. After she used the towel, Mary had to <u>fold</u> it <u>again</u>.
3. Since the color came out of his shirt when it was washed, Sam had to <u>dye</u> it <u>again</u>.

**SAMPLE ACTIVITIES**

Discuss with students that the prefix *un* means "not" and can have a strong influence on meaning. Present this example:

They were welcome at the picnic.

Then tell students to add *un-* to an important word in the sentence, and discuss what happens to the meaning of the entire sentence.

**Root Word Addition.** Write affixes on the chalkboard, and have students supply root words.

| -less (without) | -en (like) |
|---|---|
| care[less] | wool[en] |
| thought[less] | gold[en] |
| hope[less] | wood[en] |

**Affix and Root Word Hunt.** Have students look through a reading selection and circle certain prefixes, suffixes, and/or roots. Then have students present their findings, explaining how the meanings of the words would have been different if the prefix or suffix had not been used.

## Dictionaries

Although dictionary definitions are of relatively minor importance in teaching word meanings, dictionaries can be used to create vocabulary learning experiences. They are also reference sources for students during independent reading activities. However, they should not be the basis for curriculum decisions. Hirsch's (1989) *First Dictionary of Cultural Literacy* has been closely tied to assessment and is sometimes referred to as the basis for a conceptual curriculum. Unfortunately, assessing words or concepts in isolation often results in the mistaken notion that the concepts are unknown. Essentially, any attempt to judge conceptual understanding without the use of supporting context is inappropriate, especially when complex or abstract concepts are involved.

Dictionaries can be used at all grade levels: there are many attractive and useful dictionaries aimed at elementary-aged students, beginning with picture dictionaries. Such dictionaries make effective use of color, drawings, photos, and other visual aids to explain and define concepts. Popular primary dictionaries include these two:

W. D. Halsey, *First Dictionary* (New York: Macmillan, 1987)
W. A. Jenkins and A. Schiller, *My First Picture Dictionary* (Glenview, IL: Scott, Foresman, 1982)

Nonetheless, we need to remember that using a dictionary to look up an unknown word's meaning requires a number of skills. For example, a child must (1) be able to alphabetize by at least the first letter of a word; (2) be able to locate a word without turning every page of the dictionary; (3) be able to

Dictionary games can build vocabulary knowledge if children have necessary background skills.

associate word and meaning; (4) be aware that a word often has more than one meaning; and (5) use context to select one meaning from alternatives. If these skills are present, the dictionary can be a useful tool, especially as students encounter unfamiliar words in content-area subjects. However, dictionary definitions generally need to be discussed, used in meaningful examples, and related to students' prior knowledge.

To teach your students the value of using a dictionary, you can model its use and draw students' attention to the reason the dictionary is being consulted. Modeling the use of a thesaurus and a glossary is also effective. Modeling can result in students' using these tools independently when they find new words in reading assignments. Certainly, a dictionary written at an appropriate level should be available for student use in each classroom.

**Modeling.** Pick an interesting, unknown word and use it incidentally during the day. Say something like this: "Yesterday I heard someone say that he really doesn't like canines. I'd like you to help me look that up in the dictionary and see what *canine* means." Then have students help you find the word in the dictionary, read the meaning, and relate it to previous knowledge.

**Finding Correct Meanings.** Present sentences like "He put the fish on the *scale* to find out how heavy it was" and "Her wedding dress had a long *train*." Have students find the words in the dictionary and decide which of the listed meanings make sense in the sentence context.

**SAMPLE ACTIVITIES**

## Learning Centers

learning center: A class-room location where in-structional materials are used independently by stu-dents.

A **learning center** is an area in a classroom that contains a variety of instruc-tional materials dealing with a specific goal or objective. Because it is often used independently by students, provisions are usually made for self-evaluation. Such a center lends itself to vocabulary instruction, whether in thematic units or not.

A learning center, sometimes called an activity center or a learning station, contains a set of activities designed to build specific skills. Since students work independently, they must be aware of acceptable behavior at the center and must also be aware of the goal of the activities. Careful planning is required to create an effective learning center. Huff (1983) and Sherfey and Huff (1976) suggest that the following steps be considered in planning a learn-ing center.

1. Clearly define the center's purposes.
2. Consider the characteristics and the needs of students who will be using the center.
3. Define the concepts and skills to be developed in the center.
4. Outline expected learning outcomes.
5. Select appropriate activities and materials.
6. Evaluate the center.
7. Implement needed changes.

Children can use learning centers individually or in small groups but should spend no more than 15 minutes there at a time. The center should be sturdy enough to withstand classroom use and should include a variety of activities focused on the targeted concept. A learning center can be many things, rang-ing from teacher-made posterboard items through baskets of materials that children use to complete appropriate activities, to a microcomputer and soft-ware. The critical component is how the center is related to overall instruc-tional goals. When well-planned and carefully implemented, learning centers represent an efficient use of a teacher's time.

## Response Cards

response cards: Cards that provide a teacher with im-mediate information about a child's response.

Another useful and efficient activity in vocabulary instruction and evaluation uses true-false and A-B-C **response cards** to replace papers and pencils. For this activity teachers should print one to three vocabulary words on cards, along with a response choice. The single-word cards are used with true-false re-sponses; the multiple-word cards prompt a response of A, B, or C. The single-word card can also be used as a vocabulary flash card. Students can also perform response-card activities in pairs, using words from their word banks. Figure 6–5 shows both types of cards; the model lesson that follows outlines the procedure.

FIGURE 6–5
Response cards for use in vocabulary instruction

## Response Cards

1. Ask students to tear a piece of paper into either two (for true-false activities) or three (for A-B-C activities) parts and write either *true* and *false* or *A, B,* and *C* on their papers.
2. Check your vocabulary cards to be sure that the words themselves, as well as statements or clues, appear on the backs of the cards. The process needs to flow smoothly.
3. For the true-false activity, hold up a single-word vocabulary card, and provide a statement or phrase about the word that is either true or false. For example, for the word *smoke* you might say, "Something that is usually present with a fire" or "Something we eat." Have children hold up their *true* or *false* paper in response.
4. For the word-choice activity hold up a multiword vocabulary card, and provide context clues to help students choose the appropriate word from the card. Have students hold up their A, B, or C paper to match the letter under the word that they think is correct.

**MODEL
LESSON**

This simple procedure can be modified easily, yet it remains valuable for several reasons.

■ Children are not self-conscious about responding. Since the response is not oral and all students face the teacher, other students cannot see an incorrect response.
■ Teachers do not spend time grading papers or worksheets but gain an overview of student comprehension. With a class list of names handy, teachers

can quickly note the students who show problems with certain words and need individual help.

■ The cards are inexpensive, easy to make, and simple for students to copy for their word banks.

■ The activity provides a quick way to review and reinforce previously presented vocabulary.


## TWO SPECIAL CASES

### Homonyms

There is often confusion in terminology about what to call words that sound the same. Because there is a difference between words that are identical in sound and spelling and words that sound the same but are spelled differently, you should learn the following precise terms. Calling them all homonyms is inaccurate and can lead to instructional confusion. Learning the precise terms will help you when you encounter them in teacher's guides.

homophones: Words with the same pronunciation but different spellings and meanings.

| **Homophones** | Words that sound alike, are spelled differently, and mean different things (e.g., "He *led* his horse." "It looked like *lead*.") |
|---|---|

homographs: Words with the same spellings but different pronunciation and meanings.

| **Homographs** | Words that do not sound alike, are spelled alike, and mean different things (e.g., "He *read* the book." "He will *read* the book.") |
|---|---|

homonyms: Words with the same pronunciation and spelling but different meanings.

| **Homonyms** | Words that sound alike, are spelled alike, and mean different things (e.g., "the bathroom *scale*"; "the fish *scale*." |
|---|---|

Homonyms present an interesting methodological challenge to the teacher. Since neither the written (graphemic) nor the oral (phonological) form of a homonym changes between meanings, young children sometimes become confused when the two meanings are presented together, especially when a teacher focuses attention on the known meaning and then tells students to learn the new meaning (Kinzer, 1982). In fact, research has shown that children who are unable to perform cognitive tasks associated with multiple class membership do better when not asked to focus on the meaning they already know (Kinzer, 1981).

As students develop, it may be appropriate to teach new meanings for homonyms by relating each new meaning to a common word-label and an already-known meaning. But with children in the primary grades, teachers must tread carefully. If the goal is to teach a new meaning for a homonym, then learning the meaning is more important than realizing that the word is a homonym. Thus, teachers in the lower grades should teach new meanings of homonyms in the same way that they teach normal words with single meanings.

The suggestion here is not that young students cannot use words in more than one way or with more than one meaning. Children know at an early age that an airplane can fly and that a fly is a sometimes-bothersome insect. The confusion results when young children are asked to become consciously aware that the label for two separate concepts is the same; young students seem to believe instead that the two words are separate items even though they sound the same. This ability to see similarity and difference across several dimensions at the same time appears to be unavailable until children can comprehend membership in multiple classes. In time, the ability to perceive multiple meanings with similar labels develops naturally.

## Referential Terms

Certain vocabulary terms have **referential properties** and can be fully understood only through experiential knowledge (Murphy, 1986). In other words, experiences with language clarify certain references that are not explicitly stated. Consider the following examples, and try to decide where Steve is physically located.

> referential properties: Word characteristics requiring readers or listeners to use background to determine what item is being mentioned.

1. On the telephone, Steve says, "Come to my house tonight."
2. On the telephone, Steve says, "Go to my house tonight."

Now try to decide where the food is physically located.

3. Sally, Bill, and Tom are sitting at a table. Sally says to Tom, "He has the food."
4. Sally, Bill, and Tom are sitting at a table. Sally says to Tom, "The food is over here."
5. Sally, Bill, and Tom are sitting at a table. Sally says to Tom, "The food is over there."

You probably decided correctly that Steve was at home while on the telephone in the first example and not at home in the second. In 3 Bill had the food, in 4 it was near Sally, and in 5 it was not near Sally. Your ability to specify the locations in these examples indicates your facility with one kind of reference—place reference. Other forms of reference and their effects on comprehension of text are discussed in the next chapter.

For our purposes here it is important to note that referential terms can cause great difficulty for young children, and teachers must be aware that vocabulary items often have referential meanings that go beyond the words' literal use. With such terms it is not enough to explain word meanings. Discussion must develop the students' understanding of the referential nature of the terms and should include several examples of their use.

**SAMPLE
ACTIVITIES**

**Pronoun Examples.** Use examples to teach pronoun reference in a number of sentence structures. Use sentence pairs like these:

1a. The teacher gave both Sue and Joyce *erasers,* even though the girls didn't need *them.*
 b. Even though the girls didn't need *them,* the teacher gave both Sue and Joyce *erasers.*
2a. *Chris* wanted a drink of water because *she* was thirsty.
 b. Because *she* was thirty, *Chris* wanted a drink of water.
3a. Bill said *the bike was new,* but Tipp did not believe *it.*
 b. Tipp did not believe *it,* but Bill said *the bike was new.*

Discuss with the students that some referential terms can refer to items in front of them or behind them. Also, draw attention to the fact that referential terms can refer to one or more words, a phrase, a clause, or a sentence.

**Extending Sentences.** Present a gradual sentence expansion, leading ultimately to the replacement of one or more parts of the sentence with a referential term(s).

> Susie eats.
> Susie eats lunch.
> Willy eats lunch.
> Susie and Willy eat lunch.
> *They* eat lunch.
> Susie and Willy eat *it*.
> *They* eat *it*.

---

Part of the difficulty children have in understanding referential terms is related to their cognitive level and to the differences between oral and written language. We know that children's understanding of time and place does not develop fully until about the third grade (Bybee & Sund, 1982; Lowery, 1981). In addition, written language loses the physical clarifiers of oral communication. For example, in speech the sentence "The food is over there" or "He has the food" is usually accompanied by some form of head motion or gesture, such as pointing, which clarifies meaning and makes it more concrete. Saying that print is speech written down is an inaccurate simplification. In text, for instance, quotation marks are intended to aid meaning but can also cause confusion. Try to locate the food in this example:

> Sally said, "Tom said, 'The food is here.'"

Thus, cognitive development and differences between oral and written language combine to produce confusion when children are asked to comprehend referential vocabulary terms in text.

*Mary had a little lamb. Its fleece was white as snow.*

## COMMENTS FROM THE CLASSROOM ■

### Emily Dodson

I think we can all agree that vocabulary knowledge is one of the most important things for readers to develop, yet Mr. Burns, Ms. Sanchez, and I teach vocabulary very differently. I emphasize the vocabulary found in the students' reading selections and in our class experiences—field trips, for example—but I also draw from lists that contain conceptually difficult words found in second-grade reading material. Since I believe that readers use multiple strategies to acquire vocabulary, my lessons include a wide range of methods. At different times I use affixes and root words, as well as analogies, synonyms, semantic webs, and context, always trying to integrate vocabulary items into the students' background knowledge. I guess I use almost all of the techniques I know about at some point. I do believe that students acquire a lot of vocabulary knowledge from reading, but I also believe that certain vocabulary words—those that are conceptually difficult or critical to the understanding of a reading selection—have to be intensively taught.

When teaching vocabulary, I try to group students for instruction. Grouping lets me avoid unnecessary teaching of students who already know certain words and also allows me to use certain activities in cooperative learning, brainstorming situations. When I'm using procedures like feature analysis, semantic mapping, or continuums, for example, I often begin a discussion and then let students brainstorm and complete the activity on their own. When they're finished, each group presents its completed map or feature analysis to the rest of the class.

### Mr. Burns

Most of my vocabulary words come from the suggested word lists in the published reading program I use. I think I can rely on the program to identify important words and provide appropriate teaching suggestions. I'm especially glad that the program gives pretesting suggestions; I use pretests whenever they're recommended, and I group my students by the results. I do teach some other vocabulary—words from field trips, for example—but that's a small part of my program. The most important thing from my text-based perspective, is for my students to know the words they'll be meeting in upcoming reading selections.

I usually follow the activities suggested by my teacher's guide, but I also try to provide examples that are similar to the context in which the words appear in the stories. Because I think specific skills are the best way to develop reading ability, I often teach vocabulary by focusing on word parts, pointing to a word's configuration and spelling, along with its prefix, suffix, and root. I think prefixes and suffixes are so important that I teach affixes, root words, and dictionary use as separate skills to be mastered, as well as strategies for vocabulary development.

### Ms. Sanchez

In my classroom, students learn vocabulary incidentally. That is, they learn vocabulary by interacting with print—when I read to them, when they read on their own, or when we do meaningful activities related to reading and writing.

If I believe that a concept is absolutely vital to understanding a story and contextual support is lacking, I may teach vocabulary directly, but I *always* begin with the students' knowledge of related concepts. Then I expand on areas of overlap between already-known concepts and the one to be learned—often through semantic webs and analogies—until the new concept becomes part of my students' knowledge base. Synonyms also play a large part in my vocabulary instruction, and I encourage my students to use the new terms in situations that are already known to them. I rarely focus on word parts such as affixes, and I rarely use dictionary definitions in my vocabulary teaching.

A major difference between my colleagues and me is that I use most of my vocabulary time in real-language settings, usually using inductive methods. I always present vocabulary in context, using experiential techniques, demonstrations, and oral discussion as much as possible. For example, I often use a language experience approach: I might introduce a vivid picture and then teach the vocabulary that pertains to it. If the picture contained a very large building, for instance, I might teach the word *enormous* in the context of the picture. Then I'd probably encourage the children to use the word in a language experience story based on the picture. But I still rely mainly on independent reading activities.

## MAJOR POINTS

■ In the primary grades teachers generally teach the words for already-known concepts. In intermediate grades and beyond, teachers generally teach both concepts and their word-labels.

■ Before presenting an unknown word, teachers should teach the concept represented by the word.

■ Vocabulary lessons can be based on word lists, reading materials, children's oral language, or any combination of these three sources.

■ When teaching vocabulary, teachers should give concrete examples as much as possible. It is also helpful to compare the features of the unknown items to those of similar, known items.

■ Vocabulary activities should include many varied examples of the unknown concept in context.

■ Homonyms and referential terms can be difficult for children in lower elementary grades to learn.

■ Vocabulary growth continues throughout life, as known terms are refined and new terms are added.

## MAKING INSTRUCTIONAL DECISIONS

1. The following words can be categorized as function (List A), content (List B), and content-specific (List C) words.

| is | car | cat | at |
| shelf | that | cumulus | molecule |
| beaker | table | microchip | and |

Two examples of each list have already been provided, one of which comes from the words presented here. Place each of the remaining words into one of the three lists. Then explain how you might teach the words from each list differently and why.

| A | B | C |
|---|---|---|
| on | door | ledger |
| is | shelf | beaker |
| ____ | ____ | ____ |
| ____ | ____ | ____ |
| ____ | ____ | ____ |

2. Identify each of the following examples as homophones, homographs, or homonyms. Then provide two effective teaching activities for each type of multiple-meaning word.

   a. He *read* the book yesterday.
      He will *read* the book tomorrow.

   b. The metal looked like *lead*.
      *Lead* me to the table!

   c. He *led* his horse to water.
      His arms were so tired they felt like *lead*.

   d. His *heir* will inherit the estate.
      The *air* was clean and fresh.

   e. The fish *scale* looked like a speck of silver.
      He weighed himself on the bathroom *scale*.

   f. He sat in the *chair*.
      He was the *chair* of the English Department.

3. Write a brief statement relating vocabulary development to concept development. How would this relationship influence your teaching of vocabulary in elementary grades?

4. Imagine that you need to teach the following new terms to first-grade students, who already know the meanings given in the second column. Describe your lesson.

   | To Be Learned | Already Known |
   |---|---|
   | fish *scale* | weighing *scale* |
   | human *race* | run a *race* |
   | pig *pen* | *pen* to write with |

5. Why would a teacher use both positive and negative examples when teaching vocabulary?

6. How might vocabulary teaching differ in primary and intermediate grades? Why? The words in Item 4 reflect one source of difference, but there are others.

7. Look at two different levels of a published reading program. Examine the introductory material to see how new vocabulary is identified and introduced. How are instructional strategies presented in the teacher's guide? Which strategies would you use? Which would you modify or reject? Why?

**FURTHER READING**

Beck, I. & McKeown, M. G. (1983). Learning words well—A program to enhance vocabulary and comprehension. *The Reading Teacher, 36,* 622–625.

Describes a program of varied methods to teach vocabulary to fourth-grade students. Involves cognitive, physical, and affective elements.

Fry, E., & Sakiey, E. (1986). Common words not taught in basal reading series. *The Reading Teacher, 39,* 395–398.

Points out that basal series generally teach about 50 percent of the 3,000 most common English words. Suggests that teachers may want to supplement basal lists with lists provided in the article.

Johnson, D. D., & Pearson, P. D. (1984). *Teaching reading vocabulary* (2nd ed.). New York: Holt, Rinehart & Winston.

A readable paperback including many ideas and suggestions for teaching vocabulary and providing a good conceptual background.

Marzano, R. J., & Marzano, J. S. (1988). *A cluster approach to elementary vocabulary instruction.* Newark, DE: International Reading Association.

Discusses teaching vocabulary in clusters of concepts, and presents an extensive list of word clusters.

Nagy, W. E. (1988). *Teaching vocabulary to improve reading comprehension.* Newark, DE: International Reading Association.

A short monograph that presents the reasons for the failure of certain types of vocabulary instruction as well as practical suggestions for improving that instruction.

Stallman, A. C., Commeyras, M., Kerr, B., Reimer, K., Jiminez, R., Hartman, D. D., & Pearson, P. D. (1990). Are "new" words really new? *Reading Research and Instruction, 29,* 12–29.

A research-based article that examines whether second- and fifth-grade children already know the meanings of vocabulary to be taught in basal readers. Points out that there are various reasons for including vocabulary lessons in published reading programs and that direct instruction can account for only a small part of the words children learn.

**REFERENCES**

Adams, M. J., & Collins, A. M. (1979). A schema-theoretic view of reading. In R. O. Freedle (Ed.), *Discourse processing: Multidisciplinary perspectives.* Norwood, NJ: Ablex.

Anders, P. L., & Bos, C. S. (1986). Semantic feature analysis: An interactive strategy for vocabulary development and text comprehension. *Journal of Reading, 29,* 610–616.

Anderson, R. C. (1985). Role of the reader's schema in comprehension, learning, and memory. In H. Singer & R. B. Ruddell (Eds.), *Theoretical models and processes of reading* (3rd ed., pp. 372–384). Newark, DE: International Reading Association.

Anderson, R. C., & Freebody, P. (1981). Vocabulary knowledge. In J. T. Guthrie (Ed.), *Comprehension and teaching: Research reviews* (pp. 77–117). Newark, DE: International Reading Association.

Anderson, R. C. & Ortony, A. (1975). On putting apples into bottles—A problem of polysemy. *Cognitive Psychology, 7,* 176–180.

Anderson, R. C., & Pearson, P. D. (1984). A schema-theoretic view of basic processes in reading. In P. D. Pearson (Ed.), *Handbook of reading research* (pp. 255–317). New York: Longman.

Anderson, R. C., Pichert, J. W., Goetz, E. T., Schallert, D. L., Stevens, K. V., & Trollip, S. R. (1976). Instantiation of general terms. *Journal of Verbal Learning and Verbal Behavior, 15,* 667–679.

Anderson, R. C., Reynolds, R. E., Schallert, D. L., & Goetz, E. T. (1977). Frameworks for comprehending discourse. *American Educational Research Journal, 14,* 367–381.

Anderson, R. C., Spiro, R. J., & Anderson, M. C. (1978). Schemata as scaffolding for the representation of information in discourse. *American Educational Research Journal, 15,* 433–440.

Bolinger, D. L. (1961). Verbal evocation. *Lingua, 10,* 113–127.

Brown, R., & McNeill, D. (1966). The tip-of-the-tongue phenomenon. *Journal of Verbal Learning and Verbal Behavior, 5,* 325–337.

Bybee, R. W., & Sund, R. B. (1982). *Piaget for educators.* Columbus, OH: Merrill.

Carroll, J. B. (1964a). Words, meanings and concepts: Part I. Their nature. *Harvard Educational Review, 34,* 178–190.

Carroll, J. B. (1964b). Words, meanings and concepts: Part II. Concept teaching and learning. *Harvard Educational Review, 34,* 191–202.

Dale, E., O'Rourke, J., & Bamman, H. A. (1971). *Techniques of teaching vocabulary.* Palo Alto, CA: Field Enterprises.

Davidson, S., Stickney, C. P., & Weil, R. L. (1980). *Intermediate accounting concepts, methods and uses.* Hinsdale, IL: Dryden Press.

DeHaven, E. P. (1988). *Teaching and learning the language arts* (3rd ed.). Boston: Little, Brown.

Duffelmeyer, F. A. (1985). Teaching word meanings from an experience base. *The Reading Teacher, 39,* 6–9.

Eeds, M. (1985). Bookwords: Using a beginning word list of high frequency words from children's literature K–3. *The Reading Teacher, 38,* 418–423.

Elley, W. B. (1989). Vocabulary acquisition from listening to stories. *Reading Research Quarterly, 24,* 174–187.

Fry, E., & Sakiey, E. (1986). Common words not taught in basal reading series. *The Reading Teacher, 39,* 395–398.

Ginsburg, H., & Opper, S. (1969). *Piaget's theory of intellectual development.* Englewood Cliffs, NJ: Prentice Hall.

Gipe, J. (1978–1979). Investigating techniques for teaching word meanings. *Reading Research Quarterly, 14,* 624–644.

Gold, Y. (1981). Helping students discover the origins of words. *The Reading Teacher, 35,* 350–351.

Gunderson, L. (1984). One last word list. *Alberta Journal of Educational Research, 30,* 259–269.

Halff, H. M., Ortony, A., & Anderson, R. C. (1976). A context-sensitive representation of word meaning. *Memory and Cognition, 4,* 378–383.

Harris, A. J., & Jacobson, M. D. (1982). *Basic reading vocabularies.* New York: Macmillan.

Heimlich, J. E., & Pittleman, S. D. (1986). *Semantic mapping: Classroom applications.* Newark, DE: International Reading Association.

Hirsch, E. D., Jr. (1989). *First dictionary of cultural literacy.* Boston: Houghton Mifflin.

Huff, P. (1983). Classroom organization. In E. Alexander (Ed.), *Teaching reading* (2nd ed., pp. 450–468). Boston: Little, Brown.

Jenkins, J. R., Matlock, B., & Slocum, T. A. (1989). Two approaches to vocabulary instruction: The teaching of individual word meanings and practice in deriving word meanings. *Reading Research Quarterly, 24,* 215–235.

Johnson, D. D., & Pearson, P. D. (1984). *Teaching reading vocabulary* (2nd ed.). New York: Holt, Rinehart & Winston.

Comprehension "

Metacognition "

Discourse "

Syntantic "

vocabulary knowledge

decoding "

Text ʰ

Johnson, D. E., Pittleman, S. D., & Heimlich, J. E. (1986). Semantic mapping. *The Reading Teacher, 39,* 778–783.

Katz, J. J. (1972). *Semantic theory.* New York: Harper & Row.

Kinzer, C. K. (1981). *Regular vs. mixed meanings effects on second and sixth graders' learning of multiple meaning words.* Unpublished doctoral dissertation, University of California, Berkeley.

Kinzer, C. K. (1982). *Interference effects of known meanings on vocabulary learning: Encountering the unexpected during the reading process.* Paper presented at the annual meeting of the International Reading Association, Chicago, IL.

Kurth, R. (1980). Building a conceptual base for vocabulary development. *Reading Psychology, 1,* 115–120.

Labov, W. (1973). The boundaries of words and their meanings. In J. N. Bailey & R. W. Shuy (Eds.), *New ways of analyzing variations in English.* Washington, DC: Georgetown University Press.

Leech, G. (1974). *Semantics.* New York: Penguin.

Lenneberg, E. H. (1967). *Biological foundations of language.* New York: John Wiley & Sons.

Lowery, L. (1981). *Learning about learning: Classification abilities.* Berkeley: University of California, Berkeley, PDARC Department of Education Publication.

Lyons, J. (1977). *Semantics* (2 vols.). Cambridge, MA: Cambridge University Press.

Marzano, R. J., & Marzano, J. S. (1988). *A cluster approach to vocabulary acquisition.* Newark, DE: International Reading Association.

Mason, J., Kniseley, E., & Kendall, J. (1979). Effects of polysemous words on sentence comprehension. *Reading Research Quarterly, 15,* 49–65.

Murphy, S. (1986). Children's comprehension of deictic categories in oral and written language. *Reading Research Quarterly, 21,* 118–131.

Nagy, W. E. (1988). *Teaching vocabulary to improve reading comprehension.* Newark, DE: International Reading Association.

Nagy, W. E., & Scott, J. A. (1990). Word schemas: Expectations about the form and meaning of new words. *Cognition and Instruction, 7,* 105–127.

Noyce, R. M., & Christie, J. F. (1989). *Integrating reading and writing instruction.* Needham Heights, MA: Allyn & Bacon.

Rosch, E. H. (1978). Principles of categorization. In E. H. Rosch & B. B. Lloyd (Eds.), *Cognition and categorization* (pp. 27–48). New York: Erlbaum.

Shapiro, J., & Gunderson, L. (1988). A comparison of vocabulary generated by grade 1 students in whole language classrooms and basal reader vocabulary. *Reading Research and Instruction, 27,* 40–46.

Sherfey, G. & Huff, P. (1976). Designing the science learning center. *Science and Children, 14,* 11–12.

Stahl, S. A., & Vancil, S. J. (1986). Discussion is what makes semantic maps work in reading instruction. *The Reading Teacher, 40,* 62–67.

Vygotsky, L. S. (1962). *Thought and language.* (E. Haufman & G. Vokow, Trans.). Cambridge, MA: MIT Press.

Woodson, M. I. C. E. (1974). Seven aspects of teaching concepts. *Journal of Educational Psychology, 66,* 184–188.

Vocabulary Knowledge    — Deictic Terms    { location
                                             time
                                             person

△ inference

like assumption about meaning. (not in the text.)
   you got to figure it out. not specific in the text.
• Dr. Christionson make the cast quickly with the Orvis graphite.

---

syntatic: oral language - "and" ⟨ have more complex / sentence structure

discourse knowledge:

metacognitive    "    : create new opportunity

---

conceptual terms: book ferry. computer

procedural terms:

concepts
<u>classic definition</u> ⃝
(machine) ~~machine~~ calculator
(computer) — math
       record ⟩ feature
☆ (example)

procedure terms (procedure steps)
1. reservation
2. order . seat
3. eat

eating at restaurant

*reciprocal teaching:* 1. summarize
2. clarify
3. question *about that part*
4. predict

# Comprehension of Extended Text

Chapter
**7**

- How Do Inferences Contribute to Comprehension?
- Differences Between Oral and Written Language
- Developing Syntactic Knowledge
- Developing Discourse Knowledge
- Using Questioning Strategies to Develop Reading Comprehension
- Developing Metacognitive Knowledge
- Using a Comprehension Framework to Guide the Use of Extended Text

*Mrs. Rodgers came into the kitchen. "Good morning, Amelia Bedelia," she said.*

*"Good morning," said Amelia Bedelia.*

*"I will have some cereal with my coffee this morning," said Mrs. Rodgers.*

*"All right," said Amelia Bedelia.*

*Mrs. Rodgers went into the dining room. Amelia Bedelia got the cereal. She put some into a cup. And she fixed Mrs. Rodgers some cereal with her coffee. She took it into the dining room.*

*"Amelia Bedelia!" said Mrs. Rodgers. "What is this mess?"*

*"It is your cereal with coffee," said Amelia Bedelia.*

Traditional     QARs

Literal question = Right-there QARS

Inferential Questions

Text-Connecting = Putting it Together

Slot-Filling = Author-and-you

From COME BACK, AMELIA BEDELIA, pp. 6–9, by Peggy Parish. Text copyright © 1971 by Margaret Parish. Reprinted by permission of Harper Collins Publishers.

Evaluative Questions = On-your-own

U nits of writing that are at least a sentence in length are called extended text. When readers encounter extended text, three new types of knowledge become important: syntactic, discourse, and metacognitive knowledge. This chapter describes instruction that is designed to help students comprehend these elements of extended text. Our discussion then continues into the next three chapters: we look at children's literature in chapter 8, the integration of reading and writing experiences in chapter 9, and the use of content-area reading selections in chapter 10.

An important concept in this chapter is the role that inferences play in our understanding of language. Using syntactic, discourse, and metacognitive knowledge to make inferences is often difficult for young readers. Perhaps that difficulty explains their delight in Amelia Bedelia's continuing inability to make correct inferences in the series by Peggy Parish.

Chapter 7 includes information that will help you answer questions like these:

1. How do inferences contribute to comprehension?
2. Why are differences between oral and written language important to reading?
3. How is syntactic knowledge developed?
4. How is discourse knowledge developed?
5. In what ways can questioning strategies be used to develop reading comprehension?
6. How is metacognitive knowledge developed?
7. How can a comprehension framework guide the use of extended text?

KEY CONCEPTS

adverbial references
author-and-you QARs
cause and effect
discourse knowledge
drawing conclusions
DRTA
evaluative level
inference
inferential level
in-my-head QARs
in-the-book QARs
language experience sentences
literal level
metacognitive knowledge

on-your-own QARs
predicting outcomes
procedural knowledge
pronoun references
putting-it-together QARs
QARs
reciprocal questioning
reciprocal teaching
right-there QARs
sequence relationship
slot-filling inference
syntactic knowledge
text-connecting inference

for comprehension
teacher should ask kids "How do/did you figure it out." QAR

Chapter 7 ■ Comprehension of Extended Text                                    247

## HOW DO INFERENCES CONTRIBUTE TO COMPREHENSION?

Some people refer to inferential reasoning as reading between the lines (Beck, 1989). Strictly speaking, an **inference** is a reasoned assumption about meaning that is not directly stated in the text. Readers make inferences whenever they add meaning to the explicit, or stated, meaning of a text. They do this in nearly every sentence they read. There are two basic types of inferences: text-connecting and slot-filling. A **text-connecting inference** occurs when a reader connects two different pieces of information in a text. For example, most readers would make a text-connecting inference if they read the following sentences:

> The Marshall Islands consist of low coral atolls. Majuro is the capital of the Marshall Islands.

inference: A reasoned assumption about meaning that is not explicitly stated in the text.

text-connecting inference: An inference that occurs when a reader connects two pieces of textual information to make a reasoned assumption about meaning.

These sentences do not explicitly specify that Majuro lies on a low coral atoll. Nevertheless, a proficient reader is likely to make that inference since the Marshall Islands are low coral atolls and Majuro is in the Marshall Islands.

A second type of inference is a **slot-filling inference,** which occurs when a reader adds background knowledge to a text, thereby filling in missing "slots" of meaning. For example, if you happen to have the appropriate background knowledge, you can infer the correct activity in this sentence:

slot-filling inference: An inference that occurs when a reader uses background knowledge to add meaning to a text.

> Dr. Christiansen made the cast quickly with his Orvis graphite and double-taper.

With background knowledge about fly-fishing, you may have correctly inferred that Dr. Christiansen was fishing with his Orvis graphite fly rod and his double-taper fly line. Without that knowledge you may have incorrectly inferred that Dr. Christiansen was repairing a broken bone. In either case you made a slot-filling inference; you added background knowledge to the text to fill in missing information. Reading is very much an inferential process.

## DIFFERENCES BETWEEN ORAL AND WRITTEN LANGUAGE

Reading is a process that requires young children to become familiar with the differences between oral and written language. Beginning readers are already effective users of oral language (McGee & Richgels, 1990). With fairly sophisticated skill they orally communicate their needs, share their joys, and articulate their disappointments. What they have yet to acquire consists primarily of those aspects of written language that are different from oral language (Leu, 1982; Purcell-Gates, 1989).

These differences exist within each knowledge source important to the comprehension process, and teachers must understand them if they hope to meet their students' needs in becoming proficient readers and writers.

## Differences Associated with Decoding Knowledge

There is one obvious difference between oral and written language in the area of decoding knowledge: separate symbol systems are used to represent meaning. In oral language, sounds are used; in written language, letters represent meaning. Beginning readers are already familiar with how sounds are used, but they are relatively unfamiliar with how letters are used. In order to access meaning in written language, young readers must become familiar with the relationships among letters, words, and sounds. This difference between oral and written language and the consequences for instruction are described in chapter 5.

## Differences Associated with Vocabulary Knowledge

All words can be used in either oral or written language. However, some words appear more frequently in written language, and young readers need to learn those meanings and labels that they may not yet have acquired from their oral language experiences. For example, children are familiar with the word *car* in oral language but are not so familiar with the words *auto* or *automobile,* which are more common in written language. Such words usually occur in content-specific writing, which is discussed in chapter 6.

Children encounter many differences between oral and written language as they interact with print.

## Differences Associated with Syntactic Knowledge

There are at least two important syntactic differences between oral and written language. First, children must become familiar with how punctuation is used in written language to represent the stress and intonation patterns of oral language. Punctuation is important in conveying appropriate meaning, as the following examples demonstrate:

1. Now! I need your help! (Not: Now I need your help.)
2. Bob talked to the teacher with Bill and Becky. Lou wanted to talk to him, too. (Not: Bob talked to the teacher with Bill and Becky Lou wanted to talk to him too.)

Second, children must become familiar with the syntactic patterns that are common in written language. The oral language that they already know uses many coordinated patterns, often linked by *and*.

"I saw Jose *and then* I went to Bill's house *and then* I played ball."

Beginning readers use this pattern frequently in their oral language (Michaels & Cook-Gumperz, 1979). Written language contains more integrated patterns, especially to express sequence and cause-and-effect relationships, which use words like *because, consequently, before,* and *after*.

I saw Jose *before* I went to Bill's house. *After* seeing him, I played baseball.

Beginning readers develop an understanding of these written language patterns from their reading and writing experiences.

## Differences Associated with Discourse Knowledge

Two important differences between oral and written language also exist in discourse knowledge. First, written language requires that readers infer the meanings of implicit pronoun and adverbial references (e.g., *he, she, this, here, there, now*) without a visible context (Rubin, 1980). Young children are used to seeing what such terms refer to. Consequently, the text-connecting and slot-filling inferences demanded by pronouns and adverbs in written language represent an important learning task for beginning readers (Murphy, 1985).

Second, the difference in the discourse structure of oral and written language also presents difficulties for young children learning to read (Teale & Sulzby, 1986). Through oral language experiences children develop knowledge about how oral conversations are organized. However, they have few opportunities to develop an understanding of how different narrative forms are organized (Sulzby, 1982). And they have even fewer opportunities to understand how different types of informational writing are organized. Nonetheless, knowledge of these discourse forms is important to a proficient reader.

## Differences Associated with Metacognitive Knowledge

Different types of metacognitive, or strategic, knowledge are also required for oral and written language tasks. Oral language is temporary, whereas written language is permanent. And that permanence allows special strategies to assist decoding, vocabulary, syntactic, and discourse processes. Consider decoding, for example. Students need to acquire strategies that help them determine the oral equivalent of a word. Rereading a sentence to better understand the surrounding context is a strategy unique to written language. With oral language the message occurs in a single stream of sounds that disappears quickly.

This same situation exists within other knowledge sources important for reading. Within discourse knowledge, for instance, young readers need to know that reading the summary at the end of an informational article can give them a preview of the major points in the article before they read it. They also need to know how to skim a piece quickly to see whether it contains the general information they are seeking. And they need to know how to scan a piece to find the specific information they want. All of these strategies are examples of the unique metacognitive knowledge that young readers need to acquire in order to understand written language.

## DEVELOPING SYNTACTIC KNOWLEDGE

**syntactic knowledge:** The knowledge that readers have of the word order rules that determine the meaning of sentences.

**Syntactic knowledge** includes an understanding of the word order rules that determine grammatical function, meaning, and pronunciation. For example, it helps us distinguish the difference in meaning between *Tom saw Mary* and *Mary saw Tom,* two sentences with identical words but different word order. Syntactic knowledge contributes to a reader's comprehension of extended text, with three aspects being especially important for young readers as they move from oral to written language: punctuation, sequence relationships, and cause-and-effect relationships. Each is related to oral and written language differences and to the inferences that readers must make.

## Punctuation

A reader's ability to determine stress and intonation contributes to the comprehension process (Cook-Gumperz & Gumperz, 1981). Knowledge of punctuation assists a reader in determining the correct stress, intonation, and meaning of a sentence. The symbols listed in Table 7–1 are those with which proficient readers should be familiar.

**language experience sentences:** A method framework used to develop an understanding of punctuation.

**Teaching Punctuation.** Instruction in using punctuation takes place early in a reading program, usually by the end of third grade. Teachers often teach punctuation concepts by linking children's oral language to its written representation. They sometimes use a method framework referred to as **language experience sentences,** a variation of the language experience story described

TABLE 7–1
Punctuation marks often taught in the elementary grades

| Name | Punctuation Mark | Intonation/Meaning |
|---|---|---|
| Period | . | Indicates a long pause and the end of a sentence |
| Comma | , | Indicates a short pause and the end or beginning of an idea within a sentence; also separates items in a list |
| Exclamation point | ! | Indicates a long pause and an expressive statement |
| Quotation marks | " " | Used with speech to indicate what someone said or wrote; also signals special use of a word or phrase |
| Internal quotation marks | ' ' | Speaking intonation; indicates the exact words of one person repeated by another. |
| Question mark | ? | Indicates a long pause with prior "rounding," up or down, of intonation; the end of a question |
| Semicolon | ; | Indicates a short pause between two related propositions |
| Colon | : | Indicates a long pause before a list or explanation |
| Italic or boldface | *italic* **bold** | Indicates greater stress for emphasis; also signals special use of a word or phrase |
| Parentheses | ( ) | Indicate an extra thought or aside |
| Ellipsis | . . . . . . . | Indicates a long pause within a sentence or an omission in a quotation |

earlier (see chapter 2). Language experience sentences include these four procedural steps:

1. Elicit oral language containing the target punctuation.
2. Transcribe the language containing the target punctuation.
3. Read the transcribed language, modeling the use of punctuation.
4. Practice reading similar sentences.

During the first step the teacher elicits an oral sentence containing the desired stress and intonation pattern. This task is often accomplished by asking students about something they have done or said. In Step 2 the teacher transcribes that sentence, usually on the chalkboard. For a more permanent copy the sentence could be transcribed on a large sheet of card stock or other heavy paper. Step 3 requires the teacher to model the use of punctuation while reading the transcribed sentence aloud. The stress and intonation pattern represented by the punctuation mark should be clearly expressed, the punctuation mark should be identified, and its function discussed. Finally, the teacher should elicit other sentences containing the desired stress and intonation pattern, transcribe them, and have students practice reading them. In the model lesson Ms. Brown is teaching her first-grade students the stress and intonation pattern associated with a comma separating items in a list. She is using language experience sentences to teach this concept.

**MODEL
LESSON**

Teaching Punctuation Using Language Experience Sentences

**Elicit Oral Language Containing the Target Punctuation**

Ms. Brown:  Daria, tell us three things that you do before you come to school in the morning.

Daria:  Let's see. I wake up, I eat breakfast, and I brush my teeth. That's three things.

**Transcribe the Language Containing the Target Punctuation.** Ms. Brown writes the following sentence on the blackboard:

Daria wakes up, eats breakfast, and brushes her teeth in the morning.

**Read the Transcribed Language, Modeling the Use of Punctuation**

Ms. Brown:  Listen while I read this sentence [Ms. Brown reads.] Do you see that I wrote this little mark between each of the things Daria does in the morning? This mark is called a comma. Can you say that word? Comma. What happens when I'm reading and I come to a comma? Listen again. [Ms. Brown reads.]

Sam:  You kind of stop for a bit but not like at the end.

Ms. Brown:  Right. With a comma you should stop reading for just a little bit, but not as long as you do at the end of a sentence.

**Practice Reading Similar Sentences**

Ms. Brown:  Let's read some more sentences like this. Michael, what do you do when you get home after school? Tell us three or four things so we can write them down and put commas between them.

Michael:     I go home. I change my clothes and have a snack, and I ride
             my dirt bike, and I have dinner.

[Ms. Brown transcribes this series with commas and has children read it
orally: Michael goes home, changes his clothes, has a snack, and rides his
dirt bike until dinner. Then she repeats this activity with other students and
other sentences containing commas to separate items in a series.]

---

Other activities may also be used to teach punctuation, several of which are
included here.

---

**Dramatic Reading.** Encourage cooperative learning groups to choose a short
selection (one or two paragraphs) for dramatic reading to the class. Be sure
the selection contains a variety of punctuation marks. Allow each group a
short period to practice and agree on the exact intonation to use. If you use
this activity to introduce new books to your students, have them read the
most exciting part without giving away the ending.

**Same Sentence, Different Meaning.** Give students sentence pairs that are
identical except for punctuation.

**SAMPLE
ACTIVITIES**

        "Linda!" said Peter. "I need that paper now."
        Linda said, "Peter, I need that paper now."

Have students work in cooperative learning groups to read each sentence
with the correct intonation and identify the correct meanings.

**Question Pairs.** To teach question intonation, make two sets of cards. One
should contain sentence beginnings, like "Can Sandra." The other should
contain a verb and a question mark, like "swim?" (see Figure 7–1). Pick
one card from each pile, put the two cards in the correct order, and read
them to students. After explaining the role of the question mark, allow students to draw a pair of cards and read the resulting question aloud.

Can Sandra      swim?

FIGURE 7–1
Question-pair cards

Did Bill      leave?

## Sequence Relationships

sequence relationship: A relationship of time between two or more events, explicitly or implicitly stated.

A **sequence relationship** expresses the time relationship between two or more events. Often these events are mentioned in the same or adjacent sentences, sometimes in separate paragraphs. Sequence relationships can be either explicitly or implicitly stated, as shown in the following examples:

### Explicit

| Events appearing in the order in which they happened | Tom finished his work *before* he went home. |
| Events appearing in the opposite order from that in which they happened | Tom went home *after* he finished his work. |

### Implicit

| Events appearing in the order in which they happened (separate sentences) | Tom finished his work. He went home. |
| Events appearing in the order in which they happened (linked by a coordinating conjunction) | Tom finished his work, *and* he went home. |

Explicit sequence relationships contain signal words, such as *before, after, then, later, following, first, initially, earlier, afterwards, next,* or *finally*. These signal words state the time relationship between the two events and thus should make such relationships easy to comprehend. Unfortunately, however, two elements of explicit sequence relationships are difficult for young children. First, the signal words for sequence relationships are not common in the oral language of young children. Consequently, they are often unfamiliar with the meanings of signal words and must be taught both their meanings and their function in explicit sequence relationships.

A second difficulty is that relationships may appear in the opposite order from that in which they happened. In oral language, children are accustomed to events being stated in the order in which they occur, and they assume that a similar situation exists in written language. As a result, children often interpret sentences like "Tom went home after he finished his work" as "Tom went home, and then he finished his work." Children have the greatest difficulty comprehending explicit sequence relationships when the events appear in the opposite order from that in which they happened (Pearson & Camperell, 1981; Pearson & Johnson, 1978).

Sequence relationships can also be implicitly stated, requiring readers to make an inference, usually a text-connecting inference. Implicit sequence relationships may be indicated by sequentially ordered events in separate sentences or by the coordinating conjunction *and* within a single sentence. Such relationships require readers to infer the temporal relationship between events.

This type of inference presents little difficulty for young readers because sequence relationships are expressed in the same way in oral language.

**Teaching Sequence Relationships.** With younger readers sequence relationships are often taught within a language experience story, which typically contains these steps:

1. Provide students with a vivid experience.
2. Elicit oral language that describes the experience.
3. Transcribe the students' oral language.
4. Help students read what was transcribed.

Throughout a language experience story, discussion should help students identify the various events and their sequence relationships. Special attention should be devoted to helping students understand the meanings of signal words and the ways in which they identify sequence relationships. Ms. Sanchez demonstrates in the model lesson how this method framework can be used to develop an understanding of sequence relationships.

---

## Teaching Sequence Relationships in a Language Experience Story

**Provide Students with a Vivid Experience.** Today, Ms. Sanchez is taking her class to the library. She decides to build on this experience when they return to the classroom.

**Elicit Oral Language That Describes the Experience.** When they return, Ms. Sanchez has her class sit on the carpeted floor in front of the chalkboard. She elicits several sentences from the students, one for each event they experienced in the library.

**Transcribe the Students Oral Language.** Ms. Sanchez writes down each sentence on the chalkboard as the student says it.

**MODEL LESSON**

> We went to the library.
> Ms. Hamm showed us the new bookshelves.
> We sat in a circle.
> Ms. Hamm read us the story about the ox-cart man.
> We got to check out a new book.
> We came back to our room.

**Help Students Read What Was Transcribed.** Ms. Sanchez has her students read the entire sequence of sentences. Then she carries out three activities to assist her students' understanding of sequence relationships.

First, Ms. Sanchez initiates a discussion, asking sequence questions such as "What happened before we sat in a circle? What happened before Ms. Hamm read us a story? What happened before we came back to our room?" She writes the students' responses next to the story they had dictated earlier.

Ms. Hamm showed us the new bookshelves *before* we sat in a circle.
We sat in a circle *before* Ms. Hamm read us a story.
We checked out a new book *before* we came back to our room.

Secondly, Ms. Sanchez discusses the meaning of the signal word *before* and then has students read this second set of sentences. Together they discuss the sequence of the different events and the way in which certain words like *before* are used to show that order.

Third, Ms. Sanchez has her students draw pictures of two events, one happening before the other. She walks around the classroom, helping students write a sentence containing the word *before* to describe their pictures. Afterwards, students read their sentences and show their pictures in a short cooperative learning group activity.

---

Among older readers instruction in understanding sequence relationships often takes place during the discussion of a story. Questions that can be used to initiate a discussion about sequence relationships include these:

When did *X* take place?
What happened before *X*?
What happened before *Y*?
Did *X* happen before or after *Y*?

An important distinction must be made here, though, between using questions to test and to teach reading comprehension (Durkin, 1981, 1986). If you accept correct responses and reject incorrect responses and do nothing else, you are testing reading comprehension. You are simply determining whether students can answer the questions. If you follow sequence questions with a request for students to model their reasoning processes, you are teaching reading comprehension. After each sequence question, for example, you might ask, "How did you figure that out?" In order to answer you, students would have to model the reasoning processes that they used. The following suggestions will help you teach, not test, understanding of sequence relationships during the discussion of a story.

■ Avoid playing the can-you-guess-the-answer-I-have-in-mind game. Ask a sequence question to direct students' attention to particular events in a story and then initiate a discussion about the sequence relationships that exist there. Do not ask a question merely to obtain a correct response.
■ Follow a sequence question with a brief discussion. For example, ask students how they determined their answer to your question. What information did they use from the text? What information did they figure out by themselves because it was missing from the text? Have they ever used such a

*good readers are good dedectives (dɪˈtɛktɪv)*

*Lets get going.*

*[handwritten top margin:] identify 4 inferences a reader must make to comprehend this paragraph. Identify each as either a slot—filling or a text—connecting inference.*

strategy before? Is it a good one to remember? After students model their reasoning processes, model your own, and explain how you arrived at your answer. Your explanation should help students who were unable to determine the sequence relationship.

*[handwritten right margin:] put together pieces of information.*

■ Pay particular attention to sequence relationships that present events in the opposite order from that in which they occurred. Those will be most difficult for young readers to understand.

■ Before reading a story with difficult sequence relationships, use a prereading question to direct students' attention to the important information. For example, say to students, "Read and see whether you can find out which happened first—X or Y."

*[handwritten left margin:] around edge*

In addition to language experience sentences, language experience stories, and discussion techniques, these other instructional activities can be used to teach sequence relationships.

---

**Time Lines.** Use time lines like the one in Figure 7–2 to help children understand the sequence relationships in a story. Time lines are especially helpful when event sequences are complicated or lengthy. They are most commonly used after a story has been read but can also be used as a prereading activity to develop expectations and guide students as they read a story.

**Cloze Tasks.** Use sentence pairs like the following to initiate discussion of why certain words were selected and whether the sentences express the same meaning. Cooperative learning groups could provide the forum for these discussions.

**SAMPLE
ACTIVITIES**

_____ putting on his shoe, Jim tied the laces.
   (Before, After)

FIGURE 7–2
A sample time line

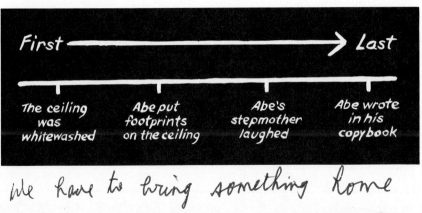

*[handwritten right margin:] hay. what is grouse swapping tales for dinner.*

*[handwritten bottom margin:] we have to bring something home*

Jim put on his shoe _____ he tied the laces.
                                 (before, after)

**Out-of-Order Orders.** Use sentence pairs like those listed in the following exercise to help students understand sequence relationships with events listed in the opposite order from that in which they happened. Be sure to discuss with your students the reasoning processes they used with each sentence pair.

> *Directions:* Read the first sentence in each pair. Then fill in the blank in the second sentence so that both have the same meaning.
>
> 1. Before eating dinner, Liz read a book.
>    _____ reading a book, Liz ate dinner.
>    (Before, After)
> 2. Jim saw his friend after he called home.
>    _____ seeing his friend, Jim called home.
>    (Before, After)

## Cause-and-Effect Relationships

cause-and-effect relationship: A causal relationship
between two or more
events, explicitly or implicitly stated.

A **cause-and-effect relationship** expresses the relationship between two events in which one event is the consequence of the other. Often the two events appear in the same or adjacent sentences; sometimes they appear in separate paragraphs. Cause-and-effect relationships can also be either explicitly or implicitly stated.

Explicit cause-and-effect relationships contain signal words such as *because* and *therefore,* which clearly indicate the causal relationship between the two events. Again, we might think that such words would make these explicit relationships easy to comprehend, but unfortunately, young children are often unfamiliar with the meanings of those words. Consequently, both the meanings of signal words and their function in explicit cause-and-effect relationships are frequently taught to young children. The cause-and-effect signal words usually taught are listed in Table 7–2.

Implicit cause-and-effect relationships require readers to infer the correct relationship between two ideas in the absence of signal words. The two events are stated in separate sentences or are connected by the coordinating conjunction *and* in the same sentence. The following examples show both explicit and implicit cause-and-effect relationships.

### Explicit

The hatch had just started, and *therefore* the fish began to feed.
        (cause)                (signal word)      (effect)

*word literacy is difficult for 1st grade*
*unfamiliar with connection*
*sounding the words out.*

TABLE 7–2
Signal words for cause-and-effect relationships

| Signal Words | Examples |
|---|---|
| because | He went home *because* he was ill. |
| so | He was ill, and *so* he went home. |
| therefore | He was ill and *therefore* went home. |
| hence | He was ill. *Hence* he went home. |
| thus | He was ill and *thus* went home. |
| since | *Since* he was ill, he went home. |
| as a result | He was ill and *as a result* went home. |
| consequently | He was ill and *consequently* went home. |
| for this reason | He was ill. *For this reason* he went home. |
| that being the case | He looked ill. *That being the case,* he went home. |
| on account of | *On account of* his illness, he went home. |
| accordingly | He looked ill and *accordingly* went home. |

Implicit

The hatch had just started. The fish began to feed.
    (cause)               (effect)

The hatch had just started, and the fish began to feed.
    (cause)                  (effect)

With implicit cause-and-effect relationships readers must have the appropriate background knowledge in order to infer the correct meaning. Without that knowledge readers may interpret the two events as being temporally, but not causally, ordered. For example, the implicit sentences just presented might be interpreted as "First, something unrelated to the fish (maybe a bird's egg) hatched. Then the fish began to feed." In that case the two events would not be thought to be causally related. However, appropriate background knowledge would lead to the correct inference, that the mayflies are hatching, and thus an understanding of the causal relationship being expressed.

**Teaching Cause-and-Effect Relationships.** With younger readers teachers often read a story aloud with or to the class. Then in the discussion that follows they help students understand causes, effects, signal words, and the way each communicates meaning. The following model lesson illustrates how Ms. Dodson taught her second graders about signal words.

**MODEL
LESSON**

Teaching the Role of Signal Words in
Cause-and-Effect Relationships

Ms. Dodson: I'm going to read you a short story about three children today. I want you to listen and find out why these children become lost at the beginning of the story.

> Once upon a time, three young children went for
> a walk on a trail that wandered through the forest
> near their cottage. They became lost because they
> left the trail. Two of the children started to cry
> since they were afraid. Then the other child dis-
> covered the path again and showed everyone the
> way home.

Does anyone know why the children became lost at the beginning of the story.

Kurt:          Yes. They left the trail.
Ms. Dodson: Good. Listen as I read the beginning again, and see if you can
hear the word that tells us why they became lost [Reads the
introduction again.]
Tama:          I think *because* is the word.
Ms. Dodson: That's right. We call words like *because* "signal words" since
they act like a signal to tell us why things happen. Does anyone remember why two of the children cried?
Erica:         Because they were afraid.
Ms. Dodson: Yes. Listen as I read that sentence again and see if you can
hear a signal word that tells us why they cried.

> Two of the children started to cry since they were
> afraid.

Tim:           I know. *Since*. That's the signal word.
Ms. Dodson: [Continues with the story, which contains a number of signal
words. She asks students to listen for words that signal cause-
and-effect relationships as she reads. Each signal word is written on the board.]

Among older readers instruction in cause-and-effect relationships often
takes place during the discussion of a story. Questions that might be used to
direct student attention to cause-and-effect relationships include these:

Why did $Z$ take place?
What happened as a result of $X$?
How are $Z$ and $X$ connected?
Which words tell us that $Z$ happened because of $X$?

As with sequence relationships, it is important to initiate discussions that teach, not test, comprehension. It is also important to direct student attention to the text so that concrete examples of causes, effects, and signal words can be seen. The following model shows how Ms. Clancy taught cause-and-effect to her sixth graders.

---

## Teaching Cause-and-Effect in the Sixth Grade

Ms. Clancy's students understand the concepts *cause, effect,* and *signal word*. They have been reading the book *The Secret Soldier* (McGovern, 1975) and have just finished a page that began with the following paragraph.

> The trouble was getting worse. In many villages, people were getting ready for war. Groups of men and young boys began training to be soldiers. They were called minutemen because they were ready to fight at a minute's notice. (p. 19)

**MODEL LESSON**

Ms. Clancy: Look up at the first paragraph. Why were these soldiers called minutemen?

Marcus: Because they could fight at a minute's notice.

Ms. Clancy: Tell us how you know that, Marcus.

Marcus: It says *because*.

Ms. Clancy: Right! *Because* is a signal word that signals a special relationship between two ideas. It tells us why something happened. Can you find the two ideas in this sentence?

Linda: "They were called minutemen" and "they were ready to fight at a minute's notice."

Ms. Clancy: Good! Can anyone find the cause and the effect statements in this sentence?

Bonnie: I can. "They were ready to fight at a minute's notice" is the cause, and "They were called minutemen" must be the effect. Being ready to fight at a minute's notice causes them to be called minutemen.

Ms. Clancy: Good! Now look at the first two sentences in this paragraph, and read them again to yourself. Sometimes signal words are missing, yet we still have a special relationship between the two ideas. One sentence can be the cause and another sentence the effect, even without a signal word. Does one of the first two sentences describe a cause?

Joan: I think people were getting ready for war, so the trouble was getting worse. "People were getting ready for war" is the cause.

Marcus: But the people didn't cause the trouble. The trouble caused the people to get ready for war. I think "The trouble was getting worse" is the cause.

> Ms. Clancy: One way to test your idea is to put these two sentences to-
> gether with a signal word like *because* at the beginning of each
> sentence. That usually tells you which one is the cause and
> which one is the effect.
>
> Joan: Because the trouble was getting worse, the people were getting
> ready for war. Yeah. That's what I mean. "The trouble was get-
> ting worse" must be the cause.

Discussions in either oral or written contexts can be used to develop an understanding of cause-and-effect relationships. In addition, there are many other appropriate activities, several of which are described here.

**SAMPLE
ACTIVITIES**

**Marking Cause-and-Effect Relationships.** Present cause-and-effect statements, and show students how to identify each component in the relationship, marking each with an appropriate letter or symbol.

ⓒ                                    ⓔ
The school bell rang for recess, <u>so</u> the children went outside.

**Cause-and-Effect Cloze Tasks.** Teach the meaning of new signal words, such as *therefore,* by using any of the methods described for vocabulary instruction in chapter 6. Then have students complete sentences like the following, either independently or in a cooperative learning group.

_____, and therefore we were late for
dinner.

The wind was too strong for our sailboat, and therefore

_____ .

To reduce the difficulty level of the task, you might provide suggested answers at the bottom of the page:

we forgot the time        it tipped over

**Signal Word Cloze Tasks.** Teach the meanings of new signal words according to methods outlined in chapter 6. Then have students practice using the new words in cloze sentences.

Debbie was ill _____ she went home.
(and thus, previously, earlier)

_____ the test, Bill was nervous and irritable.
(On the other hand, On account of, On my own time)

*discourse knowledge*

Discourse knowledge, including knowledge of organizational patterns, helps readers understand entire texts.

## DEVELOPING DISCOURSE KNOWLEDGE

**Discourse knowledge** also contributes to comprehension (Beck, McKeown, Omanson, & Pople, 1984). It includes the knowledge of language organization that helps us understand entire texts. Whereas syntactic knowledge allows us to determine meaningful relationships among words, discourse knowledge allows us to determine meaningful relationships among sentences. At least three aspects of discourse knowledge are important for young readers to acquire: pronoun and adverbial references, drawing conclusions, and predicting outcomes. Each is related to oral and written language differences and to the inferences that readers are required to make as they comprehend a text.

### Pronoun and Adverbial References

**Pronoun references** are words that are substituted for nouns or noun phrases; they include words like *I, you,* and *he.* **Adverbial references** are words that are

discourse knowledge: The knowledge that readers have of the language organization that determines meaning beyond the single-sentence level; includes knowledge of different types of writing.

pronoun references: Words that are substituted for nouns or noun phrases.

adverbial references: Words that are substituted for specific time or location designations.

substituted for specific designations of time or location; they include words such as *here, today, now, last week,* and *last month*. Both pronoun and adverbial references are very common, as we can see in the following example:

> Heather and *her* friend were determined to see the solar eclipse in *their* viewing box. *They* struggled with the box to get *it* right. *First* the hole was not big enough. *Then it* was too big. *Finally,* by putting tape across the hole and *then* poking a tiny hole in *it* with a toothpick, Heather was able to get the light to shine. *"We* can see *it here now,"* she said.

Readers must infer the meanings of pronoun and adverbial references by imagining a situation they cannot see. This task is easy for mature readers, familiar with the demands of written texts. It is much more difficult for young readers (Anderson & Shifrin, 1980; Rubin, 1980), who are accustomed to seeing, not imagining, the meanings of such words in oral language contexts.

Pronoun and adverbial references require either a text-connecting or a slot-filling inference. For example, the word *they* in the preceding paragraph requires a text-connecting inference. It requires readers to understand its logical connection to its referent in the passage—the words *Heather and her friend*. Other examples in this paragraph of references that require a text-connecting inference include *her (Heather), their (Heather and her friend), it (the box), it (the hole), it (the tape), We (Heather and her friend), it (the eclipse),* and *she (Heather)*.

When pronoun or adverbial references do not have an explicit referent in the text, they require readers to make a slot-filling inference. The word *here* in the example paragraph requires a slot-filling inference, in which readers understand the logical connection between *here* and its unstated referent—the inside wall of the box. When pronoun or adverbial references require a slot-filling inference, readers must have the appropriate background knowledge to fill in the missing meaning. Slot-filling inferences with pronoun or adverbial references are especially difficult for young readers to make.

**Teaching Pronoun and Adverbial References.** The ability to infer the meanings of pronoun and adverbial references is developed early in a reading program, usually during the first two grades, for two reasons. First, pronoun and adverbial references are among the most common words in our language. Many are included in the list of high-frequency sight words in Figure 5–2. Second, imagining the referents for pronoun and adverbial references in written language is a new task for young children.

Instruction in making text-connecting inferences for pronoun and adverbial references usually precedes instruction in making slot-filling inferences. It is easier to show students in a concrete way the connections between references and their referents. Those connections are often demonstrated by circling the references and drawing lines back to their referents. Both text-connecting and slot-filling inferences can be taught inductively but are more often taught deductively, as in the model lesson by Mr. Burns. Note in the lesson that Mr. Burns changes the directions for the practice page from those provided in the published reading program.

---

## Using Deductive Instruction to Teach Text-Connecting Inferences with Pronoun and Adverbial References

**MODEL LESSON**

Before beginning the lesson, Mr. Burns writes the following sentences on the chalkboard.

> Peter was talking to Joan on the phone. He said, "I don't know if Hal is at work today. Maybe he stayed at home. Is he there with you, Joan?"
> Joan said, "No. He isn't here. And Mark isn't here either. Do you know where he is? Maybe they are together somewhere."

**State the Skill or Rule.** Mr. Burns begins by pointing to the sentences on the blackboard and saying, "Sometimes when you read, one word will take the place of another word or phrase. Both will mean the same thing. Look at these sentences on the board. Can you read them for us, Matt?" Matt reads the sentences aloud.

**Provide Examples of the Skill or Rule.** Mr. Burns shows that pronoun and adverbial references are logically connected to their referents. He circles the first *He* on the board and draws an arrow back to its referent, *Peter*. Mr. Burns does the same thing with *I* and draws the arrow back to *Peter*. Then he circles the second *he* and draws an arrow back to *Hal*. While he does all of this, Mr. Burns explains that certain words often mean the same thing as other words in a story.

**Provide Guided Practice.** Then Mr. Burns asks the students to look at the second paragraph on the board and find similar kinds of words that mean the same thing as other words. He asks individuals to come to the board and circle each pronoun or adverb and then draw arrows back to its referent. Students follow this procedure for *he* (Hal), *here* (at work), and *they* (Hal, Mark). Mr. Burns has the students explain their decisions to the group.

**Provide Independent Practice.** Mr. Burns gives each student a copy of the page illustrated in Figure 7–3. He directs them all to read each pair of sentences and complete the starred example individually. After that he tells them to work together in two separate groups and complete a cooperative learning group activity. He explains that their task is to draw arrows from each word that appears in heavy black letters in examples 1, 2, and 3 back to its referent. When they are finished, the two groups get together with Mr. Burns and compare their answers.

---

Questioning Guidelines
1. Don't use questions simply to test comprehension.
2. Plan discussion questions in advance.

FIGURE 7–3

An example of a practice activity for pronoun references

| . Unit 14 • What Mary Jo Shared — Part 1 | PREPARE |
| --- | --- |

● Read each pair of sentences.

Underline the words that mean the same
as the word in heavy black letters.
For the last one, mark the space
for the answer.

1. That woman lost her hat.
   I will run and give it to **her**.

2. Henry did not see the puddle.
   He skated right into **it**.

3. Annie and Will are going to school.
   Fang wants to go with **them**.

★ "Here comes Gramps!" said Ana and Alex.
   "He has some flowers for **us**."
   ◯ Gramps
   ◯ Ana and Gramps
   ◯ Ana and Alex

**Comprehension:** Word Referents *her, them, us, it*          CAROUSELS

85

Houghton Mifflin Reading, 1989 Edition

**Source:** From *Houghton Mifflin Reading, Carousels* workbook by William K. Durr et al. Copyright © 1989. Reprinted by permission of Houghton Mifflin Company.

if cant answer higher
drop down

QARs

3. ask higher-level question. avoid lower-level questi

266  4. Help kids use prior knowledge to seek
knowledge and make connections with the tex

*teacher → asks question*

In addition to circling references and drawing lines back to each referent, many other techniques can be used to help students develop an understanding of pronoun and adverbial references. Several such techniques are listed here.

**Rewriting Repeated Words.** Provide students with sentences like the ones shown here. Ask them to rewrite the sentences using references for any repeated words. To make the task easier, have them cross out the second instance of any word and write the correct reference above it. You could also provide a list of possible words to use.

**SAMPLE ACTIVITIES**

Tom got on Tom's bike.

Cindy went to school at noon. Did you see Cindy?

Hello, Helene and Pat. I am at the computer. Do Helene and Pat want to come over at the computer?

**Cloze Tasks.** Follow standard cloze task procedures, but delete only pronoun and adverbial references. Then have students complete the blanks. For a variation on this task, provide students with copies of a story in which you have deleted all the references. (You might give this job to a student to complete.) Have students work together in pairs to figure out the missing references. Then bring all of the students back together, and have each cooperative learning group read its solutions.

## Predicting Outcomes and Drawing Conclusions

Both of these processes rely on the same type of schema knowledge—**procedural knowledge**—which consists of knowledge of common event sequences. Your own procedural knowledge is probably extensive. For example, you have procedural knowledge about the first day of class in a university course, and you use that knowledge to make inferences, either when you experience that first day yourself or when you read about the experiences of someone else. The first event sequence in your procedural knowledge includes your arrival. Within that sequence you probably have a location where you prefer to sit, based on previous experiences. Some students look to the front row, others to the back row, and still others to an aisle seat. Your knowledge probably includes the meanings associated with sitting in each of those locations. People often sit in the front to make an impression, they sit in the back to avoid making an impression, and they sit next to the aisle to make a quick exit. All of this knowledge is a part of the initial event sequence in your procedural knowledge of the first day of class.

Your second event sequence probably includes your professor's arrival. It may include the fact that professors are likely to be carrying a stack of syllabi, which they set down on the table or lectern at the front of the room. It may also

procedural knowledge: Knowledge of common event sequences.

5. If kids can't answer a higher-level question, ask a related, lower-level question.

include your professor's writing the title of the course and his or her name on the chalkboard. Your procedural knowledge for the first day of class probably contains a number of other event sequences that define your expectations for the remainder of that first period: passing out the syllabus, going over the syllabus, finding out where the text may be purchased, and hearing why this course is the most important course in your college career.

You possess thousands of procedural schemata such as this in your background knowledge, each containing procedural steps and event sequences. You have, no doubt, a procedural schema for eating at a restaurant, driving home, eating dinner at home, flying on an airplane, and many others. Throughout the day you use this knowledge to make inferences about what is happening or what you are reading.

The following passage and related question show how procedural knowledge is used to make inferences during reading.

> The two boys were across the street from Jose's house when they saw the ominous line of clouds approaching and heard the thunder. They were playing under a tall eucalyptus tree at the time and could see the lightning flash all along the storm front as it came closer. "Hurry," said Jose.
>
> What do you think the two boys will do?

If you have a procedural schema for what to do in a lightning storm, you are familiar with the common event sequences that accompany such a storm: getting away from trees, staying away from metal objects, heading for cover, and so on. Based on the information in the passage and your own procedural knowledge, you probably inferred that the two boys would head for shelter inside Jose's house.

predicting outcomes: A comprehension task requiring the reader to use appropriate procedural knowledge to infer a future effect from a stated cause; a forward inference.

Your inference illustrates a comprehension task referred to as **predicting outcomes,** which requires the reader to infer future effects from a stated cause. The inference in such a task is always projected into the future; it is usually a slot-filling inference about a future effect. Figure 7–4 illustrates two predicting-outcome tasks from a published reading program.

drawing conclusions: A comprehension task requiring a reader to infer an unstated cause from a stated effect; a backward inference.

A related comprehension task, **drawing conclusions,** requires the reader to infer an unstated cause from a stated effect. In this case the inference is always backward to what has been read in the text. Drawing a conclusion usually requires readers to use their procedural knowledge to make a slot-filling inference about a previous cause. Let's look at the following passage and related question to see how this process takes place.

> The team raced to the far end of the court to cut the net down. The captain climbed up to the hoop, cut the net, put it around his neck, and let out a yell. The crowd was going crazy with excitement!
>
> Why was everyone so excited?

Were you able to infer backwards from the stated effects in the passage to determine the unstated cause—that a basketball team had just won a tour-

6. Recognize the positive correlation between question level & acceptable responses.

FIGURE 7–4
A practice activity in predicting outcomes

Unit 11 · The Main Idea                    REVIEW

● Read this.

Mary and Henry went to get a dog.
They wanted a dog they both liked.

First, Henry saw a dog he liked,
but Mary didn't like the dog.
"That dog is too little," Mary said.

Then, Mary saw a dog she liked.
Henry thought the dog was too big.

So Henry and Mary looked again.
At last they found a dog that was
not too big and not too little.
They both liked the dog.
The dog liked both of them.

● Circle the words that tell
what the children will do.
look again     get a cat     get the last dog

● Now find three sentences in the story
that helped you decide.
Underline those sentences.

**Comprehension:** Predicting Outcomes                    CAROUSELS

68

Houghton Mifflin Reading, 1989 Edition

**Source:** From *Houghton Mifflin Reading, Carousels* workbook by William K. Durr et al. Copyright © 1989.
Reprinted by permission of Houghton Mifflin Company.

7. Ask question before reading a passage, not only after reading a passage.

8. Help kids learn ~~kids~~ to ask their own questions about their reading

269

nament? If so, you relied on the information in the text and your procedural knowledge of the events commonly associated with winning a basketball tournament to make a slot-filling inference and draw a conclusion. Figure 7–5 illustrates several drawing-conclusion tasks from a published reading program.

**Helping Students Predict Outcomes and Draw Conclusions.** One of the most common method frameworks used to help children predict outcomes and draw conclusions is the first phase of a **directed reading-thinking activity (DRTA).** A DRTA is an instructional procedure developed by Stauffer (1976). Its first phase consists of three procedural steps, which are repeated as students read and discuss a selection:

> predicting
> reading
> proving

During the predicting step the teacher asks students to predict the outcome and explain their inferential reasoning. At the beginning of a story, a teacher might use questions like these to initiate responses:

> What will a story with this title be about? Why do you think so?
> Who do you think will be in a story with a title like this? Why?
> Where do you think this story will take place? Why?

Each student is expected to make a prediction and support it with a reasonable explanation. Teachers should encourage different predictions as long as students can justify them logically.

The second procedural step in a DRTA is to have students read. Teachers should ask students to read silently up to a predetermined point, at which students' earlier predictions should be checked. Directions like these might be given:

> Now that you have all told me what you think this story is going to be about, who will be in it, and where it will take place, I want you to read and see if you were correct. Read up to the end of page 2, please.

The third procedural step is proving. During this step students are asked to draw conclusions and explain their reasoning process. In discussion, students are asked to evaluate the evidence in relation to their predictions. They see whether they were correct or incorrect and, most importantly, *why* they were correct or incorrect. Questions like the following can be used to begin the discussion:

> Was your guess correct? Why or why not?
> What do you think now? Why?
> Why do you think $X$ happened?
> Why did $A$ (a character) do $X$ (an event)?
> What do you think will happen next?

**directed reading-thinking activity (DRTA):** A method framework used to assist students in predicting outcomes and drawing conclusions; involves predicting, reading, and proving.

FIGURE 7–5
A practice activity in drawing conclusions

# Drawing Conclusions

Read each paragraph and the numbered questions below it. In the blank before the number of each question, write the letter of the best answer.

This summer, Lori is earning some extra money by helping her father. She takes money from people who have had their gas tanks filled. She also cleans windshields and helps people put air into their tires. She is saving her money for the special shoes that she needs for the lessons she is taking.

_____ 1. **Where do you think Lori is working?**
  a. at a gasoline service station    b. at a bicycle repair shop
            c. at a supermarket

_____ 2. **What kind of lessons do you think Lori is taking?**
  a. weaving lessons         b. dancing lessons
            c. piano lessons

Dave was hammering a nail into a board. He thought to himself, "When I get this finished, it will make a nice home for my small feathered friends. I'll hang it in the tree beside my window." He was holding the nail to keep it steady while he hammered. All of a sudden he cried, "Ouch!" Then he dropped the nail.

_____ 3. **What do you think Dave was making?**
  a. a clubhouse          b. a doghouse
            c. a birdhouse

_____ 4. **When Dave said, "Ouch!" what do you think happened?**
  a. He hit his finger with the hammer.
  b. A bird pecked him on the nose.
  c. He put his finger between two boards.

Hank knew that the swimming test would be held today. He had a funny feeling in his stomach. He took his time getting dressed and eating breakfast. Slowly he walked to the pool where the test was being given. Two hours later when his mother saw him, Hank had a big smile on his face.

_____ 5. **How do you think Hank felt about taking the swimming test?**
  a. Hank was sure that he would pass the test.
  b. Hank was nervous.
  c. Hank wanted to take the test as soon as possible

_____ 6. **Why do you think Hank had a big smile on his face?**
  a. He did not take the test.    b. He failed the test.
            c. He passed the test.

**Source:** From W. Durr et al., *Houghton Mifflin Reading Program, Weavers Teacher's Edition*. Copyright © 1985 by Houghton Mifflin Co. Used with permission.

At the end of this step the three-step procedure is repeated, beginning with making predictions about the next outcome.

This type of method framework can be used whenever children read a story together. It encourages them to continually think about what they have read and what is likely to happen next. Other instructional activities can also be used, however, to develop the ability to predict outcomes and draw conclusions.

**SAMPLE
ACTIVITIES**

**Riddle Reading and Riddle Writing.** Reading riddles provides opportunities to practice drawing conclusions in an enjoyable fashion. You may want to write a riddle on the board each day and then at the end of the day see who has figured out the answer. Older students might enjoy writing and sharing their own riddles. You could then develop a class riddle book to share with other classes in your school.

**Thematic Units.** New experiences develop procedural knowledge for students, especially when they are integrated into other subject areas. For this reason thematic units across subject areas are very helpful. Organize reading experiences around specific themes. Plan experiences in other subject areas around those themes. Chapter 9 describes how thematic units can be developed.

**Reading Mysteries.** Mysteries are especially valuable for providing practice in predicting outcomes and drawing conclusions. Be sure to select mysteries for read-aloud sessions. Have students predict outcomes, draw conclusions, and then explain their reasoning at various points in the story. You may wish to build in experiences with the following books:

> *The Case of the Cat's Meow* by Crosby Bonsall
> *Encyclopedia Brown Saves the Day* by Donald Sobol
> *Encyclopedia Brown: Boy Detective* by Donald Sobol
> *Mystery at the Edge of Two Worlds* by Christie Harris
> *Something Queer Is Going On* by Elizabeth Levy
> *The House of Dies Drear* by Virginia Hamilton

## USING QUESTIONING STRATEGIES TO DEVELOP READING COMPREHENSION

It is important for both readers and teachers to ask questions about what they are reading. For readers, questions serve to monitor comprehension, focus attention on puzzling aspects of the text, and guide the search for answers. Questions are an essential part of the comprehension process. For teachers also, questions serve a variety of functions.

When used appropriately, questions can motivate students and are a useful instructional tool.

- *Modeling the reasoning process*. Questions, along with answers and explanations of how answers were derived, can be used to model reasoning processes that are important for comprehension.
- *Initiating a discussion*. Questions can be used to trigger discussion of central information before a passage is read, thus increasing the background knowledge that readers bring to the text. Questions can also be used to initiate a discussion about what has happened or is likely to take place in the text.
- *Guiding students' reasoning*. Questions can be used to guide students' thinking. Teachers can use questions to help students replicate the reasoning strategies of proficient readers.
- *Focusing attention*. Questions can be used to focus attention on a specific portion of text for subsequent instructional purposes.
- *Providing practice in specific comprehension tasks*. Questions can be used to engage students in specific types of inferential tasks, such as cause-and-effect, sequence, pronoun and adverbial references, predicting outcomes, or drawing conclusions.

■ *Assessment.* Questions can be used to monitor students' understanding of a passage they have read.

## Comprehension Questions

There are a variety of ways to organize the questions that teachers use during reading instruction. The traditional approach identifies the levels of comprehension addressed by the questions.

**literal-level questions:** Questions asking for information explicitly stated in the text.

**inferential-level questions:** Questions asking for information that requires a reader to use background knowledge in conjunction with information explicitly stated in the text.

**evaluative-level questions:** Questions asking readers to make critical judgments about information in the text, using previous experiences or values.

**question-answer relations (QAR):** A taxonomy of relationships between questions and answers.

**right-there QARs:** One type of in-the-book QAR; questions with answers that are explicitly stated in the text.

**putting-it-together QARs:** One type of in-the-book QAR requiring readers to make a text-connecting inference.

**author-and-you QARs:** One type of in-my-head QAR requiring readers to connect background knowledge to information in the text.

**on-your-own QARs:** One type of in-my-head QAR calling for answers that are not in the text but that depend on the reader's own experiences.

**Levels-of-Comprehension Questions.** A levels approach organizes comprehension questions according to the type of information a reader must contribute to the answer. Three levels are specified: literal, inferential, and evaluative. **Literal-level questions** ask for information directly from the text. Readers can answer literal-level questions by relying on the literal, word-for-word meaning of a passage. Readers must contribute little, if any, information to answer literal-level questions because the answer is explicitly stated in the text.

**Inferential-level questions** ask for information not explicitly stated in the text. Readers must use their background knowledge in conjunction with text information and read between the lines. Inferential-level questions require readers to make either text-connecting or slot-filling inferences. **Evaluative-level questions** ask readers to make a critical judgment about information in the text. In order to answer such questions, readers must evaluate textual information in relation to their own values and experiences. Examples of each type of question can be seen in Figure 7–6.

**Question-Answer Relationships.** Raphael (1982, 1986) has suggested that it is appropriate to consider questions and their answers together. By doing so, we can be more precise in our use of questions and our understanding of why students have difficulty with certain questions. Based on an initial taxonomy developed by Pearson and Johnson (1978), Raphael has developed a system referred to as **question-answer relations,** or **QAR.**

A QAR approach organizes questions into two basic groups: questions that are "in the book" and questions that are "in my head." In-the-book questions have answers that can be found in the text. These questions come in two types: "right there" and "putting it together." **Right-there QARs** are similar to literal-level questions. They require literal recall of explicitly stated information. In other words, the answer is right there in the text. **Putting-it-together QARs** require readers to connect information stated in two or more locations; thus, they require a text-connecting inference.

The second major category includes in-my-head question-answer relationships. These questions also come in two types: "author and you" and "on your own." **Author-and-you QARs** require readers to connect information in the text with information they bring to it. The answer is not explicitly stated but requires readers to make a slot-filling inference. **On-your-own QARs** feature answers that are not in the text. Readers rely entirely on their own

FIGURE 7–6
Examples of literal, inferential, and evaluative questions

---

**Text**

Bob and Claire wanted to go out to eat, so Bob called to make a reservation. They drove to the restaurant, but when they arrived, no one was there. The door was locked, and a sign said "Closed on Mondays."

"What's going on?" Bob asked. "I just reserved a table over the phone."

Claire answered, "Are you sure you called the Steak House?"

"Oh," said Bob apologetically. "I think I may have called the Steak Place."

**Literal Questions**

1. Who wanted to go out to eat? (Bob and Claire)
2. Why did Bob call? (to make a reservation)

**Inferential Questions**

1. When did Bob and Claire drive to the restaurant? (after Bob made the reservation)
2. On what day did this story take place? (Monday)
3. At what restaurant did Bob make a reservation? (the Steak Place)
4. Where did Bob and Claire go? (the Steak House)

**Evaluative Questions**

1. What would you have done next in this situation? (All logical answers are acceptable.)
2. What do you think Bob and Claire should have done differently? (All logical answers are acceptable.)

---

experiences and can even answer on-your-own QARs without reading the text. Examples of each type of question-answer relationship can be seen in Figure 7–7.

## Guidelines for Using Questions

Questioning occurs frequently during classroom reading lessons. Therefore, it is important for you to think about how you will use questions in your own classroom. The following suggestions should help.

■ *Do not use questions solely to test comprehension.* Durkin (1979, 1981) found that teachers use questions largely to test, not teach, reading comprehension. As mentioned earlier, when teachers play the guess-the-answer-I-have-in-my-head game with students, they are testing, not teaching. To teach reading comprehension, you should model your own reasoning processes aloud to students and ask them to explain their reasoning processes

FIGURE 7-7
Examples of in-the-book and in-my-head questions

---

**Text**

Bob and Claire wanted to go out to eat, so Bob called to make a reservation. They drove to the restaurant, but when they arrived, no one was there. The door was locked, and a sign said "Closed on Mondays."

"What's going on?" Bob asked. "I just reserved a table over the phone."

Claire answered, "Are you sure you called the Steak House?"

"Oh," said Bob apologetically. "I think I may have called the Steak Place."

**In-the-Book Questions**

*Right There*
1. Who wanted to go out to eat? (Bob and Claire)
2. Why did Bob call? (to make a reservation)

*Putting It Together*
1. When did Bob and Claire drive to the restaurant? (after Bob made the reservation)
2. At what restaurant did Bob make a reservation? (the Steak Place)

**In-My-Head Questions**

*Author and You*
1. At what restaurant were Bob and Claire? (the Steak House)
2. On what day did this story take place? (Monday)

*On Your Own*
1. How would you feel if you took a friend to dinner and the restaurant was closed? (All logical answers are acceptable.)

---

as well. This procedure is sometimes referred to as "think aloud" (Davey, 1983; Fitzgerald, 1983). For example, you might follow up each comprehension question with "Can you tell us how you figured out that answer?" Making reasoning processes explicit is especially helpful for less proficient students.

■ *Help students understand that answers may come from the text or from the knowledge about the world that they have in their heads*. Students are not always aware of this distinction. Some research suggests that knowing the distinction between in-the-book and in-my-head QARs facilitates comprehension (Raphael, 1982, 1986).

■ *Ask higher-level questions*. If you take a levels approach to questions, higher-level questions are more appropriate than lower-level questions because the former provide more reasoning opportunities for readers. For example, to answer an evaluative-level question, readers must consider information at the literal, inferential, and evaluative levels. To answer an inferential-level question, readers must consider information at both literal and inferential levels. However, to answer a literal-level question, readers need to consider only information at the literal level. Higher-level questions also provide greater opportunities to model reasoning processes.

■ *If students are unable to answer a higher-level question, ask a related lower-level question*. Breaking down the reasoning task into easier elements provides a supporting scaffold, or foundation, on which students can make an inference.

■ *Accept a greater variation in responses as you ask higher-level questions*. Answers to literal-level questions or in-the-book QARs are either correct or incorrect: the answers are explicitly stated in the text. However, answers to inferential-level questions, evaluative-level questions, or in-my-head QARs rely on background knowledge, which differs among individuals. As a result, higher-level questions usually have more than one acceptable answer.

■ *Ask questions before students read a story*. This approach helps students attend to important background knowledge that is required to comprehend a passage. For example, ask students whether they have ever experienced a problem like the one in the story they are about to read. Then have a short discussion on how they solved their problem. Hansen and Pearson (1980) found this strategy to be especially helpful for students because it builds an instructional scaffold that supports students' comprehension. Evaluative-level questions and on-my-own QARs are especially appropriate for prereading activities.

■ *Plan discussion questions in advance*. Devising questions as you discuss a story with students will result in many literal-level questions or in-the-book QARs. It is nearly impossible to generate more complex questions without advance planning. Thus, before discussing a story, you should be sure that you have thought about the types of questions you will ask.

## DEVELOPING METACOGNITIVE KNOWLEDGE

**Metacognitive knowledge**—which includes the strategies we use during reading, as well as our monitoring of comprehension—also contributes to the comprehension of extended text. As texts become more complex, metacognitive knowledge is increasingly required to facilitate comprehension. Questioning strategies are often used to develop this knowledge, but in this case teachers show students how to ask questions themselves as they read an extended text. Two method frameworks are most commonly used: reciprocal questioning and reciprocal teaching.

metacognitive knowledge: A type of knowledge important for reading that includes the strategies used during reading and comprehension monitoring.

### Reciprocal Questioning

**Reciprocal questioning,** or **ReQuest,** is a method framework first developed by Manzo (1969). It was initially designed for remedial reading instruction but works equally well for developmental reading instruction. The following procedural steps are recommended to implement reciprocal questioning.

reciprocal questioning (Re-Quest): A method framework designed to improve metacognition and comprehension; involves reading and questioning by both teacher and students, predicting, and checking predictions.

1. Teacher and students read.
2. Students question teacher.
3. Teacher questions students.
4. Students predict the story's outcome.
5. Teacher and students finish reading to check predictions.

During the first step both teacher and students read a portion of the selection silently. Manzo originally suggested that this be a single sentence when working with remedial readers, and that practice may be appropriate with beginning readers. With other readers, however, longer portions of a story should be used—perhaps a paragraph, a page, or even several pages.

The second procedural step has students ask the teacher questions about what they have read. In answering these questions, the teacher might explain the reasoning process involved and should definitely share with students the evidence from the text and from personal background knowledge that went into the various answers. The teacher might want to label the different questions that are asked to encourage students to avoid right-there types of QARs and, instead, ask questions that require some degree of inferencing.

Then the teacher asks questions of the students about the same story portion. The teacher may wish to require that students explain the evidence they used to determine each answer because that process—making explicit the strategies used to determine an inference—helps develop metacognitive knowledge. These first three steps may then be repeated several times with succeeding portions of the reading selection.

Whenever an important event in the story is about to occur, the teacher should ask students to predict what will happen next. This fourth step is similar to the predicting step of a DRTA. The teacher should ask students what they think will take place or how they think the story will end. As a part of their answers, students should explain their reasoning processes. The teacher might also share his or her own prediction and give an explanation of the reasoning involved.

Finally, teacher and students should read to the end of the selection and check their predictions. A short discussion of the story's conclusion might be appropriate to end this step. Reciprocal questioning is a method framework that may be used to guide the reading of a story with a group of students. It allows the discussion to focus on comprehending the story and the metacognitive strategies that contribute to comprehension. Reciprocal questioning can be used at all grade levels. In the model lesson Ms. Dodson is using this method framework to help a small group of her students develop greater strategic knowledge and increase their understanding of inferences.

## Reciprocal Questioning

Ms. Dodson is using *Nate the Great and the Snowy Trail* by Marjorie Weinman Sharmat. The story tells how Nate the Great discovers his lost birthday present by following several clues.

**MODEL LESSON**

**Teacher and Students Read.** Ms. Dodson passes out a copy of the book to each student. Together they talk briefly about the author and look at the cover illustration. Ms. Dodson asks students to speculate and tell what they think the story might be about. Several possibilities are identified. In the course of the discussion, several important concepts in the story also emerge and are explained. Then Ms. Dodson tells her students that good readers act like detectives and look for clues to the meaning of a story. She asks her students to read the first page silently.

### Students Question Teacher

Ms. Dodson: Now, what questions do you want to ask me about what we've read? Let's try to ask questions with answers that aren't right in the story. Let's see whether I can use the clues in the story well.

Tomas: OK, how about this one: how did Nate the Great and Sludge feel?

Ms. Dodson: That's a good one. I think they were cold and wet. The story talks about the snow dog and snow detective that Nate was making and says, "They were cold, and white, and wet." That's a clue that helped me. Then Nate says, "And so were we." That's another clue. I put those two sentences together and figured out that Nate and Sludge were cold and wet.

Dominic: What was Nate the Great?

Ms. Dodson: Oh, that's easy. He was a detective. It says right there in the book, "I, Nate the Great, am a detective." Can you ask me a question with an answer that isn't right there in the book?

Dominic: What time of year was it?

Ms. Dodson: Good. I think it was winter. It doesn't say that anywhere, does it? But they were making a snow detective and a snow dog. That's the clue that made me think it was winter.

### Teacher Questions Students

Ms. Dodson: OK, my turn. I've got one that will really make you think. It's an author-and-you kind of question. What kind of stories do you think Nate likes to read?

Mike: I know. I think he likes mysteries. It says he's a detective, and detectives like to solve cases, like in *Encyclopedia Brown*.

Ms. Dodson:   Well done. That was hard, but the author did give you a clue. Now let's read by ourselves to page 21. Try to find out what you think the problem in this story is.

Ms. Dodson repeats these three steps several times as she and the students read the story. She always allows her students to ask her several more questions than she asks them because she wants them to develop the habit of asking themselves good questions as they read a story.

**Students Predict the Story's Outcome.** Just before the solution is revealed, Ms. Dodson asks her students what they think the present will be. Answers range from a sled, to a book, to a cat.

**Teacher and Students Finish Reading to Check Predictions.** Ms. Dodson has her students read the rest of the story. She asks them to find out what the present is and how Nate discovers it. Afterwards they discuss all the clues in the story that should tell a good detective what the present is. Ms. Dodson concludes by pointing out that readers need to be detectives, too. Just like Nate the Great they need to look for clues as they are reading and figure out what each one means.

## Reciprocal Teaching

reciprocal teaching: A method framework designed to improve metacognition and comprehension: summarize, clarify, question, and predict.

**Reciprocal teaching** is a second method framework often used to develop metacognition. It is especially useful in helping students develop their ability to monitor comprehension. Reciprocal teaching consists of four steps that teacher and students repeat as they read a passage:

Summarize
Clarify
Question
Predict

The goal of reciprocal teaching is to help readers internalize these steps so that they use them independently during their own silent reading. The instructional approach is to have the teacher model the use of the procedural steps first and then have students follow the teacher's lead, all while reading a story together. Students are expected to follow the steps on their own after a number of practice sessions in the group setting.

During the first step readers ask, "What did I read?" They are expected to summarize the main point(s) of what they have just read. During the second step readers ask, "Are there any parts that are not clear to me?" Then they reread portions that are not clear and attempt to clarify the meaning.

During the third step readers ask, "What question would a teacher ask about this portion of the passage?" They should ask (and answer) a comprehension question related to the main point(s) of what they have just read. During the fourth step readers ask, "What will probably happen next in this passage?" They then predict what they will read in the next portion. These four steps are repeated at regular intervals as readers work their way through a passage. Teachers usually model the steps first, as Ms. Clancy does in the model lesson. Then they have students take turns modeling the steps aloud. Ms. Clancy is using reciprocal teaching to help her seventh-grade students practice monitoring what they are reading.

## Reciprocal Teaching

Ms. Clancy has a chart on the board listing the steps for reciprocal teaching and the questions to be asked at each step. She has already introduced the informational selection called *The History of Chocolate* by James Reder and has developed an understanding of the important vocabulary concepts. Ms. Clancy and her students have read the first two pages of the selection and are now reading the following portion of the passage.

**MODEL LESSON**

> The people of Spain didn't want other people to find out about their special drink that came from Mexico. They kept it a secret for over a hundred years.
> Finally, though, other people found out about the secret. They learned where the special beans came from. Then they started growing the kakahuatl tree, or cacao tree, in other parts of the world so they could get more of the special beans. Still, only the very rich people could afford the special chocolate drink because the cacao beans were still so expensive.
> Today, cacao beans grow around the world and chocolate is not so expensive. We can all eat chocolate because so many cacao trees produce the chocolate bean.

### Summarize

Ms. Clancy:  Let's see. Let me look on our chart here. First, I need to summarize and ask myself, "What did I read?" Well, I read that Spain kept the secret of chocolate, but now it's not a secret, and we can all eat chocolate. I'm glad about that. I really like chocolate.

### Clarify

Ms. Clancy:  Now let's see. I need to ask, "Are there any parts that are not clear to me?" Yes. I'm not really clear about why there are so many cacao trees now and chocolate is not so expensive. I'd better read that part again. [Ms. Clancy reads the passage aloud.] Here it is. It says, "They learned where the special beans came from. Then they started growing the kakahuatl tree, or cacao tree, in other parts of the world so they could get more of the special beans." More and more people must have kept learning about the beans because it also says, "Today, cacao beans grow around the world and chocolate is not so expensive."

## Question

Ms. Clancy: Now I need to ask a question that a teacher would ask about this portion of the passage. Let's see. I know. Are there more cacao trees now or when the Spanish were keeping their secret?

Toni: I know. There are more now.

Ms. Clancy: Good. How did you figure that out?

Toni: I read two things in the story and put them together. First it says everyone is growing them around the world, and it also says that chocolate is not so expensive now. If we had fewer trees today, it would be more expensive, not less.

## Predict

Ms. Clancy: Great! Now I need to ask, "What will probably happen next in this passage?"

Raghib: I think we're going to read about all the different kinds of chocolate they make. At the end of this section it talks about how we all can eat chocolate. It sounds like the author will tell us next about all the different ways we use chocolate.

Ms. Clancy: Let's read the next two pages to ourselves and find out what the author does talk about next.

Ms. Clancy and her students read the next two pages silently. They discover that Raghib's guess was correct. Then Ms. Clancy guides one of her students to follow the same steps that she has just modeled. When the student finishes by making a prediction about the next portion, teacher and students read several more pages silently. Then another student becomes the teacher and completes each of the four steps. This process is repeated until the informational selection is completed.

Reciprocal questioning and reciprocal teaching are useful method frameworks for developing metacognitive knowledge. Both give students models of how proficient readers interact with texts. In addition, the following sample activities can be used to develop metacognitive knowledge.

*→ for metacognitive knowledge*

**Think-Alouds.** Try reading aloud to your students a portion of text. As you read, articulate the reading and reasoning strategies that you are employing, including any predictions you make, any questions you pose to yourself, and any inferences you make about what you are reading. Then ask students to do the same. Such explicit modeling of the reading comprehension process has been shown to contribute significantly to improved metacognitive skill (Baker & Brown, 1984).

**Cooperative Learning Groups.** After students have developed an understanding of the steps in reciprocal questioning and reciprocal teaching, try using either of these methods in cooperative learning groups. Such groups can provide a useful variation for conducting the reading of a story.

**SAMPLE ACTIVITIES**

## USING A COMPREHENSION FRAMEWORK TO GUIDE INSTRUCTION IN EXTENDED TEXT

There are two basic decisions that you will face as you consider instruction related to extended text, and your comprehension framework can assist you with both. First, you will need to decide what to teach and emphasize. Should you try to develop syntactic, discourse, and metacognitive knowledge? How much should you emphasize these types of knowledge? Your conclusion about how a person reads will guide you in these decisions.

Second, you will need to decide how you will teach the knowledge sources associated with extended text. Should you favor deductive or inductive learning experiences? Should you follow a hierarchical sequence of comprehension skills, or should you teach comprehension within reading experiences as the need arises? Should questions be used to practice and assess comprehension, or should they be used more to develop comprehension through modeling experiences? Which method frameworks should you use to teach comprehension? Your conclusion about how reading ability develops will assist you in these decisions.

### What Should I Teach and Emphasize?

To guide you in deciding what you will teach and emphasize, you should consider your assessment of how a person reads. Table 7–3 summarizes how that portion of your framework can be used to guide decision making about comprehension instruction.

**Text-Based Explanation.** Teachers who follow a text-based explanation of how a person reads spend the least amount of time developing syntactic, discourse, and metacognitive knowledge. Because they believe that meaning exists more in the text than in the prior knowledge a reader brings to that text, they spend

Teachers need to consider what knowledge is required to comprehend extended text and also how that knowledge should be taught.

more time developing decoding knowledge. When these teachers do teach elements related to the comprehension of extended text, they focus instructional time on elements that help readers comprehend the meaning that exists in the text: punctuation, explicitly signaled sequence relationships, explicitly signaled cause-and-effect relationships, signal words, literal-level questions, and in-the-book QARs. These teachers spend less time teaching elements that help readers bring meaning to a text, such as predicting outcomes.

Punctuation is taught since it helps readers "hear" the stress and intonation patterns that convey meaning in a text. Explicitly signaled cause-and-effect relationships, explicitly signaled sequence relationships, and signal words are all taught because they are elements of meaning in a text. Implicit relationships that require readers to make an inference and contribute meaning to a text are not emphasized. Literal-level questions and in-the-book QARs are used more than other types of questions, again, because they help a reader comprehend the meaning that already exists in a text.

**Reader-Based Explanation.** Teachers who follow a reader-based explanation of how a person reads spend the most time developing syntactic, discourse, and metacognitive knowledge because they believe that meaning exists more in what a reader brings to a text than in the text itself. Inferences are especially important to these teachers; therefore, predicting outcomes and drawing conclusions are encouraged since they involve inferences, either looking forward toward upcoming information or looking backward toward previous informa-

TABLE 7–3

Summary of how a comprehension framework guides decisions about what to teach regarding extended text

| Explanation of How a Person Reads | Related Assumptions | Probable Time Spent on Extended Text | Probable Emphasis |
|---|---|---|---|
| Text-based | Meaning exists more in the text. Reading is translation. Reading begins with decoding knowledge. | Little | Punctuation. Explicitly signaled relationships. Signal words. Literal questions/in-the-book QARs. |
| Reader-based | Meaning exists more in what the reader brings to the text. Reading consists of expectations of upcoming words. Reading begins with prior knowledge. | Much | Predicting outcomes. Implicitly signaled relationships. Inferential or evaluative questions/in-my-head QARs. |
| Interactive | Meaning exists in both the text and the reader. Reading is both translation and expectation. Reading uses each knowledge source simultaneously. | Moderate amount | Aspects related to both text- and reader-based explanations. |

tion. Implicit cause-and-effect and sequence relationships requiring readers to make inferences are also emphasized. In addition, inferential- and evaluative-level questions and in-my-head QARs are used more than other types of questions.

**Interactive Explanation.** Teachers who follow an interactive explanation of how a person reads spend a moderate amount of time developing syntactic, discourse, and metacognitive knowledge. But even as they develop those elements associated with what a reader brings to a text, they are also developing decoding and vocabulary knowledge wherever necessary, elements associated with the meaning that is already in a text. These teachers develop familiarity with the conventions of punctuation, and they also help youngsters draw conclusions and predict outcomes. They help students with key words and explicit cause-and-effect and sequence relationships, as well as with the inferences required in implicit cause-and-effect and sequence relationships. These teachers use the complete range of questions to develop reading comprehension: literal, inferential, and evaluative questions, in addition to in-the-book and in-my-head QARs.

## How Should I Teach?

You will also need to make decisions about how to teach the comprehension of extended text. Your conclusion about how reading ability develops should guide you in those decisions. Table 7–4 summarizes how that portion of your framework can be used in decision making.

**Specific Skills Explanation.** Teachers who follow a specific-skills explanation believe that reading ability develops as students learn specific reading skills, which should be taught in teacher-directed, deductive lessons. As a result, deductive experiences are favored, and a hierarchy of specific comprehension skills are apt to guide instruction. Questions are used mainly to practice and assess students' developing skills, and the most common method frameworks include deductive instruction and directed reading activities (DRAs).

**Holistic Language Explanation.** Teachers who follow a holistic language explanation believe that reading ability develops as students engage in holistic, meaningful, and functional experiences with print. As a result, inductive experiences are favored, and comprehension instruction always takes place, as needed, within the context of functional reading experiences. Questions are used more for modeling than for practice and assessment, and the most common method frameworks include these: language experience stories, language experience sentences, inductive instruction, DRTA, cooperative learning groups, reciprocal questioning, reciprocal teaching, and think-alouds.

**Integrated Explanation.** Teachers who follow an integrated explanation of development share both specific-skills and holistic perspectives. Inductive as well as deductive experiences are used. And even though a hierarchy of specific comprehension skills may not determine instruction, comprehension skills are developed during reading experiences. Questions are used both to assess and to develop comprehension through modeling experiences. In addition, all of the method frameworks described in this chapter are used.

TABLE 7-4

Summary of how a comprehension framework guides decisions about how to teach elements related to extended text.

| Explanation of How Reading Ability Develops | Related Assumptions | Probable Instructional Activities |
|---|---|---|
| Specific skills | Reading ability develops as students learn specific reading skills. Students learn best as a result of teacher-directed deductive experiences. | Deductive experiences Hierarchy of comprehension skills taught to mastery Questions used to practice and assess comprehension Most common method frameworks: deductive instruction and directed reading activities |
| Holistic language | Reading ability develops as students engage in holistic, meaningful, and functional experiences with print. Students learn best as a result of self-directed inductive experiences. | Inductive experiences. Instruction during reading experiences. Questions used to develop comprehension through modeling experiences. Most common method frameworks: language experience stories, language experience sentences, inductive instruction, DRTA, cooperative learning groups, reciprocal questioning, reciprocal teaching, think-alouds. |
| Integrated | Reading ability develops as students learn specific reading skills and as they engage in meaningful, functional, and holistic experiences with print. Reading ability develops as a result of both teacher-directed deductive experiences and self-directed inductive experiences. | Both deductive and inductive experiences as appropriate. Some comprehension skills targeted and taught during reading experiences. Questions used to both assess and develop comprehension through modeling experiences. Most common method frameworks: deductive method framework, directed reading activities, language experience stories, inductive instruction, DRTA, cooperative learning groups, reciprocal questioning, reciprocal teaching, think-alouds. |

## COMMENTS FROM THE CLASSROOM ■

### Mr. Burns

While I believe decoding is very important, I spend a lot of time helping my students comprehend. For me the best way to help beginning readers comprehend is to be sure they can read the words they meet. If they can't decode, no amount of inferencing will help them.

What I teach in the area of comprehension is really quite a bit. We spend time learning about punctuation, which also helps my students in their writing. In addition, I teach sequence relationships, cause-and-effect relationships, signal words, and comprehension of the stories we read in our published reading program. I ask comprehension questions with each story, often using the ones in the teacher's guide, although I do spend time before each lesson developing some of my own. Most of my questions are literal-level questions, but I also ask some inferential questions and usually include at least one evaluative question. These questions help me see whether my students understand what they have read. The questions also give my students good practice thinking about what they've read.

How I teach, as I said earlier, is mostly through the lessons in our published reading program because they give structure to the skills we work on. I usually follow the teacher's guide, but I also make up many of my own lessons. Most often my lessons follow a directed reading activity or deductive instruction.

### Ms. Sanchez

I believe that the only point to reading instruction is helping children understand what they read. That's what all of us use reading for, and that's what we should be concerned with in the classroom. So what do I teach? I'm very concerned about helping my students use their prior knowledge during reading—inferential

reasoning is what reading is all about. Children need to learn how to read between the lines, how to infer sequence and cause-and-effect relationships, and how to draw conclusions and predict outcomes when they're reading. In comprehension instruction I spend most of my time on these aspects and on developing metacognitive knowledge.

How do I teach? I see myself as helping my students develop their ability to comprehend. I help them when we're reading, not before and not after; it's important to develop comprehension within the context of actual reading experiences. I often use language experience stories and language experience sentences, especially when I notice some element of comprehension that a number of my students need help with. I also use DRTAs and cooperative learning groups a lot, along with reciprocal teaching, reciprocal questioning, and think-alouds to develop metacognitive knowledge.

### Ms. Dodson

I'm very concerned about developing comprehension among my students, but I'm also concerned about developing their decoding and vocabulary knowledge. What I teach is a little of everything. I do teach punctuation, often through our writing activities. Yet I also teach both explicit and implicit relationships in sequence and cause and effect. In addition, we work on drawing conclusions and predicting outcomes, and we spend time with the complete range of question levels and QARs.

How I teach is also a composite of different methods. Sometimes I use our published reading program with the students. At other times we read literature selections together or independently. In either case I use a full range of method frameworks, depending on what my students need and what I want to accomplish. I use both deductive and inductive experiences, directed reading activities, language experience sentences and stories, DRTAs, DRAs, and cooperative learning groups. I also use reciprocal questioning, reciprocal teaching, and think-alouds to develop metacognitive knowledge—they're really fun!

---

- An inference is a reasoned assumption about meaning that is not explicitly stated in the text. Readers make inferences by using their background knowledge to connect different pieces of information in a text and to fill in missing information. Inferential reasoning is sometimes referred to as reading between the lines.

- Young children have extensive knowledge of oral language but far more limited knowledge of written language. Understanding the differences between oral and written language can give teachers important insight into what their students must acquire in order to become proficient readers and writers.

- There are many ways to develop syntactic knowledge. The most common method frameworks include language experience sentences and language experience stories. In addition, discussion and instruction in the meaning and function of signal words are often used.

- There are also many ways to develop discourse knowledge. The most common method frameworks include deductive instruction, inductive instruction, and directed reading-thinking activities.

- Questioning strategies can be used to teach many aspects of reading comprehension. Traditional approaches use different levels of questions. More recent approaches use a taxonomy based on question-answer relationships.

- There are many ways to develop metacognitive knowledge. The most common method frameworks include reciprocal questioning and reciprocal teaching.

- A comprehension framework assists with decisions about what to teach and emphasize and how to teach it.

**MAJOR POINTS**

1. Identify at least four inferences a reader must make to comprehend the following passage. Specify whether each is a text-connecting or a slot-filling inference.

> It was raining, and they went inside the old barn. They unloaded their rifles and climbed the ladder to the loft. The hay was warm and dry. Craig and Bill sat swapping tales of their adventures

**MAKING INSTRUCTIONAL DECISIONS**

with grouse and waiting for a chance to get back outside. They both enjoyed the chance to stretch the truth a bit. Finally the rain stopped, and Bill said, ''Let's get going. We have to bring something home for dinner.'' Craig noticed, though, that it was already dark outside.

2. We can informally assess young children's knowledge of written language conventions by listening to their speech. Look at how two first-grade students told the story contained in the wordless picture book *Frog, Where Are You?* by Mercer Mayer.

### Tama

You see . . . there's a little frog, and he . . . *and* a little boy had him for a pet. *And* he had a little dog, *and* the frog was in the little bucket. *And* then they were walking, to do something, *and* the frog jumped out of . . . out of the bucket . . . *and* the frog just started looking at the flowers. *And* then they saw someone at a picnic, *and* they were having a picnic. *And* he got into their picnic basket, *and then* . . . the lady was gonna get . . . something out of her picnic basket . . . *and* the frog jumped on her hand . . . *and* . . . *and* then the lady got really mad.

### Jessica

Um . . . *once upon a time,* there was a little boy . . . who had a little frog for a pet. *After* they were walking for a while . . . the little frog jumped . . . out of the bucket *and* hopped away. The frog . . . saw two people who were having a picnic . . . *Because* he was a naughty frog . . . he hopped into their picnic basket. *After* the lady put her hand . . . into the picnic basket, the frog jumped out . . . *because* he thought . . . that she was gonna get him. The lady was scared . . . *since* she didn't like frogs.

What can you tell about each student's familiarity with written language conventions?

a. Which student is more familiar with the conventions of written language? How can you tell?

b. Which types of written language knowledge do you see in these oral language samples? decoding? vocabulary? syntactic? discourse? metacognitive? Explain.

c. Do you think sequence and cause-and-effect relationships might be difficult for one of these students to understand during reading? Why?

3. Plan a lesson using a language experience story to teach either sequence or cause-and-effect relationships. Identify which experience you will provide, how you will elicit oral language, and what you will do to teach sequence or cause-and-effect relationships.

4. Use the lesson from a published reading program in Figure 2–4 to plan a directed reading-thinking activity (DRTA). Follow the predict, read, and prove procedural steps described in this chapter. Identify the questions you would use to generate predictions as well as the beginning and ending points for each silent reading experience. Also identify the evidence in each portion of the story that could be used to answer your prediction questions.

5. Define one question each that you might use to assess comprehension of the passage in Item 1 on a literal, inferential, and evaluative level. Then develop right-there, putting-it-together, author-and-you, and on-your-own QARs for the same passage.

6. Plan a lesson using reciprocal questioning or reciprocal teaching. Base it on the lesson from the published reading program in Figure 2–4.

7. Plan a lesson using the story from the published reading program in Figure 2–4. Identify what you would teach in this lesson and how you would teach it. Specify how each decision you make is related to your comprehension framework.

**FURTHER READING**

Bauman, J. F., & Schmitt, M. C. (1986). The what, why how, and when of comprehension instruction. *The Reading Teacher, 39*(7), 640–645.
> Describes a four-step method framework for teaching comprehension in a deductive manner. More consistent with a specific-skills explanation of how reading ability develops.

Beck, I. L. (1989). Reading and reasoning. *The Reading Teacher, 42,* 676–682.
> Argues that reading is reasoning and that reading programs are ideal vehicles for developing reasoning abilities. Explains how to take advantage of the opportunities to develop reasoning that exist in reading selections.

Herrman, B. A. (1988). Two approaches for helping poor readers become more strategic. *The Reading Teacher, 42*(1), 24–28.
> Describes two methods for teaching reading comprehension processes: direct explanation and reciprocal teaching. Shows how each may be used to help readers understand how the reading process works and how they can become more strategic while reading.

Muth, K. D. (Ed.). (1989). *Children's comprehension of text*. Newark, DE: International Reading Association.
> A collection of 12 articles on helping young students to comprehend text. Contains articles related to the comprehension of narratives and other articles related to the comprehension of exposition.

**REFERENCES**

Anderson, R. C., & Shifrin, Z. (1980). The meaning of words in context. In R. J. Spiro, B. C. Bruce, and W. F. Brewer (Eds.), *Theoretical issues in reading comprehension*. Hillsdale, NJ: Erlbaum.

Baker, L., & Brown, A. L. (1984). Cognitive monitoring in reading. In J. Flood (Ed.), *Understanding reading comprehension*, Newark, DE: International Reading Association.

Beck, I. (1989). Reading and reasoning. *The Reading Teacher, 42,* 676–682.

Beck, I. L., McKeown, M. G., Omanson, R. C., & Pople, M. T. (1984). Improving the comprehensibility of stories: The effects of revisions that improve coherence. *Reading Research Quarterly, 19*(3), 263–277.

Cook-Gumperz, J., & Gumperz, J. (1981). From oral to written culture: The transition to literacy. In M. F. Whiteman (Ed.), *Writing: The nature, development, and teaching of written communication.* Hillsdale, NJ: Erlbaum.

Davey, B. (1983). Think-aloud: Modeling the cognitive processes of reading comprehension. *Journal of Reading, 27,* 44–47.

Durkin, D. (1979). Reading comprehension instruction in five basal reading series. *Reading Research Quarterly, 14,* 481–533.

Durkin, D. (1981). Reading methodology textbooks: Are they helping teachers teach comprehension? *The Reading Teacher, 39*(5), 410–417.

Fitzgerald, J. (1983). Helping readers gain self-control. *The Reading Teacher, 37,* 249–253.

Hansen, J., & Pearson, P. D. (1980). *The effects of inference training and practice on young children's comprehension (Tech. Rep. No. 166).* Urbana: University of Illinois, Center for the Study of Reading.

Leu, D. J., Jr. (1982). Differences between oral and written discourse and the acquisition of reading proficiency. *Journal of Reading Behavior, 14*(2), 111–125.

Manzo, A. V. (1969). The request procedure. *Journal of Reading, 11,* 123–126.

McGee, L. M., & Richgels, D. J. (1990). *Literacy Beginnings.* Boston: Allyn & Bacon.

McGovern, A. (1975). *The secret soldier.* New York: Scholastic Books.

Michaels, S., & Cook-Gumperz, J. (1979). A study of sharing time with first grade students: Discourse narratives in the classroom. *Proceedings of the Berkeley Linguistic Society, 5,* 87–103.

Murphy, S. (1985). Children's comprehension of deictic categories in oral and written language. *Reading Research Quarterly, 21,* 118–131.

Pearson, P. D., & Camperell, K. (1981). Comprehension of text structures. In J. T. Guthrie (Ed.), *Comprehension and teaching.* Newark, DE: International Reading Association.

Pearson, P. D., & Johnson, D. D. (1978). *Teaching reading comprehension.* New York: Holt, Rinehart & Winston.

Purcell-Gates, V. (1989). What oral/written language differences can tell us about beginning instruction. *The Reading Teacher, 42*(4), 290–295.

Raphael, T. E. (1982). Teaching children question-answering strategies. *The Reading Teacher, 36,* 186–191.

Raphael, T. E. (1986). Teaching question-answer relationships, revisited. *The Reading Teacher, 39,* 516–522.

Rubin, A. (1980). A theoretical taxonomy of the differences between oral and written language. In R. J. Spiro, B. C. Bruce, and W. F. Brewer (Eds.), *Theoretical issues in reading comprehension.* Hillsdale, NJ: Erlbaum.

Sewell, A. (1954). *Black Beauty.* Garden City, NY: Doubleday.

Stauffer, R. G. (1976). *Teaching reading as a thinking process.* New York: Harper & Row.

Sulzby, E. (1982). Oral and written mode adaptations in stories by kindergarten children. *Journal of Reading Behavior, 14*(2), 51–60.

Teale, W. H., & Sulzby, E. (Eds.). (1986). *Emergent literacy: Writing and reading.* Norwood, NJ: Ablex.

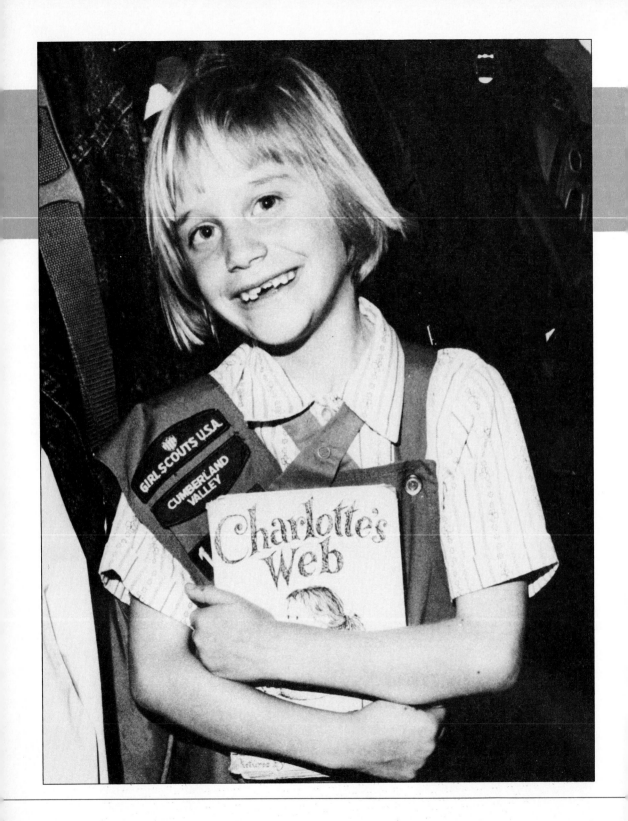

# Literature: Developing Independent Readers

- Centering a Classroom Reading Program Around Literature
- Using Literature to Develop Independent Readers
- What Is Narrative Discourse Structure?
- Developing Knowledge of Narrative Discourse Structure
- Using a Comprehension Framework to Guide Decisions About Literature in the Classroom.

*November 13*

*Dear Mr. Henshaw,*

*I am in the fourth grade now. I made a diorama of* Ways to Amuse a Dog, *the book I wrote to you about two times before. Now our teacher is making us write to authors for Book Week. I got your answer to my letter last year, but it was only printed. Please would you write to me in your own handwriting? I am a great enjoyer of your books.*

*My favorite character in the book was Joe's Dad because he didn't get mad when Joe amused his dog by playing a tape of a lady singing, and his dog sat and howled like he was singing, too. Bandit does the same thing when he hears singing.*

*Your best reader,*
*Leigh Botts*

I f you are like many adults, you can recall some of your favorite books from childhood: *Babar, Green Eggs and Ham, Where the Wild Things Are, Little House in the Big Woods, The Snowy Day, Charlotte's Web, The Velveteen Rabbit, Ramona the Pest.* These titles usually bring back warm and pleasant memories about reading. And your ability to retain those memories when you have forgotten many other childhood experiences reflects the profound effect that literature exerts on young children. As teachers, we need to consider how we can ensure that our students have similarly positive experiences with literature. This chapter introduces you to the many reasons and methods for making children's literature the center of your instructional program.

Chapter 8 includes information that will help you answer questions like these:

1. Why should literature be at the center of a classroom reading program?
2. How can I use literature to develop independent readers?
3. How does narrative discourse knowledge contribute to comprehension?
4. How can literature be used to develop narrative discourse knowledge?
5. How can a comprehension framework be used to guide instructional decisions about the use of literature?

## KEY CONCEPTS

Caldecott Medal
deductive instruction
directed reading-thinking activity
  (DRTA)
independent readers
initiating episode
interest inventory
literature
narrative discourse structure

Newbery Medal
read-aloud session
readers theatre
reading corner
setting information
story map/story mapping
succeeding episodes
sustained silent reading

## CENTERING A CLASSROOM READING PROGRAM AROUND LITERATURE

literature: A powerful vehicle for learning; includes a variety of text types, among them fiction, nonfictional narratives, and poetry.

**Literature** describes a wide variety of text types, including fiction, nonfictional narratives such as biographies and autobiographies, and poetry. Because literature is a powerful vehicle for learning, experiences with literature should be at the center of every classroom reading program (Tunnell & Jacobs, 1989). Literature's effects reach into every component of reading comprehension: emergent literacy/readiness considerations, affective considerations, decoding knowledge, vocabulary knowledge, syntactic knowledge, discourse knowledge, and metacognitive knowledge. Knowing how literature contributes to each component will help us understand why it is so important to reading instruction and how we can use it in a classroom reading program.

## Developing Emergent Literacy/Readiness Through Literature

Literature is important for developing emergent literacy/readiness both at home and at school. Parents who read to their children are preparing them for later reading experiences at school (Taylor & Strickland, 1986). Young children develop important insights from sharing a book with their parents: that print progresses from left to right, how words are related to sounds, how different types of stories begin and end, what a letter is, what a word is, and more (Clay, 1989; Cochran-Smith, 1984; Trelease, 1989, 1989b). Similar experiences with literature in preschool and elementary school classrooms continue this development (Tunnell & Jacobs, 1989). Teachers can assist the transition to literacy by encouraging parents to read frequently to their children and making literature experiences the center of reading programs at school.

## Developing Affective Aspects Through Literature

Literature has a great effect on motivation, interest, and emotional response, three affective aspects associated with comprehension. Good literature captures students' attention and increases their interest in reading, resulting in several important consequences. First, interested readers invest more of themselves in reading experiences and thus take more away from those experiences. Interested readers spend greater energy as they attempt to recognize difficult words, guess the meaning of unfamiliar words, and infer implicit relationships among several ideas. Interested readers are engaged readers who quickly learn the important elements of reading.

Second, interested readers are **independent readers**. They are more likely to read outside the classroom—finishing an exciting book on the bus ride home, reading in the living room before dinner, or even reading with a flashlight under the covers at night. Because these children choose to read independently, they have additional opportunities to develop their reading ability beyond the limited time available at school. As a result, they become better readers (Anderson, Fielding, & Wilson, 1988).

independent readers: Readers who know how to read and actually choose to read for pleasure, information, and personal growth.

Finally, literature is useful for children who are struggling to understand the realities of life. Children often find emotional support in stories about an issue they are trying to understand—death, love, fear, personal relationships, self-respect. Literature shows children that they are not alone in their emotions, and it often provides solutions to issues of personal concern (Harris & Sipay, 1990).

## Developing Decoding Knowledge Through Literature

A major goal within decoding knowledge is to develop automatic decoding skills. Because automatic decoding permits readers to focus their attention on a text's meaning, comprehension increases with the development of automatic decoding (Harris & Sipay, 1990). Literature provides opportunities for children to develop this automaticity (Rasinski, 1989). Good literature engages readers, drawing them into a book to discover how the story turns out and getting them "hooked on books" (Fader, 1976). One book by an author is just not enough for these children. And once hooked, they have greater opportunity to recognize words and, as a result, to develop automatic decoding skills more rapidly.

## Developing Vocabulary Knowledge Through Literature

Literature increases vocabulary knowledge as it captures, entertains, and enriches the lives of readers with vivid experiences that are impossible to replicate in a classroom. Literature allows a child to travel to the top of Mount Everest or to the bottom of the sea; to the edge of the galaxy or to the center of Earth; to the time of King Arthur or to the time of space traders—all without leaving a comfortable chair. And participating in these experiences, if only vicariously, enriches a child's vocabulary and conceptual knowledge. What better way is there to understand words such as *Nazi, Europe, terror,* and *diary* than to read *The Diary of Anne Frank*? What better way to understand *prairie, headcheese, journey, pioneer, hearth, covered wagon, fiddle, threshing,* or *harvest* than to read the *Little House* series by Laura Ingalls Wilder?

## Developing Syntactic Knowledge Through Literature

Literature also helps young readers enrich their syntactic knowledge. The work of our best writers provides excellent models of language use, thereby exposing children to important word order patterns and developing their knowledge about how these patterns communicate meaning. Young children develop an understanding of the syntactic patterns common to oral language through verbal interactions. Reading frequently to these children introduces them to the more complex syntactic patterns common to written language.

In addition, the vivid contexts of literature provide a supportive context for inferring implicit meanings. Such meanings are often easier to grasp in the middle of an exciting adventure story than in a workbook activity. Literature makes situations come alive in a reader's mind, thereby facilitating inferential processes.

## Developing Discourse Knowledge Through Literature

Literature helps to develop several aspects of discourse knowledge: understanding pronoun and adverb references, drawing conclusions, and predicting outcomes. The rich contexts found in literature provide opportunities for young readers to visualize the meanings of pronoun and adverb references. And mysteries, as well as other types of literature, encourage young readers to draw independent conclusions about who has done what to whom. In addition, because literature engages a reader's attention so completely, children have continuous opportunities to anticipate upcoming events and predict outcomes. Beyond these contributions literature develops the reader's knowledge of how stories are structured. This aspect of discourse knowledge is considered in greater detail later in this chapter.

## Developing Metacognitive Knowledge Through Literature

The rich contexts of literature also support the development of metacognitive knowledge, enabling readers to develop reading strategies and comprehension-monitoring abilities. When readers are entranced by a story, they often discover effective reading strategies on their own as they seek to discover how a story ends. Interested readers look for new ways to decode a word, new approaches to determining word meanings, new methods of making inferences. Literature is very useful in developing strategic knowledge.

Literature is also useful in getting students to monitor their own comprehension of a story. Engaging literature selections, by definition, provide reading experiences that prompt students to continuously check their understanding of a story. Thus, literature develops comprehension monitoring in a natural way.

Positive affective responses and independent reading are an outgrowth of interactions with quality literature.

## USING LITERATURE TO DEVELOP INDEPENDENT READERS

The fact that literature can be used to develop specific components of the comprehension process does not mean that it should be put away when instruction is completed. Literature must be integrated throughout a classroom program, becoming a part of all its seasons. The ultimate goal of any reading program is not to develop readers who know only how to read. Instead, the goal is to develop independent readers who know how to read and, in addition, choose to read for pleasure, information, and personal growth. Teaching our students to read without also developing their desire to read independently is pointless (Fuhler, 1990). If you wish to develop independent readers in your classroom through children's literature, you must do three things: become familiar with popular children's literature, identify your students' reading interest, and put children and books together in pleasurable settings.

### Becoming Familiar with Popular Children's Literature

**Newbery Medal:** An annual award given to the author of the "most distinguished contribution to American literature for children."

**Caldecott Medal:** An annual award given to the artist of the "most distinguished American picture book published in the United States."

There are many ways to become familiar with popular children's literature. You can begin by looking at books that have won the Newbery or Caldecott medals. The **Newbery Medal** is awarded annually by the American Library Association and the Association for Library Service to Children to the author of the "most distinguished contribution to American literature for children published during the preceding year." The **Caldecott Medal** is awarded annually by the same organizations to the artist of the "most distinguished American picture book for children published in the United States during the preceding year." It is important to keep in mind that Newbery and Caldecott medal winners are selected by adults, using adult criteria. Although medal-winning books meet the highest standards of the two associations that select them, they do not always meet the unique needs of individual children. Newbery and Caldecott medal winners are listed in Tables 8–1 and 8–2, respectively.

A second way to become familiar with popular children's literature is to look at books that have been selected as either Children's Choices or Teacher's Choices by the International Reading Association and the Children's Book Council. Each year, a joint committee from these two organizations coordinates a selection process involving thousands of children who read new books and vote for their favorites. The results have appeared in the October issue of *The Reading Teacher* each year since 1974. A similar process has started recently for teacher's choices. A free copy of the most recent choices can be obtained by sending a self-addressed 9-by-12-inch envelope, stamped with first-class postage for a two-ounce weight, to the International Reading Association (P.O. Box 8139, Newark, DE 19714, Attn: Children's [or Teacher's] Choices). Teachers might want to purchase copies in bulk and enclose them in the letters mailed out to parents at the beginning of the year.

A third way to become familiar with popular children's literature is to read issues of the *Horn Book Magazine,* which is the major journal in the field of children's literature. *Horn Book Magazine* reviews new children's books and contains articles on children's literature. It appears six times each year and can usually be found in a school or local library.

Another way to become familiar with popular children's literature is simply to talk to different individuals at a school. A school librarian can identify the books that are popular at a particular grade level. In addition, grade-level colleagues can share their experiences with popular literature selections, perhaps setting aside a lunch hour each week to talk about children's literature and share ideas for using literature in the classroom.

One final way to become familiar with popular children's literature is to consult an annotated bibliography. The following contain bibliographies of children's literature.

■ Association for Library Service to Children, *Notable Children's Books* (Chicago: American Library Association, annual)
■ *The Horn Book Guide to Children's and Young Adult Books* (Boston: Horn Book Inc., annual)
■ D. Norton, *Through the Eyes of a Child: An Introduction to Children's Literature* (3rd ed.) (New York: Macmillan, 1991)
■ J. Trelease, *The New Read Aloud Handbook* (New York: Penguin Books, 1989)

All of these methods are useful for developing a greater familiarity with children's literature. However, none take the place of actually reading children's literature regularly. Personal familiarity enables teachers to make appropriate choices as they build a classroom library and as they make suggestions to individual students.

As you begin to rediscover the world of children's literature, you should develop an easy-to-access filing system. It takes just a few minutes after reading each book to jot down bibliographic information, a synopsis of the story, and several questions you might use to begin a discussion. You should write this information in a consistent format on index cards or on disk, using data base management software. You will find your growing file a useful aid in selecting books. It will also be useful during student conferences when you use the method framework identified as individualized reading and described in chapter 2. A sample literature card is illustrated in Figure 8–1.

## Becoming Familiar with Students' Interests

Once you are confident that your classroom contains a wide range of interesting literature selections, you must determine the unique interests of your students, especially those who are reluctant readers. Knowing their interests will help you recommend interesting selections to them and will also help you make decisions about which literature selections to integrate into your classroom reading program.

TABLE 8–1
Award-winning children's literature: Newbery medal winners

| Year | Title | Author |
|------|-------|--------|
| 1922 | The Story of Mankind | Hendrik Willem van Loon |
| 1923 | The Voyages of Doctor Dolittle | Hugh Lofting |
| 1924 | The Dark Frigate | Charles Hawes |
| 1925 | Tales from Silver Lands | Charles Finger |
| 1926 | Shen of the Sea | Arthur Bowie Chrisman |
| 1927 | Smoky, the Cowhorse | Will James |
| 1928 | Gayneck, The Story of a Pigeon | Dhan Gopal Mukerji |
| 1929 | The Trumpeter of Krakow | Eric P. Kelly |
| 1930 | Hitty, Her First Hundred Years | Rachel Field |
| 1931 | The Cat Who Went to Heaven | Elizabeth Coatsworth |
| 1932 | Waterless Mountain | Laura Adams Armer |
| 1933 | Young Fu of the Upper Yangtze | Elizabeth Foreman Lewis |
| 1934 | Invincible Louisa | Cornelia Meigs |
| 1935 | Dobry | Monica Shannon |
| 1936 | Caddie Woodlawn | Carol Brink |
| 1937 | Roller Skates | Ruth Sawyer |
| 1938 | The White Stag | Kate Seredy |
| 1939 | Thimble Summer | Elizabeth Enright |
| 1940 | Daniel Boone | James Daugherty |
| 1941 | Call It Courage | Armstrong Sperry |
| 1942 | The Matchlock Gun | Walter D. Edmonds |
| 1943 | Adam of the Road | Elizabeth Janet Gray |
| 1944 | Johnny Tremain | Esther Forbes |
| 1945 | Rabbit Hill | Robert Lawson |
| 1946 | Strawberry Girl | Lois Lenski |
| 1947 | Miss Hickory | Carolyn Sherwin Bailey |
| 1948 | The Twenty-One Balloons | William Pène du Bois |
| 1949 | King of the Wind | Marguerite Henry |
| 1950 | The Door in the Wall | Marguerite de Angeli |
| 1951 | Amos Fortune, Free Man | Elizabeth Yates |
| 1952 | Ginger Pye | Eleanor Estes |
| 1953 | Secret of the Andes | Ann Nolan Clark |
| 1954 | . . . and now Miguel | Joseph Krumgold |
| 1955 | The Wheel on the School | Meindert Dejong |
| 1956 | Carry On, Mr. Bowditch | Jean Lee Latham |

interest inventory: A form used by teachers to gather information about student interests.

There are many methods for evaluating students' interests. The most common is an **interest inventory,** which is used by a teacher at the beginning of the year to collect information informally about each student's interests. Interest inventories contain questions for students to answer about things they enjoy. Then teachers review each student's responses to develop a better understanding of the authors and topics in which each student is most interested. Interest inventories are especially useful in putting reluctant readers and in-

TABLE 8–1
*(Continued)*

| Year | Title | Author |
|------|-------|--------|
| 1957 | Miracles on Maple Hill | Virginia Sorensen |
| 1958 | Rifles for Watie | Harold Keith |
| 1959 | The Witch of Blackbird Pond | Elizabeth George Speare |
| 1960 | Onion John | Joseph Krumgold |
| 1961 | Island of the Blue Dolphins | Scott O'Dell |
| 1962 | The Bronze Bow | Elizabeth George Speare |
| 1963 | A Wrinkle in Time | Madeleine L'Engle |
| 1964 | It's Like This, Cat | Emily Neville |
| 1965 | Shadow of a Bull | Maia Wojciechowska |
| 1966 | I. Juan de Pareja | Elizabeth Borten de Trevino |
| 1967 | Up a Road Slowly | Irene Hunt |
| 1968 | From the Mixed-Up Files of Mrs. Basil E. Frankweiler | E. L. Konigsburg |
| 1969 | The High King | Lloyd Alexander |
| 1970 | Sounder | William H. Armstrong |
| 1971 | Summer of the Swans | Betsy Byars |
| 1972 | Mrs. Frisby and the Rats of NIMH | Robert C. O'Brien |
| 1973 | Julie of the Wolves | Jean George |
| 1974 | The Slave Dancer | Paula Fox |
| 1975 | M. C. Higgins, the Great | Virginia Hamilton |
| 1976 | The Grey King | Susan Cooper |
| 1977 | Roll of Thunder, Hear My Cry | Mildred D. Taylor |
| 1978 | Bridge to Terabithia | Katherine Paterson |
| 1979 | The Westing Game | Ellen Raskin |
| 1980 | A Gathering of Days: A New England Girl's Journal, 1830–32 | Joan Blos |
| 1981 | Jacob Have I Loved | Katherine Paterson |
| 1982 | A Visit to William Blake's Inn: Poems for Innocent and Experienced Travelers | Nancy Willard |
| 1983 | Dicey's Song | Cynthia Voigt |
| 1984 | Dear Mr. Henshaw | Beverly Cleary |
| 1985 | The Hero and the Crown | Robin McKinley |
| 1986 | Sarah Plain and Tall | Patricia MacLachlan |
| 1987 | The Whipping Boy | Sid Fleischman |
| 1988 | Lincoln: A Photo Biography | Russell Freedman |
| 1989 | Joyful Noise | Paul Fleischman |
| 1990 | Number the Stars | Lois Lowry |

teresting books together. An example of one teacher's interest inventory can be seen in Figure 8–2.

Additional information can be collected informally as teachers interact with students during the day. Information about favorite activities, hobbies, games, or sports is often revealed during classroom discussions. During the first few weeks of school, teachers can discover much about their students through these informal discussions.

TABLE 8–2

Award-winning children's literature: Caldecott Medal winners

| Year | Title | Illustrator | Author |
|------|-------|-------------|--------|
| 1938 | Animals of the Bible | Dorothy P. Lathrop | Helen Dean Fish |
| 1939 | Mei Li | Thomas Handforth | Thomas Handforth |
| 1940 | Abraham Lincoln | Ingri and Edgar D'Aulaire | Ingri and Edgar D'Aulaire |
| 1941 | They Were Strong and Good | Robert Lawson | Robert Lawson |
| 1942 | Make Way for Ducklings | Robert McCloskey | Robert McCloskey |
| 1943 | The Little House | Virginia Lee Burton | Virginia Lee Burton |
| 1944 | Many Moons | Louis Slobodkin | James Thurber |
| 1945 | Prayer for a Child | Elizabeth Orton Jones | Rachel Field |
| 1946 | The Rooster Crows | Maud and Miska Petersham | Maud and Miska Petersham |
| 1947 | The Little Island | Leonard Weisgard | Golden MacDonald |
| 1948 | White Snow, Bright Snow | Roger Duvoisin | Alvin Tresselt |
| 1949 | The Big Snow | Berta and Elmer Hader | Berta and Elmer Hader |
| 1950 | Song of the Swallows | Leo Politi | Leo Politi |
| 1951 | The Egg Tree | Katherine Milhous | Katherine Milhous |
| 1952 | Finders Keepers | Nicholas Mordvinoff | William Lipkind |
| 1953 | The Biggest Bear | Lynd Ward | Lynd Ward |
| 1954 | Madeline's Rescue | Ludwig Bemelmans | Ludwig Bemelmans |
| 1955 | Cinderella, or the Little Glass Slipper | Marcia Brown | Charles Perrault |
| 1956 | Frog Went A-Courtin' | Feodor Rojankovsky | Retold by John Langstaff |
| 1957 | A Tree Is Nice | Marc Simont | Janice May Udry |
| 1958 | Time of Wonder | Robert McCloskey | Robert McCloskey |
| 1959 | Chanticleer and the Fox | Barbara Cooney | Translated by Barbara Cooney |
| 1960 | Nine Days to Christmas | Marie Hall Ets | Marie Hall Ets & Aurora Labastida |
| 1961 | Babouska and the Three Kings | Nicolas Sidjakov | Ruth Robbins |
| 1962 | Once a Mouse . . . | Marcia Brown | Marcia Brown |
| 1963 | The Snowy Day | Ezra Jack Keats | Ezra Jack Keats |
| 1964 | Where the Wild Things Are | Maurice Sendak | Maurice Sendak |

## Putting Children and Books Together in Pleasurable Settings

If you are familiar with popular children's literature and know your students' interests, you will be able to create a classroom environment rich in literature. Many children will take advantage of that environment to engage in independent reading. They will start on the road to becoming independent readers, who are able to read and choose to read on their own. Others, however, will still

TABLE 8–2

*(Continued)*

| Year | Title | Illustrator | Author |
|------|-------|-------------|--------|
| 1965 | May I Bring a Friend? | Beni Montresor | Beatrice Schenk De Regniers |
| 1966 | Always Room for One More | Nonny Hogrogian | Sorche Nic Leodhas |
| 1967 | Sam, Bangs & Moonshine | Evaline Ness | Evaline Ness |
| 1968 | Drummer Hoff | Ed Emberley | Barbara Emberley |
| 1969 | The Fool of the World and the Flying Ship | Uri Shulevitz | Arthur Ransome |
| 1970 | Sylvester and the Magic Pebble | William Steig | William Steig |
| 1971 | A Story—A Story | Gail E. Haley | Gail E. Haley |
| 1972 | One Fine Day | Nonny Hogrogian | Nonny Hogrogian |
| 1973 | The Funny Little Woman | Blair Lent | Arlene Mosel |
| 1974 | Duffy and the Devil | Margot Zemach | Harve Zemach |
| 1975 | Arrow to the Sun | Gerald McDermott | Gerald McDermott |
| 1976 | Why Mosquitoes Buzz in People's Ears | Leo and Diane Dillon | Verna Aardema |
| 1977 | Ashanti to Zulu: African Traditions | Leo and Diane Dillon | Margaret Musgrove |
| 1978 | Noah's Ark | Peter Spier | Peter Spier |
| 1979 | The Girl Who Loved Wild Horses | Paul Goble | Paul Goble |
| 1980 | Ox-Cart Man | Barbara Cooney | Donald Hall |
| 1981 | Fables | Arnold Lobel | Arnold Lobel |
| 1982 | Jumanji | Chris Van Allsburg | Chris Van Allsburg |
| 1983 | Shadow | Marcia Brown | Blaise Cendrars |
| 1984 | The Glorious Flight: Across the Channel with Louis Bleriot | Alice and Martin Provensen | Alice and Martin Provensen |
| 1985 | St. George and the Dragon | Trina Shart Hyman | Margaret Hodges |
| 1986 | The Polar Express | Chris Van Allsburg | Chris Van Allsburg |
| 1987 | Hey, Al | Richard Egielski | Arthur Yorinks |
| 1988 | Owl Moon | John Schoenherr | Jane Yolen |
| 1989 | Song and Dance Man | Stephen Gammell | Karen Ackerman |
| 1990 | Lon Po Po: A Chinese Red Riding Hood Tale | Ed Young | Ed Young |

be reluctant to select and complete a book on their own, indicating that they find books boring and uninteresting. Despite your best intentions and concerted efforts, some students will read a book only if it is required for an assignment.

What can you do about reluctant readers? You will need to actively seek out ways to put these children together with books in pleasurable settings.

FIGURE 8-1
A sample literature card

| | | |
|---|---|---|
| *Dahl, Roald* | *Charlie and the Chocolate Factory*<br>*New York: Alfred A. Knopf, 1964* | *162 pp.* |

*Synopsis:*   *Five children win a coveted prize: a tour of a mysterious*
*chocolate factory. During the tour, strange events befall*
*each of the children (and their parents). Marvelous*
*lyrical poetry in several locations!*

*Discussion Questions*

*1. How would you describe the inner workings of the magical*
*chocolate factory? (Students may wish to make a map or a*
*board game based on the factory layout.)*

*2. Describe the main characters in this story.*

*3. Do you think the five children won their prizes by*
*chance? Why or why not?*

*4. Describe the life of an Oompa-Loompa. Would you enjoy*
*working in this chocolate factory? Why or why not?*

Fortunately, there are as many ways to combine children and books in plea-surable settings as a teacher has ideas (Hiebert & Colt, 1989; Zarrillo, 1989). We describe the most common ways here.

Read-Aloud Sessions. One of the best ways to bring children and books to-gether in a pleasurable setting is relatively simple—demonstrate the pleasure of reading a good book in a **read-aloud session** each day. A read-aloud session is a method framework often used by teachers to develop independent readers. Although teachers conduct read-alouds in a variety of ways, a common set of procedural steps includes these suggestions (Trelease, 1989a, 1989b).

read-aloud session: A method framework used to develop independent read-ers; involves choosing a book, practicing reading it, creating a comfortable at-mosphere, reading the se-lection expressively, discuss-ing unfamiliar words, and letting students respond.

1. Choose a book with both your students and yourself in mind.
2. Practice reading the book.
3. Create a comfortable atmosphere for reading aloud.
4. Read the selection with feeling and expression.
5. Discuss the meanings of unfamiliar words.
6. Give students an opportunity to respond to what you have read.

It is especially important to select a book that both you and your students will enjoy. Your students will not listen for long if the story is not interesting, and you will not be able to be an effective model if you are not interested in

FIGURE 8–2

An interest inventory

Name _____ Date _____

**Books**

1. What are the titles of the last two books you have read?
   _____

2. Do you have a favorite author? If yes, who is it?
   _____

3. If you were going on a vacation and could take only one book with you, what would it be about?
   _____

4. Where do you get the books you read?
   _____

5. Which book would you most like to read again?
   _____

6. What is your favorite type of book? fiction? nonfiction? science fiction? romance? adventure?
   biography? fantasy? folk tale? historical fiction?
   _____

**After School**

1. Do you have any hobbies? What are they?
   _____

2. What do you like to do in your spare time?
   _____

3. If you had a day in which you could do anything and go anywhere you wanted, what would you do,
   and where would you go?
   _____

4. Do you have any pets? What are they?
   _____

5. Which animal would you most like to have for a pet?
   _____

6. Do you read any magazines at home? If yes, which ones?
   _____

7. Do you like sports? If yes, which ones?
   _____

8. What are your favorite TV programs?
   _____

what you are reading. A partial listing of popular books to be read aloud is listed in Figure 8–3. You will discover many others.

After you have selected an interesting book, you should practice reading it. Prepare for the intonation patterns in unusual or exciting scenes; perhaps try out different voices for each of the main characters. When you are ready, create a comfortable atmosphere for reading aloud. If possible, gather the students in front of you in a cozy part of the room where they can get comfortable. Be sure that younger children can see the story's pictures. Many

FIGURE 8–3
Good books to read aloud

## Wordless Books for Very Young Readers

*Amanda and the Mysterious Carpet* by Fernando Krahn
*Beach Day* by Helen Oxenbury
*A Boy, a Dog, and a Frog* by Mercer Mayer
*The Creepy Thing* by Fernando Krahn
*Frog on His Own* by Mercer Mayer
*The Hunter and the Animals* by Tomie dePaola
*Shopping Trip* by Helen Oxenbury
*Shrewbetinna's Birthday* by John Goodall
*Up a Tree* by Ed Young

## For Young Readers

*Alexander and the Terrible, Horrible, No Good, Very Bad Day* by Judith
  Viorst
*Brian Wordsmith's ABC* by Brian Wordsmith
*Brown Bear, Brown Bear, What Do You See?* by Bill Martin, Jr.
*Cloudy with a Chance of Meatballs* by Judi Barrett
*Corduroy* by Don Freeman
*Cranberry Thanksgiving* by Wende and Harry Devlin
*Swimmy* by Leo Lionni
*Frog and Toad Are Friends* by Arnold Lobel
*The Giving Tree* by Shel Silverstein
*Ira Sleeps Over* by Bernard Waber
*Miss Nelson Is Missing* by Harry Allard
*The Ox-Cart Man* by Donald Hall
*The Polar Express* by Chris Van Allsburg
*The Stories Julian Tells* by Ann Cameron
*Sarah's Unicorn* by Bruce and Katherine Coville
*Stevie* by John Steptoe
*The Velveteen Rabbit* by Margery Williams
*The Very Hungry Caterpillar* by Eric Carle

## For Older Readers

*Be a Perfect Person in Just Three Days* by Stephan Manes
*Bridge to Terabithia* by Katherine Paterson
*Charlotte's Web* by E. B. White
*Dear Mr. Henshaw* by Beverly Cleary
*From the Mixed-Up Files of Mrs. Basil E. Frankweiler* by E. L. Konigsburg
*Island of the Blue Dolphins* by Scott O'Dell
*James and the Giant Peach* by Roald Dahl
*Little House in the Big Woods* by Laura Ingalls Wilder
*My Side of the Mountain* by Jean George
*Mrs. Frisby and the Rats of NIMH* by Robert C. O'Brien
*Roll of Thunder, Hear My Cry* by Mildred Taylor
*The Diary of Anne Frank*
*The Lion, The Witch and the Wardrobe* by C. S. Lewis

teachers bring in a rocking chair for themselves and an old rug for the children to sit on.

When everyone is settled, read the selection with feeling and expression. Let your voice create the mood. If the story is scary, you might want to read slowly and carefully. If the story is humorous, stop and enjoy the humor with your students. If the story is sad, let your feelings show. If the story contains a predictable sentence or phrase that repeats itself, stop and have your students say it for you. Share the pleasure of the reading experience through your voice and intonation.

Often, read-aloud time is an excellent opportunity to develop an understanding of new word meanings. As you encounter words that may be unfamiliar to your students, briefly explain their meanings. However, do not disrupt the story excessively for this purpose.

Finally, be sure to give students an opportunity to respond to what you have read. This step may be accomplished in a brief discussion of listeners' reactions or through a writing experience that follows the story. If students liked the book, be sure to mention other titles by the same author and let them know where those books can be found.

Many teachers have a read-aloud session each day after lunch. Having it at that time provides a transition from the relatively unstructured lunchtime activities to the more structured activities in the classroom. For younger students you might read a single short book each day. For older students you might read one or two chapters each day from a longer selection.

In the model lesson that follows, Ms. Brown is attempting to help her first-grade students develop greater confidence in their ability to read books. She has been working with language experience stories recently, developing her students' familiarity with high-frequency sight words such as *see, can, what, you, me,* and *I.* Her students are also becoming familiar with using context to predict upcoming words, yet many of them think they cannot read until they are able to read their first book.

## A Read-Aloud Session

**Choose a Book with Both Your Students and Yourself in Mind.** Ms. Brown spoke with the school librarian about her needs. The librarian, Ms. Hamm, suggested that she look at several predictable texts, stories with a repeated phrase, sentence, or episode. Ms. Brown selected *Brown Bear, Brown Bear* by Bill Martin, Jr. This story looked easy to read because it repeated several sentences over and over.

**MODEL
LESSON**

> "Brown Bear, Brown Bear. What can you see?
> I can see a blue horse looking at me.
> Brown Bear, Brown Bear. What can you see?
> I can see a yellow duck looking at me."

tained many words that her students could recognize. And Ms. ..ked the illustrations and thought the book would be fun to read.

**...actice Reading the Book.** Ms. Brown read the book to herself that night ..n just a few minutes. She noticed the predictable pattern and decided to see whether her students could read some of the sentences for her during the read-aloud session.

**Create a Comfortable Atmosphere for Reading Aloud.** After lunch the next day Ms. Brown had her students sit on the rug in front of her rocking chair and get comfortable.

**Read the Selection with Feeling and Expression.** Ms. Brown started reading the book to her class. After several repetitions of the sentence pattern, she had her students read the last line aloud each time it appeared. Ms. Brown would read, "Brown Bear, Brown Bear. What can you see?" Then she would turn the page so that her students could see the animal and note its color. The students would then say the next sentence, such as "I can see a yellow duck looking at me." The students really enjoyed taking turns with her. When she reached the end of the story, where all of the animals were listed, Ms. Brown pointed to each word and had the class read the appropriate color and animal name.

**Discuss the Meanings of Unfamiliar Words.** Because all of the words in this story were familiar, Ms. Brown did not discuss any new word meanings. However, she did encourage students to talk about the different animals in the story.

**Give Students an Opportunity to Respond to What You Have Read.** As the class talked about the different animals in the story, Ms. Brown let the students share what they knew about each particular animal. Afterwards, she told her students that they could read this book by themselves if they wished, and she encouraged them to read it whenever they had a free moment. Ms. Brown put the book on the table in the reading corner so that it would be available. Many of her students were pleased to discover that they could read a real book. The experience was so positive that Ms. Brown hoped to bring in more predictable texts for her class.

Read-aloud sessions are a powerful way to bring children and books together in a pleasurable setting. They allow teachers to be effective advocates and role models for literature, and enthusiasm is contagious. If children see their teachers interested and enthusiastic about literature, they will be more interested in reading themselves. Read-aloud sessions can also be used as a springboard for other learning experiences, several of which are listed here.

**Counting Books.** Use counting books to develop number concepts with pre-school and kindergarten students. Consider using one of these:

> *1 Is One* by Tasha Tudor
>
> *My First Counting Book* by Lillian Moore
>
> *The Very Hungry Caterpillar* by Eric Carle

After reading a counting book aloud, encourage children to write their own counting books. Provide blank pages and help students draw numbered sets of objects on each page (one pencil, two bikes, and so on). Then write students' words at the bottom as they dictate to you. Staple the pages together, and don't forget to have students number the pages in their books, too.

**Diaries.** As you read *The Diary of Anne Frank* to upper-grade students, have them make and keep their own diaries. Encourage students to make an entry each day. You may want to make the diaries private, or you may choose to collect students' diaries once a week and write a private response to each individual.

**Recipe Reading.** Use books about food to provide an experience with recipe reading. Consider using one of these:

> *Cranberry Thanksgiving* by Wende and Harry Devlin
>
> *The Gingerbread Man* by Ed Arno
>
> *Stone Soup* by Marcia Brown
>
> *Rain Makes Applesauce* by Julian Scheer

After reading these books, have students read and follow a recipe to make the food described in the book. You may want to do this in the school kitchen with parent helpers. Duplicate the recipe, and send it home with children to share with their parents. Note that recipes have a unique discourse structure with which students may not be familiar.

**Reading Corners.** If you are committed to putting children and books together in pleasurable settings, it is essential that you establish a **reading corner** in your classroom, where students can interact with books and other reading materials in a comfortable fashion. In addition to the reading materials, a reading corner often contains a bookshelf, magazine rack, newspaper rack, carpet, comfortable chairs, pillows, and display table. It is designed to provide students with opportunities to read independently for pleasure, information, or personal growth.

reading corner: Portion of a classroom devoted solely to reading.

With the cooperation of the school library or media center, you might establish a small classroom library in your reading corner. You could develop

A pleasurable setting, such as a reading corner, provides a place where students can spend time with a favorite book.

a rotating series of displays, highlighting particular authors or categories of books. And over time you could acquire your own classroom collection of books, which could then be used to implement individualized reading, a method framework described in chapter 2. Classroom libraries can be started without great expense, using paperback editions of children's literature, which publishers make available at reasonable prices. Several are listed below:

Scholastic Book Services, 904 Sylvan Avenue, Englewood Cliffs, NJ 07632

Troll Associates, 320 Route 17, Mahwah, NJ 07430

Xerox Educational Publishers, 245 Long Hill Road, Middletown, CT 06457

In addition, publishers of paperback books for children often manage book clubs for classrooms. Once a month, classrooms receive a listing of available titles, and students may place orders through the teacher. Teachers and students are under no obligation to purchase books at any time, but teachers usually receive free books for their classroom libraries if a purchase is made.

You might also decide to have your class subscribe to one of several magazines devoted to children. If you do, be sure to announce each issue as it arrives and display it prominently in your reading corner. Popular children's magazines include the following:

*Cricket* (Cricket Magazine, P.O. Box 51144, Boulder, CO 80321–1144): stories, poetry, and informational articles

*Ebony, Jr.* (Johnson Publishing Company, 820 South Michigan Avenue, Chicago, IL 60605): articles, poetry, and stories about famous African Americans

*Kids* (Kids Publishing, Incorporated, 777 Third Avenue, New York, NY 10017): a magazine written by children for children

*National Geographic World* (National Geographic World, P.O. Box 2330, Washington, DC 20077–9955): material from *National Geographic* written for primary-grade students

*Ranger Rick* (National Wildlife Federation, Membership Services, 8925 Leesburg Pike, Vienna, VA 22180–0001): articles and stories on wildlife and conservation with color photographs

*Sesame Street Magazine* (Sesame Street Magazine, P.O. Box 52000, Boulder, CO 80321–2000): thematic issues with games, activities, and stories

A reading corner can become an important location for developing independent readers. You can organize many creative activities in such a spot, some of which are described here.

---

**Book Swapping.** Set up a swap table in your reading corner, where each student who contributes a book to the table is entitled to take one. You might also consider requiring students to bring in two books for every one they take. You could then use the extra book in your classroom library.

**Book Talks.** Each week introduce new additions to your classroom library in a book talk. Tell your students a few things about each author and book, and then read a short paragraph from the book to interest students. When you are finished, place the books on the display table in your reading corner.

**SAMPLE ACTIVITIES**

**Author of the Week.** Make an author-of-the-week bulletin board for your reading corner, and have each student be responsible for the board for one

k. Have the responsible student research a favorite author and create the
display, which might contain a short biography, the titles of important
books, and a photograph. If students select their authors early in the year,
they could write to them, telling them about their selection for the display.
The letters should be addressed to the authors' publishers. Some authors
will respond, and the responses could be displayed.

**Sustained Silent Reading.** Another way to bring students and books together
is to provide regular **sustained silent reading (SSR)**. Sustained silent reading,
or uninterrupted sustained silent reading (USSR), is a method framework that
provides uninterrupted time for both students and teachers to read self-
selected materials (McCracken, 1971). It consists of three procedural steps.

1. Introduce the purpose and procedures.
2. Be sure that everyone has something to read.
3. Read silently without interruptions.

Although SSR is usually implemented within individual classrooms, an entire
school can participate in the activity. When it does, children, teachers, and
even the school secretary and custodian will be found reading at this time.

It is important that you introduce the purpose and procedures of this
activity before beginning sustained silent reading. Several days ahead you
should explain what students will be expected to do during sustained silent
reading. Tell them that this will be a time to read self-selected materials
silently without interruption. It is especially important that students understand that they will need something to read each day there is sustained silent
reading. It is best to schedule the activity on a regular basis so that students are
always prepared with materials to read.

On the day that you begin, have students take out the materials they have
chosen to read and begin the reading session. Be sure to have several extra
reading selections to share with students who may have forgotten to bring
their own. It is very important that you, too, read something for pleasure
during this period. Completing homework assignments, grading papers, and
similar activities are not allowed. This is a time to read something for pleasure.

Initially you may wish to schedule SSR for short periods, but gradually
the time can be increased. Interruptions are not allowed during sustained
silent reading because they often result in a loss of comprehension and interest
for readers. Questions, comments, and other conversation should be held until
after the silent reading period has been concluded. In addition, no students
should be asked to report on what they have read. Sustained silent reading
must be truly free reading for pleasure if you hope to develop independent
readers.

In the model lesson that follows, Ms. Pease has decided to use SSR in her
eighth-grade class to provide more independent reading experiences for her
students.

sustained silent reading
(SSR): A method frame-
work used to develop independent readers by providing time for them to read
self-selected materials; involves introducing the process, being sure that everyone has something to read,
and reading silently without
interruptions.

## Sustained Silent Reading

**Introduce the Purpose and Procedures.** On Monday Ms. Pease announces to her students that they will begin SSR on Thursday. She explains that a 15-minute session each day will be devoted to reading whatever materials anyone chooses to read. She tells her students that there are only two rules for this activity: (1) everybody must read, and (2) there will be no interruptions. Ms. Pease explains that the purpose of SSR is to encourage students to develop independent reading interests. She reminds them that they may read whatever they wish and that they will need to have something to read each day beginning on Thursday. One student asks whether he may read a comic book. Ms. Pease explains that students may read anything they wish, including comics, magazines, and newspapers. On Tuesday and Wednesday Ms. Pease again reminds students to bring something to read for Thursday's first SSR session.

**MODEL LESSON**

**Be Sure That Everyone Has Something to Read.** Thursday afternoon Ms. Pease announces that it is now time to begin sustained silent reading. She reminds her students of the two basic rules: (1) everybody must read, and (2) there will be no interruptions. She tells students to take out what they brought to read and begin. Two students have forgotten to bring something. Ms. Pease takes out several magazines that she brought for this purpose and has the students choose. Then, Ms. Pease begins reading the book that she brought to read.

**Read Silently Without Interruptions.** When several students begin whispering, Ms. Pease reminds them of the second rule for sustained silent reading. The remainder of the period goes quietly.

After 15 minutes Ms. Pease announces that the time for sustained silent reading is over. She discusses the activity with her students; everyone seemed to enjoy it. Ms. Pease announces that the class will engage in sustained silent reading each day and that everyone should bring something to read. She mentions that she will increase the amount of time to 30 minutes as they become familiar with the activity.

**Readers Theatre.** Another way to put children and books together in pleasurable settings is to use **readers theatre**. Readers theatre is a method framework in which a group of students follow four procedural steps.

readers theatre: A method framework used to develop independent readers in four steps: reading, writing a short script, practicing, and performing.

1. Choose and read a literary selection.
2. Write a short script.
3. Practice reading the script.
4. Orally perform the script for the class.

Initially, a small group of students chooses and reads a literary selection. It may be a piece that one member of the group has discovered or a selection that the teacher suggests. In either case the first step is to read the passage and become familiar with it. Then the group writes a short script, which usually comes from one of the more exciting episodes in the story. In this process the group turns the narrative into a script for a dramatic presentation.

The next step is to practice reading the various parts in the script with intonation, expression, and eye or hand movements. Students should try different ways of reading each line and should also try out different parts until agreement is reached about who will read each part and how it will be read. Practice should continue until the group feels ready to perform the script for the class.

Usually a readers theatre performance is given without props and with readers sitting on chairs in the front of the room. Such a presentation differs from that of a play in that the message is usually communicated through the voices of the readers—their rhythm, intonation, and pace—rather than through the appearance and movement of actors. Some teachers and students, however, prefer to stage more elaborate readers theatre in which props and moving actors are used.

Readers theatre, using either prewritten scripts or scripts written by students and based on a reading selection, is a motivational way to increase students' interaction with print.

Initially, readers theatre may require teacher direction and guidance, perhaps even teacher-developed scripts. Commercially prepared scripts are available from Readers Theatre Script Service (P.O. Box 178333, San Diego, CA 92117). However, after students have had several opportunities to participate in a readers theatre presentation, they will be eager to select their own pieces, write their own scripts, and determine their own performances. In the model lesson that follows, Mr. Catney's fifth graders have already completed several readers theatre activities with prepared scripts. Now he wants them to read a literature selection and prepare their own script, which they will then practice and perform.

## Readers Theatre

**MODEL LESSON**

**Choose and Read a Literary Selection.** A group of students has been reading *The Long Winter* by Laura Ingalls Wilder. Mr. Catney suggests that the students prepare a readers theatre presentation based on an episode in the book and then share it with the class. The students discuss different portions of the story and finally settle on an episode in which the Ingalls run out of wheat in the middle of winter.

**Write a Short Script.** The group sets off to draft a script. One of the students writes a preliminary draft that night and brings it to school to share with the others. As the students read it together, they make suggestions for several changes. Another student then takes those ideas and revises the script. The next day the group makes a few minor changes and agrees that the script is ready. The students take it to Mr. Catney, who duplicates it at lunchtime and gives each group member a copy.

**Practice Reading the Script.** The following day is spent reading the parts orally and practicing for the performance. Students try out different parts and different ways of reading. Eventually, they settle on the way the piece should be read and practice several more times.

**Orally Perform the Script for the Class.** Every Friday morning Mr. Catney sets time aside for students to share the reading experiences they have had during the week. This group presents its oral reading of the script in front of the room; the performance is polished and entertaining. At the end the group identifies the source of the script in case other students want to read the book. Mr. Catney notices several students jotting the title and author down, and later that day he sees them looking for the book when the class visits the school library.

**The School Library or Media Center.** When considering pleasurable settings in which to bring children and books together, you should not be limited by the four walls of your classroom. The school library or media center should be at the center of each school's efforts to develop independent readers. Reserve time for a visit to this special place at least once a week, and coordinate the literature experiences that you and the school librarian can provide. Be sure to share what you are doing in the classroom and find out what the librarian is doing as well. In addition, ask about useful books on themes that you are developing in class. They can be borrowed, introduced in a book talk, and placed in your reading corner.

Your school library is also the perfect place to obtain books for read-aloud sessions, sustained silent reading, or readers theatre. And when students enjoy a particular story, remind them that it came from the library, and provide them with a list of related titles by the same author or on the same topic. Ask the librarian to assist you with this task. Then pass out the lists just before your regular class visit to the school library. Encourage students to locate books on the list and check them out.

If your school library is well-stocked, take full advantage of it. If you do not have a good library, advocate among your colleagues, principal, and students' parents to improve it. A good school library is important if students are to develop into independent readers.

**The Home Environment.** The pleasurable settings that are so important in developing independent readers can also extend to students' homes if you actively seek the assistance of parents. Parents are usually willing to help but sometimes do not know what to do. You need to regularly communicate the importance of a home environment that supports reading and provide clear examples of what parents can do. At open houses and back-to-school nights enlist parents as an important part of your team. Then send home a letter listing specific ways in which they can help their children become better readers. Such a letter might look like the one in Figure 8–4.

**Other Activities Promoting an Environment Rich in Literature.** As you spend time in schools, you will encounter many new and exciting instructional activities, bulletin board ideas, reading-center tasks, and other means of developing a classroom environment that is rich in literature. Some ideas will come from colleagues, others will come from professional journals, and still others will come from your own thinking about and planning for tomorrow's lesson. It will be helpful for you to keep track of these ideas, regardless of their source.

You should begin now to collect and organize the ideas that you think are useful. Some teachers keep a notebook for literature ideas; others keep their ideas on separate 3-×-5-inch cards, organized in a file box. Still others organize this information on a computer, using data base management software. However you choose to record and organize your ideas, you might want to include some of the following suggestions.

FIGURE 8–4
A sample letter sent home to parents at the beginning of the school year

September 4

Dear Parents,

The beginning of school is such an exciting time for everyone. It is a time of new beginnings, new friends, and wonderful new experiences. It is also the time when I receive many questions from parents. Most want to know what they can do to help their children in school.

The most important thing you can do is very simple—provide a home environment that supports reading. Reading independently at home will assist your child in each and every subject area, from reading to science, from math to social studies. Reading is central to everything your child does at school.

How can you create this environment? I have developed a list of six suggestions. Each is easy to do, each will make an important difference in your child's development.

1. Every day set aside a regular time to read with your child. Sharing a good book at bedtime is an enjoyable way to end the day. Reading together for 15 minutes each day is the single most important thing you can do to help your child at school.
2. If you have not already done so, take your child to the local library, and help him/her obtain a library card. Make a visit to the library a regular weekly event.
3. If you have not already done so, help your child establish a personal library. Both the necessary shelving and a beginning set of books can be acquired inexpensively. Shelving can be as simple as a freshly painted set of boards and bricks. Books can be acquired as birthday and holiday presents.
4. Create a quiet place in the home where your child can read without being interrupted—away from family traffic and television. Join your child in this place during a regular reading time.
5. Model your own reading habits for your child. When you come across something of interest as you read, show it to your child. Also, involve your child when you search for information in a phone book, TV guide, dictionary, or repair manual. Explain to your child what you are doing.
6. Encourage your child to join an inexpensive paperback book club for children. Several offer quality children's literature at inexpensive prices. Write to the Children's Book Council at 67 Irving Place, New York, NY 10003, for the names and addresses of reputable firms. Such a membership would also make an excellent birthday or holiday present.

If you have any further questions about how you can help, please call me. I welcome the opportunity to talk with you about your child.

Cordially,

*Emily Dodson*

Emily Dodson

SAMPLE
ACTIVITIES

**Book Parties.** Have a short book party several times during the year. Students can dress up as their favorite characters from books they have read in the previous month. Have students wear name tags showing their characters' names and the titles of their books. This activity is an excellent way to generate interest in and conversations about good books for future reading experiences.

**Book Cover Doors.** Turn your classroom door into a book cover each month, and use that opportunity to announce to the rest of the school what you are reading aloud to your class. In the lower grades let your students vote on their favorite read-aloud book from the past month. In the upper grades have your students design and construct the book cover for the book you are reading aloud at that time.

**Literature Motivators.** Write to the Children's Book Council at 67 Irving Place, New York, NY 10003, for a catalog of bookmarks, posters, and other promotional material.

**RIF.** Write to RIF (Reading Is FUNdamental) at the Smithsonian Institution, Department P, 600 Maryland Ave, SW, Washington, DC 20560. RIF coordinates a nationwide program to provide each child with three free books. RIF will provide 75 percent of the cost if local groups provide 25 percent. Inquire about current procedures for including your students in this program.

**Book Fairs.** Encourage your school's parent-teacher organization to sponsor a book fair. Invite book dealers to display and sell their new books each year in the school auditorium or cafeteria.

**Literature Logs.** Encourage students to keep and maintain literature logs by writing short reactions to each new book they read. Periodically collect, read, and react to students' comments in their logs. Help children design covers in the shape of a log.

## A Final Note

It is important that children leave your classroom at the end of the year as better readers. It is equally important, however, that they leave your room as independent readers. Becoming familiar with popular children's literature, identifying your students' reading interests, and putting children and books together in pleasurable settings are the tools of an effective reading program. Do not give up, however, if your first attempts do not make a dramatic change in the independent reading habits of your reluctant readers. Developing interest in and enthusiasm for reading is not a simple task when you confront a history of no interest. A continuous program of interesting books and pleasurable opportunities will ultimately yield gains in independent reading behavior.

## WHAT IS NARRATIVE DISCOURSE STRUCTURE?

Even as teachers focus on developing independent readers, they can provide their students with literature experiences that also promote an important type of discourse knowledge—knowledge about **narrative discourse structure.** Narrative discourse structure refers to the structural organization that is common to all stories and narratives. The concept also includes the special structural characteristics common to particular types of narratives, such as fairy tales, mysteries, science fiction, fables, and fantasies.

narrative discourse structure: The organizational structure common to all stories; includes setting information, a problem, and episodes that describe attempts to resolve the problem.

Knowledge of narrative discourse structure assists the comprehension of extended text in three ways. First, knowing the structure of narratives helps readers interpret correctly what they have read. The structure of a text often provides clues to interpretation. For example, both science fiction and fairy tales are associated with certain time periods, and knowledge of that structural characteristic permits readers to interpret those stories correctly.

Second, knowing the structure of narratives helps readers develop appropriate expectations of upcoming meaning. Do you remember the expectations you had in chapter 2 when you read the first sentence of a story that began, "Once upon a time. . ."? You immediately knew that the story was not true, and you knew that it took place in a kingdom long ago and far away. You also expected to see a prince and princess as characters, and you knew that a problem would appear that would require a solution. In addition, you expected a happy ending. Thus, knowing the structural characteristics of narratives helps readers develop appropriate expectations and makes reading easier.

Third, knowing the structure of narratives is important because it allows a reader to infer structural information omitted by an author. For example, an episode in a narrative is often left out because an author assumes that the reader will correctly infer what took place. Knowing that a narrative contains an episodic structure makes it easier for a reader to infer the missing information.

The exact nature of readers' knowledge of narrative discourse structure is not known. Researchers investigating this aspect of comprehension do not all agree on what it is that readers know about narrative structure. Generally, however, researchers agree that readers take advantage of two types of knowledge: knowledge of the general structure of narratives and knowledge of the structural characteristics of specific narrative forms.

## Knowledge of the General Structure of Narratives

Most researchers believe that narratives contain three basic structural elements: setting information, an initiating episode that establishes a problem to be resolved in the story, and succeeding episodes that explain how the problem gets resolved. Narratives typically contain a structure similar to the following:

I. Setting information
   A.  Character information
   B.  Location information
   C.  Time information
II. Initiating episode (story problem)
   A.  Initiating event
   B.  Goal formation
III. Succeeding episodes (including the final resolution)
   A.  Attempt
   B.  Outcome
   C.  Reaction

setting information: An element of narrative discourse structure found at the beginning of stories; includes information about the character(s), location, and time.

**Setting information** usually appears at the beginning of a narrative. It includes information about the character(s) in the story, the location where the story takes place, and the time when it takes place. Setting information often appears in the first few sentences of a story.

| Time: | Once upon a time, |
|---|---|
| Character: | there was a little girl with a red hood |
| Location: | who lived near the edge of a dark forest. |

Not all stories contain all three elements at the beginning; one or more may be missing. Nevertheless, readers who know that character, location, and time information *should* be at the beginning of a narrative use available clues to infer this information when it is missing.

initiating episode: One element of narrative discourse structure; usually the first organized sequence of actions that describe the problem to be resolved in the story.

An **initiating episode** is usually found in the first episode of a narrative. Initiating episodes specify the problem that must be resolved in the story. They describe an initiating event and the formation of a goal by one or more characters.

| Initiating event: | One day, Little Red Riding Hood's mother gave her a basket of bread and jam. |
|---|---|
| Goal formation: | She told Little Red Riding Hood to take the food to her grandmother's house in the woods. |

succeeding episodes: The element of narrative discourse structure that tells how the character solves the problem established in the initiating episode.

Initiating events and goals are not always stated in a story. Again, however, readers who are familiar with narrative structure infer this information when it is missing.

**Succeeding episodes,** including the final episode, relate how the character attempts to reach the goal or solve the problem established in the initiating episode. Succeeding episodes typically contain an attempt to accomplish the goal, the outcome of that attempt, and a reaction to that outcome. Succeeding episodes may also result in characters establishing new goals to be achieved in the course of the story.

Attempt:       Little Red Riding Hood hiked all day
               on the trail to her grandmother's house.
Outcome:       When she arrived, they sat down immediately
               and feasted on the home-baked bread and
               strawberry jam.
Reaction:      They were so content that they didn't
               even think about the wolf that had bothered
               them the week before.

Thus, readers use their knowledge of narrative discourse structure to infer missing information in a story. When a structural element is not explicitly stated, readers often supply it by making either a text-connecting or a slot-filling inference (see chapter 7). Table 8–3 shows how this takes place with a narrative selection. We can see that much missing structural information is inferred by the reader.

## Knowledge of Different Discourse Forms

In addition to the common structural characteristics of all narratives, a variety of narrative forms also have unique characteristics. Knowledge of those characteristics is important for effective comprehension of particular narrative types. For example, if we don't know that we are reading a fable, we may not infer an unstated moral or message. Similarly, if we believe that we are reading contemporary realistic fiction, we may misinterpret as fact a science fiction writer's guesses about futuristic society. Table 8–4 lists the major narrative forms and their defining characteristics, which are usually taught to students in the elementary grades.

## DEVELOPING KNOWLEDGE OF NARRATIVE DISCOURSE STRUCTURE

Instruction in narrative discourse structure is still being investigated. At least one study has concluded that teaching the structural characteristics of narrative discourse does not lead to gains in comprehension (Dreher & Singer, 1980). A number of other studies, however, suggest that several types of instructional strategies significantly improve students' ability to comprehend narratives (Davis & McPherson, 1989; Morrow, 1984; Reutzel, 1985; Spiegel and Fitzgerald, 1986). Four of those strategies are described here: questioning, directed reading-thinking activities, story mapping, and deductive instruction.

TABLE 8-3
Use of narrative discourse structure to infer missing information

| Structural Feature | Narrative Text *(Likely Inference)* |
|---|---|
| I. Setting | |
|   A. Character information | Mr. Randall had a hard time getting to the airport. |
|   B. Location information | *(This story probably took place in the United States in a metropolitan area where airports exist.)* |
|   C. Time information | *(This story probably took place in the recent past, after 1900.)* |
| II. Initiating episode | |
|   A. Initiating event | *(Mr. Randall probably needed to meet someone arriving on a plane, or else he wanted to leave on a plane himself. It is also possible that he was an airline employee.)* |
|   B. Goal formation | *(Mr. Randall wants to get to the airport.)* |
| III. Episode 1 | |
|   A. Attempt | First he took the wrong exit off the highway |
|   B. Outcome | and had to drive eight miles to get back on. |
|   C. Reaction | *(Mr. Randall was concerned that he would be late.)* |
|   Episode 2 | |
|   A. Attempt | *(Mr. Randall got back on the highway.)* |
|   B. Outcome | Then his car had a flat tire, and he had to fix it. |
|   C. Reaction | *(Mr. Randall was upset.)* |
|   Episode 3 | |
|   A. Attempt | When he was on his way again, |
|   B. Outcome | he got stuck in a traffic jam. That took more time. Now he was an hour late. |
|   C. Reaction | *(Mr. Randall was angry.)* |
|   Concluding episode | |
|   A. Attempt | *(Mr. Randall continued on his way to the airport.)* |
|   B. Outcome | When angry Mr. Randall reached the airport, he discovered that the plane he was supposed to meet was an hour late, too! |
|   C. Reaction | *(Mr. Randall was relieved.)* |

**Source:** *Golden Secrets* (Glenview, IL: Scott, Foresman, 1982), p. 41.

## Questioning

It is possible to develop narrative discourse knowledge with discussion questions (Morrow, 1984). Discussion questions can be used after a story or portion of a story is read, perhaps within a reciprocal questioning or a reciprocal teaching framework (see chapter 7). Questions should focus on the structural organization of either narratives in general or specific narrative forms. In addition, questions should be consistent with guidelines described in chapter 7.

Which questions, then, are appropriate and effective? We should remember that inferential-level or in-my-head questions are usually more useful for

TABLE 8–4
Major narrative forms and their defining characteristics

| Narrative Form | Setting Information | Episodes | Examples |
|---|---|---|---|
| **Fiction** | | | |
| Historical fiction | Characters: fictional and historical<br>Time: in the past | Fictional characters enacting historically accurate episodes | *Spies on the Devil's Belt*<br>*Searching for Shona*<br>*Island of the Blue Dolphins* |
| Modern realistic fiction | Characters: realistic<br>Time: contemporary | Realistic episodes revolving around contemporary issues | *Stevie*<br>*I Have a Sister—My Sister Is Deaf*<br>*From the Mixed-Up Files of Mrs. Basil E. Frankweiler* |
| Folk tales | Characters: average citizens or animals<br>Location: countryside<br>Time: long ago | Magical or fantastic actions, with animals talking, witches casting spells, and so on | *The Three Billy Goats Gruff*<br>*Hansel and Gretel* |
| Fairy tales | Characters: royalty<br>Location: castle or kingdom<br>Time: long ago | Magical or fantastic actions, with animals talking, witches casting spells, and so on | *Cinderella*<br>*Sleeping Beauty*<br>*Puss in Boots* |
| Fables | Characters: usually animals<br>Location: countryside<br>Time: long ago | Magical or fantastic actions, with animals taking human characteristics and a moral often stated at the end | *Aesop's Fables*<br>*Old Man Whickutt's Donkey* |
| Myths | Characters: cultural hero(ine)<br>Time: long ago | Hero(ine) demonstrating extreme courage, bravery, and skill in resolving a serious challenge | *Atalanta*<br>*Odysseus*<br>*Joan of Arc* |
| Modern fantasies | Characters: realistic<br>Time: contemporary | Magical or fantastic actions | *James and the Giant Peach*<br>*Charlotte's Web*<br>*Where the Wild Things Are*<br>*The Chronicles of Narnia* |
| Science fiction | Characters: usually realistic<br>Location: often outer space<br>Time: future | Fantastic actions logically predicted when the story was written | *A Wrinkle in Time*<br>*The Spaceship Under the Apple* |
| **Nonfiction** | | | |
| Biography | Character: historically important individual | Factual account of an individual's life | *What's the Big Idea, Ben Franklin?*<br>*Can't You Make Them Behave, King George?* |
| Autobiography | Character: historically important individual | Factual account of the author's life | *The Diary of Anne Frank*<br>*Helen Keller* |

instruction than are literal-level or in-the-book questions. Also, teaching the technical labels for structural characteristics is not necessary. Terms such as *initiating episode* may be referred to simply as "the problem in the story." Figure 8–5 lists questions that can be adapted to the information in particular stories.

on Friday or Friday Morning

Reader-theatre
1. Read a story
2. Develop a script
3. practice
   for decoding
   (intonation
    high pitch or
    low)

4. Share

Based on this picture
what do you think will happen
in this story?

Appropriate discussion
questions are one tool
for developing narrative
discourse knowledge.

## Using a Directed Reading-Thinking Activity

directed reading-thinking
activity (DRTA): A method
framework used to assist
students in predicting outcomes and drawing conclu-
sions; includes predicting,
reading, and proving.

It is also possible to develop narrative discourse knowledge by adapting a
method framework described earlier—a **directed reading-thinking activity
(DRTA).** You may remember that a DRTA includes three procedural
steps—predicting, reading, proving—which are repeated as students read and
discuss a selection. If you use a DRTA to develop knowledge of narrative
discourse structure, you should guide students in the first step—making
predictions about structural elements found in stories. Your questions should
focus students' attention on elements such as setting, a story's problem, and a
solution to the problem.

Then have students read the appropriate portion of the story to check
their predictions. This step can be accomplished either silently or orally.
Finally, have students discuss why their predictions were correct or incorrect before asking them to make predictions about the next structural element.
The model lesson on pages 328–330 illustrates how Ms. Dodson followed
the procedural steps of a DRTA to help her students develop an under-

What story does the picture tell?

FIGURE 8–5
Questions to initiate discussion about narrative discourse structure

### To Develop an Understanding of Setting Information

1. Who can tell us something about the setting of this story? What do we mean by the setting of a story? Where do we usually find this information?
2. Who are the main characters in this story? Why are they important? How can you tell who the main characters are before you even finish reading the story?
3. When did this story take place? How do you know? Could this story have taken place today? How can you tell? What time words can you find in this story? Where do they appear? If there are no time words, how did you figure out when this story took place?
4. Where did this story take place? How can you tell? Can anyone find the words in the story that tell us where the story took place? If there are no words that tell us, how can we know where the setting is located?

### To Develop an Understanding of Initiating Episodes

1. Do stories usually have a problem in them? Where do you find this information? Are problems sometimes not mentioned in a story? What do you do when a problem isn't stated. What problem (goal) did the main character have in this story? What in the story told you this was the problem? Why was this a problem for the main character?
2. What was the source of the problem? What caused the problem? How do you know?

### To Develop an Understanding of Succeeding Episodes

1. How did the main character attempt to solve his problem? Do you think this was a good solution? Would you have done the same thing?
2. What happened? What was the outcome? Did this solve the problem?
3. How did the character react to the outcome? How would you have reacted? Why?
4. How did the problem finally get solved? Was this an appropriate solution? How did the character feel afterwards? Would you have felt the same way? Why?

(小說、人生或詩歌中之) 插曲

(小說、故事等中的) 主要情節

[ˈɛpə,sod]

conformance

standing of narrative discourse structure as they read "The Rabbit and the Bear."

## Story Mapping

A **story map** is a graphic outline that expands on each structural feature of a narrative with specific information from that particular story. Thus, a story map organizes the structural information of a story for both students and teacher and provides a "map" of a story's plot. A story map can be used to guide the discussion of a story (Davis & McPherson, 1989) as well as help students

story map: A graphic outline containing the major features of narratives and the specific information in a particular story.

billet

**MODEL
LESSON**

Using a DRTA to Develop Knowledge
of Narrative Discourse Structure

### The Rabbit and the Bear

A rabbit was walking up a hill in the moonlight. She met a big bear on the hill.

The bear jumped at the rabbit. "I have you!" called the bear.

"Yes, you do," said the rabbit.

The bear looked at the rabbit. "I am very hungry," he said.

The rabbit sat very still. Then she said, "Wait! I was going to dance my spin dance. You will not see my fast, fast spin dance."

The bear did like to see a good dance. So he sat down. "I am not hungry," he said. "I'll wait. Dance your spin dance."

The rabbit did the spin dance. Around and around she went. "Can you dance as fast as that?" said the rabbit.

"Yes, I can," said the bear.

The rabbit said, "No bear can spin around as fast as I can."

"I can," said the bear. The bear went around and around. He was going very fast. He did not see the rabbit.

The rabbit ran away. She hid in the grass. Then she looked out at the bear. "Spin away, Bear," said the rabbit.

And the bear went around and around and around in the moonlight.*

Ms. Dodson has been following a DRTA format through the first four paragraphs and is now directing her students' attention to the problem in the story, the unstated goal of the rabbit, and the way in which the rabbit might achieve her goal.

### Predicting

Ms. Dodson: Let's think a little bit now about the problem in this story. Do you remember that every story has some kind of problem? I wonder what it is in this story. Any guesses?

Jose: I think the bear's problem is how he's gonna cook this rabbit. He's got it now, and he has to figure out how to cook it.

Ms. Dodson: OK. Any other ideas?

Tanya: I think the bear's problem is that he's hungry, and he wants to find something to eat.

---

*Sun and Shadow* (New York: Harcourt Brace Jovanovich, 1985), pp. 66–70. Reprinted by permission.

| Michelle: | No, he's already got the rabbit to eat. I think the rabbit has a problem, not the bear. The rabbit is caught. |
|---|---|
| Ms. Dodson: | What do you think the rabbit wants to do? |
| Jose: | It wants to get away. |
| Tanya: | Yeah. She wants to go home and be safe. |
| Michelle: | Yeah. The rabbit wants to run away. |
| Ms. Dodson: | OK. How do you think the rabbit will try to get away? What would you do if a bear caught you and you wanted to get away? |
| Jose: | I'd run away. |
| Tanya: | You can't. The bear already has you. I'd tell the bear I'd be his friend and help him if he'd let me go. You know, like that story about the lion and the mouse we read last week. |
| Michelle: | I'd give the bear a big pot of honey if he'd let me go. Bears really like honey. |
| Ms. Dodson: | Let's read the next paragraph together and see what the problem is in this story and how it's solved. |

## Reading

| Ms. Dodson: | Why don't you start reading for us, Tanya. [Tanya, Jose, and Michelle each read several paragraphs and finish the story.] |
|---|---|

## Proving

| Ms. Dodson: | OK. Now let's see who guessed the problem in the story. |
|---|---|
| Jose: | I didn't. I thought the bear wanted to cook the rabbit. |
| Michelle: | I guessed it. I thought the rabbit needed to get away, and she did. It says, "The rabbit ran away." |
| Ms. Dodson: | Good, Michelle. Did anyone guess *how* the rabbit got away? |
| Michelle: | I didn't. I thought about giving the bear a pot of honey. |
| Jose: | I guessed it right. I thought the rabbit would run away, and she did. Rabbits are fast. |
| Tanya: | Yeah, but you didn't guess that the rabbit would trick the bear. She had to trick the bear first to get away. |
| Ms. Dodson: | How did the rabbit trick the bear? |
| Tanya: | She said she could dance faster than the bear, and the bear wanted to beat her, so they had a dancing contest, and the bear put the rabbit down, and the rabbit ran away. |
| Ms. Dodson: | Can anyone read the part that tells us how the rabbit got away? |
| Jose: | I can. It says, " 'Can you dance as fast as that?' said the rabbit. 'Yes, I can,' said the bear. The rabbit said, 'No bear can spin around as fast as I can.' 'I can,' said the bear. The bear went around and around. He was going very fast. He did not see the rabbit. The rabbit ran away." |

Ms. Dodson:   Good. It doesn't say that the bear put the rabbit down,
              though. How do you know that?

Tanya:        Because the bear was dancing. He couldn't dance with the
              rabbit. No, wait. It says the bear was dancing and couldn't see
              the rabbit. If he still had the rabbit in his hand, he could've
              seen her. So he must have put the rabbit down.

---

learn the structural characteristics of narratives (Reutzel, 1985). Although it
can be used to introduce a story, it is most frequently used after students have
read the story. Figure 8–6 illustrates a story map completed after a reading of
"The Rabbit and the Bear."

**story mapping:** A method framework used to develop an understanding of narrative discourse structure; includes writing the structural headings, using them to guide questions, and filling in the story map with students' answers.

**Story mapping** is a method framework in which a teacher uses a story
map to guide discussion and develop a clearer understanding of narrative
discourse structure. It often contains three procedural steps:

1. Write the major structural headings on the chalkboard.
2. Use the chalkboard map to ask questions and guide discussion.
3. As students answer questions, fill in the story map with the students' words.

The first procedural step is usually completed before the activity begins.
The teacher writes on the chalkboard the major structural headings that pertain to the story being read: title, setting, problem (or initiating episode),
Episode 1, Episode 2, and outcome.

During the second procedural step those headings guide discussion of
what took place in the story. You may use questions such as the following:

- Where did this story take place?
- When do you think it took place?
- What was the problem in this story?
- What happened first? second? third?
- How did the main character solve the problem?

As students answer these questions, the teacher completes the map with
their words. Students should be encouraged to read aloud portions of the story
to support their answers and to indicate how they inferred missing information
whenever an inference is required.

## Deductive Instruction

**deductive instruction:** A method framework containing four steps: state the skill or rule, provide examples, provide guided practice, and provide independent practice.

**Deductive instruction** can also be used to develop an understanding of narrative discourse structure in general and different narrative forms in particular.
Do you remember the four procedural steps of a deductive method framework?

1. State the skill or rule.
2. Provide examples of the skill or rule.
3. Provide guided practice.
4. Provide independent practice.

*have multiply*      *write a story:*

FIGURE 8-6

An example of a story map

*narrative discourse structure*

*discourse ~~structure~~ knowledge:*

I. *setting information*
   A. *Time*
   B. *Characters*
   C. *Location*

II. *Initiating event (Problem)*
   A. *action*
   B. *problem*

III. *Succeeding events*
   A. *attempts*
   B. *outcome*

IV. *Happy Ending*

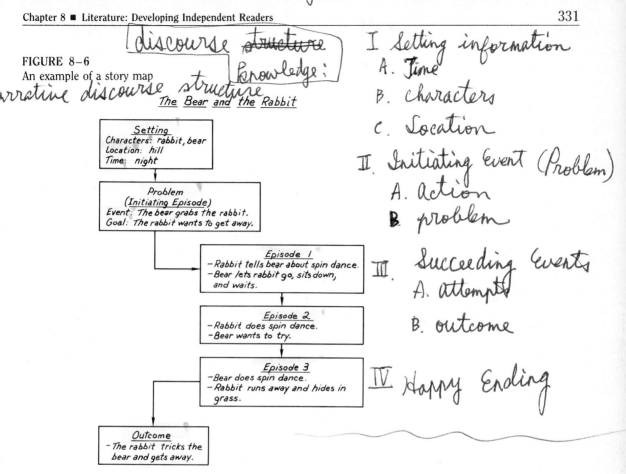

The Bear and the Rabbit

Setting
Characters: rabbit, bear
Location: hill
Time: night

Problem
(Initiating Episode)
Event: The bear grabs the rabbit.
Goal: The rabbit wants to get away.

Episode 1
– Rabbit tells bear about spin dance.
– Bear lets rabbit go, sits down, and waits.

Episode 2
– Rabbit does spin dance.
– Bear wants to try.

Episode 3
– Bear does spin dance.
– Rabbit runs away and hides in grass.

Outcome
– The rabbit tricks the bear and gets away.

When deductive instruction is used, the teacher defines for students the structural characteristics of a particular form, often listing them on the chalkboard. When teaching the structural characteristics of a fable, for example, the teacher might explain that a fable usually has four distinguishing features: (1) it is a story that is not true, (2) animals are usually main characters, (3) animals usually take on human characteristics, and (4) an explicit lesson, or moral, is often stated at the end.

During the second procedural step, students read an example of the form and discuss the way in which the story reflects the defining characteristics of the form. During the next several days students should read and discuss other examples of that narrative form in guided and independent reading experiences. Often students conclude their study with a writing experience, perhaps producing their own example of the story form they have just studied and then sharing their writing with others in the class.

In the model lesson that follows, Mr. Burns has decided to take his students out of their published reading program for a week. He wants to introduce his students to fables and the structural characteristics of that narrative form.

**MODEL
LESSON**

Using Deductive Instruction to Teach the
Structural Characteristics of a Fable

**State the Skill or Rule.** Mr. Burns begins by telling his students that they will be reading a special type of story called a fable. He tells them that a long time ago a man called Aesop told many fables to teach people how they should act. Mr. Burns writes the word *fable* on the chalkboard and asks whether anyone has ever read or heard a fable before. Several students respond, saying they think a fable has animals in it. One says that he has read a book of fables at home. As students respond, Mr. Burns lists the four characteristics on the chalkboard under the word *fable* and explains each.

1. It is not true.
2. Animals are the main characters.
3. The animals act like humans.
4. A lesson, or moral, is often stated at the end of the story.

**Provide Examples of the Skill or Rule.** Mr. Burns has his students read *The Hare and the Tortoise* by Paul Galdone. He tells them to read the story to themselves and see whether they think it is a fable.

**Provide Guided Practice.** Everyone thinks that the story is a fable. Mr. Burns initiates a discussion about why students came to that conclusion. He directs their attention to the list of characteristics on the board, and students explain how each feature was contained in the story.

**Provide Independent Practice.** Each day that week, students read and discuss a different fable from the book *Fables* by Arnold Lobel. Toward the end of the week Mr. Burns has students write their own class fable, using a language experience story method framework. He duplicates the story to read in class and to send home with the students.

## USING A COMPREHENSION FRAMEWORK TO GUIDE THE USE OF LITERATURE IN THE CLASSROOM

You have seen the many ways in which literature can function in a classroom reading program. Since literature can serve so many purposes, it should always be incorporated into classroom reading instruction, regardless of the teacher's particular comprehension framework. Nonetheless, an individual comprehension framework is useful in deciding what to teach and emphasize through the use of children's literature and how best to develop an understanding of narrative discourse structure.

## What to Teach and Emphasize with Children's Literature

As you consider the use of children's literature in your classroom, you will need to decide what to teach and emphasize with literature. Your conclusion about how a person reads should guide your decision making. Table 8–5 summarizes the relationship between this portion of your framework and decisions about using children's literature.

**Text-Based Explanation.** Teachers who follow a text-based explanation of how a person reads emphasize the importance of decoding knowledge. These teachers value literature because it helps develop fluency and automaticity in decoding. In addition, they value its ability to develop important emergent literacy/readiness aspects, promote affective aspects of reading, and develop independent readers. These teachers tend not to value the use of literature in developing those elements commonly associated with what readers bring to a text: vocabulary, syntactic, discourse, and metacognitive knowledge.

TABLE 8–5
Summary of how a comprehension framework guides decisions about what to teach with children's literature

| Explanation of How a Person Reads | Related Assumptions | Probable Focus of Children's Literature Use |
|---|---|---|
| Text-based | Meaning exists more in the text. Reading is translation. Reading begins with decoding knowledge. | Emergent literacy/readiness. Affective aspects. Fluency and automaticity in decoding. Independent reading. |
| Reader-based | Meaning exists more in what the reader brings to the text. Reading consists of expectations of upcoming words. Reading begins with prior knowledge. | Emergent literacy/readiness. Affective aspects. Expanding vocabulary knowledge. Familiarity with written syntax. Knowledge of narrative discourse structure. Metacognitive knowledge. Independent reading. |
| Interactive | Meaning exists in both the text and the reader. Reading is both translation and expectation. Reading uses each knowledge source simultaneously. | Emergent literacy/readiness. Affective aspects. Fluency and automaticity in decoding. Expanding vocabulary knowledge. Familiarity with written syntax. Knowledge of narrative discourse structure. Metacognitive knowledge. Independent reading. |

**Reader-Based Explanation.** Teachers who have a reader-based perspective, on the other hand, emphasize the prior knowledge that readers bring to a text. Therefore, they value literature because it helps develop vocabulary, syntactic, discourse, and metacognitive knowledge. In addition, these teachers, like those with a text-based perspective, value the use of literature to develop important emergent literacy/readiness aspects, to promote affective aspects of reading, and to develop independent readers. Teachers following a reader-based explanation of how a person reads, however, do not always value the use of literature to develop automaticity in decoding.

**Interactive Explanation.** Teachers with an interactive perspective value the use of literature to develop all of the elements associated with meaning in a text as well as with the meaning that readers bring to a text. These teachers use literature in classroom activities to develop emergent literacy/readiness aspects, affective aspects, decoding knowledge, vocabulary knowledge, syntactic knowledge, discourse knowledge, metacognitive knowledge, and independent reading.

## How Best to Develop an Understanding of Narrative Discourse Structure

As you consider the use of literature in your classroom, you will also need to decide how to teach narrative discourse structure. Your conclusion about how reading ability develops should guide your decision making in this area. Table 8–6 summarizes the relationship between this portion of your comprehension framework and the manner in which you develop your students' narrative discourse knowledge.

**Specific Skills Explanation.** Teachers who follow a specific skills explanation of how reading ability develops favor deductive instruction to teach knowledge of narrative discourse structure. These teachers use extensive direct instruction in the structure of narrative forms, and they use discussion questions largely to assess student understanding.

**Holistic Language Explanation.** Teachers with a holistic language perspective do not often use deductive instruction. They believe that reading is learned inductively as students engage in functional, meaningful, and holistic experiences with print. Thus, they use activities and method frameworks that rely on students' discovery of narrative structures. Read-aloud sessions are common, and a well-stocked reading corner is a central part of a holistic language classroom. In addition, these teachers use activities such as SSR, readers theatre, home reading, DRTAs, individualized reading (see chapter 2), and writing experiences (see chapter 9) to provide self-directed learning experiences with narrative discourse structures.

TABLE 8–6
Summary of how a comprehension framework guides decisions about how to teach knowledge of narrative discourse structure

| Explanation of How Reading Ability Develops | Related Assumptions | Probable Types of Instructional Activities |
|---|---|---|
| Specific skills | Reading ability develops as students learn specific reading skills. Students learn best as a result of teacher-directed deductive experiences. | Deductive instruction. Discussion questions to assess students' mastery of specific structural elements. |
| Holistic language | Reading ability develops as students engage in meaningful, functional, and holistic experiences with print. Students learn best as a result of self-directed inductive experiences. | Inductive, self-directed experiences. Discussion questions to develop narrative discourse knowledge through modeling experiences. Method frameworks and activities: read-aloud sessions, reading corner experiences, SSR, readers theatre, emphasis on home reading, DRTA, story mapping, individualized reading, and writing activities. |
| Integrated | Reading ability develops as students learn specific reading skills and as they engage in meaningful, functional, and holistic experiences with print. Reading ability develops as a result of both teacher-directed deductive experiences and self-directed inductive experiences. | Both deductive and inductive experiences. Discussion questions to assess as well as to develop narrative discourse knowledge through modeling experiences. Method frameworks and activities: deductive instruction, read-aloud sessions, reading corner experiences, SSR, readers theatre, emphasis on home reading, DRTA, story mapping, individualized reading (see chapter 2), and writing activities (see chapter 9). |

**Integrated Explanation.** Teachers with an integrated explanation of how reading develops believe that children learn best when they are exposed to both deductive and inductive learning experiences. Thus, these teachers use deductive instruction to provide direct instruction in narrative structures. However, they also use self-directed and inductive experiences as they have students read a variety of literary forms. All of the method frameworks and activities described in this chapter are apt to be used.

### Mr. Burns

I find children's literature to be an important part of my classroom program. It motivates children to read both in my class and outside my class. And that's important for two reasons. First, I believe strongly that the more students read, the better they read. As they become more automatic at recognizing words, they can focus their attention on meaning. And when they're engaged in an exciting book, they read more and they read longer.

Second, literature helps me develop independent readers. Sure, I want my students to be able to read, but I also want them to *choose* to read on their own. At our teacher's workday last week I heard a speaker talk about aliteracy, where people are able to read but tend not to in their daily lives. The speaker pointed out that aliteracy is just as serious a problem for our country as illiteracy. So developing independent readers is important to me.

All of the reading selections in our published reading program are from children's literature. I also have a classroom library in our reading corner, where students can go when they complete their regular work. These additional reading experiences help develop both automaticity and independence in reading. In addition, I spend a little time developing narrative discourse knowledge, especially an understanding of the forms we're reading right now. My unit on fables seemed to work well—I used deductive methods to teach it. But all in all, I don't spend a lot of time on this aspect of comprehension.

### Ms. Sanchez

Literature is really the heart and soul of my classroom: we *live* literature in my class. I use individualized reading and writing experiences as the core of my reading program, and both use literature as a vehicle for learning. Litera-

ture helps my students understand important concepts, become familiar with writing patterns and story forms, and develop metacognitive knowledge. But most importantly, it generates tremendous enthusiasm for reading and helps my students become independent readers. I don't know how I'd teach without literature.

I have a reading corner in my classroom, and I've acquired a fairly large library of good books over the years. But we also depend on the school library to fill in the gaps. Between the two places my students can always find a good book to get into.

I do use many different activities and method frameworks to help my students understand narrative discourse structures. I used to think that they would simply learn about these structures on their own. But recently, I've found the use of story maps to be really helpful, and the discussions that go along with the maps seem to make these structures easier to grasp. I've kind of surprised myself at how much direct teaching I've been doing in this area.

### Ms. Dodson

Literature is at the core of my reading program, too. I use it to develop each and every component of reading comprehension—everything from decoding to metacognition. I also use it to encourage independent reading, because having students choose to read is just as important as having them able to read. Literature is especially helpful in this area.

My classroom has just about all of the literature activities you can imagine. I read aloud to my students every day, and we all enjoy it. We all like SSR, too. Recently, I've been using DRTAs, story maps, and deductive instruction to teach narrative discourse structures. All three methods have been successful.

■ Experiences with literature should be at the center of every classroom reading program. Literature's effects on reading comprehension are all-encompassing; using literature develops every component of the process.

■ To develop independent readers through children's literature, teachers must become familiar with popular children's literature, identify their students' reading interests, and put children and books together in pleasurable settings. Many method frameworks and activities can help bring children and books together pleasantly: conducting read-aloud sessions, creating a classroom reading corner, using sustained silent reading, taking advantage of a school library or media center, using readers theatre, encouraging home reading, and developing other activities for a classroom environment rich in literature.

■ Knowledge of narrative discourse structure assists in the comprehension of extended text in three ways. First, knowing the structure of narratives helps readers interpret correctly what they have read. Second, knowing narrative structure helps readers develop appropriate expectations of upcoming meaning. Finally, knowledge of narrative structure allows readers to infer structural information omitted by an author.

■ Teachers can develop knowledge of narrative structure by using questioning strategies, directed reading-thinking activities, story mapping, and deductive instruction.

■ A comprehension framework can guide decisions about using children's literature. A conclusion about how a person reads can help determine what to teach and emphasize through children's literature. A conclusion about how reading ability develops can help determine how to teach narrative discourse structure.

1. Traditionally, schools assume that children learn how to read at school. Survey the students in your college classes, asking whether they learned how to read by being read to at home. Determine whether any students learned how to read in this fashion. Assuming that some students have learned to read in that way, how would you as a classroom teacher incorporate your findings into your reading program?

2. Select an interesting piece of children's literature for a read-aloud session. Practice reading it aloud until you have a clear sense of how you want it to sound. Then read your selection to a class of children or to your peers. Follow the procedural steps listed on page 306.

3. Knowledge of narrative discourse is useful for readers and for teachers. It allows teachers to understand missing portions of narratives and to anticipate the difficulty of young readers, who may not infer the appropriate

meaning because of their lack of discourse knowledge. Reread the selection "The Rabbit and the Bear" in this chapter. An important structural element is missing in this story and may not always be inferred by young readers. Is it setting information, an initiating episode, goal formation, or a final reaction by the rabbit? Knowing this information, what would you do if your students were about to read this story?

4. Make a story map for the portion of *Ira Sleeps Over* found in Figure 2–4. Which structural elements are missing in this story? What would you do to help students infer the missing information?

5. Write a description of how children's literature will be used in your classroom reading program. Be sure to describe what you plan to use literature for as well as how you will use it to accomplish your goals. Discuss the connection between your comprehension framework and these instructional decisions.

## FURTHER READING

Cullinan, B. E. (Ed.). (1987). *Children's literature in the reading program*. Newark, DE: International Reading Association.

A collection of excellent articles describing how to use children's literature in elementary classrooms. Contains sections on using literature in the primary grades, intermediate grades, and upper grades and using it in broader contexts. Presents many useful ideas.

Fuhler, C. J. (1990). Commentary: Let's move toward literature-based reading instruction. *The Reading Teacher, 43*(4), 312–315.

Argues that we need to use more literature in the classroom to allow all readers the opportunity to become literate.

Spiegel, D. L., & Fitzgerald, J. (1986). Improving reading comprehension through instruction about story parts. *The Reading Teacher, 39*(7), 676–683.

Describes how a set of specific teaching activities helped fourth-grade students gain a better understanding of story structure and, in turn, assisted comprehension.

Trelease, J. (1989). *The new read-aloud handbook*. New York: Penguin Books.

Precisely what its title claims—a handbook for conducting read-alouds. Written in a warm, entertaining style. Describes read-aloud experiences for home and classroom. Also contains an annotated listing of books that are good for read-aloud activities.

Tunnell, M. O., & Jacobs, J. S. (1989). Using "real" books: Research findings on literature-based reading instruction. *The Reading Teacher, 42*(7), 470–477.

Reviews studies investigating the effects of reading programs using literature in the classroom. Concludes that literature-based reading programs can have a profound effect on reading proficiency among all types of students.

## REFERENCES

Anderson, R., Fielding, L., & Wilson, P. (1988). Growth in reading and how children spend their time outside of school. *Reading Research Quarterly, 23*, 285–303.

Clay, M. M. (1989). Concepts about print in English and other languages. *The Reading Teacher, 42*(4), 268–277.

Cochran-Smith, M. (1984). *The making of a reader*. Norwood, NJ: Ablex.

Davis, Z. T., & McPherson, M. D. (1989). Story map instruction: A road map for reading comprehension. *The Reading Teacher, 43*(3), 232–240.

Dreher, M. J., & Singer, H. (1980). Story grammar instruction unnecessary for intermediate grade students. *The Reading Teacher, 34* 261–272.

Fader, D. N. (1976). *The new hooked on books.* New York: Putnam.

Fuhler, C. J. (1990). Commentary: Let's move toward literature-based reading instruction. *The Reading Teacher, 43*(4), 312–315.

Harris, A. J., & Sipay, E. R. (1990). *How to increase reading ability* (9th ed.). New York: Longman.

Hiebert, E. H., & Colt, J. (1989). Patterns of literature-based reading instruction. *The Reading Teacher, 43*(1), 14–21.

McCracken, R. A. (1971). Initiating sustained silent reading. *Journal of Reading, 14,* 521–524, 582–583.

Morrow, L. M. (1984). Reading stories to young children: Effects of story structure and traditional questioning strategies on comprehension. *Journal of Reading Behavior, 16,* 273–278.

Rasinski, T. V. (1989). Fluency for everyone: Incorporating fluency instruction in the classroom. *The Reading Teacher, 42*(9), 690–693.

Reutzel, D. R. (1985). Story maps improve comprehension. *The Reading Teacher, 38*(4), 400–404.

Spiegel, D. L., & Fitzgerald, J. (1986). Improving reading comprehension through instruction about story parts. *The Reading Teacher, 39*(7), 676–683.

*Sun and Shadow.* (1983). New York: Harcourt Brace Jovanovich.

Taylor, D., & Strickland, D. S. (1986). *Family storybook reading.* Portsmouth, NH: Heinemann.

Trelease, J. (1989a). *The new read-aloud handbook.* New York: Penguin Books.

Trelease, J. (1989b). Jim Trelease speaks on reading aloud to children. *The Reading Teacher, 43*(3), 200–207.

Tunnell, M. O., & Jacobs, J. S. (1989). Using "real" books: Research findings on literature-based reading instruction. *The Reading Teacher, 42*(7), 470–477.

Zarrillo, J. (1989). Teachers' interpretations of literature-based reading. *The Reading Teacher, 42*(9), 22–29.

# Connecting Reading and Writing

- The Role of Writing in a Classroom Reading Program
- Providing Appropriate Writing Experiences
- Making the Reading-Writing Connection
- Using a Comprehension Framework to Guide the Connection of Reading and Writing

*January 19*

*Dear Mr. Henshaw,*

*Thank you for sending me the postcard with the picture of the lake and mountains and all that snow. Yes, I will continue to write in my diary. . .You know something? I think I feel better when I write in my diary.*

*My teacher says my writing skills are improving. Maybe I really will be a famous author someday. She said our school along with some other schools is going to print (that means mimeograph) a book of work of young authors, and I should write a story for it. The writers of the best work will win a prize—lunch with a Famous Author and with winners from other schools. I hope the famous author is you. . .*

*Your good friend,*
*Leigh Botts the First*

Excerpt from DEAR MR. HENSHAW by Beverly Cleary. Copyright © 1983 by Beverly Cleary. By permission of Morrow Junior Books, a division of William Morrow & Co., Inc.

The discovery that Leigh Botts shares with Mr. Henshaw isn't surprising: writing makes you a better writer. But did you ever think that writing might also make you a better reader? Or that reading might make you a better writer? Increasingly, we are discovering how much children gain when we connect reading and writing. Effective teachers understand the benefits to be achieved by integrating reading and writing experiences. Consequently, they develop many method frameworks and instructional activities that allow them to integrate the two within their classrooms. This chapter will help you to make the reading-writing connection in your classroom.

Chapter 9 includes information that will help you answer questions like these:

1. Why is writing important to the development of reading proficiency?
2. What insights should guide the connecting of reading and writing in the classroom?
3. In what ways can the reading-writing connection be made for students?
4. How is a comprehension framework associated with decisions about connecting reading and writing?

KEY CONCEPTS

buddy journal
dialogue journal
drafting
editing
journal writing
macrocloze tasks
pattern stories
predictable text
prewriting

◎ process writing
publishing
reader response journal
reading/writing center
revising
story frame
thematic reading experiences
writer's workshop

## THE ROLE OF WRITING IN A CLASSROOM READING PROGRAM

In chapter 8 you discovered why literature is central to an effective classroom reading program. It is one of two vehicles that can be used to develop every component of reading comprehension. Writing is the other. Used appropriately, writing activities can promote the development of reading comprehension as significantly as the use of engaging literature selections. Writing experiences, like literature activities, can develop each of the components of reading comprehension. As a result, providing children with appropriate writing experiences is as important to effective reading instruction as using children's literature. The most effective classroom reading programs are those that regularly integrate reading and writing experiences for students.

Children develop emergent literacy/readiness aspects partly through early opportunities to write.

But how, exactly, do writing experiences promote reading comprehension? Knowing the answer to that question will help us understand why writing is so important to reading and how we should make the reading-writing connection.

## Using Writing to Develop Emergent Literacy/Readiness Aspects

Many authors have pointed out that young children develop emergent literacy/readiness aspects as a result of their early writing experiences (Chomsky, 1971; Clay, 1986; McGee & Richgels, 1990). In chapter 4 we saw that random scribbling changes to more organized left-to-right writing patterns as youngsters discover through their own writing experiences the left-to-right nature of our writing system. That discovery is an important developmental accomplishment.

Other aspects of emergent literacy/readiness also develop as youngsters compare their writing to the print around them. Letters start to appear in young children's writing as they begin to notice and replicate the symbols that we use in our writing system. Eventually, young children also begin to notice and use the spelling patterns that exist in our language as they explore the world of writing. Thus, supporting early attempts at writing helps very young children acquire insights important to emergent literacy/readiness.

## Using Writing to Develop Affective Aspects

Writers are interested and motivated readers (Smith, 1983). In fact, many teachers would argue that writing's greatest gift is the opportunity it provides for developing enthusiastic, interested, and sensitive readers. Writers are interested, of course, in reading their own writing. They are also interested, however, in reading the writing of others. They read to gather information for their writing and to see how other authors present their ideas. Thus, writing experiences hold enormous potential for increasing interest in and motivation for reading.

Writing can also be used to develop more thoughtful response patterns. Students can learn about themselves and others as they write, discuss, and reflect on their reading (Hynds, 1989). Writing can help students think critically about their feelings, reactions, and beliefs.

In addition, writing is a useful emotional outlet for dealing with life's crises. Writing about personal joys, pleasures, and difficulties can provide an important emotional outlet. As Leigh Botts observed in his letter to Mr. Henshaw, "I think I feel better when I write in my diary."

## Using Writing to Develop Decoding Knowledge

When young children write and attempt to spell words, they continually reflect on the relationships between sounds and letters (Read, 1971). In early attempts students invent their own spellings (e.g., *pichr* = *picture*) since they have not yet learned conventional spellings. However, even such inventions require students to consider carefully what they know about sound-letter relationships. As young writers develop and compare their efforts with the print around them, they begin to understand readers' needs for more conventional spellings and eventually acquire them through their writing experiences. Thus, writing experiences contribute significantly to an understanding of the relationship between print and spoken language, a central component of decoding knowledge.

## Using Writing to Develop Vocabulary Knowledge

Writing helps students develop vocabulary knowledge in at least two ways. First, writers learn the meanings of new words as they read and write about new ideas, new concepts, and new experiences. What better way to develop an understanding of the concepts associated with the Revolutionary War—the minutemen, Bunker Hill, Valley Forge, the stamp tax, the Constitution—than to read and then write about them? Writing allows us to try out new words in our language—to play with them in different sentences, practice using them, and see how they fit. Writers then come to own these new words and develop a richer, more powerful vocabulary because of their writing.

Writing also assists the development of vocabulary knowledge by helping us acquire a more precise understanding of word meanings. Have you ever found yourself trying to come up with the exact word for a particular idea in your writing? You probably ran through several similar words before deciding on the one that best fit the context. You may even have consulted a thesaurus or a dictionary. In any event this type of experience results in a more precise understanding of word meanings, which is important to the development of vocabulary knowledge. Thus, writing not only expands our vocabulary knowledge but also refines it.

## Using Writing to Develop Syntactic Knowledge

Writing experiences also allow students to experiment with different word combinations in sentences, thereby developing their syntactic knowledge. As we write, we try out different word patterns in order to communicate our exact meaning. We frequently write a sentence one way, read it, and decide that it does not quite say what we mean. Consequently, we modify the syntax of the sentence. We may change it from passive to active voice in order to be clearer; we may add a clause to modify one portion of the sentence, or we may even decide to make a complex sentence into several shorter sentences. As we experiment with these changes, we learn about the consequences of different syntactic patterns in our language. Thus, our writing experiences have helped develop our syntactic knowledge.

## Using Writing to Develop Discourse Knowledge

Writing experiences also allow students to experiment with different ways of combining sentences to form complete texts, thereby developing discourse knowledge. Writing lets students gain experience with different discourse forms. An individual's first letter to someone produces important insights into the structure of that discourse form. A flashback added to a story allows a writer to understand the positive and negative potential associated with that narrative structure. A student's first report provides a set of rich experiences and important insights into the organization of informational texts. Clearly, writing in an unfamiliar discourse form requires students to carefully attend to the structural characteristics of that form.

## Using Writing to Develop Metacognitive Knowledge

Finally, writing experiences require students to consider how their audience will read their text, thus promoting the development of metacognitive knowledge. Will the audience skim a lengthy text? If so, it becomes important to provide clear topic sentences, a clear introduction, and a strong summary. Will the audience read the text carefully to acquire new information? If so, it becomes important to make connections between ideas as explicit as possible. Writers are forced to anticipate the strategic knowledge their readers will use, thereby developing their own metacognitive knowledge.

## PROVIDING APPROPRIATE WRITING EXPERIENCES

If writing is so important to reading proficiency, how should teachers go about providing appropriate writing experiences? During the past decade much research has focused on writing and has provided us with useful information on how best to integrate writing experiences into classroom activities. The major insights from this research provide clear direction for structuring these writing experiences.

- Writing is a process.
- Writing experiences are most appropriate when they serve a communicative function.
- Writing experiences are most appropriate when they require students to create complete, extended texts.
- Reading and writing are similar types of processes.

### Process Writing

process writing: A view of writing instruction that supports each of the elements of the writing process: prewriting, drafting, revising, editing, and publishing.

Traditionally, schools have simply assigned writing tasks to students and then have evaluated their products (Applebee, 1981). By focusing on the outcome, traditional approaches treated writing as a product. In contrast, one of the most important conclusions from recent work is that writing should be viewed as a process, not a product (Calkins, 1983; Graves, 1983; Smith, 1982). **Process writing** is now rapidly replacing more traditional approaches to writing.

Teachers who take a process approach to writing do more than simply assign writing tasks and evaluate the results. Instead, they focus their attention on the complex and extensive process of writing and assist students in its basic components: prewriting, drafting, revising, editing, and publishing. Recognizing writing as a process leads teachers to support each of these elements as they design appropriate writing experiences for their students.

prewriting: One element of the writing process during which writers generate potential topics and writing ideas.

**Prewriting. Prewriting** experiences are designed to generate potential topics and writing ideas by helping students explore either personal knowledge or new information that is related to their writing task. Examples of prewriting activities include reading material related to a topic, brainstorming ideas, mapping relationships among ideas, listing sources of information, and even talking to a friend about various ideas. Appropriate prewriting experiences support students in this often-difficult beginning phase of the writing process.

At least three considerations should influence prewriting activities. First, students should explore a wide range of potential writing ideas during prewriting. Such exploration allows students to select their own topics from many possibilities and work on a writing task that is personally important and engaging. Second, it is important to provide sufficient time for this phase of the writing process. In a survey of American classrooms, Applebee (1981) concluded that students have, on average, three minutes to think of a topic during a typical writing lesson. Instead, students should have time to explore all interesting possibilities. Finally, prewriting should be viewed as an opportunity for students to discover that they have something to say about a topic. Prewriting gets ideas to flow; it is a time of beginnings. It is not a time when the final structure of a text must be decided. Examples of how prewriting activities might be used during writing instruction can be seen on page 347.

**Diary Writing.** Read together or conduct read-alouds of selections in which the main character keeps a diary. Consider these examples:

*Anne Frank: Diary of a Young Girl*

*Diary of a Rabbit* by Lilo Hess

*Penny Pollard's Diary* by Robin Klein

Tell your students that they, too, will have an opportunity to keep a diary. Brainstorm together (and list on chart paper) things that students might write about in a diary. Post this list permanently where students can refer to it when they are thinking about writing topics. After sufficient discussion give each student a small spiral notebook to use as a diary. Allow students to decorate their diaries in any way they wish before making their first entries.

**SAMPLE ACTIVITIES**

**Reader Response Journals.** Introduce the use of reader response journals (see page 357). Explain that these are used to record ideas, feelings, and responses related to what has been read. Then have students generate a list of all the different types of responses writers might include in their response journals. Keep this list posted during the first few weeks so that students can use it to generate new types of responses in their journals. The list might include items such as these:

reactions to what you have read

evaluation of characters and their actions

predictions about what will happen next

ideas for writing projects that you get from your reading

ways you would have written (and improved) a text

feelings about events

Note that reader response journals themselves may be a useful prewriting experience because they are often a source of writing ideas.

**Drafting.** The second element of the writing process is **drafting,** which consists of initial attempts to capture ideas in writing. Drafting is often messy, as writers erase, rewrite, or even start over. The goal is simply to get the writer's first attempt down on paper. There will be plenty of time later for revising.

drafting: One element of the writing process during which writers capture preliminary ideas.

**SAMPLE ACTIVITIES**

**Coauthored Writing.** Occasionally encourage two students to work on a co-authored paper in a cooperative learning group activity. After a prewriting activity, they might want to work together on one draft, talking and making decisions as they go. Alternatively, after making preliminary decisions about topic and structure, they might want to write separate drafts and then compare and combine their ideas. Students often learn much from working with someone else and seeing how others write.

**Writing Folders.** Make separate writing folders for each of your students. Keep these folders in your reading/writing center (described later in this chapter). Encourage students to keep their drafts in their folders so that they will be available for use later during revision.

revising: One element of the writing process during which writers consider what they have written and make changes in the content.

**Revising.** **Revising** is the third component of the writing process. As writers revise, they read their work, consider what they have written, and make changes in the content of their writing. Revising is an important but difficult part of the writing process. It is important because it holds great potential for developing insight into written language—possible new understanding of word meanings, syntactic patterns, discourse patterns, and other elements of writing and reading. Revising is difficult for writers, though. Younger writers focus their attention on spelling and the appearance of their writing more than its content. And writers of any age are often too close to their work to notice sections that are not clear.

To help students understand how to improve the content of their writing, teachers often use peer conferences, during which another student reads a writer's work and makes suggestions for improvement. It helps writers of all ages to have someone else read and react to their writing before they revise it. Readers can provide writers with the best suggestions for making writing clearer.

**SAMPLE ACTIVITIES**

**Peer Conferences.** Explain to students how to conduct a peer conference. First, a writer reads his or her work aloud to a listener so that both can hear it. Then, according to Crowhurst (1979), the listener should provide three types of comments: things the listener liked about the paper (praise), things that were not clear in the paper (question), and suggestions to make the paper better (polish). After the explanation, model several peer conferences in front of the entire class so that students understand how to assist a writer. Then provide a written list of questions to guide each listener's responses.

What did you like? (praise)

What did you not understand? (question)

What will make the writing better? (polish)

**Press Conferences.** Press conferences (Noyce & Christie, 1989) can also be used to provide feedback to writers for revision. These differ from peer conferences in two ways. First, press conferences involve a writer and a teacher. Second, the teacher uses such conferences to take down diagnostic information related to both reading and writing. Press conferences begin with students reading their own papers aloud. This oral reading allows them to notice some of their own writing mistakes. Then the teacher asks process-oriented questions (Graves, 1983) so that the students retain control of their writing during the conference. One sixth-grade teacher (Russell, 1983) found the following questions useful:

> What is your favorite part?
>
> What problems are you having?
>
> Does your writing end abruptly? Does it need a closing?
>
> Does your lead sentence "grab" your audience?
>
> Is each paragraph on one topic?
>
> Are there any parts you can leave out?
>
> What do you plan to do next with this piece of writing?

**Editing.** The fourth aspect of the writing process is **editing**. During editing the writer should attend to the surface characteristics of writing, including spelling, capitalization, punctuation, and usage. Editing takes place near the end of the process so that attention has first been directed to the content of the piece during prewriting, drafting, and revising.

editing: One element of the writing process during which writers make changes in the surface characteristics of their work.

**Editorial Boards.** Use an editorial board for the class. Appoint board members, and then have students with revised texts bring their work to a member of the editorial board for final editing. Regularly rotate the members of the board.

**Editing Marks.** Conduct a writer's workshop (see page 366) on the use of editing marks, as illustrated in Figure 9–1. Use either an inductive or a

SAMPLE
ACTIVITIES

| ≡ | Capitalize | ℒ | Delete something |
|---|---|---|---|
| ⊙ | Use a period | ◯ | Spell this word correctly |
| ∧ | Insert something | ¶ | Begin a new paragraph |
| ⋀ | Add a comma | / | Use a lowercase letter |
| ⌄⌄ | Add quotation marks | ∿ | Transpose |

FIGURE 9–1
Editor's marks

One method for binding books that students have written

## Required Materials

Ditto paper (8½" × 11" 6−7 pieces)
Dental floss (20")
Cardboard or posterboard (6¼" × 9½" 2 pieces)
Construction paper (9" × 12")
Rubber cement

Plastic letters (optional)
Wallpaper, adhesive-backed paper,
or material (15" × 11")
Scissors

### Making the Booklet

1. One at a time, fold 6 or 7 sheets of ditto paper in half to form book pages that are 5½" × 8½". Bring the sheets together, one inside the other. Fold the construction paper in half, forming a 6" × 9" rectangle. Place the ditto sheets inside the folded construction paper.
2. Open the booklet and lay it flat. Poke small holes through the center fold at about 1" intervals. Using the needle threaded with dental floss, sew the pages together along the fold. Begin sewing on the outside of the fold so that the knot at the end of the dental floss is not seen when the book is completely bound. Continue until the stitches cover the entire length of the fold.

### Making the Cover

1. Lay the wallpaper or other covering face down and place the two cardboard or posterboard pieces on top, leaving approximately equal overlap top to bottom and side to side and about ⅛" space in the center between the two pieces.
2. Use the rubber cement to glue the cardboard or posterboard pieces in place. Cut diagonally across each corner, and then glue down the overlap along the sides. Use the cut-off triangles to reinforce the inside corners if you wish.

### Putting the Booklet and Cover Together

1. Glue the construction paper of the booklet to the inside of the cover.
2. Use the plastic letters or some other material to add the title to the cover.

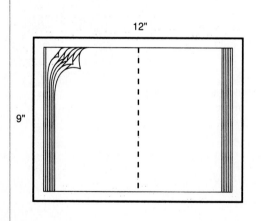

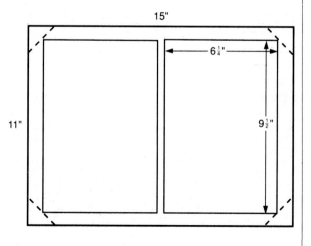

deductive method framework to teach the use of these conventions during editing. Show students how you use these marks when you edit your own work, and encourage them to use the same marks for their own editing.

publishing: One element of the writing process during which writers formally share their work with a wider audience.

**Publishing.** The final element in the writing process is **publishing,** when writers formally share their writing with a wider audience and receive recognition for their work. Sometimes publishing involves binding students' work and making it available for others to read. One method for binding books can be seen in Figure 9–2. Other suggestions for formally sharing a finished work are described in the sample activities on page 352.

**Using Process Writing in the Classroom.** Focusing on writing as a process means that we provide support to students during each phase of the process. The writing project described in the model lesson (see pp. 353–354) demon-

Here, a student is making a cover for a group book-publishing project, an important step in the writing process.

**SAMPLE
ACTIVITIES**

**Class Newspapers.** Publish stories and articles in a class or school newspaper.

**Author's Chair.** Have a special author's chair, from which students read their finished works to the rest of the class.

**Author of the Week.** Post completed work on an author-of-the-week bulletin board.

**Read-Aloud Variations.** Have completed works read regularly in the morning over the school communication system. You might also have students read their completed works to another class.

**Author Parties.** Every month set aside an hour for students to read their completed works to the rest of the class. Allow listeners to respond to the completed works. Celebrate with a small party for the authors.

---

strates how a teacher might provide support during each of these phases. However, two important points need to be made in relation to that project. First, it is important that teachers not require students to go through each phase of the writing process for every writing assignment. For example, some writing tasks, such as an entry in a journal or a diary, do not require careful editing and are rarely published, or shared publicly. Teachers may want to allow their students to decide which of their many writing projects are developed all the way to publishing.

Second, it is important to recognize that the writing process is more recursive than linear. In other words, writing does not always follow a strict sequential process of prewriting, followed by drafting, followed by revising, followed by editing, followed by publishing. When writers are drafting an article, they may also revise portions of it, or they may go back and edit word choices and spelling. They may even make plans to have their writing published. Thus, Graves (1983) points out, writing is not easily packaged into a sequence of steps. And teachers who want to support their students throughout the writing process should not expect a neat linear sequence of procedural steps.

## Communicative Writing

A second insight to guide instruction is that writing experiences are most appropriate when they serve a communicative function. Despite the common sense underlying this insight—who would want students to write something with no purpose?—classroom writing experiences often reflect only the fact that students have completed a particular task (Moffett, 1985). For example, writing a book report, which is turned in to the teacher and passed back with

A Process Writing Activity in Ms. Sanchez's Room

**MODEL
LESSON**

**Prewriting.** Ms. Sanchez's second-grade class has been reading a thematic unit on *pourquoi* tales, the "why" stories used by each culture to explain the origin of things. The students have listened to, read, and discussed *pourquoi* tales from several cultures.

> *How the Rhinoceros Got His Skin* by Leonard Weisgard
>
> *The Fire Bringer* by Margaret Hodges
>
> *Just So Stories* by Rudyard Kipling

Ms. Sanchez tells her students that they will have a chance to create their own *pourquoi* tales and publish these in a book entitled *Just Our Stories (with apologies to Rudyard Kipling)*. This book will be placed in the local library for the community to enjoy before being returned to the class. Ms. Sanchez begins with a brainstorming activity. Students share possible titles for their *pourquoi* tales: "How the Snake Lost Its Legs," "How Ms. Sanchez Got Her Smile," "How San Francisco Got the Bay," "How the Eagle Got Its Wings." As each title is shared, Ms. Sanchez writes it on the board, and a few moments are spent brainstorming explanations that might be included in the story. Once a list of titles is developed, she encourages students to decide on their own titles and begin drafting their *pourquoi* tales.

**Drafting.** Ms. Sanchez circulates around the room, providing assistance and encouragement. When she notices interesting ideas that are being developed, she has students share them with the class. Nonetheless, several students are having difficulty getting started. She calls these students together for additional brainstorming and discussion about possible stories. As each possibility is brainstormed, Ms. Sanchez maps out the story's setting, problem, episodes, and outcome on the board (see chapter 8). This support provides each student with the necessary structure to get started. At the end of each day's work, students return their drafts to their individual writing folders located in the writing center of the classroom.

**Revising.** As students finish their drafts, Ms. Sanchez assigns them to someone else in the room for peer conferencing. She has students share their work in two separate peer conferences so that they can obtain different reactions to their writing. She gives both writer and listener a paper with these procedures for peer conferencing.

1. Read the draft aloud.
2. Share your response to each of the following questions:
   - What did you like?
   - What did you not understand?
   - What will make the writing better?

After receiving comments from two listeners, students begin to revise their work in a second draft.

 **Editing.** Ms. Sanchez requires each tale to be read and edited by at least two people. The editors sign the front page of the second draft so that a list of their names can be compiled for inclusion in the final book. After two people have read and edited each story, students complete a third and final draft, taking into consideration their editors' suggestions.

 **Publishing.** After each story is completed, Ms. Sanchez has the author sit in the author's chair and read it orally to the entire class. Then she prepares it for binding with the rest of the stories.

a grade, communicates only that the student has completed reading a book. On the other hand, a book review written to guide other students in making a reading selection would serve a useful communicative function. That function would be increased if the review was read aloud to the class and then included in a collection of reviews organized by title, topic, or author for later student reference.

Writing experiences that serve a communicative function are both personal and meaningful for students. They are personal because students recognize that they are sharing a part of themselves with their readers. They are meaningful because the writing exists to communicate important information. When writing is both personal and meaningful, students invest considerable energy and attention. They are more careful because they realize that they are sharing something important about themselves with their readers; and as a result, they gain more from the experience.

As teachers, we need to create contexts in which students have functional reasons for writing. A classroom should be viewed as a literacy community, where students use writing to satisfy needs, present information, express personal thoughts and opinions, record information, interact with others, and otherwise communicate.

**SAMPLE ACTIVITIES**

**Get-well Letters.** Have students write get-well letters whenever a classmate is ill and absent from school for more than several days. Encourage students to describe what is taking place at school so that the absent student keeps posted on what is happening. Collect the letters at the end of the day, and ask a student who lives near the absent classmate to deliver them. Twenty or thirty letters from friends will always brighten someone's day.

**Letters to Visitors.** Have students write letters to classroom visitors (e.g., fire fighters, police officers, doctors, librarians, authors, and others) *before* they arrive as well as after they have come. Encourage students to list questions in their letters that they would like to have answered when the person visits. Visitors appreciate knowing in advance what is on students' minds.

**Suggestion Box.** Create a classroom suggestion box. Encourage students to share their ideas for making the classroom a better place in which to learn. Regularly post suggestions on a bulletin board, and encourage students to write their reactions to the ideas. Post student responses as well.

## Extended Writing

Writing experiences are most appropriate when they require students to create complete, extended texts such as letters, stories, or articles. Unfortunately, the writing experiences in our schools infrequently involve complete, extended texts. In an analysis of language arts textbooks used in the elementary grades, DeGroff and Leu (1987) found that, on average, students were expected to write only one piece per week that was greater than a single sentence. That level of involvement in writing is simply not enough to develop proficient readers and writers.

Complete, extended texts offer numerous benefits. First, extended writing experiences promote the development of all components of the comprehension and composing processes. More limited writing experiences make more limited contributions. For example, a task requiring students to write single-word answers demands attention only to spelling and vocabulary elements. Single sentences require only spelling, vocabulary, and syntactic knowledge. However, writing a letter, article, or story requires students to attend to all of the components associated with comprehension or composition. Thus, extended writing experiences hold greater potential for students to learn about written language.

In addition, writing a complete, extended text has much greater potential to develop critical thinking and reasoning abilities. We certainly cannot expect students to argue persuasively or explain their reasoning in a single word or sentence. And writing a complete, extended text also provides more reading opportunities at every phase of the process. Single words or sentences limit the rereading that students must do, especially during revision and editing. Finally, extended texts usually serve a greater communicative function than single words or sentences can. A single word or sentence typically reflects a student's understanding or completion of a reading assignment. Complete texts, on the other hand, permit meaningful communication.

## Similarities in Reading and Writing

It is important to keep in mind that reading and writing are similar types of processes. They have been compared by various authors as being two sides of the same coin, two wings of the same bird, or a mirror into which reader and

**SAMPLE
ACTIVITIES**

**Pattern Writing.** Read aloud a series of books containing a similar discourse structure, such as a set of fables, mysteries, or biographies. Then help students write their own stories following that same type of discourse structure. For younger students you may wish to use a single story with a predictable and repeated pattern, such as *Brown Bear, Brown Bear, What Can You See?* by Bill Martin. For older students you may wish to use an unfamiliar genre, such as science fiction. An interesting science fiction selection for older students is *This Place Has No Atmosphere* by Paula Danziger.

**Self-Evaluations.** Have students write descriptive self-evaluations of their work at the end of each marking period. Include these with their report cards to parents.

**Social Studies Journals.** Have students keep a social studies journal. Have them use it to ask questions, record interesting information, and summarize what they have read. Encourage students to use the journals to review information they have covered. Other writing activities related to social studies can also be recorded in these journals.

---

writer peer from different sides. Each of these metaphors helps us understand how closely reading and writing are related.

In both reading and writing meaning is composed. Writers compose meaning as they construct a message for their readers. Readers then compose meaning as they reconstruct the author's message. Furthermore, Tierney and Pearson (1983) point out that both writers and readers plan, draft, align, revise, and monitor as they compose meaning.

To begin, both writers and readers plan. Writers plan their messages, taking into account their goals and their audiences. Readers plan as they consider their purposes for reading, their knowledge about the topics, and the authors of the messages.

Similarly, both writers and readers engage in drafting. Writers create drafts as they refine the messages they wish to communicate. Readers create drafts as they refine the meaning that they draw from the texts. They may create one draft before they start, a second as they read and refine their initial expectations, and yet another draft after they finish reading and have thought about the text more carefully. Readers continually draft new interpretations of what they are reading, just as authors develop new drafts of what they are writing.

The process of aligning refers to the stance that writers take toward their readers and that readers take toward writers. How each views the other influences how each performs the writing or reading task.

In addition, both writers and readers revise their work. Writers revise as they attempt to make meaning clearer for their audiences. Readers revise as

*writing*

*1. read a passa[ge]*
*2. find author's stylistic featur[es]*
*3. discuss featur[es]*
*— provide examples*
*4. design writing task.*
*5. share the result[s]*

they attempt to reconstruct the meaning the authors intended. We probably notice this process most clearly when we finish a story with a surprise ending, and we are forced to revise our interpretations of the story.

Finally, both writers and readers monitor their work. Writers monitor their work as they create it, deciding when and where it needs to be revised, when and where it should be edited, and when it is complete. Readers also monitor, deciding when something makes sense, what to do when something does not make sense, and when their comprehension of a text is complete. Both writers and readers use their metacognitive knowledge during this process.

Because reading and writing are such similar types of processes, it is important for teachers to connect the two experiences for students. Reading can assist the development of writing proficiency, and writing can assist the development of reading proficiency.

## MAKING THE READING-WRITING CONNECTION

There is probably no limit to the ways in which creative teachers can make the reading-writing connection in their classrooms. Ideas range from something as simple as having very young students read their invented spelling each day after they have finished writing, to something as complex as integrating reading and writing activities within a thematically organized reading unit. Creating new and productive learning experiences for children is one of the great satisfactions of teaching.

This section describes the more common ways that teachers make the reading-writing connection. You should consider modifying those procedures to meet individual students' needs and also creating your own methods to connect reading and writing.

### Using Reader Response Journals

One of the best means of making the reading-writing connection is by encouraging **journal writing** activities. One type of journal often used for this purpose is a **reader response journal,** which was described in a sample activity earlier in this chapter. Students use such a journal to record their ideas and feelings about what they have read. Reader response journals can be used in conjunction with independent reading selections as well as with teacher-selected reading assignments. A sample entry from a reader response journal is included in Figure 9–3.

Reader response journals allow students to assume control of their responses to reading assignments. The journals combine the personal qualities inherent in a diary with a focus on facts and ideas obtained from literature (Noyce & Christie, 1989). Often, short entries in reader response journals also find their way into more extended writing pieces.

**journal writing:** An approach to writing that has students make regular entries in individual journals, telling about what they have read or thought.

**reader response journal:** A type of journal in which students record their ideas and feelings about what they have read.

reader response journal

I like the part in "This Place Has No Atmosphere" when Aurora takes the C.A.M.P. (Coordinating American Moon Pioneers) test. Everyone moving to the moon has to take one. There are a lot of silly questions on the the test, like: True or False, A crazy species of bug, found only on the moon is called a lunar tic. Also there was an Essay question—Give two facts that you have learned about the moon (one past, one present). For the past question Aurora put "Fly man to the moon in this decade." was said by John F. Kennedy in the last century. (Contrary to popular opinion, it was not said by Spider Man, who was Fly Man's brother.... ~~just kidding~~ ~~I like this part of the book the best because it's funny~~

... just kidding! A.B.W.) I like this part of the book the best because it's funny.

Teachers sometimes choose to devote a regular 10- or 15-minute period each day to writing in reader response journals. During this time all students in the class write about the selections they have been reading; they may write anything they wish, but they must write. In many ways this activity can be considered the writing equivalent of sustained silent reading (see chapter 8).

When teachers use reader response journals in relation to specific reading assignments, they sometimes provide journal starters for students. Journal starters like those in the following list provide direction and guidance for students who may be uncertain about what to write in their journals.

*[handwritten annotations at top of page: eature ① use of "and" during speech to imitate oral language ② direct quotations without assigning speaker ③ adjectival sequence for description]*

The character I like best in this story is. . .because. . .

This character reminds me of somebody I know because. . .

This character reminds me of myself because. . .

This section makes me think about. . .because. . .

This episode reminds me of a similar situation in my own life. It happened when. . .

If I were. . .at this point I would. . .(Youngblood, 1985)

## Using Dialogue Journals

A **dialogue journal** gives teachers a method framework to connect reading and writing, provide opportunities for students to solve personal difficulties, and give teachers useful insights into their students (Bode, 1989; Gambrell, 1985). In practice, dialogue journals prompt "written conversation between two persons on a functional, continued basis, about topics of. . .interest" (Staton, 1988, p. 312). Dialogue journals can be used in many ways, but the most common procedural steps in this method framework include these:

> dialogue journal: A type of journal and a method framework through which students engage in a written conversation with their teachers.

1. Students make entries in their individual dialogue journals.
2. The teacher collects the journals at the end of the day.
3. The teacher reads and writes responses in each of the journals, returning them to students the following day.

The first step in using dialogue journals is usually to have students make entries in their individual journals about any topic they choose. Students often write about what they are studying in school, events that have happened during the day, problems they are experiencing with other students, or important experiences they have had at home. It is important to allow students to select

Various types of journal-writing activities can help make the reading/writing connection.

topics of personal importance in order to create more meaningful and functional writing (and reading) experiences for them and to increase their interest and motivation.

The second step is to collect the students' journals. Some teachers require students to make regular entries and turn in their journals each day. Other teachers have students turn in their journals only when they have made new entries, and still other teachers have students write in their journals whenever they choose but turn them in once a week.

During the final step of the process the teacher reads through the students' entries and writes a short response to each student. These responses include reactions to what students have written, answers to questions they ask, and process questions the teacher asks. Process questions require students to elaborate on their writing and extend the writing process; for example, "Tell me more about. . .," "Can you explain why. . .," "What are you going to do now?" and "How did that make you feel?" An example of a dialogue journal entry can be seen in Figure 9–4.

## Using Buddy Journals

buddy journal: A type of journal through which pairs of students engage in written conversations.

Use of **buddy journals** is a method framework quite similar to that of dialogue journals. Buddy journals are kept by pairs of students, writing back and forth and maintaining a written conversation about topics of mutual interest (D'Angelo Bromley, 1989). Buddy journals provide a very functional means of connecting reading and writing in the classroom. These journals involve three procedural steps.

1. Buddy journal partners are selected.
2. Students make entries in their journals.
3. Students exchange journals, read their partner's entry, and write a response.

The selection of partners for the buddy journal experience is important. Sometimes teachers assign buddy journal partners, accepting the possibility that some students may be uncomfortable with the partners selected for them. To minimize the discomfort, teachers might limit buddy journal teams to a period of only two weeks and then assign new partners. Other strategies are to assign partners randomly by selecting names out of a hat or to let students select their own partners. Letting students help determine the method used is often useful. But regardless of the method chosen, the teacher should be prepared to serve as a buddy journal partner if there is an uneven number of students in the class.

The second step in the process is to have students make entries in their own journals. Generally, students should be encouraged to write about topics of their own choosing in order to provide ownership and increase interest and motivation. At times, however, buddy journals can be used in conjunction with specific reading selections. Under those circumstances the teacher should encourage students to converse with each other about any topics related to their

FIGURE 9–4

An example of a dialogue journal entry

reading selections. This approach increases the connection between reading and writing and provides a unique means of discussing reading experiences.

The final step is to have students exchange their buddy journals, read their partner's entry, and write a response. This step gets the written conversation started, and the teacher determines how long it should continue. Several entries from a buddy journal are shown in Figure 9–5.

FIGURE 9-5

An example of a buddy journal

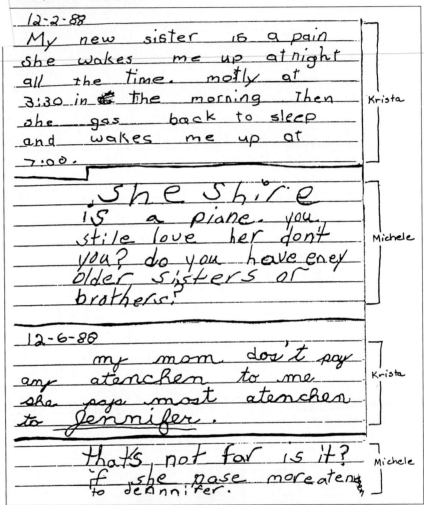

12-2-88

My new sister is a pain
she wakes me up at night
all the time. motly at
3:30 in the morning Then
she gos back to sleep
and wakes me up at
7:00.

Krista

She Shire
is a piane. you
stile love her don't
you? do you have eney
older sisters or
brathers?

Michele

12-6-88

my mom dos't pay
any atenchen to me
she pys most atenchen
to Jennifer.

Krista

that's not far is it?
if she pase more ateng
to Jennifer.

Michele

**Source:** From K. D'Angelo Bromley, "Buddy Journals Make the Reading-Writing Connection," *The Reading Teacher, 43* (1989), p. 128. Reprinted by permission.

## Developing Reading/Writing Centers

reading/writing center: A classroom location in which students participate in a series of independent activities that connect reading and writing.

A **reading/writing center** is a location in the classroom where children can participate in a series of independent, self-guided, teacher-designed activities that connect reading and writing. These centers take many forms but usually share several characteristics.

First, reading/writing centers contain all the reading and writing materials that students require to complete the activities. For example, the follow-

FIGURE 9–4
An example of a dialogue journal entry

reading selections. This approach increases the connection between reading
and writing and provides a unique means of discussing reading experiences.

The final step is to have students exchange their buddy journals, read
their partner's entry, and write a response. This step gets the written conversation started, and the teacher determines how long it should continue. Several entries from a buddy journal are shown in Figure 9–5.

FIGURE 9–5
An example of a buddy journal

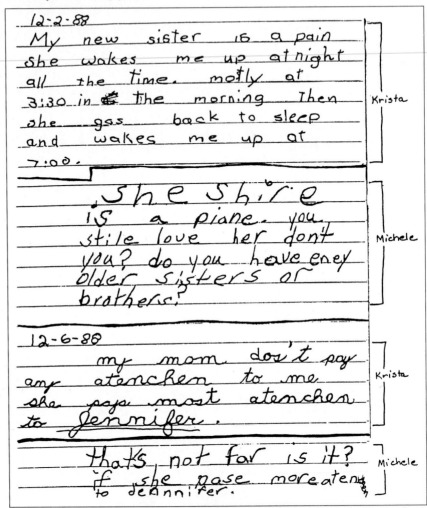

12-2-88
My new sister is a pain
she wakes me up at night
all the time. motly at
3:30 in the morning Then
she gas back to sleep
and wakes me up at
7:00.                                    Krista

She Shire
is a piane. you
stile love her don't
you? do you have eney
older sisters or
brothers?                                Michele

12-6-88
my mom. don't pay
any atenchen to me
she pay most atenchen
to Jennifer.                             Krista

that's not far is it?
if she pase more atend
to Jennifer.                             Michele

**Source:** From K. D'Angelo Bromley, "Buddy Journals Make the Reading-Writing Connection," *The Reading Teacher,* 43 (1989), p. 128. Reprinted by permission.

## Developing Reading/Writing Centers

reading/writing center: A classroom location in which students participate in a series of independent activities that connect reading and writing.

A **reading/writing center** is a location in the classroom where children can participate in a series of independent, self-guided, teacher-designed activities that connect reading and writing. These centers take many forms but usually share several characteristics.

First, reading/writing centers contain all the reading and writing materials that students require to complete the activities. For example, the following materials were available for one reading/writing center activity at the third-grade level:

1. Ten articles about exotic animals from the nature magazine *Ranger Rick*. Each had been separated from the magazine and stapled into construction-paper covers.
2. Duplicated copies of a fact sheet, which was an outline with major headings such as name of animal, size, appearance, home, food, family, and unusual facts. Students had previously learned how to use this form for recording information about animals in a science project.
3. Writing paper and felt-tip pens.
4. Students' writing folders.

Second, reading/writing centers contain clear directions for completing particular learning activities. Often the directions contain the procedural steps that students should follow (see Figure 9–6). Third, these centers contain students' writing folders, in which they keep drafts of their writing projects. Students can take their folders as they need them and return them at the end

FIGURE 9–6
An example of the directions provided for a reading/writing center activity

UNUSUAL ANIMAL STORIES

1. Look through the *Ranger Rick* articles about unusual animals from different countries. Choose one animal that you want to learn more about.

2. Read the article about the animal you have selected.

3. Look back through the article and locate the information requested by your Fact Sheet. Write this down.

4. Use the information in your Fact Sheet to write an interesting story about your animal. Share your story with a friend. Revise your story based on your friend's suggestions. Illustrate your story.

5. When finished, turn in your story to the Work Completed Box, or post it on our bulletin board.

of the day. Finally, reading/writing centers have a place to display completed work. Often this consists of a bulletin board where students may post their work and thus provide examples for other students.

## Relating Writing Activities to Thematic Reading Experiences

thematic reading experiences: Reading experiences organized around a theme and including writing activities, vocabulary study, and discussions.

An increasingly common way of making the reading-writing connection is to develop writing experiences that are related to **thematic reading experiences**. Thematic reading experiences occur when several reading selections are organized around a single theme. The theme may consist of a topic (e.g., sharing, nature, dinosaurs, friendships), an author (e.g., Laura Ingalls Wilder, Daniel Pinkwater, Beverly Cleary, Katherine Paterson, Arnold Lobel), or a genre (e.g., biography, science fiction, predictable texts, fables, mysteries). Thematic reading units produce more functional experiences because students read, discuss, and then write in order to learn more about a topic or issue, not simply to learn how to read or write.

Thematic reading units are becoming more common in published reading programs. For example, the lesson for *Ira Sleeps Over* in Figure 2–4 appears within a thematic unit entitled "Lights Out." Thematic units provide exciting opportunities to connect reading and writing, even though published reading programs do not always capitalize on them fully. Teachers should expand the writing activities found in published reading programs by adding some of their own creation. Figure 9–7 lists activities that might be used to make the reading-writing connection for first-grade students who are reading the "Lights Out" unit.

Teachers can also organize their own thematic units by reordering the selections in a published reading program around specific themes or by thematically grouping read-aloud selections. Once the thematic units have been organized, the teacher should think creatively about possible writing activities to connect the reading and writing. Figure 9–8 gives examples of reading selections and potential writing experiences that could be used within different thematic units.

## Developing Writing Activities for Published Reading Programs

Published reading programs usually contain descriptions of writing activities related to either the skill or the content of their reading lessons. These activities are most frequently found in the enrichment section of the individual lessons and should not be overlooked as a source of ideas to make the reading-writing connection. Such activities can be designed for either prereading or postreading experiences. When used before a selection is read, writing activities usually develop prior knowledge that will be useful to readers of the selection. When used after a selection is read, writing activities usually allow students to practice skills developed in the lesson or extend the reading experience in some fashion. When writing activities are not included in a published

FIGURE 9–7
Writing activities to support the reading-writing connection in the "Lights Out" unit

1. Have students keep a running list of words related to the theme "Lights Out." Encourage them to make a title for their list, like "Bedtime Words," and to add words to the list as they encounter them in their reading or listening experiences (e.g., *teddy bear, sleeping, dark, monsters, ghost story, toothbrush, night light*). You might want to keep a running list on the chalkboard, too. At the end of the unit, have the students each write a short story using as many words from their lists as they can. Alternatively, you might have them each draw an illustration of how they go to bed at night. Then have them add as many words from their lists to their illustrations as they can. Have students share their work with the rest of the class.

2. Show students a Do Not Disturb sign from the door of a hotel. Have them make one for their own rooms at home.

3. Have students make a list at home of their favorite bedtime stories. Then have them bring the list to school and read it to the rest of the class. Post their lists on a bulletin board entitled "Books to Snuggle Up To at Night." Some students might want to bring their favorites to school and either read them or have them read.

4. Have students dictate a language experience story describing how they go to bed. Write this on chart paper, and use it for additional reading experiences. Post the story during your school's open house for parents to read with their youngsters.

5. After they have read the story *Ira Sleeps Over,* have students dictate a letter that you write on the board or chart paper. It should be a letter that they might write inviting a friend to sleep over. Read the letter together, and suggest that they use it as a model when they next invite a friend over to spend the night.

reading program, activities such as those listed here might be appropriate for individual lessons. The first three might be used before reading a selection. The final four might be used after reading a selection.

**Speculative Writing.** Develop prior knowledge about a situation that students will meet in a reading selection by having them respond to the question "What would you do if. . .?" or "Have you ever. . .?" Have students write their responses the day before reading the particular selection. Then, before beginning the story, have students read their responses aloud to the group. Discuss the problem that students will encounter in the story. Have them revise their responses (if they wish) after reading the selection.

**SAMPLE
ACTIVITIES**

**Brainstorming.** Before students read a story about a particular topic, have them spend five minutes writing down everything they know about that topic. Encourage them to write their information in a list and share it with the group. Use this information to begin a discussion about key concepts in the story. Work into your discussion the meanings of important vocabulary words listed in the teacher's manual.

**Word Association.** On the chalkboard write the vocabulary words listed in the teacher's manual. Have students copy the words and write next to each the first word that comes into their minds. Have students share their responses, and use those responses to initiate a discussion of each word's meaning. You might want to use your students' responses to draw semantic maps defining each word's meaning.

**Rewriting a Story.** After students have read a narrative, have them rewrite specific story elements. For example, students might rewrite the ending to a story or rewrite the same story in a different setting. If a story is told from the perspective of one character, suggest that students rewrite the story from a different character's perspective.

**Conducting Research.** Have students conduct outside research on a topic explored in a reading selection. They might work alone or in cooperative learning groups. Have students accompany their reports with a diorama or a bulletin board display.

**Guessing Biographies.** After students have read several selections, have them write character biographies without naming their characters. Then have the students read their biographies and let other students guess their characters.

**Writing Persuasive Essays.** Have students write a persuasive essay defending or criticizing a story character's decision. Have them read their essays to a group of students who act as a jury. Let the jury decide the appropriateness of the character's action.

## Conducting Writer's Workshops

writer's workshop: A mini-lesson for a whole class or a small group on a specific aspect of writing.

A **writer's workshop** is a whole class session or a small group minilesson on a specific aspect of writing. It is developed and directed by the teacher to assist students with their writing. Writer's workshops can be used for a variety of purposes. They can be used to introduce writing-process strategies, such as brainstorming or peer conferencing. They can also be used to explain strategies that writers use to solve common writing problems. For example, a writer's workshop might show students how to make meaning clearer in informational writing by using topic sentences in paragraphs. In addition, writer's workshops can provide a time during the day when students get together to read their work and help each other solve common writing problems. Examples of topics that might be covered during a writer's workshop session are listed in Figure 9–9.

Teachers organize writer's workshops in several different ways, depending on their comprehension framework and their goal for the session. Some

FIGURE 9-8
Examples of reading selections and writing experiences to accompany certain thematic units

## Theme: Sharing

**Reading Selections**
*The Giving Tree* by Shel Silverstein
*The Gift* by Helen Coutant
*New Year's Hats for the Statues* by Yoshiko Uchida

**Writing Experiences**
Have students identify the most important thing they have to share with others and explain why they chose that particular item. Publish their essays in a book titled "What I Have to Share with Others." Have the students read and share their ideas with the rest of the class and perhaps with another class.

Have students share in writing an idea to make the classroom a better place. Then have them read their ideas aloud. Use their papers to initiate a discussion about making the class a better place to learn and grow. Post the completed papers on a bulletin board labeled "Share a Great Idea."

Conduct your show-and-tell or sharing session in writing. Have the students share something about themselves in writing without signing their names. Then collect their papers and pass them out randomly. Have the students read the papers they received, and have the rest of the class try to guess who wrote each one.

## Theme: Friendship

**Reading Selections**
*Frog and Toad Are Friends* by Arnold Lobel
*More Stories Julian Tells* by Ann Cameron
*My Grandson Lew* by Charlote Zolotow
*Maude and Sally* by Nicki Weiss
*What's the Matter with Carruthers?* by James Marshall

**Writing Experiences**
Write to a colleague, friend, or relative in another part of the country. Ask that person to check with a local school and find a class interested in exchanging pen-pal letters. Have your students write to their new pen pals.

Have the students write descriptive poems beginning with "A friend is . . ." Post these on a bulletin board labeled "Friendship."

As students read (or listen) to the reading selections, have them keep a list of words and phrases that friends like to hear. Have students read their lists at the end of the unit. Use them to initiate a discussion about making friends.

Have students select a character from these stories that they would like as a friend. Have them write a descriptive essay explaining why they would like to be friends with that person and what they would do to nurture the relationship. Have students share their essays with the rest of the class.

## Theme: Tall Tales

**Reading Selections**
*Shenandoah Noah* by Jim Aylesworth
*Paul Bunyan* by Steven Kellogg
*Sally Ann Thunder and Whirlwind Crockett* by Caron Lee Cohen
*John Henry* by Ezra Jack Keats

**Writing Experiences**
After discussing the characteristics of tall tales, help students brainstorm and then write their own. Have students read their tall tales to the rest of the class.

Have students write a story that is told in their families and has some basis in fact but may have been exaggerated or modified over the years. Publish these stories in a book for the class entitled "Family Legends."

FIGURE 9–9
Examples of topics for writer's workshop lessons

---

**Specific Writing-Process Strategies**

Brainstorming techniques
How to map writing ideas
How to outline writing ideas
How best to conduct a peer conference
Revision strategies that work
Using editing marks
How to prepare final copy for binding
How to use illustrations in the right locations

**Strategies That Writers Use to Overcome Common Problems**

Using journal ideas as sources of writing topics
Working through writer's block
Writing patterns used by good writers
Making the message clear
Letting a draft sit to acquire "distance" before revising
Using headings and subheadings to organize informational articles
Using questions (and answers) to present information

**Problems Faced by Individual Writers**

How should I end this story?
Something isn't right in this article—what is it?
Can you help me find a better title?
How can I organize my ideas better?

---

teachers rely on a deductive framework to teach specific strategies. Others use an inductive framework to organize the workshop lessons. Still others use a writer's workshop as a time to allow students to raise their own concerns and seek solutions for their individual writing problems.

In the model lesson that follows, Ms. Dodson's second-grade class has been reading a thematic unit on dinosaurs. She created the unit by combining one selection in the published reading program with these additional reading and read-aloud experiences:

*Dinosaur Time* by Peggy Parish

*Patrick's Dinosaur* by Carol Carrick

*In the Days of the Dinosaurs* by Roy Chapman Andrews

*Digging up Dinosaurs* by Aliki

*Dinosaurs, Asteroids, and Superstars: Why the Dinosaurs Disappeared* by Franklyn Branley

*The Illustrated Dinosaur Dictionary* by Helen Roney Sattler

## Inductive Instruction in a Writer's Workshop

**MODEL LESSON**

To connect reading and writing, students are preparing written reports on their favorite type of dinosaur and, with the art teacher, are creating fired clay models, which the librarian wants to display in the school library to interest other readers in books on this topic. Students have collected their information on an outline fact sheet that Ms. Dodson prepared and are currently using that information to draft their reports. Ms. Dodson has noticed that students are having difficulty presenting and organizing their information. Consequently, she has scheduled a writer's workshop to show them two different approaches: topic headings (e.g., size, appearance, favorite location) or question headings (e.g., How Big Is a Brontosaurus? What Did a Brontosaurus Look Like? Where Did Brontosauruses Live?).

**Provide Examples of the Skill or Rule.** Ms. Dodson has duplicated two pages of text for her students to look at. The first comes from one of their reading selections on dinosaurs. It uses topical section headings to organize and present information: "Plant-Eaters," "Meat-Eaters," "Dinosaur Birds," and "The Dinosaurs Disappear." The other is from the book *Sharks* by Carl Green. It uses question headings to organize and present information: "How Long Do Sharks Live?" "Do Sharks Sleep?" "What Do Sharks Eat?" She reads both pages aloud and has her students follow along, paying attention to the way each author writes.

**Help Students Discover the Skill or Rule.** Ms. Dodson asks questions to help students notice the two writing styles: "What is the same about the way these two authors wrote their articles? Yes, they both wrote facts. But how did they organize those facts? Right—in parts or sections. Now, what is at the beginning of each section? Yes, a title. We call these little titles inside a book *headings*. They tell you what each section is about. Now look and see if you notice anything different about how these two authors wrote their headings. That's right—one author used what we call a topic heading and the other used a question heading." Then Ms. Dodson shares several other examples of these two organizational patterns in other books and has one student summarize the two ways writers can organize their facts.

**Provide Guided Practice.** Ms. Dodson writes these two organizational methods on the blackboard: topic headings and question headings. Then she asks students to brainstorm what they might choose for headings if they used the first method in their own papers. They quickly notice that each heading on their fact sheet ("Size," "Appearance," "Favorite Location," "Type of Food," and "Unusual Facts") could be used as a topic heading. Ms. Dodson writes those headings on the board under "Topic Headings." Then she asks students to brainstorm questions that might be used in place of those words and writes them on the board under "Question Headings": "What Size Was the Brontosaurus?" "What Did the Brontosaurus Look Like?" "What Was Its Favorite Location?" "What Type of Food Did It Eat?" "What Are Some Unusual Facts About the Brontosaurus?" Ms. Dodson and the class talk briefly about how students might use each type of section heading to organize their reports.

**Provide Independent Practice.** After the writer's workshop, students return to their work and use one of the two types of headings to organize their information. Ms. Dodson circulates through the class, helping students who need her assistance. She notices that one student has combined the two patterns by using a topic heading ("Size") and then beginning her paragraph with the related question ("How big was the tyrannosaurus?"). Ms. Dodson has this student read her draft aloud to the class so that they can see a third pattern to use.

## Teaching Reading/Writing Patterns

Writing experiences can be especially helpful in developing an understanding of reading/writing patterns. As students think about what to write, they must reflect on the structural characteristics of a particular form. As a result, students acquire new insight into the structural characteristics of written language, which helps them with both reading and writing. Several types of writing activities can be used to focus students' attention on reading/writing patterns: macrocloze tasks, pattern stories, and story frames.

macrocloze task: A method framework through which students are asked to write and fill in a missing structural element of a story.

**Macrocloze Tasks.** **Macrocloze tasks** ask readers to fill in a missing structural unit in a story. For example, students might be asked to supply the setting for a story, an episode describing how the story's problem developed, or the resolution of the problem and the story's ending. Macrocloze tasks can effectively develop a better understanding of the structural organization of narratives. Such tasks typically contain six procedural steps.

1. The teacher selects a structural element in a discourse form that is somewhat unfamiliar to students.
2. The teacher finds a selection containing that structural characteristic and deletes it from the text.
3. The teacher or students read the selection.
4. The students write the missing portion of the selection as they think it might have been written.
5. The students share their versions of the missing portion.
6. The teacher presents the missing element so that students can compare their versions with the original.

The first step in a macrocloze task is selecting a structural element in a discourse form somewhat unfamiliar to students. Possible combinations include the setting in science fiction, the initiating episode in a fantasy, the definition of the problem in historical fiction, the resolution of the problem in a mystery, and the moral of a fable. The second step is to find an appropriate selection with that structural element and delete it from the text. For the third step most teachers simply read the selection aloud, skipping over the deleted portion. If students are to read the passage, they will need duplicated copies with the selected portion deleted.

Fourth, students write the missing portion of the reading selection as they think it might have been written. Some teachers precede this step with a brief brainstorming session to provide support for students' prewriting efforts. Normally, however, this entire task requires only the prewriting and drafting components of the writing process.

After writing, students share their versions aloud and often engage in lively discussion and debate. Thereafter, the teacher reads the missing portion of the story aloud, allowing students to see how their guesses compare to what was actually written. Macrocloze tasks are very useful in developing an understanding of discourse structure.

---

**Fables.** Read together several fables with morals at the end. Using either an inductive or a deductive method framework, discuss with your students the discourse structure of fables. Then read aloud another fable, leaving out the moral. Have your students complete a macrocloze task, writing down their guesses about the missing moral. Then read the actual moral to them, and compare it to their guesses. After completing several macrocloze tasks like this, have students write their own fables and morals. Support each of the stages of the writing process and publish the fables as described earlier in this chapter.

**SAMPLE ACTIVITIES**

**Science Fiction.** To help students recognize that science fiction contains a setting in the future, read a short science fiction selection aloud but omit the setting. Have students complete a macrocloze task, writing down their guesses about how the author described the setting. Compare students' guesses with the author's actual description.

**Mysteries.** In a thematic unit on mysteries, use a macrocloze task to develop an understanding of the resolution to a mystery, or the who-done-it explanation. Have students read a case in the *Encyclopedia Brown* series by Donald Sobol. These books each contain a series of short mysteries, with solutions listed separately at the end of the book. Have students write their solutions to one of the mysteries and then compare their versions to the author's solution. This task might also be developed into an interesting activity for a reading/writing center.

pattern stories: A story
written according to the
pattern of another story
that has been recently read.

predictable text: A story
containing a repeated pattern that makes reading the
story very predictable; may
use repeated sentences,
phrases, or structural elements.

**Pattern Stories. Pattern stories** are written by students and are structurally similar to a **predictable text** that they have recently read. Thus, the initial reading selection is used as a pattern for students to follow when writing their own, similar story. Pattern stories are especially useful with very young students, who often focus their attention on letters and sounds and not on higher-level aspects of written language organization. Pattern stories help these children understand that stories contain a regular structure, which is helpful to both readers and writers (Rhodes, 1981).

Beginning readers and writers enjoy writing pattern stories after reading counting books, such as *One Is One* by Tasha Tudor, or alphabet books, such as *City Seen from A to Z* by Rachael Isodora. Somewhat older students enjoy writing pattern stories after reading narratives with a repeated sentence or episodic pattern, such as *Too Much Noise* by Ann McGovern. Figure 9–10 lists numerous examples of these three types of books.

Beginning readers often enjoy the repetitive patterns found in predictable texts and imitated in oral and written pattern-story activities.

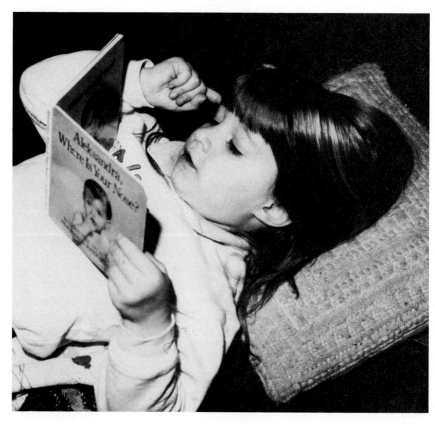

With older students nearly any book can be used as a pattern. Variations can be created in many different ways—for example, by writing the same story told by another character, by changing the time in which the tale takes place, or by changing the solution to a problem.

FIGURE 9–10
Examples of books that can be used in pattern writing activities

---

### Counting Books

*Anno's Counting Book* by Misumasa Anno
*Anno's Counting House* by Misumasa Anno
*Ten, Nine, Eight* by Molly Bang
*Up to Ten and Down Again* by L. Ernst
*Moja Means One* by Muriel and Tom Feelings
*Ten What? A Mystery Counting Book* by Russell Hoban
*A Walk in the Park* by S. Hughes
*1 Hunter* by Pat Hutchins
*Animal Numbers* by B. Kitchen
*Numbers of Things* by Helen Oxenbury
*When Baby Went to Bed* by S. Pearson
*Who's Counting?* by N. Tafuri
*One Is One* by Tasha Tudor
*Brian Wildsmith's One, Two, Three* by Brian Wildsmith

### Alphabet Books

*Anno's Alphabet* by Misumasa Anno
*Anno's Magical ABC: An Anamorphic Alphabet* by Misumasa Anno
*Alligator Arrived with Apples, a Potluck Alphabet Feast* by J. and A. Aruego
*A Farmer's Alphabet* by Mary Azarian
*Handmade ABC: A Manual Alphabet* by Linda Bourke
*A Is for Angry* by Sandra Boynton
*Ashanti to Zulu* by Leo and Diane Dillon
*Jambo Means Hello: Swahili Alphabet Book* by Tom Feelings
*The ABC Bunny* by Wanda Gag
*Dr. Seuss's ABC* by Theodore Geisel
*A, B, See!* by Tana Hoban
*26 Letters and 99 Cents* by Tana Hoban
*City Seen from A to Z* by Rachel Isadora
*Aster Aardvark's Alphabet Adventures* by Steven Kellogg
*Animal Alphabet* by Bert Kitchen
*Letters to Talk About* by Leo Lionni
*On Market Street* by Arnold Lobel
*Countin' Wildflowers* by B. McMillan
*Helen Oxenbury's ABC of Things* by Helen Oxenbury
*A Peaceable Kingdom: The Abecedarius* by Alice and Martin Provensen
*A Is for Annabelle* by Tasha Tudor
*Brian Wildsmith's ABC* by Brian Wildsmith

FIGURE 9–10
*(Continued)*

---

**Books with Repeated Sentence or Episodic Patterns**

*Why Mosquitoes Buzz in People's Ears* by Verna Aardema
*Go Tell Aunt Rhody* by Aliki
*Bertie and Bear* by Pamela Allen
*A Dark, Dark Tale* by Ruth Brown
*The Very Hungry Caterpillar* by Eric Carle
*The Grouchy Ladybug* by Eric Carle
*The Very Busy Spider* by Eric Carle
*Busy Monday Morning* by Janina Domansky
*Drummer Hoff* by Barbara Emberly
*As I Was Crossing Boston Common* by Norma Farber and Arnold Lobel
*I Unpacked My Grandmother's Trunk* by Susan Hoquet
*Goodnight, Goodnight* by Eve Ice
*When You Were a Baby* by Ann Jonas
*Where Are You Going, Little Mouse?* by Robert Kraus
*On Market Street* by Arnold Lobel
*The Rose in My Garden* by Arnold Lobel
*Brown Bear, Brown Bear, What Do You See?* by Bill Martin
*Fire! Fire! Said Mrs. McGuire* by Bill Martin
*Too Much Noise* by Ann McGovern
*The Day Jimmy's Boa Ate the Wash* by Trinka Noble
*If You Give a Mouse a Cookie* by Laura Numeroff
*Old MacDonald Had a Farm* by Tracey Pearson
*Mary Wore Her Red Dress and Henry Wore His Green Suspenders* by
    Merle Peek
*The House That Jack Built* by Janet Stevens
*Have You Seen My Duckling?* by Nancy Tafuri
*Cat on the Mat* by Brian Wildsmith

---

**SAMPLE
ACTIVITIES**

**Counting Books.** Read a counting book such as *Animal Numbers* by B. Kitchen, which uses animals to illustrate number concepts. Discuss with students that a similar book could be written using other objects to illustrate the number concepts. Then brainstorm with students the types of objects that might be used in such a counting book: toys, sports equipment, tools, food, and so on. Reach agreement on a single theme for a class counting book. Then assign each student one number to write and illustrate, using paper of a consistent size. Collate the pages in order, bind the book, and make it available for students to read.

**Alphabet Books.** Read several alphabet books to your students. As you read, discuss the similarities and differences among the books. After students have seen several alphabet books, brainstorm possible ways in which small groups might create their own alphabet books. List the possibilities on the board.

Then divide the class into cooperative learning groups and have each group decide on a theme for its alphabet book. Help each group write, illustrate, and bind its book. Then have a member from each group read it to the class. Put these books out so that students may read through them.

**Other Pattern Books.** Read *I Unpacked My Grandmother's Trunk* by Susan Hoquet to your class. Brainstorm additional book ideas that might be developed with this pattern (*I Unpacked My Lunch Box, I Unpacked My Vacation Suitcase, I Unpacked My Sister's Trunk, I Unpacked My Teacher's Desk*). Have students decide on a theme and title for their individual pattern books and then begin drafting their stories. Help your students through the drafting, revising, editing, and publishing phases of the writing process. Display the students' work on a bulletin board for everyone to read.

**Story Frames.** A **story frame** is a guided writing activity that promotes an understanding of the structural characteristics of narratives. In a story frame activity, students have an opportunity to reflect on the structural elements of narratives as they summarize a story or a portion of a story that they have read. Story frames are particularly useful for students in Grades 1 through 3 (Fowler, 1982), who are still acquiring an understanding of narrative discourse structure. An example of a story frame focusing on setting information can be seen in Figure 9–11. A story frame used to develop familiarity with the discourse structure of a fable can be seen in Figure 9–12.

> story frame: A guided writing activity that promotes understanding of the structural characteristics of narratives.

FIGURE 9–11
A story frame designed to develop familiarity with setting information

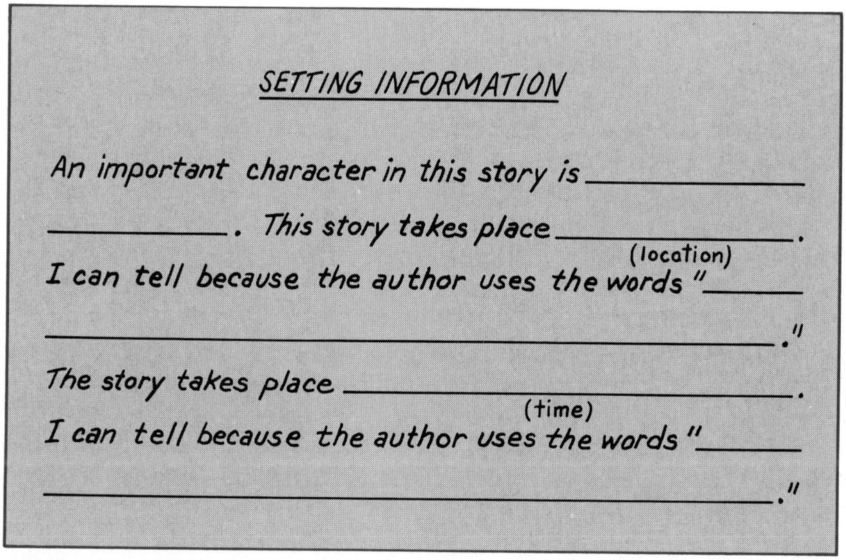

SETTING INFORMATION

An important character in this story is _____
_____ . This story takes place _____ .
(location)
I can tell because the author uses the words "_____
_____ ."

The story takes place _____ .
(time)
I can tell because the author uses the words "_____
_____ ."

FIGURE 9–12
A story frame designed to develop familiarity with the discourse structure of fables

## FABLE

The animals in this story are _____
_____ .

The problem starts when _____
_____ .

One of the animals, _____, wants to
_____ .

First, _____
_____ .

Then, _____
_____ .

After that, _____
_____ .

The problem is solved when _____
_____ .

The moral of this story is _____
_____ .

There are a number of ways in which story frames can be used. They can be a guided or independent practice activity to teach narrative discourse structure within a deductive method framework. In other words, after the structural characteristic targeted for instruction has been explained and students have been shown several examples of the characteristic through reading and discussion, a story frame activity could provide additional independent practice. Story frames can also be used to help students summarize the entire contents of a narrative they have read, thus indirectly leading to greater familiarity with narrative discourse structure in general, especially when follow-up discussion of students' work takes place.

In addition, story frames can help students plan their initial drafts of a narrative, particularly when they are writing in a narrative form that may not be familiar. For example, the story frame in Figure 9–12 might be used with students attempting to write a fable for the first time. Students could fill in the different elements in the story frame and would then have an outline of a fable that could be expanded.

## USING A COMPREHENSION FRAMEWORK TO GUIDE THE CONNECTION OF READING AND WRITING

Your explanation for how one reads can be used as you consider what to teach and emphasize when connecting reading and writing. For example, a text-based explanation would lead you to connect reading and writing in order to develop decoding knowledge. Practices like peer conferences would be seen as important because students can practice their decoding skills as they read their work aloud. If you have a reader-based explanation, however, writing would be seen as a useful tool for developing the prior knowledge important for reading, not decoding skills. Reading and writing would be connected to provide students with opportunities to learn about new concepts, try out different word order patterns, learn about new discourse structures, and acquire effective reading and writing strategies. An interactive explanation would lead you to connect reading and writing in order to develop both decoding skills and the elements of prior knowledge.

Your explanation for how reading ability develops can also be used to guide decisions as you make the reading-writing connection. Your explanation for this issue guides decisions about how to teach. If you have a specific skills perspective you will see writing as an opportunity to practice reading skills. In addition, you would favor the use of deductive instructional methods, especially during writing workshop sessions. If you have a holistic view of how reading ability develops you see writing as the perfect opportunity to create functional, meaningful, and holistic experiences with print. Writing would be seen as a means to learn insights important to reading, not as a means to practice specific reading skills. You will find several method frameworks to be useful: reader response journals, dialogue journals, buddy journals, pattern story writing, and thematic reading and writing experiences. Each uses writing in functional ways to develop important insights about reading. If you have an integrated perspective you see writing as both an opportunity to practice and to learn important insights about reading. All of the method frameworks described in this chapter will be used.

## COMMENTS FROM THE CLASSROOM ■

### Mr. Burns

As I said before, I view decoding knowledge as the key to my students' reading success. Therefore, because I have more of a text-based perspective of how someone reads, I value writing experiences for the contribution they make to decoding knowledge. I use peer conferences because my students get to practice their decoding skills as they read their own work and that of other students. Sometimes my students even have difficulty reading their *own* work out loud. So I'm pleased when I see two students trying to figure out what a particular word must be—I know they're learning how important it is to be able to decode an author's writing.

I also believe that students develop their reading ability best when I make clear presentations and provide adequate practice on specific skills. I use writing experiences a lot to provide that practice. I almost always create a writing activity for the lessons in our published reading program; I design it so the students practice the major skill of each lesson. I also use writer's workshops frequently, in conjunction with deductive instruction. And I put together a number of reading/writing center activities, each one focusing on a recently acquired skill and each one requiring the students to read their writing aloud to a partner when they finish. In addition, I teach reading/writing patterns to my students, usually deductively.

## Ms. Sanchez

Because I have a reader-based perspective of how people read, I see writing experiences as central to developing all the knowledge that readers bring to a text: vocabulary, syntactic, discourse, and metacognitive. Writing takes my students far beyond decoding. They learn new words, try out different word order patterns, learn about new discourse structures, and acquire effective reading (and writing) strategies. Writing is a marvelous tool, and I use it a lot.

Because of my leaning toward a holistic language perspective, I choose functional, meaningful, and holistic writing experiences for my students. They write in conjunction with whatever they're reading, and the writing helps them understand reading better. Every day each of my students acquires some new insight, some new understanding, as a result of writing. And they're learning what is most important for

them as individuals, especially when the writing experiences are truly functional.

I try to connect reading and writing with reader response journals, dialogue journals, and buddy journals. As I said before, I tend not to use our published reading program since it focuses too much on specific skills. Instead, I develop thematic reading experiences and then relate our writing activities to those experiences. Sometimes I conduct writer's workshops, always using an inductive method, to let students share their individual writing problems and see if the group can find solutions. I also do a lot of pattern story writing because the students seem to learn a lot about narrative discourse structure that way.

## Emily Dodson

Because of my interactive view of how someone reads, I use a reading-writing connection to develop all of the knowledge sources important to the reading process: decoding, vocabulary, syntactic, discourse, and metacognitive knowledge. I do think writing experiences help develop decoding knowledge, but I also think they're useful in developing all the other components associated with prior knowledge.

Because of my integrated understanding of how reading proficiency develops, I use most of the material and method frameworks that I know about. I use reader response journals, dialogue journals, buddy journals, pattern story writing, and thematically related reading and writing experiences, trying to give my students a functional connection between reading and writing. But I also use some of the writing activities with the lessons in our published reading program, some reading/writing center activities, and writer's workshops to focus on specific skills. I think my students benefit from the wide variety of activities they experience in my room.

▪ Writing experiences are as important to the development of reading comprehension as the use of engaging literature selections. Writing experiences, like literature selections, can be used to develop each of the components of reading comprehension.

▪ Recent research has provided four major insights that should guide our attempts to connect reading and writing: (1) writing is a process, (2) writing experiences are most appropriate when they serve a communicative function, (3) writing experiences are most appropriate when they require students to create complete, extended texts, and (4) reading and writing are similar types of processes.

▪ There are many ways to connect reading and writing in a classroom: reader response journals, dialogue journals, buddy journals, reading/writing centers, writing activities related to thematic reading experiences, writing activities for lessons in published reading programs, writer's workshops, and experiences with reading/writing patterns.

▪ A comprehension framework assists teachers in making the reading-writing connection. An explanation of how a person reads guides decisions about what to teach and emphasize in these experiences. A text-based perspective is more consistent with an emphasis on decoding knowledge. A reader-based perspective emphasizes vocabulary, syntactic, discourse, and metacognitive knowledge. And an interactive perspective gives equal emphasis to all components of the reading process. A teacher's explanation of how reading proficiency develops guides decisions about how to create the reading-writing connection. A specific skills perspective is more consistent with reading/writing centers, writing activities for lessons in published reading programs, deductive writer's workshops, and experiences with reading/writing patterns. A holistic language perspective is more consistent with reader response journals, dialogue journals, buddy journals, reading/writing centers, and writing activities related to thematic reading experiences. And an integrated perspective is consistent with all of the method frameworks and activities described in this chapter.

1. This chapter suggests that appropriate writing experiences can be used to develop each of the components of the reading process. In keeping with this understanding, evaluate the learning experience described on pages 369 to 370. Are emergent literacy/readiness aspects developed? affective aspects? decoding knowledge? vocabulary knowledge? syntactic knowledge? discourse knowledge? metacognitive knowledge? Explain how each component is or is not developed in this experience and therefore why you would or would not consider it to be an appropriate writing experience.

2. Consider the learning experience described on pages 353 to 354. Explain how this experience does or does not take into consideration each of the four major insights that should guide our attempts to connect reading and writing. Given your evaluation, do you think that this learning experience could be improved? If yes, how? If no, why not?

3. This chapter describes many different ways to make the reading-writing connection. These separate instructional practices can also be combined. Describe two combinations of instructional practices that you would consider using in your classroom, and explain in detail how you would implement them.

4. Define your own comprehension framework. Then list the instructional practices described in this chapter that are consistent with your framework. Also, list any instructional practices described here that are inconsistent with your framework. Explain why you have identified each practice as you have.

## FURTHER READING

Bode, B. A. (1989). Dialogue journal writing. *The Reading Teacher, 42,* 568–571.

Describes how dialogue journal writing can be used in both first-and sixth-grade classrooms to make the reading-writing connection.

D'Angelo Bromley, K. (1989). Buddy journals make the reading-writing connection. *The Reading Teacher, 43,* 122–129.

Explains how the use of buddy journals promotes the development of both reading and writing proficiency in elementary grades. Provides many useful suggestions for using buddy journals.

Noyce, R. M., & Christie, J. F. (1989). *Integrating reading and writing instruction in grades K–8.* Boston: Allyn & Bacon.

Describes a wide variety of method frameworks and activities for connecting reading and writing experiences in the elementary grades. Explains how reading and writing can be integrated into emergent literacy, prewriting, composing, guided-reading, skill-building, and content areas.

Tierney, R. J., & Pearson, P. D. (1983). Toward a composing model of reading. *Language Arts, 60,* 568–580.

One of the first articles to describe the similar processes shared by reading and writing. Provides a clear and compelling theoretical explanation of their similarities.

Wollman-Bonilla, J. E. (1989). Reading journals: Invitations to participate in literature. *The Reading Teacher, 43,* 112–120.

Describes case studies of three fourth-grade students who used journals as they read *Tucker's Countryside* by George Selden. Describes how each of these students developed as both a reader and a writer from their individual experiences in responding to literature.

## REFERENCES

Applebee, A. N. (1981). Looking at writing. *Educational Leadership, 38,* 458–462.

Bode, B. A. (1989). Dialogue journal writing. *The Reading Teacher, 42,* 568–571.

Calkins, L. M. (1983). *Lessons from a child.* Exeter, NH: Heinemann.

Chomsky, C. (1971). Write first, read later. *Childhood Education, 47,* 296–299.

Clay, M. (1986). Constructive processes: Talking, reading, writing, art, and craft. *The Reading Teacher, 39,* 764–770.

Crowhurst, M. (1979). The writing workshop: An experiment in peer response to writing. *Language Arts, 56,* 757–762.

D'Angelo Bromley, K. (1989). Buddy journals make the reading-writing connection. *The Reading Teacher, 43,* 122–129.

DeGroff, L. C., & Leu, D. J. (1987). An analysis of writing activities: A study of language arts textbooks. *Written Communication, 4,* 253–268.

Fowler, G. F. (1982). Developing comprehension skills in primary students through the use of story frames. *The Reading Teacher, 36,* 176–179.

Gambrell, L. B. (1985). Dialogue journals: Reading-writing interaction. *The Reading Teacher, 38,* 512–515.

Graves, D. (1983). *Writing: Teachers and children at work.* Exeter, NH: Heinemann.

Hynds, S. (1989). Bringing life to literature and literature to life: Social constructs and context for adolescent readers. *Research in the Teaching of English, 23,* 30–61.

McGee, L. M., & Richgels, D. J. (1990). *Literacy's beginnings: Supporting young readers and writers.* Boston: Allyn & Bacon.

Moffett, J. (1985). Hidden impediments to improving English teaching. *Phi Delta Kappan, 67,* 50–55.

Noyce, R. M., & Christie, J. F. (1989). *Integrating reading and writing instruction in grades K–8.* Boston: Allyn & Bacon.

Read, C. (1971). Preschool children's knowledge of English phonology. *Harvard Educational Review, 41,* 1–34.

Rhodes, L. K. (1981). I can read! Predictable books as resources for reading and writing instruction. *The Reading Teacher, 34,* 511–517.

Russell, C. (1983). Putting research into practice: Conferencing with young writers. *Language Arts, 60,* 333–340.

Smith, F. (1982). *Writing and the writer.* New York: Holt, Rinehart & Winston.

Smith, F. (1983). Reading like a writer. *Language Arts, 60,* 558–567.

Staton, J. (1988). Dialogue journals in the classroom context. In M. Farr (Ed.), *Interactive writing in dialogue journals: Practitioner, linguistic, social, and cognitive views.* Norwood, NJ: Ablex.

Tierney, R. J., & Pearson, P. D. (1983). Toward a composing model of reading. *Language Arts, 60,* 568–580.

Youngblood, E. (1985). Reading, thinking and writing using the reading journal. *English Journal, 74,* 46–48.

# Content-Area Reading

**Chapter**

**10**

- Changes in Reading Throughout the Grades
- Teaching Approaches for Content-Area Reading
- Connecting Writing and Content-Area Reading
- Reading Concerns in Specific Content Areas
- The Relationship of a Comprehension Framework to Content-Area Instruction

*"Miss Amburgy," asked Charley, "how can snakes run so fast when they don't have legs?"*

*"There are books in the library that tell all about snakes," Miss Amburgy said. . . ."I suspect they even tell how a snake can run fast when it hasn't any legs."*

*"Is that what books really do?" asked Charley. "Tell you about things?"*

*"Books tell you almost anything you will ever want to know," said Miss Amburgy. "Some things, of course, you'll have to find out for yourself."*

*"When do I go to the library again?" asked Charley.*

R. Caudill, *Did You Carry the Flag Today, Charley?* (New York: Holt, Rinehart & Winston, 1966), pp. 60–61. Reprinted by permission.

Previous chapters have noted that not all reading is alike and have shown that even good readers have difficulty reading specialized text, such as texts about accounting principles. This chapter shows that the materials that students are expected to read in different school subjects are also specialized, with varying structures that make different demands on a reader. Since textbooks are still the predominant tool used in educating children, instruction in content-area reading skills cannot be ignored. Students who are not able to read well in content areas are at a great disadvantage throughout their educational careers.

Chapter 10 includes information that will help you answer questions like these:

1. What are the structural characteristics of textbooks, and how do those characteristics affect comprehension?
2. What are the major differences between the kinds of reading material children encounter while learning to read and the kinds they encounter in various academic subject areas?
3. What are the different reading demands required in different subject areas?
4. How are textbooks structured differently in social studies, mathematics, and science?
5. Which techniques can help students better read and study required reading material in content-area subjects?

KEY CONCEPTS

advance organizer
DRA
expository text
K-W-L Strategy
marginal gloss
PQRST
scanning
semantic mapping

skimming
SQRQCQ
SQ3R
structured concept outline
study guide
text structure
think-aloud

## CHANGES IN READING THROUGHOUT THE GRADES

Let's think back to our own elementary school days and the changes in both reading ability and reading instruction as our grade level increased. If we look at how much new knowledge we gained relative to reading ability as we progressed through the grades, we might end up with a graph something like the one pictured in the margin note. Clearly, the largest increase in reading ability takes place in the earliest stages of schooling. Examples are easy to imagine. Just think of the difference between an average reader in the middle of first grade and an average reader in the middle of third grade. Then try to specify the difference between an average 10th-grade reader and an average 12th-grade reader. Differences in both curriculum and performance become more difficult to identify at higher grade levels.

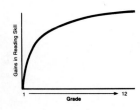

Gains in Reading Skill

1                    Grade                    12

As we might have guessed, most reading instruction takes place in the early school years, when students learn the general reading skills that allow them to decode words and arrange them in meaningful units. By about the third grade, instruction specifically related to reading tapers off, and more emphasis is placed on learning content in academic subject areas. In fact, the whole school experience is often restructured as a child moves from primary to intermediate grades. Where there was only one classroom and one teacher, there may now be different teachers and different classrooms for various subjects. Where there was previously a great deal of stability, there may now be a continually changing instructional environment, which will continue throughout the intermediate grades and become even more pronounced in secondary grades.

Along with different subject areas come different demands on readers. In science, students are required to understand and manipulate various formulas and to learn many new terms. In mathematics they must read many self-contained units, such as word problems, and comprehend many numerical examples and rules in the form of theorems and laws. In addition, different types of texts demand different strategies from the reader, in terms of both approach and interpretation as well as background knowledge and recognition of text structure. For example, readers unaware that a text is designed to persuade may interpret it as fact and use it incorrectly.

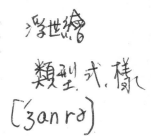

Differences in text styles seem fairly easy for people to recognize within narrative writing. After all, poetry is clearly different from dramatic scripts and both differ from stories even in visible ways. It also seems easy to note the different ways in which people read different narrative **genres.** The fact that readers read poems differently from the way in which they read plays causes no great controversy. However, the general differences between **expository** texts and narratives and the concept that expository texts in different subject areas make different demands on readers seem somewhat more difficult to recognize. Nonetheless, knowing these differences and understanding how readers comprehend different text types will make you a more effective teacher, better able to prepare your students to read the wide range of materials ahead of them.

genres: Categories of literary compositions, each having a special style, form, or content.

expository: Designed to explain or present.

---

**DECISION POINT ➤**

Normally, content-area texts are read for information, whereas narratives are read for pleasure. Content-area textbooks and expository texts in general, which permit the reader to discover new ideas or perhaps to reinforce and extend already-known concepts, form the bulk of the reading that students are required to do beyond the primary grades. Thus, it might be argued that expository material should be an early focus, allowing children to learn to read using materials like those they will encounter later. Do you agree with this argument? Would it present any difficulty for a teacher who believes strongly in using children's literature to teach reading?

## Identifying Book Parts

Textbooks are often composed of similar sections—usually a title, copyright page, preface, table of contents, reference list, index, and glossary. Likewise, a chapter within a book usually contains a title, introduction, headings, sub-headings, conclusion, and perhaps questions and activities. Although not all books and chapters have each of these parts, most books do that are not narratives (e.g., novels, plays, and so on).

Knowing about each of a book's parts helps a reader comprehend what is presented. For example, the copyright page can tell us whether the information contained in the book is out of date or whether the book was published by a special-interest group and might be biased. The preface can point out the purposes for which the book was written. And the table of contents presents an outline of what the book covers and helps set up expectations. Each book part contains important information that can help the reader.

Lessons that teach the parts of books and show how they can help the reader should be included in reading instruction. Students need to be aware of the various parts, the information each contains, and the uses of each. The following sample activities include suggestions for teaching this aspect of reading.

**SAMPLE
ACTIVITIES**

**Table of Contents.** Using the table of contents, have students predict what specific information might be found in various chapters and in various sections and subsections. Write their predictions on the chalkboard. Then have students go to the appropriate pages to check their predictions.

Provide a list of specific items or information found in various chapters, sections, and subsections. Allow students to match the items on the list with the titles in the table of contents. Have them explain and discuss the reasons for their matches, and check to see whether the matchups are correct.

**Copyright Differences.** Examine several copyright pages and tables of contents from books in one subject area but with copyright dates spanning 15 years (e.g., science books). Have students use the tables of contents to compare the topics. Then have them use the copyright pages and attempt to match copyright pages to tables of contents. Be ready to provide some guidance with this activity, pointing out which topics are relatively recent and thus would not have been included in earlier books.

**Glossary and Index Activities.** Discuss the difference between a glossary and a dictionary: a glossary contains definitions only for words that appear in that particular book, whereas a dictionary includes many other words. Find sentences that contain content-specific vocabulary in a book with a glossary, and have students look up the meanings of the specialized words in the glossary. Then read the paragraphs that contain the terms to see whether the definitions are appropriate.

Compare the pages of an index and a glossary of a book. Have students identify the differences, and write their suggestions on the chalkboard (e.g., glossary contains definitions, index contains page numbers, and so on). Discuss the purposes of each and the ways in which the differences help to meet those purposes.

## Recognizing Differences in Text Organization

説明的
[ ɪkˈspazɪˌtorɪ ] 註解的

Text structure is also an important factor in the reading process. The major structural difference between narrative and expository text is that narratives are usually written along a time sequence, whereas exposition is organized according to a **superordinate** and **subordinate concept**. This difference is easy to see, even in the partial tables of contents shown here. The example on the left comes from a mathematics textbook (Bassler, Kolb, Craighead, & Gray, 1981); the example on the right, from a fictional narrative (Defoe, 1967).

**superordinate concept:** Part of the organizational pattern in expository text; a major unit supported by subunits.

**subordinate concept:** Part of the organizational pattern in expository text; a subunit that supports a larger unit.

Table of Contents

Addition and Subtraction—Whole Numbers

>  Rounding numbers through hundred thousands
>  Finding sums and differences through 6 digits
>  Estimating sums and differences by rounding
>  Checking addition and subtraction

Multiplication and Division—Whole Numbers

>  Multiplying by 1- and 2-digit factors
>  Estimating products by rounding
>  Solving multiple-step problems

Table of Contents

I Go to Sea

On the Island

We Plan to Leave the Island

The English Ship

Home!

These examples show clearly the conceptual organization of exposition and the sequential arrangement of narratives.

Several organizational patterns are found in content-area texts, with certain patterns more common in certain subject areas. For example, the following passage demonstrates the time-order sequence usually found in the narrative materials of language arts. See whether you can find the cues that tell the reader that the organizational pattern here is a time sequence.

>  Tracy knew she would not be able to sleep. But her mother had told her to brush her teeth and put on her nightgown anyway, and Tracy did as she was told.

> Just as she got into her nightgown, a loud crack of thunder filled the air! Tracy jumped into bed and pulled the covers over her head. When Meg peeked into the room, Tracy wailed, "The last time we had a storm like this, I stayed awake all night!"
>
> Meg sat beside Tracy and tucked her little sister in. Then she started to hum softly. It was one of Tracy's favorite songs.
>
> As the song went on, Meg noticed that Tracy's eyes had closed. Meg turned off the bedroom light as she tiptoed out of the room. Tracy didn't hear the next clap of thunder as the storm continued into the night. (Carson, 1990)

Background knowledge tells children that brushing teeth happens before getting into bed, getting tucked in, and going to sleep. In addition, conjunctions such as *and* can indicate sequential order, as can specific references such as *last time, then,* and *next.* Students have less difficulty with this type of text than with other organizational patterns.

The following passage taken from a social studies textbook demonstrates how number order is used as an organizational pattern. In this case the structure of the passage outlines its content. The organizational cues lie in the enumeration of points—*first, second*—and in the two-part activity that relates to and balances the two factual statements that precede it.

> Look at the map above. It shows you two things. First, it tells you the periods in which early Islam spread. Second, it shows the areas into which Islam spread. Islam began in the cities of Mecca and Medina. Use the map key to find the name of the area in which these two cities are found. Use the map key to find the territory that Muslims had conquered by Muhammed's death in 632. (Myers & Wilk, 1983, p. 272)

Can you pick out the cues indicating that the next passage, taken from a science textbook, is organized in a comparison/contrast pattern? Notice the comparisons between radio and television and the implicit assumption that the reader's background knowledge will incorporate this new information.

> Television is the most popular form of communication in the world today. Television is very similar to radio. In radio, sound energy is changed to radio wave energy. Radio wave energy is sent through space. In television, both sound and light are changed to invisible waves. Television sets change the invisible waves back to light and sound. (Sund, Adams, & Hacket, 1980, p. 275)

The last organizational pattern discussed here is one of cause and effect. Often, events happen because of other events, especially in history textbooks, for example, where the causal relationships between historical events are a primary focus. Cause-and-effect relationships can also be subtle, as in the following example from an elementary mathematics textbook (Bassler, Kolb, Craighead, & Gray, 1981). Notice that the passage implies that a plane boundary is dependent on a plane region; therefore, the plane region can be considered the cause of the plane boundary.

> A closed plane figure together with its inside is called a plane region. The figure around the plane region is called its boundary. Plane regions are named for their boundaries. (p. 256)

This is a circle.  ◯   ⬤  This is a circular region.

Teachers must not assume that students who can read one kind of text structure can read another with similar ease. To build student awareness of the different structures, teachers might discuss how authors use language to signal the type of organization they are using. Vacca and Vacca (1986, p. 33) provide a representative list of signal words for the four organizational patterns discussed here. Obviously, not all of the words are found at all elementary grade levels. Teachers should preview the material that their students will be reading and then teach the signal words that they will encounter.

| ① Time | ② Enumeration | ③ Comparison/ Contrast | ④ Cause-Effect |
|---|---|---|---|
| on (date) | to begin with | however | because |
| not long after | first | but | since |
| now | second | as well as | therefore |
| as | next | on the other hand | consequently |
| before | then | not only/but also | as a result |
| after | finally | either . . . or | this led to |
| when | most important | while | so that |
| | also | although | nevertheless |
| | in fact | unless | accordingly |
| | for instance | similarly | if . . . then |
| | for example | yet | thus |

*structure characteristics*

**Signal Word Search.** Choose a paragraph or page in a future reading assignment that demonstrates the overall structure of the selection. Tell students about the structure being used, including the signal words appropriate to such a structure. On a copy of the chosen paragraph or page, have students mark any signal words that they find. Then discuss how each of the marked words specifically indicates the pattern in the passage.

**Sequence Completion.** Create an ordered list of the steps in a selection with a time-sequenced or a numbered, step-by-step organization. Then delete some of the steps in the sequence, give the list to students before they read the selection, and discuss the concept of a sequenced organizational pattern.

**SAMPLE ACTIVITIES**

Have students check the steps on the list as they meet them in their reading and add those that are missing.

**Sequence Reorder.** For a similar activity create an out-of-order list of the steps in a sequence. Before students read the selection, discuss the concept of an ordered sequence and have students decide how to reorder the list so that it makes logical, sequential sense. Then have students read to see whether their reordered sequence holds true, and discuss again the concept of sequence.

**Predicting in Categories.** For a superordinate/subordinate structure, discuss the pattern, and list the major categories found within a given selection. Have students guess what might be found under each category. Then have students read to see whether their predictions were accurate. In a postreading discussion, examine which of the predictions were on target, and discuss why some were not.

## Adapting Reading Rates

Reading rate depends on a number of factors, among them the reader's purpose for reading. For instance, a mathematics word problem requires a different reading rate from that required by a story read for entertainment. Within some content-area texts it is vital not to miss even one word; the directions for a science experiment are just one example. Many suggest that reading rates be consciously changed to meet the demands of each reading task (Farr & Roser, 1979; Shepherd, 1982). To build the idea that reading speed does vary and that reading materials need not always be read from beginning to end, teachers can use activities designed to enhance skimming and scanning abilities.

skimming: Reading rapidly to get a general idea of material that will be reread in detail.

**Skimming.** Many content-area reading techniques discussed in this chapter require that a student first preview the reading material. Usually this step entails **skimming,** which is quick movement through a text to discover key concepts and main ideas. Skimming gives the reader an idea of what to expect on more detailed reading; the process is aided by an awareness of headings and subheadings.

There are many reasons for skimming. We may skim a newspaper to decide what to read in depth. We may skim an encyclopedia entry to decide whether any or all of it needs careful attention. Or we may skim a journal article to determine whether it contains information relevant to a particular assignment. Skimming can save valuable time, and teachers need to help students develop that ability.

**Newspaper Page Skim.** Provide students with the front page of a newspaper, and allow only enough time for students to skim the page. Then from a list of topics, have students identify those that were on the page. Follow up with a discussion of which topics are of most interest to them.

**Skim for Sequence.** Provide a passage that has a sequenced organizational pattern. As a prereading activity, discuss which words signal sequence. Then have students skim the passage to determine the sequence.

**Skim for Main Idea.** Provide a paragraph or passage, and direct students to find the main idea. Set a time limit that allows only rapid skimming, not careful reading. After they have skimmed, have students write down the main idea and then go back and read the selection carefully, writing down supporting details.

**SAMPLE
ACTIVITIES**

**Scanning.** **Scanning** is rapid movement through a reading selection to find specific information. It is another skill that mature readers use daily. Looking through a telephone directory to find a specific telephone number is just one example. Teachers need to foster this skill by giving their students the opportunity to practice it.

scanning: Reading rapidly to find specific information.

**Scanning for Information.** Ask students to use scanning to find the following:

1. a particular date in a history selection
2. the murderer's name in a short mystery story
3. a specific heading in a science chapter
4. a specific ingredient in a recipe
5. answers to questions like "Who wrote _____ ?" found in a list of titles and authors

**SAMPLE
ACTIVITIES**

## Using Research Materials

Students in higher grades are required to study more informational material and are expected to use the library to find background or supplementary material. To perform effectively, students must use card catalogs, encyclopedias, almanacs, newspapers, books on related topics, atlases, and abstracts. Research abilities are important in content-area subjects and require skills such as organizing, alphabetizing, and summarizing, in addition to knowing about reference tools and sources, their contents, and their proper use.

Students demonstrate how to vary their reading rate to match their goal, quickly scanning several sources here to find special information.

The use of reference materials such as encyclopedias and tools such as the card catalog is usually included in a language arts program before specific content areas are encountered. Trips to the library and a discussion of what the library contains should begin early in the primary grades. In addition, picture encyclopedias specifically designed for young children should be used early to teach young readers that there are information sources available for numerous topics. The following sample activities show some ways that children can be taught needed reference skills.

**SAMPLE ACTIVITIES**

**Library Hunts.** Each week, post a question that requires students to use reference skills in the school library. Ask older students questions like "What is one book written by Judy Blume after 1979?" or "Who illustrated *Where the Sidewalk Ends?*" For younger students ask questions like "Where would you find a book by Ezra Jack Keats?" or "What are the titles of one fiction book and one nonfiction book?" Put the question up on the chalkboard just before library period, and see who can return with the answer. Place a box below the question, in which children are to submit their answers. Before the end of the day, write one or more of the correct responses below the question, and discuss how the answers were found.

**Reference Match.** After a discussion and demonstration of various types of reference materials, provide a list of reference materials and a separate list of information found in those materials. Have students match the information to the source.

Atlas         _____     a. Map

Encyclopedia   _____     b. Information about famous people

Thesaurus     _____     c. Use to find out which rivers flow through California

                                            d. Use to find out how the telephone was invented and how it works

                                            e. Use to find synonyms

**Topic Sort.** Place a number of topics in a box. On the chalkboard have an illustration of the spines of an encyclopedia set. Have students choose a topic and state which volume they would use to find information on that topic.

| 1 | 2 | 3 | 4 | 5 | 6 | 7 | 8 | 9 | 10 | 11 | 12 | 13 | 14 | 15 | 16 | 17 | 18 | 19 | 20 | 21 |
|---|---|---|---|---|---|---|---|---|----|----|----|----|----|----|----|----|----|----|----|----|
| A | B | C–Ch | Ci–Cz | D | E | F | G | H | I | J–K | L | M | N–O | P | Q–R | S–Sn | So–Sz | T | U–V | WX YZ |

**Newspaper Fact Hunt.** After a discussion of the general purpose of an index, provide newspapers to familiarize students with newspaper parts and a newspaper index. Have students use the index to find answers to questions like these: Where would you look for information about football scores? Where would you find out which movies are in town and when they are being shown? What page are the comics on? On what page would you find the weather forecast and the highest and lowest temperatures in the United States yesterday?

**Dictionary Keys.** Discuss the concept of key words in dictionaries, asking students how they know which words are on any given page of a dictionary. Write on the chalkboard the key words for a dictionary page, as well as words that would and would not appear on that page. Have students place the words in alphabetical order, stating whether or not they would be found on the page indicated by the key words.

**Atlas Information.** Have students use an atlas to find information; for example, which state borders another, which is the longest river in a particular area, which two cities are farther apart than another two, which of two European countries is farther north, and so on.

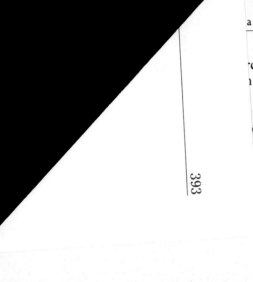

·rch. Visit the library and discuss the card catalog with stu-
1 and the three types of cards it contains (author cards,
title cards). Then present one list with information de-
with the three types of cards. Have students match the
, have students use the card catalog to find out how
)articular author are owned by the library, how many
1 given subject in the past two years are in the library,

393

_____     a. You want to find the book *The Black
             Stallion.*
_____     b. You want to find another book by Walter
             Farley.
             c. You want to find a book that tells about
             different breeds of horses.

## TEACHING APPROACHES FOR CONTENT-AREA READING

Although the general teaching strategies discussed throughout this text apply
to both narrative and expository materials, the method frameworks discussed
in this chapter are specifically appropriate to content-area reading instruction.
And even though all reading teachers should use both narrative and expository
materials, the particular approaches described here are especially important for
middle-school teachers, whose students will encounter predominantly expository texts. Ideally, a separate course in content-area reading should be a part
of your teacher preparation. However, as an introduction some representative,
readable texts in this area are listed at the end of this chapter.

### Modeling

Other chapters have pointed out the benefit of having teachers model reading
behavior and processes. In particular, the modeling of questioning strategies
and metacognitive aspects of reading can result in students' transferring those
behaviors to their own reading practices. Modeling is especially valuable in
content-area reading, where different strategies are required because of the
different text structures and the demands of subject-specific reading material.
Modeling the reading process in different subject-area texts highlights the fact
that reading strategies need to be adapted to the material being read. Modeling
also helps students acquire appropriate strategies to use with specific kinds of
text.

think-aloud: A method to
show students the thoughts
that occur as people read;
requires that teachers read
a text and tell students what
they are thinking as they
read.

An effective modeling technique is the **think-aloud** method (Davey,
1983), in which the teacher reads a passage and talks through the thought
processes that occur. Specifically, the teacher focuses on the use of predictions,
imagery (creating a picture of what is being read), links between background
knowledge and the text (i.e., creating analogies to something already known),

TABLE 10–1
A check sheet to monitor use of think-aloud strategies

| What I Did | How Often I Did It | | | |
|---|---|---|---|---|
| | Not Very Often | A Little Bit | Much of the Time | All of the Time |
| Making predictions | | | | |
| Forming pictures | | | | |
| Using *like* (analogies) | | | | |
| Finding problems | | | | |
| Using fix-ups | | | | |

monitoring to see whether understanding is taking place, and fix-up strategies to address problem areas. Teachers should model not only how to read, but also when and why to use certain strategies. After students become familiar with the approach, they can practice it with partners and then try to apply the think-aloud strategies in their silent reading. To keep them conscious of think-aloud strategies, Davey suggests that students complete a check sheet similar to the one shown in Table 10–1 after reading a passage. The model lesson that follows shows a teacher demonstrating the use of a think-aloud approach with a social studies passage (Myers & Wilk, 1983).

---

## Think-Aloud with Content-Area Material

### Herders and Nomads of the Steppe

Thousands of years ago nomads traveled the grasslands of Europe and Asia. Skilled at riding horses, they became warriors feared for their raids on settled communities. During the time of the Romans, some rode out of the north and east to attack cities of the empire. (p. 237)

**MODEL LESSON**

**Introduction.** The teacher tells the students that they will soon be reading a selection in their social studies book—"Herders and Nomads of the Steppe." First, however, she wants them to listen as she thinks aloud her own reading of the first part of the selection.

**The Think-Aloud.** The teacher reads the title, "Herders and Nomads of the Steppe." She says, "I know about herders. They're like shepherds—people who take care of animals. And I know that a nomad is a wanderer, but I'm not sure about *steppe*. I can probably use context to find out. The words *of the* probably mean that the *steppe* is where the herders do their wandering. But that doesn't really tell me what the steppe is. I'll have to look for clues as I read on, but I might need to use a dictionary or ask someone about this word. Based on the title, I predict that the passage will tell me about what kind of animals the herders kept, where they wandered, and what a steppe is."

After reading "Thousands of years ago," the teacher says, "This tells me that the passage is not about what is going on now. But maybe there are things going on now that relate to what happened thousands of years ago. I'll probably have to make these connections myself, based on what I know." After reading the rest of the second sentence, the teacher notes, "Now I know where this takes place—in Europe and Asia. I went to Italy last summer (that's in Europe!) and saw lots of grassland. I wonder if that's where these nomads roamed thousands of years ago."

After reading "During the time of the Romans, some rode out," she says, "This is confusing me. Does the 'some' who rode out refer to the Romans or the nomads? I'll look back and see. Since it says that the nomads were good at riding horses, I'll guess *some* refers to the nomads—but I'll have to change my prediction if other things don't fit."

**Purpose Setting.** After the first paragraph, the teacher reminds students that they should try to think aloud as they read silently and that they should complete their check sheets every half page.

**Reading and Follow-up.** Students read and complete their check sheets. The teacher then discusses the passage and allows students to share their check sheets. She also allows some students to practice thinking aloud on some other paragraphs in the selection they have just read.

---

Other modeling method frameworks are discussed in chapter 7. Particularly applicable here is the ReQuest procedure (Manzo, 1969; 1985), which allows teachers to model questions at all comprehension levels and allows students to acquire needed background knowledge in a supportive way.

## Directed Reading Activity

directed reading activity (DRA): A method framework containing the following steps: preparation, guided reading, skill development and practice, and enrichment.

**Directed reading activity (DRA)** is commonly associated with a formal reading program but is also applicable to content-area reading. Of the four basic steps in a traditional DRA, Steps 1, 2, and 4 are emphasized slightly more in expository texts than they are in narrative texts.

1. *Preparation.* This step involves providing needed background, preteaching necessary vocabulary (especially important in content-area reading), and providing motivation for reading.

2. *Guided reading*. With questions or outlines the readers' attention is directed as they proceed through the material. This step aids retention and comprehension of what is read.
3. *Skill development and practice*. Direct instruction in comprehension or other areas is provided, as are opportunities to practice what is taught.
4. *Enrichment*. Activities based on the reading selection often allow children to pursue topics more specifically related to their own interests.

We know that background knowledge influences the comprehension process, and that interaction is especially important with content-area material. The preparation stage, therefore, is critical. Shortly before assigning reading material, teachers must carefully read the selection with their students in mind. Prereading discussion can then center around the concepts that are covered in the reading, with background knowledge provided as needed. Teachers should also deal with unknown vocabulary and should provide students with a clear and definite purpose for reading the assigned text.

With content-area material the second DRA step requires an awareness that textbooks are to be used as instructional tools, and teacher guidance is expected. A study guide or outline, periodic help with vocabulary and concepts, and other support must be available as students read. Since readability and other analyses have consistently shown most content-area textbooks to be more difficult for students than narrative materials intended for comparable grade levels, few students should be expected to read textbooks on their own.

In content-area reading the skill-development and practice step of a DRA can provide practice with vocabulary terms and concepts that are difficult for students. Each student might keep an informal list of difficult or unknown items encountered while reading. Class discussion can then teach the needed vocabulary, as well as review main ideas and supporting details. Teachers should check students' understanding of the selection and point out relationships to previous work and knowledge, thereby setting up the enrichment step of the DRA. As in other types of reading lessons, the enrichment stage in a content-area DRA should provide activities that allow students to apply new knowledge and go beyond the text.

Several authors have addressed the application of DRA to content areas (Rubin, 1983; Thomas & Alexander, 1982). They note that, as in all teaching, the activity must take into account the special demands of the appropriate subject area and individual differences among students. A model of a content area DRA appears on page 398.

## Vocabulary and Concept Development

One of the major barriers to comprehension in content-area reading is the high number of new concepts presented. When reading in science, mathematics, or social studies, students encounter words that are familiar in everyday use but that have unfamiliar meanings within the particular subject area. They are also confronted with new words and concepts that are subject specific. Conse-

**MODEL
LESSON**

Directed Reading Activity

Preparation. The teacher states that students will be reading about Columbus discovering America and introduces vocabulary and concepts in the selection that might be difficult. The teacher notes that the popular belief at that time was that the world was flat and asks students why they think that thought prevailed. The teacher also asks students what ships were like at that time and then shows pictures of sailing ships, which lead to a discussion of the hardships associated with sailing for long periods of time. The teacher notes that Columbus set out with three ships, and the students brainstorm why. In addition, the teacher sets the purposes for reading: to find out why Columbus wanted to set sail, to find out some of the difficulties along the way, and to find out the results of his discovery.

Guided Reading. The teacher provides a study guide (see p. 399) for the students to use while reading. Then, during the reading the teacher walks around and provides help to students who need it, asking individual questions periodically. When the reading and study guide activity have been completed, the teacher leads a class discussion that addresses student understanding of the selection and reviews main ideas, as well as their relationship to students' general knowledge.

Skill Development and Practice. The teacher decides to combine a lesson on scanning with additional attention to the vocabulary and concepts introduced earlier. Students are directed to scan certain pages to find vocabulary items. Then they discuss how each word is used and what it means in this specific social studies selection. The class also discusses the potential benefits of scanning and the different types of materials in which scanning might be useful. Thereafter, students practice using the vocabulary items and concepts, and they use telephone books and newspapers for further scanning activities.

Enrichment. The teacher provides a list of three items and asks students which they are most interested in: (1) other early explorers of America, (2) Columbus's other journeys, or (3) the events of Columbus's life after his discovery. The students divide into groups and go to the library to research their interest. Each group prepares a brief report and later presents it to the rest of the class.

quently, content-area teachers must identify and teach the vocabulary and concepts that are required for their subject areas. Because students learn vocabulary best when it occurs in meaningful situations, content-specific vocabulary should be presented as part of a reading assignment. Both content-specific vocabulary and concept development are discussed further in chapter 6.

**study guides:** Teacher-designed aids that assist students in reading text.

## Study Guides

**Study guides** help students comprehend and remember what they have read. Some guides are referred to during reading; others are used after the selection has been read. A teacher should incorporate into a guide the important content of a reading selection and the organizational structure of the material. As noted by Herber (1978) and Tierney, Readence, and Dishner (1990), a study guide should have three levels, each corresponding to one of the three general levels of comprehension questions—**literal**, **inferential**, and **evaluative**. Also, the study guide must be easy to read. The guide may include specific page and paragraph references or other aids, depending on the teacher's assessment of student abilities. Study guides are not intended to stand alone but should be used as part of an overall lesson, for example, within a directed reading activity.

**literal level question:** A question that asks for information directly stated in the text.

**inferential level question:** A question that requires readers to contribute background knowledge in conjunction with literal information.

**evaluative level question:** A question that asks readers to make critical judgments about information in the text and, often, to relate that information to past or future experiences.

---

## Study Guides

Students will be reading "Food for the Future" (Buggey, 1983), which is a third-grade social studies passage discussing how food might be grown to feed the world's increasing population. The teacher wants students to learn about different ways of growing food and has constructed the following three-level guide. The parenthetical information was included because the teacher felt that the students needed additional help.

**MODEL LESSON**

Level I [literal level]

Why will we need more food in the future?

Why will we not be able to use more land? (p. 213, par. 1)

What three methods of growing food other than using farmland are discussed? (Look at subheadings.)

Why are conditions inside greenhouses "perfect for growing crops"? (p. 232, par. 2)

What does *hydroponics* mean? (p. 233, par. 2)

Will plants grow closer together in water or in soil? (p. 233, par. 2)

**Level II** [interpretive level]

Why does the author say that greenhouses can be used in many
  places where crops usually cannot grow? (p. 232, par. 2)
How does irrigation in deserts allow crops to grow? (p. 232,
  par. 1)
How are insects and weeds kept from getting inside a green-
  house?
What is the major difference between greenhousing and hydroponics?

**Level III** [evaluative level]

Why do you think plants grown in water don't need as many
  roots as plants grown in soil?
How might greenhouses control growing conditions?
Do you think it would be better to irrigate in deserts instead of
  using greenhouses? Explain. (p. 232, par. 1 & 2)

## Marginal Glosses

Another technique that is applicable to reading in all content areas is called
glossing. It provides a system of marginal notes designed to explain concepts,
point out relationships, and otherwise clarify the text as the student reads.
**Marginal glosses** are constructed by the teacher and are provided for the
student when a passage is assigned. In effect, the marginal glosses reflect the
presence of the teacher, providing a guide for the reader while demonstrating
the kinds of questions to be asked during reading. Just as questioning strategies provide a model for students to follow when reading independently,
glosses also model what should take place when students read on their own.

marginal glosses: Teacher-
constructed margin notes
that aid students' comprehension by emphasizing and
clarifying concepts, noting
relationships, and modeling
questions.

  Singer and Donlan (1989) suggest the following steps for teachers to use
in preparing a relevant and useful gloss. As an alternative, it may be desirable
in some situations to have more able students prepare the glosses for or
together with less able readers.

1. *Preview.* The teacher identifies vocabulary or other material to emphasize
   or clarify.
2. *Create the gloss.* The teacher writes the marginal notes on copies of the
   original passage (see Figure 10–1). Glosses can be used for all or part of a
   selection.
3. *Hand out the gloss.* The teacher gives copies of the passage with glosses to
   students to insert in the appropriate places in their texts and refer to as they
   read.

Figure 10–1 shows how glosses can clarify vocabulary, point out relationships,
direct attention, and emphasize important points.

FIGURE 10–1

Text with marginal glosses

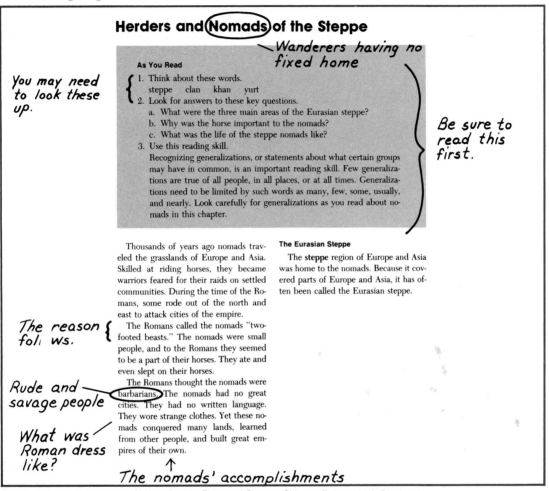

**Source:** From C. B. Myers and G. Wilk, *People, Time, and Change* (Chicago: Follett, 1983). Reprinted by permission.

## Advance Organizers

Although **advance organizers** are, technically, any prereading guide or aid that clarifies concepts, sets up expectations, or builds background, they are usually thought of as specific, brief selections or outlines that are read before a main reading assignment is attempted. Advance organizers require that teachers present a brief outline related to the assigned reading and written at the students' **independent reading level**. Organizers should always foster comprehension and thus should never be difficult to read. An advance organizer appropriate to a science textbook passage on the measurement of electricity is

advance organizers: Aids that enhance comprehension by explaining concepts, encouraging prediction, or establishing background knowledge.

independent reading level: The level at which students can read by themselves with few word recognition problems and excellent comprehension.

FIGURE 10–2
An advance organizer

> You will be reading about measuring electricity. The unit you will read has three parts. The first part will tell you about one way of measuring electricity, using a unit of measurement called VOLTS. The other two parts in the reading will tell you about measuring electricity with units called AMPERES and WATTS.
>
> When you read, try to find out why there are three different units to measure electricity. What is the purpose of each unit of measurement? Do you think we need three ways, or units, to measure electricity?
>
> Before you start reading, write down a sentence or two about what you think you might find out by reading the unit on measuring electricity.
>
> _____
>
> _____
>
> _____

shown in Figure 10–2. Advance organizers do not always appear in written form, although that is usual.

## Mapping and Other Schematic Overviews

A number of techniques visually relate important concepts in the reading selection, thereby enhancing retention and also providing a study guide. Most often, these techniques expect the reader to identify main ideas and important concepts, together with their supporting details. Because poorer readers have difficulty identifying main ideas and relationships, teachers must not only teach the techniques but must also discuss why certain concepts are identified as important and what suggests that a particular item is related to another, perhaps in a subordinate way. Students then need to practice the techniques, at the same time identifying main ideas and supporting details.

**Semantic Mapping.** Hanf (1971) has suggested semantic mapping as a method of organizing ideas to enhance note-taking and as a recall and study technique (see Ruddell & Boyle, 1989, for research with older students; also Garner, 1987). The strategy consists of identifying and recording main ideas and related supporting details in visual, graphic form. Semantic mapping requires these two steps:

1. Record the title or main idea anywhere on a piece of paper, leaving enough room so that additional information (the supporting details) can be added around the central idea.
2. Place the secondary, related ideas around the main idea in an organized pattern. Plan the placement of the secondary ideas so that their proximity to the main idea reflects the strength of the relationship.

   A semantic map can be a small-group, whole-class, or individual activity. As a prereading activity, teachers might provide a list of the main ideas and supporting details. Through guided discussion, students should then decide which item is the main, or superordinate, idea and rank order the supporting details by importance. Based on the discussion create the map on the chalkboard or chart paper and have students copy it to use as an aid to study, discussion, or recall. Then reading takes place. It is also possible for students to generate the map during reading, noting ideas as they arise, or to create the map as a postreading activity. Figure 10–3 presents a sample semantic map.

FIGURE 10–3
An example of a semantic map

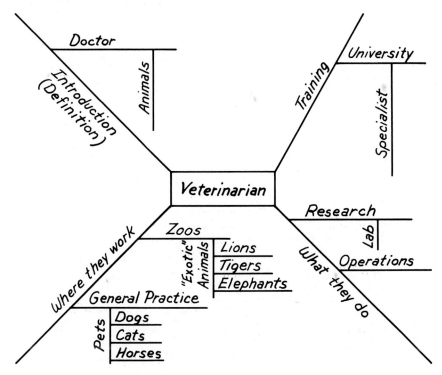

**Structured Concept Outlines.** A structured outline represents schematically the relationships among concepts in reading material. This technique requires that concepts be ordered into superordinate, coordinate, and subordinate categories. For example, the following outline might apply to a selection about growing tomatoes.

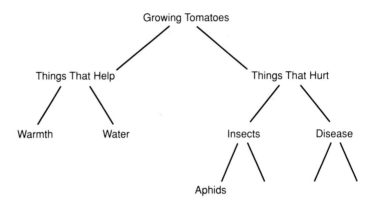

Such an outline may serve the function of an advance organizer or may be used as an aid for postreading activities. In either case it is important for teachers to point out what relationships exist and also to discuss with students how and why the various concepts are related. A structured outline is similar to the herringbone technique (Tierney, Readence, & Dishner, 1990), which tells who, what, where, when, why, and how in a schematic format that provides structure for recall and study. The following activities suggest how structured concept outlines can be used.

**SAMPLE ACTIVITIES**

**Concept Outline Discussion.** Prepare, duplicate, and distribute a structured concept outline. Use it as the basis for discussion with students prior to their reading the selection.

**Concept Outline Completion.** Omit certain parts of an outline, and tell students to complete it as they read. This activity provides a purpose for reading, as well as allowing students to make active choices while they read.

**Combined Glosses and Structured Concept Outlines.** Combine a structured concept outline with marginal glosses, leaving adequate space for students to write their responses. Instruct students to make notes or otherwise complete the outline as requested by the gloss (see Figure 10–4).

FIGURE 10-4
Marginal glosses combined with a structured concept outline

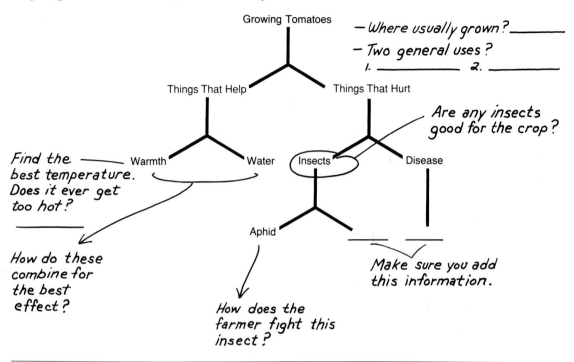

## SQ3R

Originally developed by Robinson (1961) as a study strategy for college students, SQ3R is also taught as a study tool for secondary and upper elementary–grade students. SQ3R stands for these actions:

| | |
|---|---|
| *Survey* | Quickly skim through the material. Focus on headings and titles to get a general feel for what the material covers. |
| *Question* | Based on the survey just completed, identify questions that the material will probably answer. |
| *Read* | Read the material to answer the questions previously identified. |
| *Recite* | Orally or in writing attempt to answer the identified questions. |
| *Review* | Reread portions of the material to verify the answers previously given. |

Although SQ3R has been shown to be an effective study strategy when used as described, it is rarely used spontaneously by students (Cheek & Cheek, 1983) and needs to be taught and reinforced. Some (Vacca, 1981) believe that students need more structure than is provided by SQ3R. Pauk (1984), for example, suggests a more structured method of presenting the technique and stresses setting purposes at each step. In addition, he has added *record* after *reading,* thus making his technique SQ4R. Pauk believes that students should record succinct margin notes of ideas, facts, and details from their reading, thus establishing cues for immediate and future reviews.

**MODEL
LESSON**

## SQ3R

The teacher begins with a discussion of SQ3R, reminding students of the steps involved.

**Survey.** Students are asked to survey a science passage about the invention of the telephone, quickly skimming the headings and overall content. A short period of time is allowed, and then students are asked to identify the title of the passage and the three subheadings.

**Question.** The teacher lists on the board the title and subheadings that students provide and asks what questions might be answered in each subsection. Students generate these questions:

*The Telephone: A Useful Invention*
    Q: Why is the telephone useful?
    Q: What makes the telephone useful?
    Q: How was it invented?

*Before the Telephone*
    Q: How did people talk to each other before the telephone?

*The Invention*
    Q: Who invented the telephone?
    Q: When was it invented?
    Q: How was it invented?

*After the Invention*
    Q: What happened after the invention?
    Q: How did the telephone change people's lives?

**Read.** Students are asked to read the selection, keeping the questions in mind.

**Recite.** Students actively but silently recite or write down the answers to the questions as the information is learned.

**Review.** When finished reading, students review their answers—in a large group with the teacher, in pairs or small groups, or individually. The parts of the passage that provide answers should be reread, and the passage as a whole should be discussed.

Connecting reading and writing allows teachers to incorporate many research skills such as use of the card catalog, which requires alphabetizing and indexing knowledge.

## CONNECTING WRITING AND CONTENT-AREA READING

Writing activities should be used in all types of classrooms, ranging from more traditional to whole language, to help build students' comprehension of content-area, or expository, texts. Teachers should provide practice with different text structures and should ensure that the classroom environment includes books of many types—children's literature as well as expository materials. Teachers should also ensure that writing activities move beyond stories.

Flood, Lapp, and Farnan (1986) suggest a three-step procedure that links reading and writing.

1. *Prewriting*. Students choose a topic and brainstorm what they already know about it, listing what is generated. Students are then directed to gather additional information about the topic—from reference sources, interviews, or a targeted expository selection. After they have gathered the information, students list the facts that they learned about the topic.
2. *Writing*. Students select the most important topic (the most all-encompassing) from the two lists created during the prewriting stage and list supporting details or subtopics under that main idea. Following their main topic–subtopic outline, students then write a short expository paragraph.
3. *Feedback and editing*. Partners or groups can read each other's paragraphs to determine whether a main idea and supporting details are included. Feedback or further information can be provided, which the original author can use to rewrite and strengthen the paragraph.

The language experience approach (LEA) can also be used to build familiarity with expository text structures (Kinney, 1985). The language experience is provided by the teacher, who might use a feature analysis to compare ideas or vocabulary terms or might list headings and subheadings from a text and allow students to brainstorm what might be found in the selection. Students then dictate a story or description to the teacher, based on the brainstorming or information session. The teacher can guide the students, perhaps asking for information that might fit under a specific heading or asking for a contrast or comparison sentence at some point. After the dictation is completed, students can read and discuss their writing, copy it into their notebooks, and read the target selection. An interesting follow-up to reading is a discussion that compares the dictated story to the actual selection from which the headings came.

## Summarizing, Note-taking, and Organizing

Many of the strategies and techniques discussed in this chapter require that information be summarized or organized, often in written form. These skills can be developed from the earliest stages of schooling. When students are asked to restate or paraphrase a story, their summarizing ability is enhanced, as are their note-taking skills when summary statements or main points are compiled in written form. When children are asked to categorize similar items, they are developing categorizing skills that help in organizing information.

Brown, Campione, and Day (1981) identify the following actions as helpful in summarizing:

■ deleting nonessential information
■ deleting repetitive information
■ using blanket terms to replace lists of simpler items (e.g., *pets* to replace "dogs, cats, hamsters, and goldfish")
■ selecting topic sentences or, if there are none, creating topic sentences

Tei and Stewart (1985) suggest that the first two of these actions are the most appropriate for middle school students. However, with teacher guidance and modeling, students can use all of them to write summary paragraphs.

**SAMPLE ACTIVITIES**

**Summary Statements.** Have students listen to a story or an expository reading. Then ask them to restate or paraphrase the main idea of the selection. At another time students might be asked to provide a one- or two-sentence written statement.

**Note-taking Contrasts.** Model and then allow students to practice taking notes in various forms—listing points, summarizing paragraphs, and outlining. Use a short reading selection, film, or audiotape as the basis for the note-taking activity. Be sure to discuss the students' work, focusing on their reasons for including and not including certain information.

**Outline Completion.** Provide headings and subheadings in outline for~~m~~ leave the outline incomplete. Then read a selection that pertains to t~~h~~ line, and have students complete the outline. This activity enhances note-taking and summarizing skills.

**Picture Categories.** For young students compile a set of pictures that includes items in two categories. Mix up the pictures and have students tell which belong together. Alternately, identify a category and have students tell which pictures do not belong.

**The K-W-L Strategy.** The **K-W-L** method framework (Ogle, 1989) includes both writing and reading and requires brainstorming as well as categorizing and information-gathering/note-taking activities. K-W-L stands for *k*now, *w*ant to know, and *l*earn. The procedure begins with discussion about what students already know about the topic. That information is then organized into categories, after which students raise questions that might need to be answered. During and after reading, students record what they are learning and what they still want to know. The K-W-L procedure recognizes the importance of prior knowledge, group learning, writing, and a personalized learning experience. When extended to use semantic mapping, as discussed in chapter 6, the process is called K-W-L Plus (Carr & Ogle, 1987).

## K-W-L

**Before Reading (Know).** The teacher models and then facilitates discussion and activity in four areas.

1. *Brainstorming.* The teacher asks students to brainstorm what they know about a topic and writes their responses on the chalkboard or chart paper. As conflicts or uncertainty about the appropriateness of a response arise, questions are also noted (e.g., Is _____ a part of the topic?). The questions become part of what needs to be found out.
2. *Categorizing.* The teacher encourages students to categorize items generated during brainstorming. If students have trouble with this task, the teacher models the categorizing process, using a think-aloud procedure. Another strategy is to write similar items closer together in the beginning, as they are generated.
3. *Anticipating.* The teacher facilitates discussion about what readers may discover when they read about the categorized topics.
4. *Questioning.* The teacher helps students specify certain questions to be answered during and after reading. It is important that such questions be specific.

**MODEL LESSON**

**During Reading (Want to Know).** Students are asked to read and actively look for new information and ideas, which are noted on a worksheet/table like the one shown here. Longer or more difficult reading assignments should be broken into manageable chunks.

| What We Know | What We Want to Find Out | What We Learned |
|---|---|---|
|  |  |  |

**After Reading (Learn).** As a class activity, the teacher compiles the information that the students learned and helps them relate it to what they previously knew and what they needed to find out. During discussion both teacher and students add additional information to the worksheet/table, which can then be used to generate a written summary.

## READING IN SPECIFIC CONTENT AREAS

The techniques presented earlier in this chapter can be used in any subject area. In addition, there are method frameworks appropriate for use with texts in specific subject areas. The discussion that follows presents some of the specific demands faced by readers in social studies, science, mathematics, and language arts and describes method frameworks that specifically address reading in those subjects. Those areas are not in any way superior to others, but all four use reading material as a major instructional component.

### Social Studies

**Organizational Differences.** Often students who have difficulty reading mathematics and science texts have less difficulty reading language arts and social studies materials (Muhtadi, 1977). This distinction may be due to patterns of text organization. The majority of reading materials within language arts are narrative texts, organized along a time sequence. Science and mathematics texts, on the other hand, are usually organized hierarchically. Social studies texts can be organized along either of these patterns, although history, one particular component of social studies, is usually presented in a time-sequenced format.

We can usually determine a book's general organization from its title and the headings included in the table of contents. Can you see the hierarchical organization in the following example?

Climates of the World

Arid Climatic Regions
Arid Climate Defined
Arid Regions
African Continent
European Continent
American Continents
Desert Climatic Regions
Desert Climate Defined
Desert Regions
African Continent
Asian Continent
American Continents

On the other hand, a title such as *Decline of the Dinosaurs* would imply a time-sequenced organization, moving from the evolution of dinosaurs through their most prolific period to their decline and eventual extinction.

Organizational structures can also have a mixed organization, like the time sequence within a hierarchical pattern illustrated here.

Government in the United States

Government at the Federal Level
Evolution of Federal Government
The Prerevolutionary Period
The Postrevolutionary Period
Government at the State Level
Evolution of State Legislatures

Thus, in social studies material, students are often required to contend with different organizational structures within one reading selection, and students need to be aware of that possibility.

**Graphic Elements.** Social studies readers also see graphic elements—maps, charts, and graphs—that are not normally used in narrative texts. Although other content areas include such material, the graphs and charts in social studies can incorporate fairly unique symbols. The examples in Figure 10–5 typify the graphics that students encounter in their social studies textbooks, in addition to more normal photographs, graphs, and charts. Even good readers may have difficulty interpreting graphic information and may be unable to move back and forth between textual material and graphics without losing

FIGURE 10–5
Graphic material from a representative third-grade social studies text

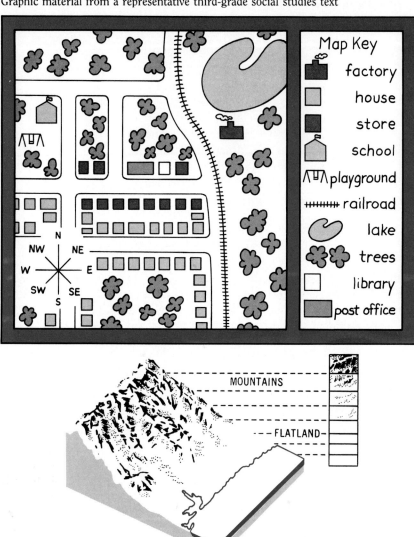

**Source:** From J. Buggey, *Our Communities* (Chicago: Follett, 1983), pp. 18, 94. Reprinted by permission.

their place. Interpretation of maps and graphs is rarely taught as a specific skill, even though the complexity of such reading has been noted (Summers, 1965; Vacca, 1981).

Fry (1981) presents a taxonomy of graphs with six main subdivisions, although almost all of the types can be combined with another type.

1. *Lineal graphs,* showing sequential data (e.g., simple time lines, parallel time lines, and flow charts)
2. *Quantitative graphs,* used for numerical data (e.g., growth curves, bar graphs, pie graphs, and multiple variable graphs)
3. *Spatial graphs,* representing area and location (e.g., two-dimensional road maps and three-dimensional contour maps)
4. *Pictorial graphs,* depicting visual concepts (e.g., realistic drawings, schematic drawings, and abstracted representations)
5. *Hypothetical graphs,* demonstrating an interrelationship of ideas (e.g., sentence diagrams or semantic maps)
6. *Intentional omissions from the taxonomy of graphs: high verbal figures* (e.g., posters and advertisements); *high numerical tables* (e.g., statistical tables); *symbols* (e.g., word equivalents like the outline of a man on a restroom door); *decorative designs* (e.g., designs whose main purpose is decorative rather than conceptual or informative)

Summers (1965) has pointed out differences between what he calls map readers and **map thinkers**. A map reader can locate information but cannot interpret the presented information, much as a student might be able to locate literal information in text yet be unable to assimilate that information into existing knowledge structures or interpret it in the general context of the text as a whole. Obviously, a teacher's goal is to move students beyond being map readers and mold them into map thinkers.

According to Summers (1965), a map thinker must be aware of these six elements:

1. *Map title.* Similar to a book title, this tells what the map depicts; it provides an introduction to the map and its features. Discussion of the title and other activities similar to those associated with a book or story title are appropriate.
2. *Legend.* Often compared to the table of contents in a book, the legend indicates what map symbols stand for and provides other information, such as the map scale. The legend usually appears in a box within the map or graph. Students should try to focus on each item in the legend and visualize whatever it represents. For example, a map thinker should try to imagine the vast oceans that a legend might equate with the color blue.
3. *Direction.* The top of a map usually, but not always, indicates north. Students must be taught to realize that north is not just a direction; it is also a concept with related understandings of true and magnetic north, intermediate distances, and polar regions.
4. *Distance scale.* Three types of scales are common: graphic, statement, and fractional scales. The scale must be kept in mind because it enables a reader to tell how far or how big something is. A small-scale map depicts a large area made smaller, whereas a large-scale map depicts a small area made larger.

map thinkers: Students who are able to locate information on a map and interpret it.

Learning to read
different kinds of maps,
charts, and graphs is
important to fully
understanding certain
types of information.

5. *Location*. This is usually depicted by a grid system that segments maps,
   most often with horizontal and vertical lines. Township range lines and
   marginal letters and numbers are common grid systems, as are parallels and
   meridians, which locate places by latitude and longitude.
6. *Types of maps*. Major map types include land, elevation, climate, vegetation
   and water features, political, economic, and population. Combinations of
   these types are often found on one map.

**Miscellaneous Concerns.** In addition to changes in structure and different
kinds of graphic information that must be actively incorporated into the text,
social studies readers face other challenges.

■ Vocabulary terms involve a larger-than-normal proportion of words with
  Latin and Greek roots, prefixes, or suffixes.
■ Social studies vocabulary and concepts reflect a variety of disciplines: an-
  thropology, sociology, economics, political science, and more.
■ Many social studies textbooks focus on details to such an extent that important major issues may be difficult to grasp. History segments often stress
  many details without drawing clear relationships to the larger picture.
■ In our world of rapid change, the material in social studies textbooks can
  become rapidly dated. Sometimes, it is obsolete or even false. As a result,
  children who have seen more recent or correct information in newspapers or
  on news broadcasts may be confused.
■ Differentiating fact, opinion, and propaganda can be difficult.

■ Some younger children may have trouble grasping time-dependent concepts. Students at certain lower **cognitive levels** have problems understanding concepts involving time, space, and distance relationships, all of which are important to social studies and appear in various kinds of maps.

cognitive levels: Stages of intellectual development.

**Instructional Techniques.** The teaching procedures noted earlier in this chapter apply to social studies material as well as to other content areas. Building student background, providing prereading activities, and implementing other techniques discussed throughout this text are certainly important activities for social studies teachers. Additionally, their students will benefit from cloze and **maze procedures,** both of which emphasize context clues to aid comprehension. Cause-and-effect activities should also be emphasized, along with crossword and word search puzzles to build vocabulary. All of these techniques have been discussed in previous chapters.

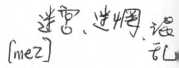

[mez]

maze procedure: A fill-in-the-blank activity to measure comprehension.

**Map Information Hunt.** After a discussion of the information that can be found in various parts of a map, provide a list of questions that students should answer while referring to a specific map.

**SAMPLE ACTIVITIES**

**Map Drawing.** Provide a summary of information in paragraph or list form. Then have students use that information to draw a map or create a graph. Discuss the advantages of the information in graphic form (e.g., better overview, visual summary, ease of seeing relationships).

**Fact and Opinion Statements.** Find statements of fact and opinion in newspapers, or create statements that would fit into those categories. Present the statements in pairs, and have students discuss and explain which is fact and which is opinion.

| Factual Statement | Opinion Statement |
|---|---|
| 1. Trans World Airlines and Western Airlines both reported losses [in income] during the first quarter. | The airlines will close down if they lose money in the next quarter. |
| 2. All land and buildings in Davidson County will be reassessed before the next taxation year. | All taxes on real estate in Davidson County will go up in next taxation year. |

**Cause and Effect Statements.** Follow the same initial procedure as that in the previous activity. Then delete either a cause or an effect, and direct students to supply the deleted item. Have students present and explain their answers.

| Cause | Effect |
|---|---|
| 1. There have been several airplane accidents recently. | Fewer people want to travel by airplane nowadays. |
| 2. Fewer people want to travel by airplane nowadays. | The airlines are making less money. |
| 3. All land and buildings in Davidson County will be reassessed before the next taxation year. | The county clerk needs to hire more staff to update Davidson County's tax records. |

These examples show that causes and effects can be transposed; that is, the effect of one cause may, in turn, be the cause of a different effect. Such transpositions serve to focus attention on the differences between causes and effects.

## Mathematics

**Differences in Content and Approach.** The exercises in Figure 10–6 are representative of reading demands in mathematics. We can see that mathematics passages contain numerous items not generally found in narrative texts. Perhaps the most obvious are the numeric symbols that must be "read." Just as a set of letters represents a concept, numbers and other symbols also represent meaning. For example, the number 50 represents a quantity of items totaling a certain amount, which could be expressed as "2 more than 48" or in innumerable other ways. Thus, just as readers must learn the specific concepts represented by letter combinations, so must they also learn the concepts for other symbol sets. Look again at Figure 10–6, and notice the other numeric arrangements and process symbols that are generally not used in narrative texts: decimals (e.g., 5.1, 6.5), fractions (e.g., ⅖, ⅞), mathematical symbols (e.g., $+$, $-$, $=$).

In addition to different symbol sets, other differences are also associated with reading mathematics materials.

- Specialized vocabulary that is content specific—for example, *division, quotient, digit, multiplication, product, numeral,* and so on.
- Specific shapes and diagrams—for example, triangle, rectangle, parallelogram, and so on.
- A slower rate of reading than is necessary in narrative texts and in some other expository texts, such as history books. Word problems and theorems must be carefully read and read more than once.
- Eye movements that deviate from the expected left-to-right sequence, as in this problem:

$$3 + 2 (6 + 1) = 17$$

**FIGURE 10–6**
A sample mathematics passage from an elementary

## PRACTICE

**Add or subtract. Write each answer in lowest t**

1. $3\frac{2}{5}$
   $-2\frac{1}{5}$

2. $6\frac{2}{6}$
   $+3\frac{2}{6}$

3. $5\frac{2}{3}$
   $-1\frac{1}{3}$

4.
   $+$

5. $8\frac{7}{8}$
   $-\frac{2}{8}$

6. $5\frac{1}{6}$
   $+3\frac{1}{6}$

7. $9\frac{3}{4}$
   $-1\frac{3}{4}$

8.
   $+$

9. $8\frac{5}{12}$
   $+\frac{3}{12}$

10. $3\frac{4}{9}$
    $+1\frac{2}{9}$

11. $6\frac{5}{7}$
    $-\frac{2}{7}$

12. $4$
    $-2\frac{1}{5}$

13. $7\frac{5}{9} + 3\frac{2}{9} = \square$

14. $5\frac{1}{2} - 2\frac{1}{2} = \square$

★ 15. $(3 + 2\frac{1}{2}) - 1\frac{1}{2} = \square$

**Follow the rule to complete.**

Rule: Add $1\frac{2}{7}$.

| | Input | Output |
|---|---|---|
| 16. | $3\frac{4}{7}$ | |
| 17. | $1\frac{1}{7}$ | |
| 18. | $2\frac{3}{7}$ | |

Rule: Subtract $1\frac{1}{8}$.

| | Input | Output |
|---|---|---|
| 19. | $1\frac{2}{8}$ | |
| 20. | $2\frac{3}{8}$ | |
| 21. | $5\frac{5}{8}$ | |

## APPLICATION

22. Ralph filled $7\frac{3}{4}$ bags with leaves. Rudy filled $5\frac{1}{4}$ bags with leaves. How many more bags of leaves did Ralph fill?

★ 23. Rosa wants to knit 2 scarves. She needs $4\frac{1}{2}$ packages of yarn for one, and $3\frac{1}{2}$ packages for the other. She has $9\frac{1}{2}$ packages. After making the scarves, how much yarn will she have left?

7.   362
     $\times$ 38

8. $17 - 2.58 = \square$

9. $48 \times 97 = \square$

10. $386 \div 25 = \square$

11. $42\overline{)847}$

12.   $6.38
     $\times$   81

13. $52.4 + 3.73 = \square$

14. $178.6 - 5.2 = \square$

15. $50 \times \$6.71 = \square$

16. $36\overline{)\$7.20}$

17. $32\overline{)946}$

18. $4.26 - 3.8 = \square$

**Source:** From L. J. Orfan and B. R. Vogeli, *Mathematics* (Morristown, NJ: Silver Burdett, 1987), p. 331. Reprinted by permission.

Mathematical rules require that $6 + 1$ be computed and the sum multiplied by 2 before that product is added to 3. Eye movements also go from up to down and from down to up in addition and division problems, as well as diagonally in the multiplication of fractions.

_nt_ approach to comprehension. For example, word problems such as __llowing_ require attention to parts of the text not normally thought _portant.

> John was going to the store. First he stopped at Mary's house.
> Mary lived 2 blocks from John. John and Mary went to the store
> together. The store was 2 blocks past Mary's house. How far did
> John go to get to the store?

Normally, children would read to find out who the people in the story were or what the action was. However, for this problem such information is unimportant. With mathematics problems students(who focus on the types of questions)asked with narrative materials)may attend to inappropriate items. In fact, reading difficulties may account for as much as 35 percent of student errors on mathematics achievement tests (O'Mara, 1981).

SQRQCQ: A study strategy for reading math word problems: survey, question, read, question, compute, and question.

**Instructional Strategies.** Fay (1965) suggests that a strategy called **SQRQCQ** be used to solve word problems.

| | |
|---|---|
| _Survey_ | Read the problem rapidly, skimming to determine its nature. |
| _Question_ | Decide what is being asked—in other words, what the problem is. |
| _Read_ | Read for details and interrelationships. |
| _Question_ | Decide which processes and strategies should be used to address the problem. |
| _Compute_ | Carry out the necessary computations. |
| _Question_ | Ask whether the answer seems correct. Check computations against the facts presented in the problem and against basic arithmetic facts. |

**MODEL
LESSON**

### SQRQCQ

Ms. Jackson knows that there are really only three things that prevent a student from correctly completing a word problem: (1) reading the problem incorrectly and thus not finding the appropriate information; (2) not per- forming the appropriate computation (e.g., subtracting when addition is needed); and (3) not performing the computation correctly (e.g., multiply- ing incorrectly). Ms. Jackson has decided to address the first point by teach- ing her students SQRQCQ. She first explains that SQRQCQ will help them better understand their mathematics problems. She then explains what the letters stand for and demonstrates how to read a mathematics problem (written on the chalkboard) using the SQRQCQ technique.

After Ms. Jackson is sure that her students know what SQRQCQ re- quires a reader to do, she tells them that they will practice the technique

*inconsiderate*

*don't know reader's need*

together. She hands out a ditto sheet of simple word problems and instructs students not to begin reading until she says to. After all students have ditto sheets, she asks several students to describe the first step in SQRQCQ. Then she directs students to skim the first problem rapidly and to turn their papers over when they have finished skimming.

When the students are finished, Ms. Jackson discusses with them what the problem is generally about. She then reminds them what the next step in the procedure is, suggests that they write down what is being asked, and again instructs them to turn over their papers when they are finished.

Ms. Jackson continues this process, discussing each step of the SQRQCQ procedure, both before and after it is attempted. She has students practice several of the problems on the ditto sheet in this way and reinforces the technique several times during the next week and periodically thereafter.

*content area reading*

Kane, Byrne, and Hater (1974) suggest a modification of the traditional cloze technique for mathematics. Their **modified cloze procedure** first specifies areas of student difficulty in textual aspects of mathematics material and in comprehension of mathematical concepts. The modification is then completed as a joint activity among students or among teacher and students. The exercise should be accompanied by discussion that focuses student attention on pertinent information that helps fill in the blanks. As the teacher models the thought processes necessary to replace the deletions, students can learn the reasoning specific to mathematics. An example of a mathematics cloze passage is shown in Figure 10–7.

modified cloze procedure: A comprehension assessment procedure that departs from the traditional routine of deleting every fifth word.

It is also necessary to teach students the specialized symbolic vocabulary of mathematics, even though this task is often forgotten. All of the process symbols have the same properties as letter- and word-based vocabulary. For example, the various multiplication or division signs represent the same concept and can be considered synonyms.

$$3 \times 2 \qquad 3 \cdot 2 \qquad 3(2)$$
$$2\overline{)3} \qquad 3 \div 2 \qquad \frac{3}{2}$$

These symbols can be taught with the same procedures used to teach synonyms that are words. Any symbols that stand for concepts can be considered vocabulary items and can be taught with the techniques presented in chapter 6.

## Science

**Technical Reading.** The following passage from an elementary science textbook (Sund, Adams, & Hackett, 1980) illustrates some of the reading demands in this content area.

FIGURE 10–7
Adaptation of the cloze procedure for mathematics

---

Following is a brief passage that could occur in a mathematics book written for upper elementary or middle school students. To the right is a cloze test constructed for the passage on the left. In actual practice, longer passages are used so that many more blanks are obtained.

Divide 20 by 5. Now, multiply 20 by $\frac{1}{5}$. Is dividing by 5 the same as multiplying by $\frac{1}{5}$? Are these sentences true?

$$36 \div 18 = 36 \times \frac{1}{18}$$
$$72 \div 8 = 72 \times \frac{1}{8}$$

Divide 20 by ___. Now multiply 20 ___ $\frac{1}{5}$. Is ___ by 5 the same ___ multiplying by $\frac{1}{}$ ? Are these sentences true?

$$\_\_6 \div 18 \_\_ 36 \times \frac{1}{18}$$
$$72 \_\_ 8 = 72 \_\_ \frac{1}{8}$$

Here are some observations you should note concerning the cloze test:

1. Both word tokens (i.e., words) and math tokens (i.e., numerical digits or process symbols) are counted in this procedure.
2. Every fifth token is deleted, starting with the fifth token.
3. Deleted tokens are replaced by blanks of two sizes. The shorter blanks are used for math tokens.
4. Tokens are ordered according to the words used to read them. For example, $\frac{1}{5}$ can be thought of as one, process symbol, five. Therefore, these tokens would be ordered as 1, /, 5. What is important is that the translation to words be consistent within a passage.

Source: From R. B. Kane, M. A. Byrne, and M. A. Hater, *Helping Children Read Mathematics* (New York: American Book, 1974), pp. 18–19. Adapted by permission.

The chart below shows several common compounds. It also shows the chemical formula and the phase of the compound.

| Compound | Formula | Phase of Matter |
|---|---|---|
| carbon dioxide | $CO_2$ | gas |
| water | $H_2O$ | liquid |
| ammonia | $NH_3$ | gas |
| salt | $NaCl$ | solid |

There are simple rules for writing chemical formulas. The formula for water is $H_2O$. The small number 2 means that a water molecule has two hydrogen atoms. The O has no number after it. No number means there is only one atom of oxygen. The number 1 is not written in chemical formulas. A molecule of water has 2 atoms of hydrogen and 1 atom of oxygen. $CO_2$ is the formula for carbon dioxide. What elements make up carbon dioxide? How many atoms of each element are in a molecule of carbon dioxide? (p. 90)

Science texts often seem more technical than other content-area texts. For example, the above explanation of the rules for writing formulas is specific and reflects technical writing. It must be carefully read, or the concept may not be grasped. The passage also includes several terms specific to science: element, molecule, compound, atom, dioxide, and formula. And, like mathematics and social studies, science uses several symbol sets. The chemical symbols and the numerical subscripts in the formulas must all be mastered in order to understand this science passage correctly.

Like social studies, science draws on several disciplines for its knowledge base. In fact, science materials show some overlap with social studies materials; units on space exploration and on weather and climate are two examples. Thus, the previous discussion of maps and charts applies to science as well. And science, too, has a great many words with Latin and Greek **morphemes**.

morphemes: The smallest meaningful linguistic units.

A further distinction in the vocabulary found in science materials is the high number of words with a meaning specific to science—that is, words that are not found in everyday speech. Whereas social studies and mathematics include many words with both general and content-specific meanings, science has a large number of words with only content-specific meanings. Thus, teach-

All content-area materials, including science texts, make specialized demands on a reader.

ers may need to preteach specific science concepts before students see the terms in text. Even though context often helps, we cannot assume that unknown words will become clear through reading alone.

A key component in understanding science material is reading to follow directions, particularly in laboratory exercises, where even the slightest departure can result in a failed experiment. In addition, science experiments follow a structure that is different from that of other textual materials.

| | |
|---|---|
| 1. Problem | 4. Observation |
| 2. Hypothesis | 5. Collection of data (results) |
| 3. Procedure | 6. Conclusion(s) |

If students are unfamiliar with this structure, it must be taught.

**PQRST.** PQRST is an effective study technique specific to science (Spache, 1963; Spache & Berg, 1966). It recommends that students reading science materials follow a five-step sequence.

PQRST: A science study technique that stresses previewing, questioning, reading, summarizing, and testing.

| | |
|---|---|
| *Preview* | Rapidly skim the selection to be read. The reader should not move on until the generalization or theory of the passage has been identified. |
| *Question* | Raise questions for study purposes. |
| *Read* | With questions in mind, read the selection and answer the questions. Sometimes experiments need to be done before the questions can be answered. |
| *Summarize* | Organize and summarize the information gathered through reading. Group relevant facts and summarize answers to each question. This step is best done in writing. |
| *Test* | Go back to the reading selection and check the summary statement for accuracy. Can the generalization or theory identified in the first step be supported through the answers and summaries? |

Forgan and Mangrum (1985) note that the difference between SQ3R and PQRST is "more than semantic" and agree with Fay (1965) that PQRST, rather than SQ3R, should be used with science material.

## Language Arts

In some ways the reading task in a language arts or English classroom can be the most demanding of all. Although the various subject areas make specific demands on a reader, a language arts reading assignment can include any or all of the demands and text structures previously discussed. Although the general reading requirements in language arts revolve around narrative text structures, once students are able to read on their own, they are required to read everything from autobiographies to historical fiction. As a result, the reading requirements are complex.

## PQRST

**MODEL
LESSON**

Mr. Hernandez, a fourth-grade teacher, has decided to teach his science class the PQRST study technique. He explains that science textbooks are structured so that a generalization or theory is stated near the beginning of a selection, the generalization is expanded and supported throughout the rest of the selection, and a summary statement of the generalization or theory is usually presented at the end. He has his students look at a section in their science textbooks that demonstrates this structure.

Mr. Hernandez then explains that a technique called PQRST helps readers consciously identify the generalization or theory and become more aware of the supporting details. He reminds his students that they should be active readers who anticipate what may come next, based on what has come before. He then presents each of the steps in PQRST, demonstrates what a reader might do at each step, and verbally tests a number of students to make sure that they know what should be done at each step.

**Preview.** Mr. Hernandez asks his students to open their books to a specific selection that has not been read before. He tells them to preview the selection, jotting down a note about the generalization or theory. When all are finished, he asks what they think the generalization is and has several students supply the reasons for their decision.

**Question.** Mr. Hernandez tells students to write down questions they might have about the generalization or theory and questions that they think might be answered as they read through the selection. He tells students not to refer to their books at this stage.

**Read.** Mr. Hernandez knows that a different class might need to continue this lesson on another day, but he thinks that this class can go ahead. He tells students to keep their questions in mind and to read the selection, writing down brief notes that might help them answer their questions.

**Summarize.** Mr. Hernandez reminds his students about the need to summarize. He suggests that they group relevant facts and also attempt to specifically answer their own questions, using their notes as a place to start.

**Test.** Because Mr. Hernandez wants to do this final step as a group activity, he has five or six students read their summaries aloud while the other students silently compare their own to those that are read. Students then discuss the accuracy of the summary statements and the answers to the questions identified earlier. During this process, students are encouraged to use the selection as a reference to justify their conclusions. Mr. Hernandez reinforces the use of PQRST on a continuing basis.

Part of the structure of a mathematics text may appear within the context of a biography of a mathematician, or that of a history text may appear in a historically based novel. In language arts reading materials, students must cope with different structures in different genre forms and also with specialized concepts, such as mood, setting, imagery, characterization, plot, foreshadowing, and other literary techniques. In addition, a literary selection may combine vocabulary from other content areas with its own, unique vocabulary demands. Thus, a wide range of vocabulary concepts can be encountered in literature, including vocabulary and language structures that are archaic or unfamiliar, as in the following passage:

> "Say, Tom, let me whitewash a little."
> Tom considered, was about to consent; but he altered his mind.
> "No—no—I reckon it wouldn't hardly do, Ben. You see, Aunt Polly's awful particular about this fence—right here on the street, you know—but if it was the back fence I wouldn't mind and she wouldn't. Yes, she's awful particular about this fence; it's got to be done very careful; I reckon there ain't one boy in a thousand, maybe two thousand, that can do it the way it's got to be done."
> "No—is that so? Oh come, now—lemme just try. Only just a little—I'd let you, if you was me, Tom." (Twain, 1982, p. 25)

The various demands of language arts materials require prereading attention to concepts and textual organization. Teachers should give particular care to literary techniques, as well as to visual imagery. The specific teaching suggestions presented in chapter 8 are appropriate for the various genres found in language arts reading.

## THE RELATIONSHIP OF A COMPREHENSION FRAMEWORK TO CONTENT-AREA INSTRUCTION

The method frameworks discussed in this chapter are most compatible with an interactive explanation of how a person reads. From that perspective meaning is not thought to reside in either text or reader but is seen as the result of their interaction. Similarly, the method frameworks presented here require readers to bring their own knowledge to bear on the text, while at the same time using the information in the text. For example, these method frameworks commonly expect readers to identify main ideas and supporting details. Thus, readers must have some knowledge about the text and must bring to bear existing world knowledge about the topic.

Another aspect of this interaction is that many of the method frameworks used in content-area reading also require readers to monitor comprehension (Baker & Brown, 1983; Markam, 1981). For example, during the reading step in SQ3R, students keep questions in mind and monitor to see when answers are found. **Comprehension monitoring** means that readers must actively attend to content, be aware of key ideas, separate important information from unimportant, and know when something has not been properly understood. In

comprehension monitoring: The ongoing process through which readers check their understanding as they read.

essence, all of the method frameworks discussed in this chapter are an attempt to foster internal comprehension-monitoring and metacognitive abilities.

Thus, the teaching suggestions in this chapter are based on interactive explanations of how people read. Nonetheless, teachers in content-area classrooms may have comprehension frameworks involving text-based or reader-based explanations of reading. Some teachers may say that students need to read a content-area selection again in order for the meaning to become clear, thus implying that meaning resides in the text. Other teachers may talk around a subject, rarely referring to the textual material actually read by students. Regardless of personal framework, however, all teachers recognize the importance of teaching appropriate reading and study strategies, even as they emphasize different procedural steps within those strategies.

## COMMENTS FROM THE CLASSROOM ■

### Emily Dodson

The method frameworks connected with content-area reading instruction are completely compatible with my personal framework, so I use all of them at one time or another. I guess what makes them especially attractive to me is that they're flexible. They can be used to develop all knowledge sources, from the lowest to the highest levels. For example, all of the methods require attention to detail and to content, as well as to background knowledge and metacognitive skills. Even opportunities for writing can be highlighted when students are asked to summarize.

Since I think that reading instruction should get students ready to read "real world" material and since most people read expository material after the primary grades, I stress different text structures and allow my second graders to experience reading and writing across a variety of those structures. I make sure they don't read *only* narrative stories—they also read short, interesting selections about science and inventions, biographies, and historical and other social studies selections (all with interesting illustrations and written at an appropriate level, of course). My second graders even use the dictio-nary and picture encyclopedia to find things that relate to our class discussions and to experience the need for research. Even though narratives are what we read and discuss most, my students really like to read expository material. It gives them a chance to talk about new ideas, and they really like hearing me model different approaches as I read those texts. When I "think aloud," I try to make it entertaining as well as instructional.

### Mr. Burns

I use all of the method frameworks associated with exposition at one time or another, but I spend more time on certain procedural steps within method frameworks like DRA or SQ3R, and I emphasize different information within marginal glosses or mapping activities. For example, within a DRA I spend more time in skill development and practice, and I often choose skills that relate to decoding. In method frameworks like SQ3R or SQRQCQ, I emphasize the survey and review steps. Those steps keep children looking for specific information in the text.

I also bring in my direct instruction bias when I'm teaching note-taking or the use of picture encyclopedias. I especially value study and research skills—the use of book parts, dictionaries, the card catalogue, and so on—because they fit in so well with alphabetizing, which I think helps decoding. In addition, during activities such as think-alouds, I model how the text relates to other reading, as well as looking at word structures and vocabulary that are specific to that one content area.

## Ms. Sanchez

I do value the method frameworks used with expository texts, but I highlight the predict and summarize steps. With predictions I stress students' use of prior experiences—what they already know—and attempt to build up their background knowledge. I usually ask students to make their predictions orally to give them practice with their oral language and listening skills. And since I also stress writing, I frequently have my students write summaries of what they've read. Of course, I make sure they *do* something with their summaries—like post them, compile them, or discuss them—so that it's a meaningful activity. All in all, I want my students to extend their own experiences, so I deemphasize activities that have them simply gather information from the text.

I must admit, I don't use expository material much in my classroom. My main focus is on children's literature, with some historical fiction and an occasional biography. I feel that children should self-select their own materials as much as possible, and they simply don't go beyond stories much, so I probably don't use different text structures as much as I should. I also give little direct instruction on alphabetizing or the use of reference sources or book parts.

I've been seriously considering adding some appropriate expository books to my classroom library, though. After all, I believe that a literacy environment furthers literacy acquisition, so having different text structures within my classroom should help my students read those materials more effectively later on.

MAJOR POINTS

- Reading and content-area teachers who expect children to read texts in specific subjects must provide students with reading instruction related to that subject area.

- Knowledge of book parts and general research skills helps children's comprehension and should be a part of reading instruction.

- The organization of narrative texts, which are generally used to teach reading, and expository texts, which students are required to read in subject areas, differs greatly. Textual organization also differs among subject areas.

- Reading rate depends largely on the purpose for reading. Flexibility in reading rate needs to be taught.

- Method frameworks used in content-area reading include frameworks that can be used in any subject, as well as frameworks specific to one subject.

- Most effective reading and study strategies are based on an interactive explanation of how a person reads.

*superordination*
*subordination*

1. Some of the method frameworks discussed in this chapter are listed here. Specify the comprehension framework explanation exemplified by each.

| Method | Explanation |
|---|---|
| SQ3R | _____ |
| directed reading approach | _____ |
| marginal gloss technique | _____ |
| advance organizers | _____ |
| semantic mapping | _____ |
| structured concept outlines | _____ |
| SQRQCQ | _____ |
| PQRST | _____ |
| K-W-L | _____ |

2. List and discuss the specific reading demands of social studies, mathematics, science, and language arts materials. Identify general differences in organizational patterns and reading requirements. Find an elementary school textbook for each subject area, provide specific examples of the items on your list, and explain the instructional implications of each.

3. Examine a published reading program intended for second-, fourth-, and sixth-grade levels. How is the issue of content-area reading addressed at those grade levels? What is the approximate proportion of narrative/literary selections to expository/content-area selections? If you were using such a program, how would that proportion of selections affect your teaching?

4. Find a reading unit in any content-area subject, and construct a directed reading activity for a reading selection. Then construct a three-level study guide and a set of marginal glosses for the same material.

5. If possible, practice using the SQ3R technique with an elementary school student. Otherwise, practice guiding a classmate through SQ3R, or use it yourself in your own reading.

6. How does a map reader differ from a map thinker? How might your instructional practices foster the development of map thinkers?

MAKING
INSTRUCTIONAL
DECISIONS

I.    *(main idea)*
   A.
   B.
   C.  1.
        2.
        3.

Monahan, J., & Hinson, B. (1988). *New directions in reading instruction.* Newark, DE: International Reading Association.

A flip-chart format that provides a summary of research-based ideas for teaching content-area reading. Includes more than 20 topics.

Moore, D. W., & Readence, J. E. (1983). Approaches to content area reading instruction. *Journal of Reading, 26,* 397–402.

Discusses four approaches to teaching content-area reading, adaptable to primary or secondary grades.

Moore, D. W., Readence, J. E., & Rickelman, R. J. (1989). *Prereading activities for content area reading and learning.* Newark, DE: International Reading Association.

Describes activities useful for pre- and post–content-area reading at all grade levels.

FURTHER
READING

Slater, W. H., & Graves, M. F. (1989). Research on expository texts: Implications for teachers. In K. D. Muth (Ed.), *Children's comprehension of text* (pp. 140–166). Newark, DE: International Reading Association.

> Provides a synthesis of research findings focusing on comprehension of expository texts, as well as a classification system that allows teachers to categorize texts in ways that aid teaching. Also discusses a model and strategies for teaching expository texts.

Smith, C. B. (1990). Vocabulary development in content area reading. *The Reading Teacher, 43,* 508–509.

> A brief discussion of several approaches to vocabulary development in content-area reading.

## REFERENCES

Baker, L., & Brown, A. C. (1983). Metacognition and the reading process. In P. D. Pearson (Ed.), *Handbook of reading research.* New York: Plenum Press.

Bassler, O. C., Kolb, J. R., Craighead, M. S. & Gray, W. L. (1981). *Succeeding in mathematics* (revised). Austin, TX: Steck-Vaughn.

Brown, A. C., Campione, J. C., & Day, J. D. (1981). Learning to learn: On training students to learn from texts. *Educational Researcher, 10,* 14–21.

Buggey, J. (1983). *Our communities.* Chicago: Follett.

Carr, E., & Ogle, D. M. (1987). K-W-L Plus: A strategy for comprehension and summarization. *Journal of Reading, 30,* 626–631.

Carson, J. (1990). Unpublished manuscript.

Cheek, E. J., Jr., & Cheek, M. C. (1983). *Reading instruction through content teaching.* Columbus, OH: Merrill.

Daines, D. (1982). *Reading in the content areas: Strategies for teachers.* Glenview, IL: Scott, Foresman.

Davey, B. (1983). Think-aloud—Modeling the cognitive processes of reading comprehension. *Journal of Reading, 27,* 44–47.

Davis, A. R. (1983). Study skills. In J. E. Alexander (Ed.), *Teaching reading* (2nd ed.). Boston: Little, Brown.

Defoe, D. (1967). *Robinson Crusoe* (abridged and adapted by Ron King). Belmont, CA: Fearon.

Dupuis, M. M. (Ed.). (1984). *Reading in the content areas: Research for teachers.* Newark, DE: International Reading Association.

Farr, R., & Roser, N. (1979). *Teaching a child to read.* New York: Harcourt Brace Jovanovich.

Fay, L. (1965). Reading study skills: Math and science. In J. A. Figurel (Ed.), *Reading and inquiry* (pp. 93–94). Newark, DE: International Reading Association.

Flood, J., Lapp, D., & Fornan, N. (1986). A reading-writing procedure that teaches expository paragraph structure. *The Reading Teacher, 29,* 556–562.

Forgan, H. W., & Mangrum II, C. T. (1985). *Teaching content area reading skills* (3rd ed.). Columbus, OH: Merrill.

Fry, E. (1981). Graphical literacy. *Journal of Reading, 24,* 383–389.

Garner, R. (1987). Strategies for reading and studying expository text. *Educational Psychologist, 22,* 299–312.

Hanf, M. B. (1971). Mapping: A technique for translating reading into thinking. *Journal of Reading, 13,* 225–230.

Herber, H. (1978). *Teaching reading in content areas* (2nd ed.). Englewood Cliffs, NJ: Prentice Hall.

Kane, R. B., Byrne, M. A., & Hater, M. A. (1974). *Helping children read mathematics.* New York: American Book.

Kinney, M. A. (1985). A language experience approach to teaching expository text structure. *The Reading Teacher, 38,* 854–856.

Manzo, A. V. (1969). The ReQuest procedure. *Journal of Reading, 11,* 123–126.

Manzo, A. V. (1985). Expansion modules for the ReQuest, CAT, GRP, and REAP reading/study procedures. *Journal of Reading, 28,* 498–503.

Markham, E. M. (1981). *Comprehension monitoring in children's oral communication skills.* New York: Academic Press.

Muhtadi, N. A. (1977). Personal communication.

Myers, C. B., & Wilk, G. (1983). *People, time, and change.* Chicago: Follett.

Ogle, D. M. (1989). The know, want to know, learn strategy. In K. D. Muth (Ed.), *Children's comprehension of text* (pp. 205–223). Newark, DE: International Reading Association.

O'Mara, D. A. (1981). The process of reading mathematics. *Journal of Reading, 25,* 22–30.

Pauk, W. (1984). The new SQ4R. *Reading World, 23,* 274–275.

Pieroneck, F. T. (1979). Using basal reader guidebooks—The ideal integrated reading lesson plan. *The Reading Teacher, 33,* 167–172.

Robinson, F. P. (1961). *Effective study.* New York: Harper & Row.

Rubin, D. (1983). *Teaching reading and study skills in content areas.* New York: Holt, Rinehart & Winston.

Ruddell, R. B., & Boyle, O. F. (1989). A study of cognitive mapping as a means to improve summarization and comprehension of expository text. *Reading Research and Instruction, 29,* 12–22.

Shepherd, D. L. (1982). *Comprehensive high school reading methods.* Columbus, OH: Merrill.

Singer, H., & Donlan, D. (1989). *Reading and learning from text* (2nd ed.). Hillsdale, NJ: Erlbaum.

Spache, G. D. (1963). *Toward better reading.* Champaign, IL: Garrard Press.

Spache, G. D., & Berg, P. C. (1966). *The art of efficient reading.* New York: Macmillan.

Summers, E. G. (1965). Utilizing visual aids in reading materials for effective reading. In H. L. Herber (Ed.), *Developing study skills in secondary schools.* Newark, DE: International Reading Association.

Sund, R. B., Adams, D. K., & Hackett, J. K. (1980). *Accent on science* (Level 6). Columbus, OH: Merrill.

Tei, E., & Stewart, O. (1985). Effective studying from text: Applying metacognitive strategies. *Forum for Reading, 27,* 36–43.

Thomas, E. L., & Alexander, H. A. (1982). *Improving reading in every class* (abridged 3rd ed.). Boston: Allyn & Bacon.

Tierney, R. J., Readence, J. E., & Dishner, E. K. (1990). *Reading strategies and practices: A compendium* (3rd ed.). Boston: Allyn & Bacon.

Twain, M. (1982). *The adventures of Tom Sawyer.* New York: Wanderer Books.

Vacca, R. (1981). *Content area reading.* Boston: Little, Brown.

Vacca, R. T., & Vacca, J. L. (1986). *Content area reading* (2nd ed.). Boston: Little, Brown.

# ASSESSMENT AND INSTRUCTIONAL NEEDS

PART

3

# Assessment of Readers and Reading Materials

- General Issues in Assessment
- Tests and Test Scores
- Evaluating Readers
- Evaluating Materials
- The Role of a Comprehension Framework in Assessment

*George looked at the test. It said:*

Rabbits eat

☐ lettuce          ☐ dog food

☐ sandwiches

*"Rabbits have to eat carrots, or their teeth will get too long and stick into them," he said.*
*The teacher nodded and smiled, but she put her finger to her lips.*
*George carefully drew in a carrot so the test people would know.*

A teacher is a type of researcher in the classroom, using a variety of data to make instructional decisions. Those data range from informal observations of students to formal, standardized tests. This chapter examines different strategies and techniques that can be used by teachers to evaluate students, reading materials, and the interaction between the two.

Chapter 11 includes information that will help you answer questions like these:

1. What are the general issues in assessment that should be of concern to reading teachers?
2. What are the differences among formal, informal, and teacher-made tests, and how are these instruments used in instructional decision making?
3. What do assessment tools measure when assessing readers and reading materials?
4. How does a comprehension framework guide the use of assessment tools and the interpretation of test results?

KEY CONCEPTS

| | |
|---|---|
| assessment program | norm group |
| cloze test | norm-referenced test |
| criterion-referenced test | passage independent question |
| diagnostic test | percentage score |
| formal test | percentile score |
| frustration reading level | portfolio assessment |
| grade equivalent score | process vs. product assessment |
| group test | raw score |
| idea unit | readability formula |
| independent reading level | relative standing |
| individual test | reliability |
| informal reading inventory (IRI) | standard error of measurement |
| informal test | standardized testing |
| instructional reading level | stanine score |
| listening comprehension level | survey test |
| management system | teacher-made test |
| miscue | validity |

## GENERAL ISSUES IN ASSESSMENT

standardized testing:
Evaluation using standardized materials and standardized procedures for administration and scoring.

Teachers sometimes find that a great deal of their time is spent testing. Often, they spend much of the first week of a new school year using different tests to determine students' instructional needs. Additionally, school districts commonly require both yearly **standardized testing,** to compare their students' progress to the progress of students in other districts or previous years, and detailed record keeping by their teachers as part of a management system. A management system specifies what students should learn and requires an ongoing **assessment program** to document progress. Although emergent literacy perspectives are causing some rethinking of such an approach to reading instruction, it still predominates. Tests are also a part of many published reading programs: students often must demonstrate mastery before moving to the next unit or lesson.

assessment program: Systematic evaluation of students' progress by various testing methods consistent with a teacher's or school district's goals.

Clearly, testing can demand substantial amounts of a teacher's time, especially when we include not just test administration time, but also preparation time, time for scoring, and time for interpretation of completed tests. Because it is important to use this time in the best possible way, choosing assessment instruments to match specific measurement objectives is critical. Test selection is largely determined by the reasons for testing, and there are many purposes for administering tests in school (Ruddell & Kinzer, 1982).

1. to provide information on the strengths and weaknesses of specific students in order to aid teachers' instructional planning
2. to discover strengths and weaknesses of students and curriculum in order to guide decisions for general program improvement
3. to provide the general public with evidence of student growth or instructional success
4. to provide data to contribute to the evaluation of special programs
5. to provide information for research into effective instructional programs
6. to provide data for budgetary planning and allocation of tax dollars

Test results are used by many people in addition to teachers: district staff, superintendents, school board members, curriculum committees, principals, and others. Each has slightly different goals and purposes, all of which influence instructional decisions and the selection of tests or types of tests. Some tests measure specific skills and are closely tied to individual students' instructional situations. Other tests provide only group or survey data, which cannot be used for specific diagnostic purposes. Still other measures are appropriate for comparing different sets of materials—perhaps before purchasing decisions are made.

Assessment instruments range from highly sophisticated tests purchased from test publishers to simple tests constructed by individual teachers. Nonetheless, there are certain factors common to all measurement instruments that determine whether a test is good or bad. Understanding these factors helps teachers choose a test or type of test to best meet their measurement objectives. Many people define a good test like this:

■ It measures what it is supposed to measure—what it says it measures.
■ It gives consistent results, not random or changing over time.
■ It is manageable in terms of administration time.
■ It is easy to score and interpret.

## Validity

validity: The ability of a test to measure what it claims to measure.

**Validity** describes whether a test measures what it is supposed to measure, what it intends to measure. If a test measures what it is supposed to, we say that it is valid. A test of oral reading ability would be valid if students were required to read orally while their reading was appropriately scored. A test using silent reading procedures to test oral reading would be invalid. Sometimes a test claims to measure a particular skill or ability, but an examination of the actual test items, procedures, or testing tasks may show that it does not. At other times a valid test might be used in a manner not intended by its authors. For example, a survey test providing information about general reading ability might be inappropriately used to infer areas of specific reading disability. However, the fact that a test is misused does not make it an invalid test, and we must be careful not to dismiss an instrument because of factors beyond the intent of the test.

content validity: One of several types of validity; assesses whether a test measures skills appropriate to the subject-area being tested.

curricular validity: One of several types of validity; assesses whether a test measures what children have been taught.

When considering validity, teachers should also be aware of the reading process. They should examine test items and procedures carefully to determine whether a test does what it claims to do and also whether it measures appropriate reading skills and therefore has **content validity**. In addition, classroom teachers are in the best position to determine whether a test has **curricular validity,** that is, whether it measures what children are taught. Most respected tests acknowledge that curricular validity depends in large part on the given curriculum and students being tested.

## Reliability

reliability: The ability of a test to provide consistent information

**Reliability** tells whether a test is consistent in the information it provides. If a test is given to a student over and over again and yields the same score each time, then it is extremely reliable. In fact, if the scores are identical each time, the test is 100 percent reliable. In reality, tests are not 100 percent reliable; differences in student learning and in affective, physical, or environmental factors, all influence the test/retest results of any given student. Teachers need to be able to assume that a test does provide consistent information. Then, if differences in pre- and posttest results are found, they can more confidently attribute the change to factors such as learning. For this reason it is very important to keep the testing situation, including both the environment and the administration, as constant as possible.

split-half reliability: A method of determining test reliability by dividing a test in half and evaluating the consistency between the two halves.

test/retest reliability: A method of determining test reliability by seeing whether two separate administrations of the same test produce similar results.

alternate-form reliability: A method of determining test reliability by seeing whether different forms of the same test produce similar results.

Reliability estimates are generally listed in the teacher's or technical manuals provided with published tests. Teachers should make a special effort to look through such manuals, requesting that they be provided if necessary. Three common methods of determining reliability are the **split-half, test/retest,** and **alternate-form** reliability estimates. Readers interested in the differences among these methods should consult any introductory text on measurement. For our purposes here, it is enough to know that all three methods are, in effect, correlations, which show the degree of relationship among factors. For example, the relationship might be among scores on different administrations of a test (i.e., test/retest reliability).

The degree of relationship between two test administrations is indicated by a **reliability coefficient,** with 1.00 indicating a perfect relationship between the two sets of scores. In other words, a coefficient of 1.00 means that a test is 100 percent reliable. Thus, a student taking the same test twice, with no increase in learning, would receive identical scores both times. In education, tests with reliability coefficients above 0.80 are considered reliable.

reliability coefficient: A statistic that indicates the degree of relationship between two scores.

Standard Error of Measurement.  Since we know that tests are not 100 percent reliable, teachers must know how widely students' scores can vary by chance. The **standard error of measurement** specifies exactly how much a score must increase or decrease before the difference is attributed to something other than chance. Such information can be viewed in plus and minus terms. For example, if a student scored 17 on a 20 item test and the test had a standard error of measurement of 2, then that student's score would really be 17 plus or minus 2. In other words, it would fall between 15 and 19. Thus, if the student was tested again and received a score of 19, it would not be appropriate to assume that improvement had been shown, because the two scores are both within the range of the standard error of measurement. That is, they are within two points of each other, and the difference could be due to chance. All high-quality tests provide information regarding the standard error of measurement.

standard error of measurement: A statistic that indicates how much a score must increase or decrease before the difference is attributed to something other than chance.

## Process vs. Product Assessment

Assessment that looks mainly at the outcomes of student performance is called **product assessment**. Assessment that attempts to interpret performance in an effort to evaluate underlying strategies, actions, or behaviors is called **process assessment**. Wittrock (1987) points out that most formal assessment instruments can answer questions about how well students do but cannot answer questions such as "What strategies does this student use to construct main ideas?" or "How does this student relate prior knowledge and experiences to the text?" (p. 734). Nonetheless, despite the fact that process measures might be more important to teachers in making individual instructional decisions, all types of tests can be useful if they are closely tied to the purposes of testing. However, standardized tests, especially multiple-choice tests, have been increasingly criticized as being harmful to minorities, as contributing to an overreliance on testing, and as hindering educational reforms (Gifford, 1990). Calfee (1987) has pointed out that standardized tests will continue to be used and can provide indications of student progress as long as those tests and test results are appropriately used.

product assessment: Assessment that evaluates primarily the outcomes of student performance.

process assessment: Assessment that evaluates primarily the strategies, actions, or behaviors underlying the products of student performance.

Assessment of products is easier to conduct than assessment of processes. To assess products, a teacher needs only to follow the guidelines in a standardized or criterion-referenced test. Process assessments, however, require reasoned decisions about a reader's underlying reading processes. For example, in a product assessment a student might be asked to read a passage and answer a question. The result—the answer—is assumed to indicate whether or not the passage was understood. In process assessment, on the other hand, a teacher must attempt to find out how the answer was arrived at and what strategies were used and/or rejected.

Process assessment has received increasing attention because of an emphasis on higher-order thought processes, such as critical thinking and problem solving (e.g., see Nickerson, 1989; Siegler, 1989). One difficulty associated with process assessment is that there are usually multiple paths to solving a problem, and individuals may process information differently. This flexibility makes it inappropriate to interpret the results of process measures in terms of a single strategy (Gardner & Hatch, 1989; Siegler, 1989). Consequently, teachers who use process-based assessments must consider multiple paths to an answer, thereby making assessment and interpretation more difficult. Such assessment is more valid, however, since students are not automatically penalized for answers that differ from an expected response. Thus, with a process measure a teacher must determine whether the test can accurately infer a reader's processes and whether that inference is reflected in scoring and interpretation. The assessment tools and procedures discussed throughout this chapter include both process and product measures.

## DECISION POINT ➤

As our knowledge of the reading process has increased, testing has changed little. Consequently, Valencia and Pearson (1987) note that reading tests and testing procedures often do not match what we know about reading. Not surprisingly, an increasing number of voices are being raised in favor of alternatives to traditional tests and testing methods, especially in favor of process assessment. However, process measures are valuable only to the extent that individual teachers understand the reading process and are able to infer students' processes based on their overt behavior. Unfortunately, not all teachers understand the reading process equally or similarly, and disagreement in interpreting process measures could lead to problems of accountability with parents and others. Thus, whereas some argue that process measures can provide important knowledge about how students do what they do, others point to the difficulty of process analysis and the inconsistency of interpretation. Will you favor product measures, process measures, or a combination of both in your classroom?

# TESTS AND TEST SCORES

## Types and Uses of Tests

Reading teachers commonly use measurement in their classrooms for a variety of reasons:

1. to find a student's general reading competency (and strategies and processes used)
2. to see whether one book is more difficult than another
3. to identify motivational material for a student or class (i.e., to find out students' interests and attitudes)
4. to match a student with appropriate materials
5. to find out whether a student has mastered a particular instructional lesson or unit

   Can you see that these **targets of assessment** differ? For example, Goals 1, 3, and 5 are student centered; that is, the student is the target and the

**targets of assessment:** Who or what is being assessed; may include the student, the text, or the student and the text together.

Making appropriate instructional decisions is a major goal in an assessment program.

assessment is conducted directly on the student. Goal 3 differs slightly from 1 and 5 in that it measures an emotional response rather than reading ability, but it still deals with the reader. Goal 2 does not measure the student; instead, it assesses the difficulty of reading material, perhaps through an analysis of factors such as print size or density of ideas. Goal 4 combines two categories: it measures both the materials and the student in combination. Thus, assessment can focus on the student, the materials, or the student and the materials together. The target and goal of assessment jointly determine the type of measurement tool needed. Several specific considerations help to further define the appropriate instrument.

**group tests:** Assessment instruments that are administered to more than one person at the same time.

**individual tests:** Assessment instruments that are administered to one person at a time.

**survey tests:** Assessment instruments that evaluate general ability in a certain area.

**diagnostic tests:** Assessment instruments that evaluate specific product and process characteristics so that instructional decisions can be made.

1. *Is the test intended for group administration?* **Group tests** are administered to several students at the same time. Such tests result in overall time savings when a class or an entire school of students needs to be evaluated.
2. *Is the test intended for individual administration?* **Individual tests** are administered in one-on-one situations. Such tests allow more controlled conditions and permit examiners to observe student behavior during test administration.
3. *Is the test intended to survey general reading ability?* **Survey tests** provide indications of general ability. Reading tests that indicate general reading level but not specific strengths and weaknesses fall into this category.
4. *Is the test intended to diagnose a specific reading deficiency?* **Diagnostic tests** assess specific abilities and provide information leading to specific instructional practices. Such tests may be group tests (e.g., Stanford Diagnostic Reading Test) or individual tests (e.g., Durrell Analysis of Reading Difficulty) but not survey tests.

Once target and goal have been clearly specified, teachers can choose from three general categories of tests: formal, informal, and teacher-made tests. Because all are valuable, it is important to know the strengths and weaknesses of each type and the circumstances of appropriate use.

■ *Formal tests.* These tests have strict guidelines for administration, scoring, and interpretation. They are purchased from test publishers and are often called standardized tests.
■ *Informal tests.* These tests allow for teacher judgment in administration, scoring, and interpretation. They may be purchased as stand-alone items or may be included as part of a larger set of materials. Although tests in this category have a general procedure that must be followed, a teacher's judgment is critical within that procedure. For example, an informal test might indicate that testing should stop when a student becomes frustrated. Clearly, the teacher's judgment would play a major part in determining when frustration occurred.
■ *Teacher-made tests.* These tests are made and used by teachers to test their students' knowledge of a particular instructional unit or lesson. For this

**Test Types**

|  | Formal Tests | Informal Tests | Teacher-Made Tests |
|---|---|---|---|
| Readers |  |  |  |
| Materials |  |  |  |

Targets of Assessment

FIGURE 11–1

A framework of test types and targets of assessment

category of test the teacher alone determines administration and scoring procedures.

The types of tests and the targets of assessment together provide a framework (see Figure 11–1) against which assessment instruments can be analyzed and evaluated.

Whichever types of tests are used, they must not be used indiscriminately. Generally, teachers gather initial information about students from cumulative records. These records follow a student throughout school, providing a compilation of information about strengths, weaknesses, teacher observations and comments, and so on. Using the cumulative record as a guide, teachers can observe students in the classroom situation and can then administer specific tests to discover or confirm areas of weakness so that instructional decisions can be made more reliably.

## Types and Uses of Test Scores

Students' scores on reading tests are commonly reported in five ways:

1. raw scores
2. percentage scores
3. percentile scores
4. stanine scores
5. grade-equivalent scores

Each of these reporting methods yields different information and can be misleading if not used properly.

**Raw scores** are determined by simply adding up the number of correct responses, regardless of the total number of items on a test. A student who gets eight items right has a raw score of 8. When a single test is given to a student or group of students, the scores can be valuable since all students are taking the same test and there are no variations in how long the test is or what the test is assessing. However, many published tests consist of a series of subtests,

raw scores: The number of correct responses on a test.

which usually measure different reading components and have different numbers of items. For example, a comprehension subtest might include 25 items, whereas a vocabulary subtest might include 40 items. Thus, a raw score of 20 on each of the subtests would not indicate relative ability in the subtest areas.

percentage scores: The percentage of correct responses on a test.

**Percentage scores** are one way to deal with some of the shortcomings of raw scores. Percentages are calculated by dividing the number of correct responses by the total possible and then multiplying the result by 100. This process yields a theoretical score out of 100 regardless of the length of the test, thus allowing more representative comparisons. In the earlier example a raw score of 20 on both the 25-item comprehension subtest and the 40-item vocabulary subtest would produce percentage scores of 80 and 50, respectively. Thus, percentage scores allow clearer comparisons across subtests.

percentile scores: Ratings that indicate the percent of the norm population scoring below a student's score.

**Percentile scores** indicate the percent of the norm population scoring below individual students' scores, thereby reflecting the relative standing of those students within the norm group. In other words, a percentile score of 80 says that 80 percent of the norm group scored below that student's raw score. In our example the raw score of 20 (or 80 percent) on the 25-item comprehension subtest probably seems fairly good. However, if the student's peer group averaged 24 (or 95 percent), then the 20 was below average when compared to students of similar ability. Unlike percentage scores, which mask an individual's rank within the peer group, percentile scores provide information about relative standing.

stanine scores: Scores related to consistent bands on a normal curve, ranging from 1 to 9.

normal curve: A bell-shaped curve that if based on enough cases, represents a naturally occurring distribution.

**Stanine scores** also allow a comparison of relative standing. Stanines indicate where in the overall distribution of scores the score in question lies, assuming that the total distribution of scores falls into a **normal curve**. The curve is then divided into nine bands, numbered 1 through 9, which correspond to predetermined percentages of scores falling into each band. A score in the fifth stanine would fall in the middle of the normal curve; scores of 4, 5, or 6 are considered average. Thus, in addition to relative standing, stanine scores also indicate the relation of a student's score to the overall distribution of scores.

grade-equivalent scores: A measure of relative standing that compares a student's raw score to average scores across grade levels.

**Grade-equivalent scores** are also commonly used to provide information about relative standing. For example, if a student receives a grade-equivalent score of 7.0, then that student's raw score is equivalent to the average score of beginning seventh graders in the norm population. Unfortunately, grade-equivalent scores can be deceptive and can inadvertently label students. Consequently, the International Reading Association is opposed to grade-equivalent scores, and test publishers have moved away from providing them.

## EVALUATING READERS

### Formal Tests: Norm-Referenced

norm-referenced tests: Tests that compare an individual or a group to a group of other, similar individuals.

norm group: The group whose test performance is used to establish levels of performance for a standardized test.

**Norm-referenced tests** compare an individual or a group to a **norm group** of similar individuals. A norm-referenced test usually contains several subtests. For example, a survey reading test might include subtests in vocabulary, reading rate, comprehension, and study skills. A diagnostic reading test might include subtests in knowledge of word parts, blending ability, inferential and literal comprehension, identification of relationships (e.g., cause and effect), oral vocabulary, and so on.

Before you choose a norm-referenced test, you should carefully examine the test manual(s) to find out about the group to which your students would be compared. You need to determine whether your students are similar enough to the norm group for valid comparison. A manual should provide norm-group information such as the following:

- number of males and females
- range of ages
- distribution across geographic regions
- representation of rural and urban areas
- number of racial and/or ethnic students

It is also important to realize that norm group scores are presented as an average or norm, making individual student comparisons less reliable than comparisons of groups to the norm. For example, comparing a class average to the norm would be more accurate than comparing the scores of an individual student. The model lesson that follows relates the experiences of one third-grade teacher with a norm-referenced test.

---

## Experience with a Norm-Referenced Test

All students in the third grade at Ms. Henshaw's school are to be given a norm-referenced test. The goal of the assessment is to compare students' achievement over several years and to see how these third graders perform relative to other third graders across the nation. The teachers and principal have determined that the test is both reliable and valid and that the school's third-grade population adequately reflects the norm group for comparative purposes.

**MODEL LESSON**

A faculty meeting is called to discuss test administration. Everyone realizes that the test instructions need to be followed to the letter. Instructions are to be read to students as stated in the test manual, a stopwatch is to be used to make sure that timed sections are accurate, subtests are to be done in order, and so on. Test booklets and answer sheets are to be collected at the end of the testing session and will be scored electronically, with the results returned to the teachers.

Several months later, Ms. Henshaw receives those results. She notices that there are several parts to the report: a section listing overall scores for her class; a section comparing her class to a norm group; a section that notes how many students missed particular items; and a section that lists her students' names along with the items each student missed. This information is clustered within question types that appeared on the test.

Since the test was given late in the school year, the results cannot be incorporated into Ms. Henshaw's instruction for the students that were tested. However, her third graders compared favorably to their peers. Ms. Henshaw does record individual students' deficiencies on her class record sheet and on the students' official cumulative record cards. She knows that her students' next teachers will be looking at these records and will thus have a better idea of general areas needing particular attention. She will also share the information the following year, when teachers tell each other about their classes from the previous year.

## Formal Tests: Criterion-Referenced

criterion-referenced test: A test that compares a student's performance to a predetermined measure of success.

A **criterion-referenced test** (CRT) does not compare a student to a norm group; its intent is simply to provide a picture of student performance by comparing it to an established criterion (Popham, 1978). In norm-referenced assessment a student's score is compared to those of a norm group of peers. In criterion-referenced assessment a student's score is compared to a predetermined criterion of success. As Mehrens and Lehman (1984) have stated, "To polarize the distinction, we could say that the focus of a normative score is on how many of Johnny's peers do not perform (score) as well as he does; the focus of a criterion-referenced score is on what it is that Johnny can do" (p. 18).

In part, the popularity of criterion-referenced assessment lies in its ability to determine whether a student has mastered a specific lesson and can be moved on to the next level of instruction. This approach has been criticized, however, because it implies that all necessary reading subskills have been correctly sequenced and identified and that a strict sequence of instruction is known to be best for all students. Unfortunately, even though much is known about reading, there is still much to learn. And even though certain skills are generally thought to be necessary in reading, they are interrelated and are difficult to separate. A difficult issue to resolve in criterion-referenced measurement is the fact that the absence of any one subskill presented in a criterion reading test does not usually reflect an inability to read. A similar situation exists for most skill areas, leaving individually tested skills on a CRT open to question (see Johnston, 1983, for a discussion of holistic vs. subskill theories of reading comprehension and their relationship to assessment).

management system: A detailed, systematic record of a student's progress through an instructional program.

Nonetheless, criterion-referenced measures are included in almost every published reading program. Their advantage over norm-referenced tests is that they can be closely tied to instruction, making them useful for a **management system.** A management system provides a detailed record of each student's progress through an instructional program and records when mastery of specific skills occurs. Such systems are attractive to school systems that are concerned with accountability issues.

Criterion-referenced assessment can monitor a student's progress through instructional materials. For example, let's assume that a reader is learning the two-letter blend *st*. The instructional program introduces the *str* blend at a more difficult level, which should not be attempted until *st* has been mastered. Five items testing *st* might be administered, with the criterion set at

3. When the student answers three of the five items correctly, instruction moves on to the *str* blend. Until then, more instruction is provided on *st,* and the test (usually in a different form) is readministered. This close tie to instruction is a major reason for the popularity of criterion-referenced assessment.

One misconception about the differences between norm- and criterion-referenced scores needs to addressed here. The statement is often made that norm-referenced assessment results in a relatively arbitrary comparison of individual students to a norm group, whereas criterion assessment examines students' performance only against their own strengths. However, criterion-referenced tests also compare student performance to an externally imposed criterion. In fact, one could argue that the criterion is more arbitrary than the norms, since norm-referenced tests provide a comprehensive and valuable discussion of the norm group and the norming procedure, whereas the rationale for a given criterion level is rarely addressed in teacher's manuals. Consequently, such questions as How is a criterion determined? are left unanswered.

Usually, a criterion is set at the level at which average students—average in relation to the students being tested—perform. Thus, the difference between a norm and a criterion is minimal. The major difference between criterion- and norm-referenced assessment lies in philosophy and in the way scores are used, rather than in any substantive difference in how appropriate performance is determined. This difference in usage is reflected in the frequency of administration of the two types of assessment. Criterion-referenced tests are used often and are usually specifically keyed to the instructional situation, whereas norm-referenced tests are generally used only once or twice a year. The model lesson that follows indicates how a criterion-referenced test leads to instructional decisions.

---

## Experience with a Criterion-Referenced Test

Mr. Washington has just completed a lesson on cause-and-effect relationships. The lesson format came from a published reading program that includes criterion-referenced tests as part of the program. The teacher's manual suggests that the appropriate criterion-referenced test be given to see whether students have mastered the concept.

The test provided in the reading program contains 10 items, with 8 as the criterion. The teacher's guide suggests reteaching if the criterion is not met, and new lessons are provided for that purpose. An additional criterion assessment, with new items, is provided for use after reteaching.

Mr. Washington administers the test to his students, and all but five meet the criterion. His teacher's aide works with this group of students, using the reteaching lesson and then retests. On the retest all five meet the criterion and Mr. Washington begins instruction on the next unit.

**MODEL
LESSON**

---

## Informal Tests: The Informal Reading Inventory

informal reading inventories (IRIs): Individualized tests that use a graded word list and passages to determine a student's reading ability and provide diagnostic information.

**Informal reading inventories** (IRIs) allow a teacher to match students and materials. They provide information that helps a teacher place students at appropriate instructional levels within a set of graded materials. The information is obtained by having students read increasingly difficult passages and stop reading when they come to a passage that is too difficult. The students' patterns of errors indicate materials that could be used appropriately with a particular student. IRIs are included as a part of most published reading programs, can also be purchased as stand-alone items, or can be teacher developed.

An informal reading inventory must be administered individually to students and requires some expertise to score and interpret. It thus requires somewhat more time to administer than some other measures, but it provides information that can be of great value in instructional decision making. Teachers typically use IRIs near the beginning of a school year as one information source to help determine instructional groupings and appropriate levels of materials for students. IRIs are also used when a teacher desires more information about some observed reading behavior.

IRIs describe the functioning level of a reader, indicating that student's independent, instructional, and frustration reading levels. These are important concepts and are mentioned often.

■ *Independent reading level*. At this level students can read on their own without teacher assistance. Their reading is fluent and free of undue hesitations. Intonation is appropriate for the punctuation and phrasing of the material.
■ *Instructional reading level*. At this level students can read if support and instruction are provided. Material at this level is challenging but not frustrating to read.
■ *Frustration reading level*. At this level students have great difficulty, even with teacher guidance and instruction. In effect, they are unable to read the selection even with support.

Typically, an IRI provides three scores, each corresponding to one of these three general levels of reading. For example, an IRI might determine that a student's independent reading level is at approximately the third-grade level, whereas that student's instructional and frustration levels might be at about the fourth and fifth grades, respectively. These scores indicate the difficulty of materials appropriate for instruction, practice, and free-reading.

miscues: Oral reading responses that deviate from the text being read.

Published informal reading inventories usually include two copies of each reading selection so that the teacher can note any **miscues** and make other comments on one copy while the student reads from the other. The teacher's copy is usually double spaced to allow written comments and includes suggested comprehension questions with space to record student responses. After each IRI passage is read, different kinds of comprehension questions are asked—for example, questions that deal with vocabulary, details, inferences, and main ideas.

Although IRIs have generally been praised for including a range of questions, Duffelmeyer and Duffelmeyer (1989) have noted that approximately 50 percent of the main idea questions in IRIs might be inappropriate because the IRI passages may not have had an explicitly stated main idea or a unified passage focus. This condition was especially prevalent among narrative passages. Thus Duffelmeyer and Duffelmeyer note that a student's poor performance on main idea questions is "as likely to be a reflection of ill suited passages as of the student's inability to comprehend main ideas" (p. 363). As a result, teachers should be cautious when scoring student responses to main idea questions in IRIs, and the questions should be examined carefully.

**Deciding Where to Start Testing.** An IRI includes passages with varying difficulty levels. Thus, teachers must decide at what level to begin the test. Passages that are either too difficult or too easy should be avoided. Published IRIs usually provide entry to the oral reading passages through a set of graded word lists. Beginning with the list suggested by the IRI being used, a student reads successive lists until a certain number of errors occur within a given list. Most IRIs suggest that the student begin reading the passage that corresponds to the highest level list that was read perfectly, or perhaps the passage one level below that list. The word lists come in two forms: one for the teacher and one for the student. The teacher's copy provides space for noting student answers. And student responses must be noted, since miscue patterns can provide valuable supplementary information.

**Noting Student Miscues on an IRI.** The marking system in Table 11–1 can be used to indicate reading behavior on the word lists as well as on subsequently administered passages. Different tests use different symbols or methods to mark reading miscues and other behaviors. However, since the miscue types are well accepted, the particular marking system is not important. It is important, though, to choose one system and use it consistently.

The scoring system in Table 11–1 can be used to mark all reading behaviors, and noting all miscues allows patterns to be more easily observed. However, when counting miscues to decide whether a student's frustration level has been reached, a teacher must decide whether a miscue is significant. IRIs such as the Classroom Reading Inventory (Silvaroli, 1990) suggest that "insignificant" miscues be noted but not necessarily counted.

Significant miscues are those that interfere with fluency or change the meaning of what was written. The following examples illustrate the difference between significant and insignificant miscues.

Text:        The boy likes the kitten. Ask him where it is.
Student 1:   The boy likes the cat. Ask him where it is.
Student 2:   The boy likes the kitchen. Ask him where it is.
Student 3:   The boy like da kitt'n. Ax him where it is. (Black English)

TABLE 11–1
Informal reading inventory marking system

| Miscue/Behavior | Mark | Example |
|---|---|---|
| **Miscues That Are Usually Significant (always counted)** | | |
| **Omission**<br>Not reading something in the text (e.g., part or whole word, phrase, punctuation) | Circle the omission. | He likes the big (yellow) car. |
| **Insertion**<br>Adding something not originally present in the text | Use caret (^) and add insertion. | He likes the big ᴧ yellow car.  *and blue* |
| **Substitution**<br>Replacing something in the text with something else (e.g., *this* for *the*) | Cross out original and add substitution. | He likes the big yellow car.  *takes* |
| **No response**<br>Substantial pause indicating inability to read the word, resulting in the teacher's pronouncing the word | Write *P* over teacher-pronounced items. | He likes the big yellow car.  P |
| **Miscues That Are Usually Not Significant (always marked, sometimes counted)** | | |
| **Repetition**<br>Repeated reading of a word or group of words | Put dome over repeated items. | He likes the big yellow car. |
| **Hesitation**<br>Pause that interrupts the flow or pattern of reading | Put checkmark at point of hesitation. | He likes the big yellow car.  ✓ |
| **Transposition**<br>Reversing order of letters in words or words in sentences | Put reverse *S* around transposed items. | He likes the big yellow car. |
| **Mispronunciation**<br>Pronunciation clearly different from normal (e.g., *k* in *knife* or *w* in *sword*) | Write phonetic pronunciation or use diacritical marks. | He likes the big yellow car.  līkĕs |
| **Self-correction**<br>Corrected by the student without teacher help | Write *C* above the miscue. | He likes the big yellow car.  *large* C |

Student 4:  The boy likes the kitten let's ask where she is.
Student 5:  The boy likes the kitten. Ask him to go where it is.

You may have noticed that some of the miscue(s) preserved the essential meaning of the text, whereas others did not. For example, substituting *cat* for *kitten* (Student 1) or combining the two sentences (Student 4) did not substantially alter the original meaning of the text, although neither student read exactly what was presented. Do you think it would be appropriate to consider those inconsistencies mistakes? If such reading occurred in your classroom, would you stop it and correct the mistakes immediately or allow the reader to go on? Although the students did not read exactly what was written, they did comprehend the text. Such occurrences should be noted for later analysis; but since the miscues were semantically correct, they should not be scored as significant.

What does Student 2's miscue tell us? Does the substitution of *kitchen* for *kitten* indicate anything more than the fact that comprehension has not taken place? Notice that the substitution makes sense in the sentence, even though the sentence now means something different from the original. Thus, the student has used syntactic cues effectively, correctly placing a noun where it belongs in the sentence, that is, after an article. Notice also that the student has used many of the letters in the original word in the substitution. Indeed, the only difference between the two words is the replacement of the second *t* in *kitten* with a *ch*. Thus, the student is not making wild guesses about what is to be read; active and logical processing is taking place. The same may be said of Student 5. Although the meaning of the original sentences has been altered, the student's miscue is not arbitrary. The **pattern of miscues** that emerges from several such instances, never from just one, permits a teacher to draw generalizations about the reader.

pattern of miscues: A group of similar miscues from which a teacher may draw generalizations about the reading process or strategies used by a reader.

But what about Student 3's reading? How did you categorize that student's miscues? Did you think that the student read incorrectly or simply reflected a normal dialect pattern? Some believe that there are times when dialect differences should be focused on to make a student aware of more-accepted standards. However, in the IRI scoring situation dialect variations do not usually impact comprehension and are not typically counted as miscues (Goodman & Buck, 1973; Harris & Sipay, 1990).

**Administering an Informal Reading Inventory.** Let's look at part of an actual IRI given to Debby, an average second-grade student (see Figure 11–2). Because Debby made no errors on the first 10 words of the initial list, she was moved to the next level. On the second-grade list she stumbled on *beautiful* but did read the word correctly. *I'm* was read as *am* but was self-corrected. Thus, her only miscue was the last word on the list. The next word list (third-grade) resulted in three miscues and one self-correction, so Debby was asked to read the words on the fourth-grade list.

The teacher allowed Debby to finish the fourth-grade list, even after five miscues (the cutoff point for this particular test), for two reasons. First, Debby went on immediately after her fifth miscue; and second, she did not exhibit signs of frustration. Thus, the teacher felt that it would have been detrimental to discontinue after *is-land,* thereby sending the message that too many mistakes had taken place. With an informal reading inventory the teacher's judgment largely determines administration and interpretation, and decisions should center around the child. If frustration is evident, the list should be discontinued; if not, the teacher can appropriately gather further information.

After the fourth-grade list Debby was told that she would be reading several short passages out loud. However, Debby told the teacher that she was uneasy reading out loud; so the teacher, who was confident of the inventory's flexibility, decided to begin at a level slightly lower than that indicated by the word lists. Figure 11–3 shows the two passages that Debby read; they correspond to grade levels 1 and 2.

Before each passage the teacher read a focusing statement and asked Debby what the passage might be about. That approach allowed Debby to activate expectations and provided the teacher with an indication of Debby's background knowledge relative to the passage. Then Debby read each passage. With Passage 1 Debby appeared to be reading for meaning: she self-corrected several miscues that did not make sense, and her reading of the last sentence was syntactically correct, preserving the text's intended meaning. She did appear to have some difficulty with the latter half of the passage. In one instance she omitted punctuation; in another, she made a question out of a statement. Word recognition miscues were scored as being between instructional and frustration levels, yet Debby's comprehension of the passage was at the independent level even though she missed one factual question.

Teacher judgment again determined whether the assessment should continue. When asked whether she wanted to read another passage, Debby answered yes. And since her comprehension was still at the independent level, the teacher decided to proceed. Another factor was Debby's admitted nervousness in reading aloud, which the teacher realized might have contributed to the number of miscues in her reading.

The second passage also indicated that Debby was actively processing the text and was trying to derive meaning from what she read. The comments that she made during the reading showed that she was interacting with what she was reading and was trying to relate the text to her existing knowledge base. Unfortunately, her answer to the third comprehension question revealed that she never did understand that Midnight was the horse's name. However, the fact that she was attempting to process what she read and was not simply reading words without thinking about meaning was important.

After this passage the teacher decided to discontinue the test. During the comprehension questioning Debby had begun exhibiting signs of frustration: she fidgeted in her chair, often looked around the room, began drumming her fingers, and showed signs of stress between questions. In addition, the scoring of Debby's miscues and comprehension questions indicated that both aspects bordered on the frustration level. At that point the teacher began reading the next passage to Debby, asking questions as before to evaluate listening comprehension. That procedure, also, was discontinued when the frustration level was reached on the comprehension questions.

After finishing the inventory, Debby's teacher completed the summary sheet shown in Figure 11–4. Published IRIs usually include summary pages as part of the inventory. This particular summary includes information about word recognition (WR) miscues from the word lists as well as Debby's comprehension (COMP) errors on the IRI passages. Additionally, a **listening capacity (LC) level** is indicated, which reflects Debby's comprehension level aside from any decoding factors. Theoretically, the difference between a student's listening capacity (or listening comprehension) and his or her reading comprehension indicates whether that student is reading to potential (Harris & Sipay, 1990). The summary sheet also notes any trends or patterns in Debby's reading.

listening capacity (LC) level: Measures a student's comprehension aside from any decoding factors.

The checklist that follows summarizes and expands on the example you have just read. These steps should help you administer any IRI effectively.

## IRI Administration Checklist

1. Have all materials ready. Type word lists on separate sheets of paper or cards, as needed. Avoid having to shuffle papers during the session with the student. Be familiar with a marking system and the passages.
2. Have a tape recorder ready. It is sometimes difficult to keep up with the reader, and most students don't mind if a tape recorder is used unobtrusively. However, don't turn the recorder on and off throughout the session, drawing undue attention to the machine.
3. Begin with a word list one or two grade levels below the student's actual grade. This selection may vary, depending on your knowledge of a student or the specific instructions of a given IRI.
4. Continue with word lists until the criterion level for miscues has been reached. Record all discrepancies between the student's reading and the words on the list.
5. Begin the IRI passages at a level one or two grades below that of the word list on which the criterion error level was reached. Use your knowledge of the student and your observation during administration of the word lists to modify the level of the initial passage as necessary. Also, consult the IRI manual guidelines regarding the entry level of the test being used.
6. Be sure to read the focusing statement to the student before allowing the student to begin reading the passage. A brief discussion can take place to activate the student's prior knowledge, but the teacher should not provide any information or clues about the passage.
7. Note any miscues during oral reading of the passages. Record any discrepancies between the student's reading and the original text.
8. Ask the student the comprehension questions for each passage, noting errors and recording the student's responses. Do not allow the student to refer to the passage. It is appropriate to give partial credit for answers.

FIGURE 11-2
Graded word lists

---

*Form A* Part 1 / Graded Word Lists

| PP | | P | | 1 | | 2 | |
|----|--|---|--|---|--|---|--|
| 1 for | _____ | 1 was | _____ | 1 many | + | 1 stood | + |
| 2 blue | _____ | 2 day | _____ | 2 painted | + | 2 climb | + |
| 3 car | _____ | 3 three | _____ | 3 feet | + | 3 isn't | + |
| 4 to | _____ | 4 farming | _____ | 4 them | + | 4 beautiful | bōw – beautiful _____ |
| 5 and | _____ | 5 bus | _____ | 5 food | + | 5 waiting | + |
| 6 it | _____ | 6 now | _____ | 6 tell | + | 6 head | + |
| 7 helps | _____ | 7 read | _____ | 7 her | + | 7 cowboy | + |
| 8 stop | _____ | 8 children | _____ | 8 please | + | 8 high | + |
| 9 funny | _____ | 9 went | _____ | 9 peanut | + | 9 people | + |
| 10 can | _____ | 10 then | _____ | 10 cannot | + | 10 mice | + |
| 11 big | _____ | 11 black | _____ | 11 eight | _____ | 11 corn | + |
| 12 said | _____ | 12 barn | _____ | 12 trucks | _____ | 12 everyone | + |
| 13 green | _____ | 13 trees | _____ | 13 garden | _____ | 13 strong | + |
| 14 look | _____ | 14 brown | _____ | 14 drop | _____ | 14 I'm | am ⌐ |
| 15 play | _____ | 15 good | _____ | 15 stopping | _____ | 15 room | + |
| 16 see | _____ | 16 into | _____ | 16 frog | _____ | 16 blows | + |
| 17 there | _____ | 17 she | _____ | 17 street | _____ | 17 gray | + |
| 18 little | _____ | 18 something | _____ | 18 fireman | _____ | 18 that's | + |
| 19 is | _____ | 19 what | _____ | 19 birthday | _____ | 19 throw | + |
| 20 work | _____ | 20 saw | _____ | 20 let's | _____ | 20 own | on |
| | _____ % | | _____ % | | 100 % | | 90–95 % |

*Teacher note:* If the child missed five words in any column—stop Part 1. Begin Graded Paragraphs, Part 2, (Form A), at highest level in which child recognized all 20 words. To save time, if the first ten words were correct, go on to the next list. If one of the first ten words were missed, continue the entire list.

FIGURE 11-2
*continued*

---

**Form A Part 1**

| 3 | | 4 | | 5 | | 6 | |
|---|---|---|---|---|---|---|---|
| 1 hour | *hoar* | 1 spoon | + | 1 whether | _____ | 1 sentinel | _____ |
| 2 senseless | *sendless* | 2 dozen | + | 2 hymn | _____ | 2 nostrils | _____ |
| 3 turkeys | + | 3 trail | + | 3 sharpness | _____ | 3 marsh | _____ |
| 4 anything | + | 4 machine | *matching* | 4 amount | _____ | 4 sensitive | _____ |
| 5 chief | + | 5 bound | *brown* c | 5 shrill | _____ | 5 calmly | _____ |
| 6 foolish | + | 6 exercise | *ex-* P | 6 freedom | _____ | 6 tangle | _____ |
| 7 enough | + | 7 disturbed | *dis-disturb* | 7 loudly | _____ | 7 wreath | _____ |
| 8 either | *other* | 8 force | + | 8 scientists | _____ | 8 teamwork | _____ |
| 9 chased | + | 9 weather | + | 9 musical | _____ | 9 billows | _____ |
| 10 robe | + | 10 rooster | + | 10 considerable | _____ | 10 knights | _____ |
| 11 crowd | + | 11 mountain(s) | _____ | 11 examined | _____ | 11 instinct | _____ |
| 12 crawl | + | 12 island | *is-land* | 12 scarf | _____ | 12 liberty | _____ |
| 13 unhappy | + | 13 hook | + | 13 muffled | _____ | 13 pounce | _____ |
| 14 clothes | + | 14 guides | + | 14 pacing | _____ | 14 rumored | _____ |
| 15 hose | *house* c | 15 moan | + | 15 oars | _____ | 15 strutted | _____ |
| 16 pencil | + | 16 settlers | *sletters* | 16 delicious | _____ | 16 dragon | _____ |
| 17 meat | + | 17 pitching | + | 17 octave | _____ | 17 hearth | _____ |
| 18 discover | + | 18 prepared | *period* | 18 terrific | _____ | 18 shifted | _____ |
| 19 picture | + | 19 west | + | 19 salmon | _____ | 19 customers | _____ |
| 20 nail | + | 20 (k)nowledge | *nowledge* | 20 briskly | _____ | 20 blond | _____ |
| | *80-85*% | | *60-65*% | | _____ % | | _____ % |

**Source:** From N. J. Silvaroli, *Classroom Reading Inventory* (6th ed.) (Dubuque, IA: Wm. C. Brown, 1990), pp. 52–53. Reprinted by permission.

FIGURE 11–3

Graded passages

---

*Form A* Part 2/*Level 1* (43 words)　　　　　　　　　　　　　　　W.P.M.

／2580

*Background Knowledge Assessment.* This story is about spiders. What can you tell me about spiders?

　　　　　　　　　　　　　　　　　adequate ☐　　　　inadequate ☐

### Plant Spiders

There are all kinds of spiders.
~~These~~ ᶜ
~~This~~ black and green one is called ~~a~~ the plant spider.
The　is/his feet are small ᶜ- whole
~~A~~ plant spider ~~has~~ small feet.　　　sent
The
~~All~~ spiders have small feet.
　　　　have the
Plant spiders ~~live in~~ nests ?
　　　　　・They
They soon learn to hunt for food ~~and~~ build new
　　　　　　　∧
nests.

**Scoring Guide** First

| SIG WR Errors | | COMP Errors | |
|---|---|---|---|
| IND | 0 | ⟨IND | 0–1⟩ |
| ~~INST~~ | ~~2~~ | INST | 1½–2 |
| FRUST | 4+ | FRUST | 2½+ |

### Comprehension Check

"humm"(F)　1. ⎓　Is there more than one kind of spider?
　　　　　　　(Yes—many more) NO.

　　　　+
(F)　2. ―　What two things do plant spiders quickly learn?
　　　　　(Hunt for food and build new nests)

(F)　3. +　What color was the spider in this story?
　　　　　(Black and green)

(F)　4. +　What did the story say about the spider's feet?
　　　　　(Small feet, little) teeny small ones!

(I)　5. +　What does this spider probably eat?
　　　　　(Insects, bugs) Bugs and things

---

*Form A* Part 2/*Level 2* (54 words)　　　　　　　　　　　　　　　W.P.M.

／3240

*Background Knowledge Assessment.* At a rodeo cowboys show their skill with wild horses and bulls. Have you ever seen a rodeo (real, movie, T.V.)?

　　　　　　　　　　　　　　　　　adequate ☐　　　　inadequate ☐

### The Rodeo

The people at the rodeo stood up.

They were all waiting for the big ride. ride at
　　　　　　　　　　　　　　midnight. Or
Everyone came to see Bob ⟨Hill⟩ ride Midnight.　is that the
　　　at the　　　　　　　　horses?
Bob Hill is ~~a~~ top rider.　　　　name?

Midnight is the best horse in the show.
　a
He is big and fast. Midnight is a black horse.
　　∧
　　　the
Can Bob Hill ride ~~this~~ great horse?
　　　　　　—"I don't know!"

**Scoring Guide** Second

| SIG WR Errors | | COMP Errors | |
|---|---|---|---|
| IND | 0 | IND | 0–1 |
| ⟨INST⟩ | ⟨3⟩ | ⟨INST⟩ | ⟨1½–2⟩ |
| FRUST | 5+ | FRUST | 2½+ |

### Comprehension Check

(F)　1. +　What did the people do?
　　　　　(Stood up, were waiting, etc.)

(I)　2. +　The people seemed to be excited, why?
　　　　　(They wanted to see this great horse and or rider.)

(F)　3. ⎓　What was the name of the horse?
　　　　　(Midnight) "Don't know" —answer provided

(F)　4. +　What did he (Midnight) look like?
　　　　　(Big, black, strong, etc.)

(F)　5. ⎓　Why do you think that Bob Hill was a good rider?
　　　　　(The story said he was a top rider. He had practice.)

　　　　　He was at the rodeo

---

**Source:** From N. J. Silvaroli, *Classroom Reading Inventory* (6th ed.)(Dubuque, IA: Wm. C. Brown, 1990), pp. 55–56. Reprinted by permission.

FIGURE 11-4
Summary sheet for an IRI

## Form A Inventory Record

### Summary Sheet

Student's Name **Debby**     Grade **2**    Age (Chronological) **7 2**
                                                                                                    yrs. mos.
Date **9/8**    School _____ Administered by _____

| Part 1 Word Lists | | | Part 2 Graded Paragraphs | | |
|---|---|---|---|---|---|
| Grade Level | Percent of Words Correct | Word Recognition Errors | SIG WR | Comp | L.C. |

Part 1 — Word Lists:

| Grade Level | Percent of Words Correct | Word Recognition Errors |
|---|---|---|
| PP | _____ | Consonants |
| 1 P | _____ | ___ Consonants |
| 1 | | ___ blends |
| | 100 | ✓ digraphs |
| | | ___ endings |
| | | ___ compounds |
| | | ___ contractions |
| | | Vowels |
| | | ✓ long |
| | | ___ short |
| | | ___ long/short oo |
| 2 | 90-95 | ___ vowel + r |
| | | ___ diphthong |
| | | ✓ vowel comb. |
| | | ___ a + 1 or w |
| | | Syllable |
| 3 | 80-85 | ___ visual patterns |
| 4 | 60-65 | ✓ prefix |
| | | ___ suffix |
| 5 | _____ | Word Recognition reinforcement and |
| 6 | _____ | Vocabulary development |

Part 2 — Graded Paragraphs:

| | SIG WR | Comp | L.C. |
|---|---|---|---|
| PP | | | |
| P | | | |
| 1 | INST/FRUST | IND | |
| 2 | INST | INST | |
| 3 | | | 90 |
| 4 | | | 90 |
| 5 | | | 75 |
| 6 | | | |
| 7 | | | |
| 8 | | | |

Estimated Levels

| | Grade |
|---|---|
| Independent | 1 |
| Instructional | 2 (range) |
| Frustration | 3 |
| Listening Capacity | 5 |

Comp Errors
  **3** Factual (F)
  **0** Inference (I)
  **0** Vocabulary (V) (none in her 2 passages)
  **N/A** "Word Caller"
    (A student who reads without associating meaning)
  **N/A** Poor Memory

Summary of Specific Needs:

MINIMAL INFORMATION ON WHICH TO BASE WORD RECOGNITION ERROR PATTERNS. SUGGEST DIAGNOSTIC TEST IF CLASSROOM OBSERVATIONS CONFIRM THE PATTERNS NOTED HERE.

Permission is granted by the publisher to reproduce pp. 51 through 62.

**Source:** From N. J. Silvaroli, *Classroom Reading Inventory* (6th ed.)(Dubuque, IA: Wm. C. Brown, 1990), pp. 51. Reprinted by permission.

9. Discontinue the student's oral reading of the IRI passages when the frustration level has been reached. Again, use your own judgment. Some students reach frustration level earlier on word recognition errors than they do on comprehension questions. Other students reverse that pattern, and still others reach frustration level simultaneously in both aspects. Discontinue if both word recognition and comprehension aspects test at frustration level; use your judgment about continuing the test if only one aspect is at this level. In any case let your observation of the student in the testing situation guide your decision about when to stop.

10. To determine listening capacity (or listening comprehension level), begin reading the next passage beyond the one on which you discontinued the student's oral reading. Ask comprehension questions as before. Listening capacity indicates the level at which students can comprehend information presented orally, rather than in written form. Discontinue testing after the frustration level has been reached, as indicated by the score on the comprehension questions.

**MODEL
LESSON**

### Informal Reading Inventory

Joann and her parents have just moved to a new neighborhood, where school has been in session for just over one month. On Joann's first day Ms. Chen welcomes her to her third-grade class and introduces Joann to her new classmates. To help place Joann in an appropriate reading group, Ms. Chen decides to administer an informal reading inventory. The testing takes place while the other students are involved in art activities under the supervision of Ms. Chen's parent-volunteer aide.

Ms. Chen uses the IRI provided with her published reading program. After administering the appropriate word lists and passages, Ms. Chen decides that Joann is able to read material just a little more difficult than that being read by the average readers in her class. However, Ms. Chen wants to confirm her assessment through some regular classroom work and also wants Joann to experience success in her new situation, so Ms. Chen places her with a group of average readers. She makes a note on her class record sheet, though, to review Joann's work after a short period of time to see whether she should be moved to more difficult material.

**Creating an Informal Reading Inventory.** There are many published IRIs readily available, and most published reading programs also include an IRI. Nonetheless, you may sometime wish to create your own. For example, you might want IRI passages to come from a specific set of materials that will be used in class. Such passages would have more curricular validity than a generic IRI. In order to create your own IRI, you will need to choose passages at various levels and will also need to know scoring guidelines to establish independent, instructional, and frustration reading levels. With published IRIs the specific number of miscues corresponding to each of the reading levels for a given passage is generally determined by the percentage of miscues within the total words read (for word recognition) or the percentage of wrong answers within the number of comprehension questions (for comprehension). However, there has been some disagreement regarding the scoring criteria for IRIs (Aulls, 1982; Betts, 1946; Cooper, 1952; Powell, 1970). This text agrees with Burns, Roe, and Ross (1988), who suggest combining the criteria proposed by Johnson, Kress, and Pikulski (1987) with those of Powell (1970). You can use the result, shown here, to determine reading levels on an IRI, but you should remember that these percentages are only approximate guidelines.

| Reading Level | Word Recognition Accuracy | | Comprehension Accuracy |
|---|---|---|---|
| independent | 99% or higher | (and) | 90% or higher |
| instructional | 85% or higher (Grades 1–2) | (and) | 75% or higher |
| | 95% or higher (Grades 3 and above) | (and) | 75% or higher |
| frustration | below 90% | (or) | below 50% |
| listening capacity | | | 75% or higher |

## Informal Tests: The Cloze Procedure

The **cloze procedure** is another way to match readers to materials. It is sometimes preferred to the IRI because it allows group rather than individual administration. A cloze task also involves a student directly with the text, without the intervening teacher questions. Table 11–2 outlines the major differences between cloze and IRI. As described earlier, a cloze procedure presents students with a passage that has blanks in place of some of the words. Students attempt to fill in the blanks with the words that were deleted from the original passage. The teacher uses the scoring procedure described later in this section to indicate whether the passage is at independent, instructional, or frustration level for the student and, thus, whether the material from which the passage came is appropriate.

cloze procedure: A fill-in-the-blank task used to estimate the level at which a child can read with assistance.

Cloze gained widespread use after its modification by Taylor (1953). With its roots in Gestalt psychology, cloze makes use of the human drive to add closure to incomplete items. In the reading cloze procedure, this inclination has been translated into the reader's use of context to complete passages from which words have been systematically deleted. It is essentially a fill-in-the-blank task (see Warwick, 1978; Rankin, 1974, 1978).

**Constructing a Cloze Test.** In order to match students and materials, cloze passages can be constructed from the material that students will be reading. The passages should be representative of that material and should not be

TABLE 11–2
General differences between cloze and IRI

|  | Cloze | IRI |
| --- | --- | --- |
| Administration | Group or individual | Individual |
|  | Written (or oral) | Oral |
|  | Passages | Word lists, passages, oral questions |
| Uses | Match students and materials | Match students and materials |
|  | Find a student's general reading level | Find a student's general reading level |
|  | Provide general readability measure | Provide general readability measure |
|  |  | Permit inferences about student's reading process |
| Type of information | Ability to use context | Word recognition score |
|  | Comprehension score | Comprehension score |
|  | Independent, instructional, frustration reading levels | Listening capacity score |
|  |  | Independent, instructional, frustration reading levels |

broken up by illustrations or other potentially distractive features. Within the chosen passages, words are systematically deleted, and blanks are substituted for the deleted words. The following steps describe the construction of a cloze test in detail, and Figure 11–5 illustrates a cloze test ready for use.

1. Choose a representative passage from the beginning, middle, and end of material (usually a book) that you wish to use with your student(s). For high reliability, each passage should contain approximately 250 words, although that length may not be possible in primary grade materials. Using a number of representative passages is strongly recommended so that the results can be averaged, thereby increasing the validity and reliability of the procedure.
2. Leave the first sentence of the passage intact to provide a contextual base.
3. Beginning with the second sentence, replace every fifth word with a blank. Be sure that your blanks are the same size so that their length does not give a clue to the length of the deleted words. Continue until 50 words have been deleted, if possible. However, do not delete the following: proper names, dates, abbreviations, or acronyms. When such words are encountered, the next word is deleted, and the every-fifth-word rule proceeds from that point.
4. Conclude with a complete, intact sentence without deletions.

FIGURE 11–5
Sample cloze passage

> That evening they all had dinner together in the enchanter's cozy
> kitchen. Then Albion took Petronella _____ to a stone
> building _____ unbolted its door. Inside _____ seven
> huge black dogs.
>
> " _____ must watch my hounds _____ night,"
> said he.
>
> Petronella _____ in, and Albion closed _____
> locked the door.
>
> At _____ the hounds began to _____ and bark.
> They showed _____ teeth at her. But Petronella
> _____ a real princess. She _____ up her courage.
> Instead _____ backing away, she went _____ the
> dogs. She began _____ speak to them in _____ quiet
> voice. They stopped _____ and sniffed at her.
> _____ patted their heads.
>
> "I _____ what it is," she _____ . "You are
> lonely here. _____ will keep you company."
>
> _____ so all night long, _____ sat on the
> floor _____ talked to the hounds _____ stroked them.
> They lay _____ to her.
>
> In the _____ , Albion came and let _____ out.
> "Ah," said he, " _____ see that you are _____ . If you
> had run _____ the dogs, they would _____ torn you
> to pieces. _____ you may ask for _____ you want."
>
> "I want _____ comb for my hair," _____
> Petronella.
>
> The enchanter gave _____ a comb carved from
> _____ piece of black wood.
>
> Prince Ferdinand _____ sunning himself and working
> _____ a crossword puzzle. Petronella _____ to him in
> a _____ voice, "I am doing _____ for you."
>
> "That's nice," _____ the prince. "What's 'selfish'
> _____ nine letters?"
>
> "You are," _____ Petronella. She went to
> _____ enchanter. "I will work _____ you once more,"
> she _____ . That night Albion led _____ to a stable.
> Inside were seven huge horses.

**Source:** From J. Williams, *Petronella* (New York: Scholastic, 1973). Reprinted by permission.

**Scoring and Interpreting a Cloze Test.** A cloze test is similar to an informal reading inventory in that it provides an indication of a reader's independent, instructional, and frustration reading levels. Cloze tests determine that level by calculating the percentage of exact replacements of deleted words. Synonyms are not counted as correct in scoring a cloze test. For the cloze test shown in Figure 11–5, the following replacements were provided by Lee, a third-grade student. Underlined numbers indicate correct replacements, making Lee's score 24 out of 50 or 48 percent.

| Original Deletion | Lee's Replacement | Original Deletion | Lee's Replacement |
|---|---|---|---|
| 1. out | away | 26. close | beside |
| 2. and | and | 27. morning | morning |
| 3. were | sat | 28. her | her |
| 4. you | we | 29. I | I |
| 5. all | all | 30. brave | alive |
| 6. went | went | 31. from | No response |
| 7. and | and | 32. have | have |
| 8. once | No response | 33. now | so |
| 9. snarl | growl | 34. what | anything |
| 10. their | their | 35. a | a |
| 11. was | No response | 36. said | said |
| 12. plucked | No response | 37. her | her |
| 13. of | of | 38. a | a |
| 14. toward | toward | 39. was | lay |
| 15. to | to | 40. at | No response |
| 16. a | her | 41. said | said |
| 17. snarling | No response | 42. low | nice |
| 18. she | she | 43. this | this |
| 19. see | know | 44. said | said |
| 20. said | said | 45. in | about |
| 21. I | No response | 46. snapped | said |
| 22. and | then | 47. the | the |
| 23. she | she | 48. for | with |
| 24. and | and | 49. said | cried |
| 25. and | then | 50. her | Petronella |

Several researchers have attempted to specify the scoring criteria for interpreting cloze results (Bormuth, 1968; Rankin, 1971; Rankin & Culhane, 1969). Although this text like Aulls' (1982), suggests the percentage bands noted by Rankin and Culhane, Bormuth's percentages are also noted here. Both scales are widely accepted.

| Reading Level | Percentage of Exact Replacements (Rankin & Culhane) | Percentage of Exact Replacements (Bormuth) |
|---|---|---|
| independent | above 60% | above 57% |
| instructional | 40% to 59% | 44% to 57% |
| frustration | below 40% | below 44% |

In our example, Lee's percentage of replacements was 48, putting his reading of the passage at the instructional level.

**Common Questions About Cloze.** *Why are only exact replacements counted and not synonyms?* The **exact replacement criterion** allows more accurate scoring and resolves the potential problem of different interpretations by different people. Some might argue, for example, that *home* and *house* are not the same—that a house is only a building, whereas a home implies much more. Because of the exact replacement criterion, however, the percentages corresponding to the various reading levels are set quite low. Thus, a student can correctly replace as few as 4 out of 10 deletions (40 percent) yet still be placed at the instructional reading level. In addition, the percentage bands for the various reading levels are quite wide—20 percent for the instructional level—so that students are not penalized. Some people do score synonyms as correct, but they must then use higher scoring percentages, and the test becomes more difficult to score, thus taking more teacher time.

exact replacement criterion: A scoring procedure that counts as correct only responses that match the precise words deleted from the text.

*How accurate is the cloze procedure?* The cloze procedure is quick and easy to use and provides approximate measurements consistently. Because teacher judgment plays a significant part in cloze interpretation, students should be given the benefit of the doubt if their percentage scores border the bands separating the different reading levels. The test is most accurate when at least three passages are used from the material under consideration.

*Should there be a time limit when administering a cloze test?* No. Generally, students are given as much time as they wish to complete the cloze passage, and they are certainly allowed to go through a passage more than once.

*Does spelling count when scoring a student's replacements?* No. This is not a spelling test.

**Other Uses of the Cloze Procedure.** The cloze test has traditionally been used to examine the match between readers and specific reading material. However, there are other ways in which the cloze procedure can benefit the reading teacher. First, the cloze test can be used with a graded set of materials to determine a student's general reading level. This approach allows the teacher to generalize the student's score beyond the material from which the cloze test was constructed. With this application a set of graded passages should be used to construct a series of cloze tests. Scoring should then provide a rough guide to the student's reading level (corresponding to the grade level of the passage) at which frustration reading level is reached. Instead of a leveled set of passages taken from a published reading program, readability formulas (discussed later in this chapter) can also be used to determine the reading grade level of the selected passages.

The other common use for cloze is as a teaching technique with several variations. For instance, teachers might delete specific parts of speech (e.g., nouns, adjectives, or verbs) or might provide choices above the blanks. As an instructional aid, however, cloze requires time for meaningful discussion of replacements. It is not enough to simply grade a student's effort; instead, students must be led to understand why given replacements are appropriate, what other options might fit, and why some replacements are not very good choices.

## Informal Tests: Additional Measures

In addition to informal reading inventories and cloze tests, there are other informal assessment tools that teachers commonly use as a part of their instructional program. Wade (1990) has suggested that oral think-alouds can be used to assess comprehension. This procedure is somewhat related to the use of retellings.

**retelling scores:** A measure of comprehension obtained by having readers tell in their own words what they have just read.

**Retelling Scores.** **Retelling scores** are derived when students are asked to read a passage and then retell in their own words what was read. Retellings are useful measures of comprehension. They have been used in informal reading inventories to supplement or, at times, replace the comprehension questions generally asked at the end of an IRI passage. Some believe that retellings are more accurate than answers to questions, because questions can sometimes be answered from general knowledge without even reading the passage. In fact, Allington, Chodos, Domaracki, and Truex (1977) have shown that approximately 30 percent of the questions asked in informal reading inventories are **passage independent**. That is, they can be answered without first reading the passage to which they refer (see also Tuinman, 1974, for a discussion of passage dependent/passage independent questions).

**passage independent:** Describes questions that can be answered from general knowledge rather than from a reading of the text.

**idea units:** Thought units used to determine comprehension.

To use retelling as an assessment procedure, the teacher should first divide the original passage into units, often called **idea units,** or thought units. The following example would be categorized as two idea units.

The boy ran / although his leg was hurt.

To increase the reliability of this procedure, two people should work together to segment the passage. Thereafter, the following procedure and scoring system can be used (Clark, 1982; Morrow, 1988)

1. Assign each unit a number from 1 through 3 in terms of its importance (1 being very important, perhaps a main idea, and 3 being of relatively little importance, perhaps an insignificant detail).
2. Make a three-columned scoring sheet with the importance ratings on the left, the units in the middle, and recording space on the right (see Figure 11–6).
3. As the child retells the passage, use the right-hand column to number the units in the order in which they are recalled.
4. Score the recall by first comparing the sequence of the recalled units with that of the original, then totaling the number of units recalled in each category of importance, and finally dividing that number by the total possible in each category.

Comparing the three categories allows inferences about how well the reader has understood and remembered the various levels in the passage.

Figure 11–6 shows a completed retelling measure for a passage introduced in Chapter 4 (Carson, 1990). An instructional reading level was determined by the degree of consistency between the retelling and the segmented passage. Generally, a 60 to 70 percent match is used as the criterion for the instructional reading level. However, that determination is influenced by teacher judgment, especially as it relates to the amount and specificity of the ideas recalled and the order and fluency of the retelling. In addition, it is important that students have an opportunity to practice the retelling procedure before it is used in evaluation. Morrow (1988) points out that students who are unfamiliar with the procedure do not know what is being asked of them and are at a disadvantage.

**Assessment of Attitudes and Interests.** One of the most powerful pieces of information available to a teacher is an awareness of student attitudes and interests. Informal measures can be used to discover motivational topics that can enhance instruction. Published reading programs provide assessment inventories, and other published inventories are also available. However, teacher-made assessments in this area are often more valuable than those commercially available.

Unfortunately, it is easy to get so involved in teaching students how to read that enhancing reading ability becomes an end in itself. This situation can lead to students who are able to read but do not want to. On the other hand, when students develop a love of reading, it becomes a lifelong activity. Thus, the most effective teachers go beyond simply teaching students how to read; they show students that reading is relevant and interesting. And materials that students find interesting lead to increased time on task and enhanced learning.

Figures 11–7 and 11–8 show items from Dulin and Chester's (1984) interest and attitude surveys (see also Dulin, 1984). Those items demonstrate

FIGURE 11-6
Completed retelling score form

| Importance | Unit | Retelling Sequence |
|---|---|---|
| 1 | Tracy | 1 |
| 1 | knew she would not | 2 |
| 1 | be able to sleep. | 3 |
| 3 | But her mother | |
| 3 | had told her | |
| 2 | to brush her teeth | |
| 2 | and put on her nightgown anyway, | |
| 3 | and Tracy did as she was told. | |
| 3 | Just as she | 4 |
| 3 | got into her nightgown, | 5 |
| 1 | a loud crack of thunder | 6 |
| 3 | filled the air! | |
| 1 | Tracy jumped into bed | 7 |
| 2 | and pulled the covers | |
| 3 | over her head. | |
| 3 | When Meg | 12 |
| 3 | peeked into the room, | 13 |
| 3 | Tracy wailed, | |
| 2 | "The last time | 8 |
| 2 | we had a storm like this, | 9 |
| 2 | I stayed awake | 10 |
| 2 | all night!" | 11 |
| 2 | Meg sat | 14 |
| 2 | beside Tracy | 15 |
| 3 | and tucked her little sister in. | |
| 2 | Then she started to hum softly. | 16 |
| 2 | It was one of Tracy's | 17 |
| 2 | favorite songs. | 18 |
| 2 | As the song went on, | |
| 2 | Meg noticed that Tracy's eyes | 20 |
| 3 | had closed. | 21 |
| 2 | Meg turned off the bedroom light | 19 |
| 2 | as she tiptoed | |
| 2 | out of the room, | |
| 1 | Tracy didn't hear | 23 |
| 1 | the next clap of thunder | |
| 2 | as the storm continued | 22 |
| 3 | into the night. | |

| | Units Recalled | Possible Units | Score (%) |
|---|---|---|---|
| Category 1: | 6 | 6 | 100% |
| Category 2: | 12 | 18 | 67% |
| Category 3: | 5 | 13 | 38% |
| Total: | 23 | 37 | 62% |

Comments: OVER 60% MATCH IN UNITS RECALLED. FAIRLY CLOSE MATCH IN SEQUENCE ORDER. HAS A GOOD SENSE OF IMPORTANT INFORMATION. INSTRUCTIONAL LEVEL.

that attitude/interest measures can examine various important aspects related to reading instruction:

- how students feel about reading
- how they feel about various instructional methods and reward systems
- how they feel about different types of materials

Note the different response methods that students can use to indicate their attitudes and interests.

The affective information gathered through interest/attitude inventories should be added to the informal classroom records previously discussed. In addition, since children's interests and attitudes change fairly quickly, these measures should be attempted several times during a year, along with ongoing anecdotal records of current trends, fads, and interests.

**Stress Factors in Reading.** A poor attitude toward reading can indicate that a student is experiencing stress resulting from poor reading skills or from a teacher's demands to read. Gentile and McMillan (1987, 1988) point out that stress is often related to reading difficulty and present a scale for assessing stress reactions to reading (see Figure 11–9). They categorize students' stress reactions as fight or flight responses. Fight responses manifest themselves in confrontations with the teacher and with reading material; they can be summarized as "I won't read, and you can't make me." With this response students condemn reading, books, school, and teachers; anxiety is directed outward, and the students are confrontational. The flight reaction can be characterized as "I can't read and no one can teach me." These students condemn themselves; anxiety is directed inward, and they retreat from teachers (Gentile & McMillan, 1988, p. 21).

To interpret the Stress Reaction Scale, teachers must count the number of $a$ and $b$ responses. A large majority of $a$ responses indicates a fight reaction; a large majority of $b$ responses indicates a flight reaction. Gentile and McMillan recommend a number of specific strategies, depending on a student's score. Their strategies focus on goal setting, personal incentives, and self-monitoring. In general, teachers working with fight-response students need to channel the students away from confrontation and into reading. Flight-response students must be drawn out and interested in successful completion of reading tasks. Normally, fight reactions are more easily dealt with because they have a force behind them that can be redirected into reading. Flight reactions are generally passive, and teachers must intervene more directly to involve students and provide them with feelings of success.

## Teacher-Made Tests

Perhaps the most common assessment instruments used in reading classrooms are teacher made. Such measures have the advantage of being closely tied to the curriculum and program being taught; they can be written to apply spe-

FIGURE 11–7

Excerpts from the Reading Interest Questionnaire

I. The first part of the inventory consists of a series of choices to be made between different leisure-time activities, some dealing with reading and others not. You're to indicate your choices by marking a series of scales, and it works like this.

At each of the two ends of each scale there'll be an activity, something you could do in your spare time if you wanted to. If you'd <u>much</u> rather do one of the activities than the other, mark the box <u>nearest to</u> that activity, like this:

| read a<br>book | X |  |  |  |  | watch<br>TV |
|---|---|---|---|---|---|---|

\*      \*      \*

II. Now, to take the next part of the inventory, you're to <u>grade</u> twenty statements in terms of how you feel about them. If you STRONGLY AGREE with a statement, give it an A; if you TEND TO AGREE with it, give it a B; if you feel FAIRLY NEUTRAL about it, give it a C; if you TEND TO DISAGREE with it, give it a D; and if you STRONGLY DISAGREE with it, give it an E. Be sure to read each statement carefully before you circle a grade for it, and be sure to grade <u>every</u> statement.

1. Reading is for learning but not for enjoyment.    A  B  C  D  E

\*      \*      \*

III. This third part of the inventory calls for a bit of math ability. Your job this time is to <u>divide up 100</u> points among the following ten things in terms of <u>how desirable</u> you feel they are as leisure activities. Remember, the total should come out to 100.

| Activities | Points |
|---|---|
| Reading books |  |
| Reading magazines and newspapers |  |
| Watching television |  |

\*      \*      \*

IV. And finally, to tell us a few things about <u>you</u> personally, please respond to the following scales by circling the answer to each which <u>best describes you</u>.

1. Compared to other people your own age, about <u>how well</u> do you think that you read?

| 1 | 2 | 3 | 4 | 5 |
|---|---|---|---|---|
| a good deal<br>better than most | somewhat<br>better than most | about as well as<br>most | somewhat less<br>well than most | a good deal<br>less well than<br>most |

2. Compared to other people your own age, about how much do you feel you <u>like</u> to read?

| 1 | 2 | 3 | 4 | 5 |
|---|---|---|---|---|
| a good deal<br>more than most | somewhat more<br>than most | about as much<br>as most | somewhat less<br>than most | a good deal<br>less than most |

**Source:** From K. L. Dulin and R. Chester, *Dulin-Chester Reading Interest Questionnaire* (Madison: University of Wisconsin, 1984). Reprinted by permission.

FIGURE 11–8

Excerpts from the Reading Attitude Scale

I. Here are possible rewards people get for reading. For each reward, circle the grade you're giving it.

1. getting a grade for how much reading you do          A   B   C   D   E
2. getting extra credit for how much reading you do    A   B   C   D   E
3. getting your name on a bulletin board for how much reading you do    A   B   C   D   E

\*     \*     \*

II. Sometimes things <u>teachers</u> do encourage us to read. Please grade the following ten things to show how much you think they'd encourage <u>you</u> to read. Again, circle the grade you're giving the activity.

1. having the teacher read a book to the class at a chapter a day    A   B   C   D   E
2. having the teacher read to the class the first few pages of books that you can then check out if you want to    A   B   C   D   E

\*     \*     \*

III. Now, here are some things you might do <u>after</u> reading a book or story in class.

1. take an oral test on a story or book you've read    A   B   C   D   E
2. use some of the new words in a story or book you've read for word-study    A   B   C   D   E

\*     \*     \*

IV. And finally, here are some <u>extra</u> things you could do after reading a story or book. Grade them with <u>these</u> grades.

     A = I'd <u>really</u> like to do this.      D = I'm <u>fairly sure</u> I wouldn't
     B = I'd <u>sort of</u> like to do this.       like <u>to</u> do this.
     C = I <u>might or might not</u> like to do this.    E = I'm <u>quite sure</u> I wouldn't like to do this.

1. make a play out of a story or book you've read    A   B   C   D   E
2. make a picture to go with a story or book you've read    A   B   C   D   E
3. have a discussion in class about a story or book you've read    A   B   C   D   E

\*     \*     \*

V. And finally, for the last part of the questionnaire, <u>divide up 100</u> points to show how much you like different <u>types</u> of reading material. Any one type <u>can</u> get from 0 to 100 points, but you should try to give at least <u>some</u> points to each.

| TYPES OF READING MATERIAL | POINTS |
|---|---|
| magazines | |
| newspapers | |
| comic-books | |
| hard-bound books | |
| paper-back books | |
| TOTAL | 100 |

**Source:** From K. L. Dulin and R. Chester, *Dulin-Chester Reading Attitude Scale* (Madison: University of Wisconsin, 1984). Reprinted by permission.

FIGURE 11–9
The Stress Reaction Scale for Reading

For each of the following phrases, circle the letter, *a* or *b,* that most accurately describes the student's reactions when asked to read or during reading. If *neither one* applies, write *N/O* on the blank to the right of each pair.

When asked to read or during reading, this student:

1. a. exhibits hostility or rage.
   b. becomes anxious or apprehensive. _____
2. a. becomes sullen or exhibits aggressive acting out behavior.
   b. appears indifferent, insecure, or fearful. _____
3. a. responds impulsively to requests or questions, blurts out answers, and offers information that is irrelevant or inaccurate.
   b. appears subdued, overly withdrawn, and depressed. _____
4. a. throws temper tantrums, cries, or becomes verbally abusive.
   b. seeks an escape or runs and hides. _____
5. a. clenches fists, becomes rigid, defiant, and angry.
   b. appears despondent, passive, and unable to concentrate. _____
6. a. becomes defensive and resistive, verbalizes or expresses an attitude of "I don't want to."
   b. lacks confidence, appears timid, verbalizes or expresses an attitude of "I can't, it's too hard." _____
7. a. demands entertaining, easy, or expedient activities, shows no tolerance for difficulty or challenge.
   b. takes no risks in challenging situations, constantly answers "I don't know," even when answers are obvious. _____
8. a. refuses to comply, does not follow directions or complete assignments.
   b. appears embarrassed, daydreams, or frets over lack of ability. _____
9. a. becomes upset with change in routine, manipulates the situation to satisfy personal needs or whims.
   b. requires constant assurance, frequently checks with teacher by asking "Did I get that right?" or "Was that good?" _____
10. a. seeks to disrupt the teacher, the lesson, or other students.
    b. expresses fear of rejection by parents, teachers, or peers for reading weaknesses. _____
11. a. uses any excuse for not being able to participate, temporizes until parent or teacher gives up.
    b. skips over material, ignores punctuation, inserts or depletes words and phrases, unable to follow structure or order. _____
12. a. demands constant supervision, attention, or guidance, refuses to do any independent reading.
    b. will try as long as parent or teacher closely monitors situation, appears helpless when left to work independently. _____
13. a. provides sarcastic, bizarre, or nonsensical answers to teachers' questions, makes weird sounds, sings, or bursts into loud, raucous laughter.
    b. becomes excessively self-critical, says things like "I'm dumb," "I never get anything right," or "I'm not a good reader." _____
14. a. declares reading is "boring," "no fun," "hard work," refuses to cooperate.
    b. tries too hard, is immobilized by perceived failure. _____
15. a. makes little or no effort to succeed, shows disdain for activities, voices anger or displeasure at parents, teachers, and students who offer assistance.
    b. verbalizes or expresses an attitude of apathy, shows no willingness to try. _____

**Source:** From L. M. Gentile and M. M. McMillan, "Reexamining the Role of Emotional Maladjustment," in S. M. Glazer, L. W. Searfoss, and L. M. Gentile (Eds.), *Reexamining Reading Diagnosis: New Trends and Procedures* (Newark, DE: International Reading Association, 1988), pp. 16–18. Reprinted by permission.

cifically to one student or a whole class. Length and number of items, testing duration, and format all vary in teacher-made tests.

Effective teachers must be aware of the wealth of information available to them and use it in an informed manner to make their daily instructional decisions. Assignments and worksheets are more than simple practice pieces for students; they are part of an overall data-gathering and decision-making process. Thus, in this context teacher-made tests go beyond quizzes or other graded items and include all the things that a teacher might ask a student to do as a part of the learning process, whether in the classroom, at home, or elsewhere. All such activities reveal student needs and capabilities.

Effective use of incidental and teacher-initiated information requires, first of all, keen observation of student behavior in all learning situations. Moreover, assessment is greatly facilitated by careful planning. For example, if a comprehension assignment or worksheet is carefully constructed to include all levels of comprehension, then a teacher can determine whether a student is having difficulty within a particular level(s) and can adjust instruction accordingly.

Monitoring all aspects of student performance requires a clear, up-to-date record-keeping system. Maintaining such a record of student strengths and weaknesses allows teachers to be much more focused in their instruction and to target specific students' individual needs. A record-keeping system for a vocabulary assignment might look like the one in Figure 11–10.

Observations of normal classroom reading tasks can be a valuable source of information for instructional decision making.

FIGURE 11–10
Sample class record sheet

---

ASSIGNMENT: *Vocabulary — write words in sentence, then use all words in story or paragraph. Words: observe, suspect, strut, elegant, modest.*

| NAME | COMMENTS | DATE: 10/12 |
|------|----------|------|

Allison   *Used words correctly. Misspelled elegant both times used "elegent"*

Bobby   *Left out strut, modest.*

Julio   *No problems.*

Kathleen   *Words used correctly. Neatness and hand-writing still a problem.*

Latisha   *modest, elegant used incorrectly*

Wanda   *modest used incorrectly.*

GENERAL COMMENTS: *Reteach modest. Have Kathleen recopy - grade only on neatness. See Bobby individually about this assignment. Add elegant, modest to spelling list*

---

## Portfolio Assessment

Especially for teachers in whole language classrooms, standardized tests may have relatively low curricular validity. That is, the tests may not match what has been taught prior to the test administration. Nonetheless, whole language programs often must match students' progress to a management system even though skills are not isolated or taught in a specified sequence in those classrooms. Teachers in both whole language and traditional classrooms are turning increasingly toward portfolio evaluation as a supplement to the assessment measures outlined earlier in this chapter. Portfolio assessment involves collecting students' work on an ongoing basis and examining it for evidence of growth in literacy. Rather than an evaluation based on norms or externally imposed criteria, portfolio assessment allows a teacher to see—and to show children, parents, and administrators—what students have done over time.

Lapp and Flood (1989) point out the difficulty of making parents understand that a student who achieves at the 50th percentile every year is making average and expected progress from grade to grade. They suggest that teachers place in student portfolios a variety of items that can be shared with parents and others as appropriate. Their suggestions are similar to the recommendations of others (e.g., see Farris, 1989; Jongsma, 1989; Pikulski, 1989) and are included in the following list:

- norm- and criterion-referenced test scores
- informal tests
- dated writing samples
- dated titles of books read voluntarily (e.g., during free reading time)
- dated samples of what students have read (photocopied pages)
- dated self-evaluations of reading ability and comments on feelings toward reading and writing.

There is increasing recognition that teachers are the experts with regard to their students and are in the best position to judge progress on a day-to-day basis (Harp, 1989; Johnston, 1987). Several checklists and specific forms have been suggested that can be used to summarize students' progress and then can be inserted into their portfolios. For example, Eeds (1988) has adapted suggestions by Gentry (1982) to aid teachers in documenting development in early writing (see Figure 11–11). Such forms can facilitate formal reporting to parents and the transfer of specific information to management forms, as required by many school districts.

Although it is not necessary to use any particular form, and teachers are encouraged to create their own evaluation summaries, it *is* important to document and summarize students' work periodically. To be effective, portfolio evaluation requires student samples or teacher comments every two to three weeks across all areas of literacy. Figure 11–12 illustrates the considerable growth in Tanisha's writing in only 4½ months. Note the longer sentences, more complete punctuation, improvement in capitalization, greater number of words, and better-formed letters. All of these features should be noted on a summary form, preferably one created by the teacher and inserted regularly into Tanisha's portfolio.

In addition to writing samples and summary sheets, portfolios should include photocopied pages from materials that students are reading fluently. Growth in reading can be easily shown when material read at the beginning of first grade (characterized by short sentences, single-syllable words, large print,

FIGURE 11–11

Checklist for developmental stages in early writing

| Name _____ Age _____ Grade _____ | | | | |
|---|---|---|---|---|
| | I | II | III | IV |
| **Precommunicative Stage**          Date | | | | |
| 1. Produces letters or letter like forms to represent a message. | | | | |
| 3. Demonstrates left-to-right concept. | | | | |
| 4. Demonstrates top-bottom concept. | | | | |
| 5. Repeats known letters and numbers. | | | | |
| 6. Uses many letters and/or numbers. | | | | |
| 7. Mixes upper and lowercase letters. | | | | |
| 8. Indicates preference for uppercase forms. | | | | |
| **The Semiphonetic Stage**          Date | | | | |
| 1. Realizes letters represent sounds. | | | | |
| 2. Represents whole words with one or more letters. | | | | |
| 3. Evidence of letter name strategy. | | | | |
| 4. Demonstrates left-to-right sequence of letters. | | | | |
| 5. Puts spaces between words. | | | | |
| **The Phonetic Stage**          Date | | | | |
| 1. Represents every sound heard. | | | | |
| 2. Assigns letters based on sounds as child hears them (invented spellings). | | | | |
| 3. Puts spaces between words. | | | | |
| 4. Masters letter formation. | | | | |
| **The Transitional Stage**          Date | | | | |
| 1. Utilizes conventional spellings. | | | | |
| 2. Vowels appear in every syllable. | | | | |
| 3. Evidence of visual as opposed to phonetic strategy. | | | | |
| 4. Reverses some letters in words. | | | | |

Comments _____

_____

_____

_____

**Source:** From M. Eeds, "Holistic assessment of coding ability," in S. M. Glazer, L. W. Searfoss, and L. M. Gentile (Eds.), *Reexamining reading diagnosis: New trends and procedures* (Newark, DE: International Reading Association, 1988), p. 56. Reprinted by permission.

many pictures, and short selections) is compared to material being read in the middle of first grade. Students like to be able to look back at their progress, and parents are able to see how far their children have come.

Self-reports by students—either through interviews or, in higher grades, through writing—should also be a part of portfolios. Wixson, Bosky,

FIGURE 11–12

Writing samples from Tanisha's first-grade portfolio: (a) September 9, ("I like to help my daddy, Leon. He's building! I like Nintendos!"); (b) January 31.

(a) Tanisha
ILIKEToHELPmYdadeLEon
HisBuilcLing !
ILiKENiNTENdoc

(b)
My Favorite Animal
By Tanisha            Jan. 31
    I like monkeys because
they are good at tricks.
I mean tricks! They are
better then a poodle.

Yochum, and Alvermann (1984) have noted that self-assessment interviews can provide much valuable information. Such reports can indicate what is being read, what reactions students have toward reading and writing, what strategies they use when they come to a hard word, how they select reading materials, what they think they are learning, how well they think they are doing, where help might be appreciated, and so on. Self-reports should be completed on a regular schedule.

Portfolios should not be viewed as a teacher's property. They change over time because of all that goes into them, and student access should be encouraged, especially to revise work or to add information about reading and writing. Furthermore, students should develop pride in their portfolios and should be encouraged to share them with others. Peer input, in turn, may prompt effective writing revision and book selection. Teachers must be careful, however, to structure sharing experiences so that they are meaningful and helpful.

Students should always know how their portfolios will be used—especially if teachers plan to use them to determine grades at the end of a formal reporting period. In such cases students should be given the opportunity to revise their work. Portfolios can also serve an important function during student-teacher conferences and can, in addition, be a place where teachers and students can communicate with each other. For example, a teacher's comments in a portfolio might include any or all of these:

- the names of students who are reading or writing about similar topics and suggestions for a sharing session
- book titles similar to a book that is currently being read
- information that might be included in a piece of writing
- a television show that might relate to an area of interest
- supportive comments about progress
- expression of personal interest in a particular topic, piece of writing, or book read by the student

Thus, a portfolio is not simply a repository of work waiting to be graded. It is a dynamic entity that is continually modified and clearly reflects ongoing progress.

## EVALUATING MATERIALS

### Readability Formulas

readability formula: A formula that indicates the difficulty of textual material in terms of a reading grade level; uses factors such as the number of syllables and sentences in a passage.

A **readability formula** provides a rough guideline for determining the difficulty level, or grade level, of reading material. Although useful, the results of a readability formula must be interpreted carefully. In fact, the International Reading Association and the National Council of Teachers of English (1984–1985) have noted that readability formulas, on their own, are insufficient for matching books with students. They suggest that teachers do the following:

- evaluate proposed texts based on knowledge of their students' prior information, experiences, reading abilities, and interests
- observe students using proposed texts in instructional settings to evaluate the effectiveness of the material
- use checklists for evaluating the readability of proposed materials, paying attention to variables such as student interests, text graphics, number of ideas and concepts in the material, length of lines in the text, and other factors that contribute to the relative difficulty of textual material

Although several readability formulas are available, all are similar in their manner of analyzing textual difficulty. Two factors are usually considered in determining difficulty level: word difficulty and sentence difficulty. To determine word difficulty, many readability formulas follow the premise that longer words are more difficult. Thus, by extension, difficult words contain more syllables than easier words. For that reason, many formulas require that the number of syllables in a given sample of text be counted. Other formulas compare the words in the sample material to a specific word list and that list guides the estimate of word difficulty.

To determine sentence difficulty, readability formulas use similar logic, reasoning that longer sentences are more difficult. Thus, many readability formulas require that the number of sentences in a given sample of material be counted. A small number suggests that the sentences are long and thus difficult. The relationship between the number of syllables and the number of sentences is often used to determine the approximate reading grade level (RGL) of the text being evaluated.

Readability formulas are more accurate at higher grade levels (i.e., above second grade) because most materials written for lower grade levels use controlled vocabulary, many words of one syllable, and relatively short sentences. In addition, reading selections for young students are usually quite short. For a readability measure to be valid, however, a continuous passage of approximately 100 words should be used, and it is strongly suggested that at least three representative passages from several sections of the material be averaged to estimate the overall reading grade level. Thus, some formulas specifically state that they are not intended for use below certain grade levels, whereas others may be used throughout a broad range of grades. (Fry [1990] has proposed a formula for use with passages as short as 80 words, but that formula may also not be completely reliable for use with beginning reading materials.)

**A Common Readability Measure.** A popular readability measure, the Fry Readability Scale, is shown in Figure 11–13, along with directions for using it. The popularity of the Fry scale results from its ease of use and its wide range of grade levels. Try using the Fry scale to estimate the reading grade level of the following passage (Williams, 1973). For your information, 100 words precede the double slash mark. (The answer is given at the end of this section.)

That evening they all had dinner together in the enchanter's cozy kitchen. Then Albion took Petronella out to a stone building and unbolted its door. Inside were seven huge black dogs.

"You must watch my hounds all night," said he.

Petronella went in, and Albion closed and locked the door.

At once the hounds began to snarl and bark. They showed their teeth at her. But Petronella was a real princess. She plucked up her courage. Instead of backing away, she went toward the dogs. She began to speak to them in a quiet voice. They stopped snarling and sniffed // at her.

## FIGURE 11–13
The Fry Readability Scale

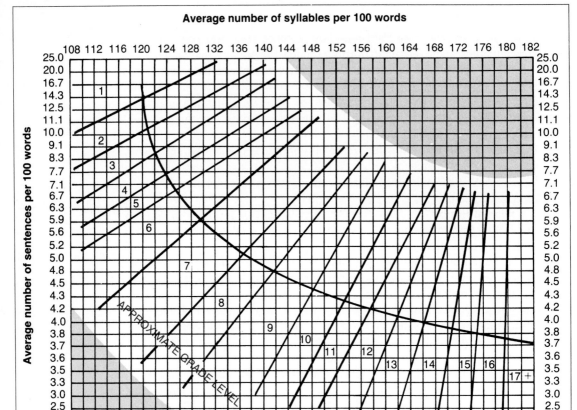

**Average number of syllables per 100 words**

### Expanded Directions for Working Readability Graph

1. Randomly select three (3) sample passages and count out exactly 100 words each, beginning with the beginning of a sentence. Do count proper nouns, initializations, and numerals.
2. Count the number of sentences in the hundred words, estimating length of the fraction of the last sentence to the nearest one-tenth.
3. Count the total number of syllables in the 100-word passage. If you don't have a hand counter available, an easy way is to simply put a mark above every syllable over one in each word, then when you get to the end of the passage, count the number of marks and add 100. Small calculators can also be used as counters by pushing numeral 1, then push the + sign for each word or syllable when counting.
4. Enter graph with *average* sentence length and *average* number of syllables; plot dot where the two lines intersect. Area where dot is plotted will give you the approximate grade level.
5. If a great deal of variability is found in syllable count or sentence count, putting more samples into the average is desirable.
6. A word is defined as a group of symbols with a space on either side; thus, *Joe, IRA, 1945,* and *&* are each one word.
7. A syllable is defined as a phonetic syllable. Generally, there are as many syllables as vowel sounds. For example, *stopped* is one syllable and *wanted* is two syllables. When counting syllables for numerals and initializations, count one syllable for each symbol. For example, *1945* is four syllables, *IRA* is three syllables, and *&* is one syllable.

**Source:** From E. Fry, "Fry's Readability Graph: Clarifications, Validity, and Extension to Level 17, *Journal of Reading,* 21 (1977), pp. 242–252. (Reproduction permitted. No copyright.)

There are, of course, other highly regarded readability formulas: for example, the formula by Spache (1953, 1976), appropriate for Grades 1 through 3; by Dale and Chall (1948), for Grades 4 through 6; and by Flesch (1948), for Grades 5 and above. Many publishers and other private businesses offer computerized estimates of readability, based on a variety of such formulas. Readability analyses can also be performed using microcomputers. There is commercially available software, as well as free or inexpensive public domain (i.e., without copyright) software, that can apply one or more formulas to a passage (see chapter 14). [The reading grade level of the Petronella passage is early fourth grade.]

**The Limitations of Readability Formulas.** The following sentence pairs illustrate some factors that make texts more or less difficult to read. Which sentence in each pair would be easier for a second grader to understand?

1. (a) The boy ran down the street.
   (b) The boy ran down the street.

2. (a) The boy ran down the street.

   (b) The boy ran down the street.

3. (a) The boy ran down the street.
   (b) Down the street ran the boy.

4. (a) The boy ran down the long, busy street.
   (b) The boy ran down the street. The street was busy. The street was long.

In each of the pairs, the first sentence is generally considered to be easier to understand than the second. Such things as print size, supportive illustrations, and word order do affect reading difficulty, yet those factors are not considered when a formula is used. In addition, short sentences do not always facilitate comprehension: 4(a) is easier for a second grader to read than 4(b) (Pearson, 1974–1975). But readability formulas usually equate length with difficulty.

Conceptual difficulty and background knowledge are other aspects of reading that formulas do not address, and misleading estimates can sometimes result. For example, since readability formulas generally assume that more syllables imply greater difficulty, a formula would consider *television* a more difficult word than *vector*, even though second graders would have much less trouble understanding *television*. Because of these limitations several proposals are being introduced that have the potential for more precise estimation of readability, both with and without the use of formulas (e.g., see Zakaluk and Samuels, 1988).

Nonetheless, readability formulas provide an easy-to-use method of estimating the relative difficulty of reading materials. If carefully and thoughtfully interpreted, readability formulas can provide an indication of the RGL of a specific piece of text. We must remember, however, that formulas can be fooled, especially at lower grade levels, where reading selections often become more difficult as the reader moves through a book. Thus, the readability of a passage at the beginning of a book might be different from that of a passage at the end—just one more reason to use multiple passages and average the results.

### Additional Considerations

When evaluating materials, teachers often supplement readability formulas with other information. A form that considers readability as well as other data is presented in Figure 11–14. Such a form should be used with the realization that not all the items apply to every type of reading material. For example, deductive and inductive presentation methods would not apply to narrative reading material. Thus, only items that pertain to the material under consideration need to be addressed. In addition, when materials are compared, it is important that they be from similar domains. For example, it is not appropriate to compare a children's literature book with a content-area textbook. The form in Figure 11–14 identifies many factors that teachers might consider important in the selection of reading materials, and it can help in decision making.

## THE ROLE OF A COMPREHENSION FRAMEWORK IN ASSESSMENT

A comprehension framework plays a significant role in test selection and interpretation of results. Teachers who follow a specific skills explanation of how reading ability develops tend to be happier with tests that assess various subskills. Teachers with a holistic language perspective tend to choose tests that present items in context, are based on what students are reading, and do not attempt to split reading into closely defined subskills. Teachers with an integrative explanation of how reading ability develops are likely to combine assessment tools, using tests that examine specific skills as well as less formal and global assessment methods.

When interpreting test results, teachers with a text-based perspective are more likely to count as inappropriate any response that deviates from the text. In tests of oral reading, for example, these teachers might count a reading of *cat* for *kitten* as incorrect. Teachers with a reader-based perspective are more likely to be flexible in scoring, focusing on whether the reader understood the intent of the passage. In a cloze test, for example, they might count synonyms as correct. Teachers with an interactive explanation of how a person reads

FIGURE 11–14
Material analysis form

Title _____

Author _____

Publisher _____

A. Readability

Formula used _____

Reading grade level _____,     which is

(1) appropriate                         5 points
(2) more than one grade off             3 points
(3) one grade off                       2 points

B. Rate all appropriate items in this section using a scale of 1 through 5, with 1 being unsatisfactory and 5 being excellent.

Literary Style

Use of topic sentences          _____
Use of technical terms          _____
Sentence complexity             _____
Appropriate summaries           _____

Content

Suitable for chosen objective         _____
Up-to-date (current and accurate)     _____
Appropriate to students' readiness    _____
Appropriate to students' interests    _____
Treatment of controversial subjects   _____
Comments:

Organization of Content

Use of underlying theme            _____
Logical units, subunits            _____
Logical chapter/heading sequence   _____
Comments:

General Appearance
Total selection size          _____
Print size and quality        _____
Eye appeal                    _____
Durability                    _____
Comments:

Illustrations
Modern, generally of high quality     _____
Useful for learning and discussion    _____
Matching the written text             _____
Comments:

Supplementary Materials/Learning Aids
Table of contents              _____
Appendices                     _____
Glossary                       _____
Suggested activities           _____
References                     _____
Teacher's guide (appropriate)  _____
Teacher's guide (easy to use)  _____
Comments:

FIGURE 11–14
*continued*

---

C. <u>Presentation of Content</u> (check primary mode of presentation)

| | | | |
|---|---|---|---|
| Authoritarian presentation | _____ | Prescriptive presentation | _____ |
| Deductive presentation | _____ | Inductive presentation | _____ |
| Type of text: expository | _____ | Narrative | _____ |

D. <u>Background Knowledge Demands</u>          E. <u>Other Comments</u>

Note background knowledge requirements
(e.g., prior knowledge, mathematical concepts,
prerequisite course work or reading)

_____

_____

F. <u>Overall Rating</u>

  1. (a) Count the number of ratings given in Section B.          _____

     (b) Multiply by 5.          $\times\ 5$

     (c) Enter the result.          _____

     (d) Add 5 (from Section A).          $+\ 5$

     (e) Enter the result. This is the total possible points.          _____

  2. (a) Add all of the numerical ratings given in Section B.          _____

     (b) Add the appropriate points from Section A.          $+$

     (c) Enter the result. This is the raw score.          _____

  3. (a) Divide 2(c) by 1(e). Enter the result.          _____

     (b) Multiply by 100.          $\times\ 100$

     (c) enter the result. This percentage can be used to
        compare similar materials.          _____ %

---

**Source:** From *Effective Reading Instruction: K–8,* Second Edition, by Donald J. Leu, Jr., and Charles K. Kinzer. Copyright 1991 by Macmillan Publishing Company. Permission is granted by the publisher to reproduce Figure 11–14 for student record-keeping purposes.

might examine both the text and the background knowledge of the reader to determine how the material, in combination with reader factors, may have led to a particular response.

Regardless of a teacher's comprehension framework, however, a test in and of itself is relatively meaningless, whether it be formal, informal, or teacher-made, a process or a product measure. It is the goal of testing, together with the use of test results, that determines a test's value to the instructional situation. Clearly understanding why a test is being given and using test results to further instructional goals can make assessment a valuable addition to any instructional program.

A wide variety of tools exist to facilitate the gathering of desired information, and careful selection will help match the measurement tool to a teacher's comprehension framework.

## COMMENTS FROM THE CLASSROOM ■

Emily Dodson    *norm referenced test*                    *IRI*

All of us at Tecumseh give the formal tests that are required by our school district. The standardized test for second graders provides subtest scores related to specific reading skills, as well as an overall score related to general reading ability. I tend to use the subtest scores as "flags" for children who need special assistance and I also look closely at the overall score. Then I observe reading behaviors in my classroom to see if any problem areas implied by the subtests actually occur in more realistic reading situations. If they do, I usually follow up with an informal reading inventory or use a retelling measure. IRIs are really helpful when school starts and also when new students transfer into my class.

I also collect students' work in portfolios and use those during conferences. With what appears in a portfolio, I can show parents their child's progress and any problem areas. Whenever there are problems, I use a diagnostic test to help identify the difficulty more specifically, and then I follow up with appropriate instruction. I use interest inventories and cloze tests periodically to match up students and materials.

I guess I use a lot of measures, but I don't depend on any one of them. I think testing should use whatever measures are available to identify patterns. Both process and product measures can provide valuable information.

## Mr. Burns

I favor formal tests that can tell me what skills are yet to be mastered. For example, on our standardized test I focus on the subtest scores because they relate to skills such as decoding, vocabulary, and the other components of comprehension. I also like to use criterion-referenced tests that tie in closely to my published reading program. They let me know when mastery has occurred so I can move students to the next level.

I do use informal reading inventories and cloze tests, but I score them fairly strictly. I count as incorrect almost anything that deviates from the text, with the exception of dialect differences. And I follow the exact replacement criterion closely when I score cloze tests. I guess my text-based/specific skills perspective influences my testing decisions, too.

I tend to use product measures, although I'm very aware of what my students do when they read. I think I'm going to start collecting their work in portfolios so that I'll have examples for conferences and the students will have a better chance to revise their work. I can also use portfolios to check formal test results.

I also use readability measures to assess materials. I try to make sure that the materials I use are appropriate for my students because it's very difficult to teach reading skills in materials that are not motivational or are too difficult. I

really depend on testing to let me know what abilities my students still need to master and what materials are appropriate for them.

## Ms. Sanchez

Because I teach from a holistic, reader-based perspective, I favor informal tests and process measures. With IRIs and cloze tests, I rarely even note a miscue unless it changes the meaning of what the student is reading, and almost never use the exact replacement criterion with a cloze test. I always count synonyms as correct, so I use different percentage bands to indicate instructional, frustration, and independent reading levels. I know I assess my students' interests and attitudes toward reading more often than most of the teachers I work with.

My favorite way to document student progress, though, is the student portfolio. I collect almost everything my students do and then spend a lot of time every two or three weeks going through the portfolios and completing summary sheets on the students' progress. I also write comments about their work and read any comments they've left for me. I encourage them to revise their work and to assess their own interests and progress, and I've found their portfolios are really motivational, especially in student conferences. I've also received good comments about the portfolios from parents during parent-teacher meetings—they really appreciate my summary sheets.

I do still use formal tests because I think all types of tests can be valuable if they're used properly. But some tests just don't match my beliefs. For example, I rarely look at the subtest scores on standardized tests. Instead, I look at the overall reading score and then match that to students' actual work. Whenever possible, I try to use process measures.

■ Validity (both content and curricular) and reliability are important in the selection or creation of a test. **MAJOR POINTS**

■ Process assessment allows teachers to infer students' underlying processes. Product assessment provides an indication of students' performance without reference to how a score was achieved.

■ Measurement instruments can be categorized as formal, informal, or teacher made. They are also categorized as either norm- or criterion-referenced.

■ Assessment instruments are used to evaluate readers, reading materials, and the interaction between readers and materials.

■ An informal reading inventory provides valuable information regarding students' reading processes and instructional needs. It can evaluate readers or, if it has been created from classroom materials, the interaction of readers with specific instructional material. Similarly, cloze tests can indicate general or specific reading ability.

■ Evaluation of materials cannot be accomplished with a readability formula alone. Factors such as complexity of ideas, visual aids, print size, and students' background are only some of the elements that must also be considered.

■ Portfolio evaluation can help document student progress and is a good way to supplement standardized testing information.

1. At some point in your teaching career, you will probably be asked to recommend a reading test for use in your classroom, or you may be asked to serve on a committee that will choose a test for your school or school district. What would your criteria be? What should a good test do? What would you look for in a test? **MAKING INSTRUCTIONAL DECISIONS**

2. Interview a teacher, a parent, and a school principal. Ask them to describe how they view testing and how they use or what they think about test results. How do the goals and uses of testing differ among these people? What implications do these differences have for you as a future teacher?

3. Interview both a primary and an intermediate grade teacher. Ask about the different kinds of measurement that are used in their classrooms. What are the purposes of each kind? How are the tests used to help in instruction?

4. Your school's curriculum library should have a file of commonly used reading tests. Choose three or four tests recommended for use with students at a particular grade level, and compare their testing of reading. How do they test word attack? vocabulary? comprehension? Which of the tests best fits your comprehension framework? Why?

5. Choose two passages from two different published reading programs, and perform a readability analysis, using the Fry scale. Compare your results with the readability information provided in the teacher's manual of each program. What are some of the reasons that a mismatch might occur?

6. Borrow a copy of a published IRI from your library. Using the checklist for IRI administration included in this chapter, practice giving that IRI to a second-grade student and a fourth-grade student. How did you have to change your administrative techniques to account for the differences in the students' grade level? Practice until you feel comfortable with the scoring system.

7. Construct a cloze test for use with elementary students or with some of your college-age friends. Choose appropriate materials for your practice group. Administer your test.

8. Try to find a teacher who uses portfolio evaluation (you might ask a professor or a principal to recommend someone). Interview the teacher, and ask how the portfolio is used in instructional decision making. Ask whether you might see a student's work. If so, try to describe that student's progress from what appears in the portfolio.

9. Describe your view of testing, and relate it to your comprehension framework. Specify how you might use assessment to make instructional decisions in your own classroom.

**FURTHER READING**

Baumann, J. F. (1988). *Reading assessment: An instructional decision-making perspective*. Columbus, OH: Merrill.

> A comprehensive paperback discussing most aspects of reading assessment. Numerous examples of tests as well as discussions of test interpretation. Includes checklists and forms for choosing tests and setting assessment goals.

Eeds, M. (1988). Holistic assessment of coding ability. In S. M. Glazer, L. W. Searfoss, & L. M. Gentile (Eds.), *Reexamining reading diagnosis: New trends and procedures* (pp. 48–66). Newark, DE: International Reading Association.

> Provides a basis for holistic evaluation of coding, including several sets of guidelines that teachers can use when examining children's writing.

Lapp, J., & Flood, D. (1989). Reporting reading progress: A comparison portfolio for parents. *The Reading Teacher, 42,* 508–514.

> Suggests items that should be placed in a portfolio that is shown to parents and discusses how portfolio assessment can provide a more complete picture of student growth than a single, traditional measure can.

Jongsma, E. (1980). *Cloze instruction research: A second look*. Newark, DE: International Reading Association.

> Discusses the history and uses of the cloze procedure, including its weaknesses and its use as a teaching tool.

Pikulski, J. J. & Shanahan, T. (Eds.). (1982). *Approaches to the informal evaluation of reading*. Newark, DE: International Reading Association.

> Describes informal assessment techniques that are useful with a range of reading materials and in instructional planning.

Pumfry, P. (1985). *Tests and assessment techniques* (2nd ed.). Newark, DE. International Reading Association.

   Describes the justification, use, and interpretation of reading tests. Includes an extensive list of tests for specified purposes and age ranges.

Valencia, S. (1990). A portfolio approach to classroom reading assessment: The whys, whats, and hows. *The Reading Teacher, 43,* 338–340.

   Outlines the benefit of portfolio assessment, describes what should be included, and discusses its use.


Allington, R. L., Chodos, L., Domaracki, J., & Truex, S. (1977). Passage dependency: Four diagnostic oral reading tests. *The Reading Teacher, 30,* 393–395.

Aulls, M. W. (1982). *Developing readers in today's elementary schools.* Boston: Allyn & Bacon.

Betts, E. A. (1946). *Foundations of reading instruction.* New York: American Book.

Bormuth, J. R. (1968). The cloze readability procedure. In J. R. Bormuth (Ed.), *Readability in 1968* (pp. 40–47). Champaign, IL: NCTE.

Burns, P. C., Roe, B. D., & Ross, E. P. (1988). *Teaching reading in today's elementary schools* (4th ed.). Boston: Houghton Mifflin.

Calfee, R. C. (1987). The school as a context for assessment of literacy. *The Reading Teacher, 40,* 738–743.

Carson, J. (1990). Unpublished manuscript.

Clark, C. H. (1982). Assessing free recall. *The Reading Teacher, 35,* 434–439.

Cooper, J. L. (1952). *The effect of adjustment of basal reading materials on reading achievement.* Unpublished doctoral dissertation, Boston University.

Dale, E., & Chall, J. S. (1948). A formula for predicting readability. *Educational Research Bulletin* (Ohio State University), *27,* 11–20; *28,* 37–54.

Duffelmeyer, F. A., & Duffelmeyer, B. B. (1989). Are IRI passages suitable for assessing main idea comprehension? *The Reading Teacher, 42,* 358–363.

Dulin, K. L. (1984). Assessing reading interests of elementary and middle school students. In A. J. Harris & E. R. Sipay (Eds.), *Readings on reading instruction* (pp. 346–357). New York: Longman.

Dulin, K.L., & Chester, R. (1984). *Dulin-Chester Reading Attention Scale/Reading Interest Questionnaire.* Madison: University of Wisconsin.

Eeds, M. (1988). Holistic assessment of coding ability. In S. M. Glazer, L. W. Searfoss, & L. M. Gentile (Eds.), *Reexamining reading diagnosis: New trends and procedures.* Newark, DE: International Reading Association.

Englert, C. S., & Semmel, M. I. (1981). The relationship of oral reading substitution miscues to comprehension. *The Reading Teacher, 35,* 273–280.

Farris, J. (1989). From basal reader to whole language: Transition tactics. *Reading Horizons, 30,* 23–28.

Flesch, R. F. (1948). A new readability yardstick. *Journal of Applied Psychology, 32,* 221–223.

Flesch, R. F. (1949). *The art of readable writing.* New York: Harper.

Fry, E. (1990). A readability formula for short passages. *The Reading Teacher, 33,* 594–597.

Gardner, H., & Hatch, T. (1989). Multiple intelligences go to school: Educational implications of the theory of multiple intelligences. *Educational Researcher, 18*(8), 4–10.

Gentile, L. M., & McMillan, M. M. (1987). *Stress and reading difficulties: Research, assessment, intervention.* Newark, DE: International Reading Association.

Gentile, L. M., & McMillan M. M. (1988). Reexamining the role of emotional maladjustment. In S. M. Glazer, L. W. Searfoss, & L. M. Gentile (Eds.), *Reexamining reading diagnosis: New trends and procedures* (pp. 12–28. Newark, DE: International Reading Association.

Gentry, J. R. (1982). An analysis of developmental spelling in GNYS AT WRK. *The Reading Teacher, 36,* 192–200.

REFERENCES

Gifford, B. R. (1990). *Report of the National Commission on Testing and Public Policy*. Chestnut Hill, MA: Boston College.

Goodman, K. S., & Buck, C. (1973). Dialect barriers to reading comprehension revisited. *The Reading Teacher, 27,* 6–12.

Harp, B. (1989). "When you do whole language instruction, how will you keep track of reading and writing skills?" *The Reading Teacher, 42,* 160–161.

Harris, A. J., & Sipay, E. R. (1990). *How to increase reading ability: A guide to developmental and remedial methods* (9th ed.). New York: Longman.

IRA, NCTE take stand on readability formulae. (December 1984–January 1985). *Reading Today, 2,* 1.

Johns, J. L., & Kuhn, M. K. (1983). The informal reading inventory: 1910–1980. *Reading World, 23,* 8–19.

Johnson, M. S., Kress, R. A., & Pikulski, J. J. (1987). *Informal reading inventories* (2nd ed.). Newark, DE: International Reading Association.

Johnston, P. H. (1983). *Reading comprehension assessment: A cognitive basis*. Newark, DE: International Reading Association.

Johnston, P. (1987). Teachers as evaluation experts. *The Reading Teacher, 40,* 744–748.

Jongsma, K. S. (1989). Portfolio assessment. *The Reading Teacher, 42,* 264–265.

Lapp, J., & Flood, D. (1989). Reporting reading progress: A comparison portfolio for parents. *The Reading Teacher, 42,* 508–514.

Mehrens, W. A., & Lehman, I. J. (1984). *Measurement and evaluation in education and psychology* (3rd ed.). New York: Holt, Rinehart & Winston.

Morrow, L. M. (1988). Retelling stories as a diagnostic tool. In S. M. Glazer, L. W. Searfoss, & L. M. Gentile (Eds.), *Reexamining reading diagnosis: New trends and procedures* (pp. 128–138). Newark, DE: International Reading Association.

Nickerson, R. S. (1989). New directions in educational assessment. *Educational Researcher, 18*(9), 3–7.

Nitko, A. J. (1980). Distinguishing the many varieties of criterion-referenced tests. *Review of Educational Research, 50,* 461–485.

Pearson, D. (1974–1975). The effects of grammatical complexity on children's comprehension, recall and conception of certain semantic relations. *Reading Research Quarterly, 10,* 155–192.

Pikulski, J. J. (1989). The assessment of reading: A time for change? *The Reading Teacher, 42,* 80–81.

Popham, W. J. (1978). *Criterion referenced measurement*. Englewood Cliffs, NJ: Prentice Hall.

Powell, W. R. (1970). Reappraising the criteria for interpreting informal reading inventories. In J. DeBoer (Ed.), *Reading diagnosis and evaluation*. Newark, DE: International Reading Association.

Rankin, E. F. (1971). Grade level interpretations of cloze readability scores. In F. Greene (Ed.), *The right to participate*. Milwaukee, WI: National Reading Conference.

Rankin, E. F. (1974). The cloze procedure revisited. In P. L. Nacke (Ed.), *Interaction: Research and practice in college-adult reading* (23rd NRC Yearbook). Clemson, SC: National Reading Conference.

Rankin, E. F. (1978). Characteristics of the cloze procedure as a research tool in the study of language. In P. D. Pearson & J. Hanson (Eds.), *Reading: Disciplined inquiry in process and practice* (pp. 148–153). Clemson, SC: National reading Conference.

Rankin, E. F., & Culhane, J. W. (1969). Comparable cloze and multiple choice comprehension test scores. *Journal of Reading, 13,* 193–198.

Ruddell, R. B., & Kinzer, C. K. (1982). Test preferences and competencies of field educators. In J. Niles & L. Harris (Eds.), *New inquiries in reading research and instruction*. Rochester, NY: National Reading Conference.

Siegler, R. S. (1989). Strategy diversity and cognitive assessment. *Educational Researcher, 18*(9), 15–20.

Silvaroli, N. J. (1990). *Classroom Reading Inventory* (6th ed.). Dubuque, IA: Wm. C. Brown.

Spache, G. S. (1953). A new readability formula for primary grade reading material. *Elementary English, 53,* 410–413.

Spache, G. S. (1976). The new Spache readability formula. In *Good reading for poor readers* (pp. 195–207). Champaign, IL: Garrard.

Taylor, W. L. (1953). Cloze procedures: A new tool for measuring readability. *Journalism Quarterly, 30,* 415–433.

Tuinman, J. J. (1974). Determining the passage-dependency of comprehension questions in 5 major tests. *Reading Research Quarterly, 9,* 207–223.

Valencia, S., & Pearson, P. D. (1987). Reading assessment: Time for a change. *The Reading Teacher, 40,* 726–735.

Wade, S. E. (1990). Using think-alouds to assess comprehension. *The Reading Teacher, 43,* 44–53.

Warwick, G. E. (1978). Cloze procedures as applied to reading. In O. K. Buros (Ed.), *Eighth mental measurements yearbook* (vol. 2, pp. 1174–1176). Highland Park, NJ: Gryphon Press.

Williams, J. (1973). *Petronella.* New York: Scholastic.

Wittrock, M. C. (1987). Process oriented measures of comprehension. *The Reading Teacher, 40,* 734–737.

Wixson, K. K., Bosky, A. B., Yochum, N., & Alvermann, D. E. (1984). An interview for assessing students' perceptions of classroom reading tasks. *The Reading Teacher, 37,* 346–352.

Zakaluk, B. L., & Samuels, S. J. (Eds.). (1988). *Readability: Its past, present, & future.* Newark, DE: International Reading Association.

# Teaching Reading to Children with Special Needs

- Special Needs: A Point of View
- Children with Unique Linguistic and Cultural Backgrounds
- Exceptional Children
- Using a Comprehension Framework to Guide Instruction of Students with Special Needs

*"They were all—all laughing—whenever I made a mistake—and I kept making mistakes. I couldn't help it.* .' *.Because I can't,"* Maybeth *wailed, "I can't—read, and I—can't learn."*

*"Who says?" James's cool voice cut across her tears.* . .*"I say—you can learn. I say, I can teach you. . . ."*

*A little smile lifted the corners of Maybeth's mouth, like a wave licking at the shore.*

*"Have you ever known me to be wrong?" James asked. He sounded so confident. . . .*

*"All right," Maybeth said, in a little voice.*

S everal recent trends require today's teacher of reading to be prepared to work with a wider range of students than ever before. We are witnessing an increasing respect for the multicultural and multilingual nature of our society and an increasing sensitivity to the unique needs of individual students. In addition, federal and state legislation requires schools to provide a free and appropriate public education for all handicapped students. Consequently, it is imperative that teachers understand the unique reading needs of students who come from special cultural and linguistic backgrounds and those who fall within federally defined categories of special education. This chapter will help develop that understanding and will provide instructional suggestions to help meet those needs.

Chapter 12 includes information that will help you answer questions like these:

1. In what way is each student a student with special needs?
2. How should you teach reading to children with unique linguistic and cultural backgrounds?
3. How should you teach reading to exceptional children?
4. How can your comprehension framework guide your instructional decisions as you teach reading to children with special needs?

KEY CONCEPTS

bilingual approaches
Black English
contract reading
cross-age tutoring
dialect
The Education for All Handicapped
   Children Act (PL 94–142)
emotionally disturbed
enrichment program
ESL approaches
exceptional children
giftedness
hearing impaired

individualized education program
   (IEP)
inquiry reading
language disorders
learning disability
least restrictive environment (LRE)
limited English proficiency (LEP)
mainstreamed
mental retardation
special education
speech disorders
Standard American English
VAKT approaches
visually impaired

## SPECIAL NEEDS: A POINT OF VIEW

Three thoughts should guide your consideration of children with special needs. The most important is that each of your students is, in fact, a student with special needs. Each and every student has unique needs that must be acknowledged as you make instructional decisions. You must always consider each student's background and abilities as you teach reading. Nothing is more important.

Reading Recovery, one of the more successful programs for children experiencing reading difficulty in the first year of instruction, demonstrates the importance of focusing on individual needs. In fact, Reading Recovery has achieved success specifically because it focuses so carefully on the unique needs of each student (Pinnell, Fried, & Estice, 1990). Specially trained teachers in the program provide a daily, 30-minute lesson for individual students, following a five-step method framework but adjusting the lesson on a minute-to-minute basis to meet an individual student's needs. This unique focus on individual needs may be difficult for you to replicate with an entire class. Nonetheless, it is the single most important thought you should keep in mind during reading instruction.

The second point is related to the first: categorical designations used for pedagogical, legal, or administrative purposes must never limit your instructional decisions regarding individual children or your expectations for their achievement. Categorical designations for different populations appear in this chapter for three reasons: (1) because they are used in legal definitions for categorical aid programs, (2) because they are sometimes used for administrative purposes, and (3) because they facilitate your learning as a new teacher. However, you must recognize that the definitions used here for individual categories are not consistently held by all educators. You must also recognize the inherent variation that exists within each category. The children who have been labeled as bilingual, learning disabled, mentally retarded, or any other designation are not identical. As a result, your instructional decisions must always take into account the unique differences of the special individuals in your classroom. The use of labels has brought significant benefits to students whose needs have too long been ignored, but we must ensure that those labels do not blind us to the individuality each of us expresses in our daily lives.

The third point is a simple but important perspective. Having children with special needs in your classroom provides an opportunity to celebrate and learn about diversity. Working with special children provides special opportunities for both you and your students, not an additional burden. If you want to prepare your students for the realities of contemporary life in a multicultural, pluralistic society, you must seek out diversity for your classroom. Diverse classrooms help each of us learn more about ourselves and our society.

# CHILDREN WITH UNIQUE LINGUISTIC AND CULTURAL BACKGROUNDS

## Speakers of Nonstandard Dialects

What is a **dialect**? Dialects are alternative language forms commonly used by regional, social, or cultural groups. Dialects can be understood by speakers of the same language group, but they feature important differences in sounds (e.g., *this* or *dis*), vocabulary (e.g., *soda* or *pop*), and syntax (e.g., "He is tired" or "He tired"). Nearly every major language has evolved a number of different

dialect: An alternative language form used by a regional, social, or cultural group and understood by speakers of the same major language.

dialects. All are equally logical, precise, and rule governed; no dialect is inherently superior to another. Usually, however, one dialect becomes the standard language form in a society because it is used by the socially, economically, and politically advantaged members of that society.

In the United States the standard language form is called **Standard American English** (SAE). Although it is difficult to define precisely, Standard American English is commonly identified as the form of English spoken by newscasters in most parts of the United States. It is thought to be most similar to the main dialect found in the midwestern states.

There are many nonstandard dialects spoken in the United States. One of the more common is **Black English**. Others include dialects common to the Appalachian region and to New England. Speakers of these dialects share certain language conventions, but there remains some degree of variation within each dialect. Thus, when we speak of a Black English dialect, we must recognize that speakers of Black English in one region may differ slightly from speakers of Black English in another region. Black English is the nonstandard dialect considered in the following discussion, but all that is said about it also applies to other nonstandard dialects.

**Dialect Differences.** When students who speak a nonstandard dialect read aloud, they often alter the sounds, words, and syntax of the writing to be consistent with their own dialect. A speaker of Black English, for example, might read the sentence "He is playing" as "He playing." Although it may appear that the child has not read the sentence correctly, there is no evidence that this behavior interferes with comprehension (Eller, 1989; Simons, 1979). Indeed, this behavior reflects an attempt to understand the text in the dialect of the reader and should not be discouraged. To do so would force the student to attend to the surface conventions of writing at the expense of comprehension.

**Standard American English:** The language form spoken by newscasters in most parts of the United States.

**Black English:** A dialect spoken in the United States by many individuals.

It is important to realize that dialect patterns within cultural groups are complex and that no dialect is more logical than or superior to any other.

At the same time it is important to encourage students to self-correct any mistakes that interfere with comprehension and are unrelated to a dialect (e.g., "He painting" instead of "He is playing"). Thus, teachers need to be aware of the dialects of their students and distinguish between oral reading errors reflecting dialect differences and oral reading errors reflecting comprehension difficulties.

To become familiar with some of the more common dialect differences between Standard American English and Black English, you should study Table 12–1. Every dialect contains similar differences that are regular and predictable. By listening to your students speak, you should be able to discover those regularities and then let your knowledge of dialect differences guide decisions during oral reading.

TABLE 12–1
A partial summary of common differences between Standard American English and Black English

| Language Trait | Standard American English | Black English |
|---|---|---|
| **Phonological Differences** | | |
| Initial | | |
| *th* (becomes *d*) | this | dis |
| *th (becomes t)* | thin | tin |
| *str* (becomes *skr*) | stream | scream |
| *thr* (becomes *tr*) | three | tree |
| Final | | |
| *sks* (becomes *ses*) | tasks | tasses |
| *sk* (becomes *ks*) | ask | aks |
| *th* (becomes *f*) | teeth | teef |
| *l* (has no sound) | tool | too |
| *r* (has no sound) | four | foe |
| General | | |
| Final consonant clusters simplified | best | bess |
| | walked | walk |
| | books | book |
| | talks | talk |
| *i* (becomes *e* before nasals) | pin | pen |
| **Syntactic Differences** | | |
| Omission of *to be* verbs | He is playing. | He playing. |
| Use of *be* for extended time | He is always here. | He be here. |
| Use of third-person singular verbs | I am going. | I is going. |
| | There were two girls. | There was two girls. |
| Change in irregular verb forms | She rode her bike. | She rided her bike. |
| Omission of indefinite article | Give him a book. | Give him book. |
| Use of *more* for comparatives | He is bigger than you. | He is more bigger than you. |
| Use of double negatives | I don't want any. | I don't want none. |

**Instruction.** Because reading is a language process and because speakers of nonstandard dialects have sometimes attained lower reading levels, it may seem reasonable to assume that nonstandard dialects interfere with reading comprehension. That assumption, which was common before 1970, is referred to as a **deficit explanation** (Eller, 1989). According to that line of thinking, nonstandard dialects are not only different from the standard dialect, but are also illogical, imprecise, and unsystematic. In an attempt to overcome the perceived deficit that nonstandard speakers faced in their use of dialect, several instructional practices were recommended.

deficit explanation: A view of nonstandard dialects as less logical, less precise, and less rule-governed when compared to the standard dialect.

- Teach the students with reading materials that match their dialect.
- Use dialect-neutral stories, that is, reading materials that do not conflict with the nonstandard dialect.
- Teach the students to speak Standard American English before teaching them to read.

None of these approaches were particularly effective in increasing the students' reading ability (Simons, 1979). In addition, because each proposal assumed that the children had deficits, they were being told implicitly that their language was inferior. The result was a negative impact on self-image and motivation.

Research during the 1970s led most educators to accept a **difference explanation** of dialect differences. In other words, nonstandard dialects are now recognized as different but equally logical, precise, and rule-governed. Moreover, we recognize that speakers of nonstandard dialects can understand Standard American English very well, even if they do not speak it. Dialect differences, by themselves, are not the cause of reading failure.

difference explanation: A view of nonstandard dialects as being different from the standard dialect but equally logical, precise, and rule-governed.

Today, five instructional practices are usually encouraged in classrooms with nonstandard dialect speakers.

1. Language experience approaches are used in the beginning stages of reading to help children see the close connection between their language and printed words.
2. Culturally relevant materials are used to provide a supportive environment for reading and to increase interest and motivation. Such materials also ensure that students' background knowledge is consistent with the background knowledge required to comprehend a text. In addition, they provide multicultural reading experiences for all of the students in a class. Literature selections portraying different cultural and ethnic groups are listed in Figure 12–1. Many reading programs now routinely incorporate such stories.
3. Children's background knowledge is carefully considered in relation to the texts they read (Maria, 1989). During vocabulary instruction, students' understanding of key concepts is probed to determine what they need to know about key terms. Instruction then helps students understand word mean-

FIGURE 12–1
Literature selections portraying different cultural or ethnic groups

---

### The Black Experience

*All the Colors of the Race* by Arnold Adoff
*Anansi the Spider* by Gerald McDermott
*Ashanti to Zulu* by Leo and Diane Dillon
*Autumn Street* by Lois Lowry
*The Boy Who Didn't Believe in Spring* by Lucille Clifton
*The Case of the Double Cross* by Crosby Bonsall
*The Drinking Gourd* by Ferdinand Monjo
*Here I Am! An Anthology of Poems Written by Young People in Some of
  America's Minority Groups* by Virginia Baron
*Jambo Means Hello: Swahili Alphabet Book* by Muriel Feelings
*Jethro and the Jumbie* by Susan Cooper
*John Henry* by Ezra Jack Keats
*Moja Means One: Swahili Counting Book* by Muriel Feelings
*More Stories Julian Tells* by Ann Cameron
*My Friend Jacob* by Lucille Clifton
*Roll of Thunder, Hear My Cry* by Mildred Taylor
*Sam* by Ann Herbert Scott
*Shadow* by Blaise Cendrars
*She Come Bringing Me That Little Baby Girl* by Eloise Greenfield
*The Slave Dancer* by Paula Fox
*The Snowy Day* by Ezra Jack Keats
*Some of the Days of Everett Anderson* by Lucille Clifton
*Stevie* by John Steptoe
*Stories Julian Tells* by Ann Cameron
*A Story—A Story: An African Tale* by Gail Haley
*Tancy* by Belinda Hurmence
*Ten, Nine, Eight* by Molly Bang
*Tough Tiffany* by Belinda Hurmence
*Wagon Wheels* by Barbara Brenner
*The Young Landlords* by Walter Dean Myers
*When Will I Read?* by Miriam Cohen

### The Hispanic Experience

*. . . And Now Miguel* by Joseph Krumgold
*Arrow to the Sun* by Gerald McDermott
*Benito* by Clyde Bulla
*The Black Pearl* by Scott O'Dell
*Born to Dance Samba* by Miriam Cohen
*Candita's Choice* by Mina Lewiton
*Child of Fire* by Scott O'Dell
*Dreams* by Ezra Jack Keats
*Families Are Like That* by Child Family Association of America
*Friday Night Is Papa Night* by Ruth Sonneborn
*Gilberto and the Wind* by Marie Hall Ets
*The Girl from Puerto Rico* by Hila Colman
*Here I Am! An Anthology of Poems Written by Young People in Some of
  America's Minority Groups* by Virginia Baron

FIGURE 12–1
*continued*

*If I Had a Paka: Poems in Eleven Languages* by Charlotte Pomerantz
*Juan* by Mary Stolz
*Louie* by Ezra Jack Keats
*Mira! Mira!* by Dawn Thomas
*My Name Is Pablo* by Aime Sommerfelt
*Nine Days to Christmas* by Marie Hall Ets
*Three Stalks of Corn* by Leo Politi
*Victor* by Clare Galbraith
*Viva Chicano* by Frank Bonham

### The Native American Experience

*Alice Yazzie's Year* by Ramona Maher
*Bright Fawn and Me* by Jay Leech and Zane Spencer
*Caddie Woodlawn* by Carol Ryrie Brink
*Dakota Sons* by Andree Distad
*Four Corners of the Sky: Poems, Chants, and Oratory* by Theodore Clymer
*High Elk's Treasure* by Virginia Driving Hawk Sneve
*In the Trail of the Wind* by John Bierhorst
*Island of the Blue Dolphins* by Scott O'Dell
*Lone Bull's Horse Raid* by Paul Gobel
*Long Claw: An Arctic Adventure* by James Houston
*Moonsong Lullaby* by Jamake Highwater
*Our Cup Is Broken* by Florence Crannell Means
*Our Fathers Had Powerful Songs* by Laszlo Kubinyi
*Rattlesnake Cave* by Evelyn Sibley Lampman
*Raven's Cry* by Christie Harris
*Red Hawk's Account of Custer's Last Battle* by Paul and Dorothy Gobel
*River Runners: A Tale of Hardship and Bravery* by James Houston
*Sarah Bishop* by Scott O'Dell
*Shadi* by Margaret Embry
*Shoeshine Girl* by Clyde Bulla
*Sing Down the Moon* by Scott O'Dell
*Snorri and the Strangers* by Nathaniel Benchley
*Songs of the Dream People* by James Houston
*The Amethyst Ring* by Scott O'Dell
*The Bloody Country* by James and Christopher Collier
*The Captive* by Scott O'Dell
*The Desert Is Theirs* by Byrd Baylor
*The Girl Who Loved Wild Horses* by Paul Gobel
*The Sacred Path: Spells, Prayers, and Power Songs of the American Indians* by John Bierhorst
*The Scared One* by Dennis Haseley
*The Sign of the Beaver* by Elizabeth George Speare
*The Talking Earth* by Jean George
*The Two Uncles of Pablo* by Harry Behn
*You Go Away* by Lois Axeman
*Wagon Wheels* by Barbara Brenner
*Waterless Mountain* by Laura Adams Armer
*Whirlwind Is a Ghost Dancing* by Leo and Diane Dillon

ings with which they are unfamiliar (appropriate techniques are described in chapter 6). Semantic mapping activities are especially useful, also.

4. Cooperative learning group activities are frequently used, again to provide a supportive environment in which students can accomplish tasks that they might be unable to complete alone (techniques are described in chapter 2). Discussion and debate often serve to clarify understanding.

5. During oral reading, teachers ignore reading errors when they do not alter the underlying meaning of a text but merely reflect a student's dialect.

---

## Responding to Dialect Errors During Oral Reading

Mr. Stanton is reading and discussing a story with a small group of his sixth-grade students. Darleen, who speaks Black English, reads the following sentences:

**MODEL LESSON**

Text:      They won't ask for the two books. They are afraid.
Darleen:   Dey woan aks for duh two book. Dey [pause] after?

As Darleen reads, Mr. Stanton must quickly decide how to respond. He does not want to correct a word that simply reflects a pattern in Darleen's dialect and does not interfere with comprehension. On the other hand, if a word changes the meaning of the story, Mr. Stanton needs to point that out to her.

Mr. Stanton ignores Darleen each time she reads *they* as *Dey*. Darleen's dialect uses /d/ to represent the /th/ sound in Standard American English. He also ignores Darleen's reading of *the* as *duh* and *ask* as *aks*. None of these deviations interfere with comprehension, and each reflects the pronunciation patterns of Darleen's dialect.

Mr. Stanton also ignores the reading of *won't* as *woan* because Darleen's dialect simplifies final consonant clusters such as /nt/. The same basic principle applies to her reading of *books* as *book;* the final consonant cluster /ks/ was simplified to /k/. Mr. Stanton is confident that this change did not alter Darleen's comprehension because she correctly read the word *two* just before she read *book*. Mr. Stanton also ignores Darleen's omission of the word *are: to be* verbs are sometimes dropped in her dialect.

However, Mr. Stanton is concerned about the last word. Darleen reads *afraid* as *after,* and the question intonation gives Mr. Stanton a clue that Darleen is uncertain of that word. He also notices that this error is not based on a pronunciation rule in her dialect. And most importantly, this error changes the meaning of the sentence. Consequently, he asks Darleen to look at the ending sound of the word, especially the last four letters. When she notices the word *raid,* he asks her to read the sentence again. Darleen reads the final sentence correctly in her dialect: "Dey afraid."

Does all of this mean that teachers should never try to develop oral competency in the standard dialect? On the contrary, teachers should provide learning experiences that promote such competency because the standard dialect provides access to power and influence in any society. However, the appropriate time for such efforts is not when students are demonstrating competence in comprehension. Activities such as the following can be used to direct students' attention to the conventions of the standard dialect.

**SAMPLE ACTIVITIES**

**Writing Conferences.** Use writing conferences, as suggested in chapter 9, to direct students' attention to the conventions of the standard dialect. Because writing makes language permanent and concrete, it is easier to discuss differences between standard and nonstandard dialects during writing experiences.

**Read-Aloud Sessions.** Incorporate culturally appropriate materials into read-aloud sessions. Use these to generate discussions of dialect differences. You might want to write down examples of how each dialect communicates the same message.

**Two-Sided Stories.** Have students write stories in dialect, putting a few sentences and an illustration on one side of each page. Then help them rewrite the story in standard dialect on the reverse side of each page. This activity could also be carried out as a language experience story, for which you write down the sentences as the students dictate them.

## Students with Limited English Proficiency

limited English proficiency (LEP) students: Students whose first language is not English and who have not yet developed fluency in English.

It has been estimated that at least 7½ million school-age children in the United States are nonnative speakers of English (Gonzales, 1981). Many of these are **limited English proficiency (LEP) students,** whose first language is not English and who have not yet developed fluency in the English language. LEP students come from a variety of linguistic backgrounds: Spanish, Cajun, Vietnamese, Cambodian, Haitian, Korean, Cantonese, Mandarin, or one of several Native American languages. At least one public school district on the West Coast has students who speak more than 80 different primary languages (McNeil, Donant, & Alkin, 1980).

It is important for teachers to understand the needs of these students. It is also important for teachers to develop instructional practices to meet their special needs. Although many of these students are provided with special educational services, many LEP students still receive most of their instruction from the regular classroom teacher (Feely, 1983; Gonzales, 1981).

TABLE 12–2
A partial listing of differences between Standard American English and Spanish

| Language Trait | Standard American English | Spanish |
|---|---|---|
| **Phonological Differences** | | |
| *i* (becomes *ē*) | bit | beet |
| *ă* (becomes *ĕ*) | pat | pet |
| *ā* (becomes *ĕ*) | late | let |
| *b* (becomes *p*) | bar | par |
| *z* (becomes *s*) | buzz | bus |
| *j* (becomes *ch* or *y*) | jam | cham or yam |
| *th* (becomes *s*) | thank | sank |
| *th* (becomes *d*) | this | dis |
| **Syntactic Differences** | | |
| Negatives | Bill is not here. | Bill is no here. |
| | They do not go to school. | They no go school. |
| | Don't go. | No go. |
| Use of *be* | I am eight. | I have eight years. |
| | I am hungry. | I have hunger. |
| Tense | I will see you later. | I see you later. |
| | I needed help yesterday. | I need help yesterday. |
| Omission of determiner | He is a teacher. | He is teacher. |
| Omission of pronoun | Is it time to go? | Is time to go? |
| | It is time. | Is time. |

**LEP Differences.** Two important differences exist between LEP students and students who speak nonstandard dialects. First, LEP students lack the knowledge of spoken English that is necessary to comprehend what they read. Acquiring the ability to speak English, therefore, is crucial to their developing reading proficiency. Time must be devoted to helping these students learn to communicate orally in English.

The second difference stems from the fact that nonstandard dialects do not impede reading comprehension of the standard dialect, whereas differences between English and another language often do impede comprehension. Thus, it is important to become familiar with the differences between English and a student's native language. The major differences between English and Spanish, one of the more common languages of LEP students, are listed in Table 12–2.

To understand the conflicts between other languages and English, you might seek information from three sources—(1) a speaker of the other language who also speaks English, (2) your local or state coordinator of bilingual education services, and (3) either of the organizations:

Center for Applied Linguistics
1611 North Kent Street
Arlington, VA 22209

Dissemination Center for Bilingual Bicultural Education
6504 Tracor Lane
Austin, TX 78721

**Instruction.** Research into reading instruction with LEP students is still in its infancy, and consistent findings are limited. However, several instructional approaches are commonly found in schools: immersion, English as a Second Language (ESL), and bilingual approaches. **Immersion approaches** make no special provision for LEP students. They are expected to pick up as much as they can, as fast as they can, during regular classroom lessons. This practice assumes that immersion in English will contribute to learning. Although this has been the traditional form of instruction for LEP students in the United States, it is not necessarily the most effective.

**ESL approaches** teach LEP students oral English skills before their reading instruction begins. Special ESL teachers work with students, usually in structured oral drills and usually outside the regular classroom, to develop fluency in oral English. Reading instruction in the regular classroom begins only after students have established an understanding of oral English. **Bilingual approaches** teach reading and writing skills in a student's native language at the same time that they teach oral language skills in English. Reading instruction in English begins only after students have learned to read and write in their own language and have acquired fluency in oral English. Bilingual approaches often involve teachers who are fluent in the native language of their students.

Regardless of approach, you should keep the following suggestions in mind as you work with students who are just learning to speak English.

1. Encourage discussion among all your students, but especially between LEP students and others. Speaking and listening experiences develop important prerequisites for reading and writing. Thus, LEP children need a language-rich environment in order to develop greater proficiency in English (Krashen & Terrell, 1983).
2. Make frequent use of cooperative learning group activities. This method framework provides a supportive environment for LEP students—a group learning situation with extensive use of oral English. LEP students are able to participate successfully in cooperative learning groups, thereby increasing their self-perceptions.
3. Try to reduce the anxiety level of LEP students as much as possible. These students appear to learn best in classrooms in which anxiety levels are reduced (Dulay, Burt, & Krashen, 1982).
4. Pay less attention at the beginning to your students' pronunciation and accent. Concentrate on meaning and communication.

**immersion approaches:** An instructional practice that challenges LEP students to learn English as rapidly as they can without special intervention.

**ESL approaches:** An instructional practice that teaches LEP students oral English in structured lessons before they learn how to read and write in English.

**bilingual approaches:** An instructional practice through which LEP students learn reading and writing in their native language concurrently with instruction in oral English.

5. Understand the difficulty that your students face in learning a second language, and help your other students to appreciate this challenge, also. LEP students may require as many as five to seven years of instruction in English before they can read English textbooks effectively (Cummins, 1981).
6. Select books for read-aloud sessions that are culturally appropriate for your LEP students. Use those opportunities to encourage their participation in oral discussions.
7. Respect your students' linguistic and cultural heritage. Work those aspects of diversity into classroom activities.
8. Use language experience activities as much as possible to teach beginning reading skills. Language experience activities allow LEP students to simultaneously improve their oral and written English language skills. They also allow students to use their background knowledge to maximum advantage.

---

**Picture Dictionaries.** Have your LEP students write and publish a picture dictionary. Include common school objects and activities. Have other students help them in this task.

**Thematic Units on Culture.** Develop a thematic unit on the country or culture of each LEP student in your class. Integrate reading and writing experiences into this unit. Teach new vocabulary words in English to LEP students during the unit, and have them share their native words for these concepts. Plan many cooperative learning group activities within the unit.

**Peer Tutoring.** Have one student regularly work with each LEP student in your classroom. They can complete many enjoyable and productive tasks together.

■ reading a storybook together and talking about the pictures
■ writing and illustrating a story together
■ writing buddy journals together (see chapter 9)
■ playing Simon Says together

**Readers Theatre.** Readers theatre experiences are useful as students develop their ability to read and write in English. This activity provides them with many practice opportunities before they have to read their parts in public.

**SAMPLE ACTIVITIES**

---

## EXCEPTIONAL CHILDREN

**Exceptional children** are unable to reach their full potential without services, instructional materials, and/or facilities that go beyond the requirements of the average child. Typically, exceptional children include those who are mentally

exceptional children: Children unable to reach their full potential without services that go beyond the requirements of the average child.

retarded, learning disabled, emotionally disturbed, hearing impaired, visually impaired, speech or language disordered, and gifted. According to federal estimates, approximately 13 to 16 percent of school-age children fall into at least one of these categories (Hallahan & Kauffman, 1982; Lerner, 1985; U.S. Department of Education, 1984).

**special education:** Services, materials, and/or facilities provided to help exceptional children reach their full potential.

**Special education** encompasses the educational services, materials, and/or facilities provided to help exceptional children reach their full potential. The specific nature of special education varies along a continuum ranging from the least to the most restrictive environments, as shown in Figure 12–2. You can see from the figure that regular classroom teachers have opportunities to work with exceptional students in at least half of the environments described. Increasingly, these teachers provide at least a portion of the special education services for exceptional children. Therefore, it is important that all teachers understand special education and the needs of special education students.

## PL 94–142: The Education for All Handicapped Children Act

The most important influence in the education of exceptional children has been a federal law passed in 1975—The Education for All Handicapped Children Act, or **PL** (Public Law) **94–142.** The most important provision of PL 94–142 states:

**PL 94–142:** Federal legislation mandating a free and appropriate public education for all children, regardless of handicap.

> In order to receive funds under the act every school system in the nation must make provision for a free, appropriate public education for every child. . .regardless of how, or how seriously, he may be handicapped.

This law contains two other provisions affecting classroom teachers of reading: required individualized education programs and placement in least restrictive environments.

**individualized education program (IEP):** Instructional plans for each exceptional child that are used to guide instruction and monitor progress.

**Individualized Education Programs.** PL 94–142 requires that a multidisciplinary team of trained specialists evaluate each exceptional student and each potential exceptional student. This team submits a report to a case conference meeting, at which a representative from the school, the teacher, the parents, and other appropriate individuals develop an **individualized education program (IEP)** for each exceptional child. The IEP is used to guide instruction and monitor student progress. According to federal guidelines, an IEP must contain the following components:

- a statement of the present levels of educational performance
- a statement of annual goals, including short-term instructional objectives
- a statement of the specific educational services to be provided. . .and the extent to which [each] child will be able to participate in regular educational programs
- the projected date for initiation and anticipated duration of such services, and appropriate objective criteria and evaluation procedures and schedules for

FIGURE 12–2
A continuum of special educational environments and services

| | |
|---|---|
| **Least Restrictive** → <br><br><br><br><br><br><br><br> **Most Restrictive** ← | 1. Classroom instruction by a regular classroom teacher, who is provided with special materials or who adapts existing materials to meet individual needs. <br> 2. Classroom instruction by the regular classroom teacher in consultation with a specialist in special education. <br> 3. Itinerant services provided by a special educator who regularly visits and teaches the exceptional child within the regular classroom. Itinerant teachers also make instructional suggestions to the regular classroom teacher. <br> 4. Resource services provided by a special educator outside the classroom. Exceptional children receive instruction in a resource center for a portion of the day. The resource teacher also consults with the classroom teacher regarding instruction within the classroom. <br> 5. Self-contained special education classrooms within the regular school for homogeneous classes of exceptional children. <br> 6. Special day schools for homogeneous groups of exceptional children. <br> 7. Hospital or home-bound instruction by itinerant special education teachers. <br> 8. Residential school in a segregated institution. |

determining, on at least an annual basis, whether instructional objectives are being achieved (Education for All Handicapped Children Act of 1975, p. 3).

**The Least Restrictive Environment.** One of the most important decisions made at the case conference is the recommended instructional environment. Participants in that conference must state in the IEP the extent to which a handicapped child will be **mainstreamed** into the regular classroom. PL 94–142 requires that handicapped children be placed in the **least restrictive environment (LRE)** possible, where maximum opportunity is provided for those students to engage in the full measure of school life, consistent with their educational needs. Thus, children should not be educated in a separate special education classroom if their needs can be adequately met in a regular classroom with outside instruction provided by a special educator. Other children should not leave the regular classroom for special assistance if their needs can be adequately met by the regular classroom teacher. In short, exceptional children are to be included in the mainstream of educational life.

The principle of LRE has been given a recent boost by an initiative of the federal government. This "regular education initiative" is an effort to review, coordinate, and improve mainstreaming in schools (Stainback & Stainback,

mainstreamed: Placement of exceptional students in integrated learning environments with other students.

least restrictive environment (LRE): A learning environment in which maximum opportunity is provided for exceptional students to engage in the full measure of school life, consistent with their educational needs.

1989). As a result, the education of special education students is increasingly taking place in the regular classroom.

How will all of this affect you as a classroom teacher of reading? Should you have the opportunity to have an exceptional child in your classroom, you will be affected in three ways. First, you will be required to attend the case conference meeting and assist in planning the student's IEP.

Second, if the multidisciplinary team decides to mainstream your student for reading instruction, you will be responsible for implementing the IEP in your classroom. You may be totally responsible for reading instruction, or you may provide the instruction in consultation with a special education teacher, who may advise you about materials and methods. If the multidisciplinary team decides not to mainstream your student for reading instruction, you will be responsible for coordinating the classroom visits of a special reading teacher or your student's trips away from the classroom for special assistance. Third, you will be responsible for evaluating the degree to which your student has met the specified instructional objectives. With the multidisciplinary team you will then decide on new instructional objectives.

An individualized education program (IEP) for each exceptional child is developed at a case conference meeting.

DECISION POINT ➤

Support for children with special needs is often provided in either a pull-out or a push-in program. Pull-out programs take students out of their regular classrooms to provide special services, such as ESL instruction, bilingual education, special education, or remedial reading. Push-in programs provide such services to students within their regular classrooms, working with those students and their teachers in an integrated classroom setting. Which model of support services do you favor? Why? What relationship do you see between this decision and your belief about how reading ability develops?

## General Guidelines

Beyond accommodating a child's particular handicap, reading instruction for special education students does not differ substantially from the materials, methods, and activities described in previous chapters. Reading instruction for every student requires judicious selection from the range of instructional suggestions presented in this text. Nonetheless, the following suggestions should guide you as you integrate special education students into your classroom reading program.

1. *Prepare your other students for exceptional children.* Include literature selections about exceptionalities in your students' reading experiences and in your read-aloud sessions. Use these opportunities to initiate discussions about the concerns and feelings of exceptional children. This focus will help your students respect the unique qualities of each member of the class. A list of appropriate selections can be found in Figure 12–3.

2. *Capitalize on individual strengths.* When necessary, work around a handicap by taking advantage of an individual's strengths. A hearing impaired child, for example, may require a more visual approach than a hearing child. Pictures might be needed to complement verbal definitions during vocabulary instruction.

3. *Ensure successful learning experiences.* Try to build success into your instruction by carefully considering what each child can be expected to do.

4. *Record and chart individual growth to demonstrate gains to students and parents.* Make individual growth more visible by listing individual achievement and keeping examples of work in a portfolio. Recording growth makes it concrete and tangible.

5. *Establish an accepting and positive environment.* Praise success with enthusiasm; accept failure with tolerance. Realize that mistakes are an important part of learning. Try to compliment each child in your class each day, and encourage your students to do the same.

6. *Discuss your students' progress regularly with parents, special educators, and other teachers.* It is important to keep others informed of your work.

FIGURE 12-3

A selected bibliography of children's literature and special education selections

## General

H. Bornstein (Ed.), *The Comprehensive Signed English Dictionary* (Washington, DC: Gallaudet College Press, 1983)

B. B. Osman, *No One to Play with: The Social Side of Learning Disabilities* (New York: Random House, 1982)

J. Quicke, *Disability in Modern Children's Fiction* (Cambridge, MA: Brookline Books, 1985)

## Physical Disability

P. D. Frevert, *It's OK to Look at Jamie* (Mankato, MN: Creative Education, 1983)

M. W. Froehlich, *Hide Crawford Quick* (Boston: Houghton Mifflin, 1983)

L. Henriod, *Grandma's Wheelchair* (Niles, IL: Whitman, 1982)

R. C. Jones, *Angie and Me* (New York: Macmillan, 1981)

B. Rabe, *The Balancing Girl* (New York: Dutton, 1981)

R. Roy, *Move Over, Wheelchairs Coming Through!* (Boston: Houghton Mifflin, 1985)

## Mental Retardation

A. Baldwin, *A Little Time* (New York: Viking Press, 1978)

B. Byars, *Summer of the Swans* (New York: Viking Press, 1970)

P. Hermes, *Who Will Take Care of Me?* (New York: Harcourt Brace Jovanovich, 1983)

N. Hopper, *Just Vernon* (New York: Dutton, 1982)

H. Sobol, *My Brother Stephen Is Retarded* (New York: Macmillan, 1977)

B. R. Wright, *My Sister Is Different* (Milwaukee, WI: Raintree, 1981)

## Learning Disabilities

L. Albert, *But I'm Ready to Go* (Scarsdale, NY: Bradbury Press, 1977)

J. Gilson, *Do Bananas Chew Gum?* (New York: Lathrop, 1980)

E. Hunter, *Sue Ellen* (New York: Houghton Mifflin, 1969)

J. Lasker, *He's My Brother* (Chicago: Albert Whitman, 1974)

D. B. Smith, *Kelly's Creek* (New York: Crowell, 1975)

## Hearing Impairment

R. Charlip and M. B. Charlip, *Hand Talk: An ABC of Finger Spelling and Sign Language* (New York: Four Winds Press, 1980)

J. W. Peterson, *I Have a Sister. My Sister Is Deaf* (New York: Harper & Row, 1984)

M. Riskind, *Apple Is My Sign* (Boston: Houghton Mifflin, 1981)

L. Rosen, *Just Like Everyone Else* (New York: Harcourt Brace Jovanovich, 1981)

B. Wolf, *Anna's Silent World* (Philadelphia, PA: Lippincott, 1977)

## Visual Impairment

C. Brighton, *My Hands, My World* (New York: Macmillan, 1984)

M. Cohen, *See You Tomorrow, Charles* (New York: Greenwillow, 1983)

H. Coutant, *The Gift* (New York: Knopf, 1983)

J. Little, *Listen for the Singing* (New York: E. P. Dutton, 1977)

P. MacLachlan, *Through Grandpa's Eyes* (New York: Harper & Row, 1979)

J. Yalen, *The Seeing Stick* (New York: Thomas Y. Crowell, 1977)

## Speech and Language Disorders

M. Christopher, *Glue Fingers* (Toronto: Little, Brown, 1975)

P. Fleischman, *The Half-a-Moon Inn* (New York: Harper & Row, 1980)

E. B. White, *The Trumpet of the Swan* (New York: Harper & Row, 1970)

It is also important to learn about ideas that may work from others. Keep a list of the ideas that others have found successful.

7. *Use background knowledge to make difficult learning tasks easier.* When a student experiences difficulty, redefine the content of the task to match the child's background knowledge. This modification will make the task easier and will lead to initial success. Once children have been successful and understand the nature of the task, have them try it with less familiar content.

8. *Do not continuously repeat unsuccessful learning experiences.* Be willing to change materials, strategies, and activities when a student has not been successful. Find other approaches that work and maintain them.

9. *Do not search for a single solution to reading failure.* Reading is a complicated developmental process. No single set of materials or activities will ever solve a reading problem.

10. *Provide independent reading opportunities.* Do not neglect independent reading experiences. All children need time to read for pleasure or personal information.

## Students with Mental Retardation

The American Association on Mental Deficiency (AAMD) has defined **mental retardation** as follows:

> Mental retardation refers to significantly subaverage general intellectual functioning existing concurrently with deficits in adaptive behavior and manifested during the developmental period. (Grossman, 1973, p. 11)

According to the AAMD, "significantly subaverage general intellectual functioning" requires an IQ score of 69 or below on the most commonly used test, Wechsler Intelligence Scale for Children—Revised (WISC-R). Children with IQ scores between 70 and 85 may learn more slowly than their peers and may be called slow learners. Typically, however, they are not formally labeled as mentally retarded. Figure 12–4 illustrates the various categories of mental retardation used by the AAMD.

When "deficits in adaptive behavior" are evaluated, the AAMD suggests that the age of the child be considered. In early childhood, sensorimotor, communication, self-help, and socialization skills are evaluated. In middle

mental retardation: The condition of individuals with inadequate adaptive behavior and intellectual functioning significantly below average.

FIGURE 12–4
Categories of mental retardation used by the AAMD

| IQ | 100 95 90 85 80 75 70 65 60 55 50 45 40 35 30 25 20 15 | | | | |
|---|---|---|---|---|---|
| Categories of Mental Retardation | | Mild | Moderate | Severe | Profound |

childhood and early adolescence, learning processes and interpersonal social skills are evaluated. According to federal estimates, approximately 1.9 percent of school-age children are mentally retarded (U.S. Department of Education, 1984).

**Learning Characteristics.** Mentally retarded students tend to progress through the same developmental stages that normal students experience, but their rate of progress is much slower. This difference is especially evident in academic learning tasks such as reading. Other important characteristics that need to be accommodated during instruction include the following:

- *Short attention spans.* Mentally retarded students may be easily distracted, especially when there are many visual and auditory signals to distract them.
- *Poor short-term memory.* The ability to remember words, numbers, and ideas for short periods of time is limited. Long-term memory is less of a problem.
- *Delayed language development.* Language development is often slower than normal, although it progresses in a sequence that is similar to that of most children. A higher frequency of language and speech problems can be anticipated.
- *Difficulty in grasping abstract ideas.* Mentally retarded children tend to have more difficulty with abstract concepts. They do better with concrete concepts.

**Instruction.** The most important instructional consideration with mentally retarded students is that their development lags behind that of other children of the same chronological age. Thus, while normally developing second graders are learning new vocabulary meanings, the structure of various narrative and expository forms, and useful reading strategies, mentally retarded children of the same age might still be consolidating important emergent literacy/readiness skills. In fact, emergent literacy/readiness skills are often a major aspect of reading programs for mildly retarded students in the early elementary years. Acquiring oral language skills, learning letter names, listening to stories, completing language experience activities, and learning to read and write their own names might all be appropriate. Learning sight words through language experience activities might be especially useful (Raver & Dwyer, 1986).

The use of cooperative learning group experiences is also appropriate. These provide supportive environments in which children can interact with print. In addition, cooperative learning group tasks have been found to be particularly effective in increasing social acceptance and positive social behavior among children (Slavin, 1984).

Reading instruction with mentally retarded children should emphasize **functional reading skills,** which include the reading abilities required for daily life. Such skills enable individuals to read signs, follow simple written directions, use the yellow pages, read and order from catalogs, read names, locate bus routes on a map, and read recipes.

functional reading skills: Reading skills required to successfully interact with written language during daily life.

**Learning to Understand Environmental Print.** Teach children to understand the environmental print that they experience daily. Such print includes street signs, traffic signals, labels, children's names, and bus or transit signs. Include important safety words such as *Danger, Poison, Keep Out,* and *Caution.* Put each such word on a card, and use it in a sight word recognition game.

**SAMPLE ACTIVITIES**

**Catalog Reading.** Show children how to read a catalog to determine the name and price of items. Provide duplicate copies of the order form, and have students complete it. Structure this as a cooperative learning group task.

**Reading Students' Names.** Give students frequent opportunities to read the names of other children in the class. For example, have students return papers that have been corrected.

**Reading and Writing Personal Information.** Teach children how to read and write their names, addresses, and phone numbers. Let them practice by filling out employment forms for favorite classroom jobs.

**Reading TV Guides.** Bring in program listings for TV, and show children how to read them. Have students make a TV viewing schedule for the week, allowing only one or two hours of television each day. This task could be effectively completed in cooperative learning groups.

## Students with Learning Disabilities

The term **learning disability** was first used in 1963 by Samuel Kirk to refer to children who, despite normal intelligence, had great difficulty learning in school. Since then, a variety of definitions have evolved, including these most common characteristics:

learning disability: A substantial gap between expected and actual achievement levels, which cannot be attributed to mental retardation or emotional disturbance.

- a substantial gap between expected achievement levels (based on intelligence scores) and actual performance in at least one academic subject area
- an uneven achievement profile, with achievement very high in some areas and very low in others
- low achievement levels that are not due to environmental factors
- low achievement levels that are not due to mental retardation or emotional disturbance

The federal definition is the most widely used.

"Specific learning disability" means a disorder in one or more of the basic psychological processes involved in understanding or in using language, spoken or written, which may manifest itself in an imperfect ability to listen, think, speak, read, write, spell, or do mathematical calculations. The term includes such conditions as perceptual handicaps, brain injury, minimal brain dysfunction, dyslexia, and developmental aphasia. The term does not include children who have learning problems which are primarily the result of visual, hearing, or motor handicaps, of mental retardation or emotional disturbance, or of environmental, cultural, or economic disadvantage. (*Federal Register* 42, p. 65083)

Approximately 5 percent of school-age children are considered learning disabled (U.S. Department of Education, 1984).

**Learning Characteristics.** Learning disabled students do not all share a common set of learning characteristics because different psychological processes are impaired in different children. The most common characteristic found in children who are learning disabled is some disruption in language processing. Because reading is a language-based process, learning disabled children frequently have extreme difficulty learning how to read. Consequently, they may be more than two years behind grade level in reading achievement. Often they have trouble with automatic decoding and need additional instruction to acquire that skill (Harris & Sipay, 1990).

Other characteristics are also likely to appear and should be accommodated during instruction.

- *Perceptual-motor problems*. Students may lack both fine-and gross-motor coordination. They may appear clumsy. Writing is often labored and hard to read. Many reversals appear in letter formation (e.g., *d* for *b*, *z* for *s*) and letter order (e.g., *tac* for *cat*), persisting beyond the age of seven or eight.
- *Attention problems*. Students may have short attention spans. They may be easily distracted and have difficulty completing regular class assignments on time.
- *Lack of effective learning and problem-solving strategies*. Students may not be aware of effective strategies for learning and problem solving.

**Instruction.** At least three general categories of instructional approaches have been used to teach reading to learning disabled children: visual, auditory, kinesthetic, and tactile (VAKT) approaches; behavior modification approaches; and language-based approaches. When **VAKT approaches** are used, children receive information simultaneously through visual, auditory, kinesthetic (movement), and tactile (touch) modalities. Receiving information through multiple channels of sensory input is thought to make learning more likely.

VAKT approaches: Methods of teaching reading to children through visual, auditory, kinesthetic, and tactile modalities.

The most common VAKT method is one originally developed by Fernald (Fernald, 1943; Tierney, Readence, & Dishner, 1985). With that method, letters and words are first taught to students by having them simultaneously see (visual), hear (auditory), and trace (kinesthetic and tactile) words with their fingers. Sometimes sandpaper letters are used to enhance tactile input. After the letters and some words are learned, children receive reading instruction based on what they write themselves, much like language experience methods. Such writing experiences provide important language input through each of the identified modalities and thus contribute to the development of reading.

**Behavior modification** approaches attempt to overcome the attentional problems that some learning disabled readers exhibit. Behavior modification involves identifying valued behaviors and the conditions under which such behaviors take place and then immediately reinforcing those behaviors with praise or tokens (Hallahan & Kauffman, 1982). Gradually, a set of discreet behaviors is developed that contributes to successful learning. Behavior modification was especially popular during the 1960s and 1970s and is seen occasionally today.

**Language-based approaches** have recently been suggested for children experiencing reading disabilities. Such approaches provide functional reading experiences in motivating and pleasurable environments, usually with children's literature and extensive writing experiences. The most practical and clear set of recommendations for classroom teachers has been provided by Ford and Ohlhausen (1988), who make the following suggestions:

- Focus on real, meaningful learning through the use of themes.
- Maximize the participation of disabled readers by using whole language activities which capitalize on their strong oral language skills.
- Implement whole room activities which have built-in individualization. . . [such as] Sustained Silent Reading and journal writing.
- Use open ended projects which allow students to contribute at various levels with various skills. . .[such as] the publication of a class newspaper and the production of a drama.
- Plan writing activities which allow individuals to respond at their own levels. . .[such as] using patterned stories and poetry. . . .
- Use group incentives and internal competition to motivate disabled readers.
- Implement a cross-grade arrangement with a group of younger students.
- Obtain the help of a school psychologist to implement relaxation techniques in the classroom.
- Organize and participate in a support group with other teachers who work with disabled readers. (pp. 18–22)

Learning disabled students typically receive additional reading instruction from a resource teacher, a learning disability specialist, or a reading specialist. The goal is to maintain the child as much as possible in a regular classroom reading program (Lerner, 1985). When an outside person and a classroom teacher are both working with a youngster, it is important that instruction be consistent (Allington & Shake, 1986; Walp & Walmsley, 1989). Otherwise children can become confused. Teacher and specialist need to communicate regularly regarding instructional approaches and materials, sharing teaching strategies that seem to be especially productive.

## Students with Emotional Disturbances

There is no widely accepted definition of children who are **emotionally disturbed**. However, three features are found in most definitions of emotional disturbance:

**behavior modification:** Instruction that identifies valued behaviors, defines conditions where valued behaviors will take place, and immediately reinforces positive behaviors with praise or tokens.

**language-based approaches:** Instruction that provides functional reading experiences with extensive writing and oral language opportunities.

**emotionally disturbed:** Describes individuals with normal intelligence who achieve substantially below expected levels because of chronic withdrawal, anxiety, and/or aggressive behavior.

1. behavior that goes to an extreme, that is, behavior that is not just slightly different from the usual
2. a problem that is chronic, that is, one that does not disappear
3. behavior that is unacceptable because of social or cultural expectations

According to federal estimates, approximately 1 percent of the school-age population is emotionally disturbed (U.S. Department of Education, 1984). Kauffman (1981), however, has put the actual estimate at 6 to 10 percent. Thus, teachers are likely to encounter children who experience serious and persistent emotional and behavioral problems but who have not been formally identified.

**Learning Characteristics.** Emotionally disturbed children have at least normal intellectual ability but achieve substantially below expected levels because of withdrawal, anxiety, and/or aggressive behavior. Each of those behaviors reflects a different set of learning characteristics, often in combination, that need to be accommodated during instruction.

### Withdrawal

1. May be without friends and may have difficulty working cooperatively in groups
2. Often daydreams more than is normal for a particular age group
3. May appear secretive

### Anxiety

1. May cry much more frequently than is normal
2. Often appears tense and nervous; may be easily embarrassed and overly sensitive to criticism
3. May appear depressed, sad, or troubled
4. Frequently is reluctant to attempt new tasks independently
5. May be afraid of making mistakes

### Aggression

1. May disrupt the classroom environment frequently
2. May be frequently involved in physical aggression
3. May intentionally destroy the property of others

**Instruction.** Several instructional approaches are often used with children experiencing emotional turmoil: contract reading, bibliotherapy, and cross-age tutoring. These approaches usually supplement or modify the regular reading program in the classroom but do not, except in extreme cases, replace it. Such approaches are not limited to emotionally disturbed students; they can be used with other students as well.

contract reading: An approach in which teacher and student agree to a document defining a set of reading experiences to be completed in a fixed time period.

**Contract reading** requires both teacher and student to agree that a defined set of reading experiences will be completed in a fixed time period. Usually, a reading contract is written by the teacher and then signed by the student. Upon completion, it is evaluated by the teacher or by both the teacher and the student and sometimes by the parents also. Reading contracts can cover a single reading period or can extend over a number of periods. Contract reading can be useful in helping aggressive students control disruptive behavior and complete work on time. It can also help anxious students meet with success or can assist withdrawn children in interacting with others to complete learning experiences. An example of a contract used in conjunction with **individualized reading** is shown in Figure 12–5.

individualized reading: A method framework that consists of selecting a book, reading it independently, having a conference, and completing a project (see chapter 2).

FIGURE 12–5
A sample reading contract used in conjunction with individualized reading

```
                        READING CONTRACT

  Date:  October 5


  Description of the work to be completed:

   I will read Sarah's unicorn. Then I will
  make an ad for it and put it up on our
  Good Books bord.



  This work will be completed on:  October 8


  Signed:  Michael T.        Debbie Smith



  Self evaluation:  I think I did good. Maria and
  Sarah liked my ad. Sarah read the book
  becaus it had her name.


  Teacher evaluation:  Your ad encouraged someone else
  to read your book. That's the best kind
  of ad. GREAT!


  Parent Comments and Signature(s):  Thank you for all the
  special things you do. Mike read this to us at home
  and we all enjoyed it.  Bob Tanner
```

bibliotherapy: Using literature to promote mental and emotional health.

**Bibliotherapy** refers to an "attempt to promote mental and emotional health by using reading materials to fulfill needs, relieve pressure, or help an individual in his development as a person" (Harris & Sipay, 1990, p. 682). A reader might find comfort or a solution to a real-life problem by interacting with literature that is related to an emotional difficulty being experienced. Reading about others with similar problems and seeing how they solve their difficulties often provides important therapy.

A program of bibliotherapy requires literature selections related to the emotional difficulties that students are experiencing. A librarian might be able to suggest selections, and bibliographies by Coody (1983) and Sutherland and Arbuthnot (1986) might be helpful. Bibliotherapy also requires special care in putting children in touch with appropriate materials. Self-selection is a possibility, as is introducing a number of related books to the entire class and hoping that target children are attracted to them.

Consultation with a school psychologist should precede any program of bibliotherapy. That specialist should be informed of plans and should be encouraged to give professional guidance throughout the program. Bibliotherapy should then be followed up with discussions, retellings, journal responses, role-playing, art projects, or other activities that allow students to respond to what they have read.

cross-age tutoring: Involvement of older or more proficient students in assisting younger or less proficient students.

**Cross-age tutoring** is a third approach to working with children experiencing emotional difficulties. With cross-age tutoring, older children assist younger children with reading activities, perhaps reading stories aloud to a group of younger children, listening to their oral reading, or participating in buddy journal activities. Children experiencing emotional problems can benefit from either tutoring younger children or receiving instruction from an older tutor. Children often feel special in the new roles and relationships that develop through cross-age tutoring. However, teachers must carefully choose, train, and supervise any students who work as tutors with younger children. Clear directions regarding specific responsibilities increase their chances of success.

In addition to the use of contract reading, bibliotherapy, and cross-age tutoring, there are important guidelines to follow while working with children who are experiencing emotional difficulties.

1. Be sure to complete an interest inventory before beginning reading instruction; motivation and interest are critical for these children. Then use reading materials that are interesting and engaging.
2. Communicate regularly with the specialist who provides services to your student(s). Use consistent management and instructional approaches, and share observations regularly.
3. Communicate regularly with the parents or guardians of your student(s). Ask that you be kept informed if problems occur at home.
4. Explain clearly the rules in your classroom. Children need to understand exactly what is expected of them.

5. Provide reading instruction at the student(s) instructional level. Begin with experiences with which your student(s) can be successful, and gradually increase the difficulty of reading tasks.
6. Praise children in public. Reprimand them in private.
7. Maintain your classroom as a happy, calm, orderly, and protective environment for children. Model your concern for others, and expect students to treat each other with respect.

## Students with Hearing Impairments

**Hearing impaired** children have permanently reduced sensitivity to the sounds in their environment because of genetic factors, illness, or trauma. Usually, these children are not sensitive to sounds softer than about 26 decibels (dB). It is important for teachers working with hearing impaired children to know the extent of the hearing loss. One categorization system used by the Conference of Executives of American Schools for the Deaf defines degrees of hearing impairment as follows:

hearing impaired: Describes individuals with permanently reduced sensitivity to sounds softer than 26 dB.

| Category of Impairment | Amount of Loss |
|---|---|
| mild | 26–54 dB |
| moderate | 55–69 dB |
| severe | 70–89 dB |
| profound | >90 dB |

Individuals with hearing losses greater than 90 dB are usually considered deaf; those with a lesser loss are considered hard of hearing.

It is also important for teachers to know when the hearing loss took place. The earlier a loss occurs, the more likely it is that a child will have inadequately developed language. And since reading depends on language knowledge, a child with an early hearing loss may have great difficulty acquiring higher levels of reading comprehension, especially if the loss went undetected for a long time. Approximately 0.2 percent of school-age children are considered to be deaf and hard of hearing (U.S. Department of Education, 1984).

**Learning Characteristics.** Depending on the degree of hearing loss, hearing impaired children compensate by using amplifying devices, speechreading (lipreading), sign language, or a combination of these methods to assist them. Teachers must realize that these students are very dependent on the visual information in a classroom, which includes facial expressions, lip movements, and writing. In addition, the following considerations should be kept in mind:

■ The language of hearing impaired children is often less completely developed than the language of hearing children.

■ Hearing impaired children must concentrate very carefully on learning tasks that are presented orally. Fatigue can develop quickly, leading to inattentive behavior.
■ Hearing impaired children with amplifying devices are distracted by extraneous noises in the environment. Such devices amplify both target and background sounds.

Even though most schools screen children for hearing impairment, some children have mild or moderate hearing losses that go undetected. Consequently, teachers should be aware of classroom behaviors associated with hearing loss and should request a hearing evaluation for a child displaying some of the following symptoms:

■ frequent earaches, head colds, or sinus difficulties
■ difficulty following directions or frequent requests to have explanations repeated
■ quick fatigue during learning tasks
■ easy distraction by external noises
■ frequent mispronunciation of words
■ clearly immature language

**Instruction.** Increasingly, children with hearing impairments are being mainstreamed into regular classrooms. Of those who are mainstreamed, the majority have mild or moderate hearing losses. Most mainstreamed children with profound or severe hearing losses have sign language interpreters who accompany them in the classroom. Teachers working with children who have hearing losses should consider these instructional suggestions:

1. Phonics instruction presents special problems to hearing impaired children. Therefore, teachers should depend more on contextual analysis and sight word instruction and should present all new words in context.
2. Hearing impaired children should always sit close to the teacher, where they can clearly see the teacher's face and lips.
3. Lipreading is easier for students if teachers speak normally, not with exaggerated lip movements and not too quickly or too slowly. Teachers should maintain eye contact with students and should stand still when speaking. Movement makes lipreading more difficult.
4. Because an amplifying device amplifies all sounds, teachers should attempt to limit extraneous noise in the classroom, especially during verbal instruction.
5. Periods of oral instruction should be limited. Several short sessions, separated by independent work, are better than a single long session.
6. Visual aids should be used as much as possible during vocabulary instruction and explanation of directions.

## Students with Visual Impairments

**Visually impaired** students may be legally blind or partially sighted. Individuals who are legally blind have visual acuity that is less than 20/200. That designation means that with their best eye those individuals can see at 20 feet (or less) what a normally sighted individual can see at 200 feet, even with correction. Partially sighted individuals have visual acuity in their best eye that falls between 20/70 and 20/200, even with correction.

visually impaired: Describes individuals who are legally blind (>20/200) or partially sighted (20/70 to 20/200), even with correction.

Contrary to popular opinion, being legally blind does not require being totally blind. Eighty-two percent of those who are legally blind have some vision. Often it is enough to be able to read print in large-print books or with the aid of magnifying devices (Stephens, Blackhurst, & Magliocca, 1988). Only about one in five legally blind individuals depend solely on Braille for reading. More than half use large- or regular-print books for most or all of their reading. One out of ten school-age children (10 percent) are thought to be visually impaired (U.S. Department of Education, 1984).

**Learning Characteristics.** It is important for teachers to recognize behaviors that indicate visual difficulty. Vision testing usually occurs in elementary schools but does not identify all vision problems, some of which go undetected. Teachers should recommend more thorough testing for children who display these symptoms:

- squinting
- holding reading materials very close or very far away from their eyes
- having red or watery eyes
- rubbing their eyes frequently
- covering one eye while reading
- having crusty material around their eyes and lashes

There are several ways in which visually impaired students compensate for their handicap: tactile sensation, listening skills, and greater attention. Some formal training may be required to take maximum advantage of each compensatory strategy.

**Instruction.** Visually impaired students are typically mainstreamed into elementary classrooms. If you have the opportunity to work with a visually impaired child, you should first consult your school's specialist to learn the extent of the impairment. You should also determine the most appropriate instructional methods to use, and you should find out which optical and mechanical devices your student may require when reading.

In your classroom you should try to maintain a relatively constant physical environment to help the visually impaired child move about. And you should always introduce the visually impaired child to any changes in the location of materials or furniture. Classmates can help with this task, too.

New concepts often need to be more extensively defined for visually impaired children, taking advantage of their tactile and auditory strengths. Although visually impaired students may have had identical background experiences, their interpretation of those experiences is different because it has been determined more by nonvisual senses. One important way to develop conceptual knowledge is to provide a rich listening environment. Tape recordings of favorite literature selections are particularly useful for younger children, and you may wish to develop a listening center for all of your students, including a central tape player and individual headphones. Most publishers make audio cassettes of popular children's literature, and books on tape can be obtained through your local public library or from Recordings for the Blind, 214 East 58th Street, New York, NY 10022.

## Students with Speech or Language Disorders

speech disorders: Abnormal oral language behavior due to phonological, voice, or other disorders.

Children with **speech disorders** produce oral language that is abnormal in how it is said, not in what is said. Several categories of speech disorders exist: phonological disorders, such as substituting /w/ for /r/; voice disorders, such as speaking with unusual pitch or loudness; disorders associated with abnormalities in the mouth and nose, such as orofacial clefts; and disorders of speech flow, such as stuttering. Speakers of nonstandard English dialects and children who speak English as a second (or third) language do not typically have speech disorders. Their speech needs to be compared to the speech of their language-related peers to determine whether a speech disorder exists. A speech pathologist can help make that determination.

language disorders: Difficulty expressing ideas in oral language or understanding the ideas expressed by others.

Children who have **language disorders** have difficulty expressing their ideas in oral language or have difficulty understanding the ideas expressed by others. Students with language disorders may not have developed oral language capabilities or may use words in abnormal ways, perhaps echoing words that are spoken to them. They may also have varying degrees of delayed or interrupted language development. Again, children who speak nonstandard dialects or who are acquiring English as an additional language typically do not have language disorders. According to federal estimates, about 3 percent of the school-age population has speech disorders; approximately 0.5 percent has language disorders (U.S. Department of Education, 1984).

**Learning Characteristics.** Children with speech disorders often do quite well in reading since their difficulty is associated with speech production, not comprehension. Not surprisingly, they do especially well in silent reading, rather than in oral reading experiences. Children with language disorders often have a more difficult time with reading, which is so dependent on adequate language proficiency.

At some time you may need to refer a child for formal speech and language assessment by a speech pathologist, who will appreciate specific information about the child's speech or language difficulties. Statements such as

"Karen's language seems to be different" are not especially helpful. Consider the following questions before making a referral:

- Is the child's language substantially less mature than that of peers? How does the child use vocabulary and syntax differently from peers? Can the student tell a complete story with all of the appropriate elements?
- What sound substitutions or omissions does the child regularly make? These are some of the more common substitutions:

    /w/ for /r/ or /l/ as in *wead* for *read* or *lead*
    /b/ for /v/ as in *berry* for *very*
    /t/ for /k/ as in *tat* for *cat*
    /f/ for /voiceless th/ as in *wif* for *with*
    /voiceless th/ for /s/ as in *thith* for *this*
    /d/ for /voiced th/ as in *dis* for *this*
    /voiced th/ for /z/ as in *thew* for *zoo*

- Do other students in the class often have trouble understanding what the child is saying? Why?
- Does the child speak so fast that intelligibility suffers?
- Does the child use normal intonation patterns?
- Does the child experience difficulty following directions?

**Instruction.** Classrooms provide excellent opportunities for youngsters with speech and language disorders to improve their communication skills, especially when the use of oral language is encouraged, valued, and well integrated into the daily schedule. Regular sharing times, formal oral presentations, informal conversations, group discussions, and cooperative learning group tasks can all be used to foster development of effective communication skills.

Younger students with speech disorders benefit greatly from reading experiences with predictable texts. Students can practice their rhyming or rhythmic patterns while enjoying a good story (see chapters 8 and 9). For the child who stutters, both teacher and classmates need to adhere to certain specific behavior.

- Attend carefully to what the child has to say.
- Let the child finish talking before you respond or interrupt.
- Do not become tense or frustrated at waiting for the entire message.
- Do not tease or ridicule the child's condition.

It is perfectly acceptable to talk about a disorder with a child. It helps greatly, though, if the condition is discussed in a matter-of-fact manner. For the stutterer, anxiety is likely to exaggerate the difficulty.

## Students Who Are Gifted

A universally accepted definition of **giftedness** has yet to emerge. Creativity, intelligence, motivation, artistic talent, verbal ability, curiosity, and the ability

giftedness: The condition of individuals with high cognitive ability, creativity, and/or motivation.

to see unique relationships might all be used to define giftedness. However, each would identify a different population of gifted students.

Renzulli's (1978) definition of giftedness includes three characteristics: high cognitive ability, creativity, and motivation. Alone or in combination, these factors distinguish gifted children sufficiently from their peers to make it possible for them to contribute something of exceptional value to society. Hallahan and Kauffman (1982) estimate that approximately 2 to 5 percent of school-age students might be labeled as gifted according to this definition. The federal definition is somewhat different.

> "Gifted and talented children" means children and, wherever applicable, youth, who are identified at the preschool, elementary, or secondary level as possessing demonstrated or potential abilities that give evidence of high performance capa-bilities in areas such as intellectual, creative, specific academic, or leadership ability, or in the performing and visual arts and who by reason thereof require services or activities not ordinarily provided by the school. (Gifted and Talented Children's Act of 1978, PL 95–561, section 902.)

Learning Characteristics. Gifted children tend to demonstrate exceptional per-formance with most cognitive and linguistic tasks. Indeed, a teacher's first observation of a gifted child is often to note the student's precocious language use. Gifted children talk about topics that are advanced for their ages, and the way that they talk is noticeably more mature. Some individuals believe that early reading is a mark of giftedness. However, even though early reading is often found among gifted children, not all gifted children read at an early age.

enrichment program: Learning activities provided to gifted students, often outside the regular class-room.

Instruction. The most common form of instructional accommodation for gifted children is an **enrichment program,** which provides opportunities for gifted students to pursue special interests inside and outside the regular class-room. A popular enrichment program defined by Renzulli (1978) consists of three types of activities. Type I activities are designed to help children learn about their environment and develop particular interests. Type II activities are developed around group process tasks, such as gaming and simulations. These are designed to enhance problem-solving skills, critical thinking, and creative thinking. Type III activities allow individual or group study of actual problems, such as community reaction to a new shopping center, preservation of tradi-tional folk knowledge, or changes in the local environment. Reading and writ-ing experiences are a natural part of each of these tasks. In addition, research skills are often developed with Type II tasks and then applied to the solution of real-life problems with Type III tasks.

A unique aspect of this enrichment program is the "revolving door" through which students enter and leave the program. Renzulli argues that children are gifted for particular tasks and at particular times. He advocates that children be included in a gifted program when they show an interest in and talent for the topic being covered. If they are successful and make an important contribution to the project, they may remain. If they lose interest or do not succeed in making a substantive contribution, other children are allowed to take their places. This approach opens enrichment programs to a wider population.

Cassidy (1981) has described another approach to gifted students, one referred to as **inquiry reading**. Inquiry reading follows a week-by-week sequence of activities, allowing students in Grades 3 through 6 to define, research, and then report on a project of personal interest. This method framework, which follows a procedural sequence consisting of four steps, can be used in the classroom with all students.

inquiry reading: An approach to gifted education that has students define, research, and then report on a project of personal interest.

1. Develop a contract (Week 1).
2. Research the topic (Weeks 2 to 3).
3. Prepare the project for presentation to the class (Week 4).
4. Present the project to the class (Week 4).

During the first week children learn the procedures, purposes, and goals of inquiry reading. Then they identify a topic of personal interest, locate the necessary resources, and specify a project that can be completed. All of this information is defined, along with a due date, in a contract developed by the student with assistance from the teacher.

During Weeks 2 and 3 students research their topics independently or in small groups. Often this step requires independent library work and sometimes interviews with members of the community. Students read, listen, take notes, and otherwise acquire the necessary resources to complete their projects. Often the teacher sets aside time during this step to confer with students and review their progress.

The final week is spent completing the project and preparing it for presentation to the class. Students can present the results of their work in a variety of ways. They might choose an oral report, a play, a written report, an art project, a diorama, a slide show, or one of many other creative formats.

**Establishing Mentor Relationships.** Locate local experts in areas in which your students are interested. See whether they can contribute an hour or so each week to work on an independent project with your students. Then design a contract around the project, and display the final results in your classroom.

**Publishing a Classroom Magazine.** Have a rotating group of students be responsible for gathering, editing, and printing articles written by members of the class. Encourage students to include stories, poetry, crossword puzzles, and other features, too. Consider using a computer since software is available for laying out and printing the results. Make arrangements to use the school's duplicating machine, and produce copies for each student in the class. Suggest that they share their magazines with their parents.

**SAMPLE ACTIVITIES**

**Cross-Age Tutoring.** Involve students in tutoring situations with students in younger classes. Explain that each member of a society is obligated to contribute something of value and that tutoring younger children is one way of contributing. Help students to carefully plan and evaluate their tutoring activities.

## USING A COMPREHENSION FRAMEWORK TO GUIDE INSTRUCTION OF STUDENTS WITH SPECIAL NEEDS

Teaching reading to children with special needs presents the same types of instructional decisions that must be faced when you teach any children. You must still decide what and how to teach. As a result, you will use your comprehension framework in a similar way. If, for example, you have a text-based explanation of how a person reads, you will tend to emphasize aspects such as decoding knowledge and fluent oral reading with most children with special needs. If, on the other hand, you follow a reader-based explanation, you will emphasize aspects such as inferential reasoning, vocabulary knowledge, and other elements of prior knowledge. With a specific skills explanation of how reading ability develops, you will use more deductive instructional practices when you work with children with special needs. With a more holistic language

Teachers must realize that all students have special strengths and needs, regardless of labels and categories.

explanation you will depend on students to learn what is important through inductive and self-selected reading experiences.

It is important to note that these generalizations do not mean that all children with special needs will receive identical instruction from one teacher. These children require individualized attention to their unique strengths and weaknesses. The approaches described in this chapter should be valuable resources.

## COMMENTS FROM THE CLASSROOM ■

### Mr. Burns

I believe strongly that all my students have their own special needs, and I try to accommodate those needs during reading instruction as best I can. I think I do a good job of meeting most of them.

I have several students in my class who speak a variation of Black English. I do two things to accommodate the special needs of those students. First, I always check to be sure that oral reading errors are really errors—interfering with comprehension. I only correct oral reading errors that change the meaning of the story, and that's important because I do a lot of oral reading to develop fluency in decoding skills.

Second, during read-aloud sessions I include a number of books that are culturally relevant for these students. I have students with both African-American and Haitian backgrounds in my class, so I include reading selections from both of those cultures to increase interest and motivation. Last month I read *Stories Julian Tells* by Ann Cameron, *The Drinking Gourd* by Ferdinand Monjo, and *The Magic Orange Tree and Other Haitian Folktales* by Diane Wolkstein. We've also read several Native American stories by Paul Gobel; *The Girl Who Loved Horses* was the class favorite. I like to bring multiculturalism into my class.

My Haitian student is not very proficient in English, and we don't have enough other Hai-

tian students in our school to have a bilingual program for them. We don't have an ESL teacher either, so the English she learns comes largely from her classroom experiences. Since Sherri arrived just two months ago, she's written and published a French (Creole)-English dictionary, and she's very proud of it. My other students have learned a lot of new words in Haitian, too, so it's been a great experience for everybody. Right now, Sherri is working with a group on a readers theatre activity, and that gives her lots of opportunities to practice her oral reading.

I also have a child who's been formally labeled as emotionally disturbed. He acts out quite a bit in class and has been unable to complete much of his assigned work. At our last IEP meeting we decided to try using daily contracts with him, and they seem to be working. He is attending to tasks better and completing more of his assignments. He's also receiving additional assistance from our school psychologist outside the classroom.

### Ms. Sanchez

We celebrate differences in our classroom through literature. Our reading and writing experiences allow us to explore and appreciate all the individual differences that exist in our class, and we do have a lot of unique students.

One of my students, Pat, has Down's syndrome and is mildly retarded. He's mainstreamed in our class, but Ms. Hunly, our school's special educator, comes in to work with him during reading. She's trying to develop Pat's emergent literacy/readiness through language experience stories, and she's also working on environmental print. Pat really enjoys our read-aloud sessions and is an active member of our cooperative learning groups.

We also have several Chicano children for whom English is a second language. Each of them speaks English reasonably well, but they're a little behind in reading. For their buddy journal activities I've paired them with students for whom English is their first language, and that seems to have really helped—they're all writing a great deal and learning a lot about English. I've also encouraged the Chicano students to read predictable texts during individualized reading and sustained silent reading. Those stories provide such a supportive environment for students, and they're really enjoyable.

Because there are several cultural and ethnic groups in my class, I like to create thematic units representing each culture for whole-class reading experiences. In the past two years I've created Hispanic, African-American, and Native American units, and I've managed to get multiple copies of the reading selections I need from one of the paperback book clubs. The books prompt important reading and writing experiences and great discussions about diversity.

## Ms. Dodson

Literature really allows us to bring diversity into the classroom so that we can learn about it and from it. I have two students who have been screened into the learning disability program at our school. Once each day these two students go to the learning disability teacher, Mr. Jonas, for an hour of outside work on math and reading. We're trying to arrange it so that he can

work with these students in our own classroom; but for the time being, I've asked him not to schedule his sessions during my reading period. Reading is just too important for any of my students to miss.

If we're reading a selection together in a whole-class activity, I often develop cooperative learning group activities because they're so supportive. In addition, my two LD students receive cross-grade tutoring from two fifth graders in Ms. Gallagher's class. My two students really enjoy that activity, so I've told them to get ready to do some cross-grade tutoring of their own with two first graders. They're excited about that opportunity and are reading several predictable texts to prepare for it. I want them to do several read-alouds with two first graders in Ms. Brown's room.

I've also developed several thematic units on cultural groups. The one on Native Americans I worked on with Ms. Sanchez. I really enjoy these units and have integrated them into our reading program.

Another thing I do I learned several years ago from an experience with one of my gifted students. Three years ago Wayne completed a unit on inquiry reading in the gifted program. He did a marvelous project about the need to recycle waste in the community, brought it back to class, and got everyone excited about inquiry reading. So I spoke with our gifted and talented teacher, Ms. Hall, and learned how to do it. We were one month away from our school's open house, and I decided to try it. It was a huge success. We presented our reports, dioramas, maps, posters, and projects to the parents when they came to school. Everyone learned a lot from the experience, and ever since, I've stopped working in our published reading series a month before our open house night and have gotten everyone into inquiry reading. It's been a wonderful success each year—for everyone, not just the gifted students.

■ Every student has unique needs that must be acknowledged in instructional decisions. Each student's background and abilities must be considered in reading instruction. Having children with special needs in the classroom provides an opportunity to celebrate and learn about diversity.

■ Teachers can help children with unique linguistic and cultural backgrounds in several ways: using language experience approaches, using culturally relevant materials, carefully considering background knowledge in relation to the texts being read, using cooperative learning group activities, ignoring oral reading errors when they do not alter the underlying meaning of a text, and respecting students' linguistic and cultural heritages.

■ Teachers can help exceptional children develop reading proficiency in several ways: preparing other students for exceptional children, capitalizing on individual strengths, ensuring successful learning experiences, building success into instruction by carefully considering what each child can be expected to do, recording and charting individual growth to demonstrate gains to students and parents, establishing an accepting and positive environment, regularly discussing student progress with others, and adjusting background knowledge to reduce the difficulty of learning tasks.

■ Teachers face the same types of instructional decisions with children with special needs that they face with other children. As a result, a personal comprehension framework functions in a similar way.

MAJOR POINTS

1. Interview specialists who work with exceptional children in an elementary school. Prepare a list of questions in advance, and use them to guide your interviews. Have the specialists define their roles and the learning characteristics of the children with whom they work. Find out what they do in reading instruction or how they assist classroom teachers in that area. Write up the results of your interviews, summarizing the major points.

2. The second sentence in each of the following pairs was read aloud by a speaker of Black English. Identify the deviations from the text that you would not correct because they result from the child's dialect and do not impede comprehension. Also identify the deviations that you would correct because they impede comprehension.

   a. Text:   One day five children went out to play.
      Child:  One day five childrens went out to play.

   b. Text:   The children laughed.
      Child:  The children laugh.

   c. Text:   The children were waiting for the parade.
      Child:  The childrens were watching for the parade.

   d. Text:   She wants to play. One morning a boy made a boat.
      Child:  She want to play. One morning a boy made a bus.

MAKING INSTRUCTIONAL DECISIONS

3. Imagine that it is the beginning of the school year, and your school psychologist has just informed you that you will have a new student in your room. This student was tested for mental retardation but was not admitted into the district's special education program. The school psychologist explains that the student has below-average intellectual functioning, but it is not low enough to qualify for special assistance. Identify several learning characteristics that you might look for during the first few weeks of school. Also, specify the major instructional consideration you will probably need to incorporate into your reading plans for this student. Finally, describe how you will provide appropriate instruction for this student without developing expectations that are too low and thereby preventing the student from developing her full potential.

4. Students with learning disabilities sometimes receive instruction from a classroom teacher with one type of comprehension framework and a specialist with another type of comprehension framework. What might that teacher and that specialist do to avoid confusing the child about the nature of reading?

## FURTHER READING

Chang, Y., & Watson, D. J. (1988). Adaptation of prediction strategies and materials in a Chinese/English bilingual classroom. *The Reading Teacher, 42*(1), 36–44.

Describes how prediction strategies and predictable texts in Chinese were used to teach ethnic Chinese children in the United States to read Chinese. Supports the idea that reading processes are similar in languages other than English.

Eller, R. G. (1989). Johnny can't talk, either: The perpetuation of the deficit theory in classrooms. *The Reading Teacher, 42*(9), 670–674.

Explains that the deficit theory may still be operating in the classroom. Argues that we need to listen more closely to the linguistic competence of our students who might be labeled verbally deficient.

Maria, K. (1989). Developing disadvantaged children's background knowledge interactively. *The Reading Teacher, 42*(4), 296–300.

Describes how teachers can assist children from different cultural backgrounds by looking at the central ideas in a text and finding out what children know about those ideas. Provides several useful prereading strategies.

Pinnell, G. S., Fried, M. D., & Estice, R. M. (1990). Reading recovery: Learning how to make a difference. *The Reading Teacher, 43*(4), 282–295.

Describes Reading Recovery, an early intervention program for young readers experiencing difficulty in their first year of reading instruction. Explains the five procedural steps of this method: reading familiar stories, keeping a running record of text read, working with letters, writing a message or story, and reading a new book.

## REFERENCES

Allington, R. L., & Shake, M. C. (1986). Remedial reading: Achieving curricular congruence in classroom and clinic. *The Reading Teacher, 39,* 648–654.

Cassidy, J. (1981). Inquiry reading for the gifted. *The Reading Teacher, 35,* 17–21.

Coody, B. (1983). *Using literature with young children* (3rd ed.). Dubuque, IA: W. C. Brown.

Cummins, J. (1981). *Bilingualism and minority language children*. Ontario, Canada: OISIE.

Dulay, H., Burt, M., & Krashen, S. (1982). *Language two*. New York: Oxford University Press.

Eller, R. G. (1989). Johnny can't talk, either: The perpetuation of the deficit theory in classrooms. *The Reading Teacher, 42*(9), 670–674.

*Federal Register* 42, No. 250, December 29, 1977.

Feely, J. T. (1983). Help for the reading teacher: Dealing with the limited English proficient (LEP) child in the elementary classroom. *The Reading Teacher, 36,* 650–655.

Fernald, G. (1943). *Remedial techniques in basic school subjects*. New York: McGraw-Hill.

Ford, M. P., & Ohlhausen, M. M. (1988). Tips from reading clinicians for coping with disabled readers in regular classrooms. *The Reading Teacher, 42*(1), 18–22.

Gonzales, P. C. (1981). Beginning English reading for ESL students. *The Reading Teacher, 35,* 154–162.

Grossman, H. J. (Ed.). (1973). *Manual on terminology and classification in mental retardation*. Washington, DC: American Association on Mental Deficiency.

Hallahan, D. P., & Kauffman, J. M. (1982). *Exceptional children* (2nd ed.). New York: Prentice Hall.

Harris, A. J., & Sipay, E. R. (1990). *How to increase reading ability* (9th ed.). New York: Longman.

Kauffman, J. M. (1981). *Characteristics of children's behavior disorders* (2nd ed.). Columbus, OH: Merrill.

Krashen, S. D., & Terrell, T. D. (1983). *The natural approach: Language acquisition in the classroom*. San Francisco: Alemeny Press.

Lerner, J. (1985). *Learning disabilities: Theories, diagnosis, and teaching strategies* (4th ed.). Boston: Houghton Mifflin.

Maria, K. (1989). Developing disadvantaged children's background knowledge interactively. *The Reading Teacher, 42*(4), 296–300.

McNeil, J. D., Donant, L., & Alkin, M. C. (1980). *How to teach reading successfully*. Boston: Little, Brown.

Pinnell, G. S., Fried, M. D., & Estice, R. M. (1990). Reading recovery: Learning how to make a difference. *The Reading Teacher, 43*(4), 282–295.

Raver, S. A., & Dwyer, R. C. (1986). Teaching handicapped preschoolers to sight read using language training procedures. *The Reading Teacher, 40,* 314–321.

Renzulli, J. S. (1978). What makes giftedness? Re-examining a definition. *Phi Delta Kappan, 60*(3), 180–184, 261.

Simons, H. D. (1979). Black dialect, reading interference and classroom interaction. In L. B. Resnick & P. A. Weaver (Eds.), *Theory and practice of early reading* (Vol. 3). Hillsdale, NJ: Erlbaum.

Slavin, R. E. (1984). Effects of cooperative learning and individualized instruction on mainstreamed students. *Exceptional Children, 50*(5), 434–443.

Stainback, S., & Stainback, W. (1989). Integration of students with mild and moderate handicaps. In D. Kerzner & A. Gartner (Eds.), *Beyond separate education*. Baltimore, MD: Paul H. Brookes.

Stephens, T. M., Blackhurst, A. E., & Magliocca, L. A. (1988). *Teaching mainstreamed students*. Oxford: Pergamon Press.

Sutherland, Z., & Arbuthnot, M. H. (1986). *Children and books* (7th ed.). Glenview, IL: Scott, Foresman.

Tierney, R. J., Readence, J. E., & Dishner, E. K. (1985). *Reading strategies and practices: Guide for improving instruction* (2nd ed.). Boston: Allyn & Bacon.

U. S. Department of Education. (1984). *To assure the free, appropriate public education of all handicapped children*. Sixth Annual Report to Congress on the Implementation of PL 94–172. Washington, DC: Author.

Walp, T. P., & Walmsley, S. A. (1989). Instructional and philosophical congruence: Neglected aspects of coordination. *The Reading Teacher, 42*(6), 364–368.

# INSTRUCTIONAL PATTERNS AND TECHNOLOGY

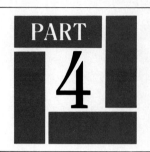

PART 4

Chapter 13
Classroom Organization

Chapter 14
Microcomputers and Related Technologies

# Classroom Organization

- Individual Differences: The Challenge and the Opportunity
- Interclass Organization
- Intraclass Organization
- Using a Comprehension Framework to Guide Decisions About Classroom Organization

*And Abe put on his buckskin breeches, washed his face and hands in the brook, and went off to school with his sister, Sally. . .There they sat together, big and small, reading and writing and reckoning aloud, all at one time together. There was such a chatter that it could be heard a long way off. But when Abe was six years old he had learned both to read and to write.*

*paired reading*
*cross-age tutoring*

How can you best organize your classroom for reading instruction? Should you teach reading to the whole class? Or should you work with separate interest groups, cooperative learning groups, or achievement groups? Should you have each student pursue an individualized reading project? Or should you develop experiences for the whole class, small groups, and individuals, too? In Abraham Lincoln's day, teachers did not make many decisions related to classroom organization. Everyone simply learned "all at one time together." The situation is very different now. Organizational decisions have become more complex as we have begun to value and accommodate individual differences.

In this chapter you will learn how informed decisions about classroom organization can nurture those natural differences. Chapter 13 includes information that will help you answer questions like these:

1. Which individual differences make a difference in reading?
2. What organizational patterns do schools use to accommodate individual differences in reading?
3. What organizational patterns do teachers use to accommodate individual differences in reading?
4. How can a comprehension framework guide decisions about classroom organization and integrate instruction focused on individuals, small groups, and the whole class?

## KEY CONCEPTS

achievement groups
cooperative learning groups
cross-age tutoring
cross-grade grouping
departmentalized reading instruction
homogeneously grouped classrooms
individualized reading
interclass accommodations
interest groups

intraclass organizational patterns
paired reading
reading/writing center
split-half classes
strategy groups
team teaching
thematic reading experiences
tracking
yearly plan

## INDIVIDUAL DIFFERENCES: THE CHALLENGE AND THE OPPORTUNITY

individual differences: Ways in which students vary; in reading, specifically background knowledge, reading interests, reading achievement levels, and reading skills.

As a developing professional, you are familiar with the concept of **individual differences** in educational settings. You know that each child in your classroom is unique in many ways. You also know that instruction must attempt to meet the unique needs of each student. Those individual differences within your classroom provide both a challenge and an opportunity. The challenge, of course, is to make instructional decisions that take into account the unique characteristics of each child in your class. The opportunity is to nurture the diversity in your classroom, modeling the respect for individual differences that is so important to our pluralistic society.

As chapter 12 pointed out, individual students differ along many dimensions. In terms of reading instruction, however, four types of individual differences are most important.

- background knowledge
- reading interests
- reading achievement level
- reading skills

These differences contribute in important ways to a student's interaction with a text. Consequently, each needs to be recognized in the organization of a reading program.

Let's look first at individual differences in background knowledge. Each child's previous experiences are unique; as a result, each has different background knowledge to assist with comprehension. If two readers are identical in every respect but background knowledge, they will comprehend the same story in very different ways. One child might make the required inferences, while the other struggles to understand. Classroom organization needs to recognize individual differences in background knowledge.

Reading interests also vary among students. Some prefer to read narratives; others enjoy exposition. Some prefer stories about animals; others enjoy stories about sports. Even students with the same background knowledge would comprehend the same story differently if one was interested in the topic and the other was not. Classroom organization needs to recognize individual difference in reading interests.

In addition, students vary in their reading achievement levels. What range of reading achievement do you think a teacher might expect in an average fourth-grade class? A conservative rule of thumb is that the variation in reading achievement levels equals the grade level of the class. According to Harris and Sipay (1990), we can expect to find at least four years' difference in achievement between the highest and the lowest achieving readers in a fourth-grade class. Thus, the lowest achieving reader might be reading at a second-grade level while the highest achieving reader is reading at a sixth-grade level. Because reading achievement levels vary so much within classrooms, no teacher can expect to accommodate individual differences by teaching all students with the same set of materials. Classroom organization needs to recognize these individual differences in reading achievement.

A final dimension of individual difference within the classroom is reading skill knowledge. Each student brings a unique combination of reading skills to instructional lessons. Some students may have comprehensive vocabulary knowledge but poorly developed decoding knowledge. Others may have comprehensive decoding knowledge but poorly developed metacognitive knowledge, or any one of many other combinations of well-developed and poorly developed knowledge sources. Multiplying the number of possible combina-

Classroom organization attempts to accommodate individual differences in reading achievement level, reading interests, and background knowledge in order to provide more appropriate, individualized instruction.

tions by the number of students in a class helps us appreciate the importance of accommodating each child's instructional needs in specific skill areas.

Students are clearly unique in the background knowledge, reading interests, achievement levels, and specific skills each brings to the reading task. The challenge is to determine how best to address that diversity to further each child's development. Both schools and teachers meet this challenge through organizational decisions, attempting to accommodate the wide range of differences to provide more appropriate reading experiences for individual students. Schools work through interclass organizational patterns; teachers utilize intraclass organizational patterns.

## INTERCLASS ORGANIZATION

interclass accommodations: Modifications in the organizational patterns among classes to accommodate individual differences.

Schools sometimes organize classes to accommodate individual differences in reading. However, these **interclass accommodations** address differences only in reading achievement. They do nothing to recognize differences in other areas important to reading, such as background knowledge, reading interests, or specific skill knowledge. Consequently, considerable variation among individuals still remains within each classroom. A variety of interclass accommodations exist and are described below.

### Homogeneous Grouping (Tracking)

Most elementary classrooms are heterogeneous; they contain children with a wide range of reading achievement levels (Hiebert, 1983; Slavin, 1987). To reduce the range of achievement differences within any single class, schools sometimes form **homogeneously grouped classrooms**. For example, a school with three homogeneously grouped classrooms at the fourth-grade level might have one class of high-achieving readers, one class of average-achieving readers, and a third class of low-achieving readers. This approach to individual differences is sometimes called **tracking** since children are placed in different educational tracks, depending on reading achievement level.

homogeneously grouped classrooms: An interclass organizational pattern in which classes are formed around students who are similar in at least one dimension, such as reading achievement level.

Homogeneous grouping is more frequently found in Grades 4 through 8, seldom in kindergarten through third grade. There is not much evidence supporting its use. Low-achieving students do not do any better in such settings, although limited evidence suggests that high-achieving readers do benefit from homogeneous grouping (Harp, 1989).

tracking: An interclass organizational structure using classes that are homogeneously grouped according to achievement levels.

## Departmentalized Reading Instruction

Occasionally schools use **departmentalized reading instruction**. This approach makes one or several teachers solely responsible for reading instruction while other teachers are responsible for other subject areas. With this arrangement, which is essentially the traditional high school format, students move from one subject-area classroom to another during the day, receiving instruction from each subject-area teacher. This type of interclass accommodation is almost always limited to Grades 4 through 8 and is seldom, if ever, found in kindergarten or Grades 1 through 3.

departmentalized reading instruction: An interclass organizational pattern in which one teacher teaches reading while other teachers teach other subject areas.

By itself, departmentalized reading instruction does not meet the challenge posed by individual differences. Often, however, it is combined with some form of homogeneous grouping. For example, the teacher responsible for reading at the fourth-grade level might teach reading to classes that have been homogeneously grouped on the basis of reading achievement.

## Team Teaching

There are probably as many different definitions of **team teaching** as there are groups of teachers who decide to share instructional ideas and students. Team teaching usually involves several teachers who pool their students for instruction, each teacher assuming responsibility for a specific subject area. This form of team teaching usually involves two or more teachers at the same grade level. For example, two sixth-grade teachers might decide to team teach mathematics and reading. Each teacher would then teach one of those subject areas to all the students in both classes. Typically, half the students would receive instruction in reading from one teacher while the other half were receiving instruction in mathematics from the other teacher. After that, the students would switch classrooms and receive instruction in the other subject area. Both teachers would remain responsible for teaching their own students in all other subjects.

team teaching: An interclass organizational pattern in which two or more teachers cooperate for instructional purposes, sharing ideas and students.

Like departmentalized reading instruction, team teaching by itself does not really meet the challenge of individual differences. Again, however, team teaching usually takes place in conjunction with some form of homogeneous grouping based on achievement levels. In the previous example the sixth graders might be grouped according to a combined achievement level in reading and mathematics. During one period the high-achieving students would receive reading instruction while the low-achieving students received mathematics instruction. Then, the same groups would switch subjects and teachers.

## Cross-Grade Grouping

cross-grade grouping: An
interclass organizational
pattern in which a school
regroups students across
several grades for reading
instruction.

**Cross-grade grouping** for reading instruction requires a school to homogeneously regroup students across several grades according to reading achievement levels. This plan affects only reading instruction. Students receive instruction in all other areas within their regular classrooms. According to this scheme, children in all classes leave their regular classrooms at the same time each day to go to their assigned classrooms for reading instruction. Thus, in each classroom, reading is taught to students who are reading at about the same grade level, even though their nominal levels might be anywhere from kindergarten to sixth grade. Sometimes cross-grade grouping is referred to as the Joplin Plan, after the Missouri town where it first received notice.

## Split-Half Classes

split-half classes: An interclass organizational pattern
in which each classroom is
divided into two halves
based on reading achieve-
ment levels.

Schools that use **split-half classes** divide each classroom into groups of higher-achieving and lower-achieving readers. One group comes to school an hour before the other group and receives reading instruction at the beginning of the day. After that period the remaining students arrive, and the school day proceeds normally with both groups in attendance. Then, one hour before the end of school, the early-arriving students leave, freeing the teacher for reading instruction with the late-arriving students.

Split-half classes create scheduling problems for families with several children in school and both parents working. Since children leave and return home from school at different times, busy schedules must accommodate additional juggling. In addition, split-half classes require that a school devote an additional period each day to reading.

## Retention and Acceleration

retention and acceleration:
An interclass organizational
pattern in which students
either repeat or skip a grade
level, based on achievement.

Retaining lower-achieving students for another year at the same grade level while accelerating higher-achieving students to a higher grade level was one of the earliest types of interclass accommodation (Harris & Sipay, 1990). In most cases of **retention and acceleration,** achievement was based on reading performance. More recently, retention has found increasing favor, despite evidence that neither retention nor social promotion have been consistently successful responses to the challenge of individual differences. Whenever retention or acceleration is being considered, it is important for the teacher to carefully review the child's situation with parents, principal, and school psychologist.

## Assistance by Reading Specialists or Special Educators

In many classrooms children who achieve at lower reading levels are provided with additional assistance, which is the final form of interclass accommodation. Under this arrangement children receive remedial reading instruction from a **reading specialist,** a teacher with special training in diagnosing and teaching children with reading difficulties. Other children may be formally identified as exceptional students and will then receive instruction from a special educator trained to work with exceptional students.

reading specialist: A teacher specially trained to diagnose and provide remedial assistance to children with reading difficulties.

## The Weaknesses of Interclass Accommodations

Interclass accommodations of individual differences suffer from two weaknesses. First, they tend to give the false impression that achievement differences among students have ceased to exist when, in fact, significant achievement differences still remain. Teachers of homogeneously grouped classes often believe that since all students in the class are high-, average-, or low-ability readers, they should receive identical instruction. Seldom is that response appropriate. Nearly every classroom, despite the best attempts at homogeneous grouping, will contain a range in reading achievement of at least two years (Harris & Sipay, 1990).

A second problem is that interclass accommodations recognize only one type of individual difference that is important to reading—differences in reading achievement levels. None of the interclass accommodations address variations in background knowledge, reading interests, or reading skills. These differences will always exist in a classroom and are also important to accommodate during reading instruction.

## INTRACLASS ORGANIZATION

Teachers often use **intraclass organizational patterns** to accommodate additional differences within their classes. There are three types of patterns that teachers use: individualized patterns, small-group patterns, and whole-class patterns.

intraclass organizational patterns: Modifications in organizational patterns within classes, designed to accommodate individual differences.

## Individualized Patterns

Individualized patterns provide an organizational framework to meet the multiple needs of students within a classroom. Such patterns can be used to accommodate all types of individual differences important to reading: background knowledge, reading interests, achievement levels, and reading skills. Because individualized patterns usually allow students to select their own reading materials, individual differences among students are easily accommodated. Students choose to read something that is appropriate for their own background knowledge, reading interests, achievement level, and reading skills. Individualized patterns include several different approaches.

Individualized reading: A method framework that involves the following steps: (1) selecting a book, (2) reading it independently, (3) having a conference, and (4) completing a project.

**Individualized Reading.** **Individualized reading** is described in chapter 2 as a method framework often used to replace or supplement a published reading program. Individualized reading uses self-selected reading experiences with children's literature, a practice that has demonstrated positive results (Tunnel & Jacobs, 1989). The process includes the following steps:

1. selecting a book to read
2. reading the book independently
3. having a conference with the teacher
4. completing a culminating experience (optional)

During individualized reading, students have an opportunity to select their own reading materials and read at their own pace. Thus, students are able to read materials that are consistent with their background knowledge, reading interests, achievement levels, and reading skills. After students complete their books, they briefly discuss with the teacher what they have read. During this conference they might be asked to read a short excerpt aloud and discuss the most interesting parts of the story. Teachers might also suggest that students complete a project based on the book (lists of possible projects are presented in chapter 2).

Individualized reading can be combined with reading contracts, which are helpful reminders for students of what needs to be done. A reading contract identifies the book a child selects to read, specifies the projected completion date, and defines how the book will be presented to the class in a culminating project, when appropriate. An example of a contract used with an independent book project is illustrated in Figure 13–1.

reading/writing center: A location in a classroom where students participate in a series of independent activities that connect reading and writing.

**Reading/Writing Centers.** A **reading/writing center** is a location in the classroom where students may engage in a series of independent, self-guided, teacher-designed activities that connect reading and writing. Reading/writing centers take many different forms but usually share several characteristics. First, reading/writing centers usually contain all of the materials required to complete an activity. For example, the following materials were needed for one reading/writing center activity used at the third-grade level.

1. Four books containing tall tales: *Shenandoah Noah* by Jim Aylesworth, *Paul Bunyan* by Steven Kellogg, *Sally Ann Thunder and Whirlwind Crockett* by Caron Lee Cohen, and *John Henry* by Ezra Jack Keats.
2. Writing paper, pencils, and felt-tip pens.
3. Students' writing folders.
4. A box to collect students' finished work.

Second, reading/writing centers have clear directions detailing the procedures for completing each learning activity. These directions are often displayed prominently on a bulletin board or wall. Figure 13–2 shows the directions for the reading/writing center activity just described.

FIGURE 13–1

A sample contract used with an independent book project

---

CONTRACT

I _Megan Fredricks_ plan to read the following book and complete my independent book project by _May 15_.

Book: _The Little Prince_

My independent book project will include:

_making a paper-mâché model of the asteroid and giving an oral report on my book._

Signed _Megan Fredricks_ _Ms. Keeney_
(Student)                               (Teacher)

Date _April 25_

---

Third, reading/writing centers hold students' writing folders, where students can keep drafts of writing projects. Often, a manilla folder is provided for each student and is organized alphabetically in a small box.

Finally, reading/writing centers often have a place to turn in or display completed work. There may be a collection box, as in the example, and perhaps

FIGURE 13–2

The directions for a reading/writing center activity

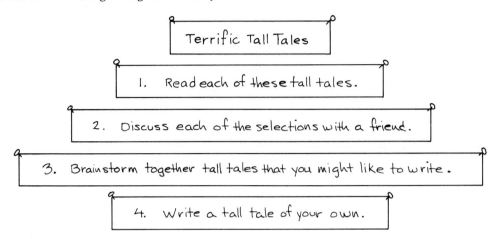

a bulletin board nearby. Displaying completed work gives other students an idea of what can be done. Usually a teacher has a single reading/writing center and rotates the activities there. Students are expected to complete center activities as they have time.

**Cross-Age Tutoring.** With **cross-age tutoring,** an older, more proficient reader assists a younger, less proficient reader in activities that are carefully organized by a teacher. Cross-age tutoring provides an opportunity to individualize reading experiences and provide a supportive reading environment for students, especially those who may require additional assistance. It is usually recommended that the older student be about two grade levels beyond the younger student.

cross-age tutoring: An approach using older, more proficient students to assist younger, less proficient students.

Cross-age tutoring is usually associated with increases in time on task, interactive learning, positive self-concepts, and positive attitudes about reading (Topping, 1989). There is also evidence that tutors gain in reading achievement at least as much as, if not more than, the students they tutor (Sharpley & Sharpley, 1981). Topping (1989) suggests that a minimum of three periods per week for at least six weeks' duration be set aside for cross-age tutoring. Usually, each session lasts from 15 to 30 minutes.

**Paired Reading.** In **paired reading** a tutor and a student read a text together. On easy sections the tutor allows the student to read out loud independently. When a mistake is made, the tutor pronounces the word correctly and has the student do the same before continuing. On more difficult sections the two read out loud together. Then, when easier sections appear again, the student might signal the tutor to stop reading, and the student would continue reading independently.

paired reading: An approach in which a tutor and a student read a text together.

Under careful teacher supervision, cross-age tutoring can benefit both the younger and the older student.

Paired reading provides a scaffold that supports a student, especially when more challenging reading materials are encountered. It requires less training than cross-age tutoring and results in similarly positive outcomes. Paired reading is typically used at frequent intervals, with each period of use lasting at least six weeks. In addition, it is often used in conjunction with a contract that outlines both the period and frequency of use.

## Small-Group Patterns

Small-group patterns provide an organizational framework designed to meet individual needs within a group of peers. Like individualized patterns, small-group patterns can be used to accommodate all types of individual differences important to reading: background knowledge, reading interests, achievement levels, and reading skills. Differences in background knowledge are usually addressed by providing a group with a common task and encouraging all group members to contribute their unique background knowledge to solving the task. Differences in reading interests, achievement levels, and reading skills are usually handled by developing groups around common interests, achievement levels, or skill needs. A variety of small-group patterns exist to meet these individual differences.

**Interest Groups.** It is often useful to group students by reading interests. Such **interest groups** allow students to explore topics that are personally interesting. For example, the sixth-grade class in one elementary school had been learning in social studies about the exploration of the western United States. Consequently, the teacher decided to let students select their favorite western state and then work with others who also selected that state. For one week during their reading period, students worked in their interest groups, reading, collecting information, and finally reporting to the class about their states. At the

interest groups: An intra-class organizational pattern that allows students to explore topics that are personally interesting.

same school the third-grade class was learning about different types of mammals in science, and that teacher decided to have students get together in groups to study their favorite mammal. Each group read, collected information, and then created a bulletin board display on their favorite mammal. Other interest groups might last longer but meet less frequently. Perhaps once a week or once a month different interest groups might get together to share information and books about their favorite topics: sports, pets, science fiction, music, or computers. In each case grouping decisions are based solely on students' interests.

Interest groups can serve several different purposes in a classroom reading program. A teacher might consider it important to regularly engage students in functional reading experiences, and opportunities to discover and share new information about an interesting topic can create important learning experiences. A teacher might also want to increase interest in and motivation for reading, developing students who not only can read, but also choose to read on their own. Or a teacher might be concerned about the negative effects on self-concept that might result from the regular use of achievement groups. With interest groups even the weakest readers have a chance to contribute to a topic that they find personally interesting.

There are several ways to form interest groups in a class. Perhaps the most common is to simply set up groups on several topics and allow students to select the area that they want to pursue. Often teachers administer a reading inventory at the beginning of the school year to determine students' interests (see chapter 8). The results of that inventory can then be used to make initial decisions about interest groups. Another approach is to ask students what areas they would like to explore that are related to a discussion topic just being completed. After students have had several experiences working in interest groups, this strategy can be an effective method of turning control over to students and developing greater independence in reading.

What is a teacher's role once interest groups are functioning? Instead of providing direct instruction, a teacher should guide students, providing resources for and direction to their reading. A teacher might circulate around the room, listening to ideas, offering suggestions, and helping children implement their own plans by directing them to appropriate resources.

cooperative learning groups: An intraclass organizational pattern that uses small groups and a cooperative learning method framework.

**Cooperative Learning Groups.** A second type of small-group pattern is the use of **cooperative learning groups,** which are described in chapter 2. Cooperative learning groups provide learning experiences for students in a supportive, collaborative environment, as small groups of students work together to gather information and complete a learning task. Examples of learning tasks that might be completed in cooperative learning groups are listed in Figure 2–5.

Cooperative learning is a method framework consisting of several procedural steps:

1. The teacher defines a learning task.
2. The teacher assigns students to groups.
3. Students complete the learning task together.
4. The results of the learning task are shared with the entire class.

The model lesson that follows reviews those steps in operation.

---

## Using Cooperative Learning Groups

**MODEL LESSON**

Mr. Graham uses individualized reading projects a lot with his sixth-grade class. He is concerned, though, that individualized reading is limiting interactions among students; he believes that his students benefit both socially and intellectually when they work together on joint projects. Consequently, Mr. Graham has decided to spend two weeks during each nine-week marking period in cooperative learning groups.

**The Teacher Defines a Learning Task.** Mr. Graham's class is studying Europe in social studies, and he decides to integrate social studies and reading for several weeks by using cooperative learning groups. He explains to the class that each group will study one European country in detail, exploring the history of the country as well as its economy, geography, political system, and famous people. Mr. Graham is especially excited about the potential this project has to motivate students to read newspapers and news magazines. The changes taking place in Europe will require that they read about current events. Mr. Graham explains that each group will read about its country and prepare a bulletin board display with a map of physical features and written reports on the country's history, economy, political system, and famous people.

**The Teacher Assigns Students to Groups.** Mr. Graham puts up a list of European countries on the bulletin board and asks students to sign up for their three favorite countries. Using that list for guidance, he puts students together in groups of four or five.

**Students Complete the Learning Task Together.** For the next two weeks each group gathers information and puts it together for a bulletin board display. Some groups work as a unit on each element of the task. Other groups split up, with one person responsible for the map and one person responsible for each of the reports. Mr. Graham encourages all groups to spend 10 minutes at the beginning of each work period sharing the information collected the previous day. He notices that students are gathering information for each other as they come across it in their reading. The last two days are a flurry of work, excitement, and debate as each group puts the finishing touches on its bulletin board display.

**The Results of the Learning Task Are Shared with the Entire Class.** On the final day the recorder/reporter designated by each group makes a formal presentation to the class. Individual group members also contribute their expertise, and then members of the class get to ask questions about the group's country.

---

achievement groups: An intraclass organizational pattern that provides students of similar achievement levels with an opportunity to work together.

**Achievement Groups.** A third type of small-group pattern is the use of **achievement groups** during reading instruction, thereby providing students of similar achievement levels an opportunity to work together. Groups of high-, average-, and low-achieving readers often use published reading programs to provide developmental reading instruction. Even though the utility of achievement groups has been questioned (Harp, 1989; Slavin, 1987), this grouping pattern remains one of the most common in schools today.

The first step in forming achievement groups is to gather information and determine achievement levels in the class. Two common sources of information include students' cumulative files and the informal assessment of reading achievement completed during the first few weeks of the school year.

cumulative file: A school file that contains a student's achievement and health records.

Each student has a **cumulative file,** which contains achievement and health records. Cumulative files are typically located in the school office, but classroom teachers have access to the information and often choose to review incoming students' files before the beginning of the year. At least two types of information might be useful: placement recommendations from last year's teacher and formal and informal test scores in reading.

In schools that use published reading programs, teachers are expected to record the materials that each student completes by the end of the year. The next year's teacher often combines that information with additional data and places it all on a single form. Table 13–1 includes the information collected by a fourth-grade teacher from the previous year's records of two third-grade teachers. The five students without such information are new students who transferred into the school at the beginning of the year.

stanine scores: Norm-referenced test scores that range from 1 to 9 and allow a comparison of relative standing.

The second type of achievement information can also be found in cumulative files—formal and informal test scores in reading. Table 13–1 lists **stanine scores** for decoding knowledge, vocabulary knowledge, and comprehension. These scores came from a test administered at the end of the third grade.

Because no single test score should ever be used to make decisions about youngsters, teachers should also gather informal assessment information on each student's performance within the context of the classroom. This type of assessment is especially important at the beginning of the year: some students read widely and make gains in reading achievement over the summer vacation, whereas others do not read anything at all and lose ground. Teachers might want to administer an informal reading inventory (IRI) at the beginning of the year to obtain informal data on achievement levels, or they might want to simply listen to children read during the first few weeks of school.

TABLE 13–1
Classroom assessment data collected at the beginning of the year by one fourth-grade teacher

| Name | Materials Completed | Stanine Decod/Voc/Comp | IRI Instructional Level | Informal Observation | Interests |
|------|--------------------|------------------------|-------------------------|----------------------|-----------|
| **FROM MR. NELSON** | | | | | |
| Tommy | *Flights* (4th) | 8/9/8 | *Explorations* (5th) | Fluent, read *The Hobbit* | Myths & legends |
| Anne | *Flights* (4th) | 9/9/9 | *Explorations* (5th)/ *Celebrations* (6th) | Spends lunch in library | Olympics, ballet |
| Tama | *Journeys* (3–2) | 3/9/6 | *Flights* (4th)/ *Explorations* (5th) | Excellent comprehension | Poetry |
| Sharon | *Journeys* (3–2) | 8/4/7 | *Explorations* (5th) | Summer library reader | Basketball, sports |
| Brian | *Journeys* (3–2) | 8/6/8 | *Flights* (4th) | Summer library reader | Mysteries |
| Jo | *Journeys* (3–2) | 5/5/5 | *Flights* (4th) | Exposition a problem | Sports |
| Katie | *Journeys* (3–2) | 6/4/5 | *Flights* (4th)/ *Journeys* (3–2) | Good reader | Horses, skiing |
| Sarah | *Journeys* (3–2) | 7/5/5 | *Flights* (4th) | Fluent reader | Science, computers |
| **FROM MRS. BLASIUS** | | | | | |
| Kathy | *Journeys* (3–2) | 6/7/7 | *Explorations* (5th) | Excellent inferences, good vocabulary | Mysteries |
| Nelima | *Journeys* (3–2) | 7/5/7 | *Explorations* (5th) | Summer library reader | Computers |
| Billy | *Journeys* (3–2) | 6/4/5 | *Explorations* (5th)/ *Celebrations* (6th) | Excellent vocabulary | Ballet, sports |
| Jesus | *Journeys* (3–2) | 6/8/7 | *Explorations* (5th) | Excellent vocabulary | Basketball, poetry |
| Tim | *Journeys* (3–2) | 5/8/7 | *Explorations* (5th) | Fluent, excellent vocabulary | Computers, sports |

TABLE 13-1
*continued*

| Name | Materials Completed | Stanine Decod/Voc/Comp | IRI Instructional Level | Informal Observation | Interests |
|------|---------------------|------------------------|-------------------------|----------------------|-----------|
| Roberto | *Journeys* (3–2) | 5/4/5 | *Flights* (4th) | Weak vocabulary, exposition a problem | Mysteries, Olympics |
| Jessica | *Journeys* (3–2) | 4/6/5 | *Flights* (4th)/ *Journeys* (3–2) | Good inferences, weak vocabulary | Reading, sports |
| Vanessa | *Journeys* (3–2) | 5/3/3 | *Caravans* (3–1) | Weak vocabulary knowledge | Pets, baseball |
| Jeff | *Journeys* (3–2) | 5/3/3 | *Caravans* (3–1) | Exposition a problem | Bowling, pets |
| Kurt | *Discoveries* (3–2) | 4/3/4 | *Caravans* (3–1) | Poor vocabulary, weak in exposition | Olympics |
| Warren | *Discoveries* (2–2) | 3/2/3 | *Discoveries* (2–2) | Poor decoding skills, halting reader | Basketball, dirt bikes |
| Becky | *Discoveries* (2–2) | 2/3/4 | *Caravans* (3–1) | Weak decoding skills | Magic, travel |
| **NEW STUDENTS** | | | | | |
| Erica | _____ | ____ | *Explorations* (5th) | Writes own stories at home | Adventure stories |
| John | _____ | ____ | *Flights* (4th) | Weak vocabulary | Science fiction |
| Vanita | _____ | ____ | *Explorations* (5th)/ *Celebrations* (6th) | Excellent vocabulary | Ballet, sports |
| Gene | _____ | ____ | *Flights* (4th) | Lacks prefix/ suffix knowledge | Dirt bikes |
| Daniel | _____ | ____ | *Carousels* (1–2) | Poor decoding skills, little comprehension | Hamsters, baseball |

Table 13–1 indicates the instructional level for each child according to an IRI administered at the beginning of the year. This particular teacher used passages from each level in the school's published reading series, and some students' instructional levels bridged two levels in the series. Table 13–1 also includes the results of informal classroom observations made during the first few weeks of school. This information, along with IRI scores, is especially important for new students, whose cumulative files are not likely to have been transferred by the beginning of the year.

---

## DECISION POINT ➤

Using the information in cumulative files at the beginning of the school year is somewhat controversial. Some professionals argue that the use of this information biases a teacher's perception of a child and results in a self-fulfilling prophecy (Rosenthal & Jacobson, 1968). They consider this practice most damaging to the least able and suggest that achievement information in cumulative files not be used to form achievement groups. Others argue that achievement scores, used correctly, are just one source of information that a teacher should consider. These professionals consider it inappropriate to ignore any information when making a decision as important as achievement group placement. What do you think? Will you use the achievement information in a child's cumulative file? If you decide to use it, what might you do to reduce the possibility of creating self-fulfilling prophecies for your students?

---

Once achievement data have been gathered, teachers must consider how many groups they want to form. The most common number is three (high, average, and low). However, teachers, especially new teachers, should consider several important factors before making that decision. First, what previous experience have students had with small-group instruction? Students with considerable small-group experience are able to handle more groups. Second, what experience has the teacher had managing several reading groups? Extensive experience makes it easier to manage more groups. Finally, what amount and quality of supplemental materials are available? Again, extensive materials for students make it easier to manage additional groups.

Teachers should also consider how many students they want to have in each group. This decision hinges on students' ability to work independently. Often it is best to reduce the number of students in a group that requires more individual attention. Thus, the lowest-achieving group in a classroom is often the smallest because those students frequently require more guidance and support from the teacher.

Any of the decisions made about placement in achievement groups at the beginning of the year should be considered tentative and open to revision. Teachers should use the first month or two to see how well individual students fit into the organizational scheme of the classroom. In addition, teachers should be conservative when making those initial placements. Placing students in a lower-achieving group lets a teacher evaluate their performance and move them to a higher group at a later time. It is much harder to move students down without disturbing their confidence and motivation. As the year progresses, teachers should continuously reevaluate their grouping decisions and be prepared to accommodate students who might benefit from a change in group assignment.

Finally, it is essential to use alternate grouping patterns during the year—perhaps interest groups, cooperative learning groups, and/or individualized organizational patterns. Flexibility is important if students' individual differences are to be accommodated.

**Skill or Strategy Groups.**  One final small-group pattern that attempts to meet individual differences is the use of **skill** or **strategy groups**. Teachers often find it useful to organize their classrooms for short periods of time on the basis of specific skill or strategy needs. For example, a teacher might provide instruction to one group on vocabulary knowledge, to another group on decoding knowledge, and to yet another group on the use of SQ3R when reading content-area selections. This type of grouping is appropriate when skill and strategy needs cut across established achievement groups in a class or when several students in individualized reading display similar skill or strategy needs. In such situations a teacher might regroup students temporarily on the basis of skill or strategy needs or might pull together certain students for a short workshop on particular reading skills or strategies.

Sometimes a school district mandates a set of minimal skill competencies that must be mastered by each student at a given grade level. In those situations it is common to find an elaborate set of pretests, instructional activities, and posttests that are used to test and then teach each skill to a specified criterion level. Teachers involved in such a process will probably need to set aside time to group students periodically on the basis of specified skill or strategy needs.

Decisions about how many groups to use and how many students to have in each group closely parallel the decisions made with achievement groups. The number of groups will depend on students' previous experience with group work, the teacher's experience, and the amount and quality of supplemental materials available. The number of students in each group will be determined by the number of students with similar skill or strategy needs.

Despite these similarities, two important differences distinguish the use of skill and strategy groups from the use of achievement groups. First, skill and strategy groups typically last for only a few reading periods before children are regrouped for instruction on new skills or strategies. Second, not all students will require instruction in the targeted areas. As a result, teachers should plan to use individualized reading activities with the students who are not placed in a skill or strategy group.

skill or strategy groups: An intraclass organizational pattern in which students are grouped for a short period of time according to skill or strategy needs.

## Whole-Class Patterns

Whole-class experiences can be valuable in many instances of reading instruction. They are especially useful when they take advantage of the diversity inherent in any classroom.

**Thematic Reading Experiences with the Entire Class.** As noted in chapter 9, **thematic reading experiences** are being used increasingly in elementary and middle school classrooms. Thematic reading experiences result when either a teacher or a published reading program organizes several reading selections around a single theme. In addition, writing activities, vocabulary study, and discussions are used to expand on the theme and generate new understanding.

thematic reading experiences: Reading experiences that include writing activities, vocabulary study, and discussions, all of which are organized around a theme.

Thematic experiences can be organized in numerous ways: around a topic, such as solving problems, helping others, winter adventures, friendship, or animal pets; around an author, such as Daniel Pinkwater, Judith Viorst, Paul Goble, or Laura Ingalls Wilder; or around a type of writing, such as science fiction, biographies, fables, or mysteries. The advantage of thematic reading experiences is that reading focuses on content. As a result, reading experiences become more meaningful and functional. Students read, discuss, and write about a theme in order to learn more about it, not simply to learn how to read.

Movable desks allow teachers to flexibly change instructional patterns, from whole-class to various small-group arrangements, as appropriate to instructional goals.

In a thematic unit the entire class usually reads the same selections so that all students share a similar body of content. However, these experiences often include cooperative learning group activities and individualized writing assignments to better accommodate individual differences.

**MODEL LESSON**

## A Thematic Unit on Sharing

Mr. Dewey has organized a unit on sharing for his entire class to enjoy. Three reading selections form the core of the unit.

*The Giving Tree* by Shel Silverstein
*The Gift* by Helen Coutant
*New Year's Hats for the Statues* by Yoshiko Uchida

Before each reading selection Mr. Dewey initiates a discussion about sharing that prepares students for the story. He also introduces any new vocabulary words from the selection that might be unfamiliar to students. After each selection Mr. Dewey uses cooperative learning groups to discuss it. He presents each group with a thought-provoking question about the story. After students read *The Giving Tree,* for example, he has cooperative learning groups consider the following:

> Do you think the boy in this story was too selfish or that the apple tree was too generous? Why do you think so? Be able to explain your point of view to the class.

During this thematic unit Mr. Dewey also conducts read-aloud sessions from the book *Chester Cricket's Pigeon Ride* by George Selden. During each session the class discusses the read-aloud story in relation to the selections they are reading themselves about sharing. Students begin to make comparisons between the characters and to apply the characters' experiences to their own experiences in the classroom and outside school.

Mr. Dewey also introduces a writing experience in order to connect the reading and the writing. He suggests that everyone in the class share an important idea for making the class a better place in which to learn and to grow. He encourages students to brainstorm a list of possible ideas, and writes the list on the board. After students finish drafting, editing, and revising their work, Mr. Dewey has them all read their papers out loud from the author's chair in the room. Their ideas generate lively discussion about improving the classroom. Finally, Mr. Dewey posts each paper on a bulletin board labeled Share a Great Idea.

**Additional Whole-Class Patterns.** Any reading activity that requires an audience is a perfect opportunity for a whole-class experience. Oral book reports, for example, can be presented by students when they finish reading a book that they think others might enjoy. Readers theatre presentations are also especially appropriate, as are read-aloud sessions. All of these activities encourage students in the audience to extend themselves on their own—to read a recommended book by an interesting author, to put together their own oral report, or prepare their own readers theatre presentation.

Short sessions in which students are introduced to new materials are also perfect opportunities for a whole-class activity. The teacher might conduct a book talk to introduce a new set of books in the reading corner. Or a student might introduce the author-of-the-week bulletin board and acquaint students with a favorite author. Perhaps a new activity at the reading/writing center could be explained. Each of these provides a useful encounter with reading materials in a whole-class pattern.

Another opportunity for a whole-class experience may occur when you wish to teach a reading skill to all students together—for example, the use of references in the library, map reading before a field trip, the use of a thesaurus as a writing aid, or a new poetic form. Another opportunity comes with current events. Often teachers have their classes subscribe to a weekly newspaper so that students can read and discuss current events together. In addition, sustained silent reading (SSR), which is often incorporated into a daily reading schedule, is an important whole-class reading experience. And choral reading provides an entire class with an opportunity to appreciate rhythm, poetry, and the stylistic conventions of unique discourse forms.

## USING A COMPREHENSION FRAMEWORK TO GUIDE DECISIONS ABOUT CLASSROOM ORGANIZATION

Decisions about classroom organization are decisions about how learning experiences will be structured for students. Will you use achievement groups to provide students with more direct instructional experiences? Will you use individualized reading, interest groups, and thematic reading experiences to provide meaningful, holistic, and functional opportunities for students to learn inductively? Or will you integrate achievement groups with individualized reading, interest groups, and thematic reading experiences? Because organizational decisions determine how learning experiences will be structured, your belief about how reading ability develops can be used as a guide. The organizational plans described here represent three specific beliefs. If your beliefs fall somewhere else on the continuum, you will need to modify your plans accordingly.

### Specific Skills Explanation

Teachers with a specific skills perspective believe that reading ability develops as students learn specific reading skills through teacher-directed, deductive lessons. As a result, these teachers organize their classrooms to maximize instruction on specific reading skills. A **yearly plan** for reading that is consistent with a specific skills explanation is outlined in Table 13–2. Yearly plans can be used by teachers to outline organizational patterns on a weekly basis. The plan in Table 13–2 specifies the primary grouping pattern for each week

yearly plan: A schedule of organizational patterns to be used during the year to accommodate individual differences.

TABLE 13–2

A schedule of organizational patterns in keeping with a specific skills perspective

| Weeks 1 & 2 | Introduce and begin reading contracts for first independent book project. Administer IRI and interest inventory. Collect informal assessment information. Check cumulative files for assessment information. Make tentative decisions about achievement groups. Begin read-aloud sessions. |
|---|---|

| Week | Primary Grouping Pattern | Read-Aloud Sessions | SSR | Independent Book Projects | Reading/Writing Center Activities |
|---|---|---|---|---|---|
| 3 | Achievement (tentative) | 15 min. | — | | Introduce center and contracts |
| 4 | Achivement (tentative) | 15 min. | Introduce | | Continue center |
| 5 | Achievement (regroup) | 15 min. | 5 min. | | Continue center |
| 6 | Achievement | 15 min. | 10 min. | | Continue center |
| 7 | Achievement | 15 min. | 15 min. | Contract # 1 due | Continue center |
| 8 | Achievement | 15 min. | 15 min. | | Continue center |
| 9 | Achievement | 15 min. | 15 min. | | Continue center |
| 10 | Skills | 15 min. | 20 min. | | New contract |
| 11 | Achievement | 15 min. | 20 min. | | Continue center |
| 12 | Achievement | 15 min. | 20 min. | | Continue center |
| 13 | Achievement | 15 min. | 20 min. | Contract # 2 due | Continue center |
| 14 | Interest | 15 min. | 20 min. | | No center activities |
| 15 | Interest | 15 min. | 20 min. | | No center activities |
| 16 | Achievement | 15 min. | 20 min. | | Continue center |
| 17 | Achievement | 15 min. | 20 min. | | Continue center |
| 18 | Achievement (regroup if necessary) | 15 min. | 20 min. | Contract # 3 due | Continue center |
| 19 | Skills | 15 min. | 25 min. | | New contract |
| 20 | Achievement | 15 min. | 25 min. | | Continue center |
| 21 | Achievement | 15 min. | 25 min. | | Continue center |
| 22 | Achievement | 15 min. | 25 min. | Contract # 4 due | Continue center |
| 23 | Interest | 15 min. | 25 min. | | No center activities |
| 24 | Interest | 15 min. | 25 min. | | No center activities |
| 25 | Achievement | 15 min. | 25 min. | | Continue center |
| 26 | Achievement | 15 min. | 25 min. | Contract # 5 due | Continue center |
| 27 | Achievement (regroup if necessary) | 15 min. | 25 min. | | Continue center |
| 28 | Skills | 15 min. | 30 min. | | New contract |
| 29 | Achievement | 15 min. | 30 min. | Contract # 6 due | Continue center |
| 30 | Achievement | 15 min. | 30 min. | | Continue center |
| 31 | Achievement | 15 min. | 30 min. | | Continue center |
| 32 | Interest | 15 min. | 30 min. | Contract # 7 due | No center activities |
| 33 | Interest | 15 min. | 30 min. | | No center activities |
| 34 | Achievement | 15 min. | 30 min. | | Continue center |
| 35 | Achievement | 15 min. | 30 min. | Contract # 8 due | Continue center |
| 36 | Achievement | 15 min. | 30 min. | | Continue center |

and also indicates how much time will be devoted to other organizational patterns, such as read-aloud sessions and sustained silent reading. In addition, it shows how independent book projects and reading/writing center activities are integrated into the class schedule.

Teachers with a specific skills perspective would probably generate a yearly plan similar to the one in Table 13–2. They would spend the first two weeks getting acquainted with students' abilities and letting students become familiar with the organization of their new classroom. These teachers might also introduce students to reading contracts for independent book projects. And as students are reading independently, these teachers might evaluate them individually with an IRI. They might also administer an interest inventory and begin collecting informal information on reading interests. At the same time they would be gathering achievement information from students' cumulative files and use all of this information to make preliminary decisions about achievement groups. These teachers would probably initiate read-aloud sessions during the first two weeks of school also. They might read quality children's literature to the students for 15 minutes each day after the lunch period.

Teachers with a specific skills perspective would rely on a published reading program for the core of their reading instruction, thereby leading to the use of achievement groups as their primary grouping pattern. According to Table 13–2, instruction would begin during Week 3. Then, during Weeks 3 to 5 these teachers would observe their students' performance and make any changes in group assignments by the end of Week 5.

We can see from the table that achievement groups are used during the first nine-week period. After that, the first week in each nine-week block is devoted to skills groups, for which students would be regrouped according to specific skill needs and provided with appropriate instruction. The next three weeks are then spent in achievement groups before switching into interest groups for two weeks. The final three weeks are again spent in achievement groups. The use of interest groups breaks up the continual use of the published reading series, increases motivation and interest in reading, and helps to develop independence.

Sustained silent reading is also integrated into the organizational plan shown in Table 13–2. It is introduced during Week 4, and students begin reading for short periods during Week 5. As they become familiar with the process, the amount of time devoted to the activity is increased, until students are reading 30 minutes on their own each day. This activity might follow the daily read-aloud session.

Independent book projects are used in this plan to provide opportunities for independent reading. Contracts are used to monitor the completion of those reading experiences. Contracts are also used to monitor the completion of reading/writing center activities. Each week the center activity is changed, and students make a contract with the teacher to complete a certain number of activities during each nine-week period. Contracts allow the teacher to monitor the number and types of learning experiences that students complete.

## Holistic Language Explanation

Teachers with a holistic language perspective believe that reading ability develops as students engage in holistic, meaningful, and functional experiences with print. A yearly plan for such a teacher would reflect those assumptions. Table 13–3 shows one possible arrangement.

Again, the first two weeks would be spent developing an understanding of students' abilities and interests and introducing students to each of the organizational aspects of the class. However, there are several important differences in the organization of this class. First, individualized reading is conducted without the use of contracts. Teachers with a holistic perspective look for more natural ways to get students reading and writing. Another difference is that students in this class are introduced to various types of journals: reader response, dialogue, and buddy journals. Journals become a vehicle for functional reading and writing experiences.

Teachers with a holistic perspective would rely largely on three grouping patterns during the year: whole-class experiences with thematic units, individualized reading, and interest groups. Table 13–3 suggests how these primary grouping patterns might be scheduled during the year. Read-aloud sessions and SSR would be used just as they would be from a specific skills perspective. Both types of teachers would want to develop independent readers.

The use of reading/writing centers would vary somewhat, however. Contracts would not be used to monitor students' completion of center activities. Instead, individual writing portfolios would be kept for students' writing. All completed works would go into those portfolios and be available to the teacher, student, or parents.

## Integrated Explanation

Teachers with an integrated explanation of development would include both specific skills and holistic perspectives in their decisions about classroom organization. Table 13–4 shows one way in which an integrated classroom might be organized.

During the first two weeks, time would be spent collecting achievement and interest data on the students and introducing them to the organizational patterns in the classroom. Table 13–4 shows that several of those patterns are consistent with a holistic perspective. First, individualized reading projects and reading/writing center activities do not involve the use of contracts. Second, journals are used extensively to facilitate students' responses to what they have read. In addition, thematic reading experiences with the entire class and individualized reading experiences are used periodically throughout the year as the primary grouping pattern. However, one important pattern in Table 13–4 is consistent with a specific skills perspective: the use of achievement groups in conjunction with a published reading program.

TABLE 13–3

A schedule of organizational patterns in keeping with a holistic language perspective

| Weeks 1 & 2 | Introduce and begin individualized reading.<br>Administer IRI and interest inventory.<br>Collect informal assessment information.<br>Check cumulative files for assessment information.<br>Begin read-aloud sessions.<br>Introduce reader response, dialogue, and buddy journals. |
| --- | --- |

| Week | Primary Grouping Pattern | Read-Aloud Sessions | SSR | Journal Experiences | Reading/Writing Center Activities |
| --- | --- | --- | --- | --- | --- |
| 3 | Individualized reading | 15 min. | — | Continue | Introduce center |
| 4 | Individualized reading | 15 min. | Introduce | Continue | Continue center |
| 5 | Individualized reading | 15 min. | 5 min. | Continue | Continue center |
| 6 | Individualized reading | 15 min. | 10 min. | Continue | Continue center |
| 7 | Individualized reading | 15 min. | 15 min. | Continue | Continue center |
| 8 | Interest | 15 min. | 15 min. | Continue | Continue center |
| 9 | Interest | 15 min. | 15 min. | Continue | Continue center |
| 10 | Whole-class/thematic | 15 min. | 20 min. | Continue | Continue center |
| 11 | Whole-class/thematic | 15 min. | 20 min. | Continue | Continue center |
| 12 | Individualized reading | 15 min. | 20 min. | Continue | Continue center |
| 13 | Individualized reading | 15 min. | 20 min. | Continue | Continue center |
| 14 | Individualized reading | 15 min. | 20 min. | Continue | Continue center |
| 15 | Individualized reading | 15 min. | 20 min. | Continue | Continue center |
| 16 | Individualized reading | 15 min. | 20 min. | Continue | Continue center |
| 17 | Interest | 15 min. | 20 min. | Continue | Continue center |
| 18 | Interest | 15 min. | 20 min. | Continue | Continue center |
| 19 | Whole-class thematic | 15 min. | 25 min. | Continue | Continue center |
| 20 | Whole-class thematic | 15 min. | 25 min. | Continue | Continue center |
| 21 | Individualized reading | 15 min. | 25 min. | Continue | Continue center |
| 22 | Individualized reading | 15 min. | 25 min. | Continue | Continue center |
| 23 | Individualized reading | 15 min. | 25 min. | Continue | Continue center |
| 24 | Individualized reading | 15 min. | 25 min. | Continue | Continue center |
| 25 | Individualized reading | 15 min. | 25 min. | Continue | Continue center |
| 26 | Interest | 15 min. | 25 min. | Continue | Continue center |
| 27 | Interest | 15 min. | 25 min. | Continue | Continue center |
| 28 | Whole-class/thematic | 15 min. | 30 min. | Continue | Continue center |
| 29 | Whole-class thematic | 15 min. | 30 min. | Continue | Continue center |
| 30 | Individualized reading | 15 min. | 30 min. | Continue | Continue center |
| 31 | Individualized reading | 15 min. | 30 min. | Continue | Continue center |
| 32 | Individualized reading | 15 min. | 30 min. | Continue | Continue center |
| 33 | Individualized reading | 15 min. | 30 min. | Continue | Continue center |
| 34 | Individualized reading | 15 min. | 30 min. | Continue | Continue center |
| 35 | Interest | 15 min. | 30 min. | Continue | Continue center |
| 36 | Interest | 15 min. | 30 min. | Continue | Continue center |

TABLE 13-4
A schedule of organizational patterns in keeping with an integrated perspective

| Weeks 1 & 2 | Introduce and begin individualized reading. Administer IRI and interest inventory. Collect informal assessment information. Check cumulative files for assessment information. Make tentative decisions about achievement groups. Begin read-aloud sessions. Introduce reader response, dialogue, and buddy journals. |
|---|---|

| Week | Primary Grouping Pattern | Read-Aloud Sessions | SSR | Journal Experiences | Individualized Reading Projects | Reading/Writing Center Activities |
|---|---|---|---|---|---|---|
| 3 | Individualized reading | 15 min. | — | Continue | Continue | Introduce center |
| 4 | Individualized reading | 15 min. | Introduce | Continue | Continue | Continue center |
| 5 | Achievement (tentative) | 15 min. | 5 min. | Continue | Continue | Continue center |
| 6 | Achievement (tentative) | 15 min. | 10 min. | Continue | Continue | Continue center |
| 7 | Achievement (regroup) | 15 min. | 15 min. | Continue | Continue | Continue center |
| 8 | Interest | 15 min. | 15 min. | Continue | Continue | Continue center |
| 9 | Interest | 15 min. | 15 min. | Continue | Continue | Continue center |
| 10 | Whole-class/thematic | 15 min. | 20 min. | Continue | Continue | Continue center |
| 11 | Whole-class/thematic | 15 min. | 20 min. | Continue | Continue | Continue center |
| 12 | Achievement | 15 min. | 20 min. | Continue | Continue | Continue center |
| 13 | Achievement | 15 min. | 20 min. | Continue | Continue | Continue center |
| 14 | Achievement (regroup) | 15 min. | 20 min. | Continue | Continue | Continue center |
| 15 | Individualized reading | 15 min. | 20 min. | Continue | Continue | Continue center |

| | | | | | | |
|---|---|---|---|---|---|---|
| 16 | Individualized reading | 15 min. | 20 min. | Continue | Continue | Continue center |
| 17 | Interest | 15 min. | 20 min. | Continue | Continue | Continue center |
| 18 | Interest | 15 min. | 20 min. | Continue | Continue | Continue center |
| 19 | Whole-class/thematic | 15 min. | 25 min. | Continue | Continue | Continue center |
| 20 | Whole-class/thematic | 15 min. | 25 min. | Continue | Continue | Continue center |
| 21 | Achievement | 15 min. | 25 min. | Continue | Continue | Continue center |
| 22 | Achievement | 15 min. | 25 min. | Continue | Continue | Continue center |
| 23 | Achievement (regroup) | 15 min. | 25 min. | Continue | Continue | Continue center |
| 24 | Individualized reading | 15 min. | 25 min. | Continue | Continue | Continue center |
| 25 | Individualized reading | 15 min. | 25 min. | Continue | Continue | Continue center |
| 26 | Interest | 15 min. | 25 min. | Continue | Continue | Continue center |
| 27 | Interest | 15 min. | 25 min. | Continue | Continue | Continue center |
| 28 | Whole-class/thematic | 15 min. | 30 min. | Continue | Continue | Continue center |
| 29 | Whole-class/thematic | 15 min. | 30 min. | Continue | Continue | Continue center |
| 30 | Achievement | 15 min. | 30 min. | Continue | Continue | Continue center |
| 31 | Achievement | 15 min. | 30 min. | Continue | Continue | Continue center |
| 32 | Achievement | 15 min. | 30 min. | Continue | Continue | Continue center |
| 33 | Individualized reading | 15 min. | 30 min. | Continue | Continue | Continue center |
| 34 | Individualized reading | 15 min. | 30 min. | Continue | Continue | Continue center |
| 35 | Interest | 15 min. | 30 min. | Continue | Continue | Continue center |
| 36 | Interest | 15 min. | 30 min. | Continue | Continue | Continue center |

## COMMENTS FROM THE CLASSROOM ■

### Mr. Burns

I've found that putting a yearly plan together at the beginning of the year really helps me organize my classroom to meet my students' needs. It's like a road map that guides my teaching during the year.

The first two weeks are probably the most important time of the year for me. I use that time to learn as much about my students as I can. I collect and organize achievement data, I discover the range of interests each child has, and I introduce my students to the rules and procedures of the classroom. Those two weeks are really central to everything else that happens during the year.

I like to use a mixture of skill groups, achievement groups, and interest groups with my students. I use the criterion-referenced skills test in our published reading program to assess and monitor their growth during the year, and that gives me useful information as I work with them in achievement groups. I do use achievement groups during most of the school year, but I switch to interest groups for several weeks in each marking period. Those are always fun, and they encourage independent reading, as well as give students a chance to practice and consolidate their reading skills.

I also use read-aloud sessions and SSR to promote independent outside reading. Our read-aloud sessions always take place after lunch. They help settle students back down into classroom routines, and I really enjoy those moments. SSR sessions take place every other day. I used to have them every day, but this year I just don't seem to have enough time. Our district has increased the time we have to spend on a new health program.

Contracts help me monitor and structure my students' experiences with independent book projects and reading center activities. The students work on those activities when they complete their regular reading tasks in the published reading program and when they have free time during the rest of the day. Contracts are the best way I've found to stay on top of my students' independent reading and writing experiences.

### Ms. Sanchez

I find a yearly plan especially helpful for my style of teaching. When visitors walk into my class, sometimes they think that my students aren't learning, just because I'm not standing in front of the class teaching a particular lesson. At times like that, I like to show visitors my yearly plan and explain that we're working on individualized reading projects or interest groups during that particular week. Then I take them around the room and introduce them to our journals, our bulletin boards, our reading/writing center, and our reading corner. Finally, I explain that we even build in time for SSR and read-aloud sessions each day. They always leave amazed at the amount of learning that's taking place.

I'm sure my yearly plan is very similar to that of most teachers with a holistic framework. But I do add in a lot of extra activities. For instance, on Fridays we all read and discuss the newest edition of our weekly newspaper. And our readers theatre presentations are always scheduled for Friday mornings. We also use our author's chair whenever someone has the final version of a writing project to present to the class. And of course, book talks are also scheduled for Fridays, along with presentations of an author-of-the-week bulletin board display. We *are* busy.

## Ms. Dodson

My yearly plan is a blend of the formats my colleagues use. I guess I use just about all possible arrangements—individualized reading, achievement groups, interest groups, thematic units—in addition to a lot of extra activities. I've shifted my emphasis a little this year, though, by decreasing the number of weeks spent in achievement groups and increasing the number of weeks spent in interest groups. Each year I try to get my students to propose, organize, and complete their own interest group projects before the end of the year. That takes preparation, care, and a little bit of trust on my part, but last year my students were able to carry it out by the middle of the year, so I've added an additional two weeks of interest group work this year.

My yearly plan lets outsiders see that there's a clear organizational structure behind all that goes on in class. It also helps me handle all the individual differences that exist in my students.

With all the challenges that come with teaching reading, there's also a lot of opportunity for satisfaction. In fact, I can't think of another career that would have been this fulfilling.

MAJOR POINTS

■ Reading instruction should attempt to meet the individual needs of each student in the classroom. Four types of individual differences are most important to reading instruction: background knowledge, reading interests, reading achievement levels, and reading skills.

■ Schools accommodate individual differences important to reading through interclass organizational patterns, such as homogeneous grouping (tracking), departmentalized reading instruction, team teaching, cross-grade grouping, split-half classes, retention and acceleration, and assistance by reading specialists or special educators.

■ Teachers accommodate individual differences important to reading through intraclass organizational patterns. These include individualized patterns, such as individualized reading, reading/writing centers, cross-age tutoring, and paired reading. Small-group patterns include interest groups, cooperative learning groups, achievement groups, and skill or strategy groups. Whole-class patterns include thematic reading experiences and other whole-class reading experiences.

■ Because organizational decisions are decisions about how to structure learning experiences, a belief about how reading develops can be used to guide decision making. A specific skills perspective will favor achievement groups as the primary grouping pattern. A holistic language perspective will favor individualized reading, interest groups, and thematic reading experiences. An integrated perspective will favor using achievement groups as well as individualized reading, interest groups, and thematic reading experiences.

MAKING
INSTRUCTIONAL
DECISIONS

1. Interview two students in an elementary grade classroom. Find out as much as possible about their background knowledge and reading interests. Then interview their teacher and find out as much as you can about their reading achievement levels and skill needs. Write a description of each student (without using real names), explaining how similar or different they are in areas important to reading instruction: background knowledge, reading interests, reading achievement levels, and reading skills. What can you conclude about the nature of individual differences in a classroom of 25 students?

2. According to Harris and Sipay (1990), you can expect a minimum of eight years' difference in reading achievement at the eighth-grade level. In reality, the difference is likely to be more than eight years. Let's assume that your school has departmentalized reading instruction for Grade 8, and you are responsible for assigning students to classes. You have begun by organizing three separate classes: one of lower-achieving readers, one of average-achieving readers, and one of higher-achieving readers. What is the minimum difference you should expect in reading achievement levels in each of your classes? Has a departmentalized reading program solved the challenge presented by individual differences? Why or why not?

3. Imagine that it is the beginning of the school year, and you have collected the data in Table 13–1. Use that information to form three achievement groups in your class. How confident are you in your decisions? Are there any students you should observe more carefully during the first week or so of achievement groups? Explain any concerns that you have.

4. Use the data in Table 13–1 to form several different interest groups. Describe several different reading projects that each group could complete.

5. Define your current comprehension framework. If you were to begin teaching next week, what yearly plan would you follow in your classroom reading program? Describe how you would meet your students' individual differences in background knowledge, reading interests, achievement levels, and reading skills.

FURTHER
READING

Harp, B. (1989a). When the principal asks: "What do we know now about ability grouping?" *The Reading Teacher, 42* (6), 430–431.
   Summarizes recent research into the use of reading achievement groups. Concludes that the disadvantages outweigh the advantages.

Harp, B. (1989b). When the principal asks: "What do we put in the place of ability grouping?" *The Reading Teacher, 42* (7), 434–435.
   Describes two methods that can be used to replace achievement groups: flexible grouping and cooperative learning groups. Explains how each method can be used to promote reading development in the classroom.

Topping, K. (1989). Peer tutoring and paired reading: Combining two powerful techniques. *The Reading Teacher, 42* (7), 488–494.

> Describes how peer tutoring and paired reading can be used in a classroom to meet individual differences. Points out that good organization is important in using these approaches.

Wesson, C. L., Vierthaler, J. M., & Haubrish, P. A. (1989). An efficient method for establishing reading groups. *The Reading Teacher, 42* (7), 466–469.

> Describes an easy method of creating achievement groups by using a curriculum-based measure.

**REFERENCES**

Harp, B. (1989). When the principal asks: "What do we know now about ability grouping?" *The Reading Teacher, 42* (6), 430–431.

Harris, A. J., & Sipay, E. R. (1990). *How to increase reading ability* (9th ed.). New York: Longman.

Hiebert, E. H. (1983). An examination of ability grouping for reading instruction. *Reading Research Quarterly, 18*(2), 231–255.

Rosenthal, R., & Jacobson, J. (1968). *Pygmalion in the classroom*. New York: Holt, Rinehart & Winston.

Sharpley, A. M., & Sharpley, C. F. (1981). Peer tutoring—A review of the literature. *Collected Original Resources in Education, 5*(3), 7–11.

Slavin, R. E. (1987). Ability grouping and student achievement in elementary schools: A best evidence synthesis. *Review of Educational Research, 57*(3), 293–336.

Topping, K. (1989). Peer tutoring and paired reading: Combining two powerful techniques. *The Reading Teacher, 42* (7), 488–494.

Tunnell, M. O., & Jacobs, J. S. (1989). Using "real" books: Research findings on literature based reading instruction. *The Reading Teacher, 42*(7), 470–477.

# Microcomputers and Related Technologies

**Chapter 14**

- A Model of Microcomputer Use in Reading Instruction
- Specific Applications of Technology in Reading Instruction
- Finding, Choosing, and Evaluating Software
- Using a Comprehension Framework to Guide Technological Applications

*"Wait a minute! This is exactly like something I saw on television. . . .See," Linda went on, pausing to get a tray, "this boy and girl started communicating by computer, and they met at McDonald's and fell in love. . . ."*

*"Linda, this is nothing like that program. I don't know who sent this message. It could have been a girl or a boy or a ninety-year-old man. You don't understand—"*

*"Of course I don't understand. How could I? I have never in my life touched a computer that it didn't go, 'ILLEGAL COMMAND.'"*

**M**any teachers share Linda's frustration with microcomputers. In fact, many are somewhat intimidated by most of our emerging technology. Nonetheless, teachers are also generally aware that the wide range of available aids offers potential benefits for instructional practices.

This chapter discusses the use of various technologies in reading instruction. It presents a five-part model of microcomputer use, followed by a discussion of other technologies that can enhance reading instruction—for example, videodiscs, television, hypermedia, and answering machines. Chapter 14 includes information that will help you answer questions like these:

1. What is an appropriate model for microcomputer use in reading instruction?
2. How can microcomputers and related technologies be used to enhance reading instruction?
3. What should be considered when choosing or evaluating software?
4. How does a comprehension framework guide a teacher's use of microcomputer technology?

KEY CONCEPTS

application software
drill-and-practice software
graphics
hardware
learning about thinking with
    computers
learning with computers
Logo

managing learning with computers
program
simulations
(speech-based) software
spreadsheet
tutorial software
videodisc

## A MODEL OF MICROCOMPUTER USE IN READING INSTRUCTION

The reading teacher's job is a demanding one. It requires careful decision making while high-level cognitive processes are being constructed. Nonetheless, some view microcomputer technology as a force that will radically change instructional practice, almost replacing teachers. Others believe that microcomputers are an expensive fad that will die out as school systems acknowledge that instruction requires a human quality.

Neither of these views adequately reflects the potential benefits of a thoughtful implementation of microcomputers in the reading curriculum. Microcomputers are an educational tool that can be well used or badly misused, like all other technology and teaching materials. For example, neither published reading programs nor the use of children's literature provide any greater guarantee of effective instruction than do microcomputers. In all cases, teachers must make appropriate instructional decisions.

DECISION POINT ➤

The two following quotations reflect the diverse opinions about the impact of computers on education.

> There won't be schools in the future. . . .I think the computer will blow up the school. . . .The whole system is based on a set of structural concepts that are incompatible with the presence of the computer. (Papert, 1984, p. 38)

> Where favorable conditions exist, teacher use [of computers] will increase but seldom exceed more than 10 percent of weekly instructional time. . . .Where unfavorable conditions exist. . .schoolwide use will be spotty. . . .I predict no great breakthrough in teacher use patterns at either level of schooling. The new technology, like its predecessors, will be tailored to fit the teacher's perspective and the tight contours of school and classroom settings. (Cuban, 1986, p. 99)

However, even the more pessimistic view acknowledges that technology will, to some extent, continue to appear in schools and that the use of technology depends on a teacher's instructional framework. Given your own comprehension framework, how will you incorporate technology into your reading instruction?

Taylor (1980) suggests that the computer has three potential functions: tutor, tool, and tutee. By tutor he means that the computer can be a patient instructor, providing practice exercises or information. Used as a tool, the computer can be an aid to the teacher, perhaps helping with recordkeeping or other functions. Finally, as a tutee the computer can be programmed or "educated." Taylor's classification system was modified by Luehrmann (1983), who relabeled the functions:

1. learning about computers
2. learning from computers
3. learning with computers

These categories were then expanded by Goldberg and Sherwood (1983):

4. learning about thinking with computers
5. managing learning with computers

This text presents that five-part model of computer use, as highlighted in Table 14–1.

## Learning About Computers

This category of computer use deals mainly with computer literacy. When students first use a computer, they need to learn about its components, as well as its common peripheral equipment, such as printers. Also included in this category is learning to **program** computers in any one of many computer languages—usually **BASIC, Logo,** or **HyperCard** in education. In addition,

(to) program: Write instructions that tell a computer what to do.

BASIC: A programming language commonly taught to beginning users.

Logo: A computer language that uses simple commands and is easy to use for graphics.

HyperCard: A computer language being used increasingly for educational programming.

TABLE 14–1
A classification system of computer use

| Classification | Examples |
|---|---|
| Learning about computers | Computer literacy: includes learning about the equipment as well as learning programming languages |
| Learning from computers | Drill and practice: includes most games and tutorial software |
| Learning with computers | Simulations: includes software that models a real-world situation and attempts to enhance problem-solving abilities |
| Learning about thinking with computers | Problem solving: includes the potential influence on students' thinking skills that results from working with computers and some types of software |
| Managing learning with computers | Classroom management: includes record keeping, filing, and other such functions |

applications software: Programs that are useful in everyday life, for example, word processing software.

spreadsheet: A type of applications software that allows entry of data in rows and columns for later manipulation.

this category includes an introduction to the most useful **application software:** word processing, filing, and **spreadsheet** programs. Such software demonstrates the potential usefulness of computers in everyday life, and programs are available in each of these applications areas that can be used with children in primary grades.

Learning about computers will not be the main focus in a reading classroom. However, students must know enough about the equipment to use it intelligently. For example, they need to know how to turn on and off a particular microcomputer, how to load and run specific software, how to use a printer, how to handle and store diskettes, and so on.

## Learning from Computers

In this category the computer acts as an instructor, with communication being essentially a one-way affair—from microcomputer to student. Most of the applications in this area are drill-and-practice software, but tutorial and gaming software also falls within this category.

drill-and-practice software: Nonteaching programs that present activities intended to reinforce knowledge.

**Drill-and-Practice Software.** **Drill-and-practice software** most often presents students with a series of questions. A correct response results in some form of feedback and a new question; an incorrect response results in feedback and the opportunity to try again. If the answer is still incorrect, most drill-and-practice programs give the answer and move on to a new question. Such software usually keeps track of a student's responses and provides the student, the teacher, or both with the student's overall score. Drill-and-practice software is available in all areas of reading, from decoding to vocabulary, main idea comprehension, and so on. The following lesson gives a typical session that a student might have with a drill-and-practice program.

When computers are located in a laboratory, sometimes linked in a network, intact classes visit at regular intervals, and students work individually or in pairs at their own pace.

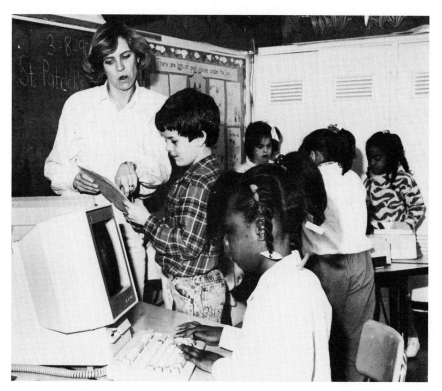

## Software for Drill and Practice on Prefixes

**MODEL LESSON**

```
This is a lesson on PREFIXES.
Please tell me your name: <Student enters Tony>

Hello, Tony. I will show you a sentence with a
word underlined. That word will have a PREFIX.
You will have to tell me the prefix and choose
what it means from a list of choices. Here is
your first question:

    That water is impure.

    The prefix in impure is <Student enters response>
```

(If incorrect, student is told that the answer is not right and is asked to try again. If correct, the program continues....)

```
Good for you! You're right! The prefix in impure
                                          ‾‾‾‾‾‾
is im.
   ‾‾

    In impure the prefix im means
       ‾‾‾‾‾‾           ‾‾
    a. with
    b. in
    c. not
Choose one of the meanings: <Student responds>
```

(If incorrect, the student is told that the answer is not right and is asked to try again. If correct, the student receives feedback, and the program continues with the drill-and-practice exercise. At the conclusion of the program, the student is presented with the number correct and number attempted.)

---

Drill-and-practice software is the most common software marketed specifically for reading instruction. By definition it does not teach; like regular paper-and-pencil worksheets, it only allows students to practice what has already been taught. However, practice can be an important step after teaching and initial learning have taken place. The question for teachers is whether drill-and-practice programs, which are often little more than computerized worksheets, offer an advantage over a regular worksheet.

In the drill-and-practice area, microcomputers may have at least three advantages over worksheets, although each drill-and-practice program must be evaluated to see whether these or other desired features are present.

1. *Motivational presentation*. Microcomputers appear to stimulate and motivate students to a greater extent than workbooks do. Even when tasks are similar, students spend more time on computer drill-and-practice activities than they do on worksheets. It is possible that this increased attention is a response to novelty rather than to some inherently motivational aspect of the microcomputer.
2. *Record-keeping functions*. The microcomputer can quickly capture and tabulate student scores, which are then usually placed in a file where teachers can easily see who has done well and who might need additional instruction. Thus, computerized recordkeeping can provide information needed for instructional decisions, thereby relieving teachers of the need to check students' answers manually.
3. *Branching capabilities*. The microcomputer can present drill-and-practice activities more closely matched to student ability levels than those presented in a workbook. For example, if a student answers three consecutive problems incorrectly, software can branch to similar items of less difficulty.

It can also branch to items of greater difficulty if a student responds correctly a given number of times.

An additional advantage of some drill-and-practice software is that a teacher can customize what is presented, thereby matching specific instructional objectives quite closely. For example, some drill-and-practice software in the vocabulary area allows a teacher to enter the vocabulary words and meanings to be presented. Other software provides a series of prompts that help a teacher customize a program. For instance, if a teacher wants to create a multiple-choice test, the software might ask how many items and how many choices per item are desired. The teacher might then type in the first item, followed by the multiple choices. Then the correct choice would be indicated, along with any feedback desired for either correct or incorrect answers. This process would continue until the entire test had been entered. At that point the software would compile and format the entries so that correct screen displays and tabulations of responses would be presented to students. Other software is available that allows a teacher to input a list of words and to receive, in return, a crossword puzzle based on that list.

**Tutorial Software.** **Tutorial software** is designed so that a student can learn as well as practice. The model lesson that follows, again on prefixes, provides an example of tutorial software (Hasselbring & Cavanaugh, 1986).

tutorial software: Programs that attempt to teach as well as reinforce concepts.

---

## Software for Tutorial on Prefixes

**MODEL LESSON**

```
This is a lesson on PREFIXES.
Please tell me your name: <Student enters Tony>

Hello, Tony. Let me tell you about prefixes.
A prefix is found at the beginning of a word.
It almost always changes the meaning of the word.

Re is a prefix.
Re means back or again.

Replace means to place back.
Replay means to play again.

Tony, read this sentence:
    Sue repaid the money she owed Mary.

It means:
    Sue paid back the money she owed Mary.

Repaid means paid back.
Re means back.
```

```
Read this sentence:
    The corn must be replanted.

It means:
    The corn must be planted again.

Replanted means planted again.
Re means again.

Try these activities, Tony.
Draw a line under all the letters in a
prefix by pressing the → key.

Underline the Prefix

repaint
```

(If the student correctly underlines *re,* the program responds:)

```
THAT'S RIGHT, Tony.
Repaint means to paint again.
```

(If the student incorrectly underlines the prefix, the program responds:)

```
TRY AGAIN, Tony.
```

(If the response is still incorrect, the program responds:)

```
No, the answer is re.
Repaint means to paint again.
```

(The program continues until there are no more items in the lesson or, in some programs, until the student elects to stop. Most tutorial programs provide the student and/or the teacher with an indication of number correct, number attempted, and overall progress.)

---

Thus, tutorial software goes beyond a simple presentation of items to which a student responds. Tutorial programs are written so that a concept or fact is first taught and then practiced. This type of software almost always includes branches that change the difficulty of items or that provide additional instruction depending on the student's performance. In addition, explanations are included, as well as feedback.

Although tutorial software is preferred to simple drill-and-practice offerings, it, too, can be misused. The computer can patiently present a tutorial, but it cannot decide whether that tutorial includes content that is important to a student's reading development. The teacher must determine whether software content, format, sequencing of concepts, pacing, and other factors are appropriate to the instructional program, the reading process, and reading instruction in general.

**Gaming Software.** Most **gaming software** uses the color, sound, and animation capabilities of microcomputers to catch and hold student attention. Such software presents instruction in a format that allows a student to play against others or the computer while learning. The student is challenged to compile a high score. Software that teaches in a game format is becoming more and more prevalent, as are microcomputers that feature advanced **graphics** and sound capabilities. Although teachers need to be careful that the concepts being presented are not overshadowed by the peripheral aspects of the presentation, well-constructed gaming software can be pedagogically sound and is popular with both students and teachers.

gaming software: Computer programs that use games or gamelike formats to teach and reinforce concepts.

graphics: Computer displays that are drawings rather than text or numbers.

Awareness of several problems associated with gaming software should help ensure that it is chosen for its educational rather than its gaming value.

- Gaming software often has violent overtones. These programs must be carefully evaluated and their consequences considered.
- Problems with reinforcement can occur if getting a wrong answer is more interesting than getting a correct one. For example, seeing something explode in full color and with sound could motivate errors.
- Gaming software is sometimes used far beyond its value. Students who like to play a particular game may continue to use the software long after mastering its concepts. In that case instructional time would be used inappropriately because students should have moved on to new items.
- Gaming software often involves eye-hand coordination and reflexes, which may prompt incorrect responses due to factors unrelated to the reading process.

To understand the appeal of gaming software, try to imagine learning prefixes in a format modeled after the Space Invaders video game. At the top of the screen, several prefixes appear, enclosed in various shapes and in different colors, and begin to move down the screen. At the bottom of the screen a definition is presented inside a cannon. The student must fire the definition at the appropriate prefix. The object is to shoot all the prefixes with their correct definitions before they reach the bottom of the screen. Such a format is also used to teach typing: different letters float to the bottom of the screen, but if a student successfully presses the proper keys in the correct order, the letters disappear and the student wins the game.

## Learning with Computers

Software in this category also attempts to teach, but it provides a much richer context for the student in the form of **simulations,** which are models of real-world events or situations. Microcomputer simulations place students in sit-

simulations: Presentations of events similar to those found in the real world.

uations that are similar to those they would experience in reality; simulations also model events and processes. Although simulation software is less prevalent in reading education than in other subject areas, it holds tremendous potential. For example, some simulation software allows a student to learn that plot development depends on a series of decisions. That is, the student learns that later developments in a story are constrained by what happens earlier. These simulations allow the student to become a character in a story and to make decisions about that character's actions. As the plot changes according to the choices made by the student, awareness of plot development builds.

Other software simulates the writing of a newspaper article, making the student a reporter who is sent out to get a story. The student searches for pertinent facts and writes the story, submitting it to the editor (the computer), who checks key words in the story to determine whether the appropriate facts have been presented. The editor then provides feedback about the logic of the facts chosen and gives hints about rewriting the story. A specific objective of this software is to teach who, why, what, when, where, and how questions.

Some software uses what we know about the reading process to require a student to approximate what a reader does. For example, we know that a reader uses context to help find the meanings of unfamiliar words or looks them up in a dictionary or glossary. We also know (1) that readers predict upcoming events, (2) that they look back to confirm their predictions, (3) that they can sometimes understand spoken words but not written words, (4) that they use syntax to aid comprehension, and (5) that quality literature is motivating. Software such as Reading Comprehension (Houghton Mifflin) incorporates these features.

That program allows a student to look up or hear a word while reading literature selections. Color illustrations and animation are included to enhance the story. Comprehension questions are asked at all levels and include questions about upcoming text, text that has just been read, and text that was read several pages before. Feedback is provided not only through the indication of a correct or incorrect response, but also through reference to the text, where syntactic and semantic connections are highlighted to make the relationships between concepts and causes explicit. The reader can reread or preview within the selection, which is longer than just a single screen of text. In addition, such integrated packages provide record-keeping functions, the capability of printing story selections, opportunities for practice, and personalized letters that can be sent to parents to indicate progress. Clearly, such programs have moved far beyond simple drill-and-practice offerings and are bordering on the realm of simulations.

Simulations intended for other subject areas can also be useful to a reading teacher. For example, Oregon Trail (MECC), a simulation intended for social studies, might be used to build background knowledge before students read stories about settlers on the American frontier. Oregon Trail puts the student in the place of an explorer moving through the frontier to a fort. The student must make decisions about where and how to travel, what supplies to buy, when and where to camp, and how to deal with dangers confronted along the way. Thus, relevant computer simulations can result in increased background knowledge and heightened interest in specific stories. Of course, appropriate prediscussion and a clear goal are important. But since simulations are most appropriate as small- or large-group activities, discussion is facilitated, and class time is used effectively even as the goal of prereading activity is met.

Simulations generally use all of the color, sound, and graphics capabilities available to the microcomputer, as well as provide record-keeping functions for the teacher. However, the same cautions that applied to tutorial software apply here. The teacher must decide whether the content is appropriate to students' needs and to the instructional program.

## Learning About Thinking with Computers

There have been claims that working with computers and with certain programming languages enhances the problem-solving strategies of the user (Papert, 1980). Such claims are closely related to the tutee function originally identified by Taylor (1980). The proponents of this view argue that either the computer dominates (in effect, controlling the student) or the student dominates (thus controlling the computer). In the former case the computer can be viewed as teaching the student—presenting content, questions, and feedback, as well as branching to appropriate difficulty levels. In the latter case the student "teaches" the computer, usually through programming, and this teaching influences students' thought processes.

Among the main advocates of the potential of microcomputers to influence thinking and problem-solving abilities are Seymore Papert and his colleagues, developers of the Logo computer language. Many who advocate using Logo in schools believe that such usage would have positive effects across an entire school curriculum, although such claims are heard more often for mathematics than for other areas. Similar claims have been made for teaching students to program and work with microcomputers using **structured BASIC,** another common computer language. In fact, Luehrmann (1983, 1984a, 1984b, 1984c) advocates using structured BASIC programming precisely because he believes that such usage can influence the development of logical thinking skills. These claims must still be carefully considered. There are, as yet, few consistent research findings and some conflicting evidence regarding these viewpoints (see Delclos, Littlefield, & Bransford, 1985; Littlefield, Delclos, Bransford, Clayton, & Franks, 1989).

structured BASIC: A common computer language that uses logical modules within programs.

For an illustration of how programming might be related to reading skills, let's consider this sample program:

```
10 PRINT ("HOW OLD ARE YOU?")
20 INPUT A
30 IF A < 10 THEN PRINT "THAT'S NICE!"
40 IF A > 11 THEN PRINT "GREAT!"
RUN
```

This program asks the user's age, waits for a response, and then, depending on whether the response is more than 10 or less than 11, prints either "That's nice!" or "Great!" The programmer used IF-THEN statements in the program to force a particular response from the computer. However, such IF-THEN statements are similar to cause-and-effect relationships in reading. Consequently, teachers might find that relating such simple programs to cause-and-effect sequences in stories could help clarify the literature concept for some students.

Another example of similarity between programming and reading and writing is the need to be aware of possible outcomes. In programming, students must keep in mind the expected outcomes of their programs, and they learn quickly that what they are able to do later in a program is determined by earlier decisions. This understanding parallels what readers and writers do when they anticipate and predict possible outcomes during reading and writing.

Simulations may also be a part of this category of computer usage. They have traditionally been developed to teach specific content, yet they require students to make decisions and anticipate the consequences of their actions. Thus, it may be that general thinking skills are also being developed and that simulation software goes beyond simply imparting information. If simulation software does in fact teach specific content and expand general thinking skills, then the usage category in which it belongs depends on the instructional goal of the simulation.

## Managing Learning with Computers

Teachers who have access to a microcomputer often set it aside for student use only. They forget that the machine can be used to make a teacher's job easier.

Although microcomputer technology can be motivational, teachers need to ensure that use goes beyond drill and practice.

An increasing amount of software is available to keep student records, indicate student progress, track lunch money, write form letters to parents, find information and references useful for lesson development, and perform other time-consuming functions.

Almost all published reading programs now have microcomputer management systems available. Such systems are generally tied into the program's criterion-referenced testing plan so that the system can indicate to the teacher which students have mastered specific concepts and which might need additional help. Additionally, the system can identify which lessons in the published reading program can be used to teach the skills needed by specific students. With a printer attached, the management system can even write personalized notes to students or parents, provide encouragement, or indicate progress.

When coupled with filing system software, a microcomputer can also be used to keep track of anything that would normally require time-consuming entries on file cards. For example, a classroom library can be easily and quickly entered into a computerized filing system, including information about author(s), title, reading difficulty level, topic area(s), genre, and so on. Similarly, a file can be made of students' attitudes and interests, as collected on attitude/interest inventories. Figure 14–1 illustrates an entry into each of these types of files. Such a file system allows a teacher to quickly and easily choose or recommend reading material. For example, the computer could search for any books in the class library that are about pets or for any student(s) who might be interested in pet stories. Thus, the teacher can personalize supplementary reading for any student or group of students in the class. The class as a whole

FIGURE 14–1
Sample entries in a computerized filing system

```
AUTHOR      Silverstein, Shel
TITLE       Where the Sidewalk Ends
GENRE       Poetry
RDGLEVEL    All
DESCRIPTOR  Appropriate for all students.
COMMENT     No reading level or descriptors because the
            book has a variety of poems. In previous
            use, has been of high interest across all
            students/grades.


STUDENT     Alex Smith
AGE         8
INTERESTS   Pets, Science Fiction, Poems, Cars, TV
RDGLEVEL    3.0
COMMENTS    Likes to read aloud to friends—espe-
            cially poems.
```

might decide on the categories to be included in the file system and might enter the data if that information is not confidential. If students are too young to enter data, older students might enjoy a real-world activity as a part of their computer class assignment and might help set up the class data base and enter the data.

For one more example of microcomputer assistance in lightening teacher loads, think back to the discussion of cloze tests and readability formulas in chapter 11. Several software programs help teachers create cloze tests, either on the screen or on paper. A teacher simply types in a passage, and the computer then deletes the appropriate words and replaces them with blanks. Most such software allows the teacher to specify which words to delete (e.g., every fifth or seventh). However, a cloze test can also be customized, with specific words deleted. In either case the test is then printed for student use or appears on the screen. If students take the test on the screen, then the program scores each test (the microcomputer "remembers" the deletions) and provides the teacher with a printout of each student's rating.

Readability analyses are also facilitated with a microcomputer. A teacher needs only to type in a passage, and the computer provides an analysis, often based on a choice of more than one readability formula. In addition, a listing of the number of syllables, the number of sentences, and other data on the passage is often presented (see Figure 14–2). Both cloze and readability software is available commercially but can also be found in the **public domain**.

**public domain:** A term used to indicate an absence of copyright restrictions; describes software that is usually inexpensive, although frequently of high quality, and often without manuals or guarantees.

**Facilitating Parental Involvement.** Parents often feel helpless in the face of curricula that may be substantially different from what was in place when they were students, and some parents feel alienated from (and somewhat threatened by) schools as a result of their own negative experiences from the past. Nonetheless, many parents say that they would do more to help their children learn and to support teachers and schools if they knew what to do. Technology can be especially helpful in communicating with parents. Several schools have purchased automatic telephone dialing equipment that is interfaced with a microcomputer. Such a system is used by teachers and administrators to leave messages for parents: the microcomputer can be set to dial a parent's phone number within certain hours and to keep dialing until contact is made. In this way parents can be told of upcoming field trips, student tardiness, and so on. With this technology, parents also have an opportunity to leave messages.

Even without a computerized system, some schools have devised an effective alternative. Telephone lines are purchased for each grade level or each classroom, and a low-cost answering machine is hooked up to each telephone line. (Schools have been relatively successful at partnering with businesses and telephone companies to provide these resources at substantial discounts.) Then each day teachers record a message about their students—for example, upcoming assignments, homework, or class achievements—and parents can listen to the messages at their convenience, leaving their own messages if they

FIGURE 14–2
Sample screens from readability software

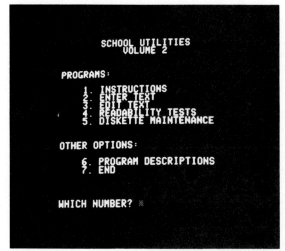

Screen 1

Screen 2

Screen 3

**Source:** From *School Utilities Disk* (vol. 2) (St. Paul, MN: MECC). Reprinted by permission.

wish. In Figure 14–3 Emily Dodson relates her first experience with telephone technology.

Bauch (1988, 1989) has studied the use of inexpensive answering machine technology in a variety of schools. Without such technology he notes that the national average of parent-to-teacher contacts is approximately two per day in schools averaging 300 students. Bauch's data indicate that a tele-

FIGURE 14–3
Implementing telephone technology

> It was just two years ago that I talked to our principal early in the school year about getting some additional telephone equipment. She agreed to contact the telephone company about a line for the second-grade teachers if we could find the funds to buy an answering machine. The three of us decided to contact several local businesses about the possibility of donating one to the school. We put together a brief but fairly detailed description of how the machine would be used and what it would do for us. Happily, three separate businesses agreed to donate it—two department stores and the bank our school uses. So we asked the bank to buy the machine, and the two stores, instead, to underwrite the cost of the telephone line for a year. They agreed, and we promised to report back at the end of the school year to let them know how it had worked out. Our principal was thrilled not to have to spend any school funds for our project.
>
> Now that we've had our system operating for two years, we all wonder how we ever managed without it. Just this morning I listened to the messages several parents left for me last night. One parent said that her son was becoming interested in the basketball playoffs, and she wondered if I could suggest any books for him. So before school started, I entered that information into our microcomputer's filing system and found we had several appropriate books right in our own classroom library. Another parent had called to say that his daughter had the chicken pox and wouldn't be in school for about a week. I called him back at lunch time and talked about catch-up activities. Right now I've just finished writing out the message I'm going to put on tonight's tape.

> > This is Emily Dodson. Our class will soon be reading a set of stories about pets, and I'll be asking students to bring pictures of pets to school. If your family doesn't have a pet, your child can cut out magazine pictures of a pet he or she might like to have. I have some magazines that I can send home with your child if you would like. Just let me know. It would also help if you could discuss with your child his or her feelings about your family pet and/or the responsibilities that having a pet brings. I'll be sending home a few short stories about pets, and you might want to talk about those with your child, too.
> >
> > Today I've asked the students to finish writing stories that were started in class. You might ask to see the story and have your child tell you what it's about. The story should be finished by Friday, and you might suggest that your child draw a picture to go along with it. If you would like your child to bring home some crayons, please leave me a message.
> >
> > In about a month we'll have a unit on Egypt. Please let me know if you or someone you know has traveled to Egypt and could share some pictures or could come and tell us about the trip.
> >
> > Thanks for your support.

phone message system increases that average to approximately 60 per day, and the 60 calls are not all from the same parents each day. However, the majority of parents do call at least once a week.

An additional and important finding is that parents from low socioeconomic levels call just as often as do parents from average and above-average socioeconomic levels. Other data indicate that low-socioeconomic families generally do have a telephone and are most appreciative of this nonthreatening way to find out about homework and class activities and to make contact with teachers. Low-socioeconomic and single parents often have great difficulty finding time to see teachers in person, yet data indicate that they are supportive of schools and are concerned that their children achieve success.

## SPECIFIC APPLICATIONS OF TECHNOLOGY IN READING INSTRUCTION

### General Guidelines

This chapter tries to avoid discussing specific software because it is frequently updated and improved and sometimes becomes unavailable after a period of time. Any programs mentioned by name are used only as examples within a category. Local computer stores, educational computer publications, or a school district resource and curriculum center can recommend specific software titles for the uses mentioned here (see also appendices A and B). Software does exist for use at all grade levels and for all major components of reading (e.g., see Whitaker, Schwartz, & Vockell, 1989; Wresch, 1987).

Teachers often wonder how to fairly distribute access to only one or two microcomputers among 25 or more students. In such situations teachers can allow students to work at the microcomputer in much the same way that they work at a learning center. Many people advocate that students work in groups of two or three per microcomputer (Berger, 1984; Bransford, 1984). The resulting discussion within the small group as problems are encountered and solved is valuable and can enhance learning. Small-group work is especially valuable when simulation software is being used.

Whatever arrangement is worked out, teachers must guard against allowing certain students more access to the microcomputer. For example, it is poor practice to allow microcomputer time as a reward for finishing assigned work. Since more advanced students often complete assignments faster than average or below-average achievers, there is a danger of increasing the gap between high and low groups. Inequities in computer use can also occur between males and females, as well as between students at high and low socioeconomic levels. Teachers must guard against the mistaken notion that males are more mechanically or mathematically inclined than females and, therefore, more appropriate for computer work. In addition, teachers must ensure that those with microcomputers at home do not monopolize microcomputer time in the classroom, simply because of greater background knowledge.

Finally, reading teachers must understand that microcomputers are appropriate for use at any grade level; they are not solely the domain of students in intermediate grades and above. Younger students may have some difficulty using keyboards to input information, but most software intended for their use requires only yes/no responses or a particular letter to indicate their choice. Computers that allow the use of a mouse or a touch pad might also be a good choice for younger children. Regardless of the equipment, however, keyboarding skills should never be the major concern in deciding whether to use a microcomputer. More important is the appropriateness of the material presented by the software—the task itself and the reading skills required.

## Word Processing

Although much software is available specifically for use in reading instruction, software intended for other applications is also valuable to a reading teacher. For example, word processing software can be used in language experience applications. As the student(s) dictate a story, it can be typed directly into the microcomputer and then quickly printed for each student, a highly motivational output. A word processor also allows students to revise or add to their stories easily. Changes can be incorporated into the original and a "clean" copy provided promptly. Printed stories can then be illustrated and either posted or made into class books. Later, teachers can create vocabulary lessons from the words that students use in their language experience stories. For a lesson on -*ing* words, for instance, the word processor can search a student's story for all words ending in -*ing,* thus making the lesson more personal and relevant.

Despite these software applications, however, students should still be provided with many opportunities to see their teachers write. Using a word processor in language experience activities should not replace that more traditional procedure. Many teachers first write their students' stories on chart paper or notebook paper and then transcribe them into the computer for distribution. At higher grade levels students often enjoy entering their stories themselves.

Students can also use word processing software to create their own stories or to access and read stories written by other class members. They might then leave messages to the other students, using the microcomputer as a form of bulletin board. They can share their reactions to other students' stories or simply leave conversational messages. As students read and respond to such messages, they develop audience awareness in their writing and are highly motivated to read any further messages written specifically to them.

In addition, word processing software can help teachers make cloze tests if specific software for that purpose is unavailable. Teachers simply type a passage and then replace specific words with a blank, using a word processor's search-for-and-replace function. Software that checks spelling, which is a part of most word processing software, can also be used to generate spelling lessons. Most spelling-checker programs can create a file of words that were used in students' entries but were not recognized as correct. Teachers then access those word lists and use them as the basis of periodic spelling lessons on the words most frequently misspelled by students.

## Spreadsheets

Other software that has been written for business use, such as spreadsheets, can also be successfully used in reading instruction. Spreadsheets present the user with a series of rows and columns (see Figure 14–4). The information entered in those rows and columns can then be manipulated in a number of ways. Mathematical formulas can be applied to numerical entries, allowing spreadsheets to be used as a gradebook or for other purposes that require numerical information. For reading instruction, however, the mathematics functions are less important than the row-and-column format.

One part of reading instruction is teaching the relationships among items. The rows and columns of a spreadsheet allow students an opportunity to classify in easily visible categories and to correct errors easily. For a lesson on

FIGURE 14–4
Spreadsheet with entries

```
  !   a   !   b   !   c   !   d   !   e   !   f   !   g   !   h   !
  2                                 NOT
  3                     ACTION       ACTION
  4                     WORDS        WORDS
  5                     _____       _____
  6
  7                     RUN          THE
  8                     JUMP         SHE
  9                     SIT          FLOOR
 10
 11
 12          Taken from the following exercise:
 13
 14          Which of the following underlined words are action words?
 15          Which are not?
 16
 17          1. He will run to the store.
 18
 19          2. She will jump down from the chair.
 20
 21          3. Sit down on the floor.
 22
 23
```

action words, for example, the teacher might write on the chalkboard or on a piece of paper beside the microcomputer a series of words containing both action and nonaction words. Then at various times during the day, students could use the spreadsheet to sort the list of words into appropriate columns headed Action Words and Not Action Words. They might also be encouraged to add several of their own words to each column. The students' categorizations would then allow the teacher to determine instructional needs and to teach accordingly.

## Enhanced Applications

**Telecommunications: Accessing Bulletin Boards and Data Bases.** More and more computer buyers are including a **modem** in their purchase. A modem is an inexpensive attachment that allows communication with other computers via telephone lines. This capability makes it possible to access computer bulletin boards and electronic data bases. Bulletin boards provide opportunities to leave messages for others, to browse through information that has been posted, or to ask questions that others will read and respond to. Teachers have found this capability helpful, especially when evaluating software. Data bases that index and evaluate software include these two:

> Educational Products Information (EPIE)
> Box 839
> Water Mill, NY 11976
>
> Online Database
> Northwest Regional Education Laboratory
> Portland, OR 97204

**modem:** An attachment to a computer that allows communication with other computers via telephone lines.

Other bulletin boards and data bases (e.g., DIALOG and CompuServe) allow modem access to information from sources such as the *New York Times,* encyclopedias, travel agencies, and so on. More specialized data bases, such as that of NASA, provide teachers with resources to develop thematic units. A modem also allows teachers and students to share work or comments or to become electronic pen pals with students and teachers in other classrooms. That kind of direct communication can also occur through bulletin boards such as KidsNet, which is supported by the University of Pittsburgh and is intended specifically for students' use.

**Video Technology in the Classroom.** In 1922 Thomas Edison stated,

> The motion picture is destined to revolutionize our educational system. . .in a few years it will supplant largely, if not entirely, the use of textbooks. . . .
> we get about two percent efficiency out of schoolbooks as they are written today. The education of the future, as I see it, will be conducted through the medium of the motion picture. . .where it should be possible to obtain one hundred percent efficiency. (Cuban, 1986, p. 9)

Edison's prediction did not come to pass, yet there is increasing evidence that television and video technology are now playing a role in education and may have an increasing impact in the future.

One reason that film did not have a significant impact is that it is a relatively linear medium. Even though students could watch an event occurring, it was difficult to revisit specific scenes for class discussion or to study in depth a specific item within a film. Even videotape—because of the time required for rewinding, inaccurate access to specific scenes, and poor freeze-frame capabilities—does not really allow more than a simple run-through of an entire film.

**Videodisc** technology, however, is becoming increasingly available for educational purposes and allows rapid, random access to any part of the disk. It also allows clear freeze-frame images and, with its large capacity, permits the showing of approximately 50,000 still-frame pictures. The cost of videodisc players is now about equal to that of high-quality videotape players, and there is no difference in the cost of a videodisc as opposed to that of a videotape. In addition, a videodisc will not tear, stretch, or deteriorate in quality.

videodisc: A disk on which images are stored, allowing for easy access to specific scenes and a clear freeze-frame image.

Many titles are now available on videodisc: National Geographic, Nova, and NASA all have videodisc offerings. General movies are available and can often be adapted for instructional use. In addition, specific instructional materials can frequently be applied to areas other than those for which they were created. For example, *VOTE '88, The Middle East,* and *Martin Luther King, Jr.* (available through Optical Data) are intended for social studies use but can also be used in reading instruction, much as simulations from other content areas. The *Laser Disc Newsletter* (Suite 428, 496 Hudson Street, New York, NY 10014) provides monthly critiques of videodisc offerings and comprehensive lists of available titles.

The power of videodisc technology is enhanced even further when it is linked to a microcomputer. This combination allows specific scenes on videodisc to be accessed and shown to illustrate textual content. For example, with the disk *Designing Invitations to Thinking,* short scenes can be played that illustrate a vocabulary word being taught, thus giving the student a clearer idea of the word's meaning. This procedure is also used to teach character traits, as shown in Figure 14–5. The student indicates which word or character trait should be illustrated, and the microcomputer tells the disc player to play the appropriate scene. Available research indicates that (1) this approach enhances vocabulary learning and retention and (2) more fully developed character traits appear in students' writing when they have learned about character and plot development through videodisc presentations coupled with text (Bransford, Kinzer, Risko, Rowe, & Vye, 1989; Kinzer & CTG Vanderbilt, 1990).

A videodisc can also be used to integrate learning across a curriculum, thus providing a larger context for instruction and a common, shared background for teacher and students (Bransford, Vye, Kinzer, & Risko, 1990). Using the video as a common reference point and relating instruction to that anchor appear to facilitate students' participation as well as improving their writing

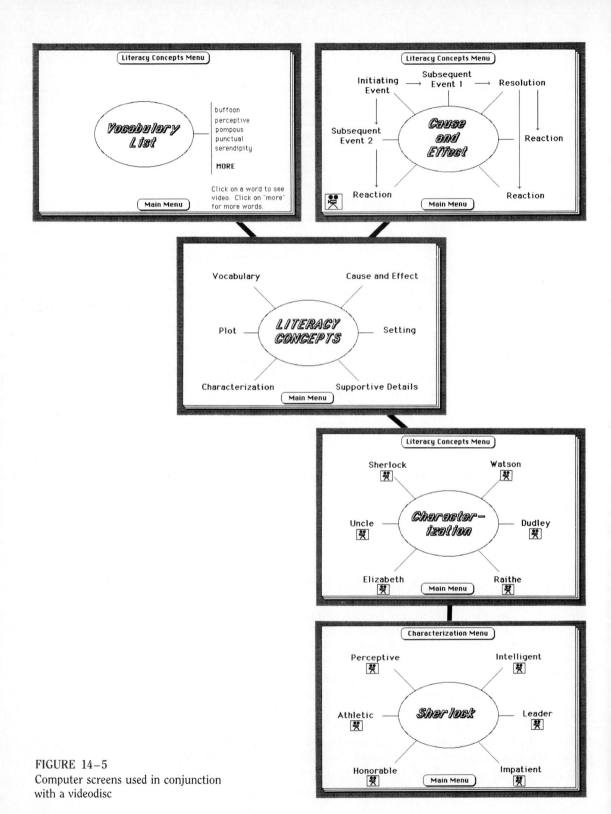

FIGURE 14-5
Computer screens used in conjunction
with a videodisc

584

Videodisc technology, often coupled with computers, can enhance group or individual instruction in reading.

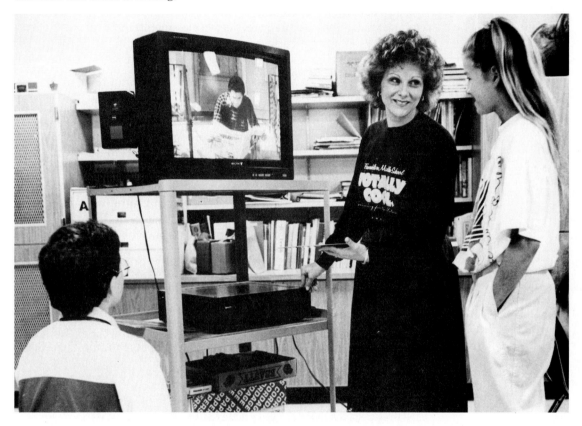

and research skills (Bransford, Sherwood, Hasselbring, Kinzer, & Williams, in press).

Another influence on the use of video technology in the schools is the entry of commercial vendors, who view the schools as a new market. Whittle Communication, for example, makes available to schools a satellite dish as well as a television for each classroom. Each day, news programs, as well as educational offerings, can be beamed to the schools by Whittle and by other communication networks. The sticking point is that Whittle pays for its equipment and installation costs with commercials targeted specifically at school-age children. Many school boards have rejected Whittle's proposal for this reason; they do not believe that school children should be captive audiences for commercials. However, other school districts believe that the Whittle approach is the only way to get such equipment into the schools because of increasingly tight budgets. For schools that already have television equipment, other agencies—for example, CNN (the Cable News Network)—offer a similar package without commercial content.

Thus, the increasing commercial presence, the availability of videodisc technology, the possible link between computers and video equipment, and the specific educational programming that is becoming available indicate that video technology will be more prevalent in classrooms in the future. Although Thomas Edison was not correct in envisioning the role of motion pictures in schools, the potential of video technology is now increasingly a factor.

HyperCard: A programming language that is easy to learn and use and that allows users to follow their own, nonlinear paths through a program; currently available for use on Apple's Macintosh computers.

**Hypermedia.** An increasingly popular computer language for developers of educational software is Apple Computer's **HyperCard**. HyperCard and similar programs (e.g., HyperPad and Linkway for the IBM and compatible computers) allow a user to pick an independent path through material more easily. With these programs items appearing on individual computer screens are usually called cards; an entire program, or set of hypercards, is called a stack. Once the stack is created, the user can pick and choose what part of the stack to look at, where to go next, and so on. Also, HyperCard can control videodisc players, allowing text and video to interact, as described earlier. The general term *hypermedia* is often used to refer to programs that combine text and video in graphic-based animated presentations.

HyperCard and similar programs allow the use of tools to draw graphics, and programming at a basic level is relatively easy. Thus, teachers can create simple, personalized lessons for their classes or can purchase HyperCard stacks with a wide array of possibilities. A number of stacks are available that move through pieces of literature, such as *Charlotte's Web*. Those stacks are often free or are distributed at low cost, and children appear to find them highly motivating.

## FINDING, CHOOSING, AND EVALUATING SOFTWARE

Literally thousands of software programs are marketed for reading instruction. Some software is intended for use on a single computer, as part of a larger reading program. Other packages (e.g., IBM's *Writing to Read*) constitute a core reading program and require a number of computers in a laboratory, where intact classes go on a regular basis for reading instruction. With all the software available, teachers often ask where they can find programs that are appropriate to meet their particular instructional programs. Appendices A and B at the end of this chapter list representative software and software publishers. In addition, a software catalog can be helpful. Those resources are published monthly or yearly by general publishers and by computer software reviewers. Most educational publishers also produce software and include those offerings in their general catalogs. Such catalogs briefly describe available educational software, but usually do not evaluate what is listed. They are available from publishers on request and are automatically sent to school and university libraries and to curriculum and resource centers. Journals, too, often list and evaluate educational software. For example, *The Reading Teacher* includes a monthly column that presents microcomputer issues in literacy education and often discusses available software. The following publications feature new product announcements, software evaluation, or similar columns.

*Classroom Computer News*

*Computers in Reading and Language Arts*

*Creative Computing*

*Digest of Software Reviews: Education*

*Educational Technology*

*Electronic Learning*

*Microcomputers in Education*

*Teaching and Computers*

*T.H.E. Journal (Technological Horizons in Education)*

*The Computing Teacher*

One of the largest distributors of educational software is the Minnesota Educational Computing Consortium (MECC), which produces an extensive software catalog (available from 3490 Lexington Avenue, N., Saint Paul, MN 55126). MECC also offers a subscription service to school systems and other educational users that automatically provides every piece of software that it distributes and forwards new offerings as they appear. Many school districts subscribe to MECC, maintaining a software depository in their district resource center from which individual schools and teachers can borrow software for use in their classrooms.

Once teachers find software that interests them, they must decide whether it is appropriate for their students and their instructional program. Some software publishers will send a program (or a compressed demonstration copy) on approval so that it can be evaluated. Other publishers do not allow the return of used software. In those cases teachers should find one or more independent reviews of the software before ordering it. Reviews and articles are available in the journals mentioned previously and from agencies that evaluate educational software. EPIE (Educational Products Information Exchange, Box 260, Stonybrook, NY 11790) evaluates software and distributes those evaluations cataloged by skill and subject area. Computer bulletin boards can also be used to ask others' opinions regarding an intended software purchase or to view compilations of reviews. Additionally, most state departments of education and many school districts have collected software evaluations and make them available to teachers.

Of course, the most relevant evaluation is that of the individual teacher who may use the software. When you find yourself considering software, there are two things that you should assess. First, you must ask whether the software is appropriate to your hardware, that is, the equipment that you have available. Second, you must consider aspects of the software itself as they relate to your instructional program. Before you order any software, you should work through the following hardware-specific evaluation checklist (Kinzer, Sherwood, & Bransford, 1986). It can help identify inappropriate software before further time, effort, and money are expended, and it does not require that the software be in hand (the questions can usually be answered from information provided in catalogs or advertising brochures). A more comprehensive treatment of software evaluation is presented by Sloane, Gordon, Gunn, and Mickelsen (1989).

### Hardware-Specific Software Checklist

1. Is the software available in your diskette format? For example, if your computer accepts only 3.5-inch diskettes, is the software available on such diskettes, or is it available only on 5.25-inch diskettes?
2. Does the software require one or two disk drives? Sometimes software programs require that a command or executive program stay in one drive, while the user's files (perhaps your gradebook or students' stories) are stored and accessed in another.
3. Is the software compatible with your brand and model of computer? Even if the software is available with your particular brand of microcomputer (e.g., an Apple), it must still be compatible with the model that you have (e.g., Apple II, Apple GS, or Apple Macintosh).
4. Does the software require a certain amount of computer memory? Some software must be loaded into memory before it can be used and may require additional memory during use. Find out how much memory is required for operation and whether your computer has the necessary amount.
5. Does the software require any programmable, function, or special keys to run? Is a special or enhanced keyboard necessary?
6. Does the software require any specific output device? Some software sends output directly to a printer and stops or "hangs up" if a printer is unavailable.
7. Does the software require any specific output capabilities? For example, a printer with graphics capabilities or an external speaker is sometimes required before the full capabilities of the software are available.
8. Does the software require any other software to be useful? For example, some programs (e.g., spelling checkers) require word processing software to input information. Thus, the software might be useless without a word processing package.

Once you have determined that the targeted software is suitable for your classroom microcomputer system, you should answer the questions in the following list (Kinzer, Sherwood, & Bransford, 1986). They require that you have the software in hand and will help you examine it carefully. Some software may be inappropriate for the reading level or typing skills of your students. In other cases the microcomputer's graphics and sound capabilities may draw attention to wrong answers. If your school district or school library catalogs software evaluations, you should forward yours for inclusion when it is completed. (Be sure to include title and version, publisher and address, and perhaps cost.) Additionally, because some software is developed and distributed without adequate **field testing,** you should send any suggestions for improvements or complaints regarding the software to the publisher so that modifications can be made. Hands-on evaluation is your only real safeguard.

field testing: Presale experimentation by people who typically would use a product.

### Questions for Evaluating Reading and Writing Instructional Software

1. Do you have the proper equipment to run the software?
2. What skills are targeted, according to the publisher? Do you agree?
3. Are the skills targeted by the software appropriate to your students and to your curriculum? For how many of your students would the software be useful?
4. What is the intended age/grade level, according to the publisher? Do you agree?
5. How do you intend to use the software? What would its purpose be in your overall program?
6. How many of your students are at a level at which the software would be useful?
7. In what area does the software fall: (a) learning from computers, (b) learning with computers, (c) managing learning with computers, or (d) some other area or combination or areas.
8. Does the software do more than a text could do in the same skill area? In what way?
9. Would the software be easy for your students to use and understand? Are the commands, required typing skills, or complexity of screen displays within your students' abilities?
10. Does the software make appropriate use of graphics, color, and sound to enhance motivation and learning? Are these elements necessary, given your intended use of the software?
11. Does the software make use of branching to provide instruction when errors are made? Is branching necessary, given your intended use?
12. How long would it take one of your students to go through the program? Is that an appropriate amount of time, given your goals and instructional situation?
13. Would your students have to go through the entire program, perhaps in some predetermined sequence, or would they be able to stop and start at various points?
14. Does the software provide a pretest so that students can begin at an appropriate level of difficulty? Is there a posttest to measure learning? Are these tests important, given your intended use?
15. Could your students load and use the software by themselves? How much teacher support would be needed? Is that involvement appropriate to your instructional situation?

16. Does the software provide a dictionary or glossary to explain words and/or concepts that students find difficult? Could students ask the computer for a more detailed explanation if they did not understand a word? Does the software provide help if commands are not easily understood?

17. Does the software use the computer's sound capabilities to provide speech support for unknown words? For example, can the user highlight a word or a larger part of the text and ask that it be read? If yes, which form is used: synthesized (more difficult to understand) or digitized (a good approximation of natural speech)?

18. If the software targets longer pieces of text, does it use selections that are interesting and/or drawn from good children's literature?

19. Does the software score students' work and file the results by individual names for later access by the teacher (i.e., does it include record-keeping capabilities)?

20. Can the software be used by more than one student at a time? Would this usage detract from your intended use?

21. Is there overt gender, racial, or socioeconomic bias in the software?

22. What suggestions for improvement should be communicated to the publisher?

## USING A COMPREHENSION FRAMEWORK TO GUIDE TECHNOLOGICAL APPLICATIONS

Your comprehension framework will determine how you use microcomputers, other technology, and associated software in your instructional program. It will also result in an emphasis on one part of the five-part model discussed at the beginning of this chapter. Teachers with a specific skills explanation of how reading ability develops tend to choose drill-and-practice or tutorial software that relates to specifically defined skills. Teachers with a reader-based view of how we read or a holistic explanation of how reading ability develops may find simulations useful or may use word processors to enhance language experience activities. Comprehension frameworks based on an interactive explanation of how we read or an integrative explanation of how reading ability develops tend to incorporate a variety of software appropriate for specific learners. They may use drill-and-practice programs for some purposes and software that targets high-level knowledge sources for other purposes—for example, the selection of story endings, which uses high-level discourse knowledge.

Computers are simply tools for teachers to use in reading instruction. They are governed by the same kinds of philosophical considerations that we applied to printed materials earlier. With both new and traditional technologies you will be on the forefront of educational opportunities. Supported by the concepts, theories, and methods suggested throughout this text and guided by your own personal comprehension framework, you should be ready to become a professional and effective teacher of reading.

## COMMENTS FROM THE CLASSROOM ■

### Emily Dodson

I must admit that I was somewhat anxious when I was told that each classroom was going to get a microcomputer. After all, my teacher training did not include anything about computers. But a few other teachers who knew a lot about them offered to set up all the equipment and give the rest of us a half-day workshop. The school district also sent their computer consultant out to our school to tell us about district software—resources, evaluations, and procedures for borrowing or copying.

As I learned about the equipment, I realized that it was actually pretty easy to use—easier than some teacher's manuals I've seen! After all, I couldn't break anything through normal use, and if I made a backup regularly, I couldn't lose much data. I also learned that there's a huge amount of software available, and I knew right away that I'd like some of the programs better than others.

Within several months I was including the microcomputer in our classroom routine fairly regularly. It actually became another learning center in the room. Students moved through the computer station just as they did through the other centers, and I changed the software depending on which students were using the equipment and what I wanted them to learn. My favorite programs are the ones that use the computer's full capabilities and also match what we know about the reading process. They ask prequestions and questions midway through a selection, they provide synthesized speech support, and they use color and animation to emphasize appropriate concepts.

For my end-of-year report I had to look back on how I had used the microcomputer during the year. I discovered that I'd actually used quite a range of software with my students. Sometimes I used drill-and-practice software

with a decoding or vocabulary lesson, and I often used integrated comprehension packages that included decoding, word attack, vocabulary, and reading children's literature. At other times I used software that let students brainstorm as a prewriting activity, and I also used word processing software in some language experience lessons. Other programs allowed the students to read and make decisions about plot; the story changed as they made their decisions. In addition, software helped me make up multiple-choice tests, cloze tests, games, and puzzles; and it let me personalize the students' stories and print them in book form. The microcomputer has been a real asset.

### Mr. Burns

I really enjoy having a microcomputer available in my room. Mostly, I use drill-and-practice software, especially the programs that help my students learn to decode. I was surprised at how many good products there are that deal with decoding and word attack skills.

I also like having the microcomputer to help me with specific activity sheets. It's nice to be able to customize puzzles and games for individual students. And it's nice to have record-keeping and gradebook functions on the computer—they save a lot of time and allow me to match up students with books that I have in class. All in all, I look at the computer as another good instructional tool.

### Ms. Sanchez

My choice of software for our classroom microcomputer goes right along with my understanding of the reading process. My selections lean toward programs that include children's literature and enhance writing activities. Specifically, I use word processing software in language experience activities, prewriting and outlining idea software, story starter software, bookmaking software to help make book covers and print students' stories, sometimes with illustrations we've chosen from a graphics catalog, and so on. Some of the software compiles students' responses or stories and prints personalized notes that students can take home to their parents. I really like that feature. At the same time I don't use any of the software intended to drill isolated skills, and I don't use testing software.

I've really appreciated the computer's data base and filing capabilities. I have so many books and magazines around the room that it's hard to keep track of everything. The computer has made this task a lot easier. All in all, computer technology has been very helpful and has fit in well with what I try to do.

**MAJOR POINTS**

■ The use of microcomputers in reading instruction falls into five general categories: learning about computers, learning from computers, learning with computers, learning about thinking with computers, and managing learning with computers.

■ In addition to microcomputers and their software, various other technologies—including videodiscs, answering machines, and television—are useful in reading instruction. These other technologies can be effectively used independently or can be linked to microcomputers.

■ All types of software—including drill-and-practice, tutorial, gaming, simulation, and programming software—can have a place in reading instruction, if appropriately used.

■ If thoughtfully applied, software intended for use in other areas can also be used in reading instruction.

■ Teachers should carefully evaluate software before using it in reading instruction.

**MAKING INSTRUCTIONAL DECISIONS**

1. What are the role and value of drill and practice in a reading lesson? For what purpose(s) might you assign students to computer software for drill and practice?

2. Imagine the management functions that will face you as a reading teacher. Explain how a microcomputer could be used to help you with those tasks.

3. Interview several teachers who use microcomputers in their reading instruction. Ask how they use the system specifically in their reading lessons and how they perceive the microcomputer in comparison to more traditional instructional practices, like workbooks.

4. Interview several students who have been allowed to use microcomputers as a part of their reading instruction. Ask how they feel about the microcomputer and how it has helped them learn.

5. Your curriculum library or microcomputer laboratory probably has software that is marketed as being appropriate for reading instruction. (If not, check a computer store.) Evaluate several software packages using the checklists in this chapter. How might the software be used in reading instruction?

6. How might microcomputers and related technologies fit into your instructional program and, specifically, your comprehension framework?

**FURTHER READING**

Balajthy, E. (1986). *Microcomputers in reading and language arts*. Englewood Cliffs, NJ: Prentice Hall.

Includes chapters on evaluating software as well as applications in emergent literacy/readiness, word recognition, vocabulary, comprehension, and study skills. Also discusses other general issues of microcomputer use in reading instruction.

Blanchard, J. S., Mason, G. E., & Daniel, D. (1987). *Computer applications in reading* (3rd ed.). Newark, DE: International Reading Association.

A popular publication by the International Reading Association. A brief but good introduction and resource for teachers wishing to implement microcomputers in their reading programs.

Blanchard, J. S., & Rottenberg, C. J. (1990). Hypertext and hypermedia: Discovering and creating meaningful learning environments. *The Reading Teacher, 43,* 656–661.

Discusses and defines hypertext and hypermedia and explores potential benefits and uses in reading instruction.

Whitaker, B. T., Schwartz, E., & Vockell, E. (1989). *The computer in the reading curriculum*. New York: McGraw-Hill.

A comprehensive paperback that discusses computer applications for each component of the reading process. Includes extensive software lists, evaluations, and publishers' addresses.

**REFERENCES**

Awad, E. M. (1983). *Introduction to computers (2nd ed.)*. Englewood Cliffs, NJ: Prentice Hall.

Bauch, J. P. (1988). Communicating with parents through technology. In J. Collins et al. (Eds.), *Proceedings of the Fifth International Conference on Technology and Education*. Edinburgh, Scotland: CEP Consultants.

Bauch, J. P. (1989). The trans*parent* school model: New technology for parent involvement. *Educational Leadership, 47*(2), 32–34.

Berger, C. (1984, April). *Assessing cognitive consequences of computer environments for learning science: Research findings and policy implications*. Paper presented at the National Association for Research in Science Teaching, Lake Geneva, WI.

Bransford, J. (1984, April). Personal communication.

Bransford, J. D., Kinzer, C. K., Risko, V. J., Rowe, D. W., & Vye, N. J. (1989). Designing invitations to thinking: Initial thoughts. In S. McCormick & J. Zutell (Eds.), *Cognitive and social perspectives for literacy research and instruction* (38th NRC Yearbook, pp. 35–54). Chicago: National Reading Conference.

Bransford, J. D., Sherwood, R. D., Hasselbring, T. S., Kinzer, C. K., & Williams, S. M. (in press). Anchored instruction: Why we need it and how technology can help. In D. Nix & R. Spiro (Eds.), *Advances in computer-video technology*. Hillsdale, NJ: Erlbaum.

Bransford, J. D., Vye, N., Kinzer, C. K., & Risko, V. J. (1990). Teaching thinking and content knowledge: An integrated approach. In B. F. Jones & L. Idol (Eds.), *Dimensions of thinking and cognitive instruction* (pp. 381–413). Hillsdale, NJ: Erlbaum.

Cuban, L. (1986). *Teachers and machines: The classroom use of technology since 1920*. New York: Teachers College Press.

Delclos, V. R., Littlefield, J., & Bransford, J. D. (1985). Teaching thinking through LOGO: The importance of method. *Roeper Review, 7*, 153–156.

Goldberg, K., & Sherwood, R. D. (1983). *Microcomputers: A parent's guide*. New York: Wiley.

Hasselbring, T., & Cavanaugh, K. (1986). Computer applications for the mildly handicapped. In C. Kinzer, R. Sherwood, & J. Bransford (Eds.), *Computer strategies for education: Foundations and content-area applications*. Columbus, OH: Merrill.

Kinzer, C. K. (1986a). Universals of computer systems. In C. K. Kinzer, R. Sherwood, & J. D. Bransford (Eds.), *Computer strategies for education: Foundations and content-area applications*. Columbus, OH: Merrill.

Kinzer, C. K. (1986b). A five-part categorization for use of microcomputers in reading classrooms. *The Reading Teacher, 30*, 226–232.

Kinzer, C. K., with the Cognition and Technology Group at Vanderbilt. (1990). Anchored instruction and its relationship to situated cognition. *Educational Researcher, 19*, 2–10.

Kinzer, C. K., Hynds, S., & Loufbourrow, M. (1986). Applications of microcomputers in reading and writing. In C. Kinzer, R. Sherwood, & J. D. Bransford (Eds.), *Computer strategies for education: Foundations and content-area applications*. Columbus, OH: Merrill.

Kinzer, C. K., Sherwood, R. D., & Bransford, J. D. (Eds.). (1986). *Computer strategies for education: Foundations and content-area applications*. Columbus, OH: Merrill.

Littlefield, J., Delclos, V. R., Bransford, J. D., Clayton, K. N., & Franks, J. J. (1989). Some prerequisites for teaching thinking: Methodological issues in the study of LOGO programming. *Cognition and Instruction, 6*, 331–366.

Luehrmann, A. (1983). *Computer literacy: A hands-on approach*. New York: McGraw-Hill.

Luehrmann, A. (1984a). Structured programming in BASIC: Part I. Top-down BASIC. *Creative Computing*, 152–156.

Luehrmann, A. (1984b). Structured programming in BASIC: Part II. Control blocks. *Creative Computing*, 152–163.

Luehrmann, A. (1984c). Structured programming in BASIC: Part III. An application. *Creative Computing*, 125–136.

Mageau, T. (1990). Software's new frontier: Laser-disc technology. *Electronic Learning, 9*(6), 22–28.

Papert, S. (1980). *Mindstorms: Children, computers, and powerful ideas*. New York: Basic Books.

Papert, S. (1984). Trying to predict the future. *Popular Computing*.

Sloane, H. N., Gordon, H. M., Gunn, C., & Mickelsen, V. G. (1989). *Evaluating educational software: A guide for teachers*. Englewood Cliffs, NJ: Prentice Hall.

Taylor, R. P. (Ed.). (1980). *The computer in the school: Tutor, tool, tutee*. New York: Teachers College Press.

Whitaker, B. T., Schwartz, E., & Vockell, E. (1989). *The computer in the reading curriculum*. New York: McGraw-Hill.

Wresch, W. (1987). *A practical guide to computer uses in the English/language arts classroom*. Englewood Cliffs, NJ: Prentice Hall.

## APPENDIX A ■ Representative Software List

| Decoding (Alphabet/ Letter Recognition and Phonics) | Alphabet Circus | Practice: alphabet and keyboarding skills (Pre through 2) | DLM |
| --- | --- | --- | --- |
| | Animal Alphabet and Other Things | Practice: graphics-based letters (Pre through 2) | Random House |
| | Charlie Brown's ABCs | Practice: letter recognition (K through 2) | Random House |
| | Letter Recognition | Practice: alphabet and keyboarding skills (K through 1) | Hartley |
| | Stickybear ABC | Practice: letter recognition (Pre through 1) | Weekly Reader Software |
| | Game of Hard/Soft Consonants | Practice: consonants in a game format (3 through 7) | Edutek |
| | Gamepower for Phonics (Plus) | Practice: phonics in a game format; extensive manual (K through 3) | Spin a Text |
| | Phonics Pinball | Practice: phonics in a game format (K through 4) | Southwest EdPsych Services |
| | Reader Rabbit and Fab Word Factory | Practice: vowels and consonants in a game format (K through 2) | The Learning Company |
| | Reading Machine | Practice: phonic drills (K through 3) | Southwest EdPsych Services |
| | Snoopy's Reading Machine | Practice: word families (K through 3) | Random House |
| | Sound Ideas | Tutorial: vowel, consonant, word attack; speech synthesis (K through 3) | Houghton Mifflin |
| | Using Phonics in Context | Tutorial: phonics (2 through 4) | Educational Activities |
| | Word Families | Tutorial: word families (1 through 4) | Hartley |
| | Word Mount | Practice: rhyming (2 through 6) | Random House |

| | Word Munchers | Practice: phonics drill in a game format (1 through 5) | MECC |
|---|---|---|---|
| | Writing to Read | Tutorial: initial teaching alphabet; phonics emphasis; requires computer workstation lab environment (K through 3) | IBM |
| **Decoding (Word Recognition)** | Cloze Vocabulary and More | Tutorial: word shapes and cloze (2 through 5) | A/V Concepts |
| | Syllable Count | Practice: syllables in a game format (3 through 8) | Edutek |
| | Wizard of Words | Practice: 5 different word games (K through 8) | Advanced Ideas |
| | Word Break-Up | Practice: syllables (3 through 8) | Edutek |
| | Word Factory | Practice: affixes, contractions, rhymes (3 through 6) | Orange Cherry Software |
| | Wordzzzearch | Practice: word recognition through word-search puzzles (3 through 12) | Mindplay |
| **Vocabulary** | Cloze Tree | Tutorial: synonyms and antonyms (3 through 7) | Sierra On-Line |
| | Cloze-Plus | Tutorial: context clues for meaning (3 through 6) | Milliken |
| | Crozzzwords | Practice: vocabulary crossword puzzles (3 through 12) | Mindplay |
| | Definitions Review | Practice: word/definition matching (5 through 12) | Collegiate Software |

| | | |
|---|---|---|
| Figurative Language | Tutorial: figures of speech through context (3 through 6) | Random House |
| Synonyms and Antonyms Game | Practice: synonyms and antonyms (3 through 8) | Edutek |
| Homonyms in Context | Practice: homonyms in context; game format (3 through 6) | Random House |
| Homonyms, Antonyms, Synonyms | Practice: game format (4 through 8) | Gamco |
| Language Arts Bingo | Practice: vocabulary through 6) | Ecole Associates |
| On Target | Practice: vocabulary definitions (3 through 8) | Micromedia |
| Riddle Magic | Practice: context clues; teacher-created riddles (3 through 12) | Mindscape |
| Semantic Mapper | Tutorial: vocabulary development through associations (3 through 6) | Teacher Support Software |
| Stickybear Reading | Practice: vocabulary and sentence structure (K through 3) | Weekly Reader Software |
| Tradewords | Practice: vocabulary with different word lists; game format (3 through 12) | NTS Software |
| Vocabulary Detective | Practice: vocabulary clues in a game format (2 through 12) | Southwest EdPsych Services |
| Word Bank | Practice: word classification (1 through 4) | Mindscape |
| Word Detective | Practice: creating words from letters; game format (3 through 12) | Sunburst |

| Comprehension | Author! Author! | Simulation: writing drama (2 through 6) | Educational Activities |
|---|---|---|---|
| | Ace Reporter | Practice: details and main ideas in a game format (3 through 6) | Methods and Solutions |
| | Adventures Around the World | Practice: comprehension using adventure texts (3 through 6) | Orange Cherry Software |
| | Cause and Effect | Tutorial: cause and effect (3 through 6) | Hartley |
| | Cloze for Developing Comprehension | Practice: context through cloze (3 through 6) | Orange Cherry Software |
| | Computer Crossroads | Practice: adventure with branching (2 through 5) | Educational Activities |
| | Hide 'N Sequence | Tutorial: sequencing; stories that can be modified (3 through 8) | Sunburst |
| | Little Riddles | Practice: inference and prediction (1 through 2) | Hartley |
| | Micro Mysteries | Tutorial: software and books (2 through 4) | Troll Associates |
| | Reading Comprehension | Tutorial: comprehension of quality children's literature; uses speech-based comprehension support (1 through 3) | Houghton Mifflin |
| | Reading for Information | Practice: graphs and charts (2 through 12) | IBM |
| | Sherlock Holmes Masters of Mysteries | Practice: problem solving/comprehension (5 through 8) | Data Command |
| | Storymaker | Practice: writing branching stories (3 through 8) | Orange Cherry Software |
| | Storyteller | Practice: writing branching stories; personalized (4 through 6) | Educational Activities |

| | | | |
|---|---|---|---|
| | Twistaplot | Practice: plot development through branching stories (4 through 8) | Scholastic |
| | Who, What, Where, When, Why | Practice: questions and titles (1 through 5) | Hartley |
| **Management and "Tool" Software** | Bank Street Writer | Word processor, spelling checker, thesaurus (2 through 12) | Scholastic |
| | Bookmate | Data base to match student interests to book titles (4 through 6) | Sunburst |
| | Byte into Books | Data base of 500 children's books (1 through 8) | Calico |
| | Crossword Magic | Creates crossword puzzles (2 through 12) | Mindscape |
| | EB: Computer-Managed Reading Program | Manages individualized reading programs (3 through 12) | Calico |
| | Fredwriter | Word processor (public domain; 3 through 12) | Cue Softswap |
| | Kidwriter | Word processor for young children (Pre through 3) | Spinnaker |
| | My Words | Word processor for young children; speech enhanced (1 through 4) | Hartley |
| | Prewrite | Brainstorming guide for writing (3 through 6) | Hartley |
| | Puzzles and Posters | Creates word-search and crossword puzzles and posters (1 through 12) | MECC |
| | Readability Analysis | Tests readability with a variety of formulas (1 through 12) | Gamco |

| | | |
|---|---|---|
| Readability Index | Tests readability with the Bormuth formula (1 through 12) | Educational Activities |
| Story Builder | Puts story elements together to make stories (2 through 6) | Random House |
| Story Time | Prints personalized stories (2 through 6) | Compuware |
| Story Tree | Gives prompts for writing branching stories (4 through 12) | Scholastic |
| Story Writer | Prewriting, outlining, and writing; includes illustrations (3 through 8) | Mindscape |
| Student Stories | Writes personalized stories (1 through 3) | MECC |
| Utility | Context clues for vocabulary and word lists (K through 6) | Teacher Support Software |

# APPENDIX B ■ Representative Software Publishers

A/V Concepts Corporation
30 Montauk Blvd.
Oakdale, NY 11769

Advanced Ideas
2902 San Pablo Ave.
Berkeley, CA 94702

Broderbund Software
17 Paul Drive
San Raphael, CA 94903

CALICO
P.O. Box 15916
St. Louis, MO 63114

Compuware
15 Center Rd.
Randolph, NJ 07869

CUE Softswap
P.O. Box 271704
Concord, CA 94527–1704

Data Command
P.O. Box 548
Kankakee, IL 60901

Developmental Learning
  Materials (DLM)
One DLM Park
Allen, TX 75002

Ecole Associates
P.O. Box 115T
Fairless Hill, PA 19030

Educational Activities
P.O. Box 392
Freeport, NY 11520

Edutek Corporation
P.O. Box 60354
Palo Alto, CA 94306

Gamco Industries
Box 1911
Big Spring, TX 79720

Hartley Courseware
123 Bridge
Dimondale, MI 48821

Houghton Mifflin Educational
  Software Division
One Beacon St.
Boston, MA 02107

IBM
P.O. Box 1329
Boca Raton, FL 33432

MECC (Minnesota Educational
  Computing Consortium)
2520 Broadway Dr.
St. Paul, MN 55113

Methods and Solutions
82 Montvale Ave.
Stoneham, MA 02180

Micromedia
170 East 1000, S.
Orem, UT 84058

Milliken Publishing Company
P.O. Box 21579
St. Louis, MO 63132

Mindplay
82 Montvale Ave.
Stoneham, MA 02180

Mindscape
3444 Dundee Rd.
Northbrook, IL 60062

NTS Software
141 W. Rialto Ave.
Rialto, CA 92376

Optical Data Corporation
30 Technology Drive, Box 4919
Warren, NJ 07060

Orange Cherry Media
7 Delano Dr.
Bedford Hills, NY 10507

Random House School
  Division
201 E. 50th St.
New York, NY 10022

Scholastic
730 Broadway
New York, NY 10003

Sierra On-Line
36575 Mudge Ranch Rd.
Coarsegold, CA 93614

Southwest EdPsych Services
P.O. Box 1870
Phoenix, AZ 85001

Spin-a-Test Publishing
  Company
3177 Hogarth Dr.
Sacramento, CA 95827

Spinnaker Software
One Kendall Square
Cambridge, MA 02139

Sunburst Communications
39 Washington Ave.
Pleasantville, NY 10570

Teacher Support Software
502 N.W. 75th St., Suite 380
Gainesville, FL 32601

The Learning Company
545 Middlefield Rd., Suite 170
Menlo Park, CA 94025

Troll Associates
100 Corporate Drive
Mahwah, NJ 07430

Weekly Reader Family
  Software
245 Long Hill
Middletown, CT 06457

# Name Index

# Subject Index

**Donald J. Leu** is associate professor of education and director of graduate programs in Reading and Language Arts at Syracuse University. He teaches graduate and undergraduate courses at Syracuse University's Reading and Language Arts Center. He has served in the Peace Corps, teaching English in the Marshall Islands of Micronesia. He has also been an elementary teacher and a reading specialist in California. He received an Ed.M. degree in Reading at Harvard and a Ph.D in Language and Literacy at the University of California, Berkeley. Professor Leu's current research includes work on predictable texts, teacher's cognitive processes in literacy context, and the development of reading/writing software. He has published articles on reading in a variety of journals, including *Reading Research Quarterly, The Journal of Educational Psychology,* and *Curriculum Review.* He currently serves on the editorial review boards for *The Journal of Educational Psychology* and *The Journal of Reading Behavior.* He enjoys dressage, fly fishing, and spending time with his family.

**Charles K. Kinzer** is associate professor of education and research scientist at the Learning Technology Center, Peabody College of Vanderbilt University, where he teaches graduate and undergraduate courses in reading education and language arts. He has taught reading and remedial reading in middle and junior high schools, and has served as Language Arts Consultant (K–12) at the school district level. He received his M.A. in Education from the University of British Columbia, Canada, and his Ph.D. in Language and Literacy at the University of California, Berkeley. Professor Kinzer's research includes reading comprehension, vocabulary acquisition, teacher cognition, and the application of technology in education. He has published articles about reading education, technology, and expert systems development in journals such as *The Journal of Reading Behavior, The Journal of Reading, Reading Research and Instruction, The International Journal of Intelligent Systems,* and *Applied Cognitive Psychology.* He currently serves on the editorial boards of the *Reading Research Quarterly, The Journal of Reading Behavior,* and *The Journal of Special Education Technology.* He enjoys photography, traveling, and spending time at the beach with his wife and daughter.